Teaching Study Strategies in Developmental Education

Readings on Theory, Research, and Best Practice

Other Bedford/St. Martin's Professional Resources

The Bedford/St. Martin's Series in Rhetoric and Composition

Disability and the Teaching of Writing: A Critical Sourcebook, by Cynthia Lewiecki-Wilson and Brenda Jo Brueggemann

Literacy: A Critical Sourcebook, by Ellen Cushman, Eugene R. Kintgen, Barry Kroll, and Mike Rose

An Open Language: Selected Writing on Literacy, Learning, and Opportunity, by Mike Rose

Second-Language: Writing in the Composition Classroom, by Paul Kei Matsuda, Michelle Cox, Jay Jordan, and Christina Ortmeier-Hooper

Teaching Advice and Blogs

Assigning, Responding, Evaluating: A Writing Teacher's Guide, Fourth Edition, by Edward M. White

Bits Blog, at blogs.bedfordstmartins.com/bits

The Elements of Teaching Writing: A Resource for Instructors in All Disciplines, by Katherine Gottschalk and Keith Hjortshoj

Portfolio Teaching: A Guide for Instructors, Second Edition, by Nedra Reynolds and Rich Rice

A TA's Guide to Teaching Writing in All Disciplines, by Beth Finch Hedengren

Take 20: Teaching Writing (DVD), by Todd Taylor

Background Readings

Teaching Composition: Background Readings, Third Edition, by T. R. Johnson

Teaching Developmental Reading: Historical, Theoretical, and Practical Background Readings, by Norman A. Stahl and Hunter Boylan

Teaching Developmental Writing: Background Readings, Third Edition, by Susan Naomi Bernstein

Bibliographies

The Bedford Bibliography for Teachers of Basic Writing, Third Edition, by Gregory R. Glau and Chitralekha Duttagupta

For more information, contact your local sales representative, e-mail us at sales_support@bfwpub.com, or visit Teaching Central at www.bedfordstmartins .com/teachingcentral.

Teaching Study Strategies in Developmental Education

Readings on Theory, Research, and Best Practice

Russ Hodges
Texas State University-San Marcos

Michele L. Simpson
University of Georgia

Norman A. Stahl
Northern Illinois University

Bedford/St. Martin's   Boston ◆ New York

For Bedford/St. Martin's

Developmental Editors: Stephanie Naudin, Shannon C. Walsh
Marketing Manager: Christina Shea
Project Management: DeMasi Design and Publishing Services
Text Design: Claire Seng-Niemoeller
Cover Design: Andrea Corbin
Production Associate: Samuel Jones
Composition: Jeff Miller Book Design
Printing and Binding: Haddon Craftsmen, Inc., an RR Donnelley & Sons Company

President: Joan E. Feinberg
Editorial Director: Denise B. Wydra
Editor in Chief: Karen S. Henry
Director of Marketing: Karen R. Soeltz
Director of Production: Susan W. Brown
Associate Director, Editorial Production: Elise S. Kaiser
Manager, Publishing Services: Andrea Cava

Library of Congress Control Number: 2010940732

6 5 4 3 2
f e d c b

For information, write: Bedford/St. Martin's, 75 Arlington Street, Boston, MA 02116 (617-399-4000)

ISBN: 978-0-312-66274-5

Preface

We would like you to think back to the days when you were still a student. Do you recall how you learned to study? Most of our colleagues to whom we've posed this question could not come up with a quick answer. So, let's probe a little deeper.

Did you receive any formal instruction in how to study in elementary school? in middle school? in high school? When you entered college, did you take a study strategies course? If not, did you encounter research- or theory-driven study strategies anywhere else — say, in first-year psychology or in an undergraduate education course?

If your experience was like that of most college students in the nation today, you probably did not receive formal instruction in study strategies until college — if, in fact, you encountered it then. (A surprisingly large number of our colleagues report having had *no* knowledge of formal study strategies until they found themselves preparing to teach their first study-skills course.) Any instruction you did receive was likely to be hit-or-miss, rather than research- or theory-driven: The promises made to you may have been great, but the actual results were probably disappointing.

Your story was probably no different than our stories. Since what we learned and how we learned it obviously influence what we do today in our own classrooms, we would like to share some of our own experiences in learning to learn — experiences that helped to shape our careers and that led to a shared belief in the value of teaching study strategies.

Origins of *Teaching Study Strategies in Developmental Education*

Norm relates the following story about learning to learn:

> It was not until my senior year at Lincoln High School, while on the community college preparatory track, that I learned to study. I'd like to say that a teacher took me under his or her wing and opened up the wonders of strategic learning, but, no — my mentor was a fellow student, Ronald Blair. When we met, Ron was a student and a particularly talented one. I was a surfer and not a particularly talented one. To this day, Ron doesn't

realize that I owe him for much of my success, as he sent me down the path of learning to learn.

Ron seemed to earn A's in Advanced Biology with ease, while I battled for C– grades. One day as we were looking over our most recent test scores, he asked how I studied for tests. My answer was simple: I read the chapters, usually the night before the test. Ron smiled and explained that I needed to start reading and outlining the chapter the very day the instructional unit began. Then, when it came time to take the test, I should study my outline of the text's information. Furthermore, I should review my class notes every night. I'm not sure why Ron's simple advice struck a chord with me: I thought it just might make sense to try out that "student" thing.

Now, I understand that any great narrative would say that I followed Ron's advice and turned into an A student. That was not the case. However, I followed Ron's advice and C– grades turned into honest B grades. Ron had taught me the way to study. I admit that when the waves were breaking down at Sloat Beach, I did not always demonstrate the will to study for classes in high school or at City College of San Francisco. But a bit of maturity and a commitment to a major area of study eventually provided the necessary direction. More often than not, the *will* and the *way* were integrated to make me a successful student, although not always a stellar one.

Michele's story is somewhat different:

Long before the concept of strategic learning permeated the literature, I understood the importance of approaching a new academic task with a logical plan. I did not necessarily know that I was following a plan of effective cognitive actions, but somehow I internalized the *art* of study such that, even then, my interest in the *science* of study was beginning to percolate. By all accounts, I was a highly successful student.

Years later, when I was trying to teach my students in the developmental education program at the University of Georgia how to prepare for essay tests, the platitudes found in test-taking guides did not seem to resonate with the students. Instead of persisting with what obviously wasn't working, I asked myself how I had undertaken the preparation for essay tests during my student years. Through reflection, I reconstructed my personal strategy for test preparation. My work led to the design of the now well-known PORPE strategy, comprising the steps Predict, Organize, Rehearse, Practice, and Evaluate.

In undertaking this activity, I engaged in what we might call the *art of study*. Many of the authors of the texts on the art of study from the early 1900s based the recommendations found in their texts on their observations of the work-study skills employed by successful students. I took the art of study one step further as my colleagues and I carefully reviewed current and historical theory and then undertook the research to validate the PORPE strategy. In other words, from the *science* of study, the field gained a successful strategy that students might employ in total or adapt as they prepared for essay tests.

Finally, Russ shares his story as follows:

> I have had many exceptional teachers throughout my educational tenure,
> but none as inspirational as Dr. Brian Kovacs. When I first met Brian, he
> seemed a bit quirky. And I call him "Brian" out of no disrespect. Dr. Kovacs
> insisted that we all call him Brian. He was mostly bald except for the
> sides of his head, which proudly displayed long, stringy hair. Brian looked
> the part of a young, absent-minded professor. I never would have guessed —
> at least by first impressions — that this humble educator would literally
> change my life. After his first lecture, something had changed within me.
> I could not wait for his second lecture. Never before had I experienced
> such a perfect match between student and teacher.
>
> Brian never lectured from notes. He simply walked into the room and
> began talking. I was on the edge of my seat. I was enthralled by his words,
> stories, and lessons. I took notes feverishly, trying never to miss a word.
> I soon learned that in order to pass his exams and write successful papers
> in his course, I had to condense what he was saying and find a way to or-
> ganize and analyze the major points he made. He expected us to elaborate
> and to defend our points of view on each essay topic. His exams were not
> only an assessment of our knowledge and critical thinking skills — they
> were also exams in endurance lasting for hours. We would fill three or four
> blue books for each exam, never feeling that we had written enough.
>
> What was different about Brian is that I had a sense he was preparing
> me for life. Through his exams and assignments, he taught me to read
> with a critical eye, to write and to support many different points of view,
> and to speak with confidence and conviction. Under his guidance, I felt
> for the very first time that I was truly learning to learn. After taking my
> first class with Brian, I changed my major to sociology. Never before had
> I loved learning so much. Actually, never before had I expected so much
> from myself.

Such experiences have helped to shape our careers. They have also
lead to a shared belief that learning to study, integrated with the act of
critical reading, is something that should not be left to chance. Students
deserve to have direct instruction in learning to be effective learners
from the earliest grade levels. Unfortunately, elementary and middle
school teachers tend to focus on isolated skills; high school and college
English teachers on narrative texts; and teachers in content fields on
content, to the exclusion of academic literacy skills. For these reasons,
we believe that it is imperative that postsecondary reading/learning
specialists be well versed in the theory, research, and best practices of
learning to study.

Goals of *Teaching Study Strategies in Developmental Education*

This text along with its companion volume, *Teaching Developmental
Reading: Historical, Theoretical, and Practical Background Readings*

(Stahl & Boylan, 2003), continues Bedford/St. Martin's commitment to the professional development of the professoriate and to the students in the fields of developmental education and learning assistance. It is the goal of this book to present the best practices in learning to learn as drawn from classic and contemporary theory and research.

The first chapter, "Historical Background on Study Strategies of the Twenty-First Century," examines past practice, theory, and research, and discusses its relationship to current trends. The second chapter, "Developmental Education and Learning Assistance Today," explores developmental education and learning assistance programs as constructs and discusses the needs of the student populations they serve. We delve deeper into the various populations served by these programs across the nation in Chapter 3, "Diverse Populations in the Classrooms." Chapter 4, "Students' Beliefs about Study Strategies," examines current psychological and sociological propositions and principles — self-regulation theory, epistemological beliefs, and metacognition — and explains how and why our students approach the activity of study in unique and personal ways. The fifth chapter, "Theory, Research, and Best Practices," evaluates different learning theories and strategies, including metacognitive awareness, self-regulated learning, the strategic reading heuristic PLAN (Predict, Locate, Add, Note), and the theory-based NORM strategy (Note taking, Organizing, Relating, Monitoring). Finally, Chapter 6, "Assessment and Evaluation," discusses the role that assessment plays in effective instruction and student learning: Articles cover traditional study strategy inventories, formative assessment, the Survey of Reading Strategies, learning portfolios and logs, and the importance of program evaluation.

Our goal in composing this text was to share with you a set of articles that we have found to be particularly helpful in our own professional development across the years. Reprinted from the *Learning Assistance Review*, the *Journal of College Reading and Learning*, the *Journal of Developmental Education*, and other journals, these articles have instructed and inspired us in our endeavors to make postsecondary education viable across the nation.

We urge you to join us in our continuing professional development not only by reading and responding to these articles, but by uniting with us and your other colleagues in one of the national organizations serving the fields of developmental education and learning assistance. We have found great personal and professional value through our membership in organizations such as the College Reading and Learning Association, the National Association for Developmental Education, and the National College Learning Center Association. (For a full list of recommended professional organizations and journals, see the Professional Resources section on page 409.)

Acknowledgments

We would like to take this opportunity to thank those instructors who reviewed our draft manuscript for *Teaching Study Strategies in Developmental Education*: Jeanne L. Higbee, University of Minnesota–Twin Cities; Irvin Peckham, Louisiana State University; and Jennifer Rockwood, University of Toledo. Their insights and advice were invaluable in the development of this book. At Bedford/St. Martin's, we would like to thank Joan E. Feinberg, president; Denise B. Wydra, editorial director; and Karen S. Henry, editor in chief, for their commitment to providing teachers with the best possible tools to better serve students across the nation. We are also grateful to Andrea Cava, publishing services manager, for her attention to detail and her organization throughout the project; Nick Murphy, editorial assistant, for managing the review and researching contributor biographies; and Stephanie Naudin, our developmental editor, for offering guidance, useful feedback, and skillful editing during all stages of development.

Russ Hodges
Michele L. Simpson
Norman A. Stahl

Contents

Isaac Watts
Of Study or Meditation   **3**

Reverend Isaac Watts's *The Improvement of the Mind* was first published in 1741. It could be referred to as the very first reading and learning strategy text. The chapter excerpted here covers 16 still-valuable recommendations for the act of studying.

Michele L. Simpson, Norman A. Stahl, and Michelle Anderson Francis
Reading and Learning Strategies: Recommendations for the Twenty-First Century   **12**

The now-classic article "Ten Recommendations from Research for Teaching High-Risk College Students" (1992) defined the best practices for the 1990s. The 10 recommendations found in this updated article provide a theory- and research-based foundation for best practices in the current reading and learning strategy program.

Norman A. Stahl and William A. Henk
Tracing the Roots of Textbook-Study Systems: An Extended Historical Perspective   **37**

A textbook-study system is a set of study strategies that have been integrated into a system designed to promote a unified approach to the act of reading and learning content materials. This article traces the development of the ubiquitous Survey Q3R from its progenitors across the first half of the twentieth century.

David R. Arendale
A Glossary of Developmental Education and Learning Assistance Terms   **47**

For a community of academic professionals to grow in the pursuit of new knowledge and the practice of quality instruction, it must speak a common language. David R. Arendale presents the common terminology that binds together the field of developmental education and learning assistance.

Jeanne L. Higbee

From the historical perspective the college reading and learning program has been saddled with the negative connotations associated with remedial education. This commentary shows convincingly that developmental education programs are so much more in the twenty-first century and that developmental education students are often mislabeled as remedial students.

Kathryn Bartle Angus and JoAnne Greenbaum

The College Reading and Learning Association (CRLA) adopted a position statement providing guidance for adult and postsecondary educators as they seek to improve the quality of education offered to all students in postsecondary education, whether they are classified as traditional, nontraditional, posttraditional, reentry adults, or stopouts/returning students. Adult students' rights in the areas of quality instructors, instruction, materials, and assessment are addressed.

Hunter R. Boylan

The cost and time investment of providing remedial courses to college students has been an issue in higher education for over a century. Criticisms of developmental education are examined and countered with evidence from research in this work. The author also outlines current practices and then describes alternative approaches, including freshmen seminars, supplemental instruction, learning communities and collaborative learning, paired courses, critical thinking instruction, and strategic learning courses.

David R. Arendale

The author first differentiates between collaborative learning, cooperative learning, and learning communities. His work reviews six postsecondary peer collaborative learning programs: (a) Accelerated Learning

Groups, (b) Emerging Scholars Program, (c) Peer-Led Team Learning, (d) Structured Learning Assistance, (e) Supplemental Instruction, and (f) Video-Based Supplemental Instruction. Each of the programs is placed into "Keimig's Hierarchy of Learning Improvement Programs" to assist educators in selecting programs to meet their institution's needs.

3 Diverse Populations in the Classroom 122

Ross B. MacDonald and Monica C. Bernardo
Reconceptualizing Diversity in Higher Education: Borderlands Research Program 123

The population of students served by learning enhancement programs grows more diverse each decade. Hence, programs should move beyond the models born of the open-door era and view diversity as a continually expanding dynamic of social power, personal perceptions, and judgments about others.

Donna McKusick and Irving Pressley McPhail
Walking the Talk: Using Learning-Centered Strategies to Close Performance Gaps 138

Faculty and staff at postsecondary institutions should understand that having a diverse population of students means that individuals will bring with them cognitive learning preferences that often differ according to a learner's culture. The authors share a set of five successful practices employed at a community college to close the achievement gap between African American and white students.

Kate Wilson
Note-Taking in the Academic Writing Process of Non-Native Speaker Students: Is It Important as a Process or a Product? 153

Note-taking has been studied extensively over the years with particular attention to the encoding hypothesis and the external storage hypothesis. However, the note-taking research with non-native speakers (NNS) has been limited. This qualitative study examines six NNS students' note-taking as they undertake an authentic writing task.

Shari Harrison
Creating a Successful Learning Environment for Postsecondary Students with Learning Disabilities: Policy and Practice 166

This article provides college learning specialists with suggestions for creating a responsive and diverse lifelong learning environment for all students, including those with learning disabilities.

Russ Hodges, De Sellers, and Carol W. Dochen

Learning framework courses integrate theory and practice from a diverse array of educational and psychological theories, and the courses are increasingly successful in helping students achieve academic goals and persist to graduation. The authors describe the evolution of such a course from 1973 through its current status using a four-component model: self-assessment, self-regulation, cognitive theories and strategies, and self-change. Also presented is a matrix of academic success courses offered at the nation's postsecondary institutions.

Noel Entwistle and Velda McCune

Although these instruments use similar formats and psychometric principles (Likert scales), they were developed for rather different purposes, derived from contrasting theoretical perspectives and labeled in differing ways.

Carol Boston

While state tests provide a snapshot of a student's performance on a given day under test conditions, formative assessment allows teachers to monitor and guide students' performance over time in multiple problem-solving situations.

Kouider Mokhtari and Ravi Sheorey

The article describes the development of the *Survey of Reading Strategies* (SORS), an instrument designed to measure adolescent and adult ESL students' metacognitive awareness and perceived use of reading strategies while reading academic materials such as textbooks.

Nannette Evans Commander and Marie Valeri-Gold

The Learning Portfolio is a method for students to participate in self-assessment, allowing them to demonstrate what they have learned about learning.

Mary P. Deming
**Learning Logs: A Vehicle for Student Learning and
Reflective Teaching**   378

Learning logs, in unique and intimate ways, assist teachers to monitor
their students' reading and writing processes, assess their students'
understanding of texts and strategies, and reveal their students' particular needs and interests.

Michele L. Simpson
**Program Evaluation Studies: Strategic Learning
Delivery Model Suggestions**   391

Although strategic learning delivery models such as study strategy
courses or paired courses are essential in assisting college freshmen
with their challenging academic tasks, very few program evaluation
studies have been conducted on their efficacy. The author focuses on
important questions that should be asked, instruments that might be
used, data analyses methods to be employed, and tips for collecting
data and writing reports.

Teaching Study Strategies in Developmental Education

Readings on Theory, Research, and Best Practice

1

Historical Background on Study Strategies of the Twenty-First Century

O ur understanding of the concept of study has evolved over the centuries. The modern terms *study, studying,* and *student* have a shared etymology tracing back to the Latin word *studium,* meaning zeal, affection, and study. *Studium* is in turn related to *studere,* which means to be zealous, seek to be helpful, and apply one's self. A careful review of the *Oxford English Dictionary Online* reveals no fewer than 24 definitions of the term *study* used as a noun and another 29 definitions of the word used as a verb. While there are definitions that touch upon affection/friendliness, occupational pursuit, the state of mental perplexity, the state of abstraction, mediation directed to the accomplishment of a purpose, or a place in a house or school, the definitions chosen by an instructor of a study strategies class or by a learning specialist in an academic assistance center would likely include:

1. The application of mind to the acquisition of learning; mental labor; reading and reflection directed to learning, literacy composition, invention, or the like;

2. The action of studying something specified or implied; mental effort in the acquisition of some kind of learning; attentive reading of a work or careful examination or observation of an object, a question, or other.

For both definitions the lexicographers for the *OED* trace the usage of the term to texts dating back to the 1300s. Still, the case can be made that it was not until the advent of Johannes Gutenberg's movable-type printing press, along with the release of the Gutenberg Bible in 1456, that the relationship of the act of reading and the act of study became truly linked. Then, during the next 50 years, a revolution occurred in the production of books: some 30,000 texts were printed, and the relationship of literacy to learning was solidified.

The question thus arose as to whether the two acts — reading and study — were one and the same. In one of the earliest texts on the art of study, B. A. Hinsdale (1900) proposed that both reading and studying are cognitive actions with initially similar actions, but they are also different by degree. Both actions attempt to obtain thought or meaning from the printed page. However, the individual who seeks to study a text directs greater attention to the act, processes the information more thoroughly, and strives to have a greater degree of recall or mastery of the content. In other words, successful study of a text leads to learning the material. Such is not necessarily the goal of reading. Furthermore, in Hinsdale's case, study was viewed to the exclusion of oral instruction or direct investigation.

During the past century, our understanding of the act of study, as well as instruction in the art of study, was to grow along with the curricular changes in higher education, such as the birth of the elective system in the 1920s and 1930s. The field moved beyond the traditional receptive mode of learning from the printed text to include other receptive activities, such as listening, and then observation. Expressive activities such as self-recitation, whether oral or written, began to be viewed as self-study activities within the next two decades. By the 1950s and during the subsequent 50 years, the systems approach, which can be traced back to scientific management theory, held sway. In the last 20 years of the twentieth century, there emerged a greater interest in strategic learning approaches, born of the cognitive revolution. Now we find the field moving toward approaches to study that evolve out of specific content fields, such as biology, history, and so forth. The concept of studying will evolve further in the years ahead as technology continues to have an ever-greater impact on the learning environment, and students are expected to have greater competency with the new literacies.

The terminology we have used to address the process of study has changed throughout the years as well: work skills, work-study skills, study skills, or study strategies. In some cases the labels have been used to specify new theoretical understandings, while in other cases the new terms simply became new labels for traditional activities. Ironically, in some cases the former simply devolved into the latter.

The point is that the field is dynamic. We do have greater cognitive understanding of the act of study than we had in the past. Furthermore, we have a greater understanding of and commitment to the diversity of students participating in the higher education experience, as well as the cognitive, ethnic, economic, and pedagogical variables that promote or hinder studying. We clearly understand that the act of studying in all its myriad forms is much more than the simple act of reading. Today we strive to understand the concepts of the *will* versus the *way*, the *process* versus the *product*, *surface* learning versus *deep structure* learning, the use of *strategies* versus *tactics*, and so on.

The articles in this chapter provide a foundation for the field based on theory, research, and best practices across the last years of the previous century and the first years of the twenty-first century. "Of Study or Meditation," by Isaac Watts, is a centuries-old text of important historical yet current value to teachers as it demonstrates that the field has a time-honored legacy. Michele Simpson, Norman Stahl, and Michelle Francis offer best practices for the twenty-first century. The work by Norm Stahl and William Henk presents a model for historical investigations of study systems that are sorely needed for our profession. Finally, every field has a register that allows the professionals within it to communicate with precision and meaning. The article by David Arendale provides a foundational glossary of terminology for those who serve students through the learning assistance and developmental education fields.

References

Hinsdale, B. A. (1900). *The art of study: A manual for teachers and students of the science and the art of teaching*. New York: American Book Co.

Of Study or Meditation

Isaac Watts

The Reverend Isaac Watts may best be known as the father of English hymnody, having written over 600 hymns, including "Joy to the World." Often overlooked, however, are his important contributions to the fields of reading and study including The Art of Reading and Writing English *(1721),* Logic, or the Right Use of Reason in the Enquiry after Truth *(1725), and* The Improvement of the Mind *(1741).* The Improvement of the Mind *went through 72 editions/printings before it was last issued in the United States in 1885. Now, with advances in technology, two versions of the 1837 edition are once again available. What follows is Watts's chapter titled "Of Study or Meditation," which covers sixteen recommendations for the act of study. While one must consider his recommendations within the historical context, one cannot help but postulate that many of the study strategy texts available in the twenty-first century have roots that can be traced back to* The Improvement of the Mind, *which might be called the first reading and study strategy book.*

I. It has been proved and established in some of the foregoing chapters, that neither our own observations, nor our reading the labours of the learned, nor the attendance on the best lectures of instruction, nor enjoying the brightest conversation, can ever make a man truly knowing and wise, without the labours of his own reason in surveying, examining, and judging concerning all subjects upon the best evidence he can acquire. A good genius, or sagacity of thought, a happy judgment, a capacious memory, and large opportunities of observation and converse, will do much of themselves towards the cultivation of the mind, where they are well improved; but where, to the advantage of learned lectures, living instructions, and well-chosen books, diligence and study are superadded, this man has all human aids concurring to raise him to a superior degree of wisdom and knowledge.

Under the preceding heads of discourse it has been already declared how our own meditation and reflection should examine, cultivate, and improve all other methods and advantages of enriching the understanding. What remains in this chapter is to give some further occasional hints how to employ our own thoughts, what sort of subjects we should meditate on, and in what manner we should regulate our studies, and how we may improve our judgment, so as in the most effectual and compendious way to attain such knowledge as may be most useful for every man in his circumstances of life, and particularly for those of the learned professions.

II. The first direction for youth is this, learn betimes to distinguish between words and things. Get clear and plain ideas of the things you are set to study. Do not content yourselves with mere words and names, lest your laboured improvements only amass a heap of unintelligible phrases, and you feed upon husks instead of kernels. This rule is of unknown use in every science.

But the greatest and most common danger is in the sacred science of theology, where settled terms and phrases have been pronounced divine and orthodox, which yet have had no meaning in them. The scholastic divinity would furnish us with numerous instances of this folly; and yet for many ages all truth and all heresy have been determined by such senseless tests, and by words without ideas: such Shibboleths as these have decided the secular fates of men: and bishopricks or burning, mitres or faggots, have been the rewards of different persons, according as they pronounced these consecrated syllables, or not pronounced them. To defend them was all piety, and pomp, and triumph; to despise them, or to doubt or to deny them, was torture and death. A thousand thank-offerings are due to that Providence which has delivered our age and our nation from these absurd iniquities! O that every specimen and shadow of this madness were banished from our schools and churches in every shape.

III. Let not young students apply themselves to search out deep, dark, and abstruse matters, far above their reach, or spend their labour in any peculiar subjects, for which they have not the advantages of necessary antecedent learning, or books, or observations. Let them not be too hasty to know things above their present powers, nor plunge their inquiries at once into the depths of knowledge, nor begin to study any science in the middle of it; this will confound rather than enlighten the understanding; such practices may happen to discourage and jade the mind by an attempt above its power; it may baulk the understanding, and create an aversion to future diligence, and perhaps by despair may forbid the pursuit of that subject for ever afterwards: as a limb overstrained by lifting a weight above its power, may never recover its former agility and vigour; or if it does, the man may be frighted from ever exerting its strength again.

IV. Nor yet let any student, on the other hand, fright himself at every turn with insurmountable difficulties nor imagine that the truth is wrapt up in impenetrable darkness. These are formidable spectres which the understanding raises sometimes to flatter its own laziness. Those things which in a remote and confused view seem very obscure and perplexed, may be approached by gentle and regular steps, and may then unfold and explain themselves at large to the eye. The hardest problems in geometry, and the most intricate schemes or diagrams, may be explicated and understood step by step: every great mathematician bears a constant witness to this observation.

V. In learning any new thing, there should be as little as possible first proposed to the mind at once, and that being understood and fully mastered, proceed then to the next adjoining part yet unknown. This is a slow, but safe and sure way to arrive at knowledge. If the mind apply itself at first to easier subjects, and thinks near akin to what is already known, and then advance to the more remote and knotty parts of knowledge by slow degrees, it would be able in this manner to cope with great difficulties, and prevail over them with amazing and happy success.

Mathon happened to dip into the two last chapters of a new book of geometry and mensuration; as soon as he saw it, and was frighted with the complicated diagrams, which he found there about the frustums of cones and pyramids, etc., and some deep demonstrations among conic sections; he shut the book again in despair, and imagined none but a Sir Isaac Newton was ever fit to read it. But his tutor happily persuaded him to begin the first pages about lines and angles; and he found such surprising pleasure in three weeks time in the victories he daily obtained, that at last he became one of the chief geometers of his age.

VI. Engage not the mind in the intense pursuit of too many things at once; especially such as have no relation to one another. This will be ready to distract the understanding, and hinder it from attaining perfection in any one subject of study. Such a practice gives a slight smattering of several sciences, without any solid and substantial knowledge of them, and without any real and valuable improvement: and though two or three sorts of study may be usefully carried on at once, to entertain the mind with variety, that it may not be overtired with one sort of thoughts, yet a multitude of subjects will too much distract the attention, and weaken the application of the mind to any one of them.

Where two or three sciences are pursued at the same time, if one of them be dry, abstracted, and unpleasant, as logic, metaphysics, law, languages let another be more entertaining and agreeable, to secure the mind from weariness, and aversion to study. Delight should be intermingled with labour as far as possible, to allure us to bear the fatigue of dry studies the better. Poetry, practical mathematics, history, etc. are generally esteemed entertaining studies, and may be happily used for this purpose. Thus while we relieve a dull and heavy hour by some alluring employments of the mind, our very diversions enrich our understandings, and our pleasure is turned into profit.

VII. In the pursuit of every valuable subject of knowledge, keep the end always in your eye, and be not diverted from it by every petty trifle you meet with in the way — Some persons have such a wandering genius that they are ready to pursue every incidental theme or occasional idea, till they have lost sight of their original subject. These are the men who, when they are engaged in conversation, prolong their story by dwelling on every incident, and swell their narrative with long parentheses, till they have lost their first designs; like a man who is sent in quest of some great treasure, but he steps aside to gather every flower he finds, or stands still to dig up every shining pebble he meets with in his way, till the treasure is forgotten and never found.

VIII. Exert your care, skill, and diligence, about every subject and every question, in a just proportion to the importance of it, together with the danger and bad consequences of ignorance or error therein. Many excellent advantages flow from this one direction.

1. This rule will teach you to be very careful in gaining some general and fundamental truth both in philosophy, in religion, and in human life; because they are of the highest moment, and conduct our thoughts with ease into a thousand inferior and particular propositions. Such is that great principle in natural philosophy — the doctrine of gravitation, or mutual tendency of all bodies towards each other, which Sir Isaac Newton has so well established, and from which he has drawn the solution of a multitude of appearances in the heavenly bodies as well as on earth.

Such is that golden principle of morality which our blessed Lord has given us — Do that to others which you think just and reasonable that others should do to you, which is almost sufficient in itself to solve all cases of conscience which relate to our neighbour.

Such are those principles in religion — that a rational creature is accountable to his Maker for all his actions — that the soul of man is immortal — that there is a future state of happiness and of misery depending on our behaviour in the present life, on which all our religious practices are built or supported.

We should be very curious in examining all propositions that pretend to this honour of being general principles: and we should not without just evidence admit into this rank mere matters of common fame, or commonly received opinions no, nor the general determinations of the learned, or the established articles of any church or nation, etc., for their are many learned presumptions, many synodical and national mistakes, many established falsehoods, as well as many vulgar errors, wherein multitudes of men have followed one another for whole ages almost blindfold. It is of great importance for every man to be careful that these general principles are just and true; for one error may lead us into thousands, which will naturally follow, if once a leading falsehood be admitted.

2. This rule will direct us to be more careful about practical points than mere speculations, since they are commonly of much greater use and consequence: therefore the speculation of algebra, the doctrine of infinites, and the quadrature of curves in mathematical learning, together with all the train of theorems in natural philosophy, should by no means intrench upon our studies of morality and virtue. Even in the science of divinity itself, the sublimest speculations of it are not of that worth and value, as the rules of duty towards God and towards men.

3. In matters of practice we should be most careful to fix our end right, and wisely determine the scope at which we aim, because that is to direct us in the choice and use of all the means to attain it. If our end be wrong, all our labour in the means will be vain, or perhaps so much the more pernicious as they are better suited to attain that mistaken end. If mere sensible pleasure, or human grandeur, or wealth, be our chief end, we shall choose means contrary to piety and virtue, and proceed apace towards real misery.

4. This rule will engage our best powers and deepest attention in the affairs of religion, and things that relate to a future world; for those propositions which extend only to the interest of the present life, are but of small importance when compared with those that have influence upon our everlasting concernments.

5. And even in the affairs of religion, if we walk by the conduct of this rule, we shall be much more laborious in our inquiries into the necessary and fundamental articles of faith and practice, than the lesser appendices of Christianity. The great doctrines of repentance towards God, faith in our Lord Jesus Christ, with love to men, and universal holiness, will employ our best and brightest hours and meditations, while the mint, anise, and cummin [sic], the gestures, and vestures, and fringes of religion, will be regarded no farther than they have a plain and evident connexion with faith and love, with holiness and peace.

6. This rule will make us solicitous not only to avoid such errors, whose influence will spread wide into the whole scheme of our own knowledge and practice, but such mistakes also whose influence would be yet more extensive and injurious to others as well as to ourselves: perhaps to many persons or many families, to a whole church, a town, a country, or a kingdom. Upon this account, persons who are called to instruct others, who are raised to any eminence either in church or state, ought to be careful in settling their principles in matters relating to the civil, the moral, or the religious life, lest a mistake of their should diffuse wide mischief, should draw along with it most pernicious consequences, and perhaps extend to following generations.

These are some of the advantages which arise from the eighth rule, viz. Pursue every inquiry and study in proportion to its real value and importance.

IX. Have a care lest some beloved notion, or some darling science, so far prevail over your mind as to give a sovereign tincture to all your other studies, and discolour all your ideas, like a person in the jaundice, who spreads a yellow scene with his eyes over all the objects which he meets. I have known a man of peculiar skill in music, and much devoted to that science, who found out a great resemblance of the Athanasian doctrine of the Trinity in every single note, and he thought it carried something of argument in it to prove that doctrine. I have read of another who accommodated the seven days of the first week of creation to seven notes of music, and the whole creation became harmonious.

Under this influence, derived from mathematical studies, some have been tempted to cast all their logical, their metaphysical, and their theological and moral learning into the method of mathematicians, and bring every thing relating to those abstracted, or those practical sciences, under theorems, problems, postulates, scholiums, corollaries, etc., whereas, the matter ought always to direct the method; for all subjects or matters of thought cannot be moulded or subdued to one form. Neither the rules for the conduct of the understanding, nor the doctrines nor duties of religion and virtue, can be exhibited naturally in figures and diagrams. Things are to be considered as they are in themselves; their natures are inflexible, and their natural relations unalterable; and, therefore, in order to conceive them aright, we must bring our understandings to things, and not pretend to bend and strain things to comport with our fancies and forms.

X. Suffer not any beloved study to prejudice your mind so far in favour of it as to despise all other learning. This is a fault of some little souls, who have got a smattering of astronomy, chemistry, metaphysics, history, etc. and for want of due acquaintance with other sciences make a scoff at them all in comparison of their favourite science. Their understandings are hereby cooped up in narrow bounds, so that they never look abroad into other provinces of the intellectual world, which are more beautiful, perhaps, and more fruitful than their own: if they would search a little into other sciences, they might not only find treasures of new knowledge, but might be furnished also with rich hints of thought, and glorious assistances to cultivate that very province to which they have confined themselves.

Here I would always give some grains of allowance to the sacred science of theology, which is incomparably superior to all the rest, as it teaches us the knowledge of God, and the way to his eternal favour. This is that noble study which is every man's duty, and every one who can be called a rational creature is capable of it.

This is that science which would truly enlarge the minds of men, were it studied with that freedom, that unbiassed love of truth, and that sacred charity which it teaches: and if it were not made, contrary to its own nature, the occasion of strife, faction, malignity, a narrow spirit, and unreasonable impositions on the mind and practice. Let this, therefore, stand always chief.

XI. Let every particular study have due and proper time assigned it, and let not a favourite science prevail with you to lay out such hours upon it, as ought to be employed upon the more necessary and more important affairs or studies of your profession. When you have, according to the best of your discretion, and according to the circumstances of your life, fixed proper hours for particular studies, endeavour to keep to those rules; not indeed with a superstitious preciseness, but with some good degrees of a regular constancy. Order and method in a course of study saves much time, and makes large improvements. — Such a fixation of certain hours will have a happy influence to secure you from trifling and wasting away your minutes in impertinence.

XII. Do not apply yourself to any one study at one time longer than the mind is capable of giving a close attention to it without weariness or wandering. Do not over fatigue the spirits at any time, lest the mind be seized with a lassitude, and thereby be tempted to nauseate and grow tired of a particular subject before you have finished it.

XIII. In the beginning of your application to any new subject, be not too uneasy under present difficulties that occur, nor too importunate and impatient for answers and solutions to any questions that arise. Perhaps a little more study, a little further acquaintance with the subject, a little time and experience, will solve those difficulties, untie the knot, and make your doubts vanish: especially if you are under the instruction of a tutor, he can inform you that your inquiries are perhaps too early and that you have not yet learned those principles upon which the solution of such a difficulty depends.

XIV. Do not expect to arrive at certainty in every subject which you pursue. There are a hundred things wherein we mortals in this dark and imperfect state must be content with probability, where our best light and reasonings will reach no further. We must balance arguments as justly as we can, and where we cannot find weight enough on either side to determine the scale with sovereign force and assurance, we must content ourselves perhaps with a small preponderation. This will give us a probably opinion, and those probabilities are sufficient for the daily determination of a thousand actions in human life, and many times even in matters of religion.

It is admirably well expressed by a late writer,

> When there is a great strength of argument set before us, if we will refuse to do what appears most fit for us, till every little objection is removed, we shall never take one wise resolution as long as we live.

Suppose I had been honestly and long searching what religion I should choose, and yet I could not find that the argument in defence of Christianity arose to complete certainty, but went only so far as to give me a probable evidence of the truth of it; though many difficulties still remained, yet I should think myself obliged to receive and practise that religion; for the God of nature and reason has bound us to assent and act according to the best evidence we have, even though it be not absolute and complete; and as he is our supreme judge, his abounding goodness and equity will approve and acquit the man whose conscience honestly and willingly seeks the best light, and obeys it as far as he can discover it.

But in matters of great importance in religion, let him join all due diligence with earnest and humble prayer for divine aid in his inquiries; such prayer and such diligence as eternal concerns require, and such as he may plead with courage before the judge of all.

XV. Endeavour to apply every speculative study, as far as possible, to some practical use, that both yourself and others may be the better for it. Inquiries even in natural philosophy should not be mere amusements, and much less in the affairs of religion. Researches into the springs of natural bodies and their motions should lead men to invent happy methods for the ease and convenience of human life; or at least they should be improved to awaken us to admire the wondrous wisdom and contrivance of God our creator in all the works of nature.

If we pursue mathematical speculations, they will inure us to attend closely to any subject, to seek and gain clear ideas, to distinguish truth from falsehood, to judge justly, and to argue strongly; and these studies do more directly furnish us with all the various rules of those useful arts of life, viz. measuring, building, sailing, etc.

Even our very inquiries and disputations about vacumm or space, and atoms, about incommensurable quantities, and infinite divisibility of matter, and eternal duration, which seem to be purely speculative, will shew us some good practical lessons, will lead us to see the weakness of our nature, and should teach us humility in arguing upon divine subjects and matters of sacred revelation. This should guard us against regarding any doctrine which is expressly and evidently revealed, though we cannot fully understand it. It is good sometimes to lose and bewilder ourselves in such studies for this very reason, and to attain this practical advantage this improvement in true modesty of spirit.

XVI. Though we should always be ready to change our sentiments of things upon just conviction of their falsehood, yet there is not the same necessity of changing our accustomed methods of reading or study and practice, even though we have not been led at first into the happiest method. Our thought may be true, though we may have hit upon an improper order of thinking. Truth does not always depend upon the most convenient method. There may be a certain form and order in which we have long accustomed ourselves to range our ideas and notions, which may be best for us now, though it was not originally best in itself. The inconveniences of changing may be much greater than the conveniences we could obtain by a new method.

As for instance, if a man in his younger days, has ranged all his sentiments in theology in the method of Ames's Medulla Theologiæ, or Bishop Usher's Body of Divinity, it may be much more natural and easy for him to continue to dispose all his further acquirements in the same order, though perhaps neither of those treatises are in themselves written in the most perfect method. So when we have long fixed our cases of shelves in a library, and ranged our books in any particular order, viz. according to their languages, or according to their subjects, or according to the alphabetical names of the authors we are perfectly well acquainted with the order in which they now stand, and we can find any particular book which we seek, or add a new book which we have purchased, with much greater ease than we can do in finer cases of shelves where the books were ranged in any different manner whatsoever; any different position of the volumes would be new and strange, and troublesome to us, and would not countervail the inconveniences of a change.

So if a man of forty years old has been taught to hold his pen awkwardly in his youth, and yet writes sufficiently well for all the purposes of his station, it is not worthwhile to teach him now the most accurate methods of handling that instrument; for this would create him more trouble without equal advantage, and perhaps he might never attain to write better after he has placed his fingers perfectly right with this new accuracy.

Reading and Learning Strategies: Recommendations for the Twenty-First Century

Michele L. Simpson, Norman A. Stahl, and Michelle Anderson Francis

The authors of this article present a set of 10 instructional and programmatic recommendations drawn from extant theory and research of the past decade for postsecondary reading and learning specialists. As their earlier work titled "Ten Recommendations from Research for Teaching High-Risk College Students" (1992) defined best practices for the 1990s, the following article provides a similar function for current practices. The 10 recommendations that follow cover the topics of programmatic models, strategy transfer and modifications, flexible use of cognitive processes, the influence of epistemologies on learning, the significance of analyzing academic tasks, approaches to vocabulary learning, procedures for mastering intertextuality, use of assessment and diagnostic procedures, the need for evaluation practices, and the importance of policy implications. This article provides an effective advance organizer for the articles that are presented throughout the rest of this book.

As the landscape of developmental education and academic assistance continues to shift, both politically and economically, time-honored professionals and those new to the field consistently search for practical ideas they know are embedded in sound theory and research. Although such ideas or recommendations provide many professionals a framework and rationale for their program development, instruction, and program evaluation endeavors, such recommendations are often difficult to unearth, especially for beginners who are less aware of professional organizations and scholarly journals. Over a decade ago we published an article, "Ten Recommendations from Research for Teaching High-Risk College Students," that was intended to address this issue (Stahl, Simpson, & Hayes, 1992). Given the promising research trends and best practices that have emerged since 1992, we knew it was important to update our original 10 recommendations. After reviewing the literature and discussing important trends with a variety of individuals, we identified 10 recommendations pertinent to the twenty-first century. In order to provide the most current and relevant research and theory, we decided to direct these recommendations toward instructors who, like ourselves, teach developmental reading and learning strategies courses. To capture that intent we refer to these individuals, our colleagues, as academic assistance professionals.

The first eight recommendations focus on what the extant theory and research suggest in terms of what should be taught and how. The last two recommendations focus on issues involved in successful programs. As we noted in that first article, these recommendations, though not comprehensive, are meant to provide a starting point for discussion and reflection. Moreover, the extensive references in this second article, as they were in the first, are an intentional effort to provide credible sources for future reading. If the original reference list captured the history of the field during the 1980s, this list will serve the same function for the last years of the twentieth and the first decade in the twenty-first century.

The Recommendations

Adopt a Programmatic Model That Emphasizes the
Cognitive Development of Students

In our first article we began by stressing the importance of adopting a cognitive-based philosophy that emphasizes the development of active learners who are in control of their learning. Even though a decade has passed and various models have been advocated (Farmer & Barham, 2001), this recommendation is still very important and needs to be revisited during these times of shifting philosophical boundaries and financially motivated cuts in programs. That is, a program that aligns itself exclusively to improving students standardized test scores tends to be more vulnerable to budget cuts by administrators who view remediation as superfluous and nonessential.

As pointed out by several different individuals, many academic assistance programs still define their delivery model and objectives around state-mandated reading tests (Bower, Caverly, Stahl, & Voge, 2003; Simpson, Hynd, Nist, & Burrell, 1997). Thus, these atheoretical programs emphasize, sometimes exclusively, goals that focus on reading skills that appear on these tests, skills such as drawing inferences, identifying main ideas, and understanding contextual clues. Students typically practice these skills in materials that decontextualize the reading experience to brief narrative or expository passages that are followed by multiple-choice questions, questions similar to the mandated exams (Nist & Holschuh, 2000b). It is acknowledged that such practice may lead to growth on tests while promoting a gatekeeping function, but it must be questioned whether these activities lead students to becoming active readers and learners.

Rather than emphasizing students' deficits, many academic assistance professionals have found it more advantageous to teach their students to become active, strategic learners. After three decades of research, the field has a rather definitive sense of the characteristics of strategic learners. These characteristics are embedded in theories and models authored by individuals such as Pressley (2000), Weinstein, Husman, and Dierking (2000), and Zimmerman (2000). What these theories share is the belief that reading and studying are dynamic and context-dependent tasks, and active learners have a command of the essential cognitive, metacognitive, and self-regulatory processes. These processes include selecting, summarizing, organizing, elaborating, monitoring, self-testing, reflecting, and evaluating (Nist & Simpson, 2000). When instructors adopt cognitive-based models for their reading and learning strategy courses, they teach their students a repertoire of techniques and strategies that embody these important processes (Alexander, 2004; Winne, 1997).

At first glance it might appear that this recommendation is a bit ethereal and impractical for the academic assistance professional facing hordes of students every semester. However, there are many advantages of having a cognitive-based model that both unifies and guides a program on a long-term basis. When a program has an encompassing conceptual framework or model, pedagogical choices such as what materials to buy, what activities to include, or what program evaluation instruments to use become much easier. Moreover, when there is a model that guides a program, the objectives become easier to identify and evaluate. In sum, a cognitive-based model can provide academic assistance professionals a program that generates credibility and support on almost any campus, whether it be with the students, other faculty members, or overly zealous administrators searching for ways to capture additional sources of money.

Emphasize Strategy Transfer and Modification across the Academic Disciplines

The main goal of any academic assistance program is for students to modify and apply the strategies and processes it teaches them to their own academic tasks. As Weinstein, Husman, and Dierking (2000) pointed out, "if transfer to other academic coursework and future learning tasks does not occur, these programs are of little value to the students or the institution" (p. 735). Yet, the research suggests that students do not automatically or immediately transfer strategies in a flexible manner (Boylan, 2002; Hadwin, Winne, Stockley, Nesbit, & Woszczyna, 2001; Simpson & Nist, 2000). Consequently, academic assistance professionals who are teaching their students how to annotate a textbook or create a map should not be surprised if their students are not using these strategies in their history or biology courses.

According to the extant literature, strategy transfer and modification can be facilitated if academic assistance professionals focus on four research-based principles. The first principle stresses that students will transfer a strategy to their tasks if they possess the "how to employ" or procedural knowledge of that strategy and the "why and when to use" or conditional knowledge. For example, with the preview strategy, students' procedural knowledge would help them understand the steps to previewing (e.g., I should read the headings and subheadings and the introduction) and how to modify those steps when they encounter different types of texts (e.g., if the text has no boldface headings, I could read the first sentence of each paragraph). Students' conditional knowledge of the preview strategy would help them understand why previewing is appropriate (e.g., it helps me see the big picture) and when they should use it (e.g., I should preview before I read or before I go to a lecture). Research studies have found that conditional knowledge is especially important to strategy transfer, especially if students are expected to abandon their usual approaches such as rereading and/or highlighting that are typically more comfortable and accessible (Hofer, Yu, & Pintrich, 1998; Weinstein, Husman, & Dierking, 2000; Winne, 1997).

The second principle states that students' strategy transfer takes a sustained amount of time to develop. In other words, students will not immediately embrace a new strategy and discard their time-honored approaches just because they heard a brief presentation on studying in college or completed a few workbook pages. As noted by Hadwin, et al. (2001), strategic learning is "enacted over time through a series of unfolding events" (p. 10). Hence, it is important to allow for that time and plan for recursive instruction (Alexander, 2004) by providing for multiple passes and scaffolding.

The third principle suggests that transfer can be enhanced if students receive explicit instruction. Explicit instruction is characterized by instructors modeling essential reading processes and providing students guided practice in texts that are authentic and represent the kinds of tasks they will encounter during their college career. As noted by Garner in 1990 and reaffirmed 10 years later by researchers such as Schunk and Ertmer (2000) and Pressley (2000), strategy instruction must be embedded within a disciplinary context and should never "occur in a vacuum" (p. 252). In addition, explicit instruction should provide students multiple opportunities for independent practice, prompt and specific feedback on their strategy attempts, and class time for strategy debriefing sessions. During those debriefing sessions students should pose their questions or concerns about a strategy and the instructor and other classmates should offer answers and possible solutions. To illustrate, during a debriefing session on the preview strategy students might ask: (a) Can you preview when your textbook has no boldface headings? (b) Does it take a long time to preview a text? or (c) Can you preview narrative text?

The fourth principle centers on the importance of teaching students how to reflect on and evaluate their performance and the strategies or approaches they used in selected learning environments (Campione, Shapiro, & Brown, 1995; Hubbard & Simpson, 2003; Zimmerman, 2000). Students who are taught how to reflect and evaluate are the ones more likely to use a strategy and modify it to fit their tasks (Simpson & Nist, 1997, 2002). The research also suggests that they will also perform better on exams (Hubbard & Simpson, 2003). One way instructors can encourage students to evaluate and reflect is to ask them to explain how they studied for an exam. For example, after each exam over a simulation unit, instructors could ask students, before they see their score and review the actual exam, to answer the following questions: (a) How long did you study? (b) When did you begin your studying? (c) How did you study? What techniques did you use? (d) What percentage do you predict you received on the exam? Why do you predict this percentage? After collecting the students' responses, the instructor could then analyze the trends and share them with the students, making sure to emphasize the strategies and plans of A and B students in contrast to the D and F students. The ultimate goal is for students to evaluate their performance in terms of their strategic actions or lack thereof rather than attributing their performance to luck, ability, or the professor.

In sum, this recommendation is dedicated to academic assistance professionals who have struggled with the challenges of encouraging their students to view the strategies they are taught as something productive and useful in their college career. Obviously, strategy transfer and modification are extremely complex and involve far more than good teaching.

Emphasize Students' Flexible Use of the Processes Embedded within a Strategy

The third recommendation addresses the tendency for academic assistance professionals to focus almost exclusively on a single set of strategies such as annotating, mapping, or SQ3R rather than the processes embedded in them. Moreover, many course evaluation procedures ask the students to report on a questionnaire or checklist whether they specifically employ mapping or annotating during their own reading and studying. If enough students check "yes," the tendency is to judge the instruction or unit successful. Conversely, if students report "no," the tendency is to feel that the unit was a failure. Often forgotten in this quest are the underlying processes embedded in these strategies. As noted earlier, these cognitive, metacognitive, and self-regulatory processes include selecting, summarizing, organizing, elaborating, monitoring, self-testing, reflecting, and evaluating. Ultimately, the goal or touchstone of any program is for students to develop a personal theory of these essential metacognitive processes in selecting and using strategies, in a flexible manner, with their own tasks and texts (Alexander, 2004; Boylan, 2002; Zimmerman, 2000). In other words, it is quite possible that students may not be choosing to annotate their own textbooks, but they could be selecting or summarizing when they read. This is more important than whether the students' maps look like the instructor's maps or whether the students report that they are annotating when they read and study.

These cognitive, metacognitive, and self-regulatory processes, often called deep-level processes, have been studied in a variety of ways and have been linked to students' academic performance. Pintrich and Garcia (1994) concluded from their large-scale study at the University of Michigan that students who were engaged in deeper levels of processing, such as elaboration and organization, were more likely to do better in terms of grades on assignments or exams, as well as overall course grades. Hubbard and Simpson (2003) found in their qualitative case study of a history course that students who were reflecting on their performance and calibrating their strategies were the ones who received As and Bs on their exams and earned As and Bs for their course grades.

Students should not perceive the processes taught to them as fixed, inflexible entities that are represented in some sort of useless, time-intensive artifact. Hence, it is important to make sure that students understand the conditional knowledge of a strategy and the processes that are embedded in them. For example, when students annotate a text selection, they should understand that they are selecting, summarizing, organizing, and monitoring their understanding. Also implicit in this recommendation is that students need to decipher the academic tasks assigned them by their professors across the campus. For example, if a history class requires students to read several sources, understand how the viewpoints are alike and different, and forge their own generalizations, they will be involved in deep-level processes such as synthesizing and elaborating. If academic assistance professionals have done an exemplary job of teaching, these students would understand that they have a variety of strategy options that will help them synthesize and elaborate for this history course. That is, they could use charts, study sheets, or maps as they read and study because all of these activities are task appropriate.

It is important to remember that artifacts such as a map or chart are merely that: artifacts. They are merely a means to an end (Hart, 1967). The ultimate end is for students to have control of the cognitive, metacognitive, and self-regulatory processes essential to reading, studying, and learning.

Understand the Impact of Students' Beliefs about Reading and Learning on Their Performance in College

For our fourth recommendation we turn to an area that has been researched rather intensively during the past decade: students' epistemologies or belief systems. Based on the work of Perry (1970) and others, these personal theories include students' beliefs about the certainty of knowledge, the organization of knowledge, and the control of knowledge acquisition (Hofer, 2001; Hofer & Pintrich, 1997; Schommer & Walker, 1995). That is, it is not atypical for college freshmen to believe that learning should be easy, completed quickly (i.e., the night before in a cramming session) and should happen to them because of what others do for them (i.e., the professor did not teach me how to solve that problem). Hofer (2001) and others have indicated that students' theories or beliefs are an aspect of metacognition since the core definition of an epistemology is knowledge about knowledge and knowing. The extant literature also suggests that college students have formed their personal theories about reading and learning by the time they graduate from high school (Hofer & Pintrich, 1997; Schommer, 1994; Schommer-Atkins, 2002) and that these personal theories are context specific, varying across academic disciplines (Hofer & Pintrich, 1997).

The impact and relevance of students' personal belief systems is quite significant, especially for those academic assistance professionals hoping that their students will adopt more effective and efficient ways to read and study. First of all, students' beliefs are important because they serve as the filter through which they decipher and interpret their academic tasks (Nist & Simpson, 2000; Simpson & Nist, 2002; Thomas & Rohwer, 1986). For example, many college freshmen fail their first chemistry exam because their beliefs about learning have filtered and reinterpreted their task to be nothing more than memorizing formulas, a task definition rarely accurate for a college-level chemistry exam.

Second, it appears from the research literature that students' beliefs can influence other factors, such as their motivation, strategy use, and performance (Hofer, 2001; Schommer, 1994; Schommer-Atkins, 2002). Schommer (1994), for example, found significant relationships between certain scales on the epistemological questionnaire she developed and students' performance and motivation. Simpson and Nist (1997) found some intriguing trends concerning students' beliefs in two different case studies conducted in history courses. Successful students' (i.e., those who received As and Bs) theories about learning and their theories about what should be learned in history were very much different from those of the less-successful students (i.e., those who received Ds and Fs). The successful students seemed to believe that they were totally or partially responsible for their learning and knowledge acquisition and employed more task-appropriate and elaborative strategies. In contrast, the less-successful students viewed the professor as the person who not only controlled what they would learn but also whether they would learn; they also selected strategies that emphasized rote memorization.

Finally, some researchers have found that skilled and expert readers have beliefs about text that cause them to respond to and interpret texts in ways different from less-skilled readers. For example, when Wineburg (1998) examined novices' and experts' beliefs about history texts, he found that the experts in history have an "epistemology of text" that permitted them to understand the writer's point of view and detect the subtexts that less-skilled readers missed. Many students in academic assistance programs are from high schools or from academic tracks in secondary schools that did not require the same depth of understanding required in college. Hence, they will read and think as novices who do not perceive alternative perceptions stated explicitly and implicitly. Wineburg also determined what many academic assistance professionals already suspected: College students treat their texts as indisputable sources of information rather than ideas posited by a particular individual. In fact, many college students believe that what they read in textbooks is more trustworthy than primary-source documents (Britt & Aglinskas, 2002; Stahl & Hynd, 1994).

Hence, it is important for academic assistance professionals to be aware of students' beliefs or personal theories about reading and learning. Writing probes (e.g., What does it mean to read?) or case studies are excellent ways to delineate these beliefs and should be done on a routine basis if instructors hope to nudge their students' beliefs about reading, studying, and learning.

Understand the Academic Tasks Students Encounter during College and Teach Students How to Define These Tasks

Our fifth recommendation focuses on the critical role that academic tasks play in terms of students' strategic learning (Weinstein, Husman, & Dierking, 2000; Zimmerman, 2000). As noted earlier, contextualization of strategy instruction is the best approach to help students learn to employ the strategies and techniques study-skills classes teach (Alexander, 2004; Pressley, 2000). In order to embed instruction in a context, academic assistance professionals must know that context or the academic tasks required of their students. Due to its importance, we will examine the fifth recommendation in two different ways.

First, it is important that academic assistance professionals understand the academic tasks required of their students (Boylan, 2002). That is, what are the products that students must produce — tests, papers, projects — in those required core courses such as biology, history, or geography? Moreover, what are the processes embedded in those products; do students have to apply concepts to new situations or merely memorize facts? In order to assist students in transferring and modifying the processes taught to them, instructors must have a sense of what their students are encountering outside the reading or learning strategy classroom. Such knowledge is also motivating for students because they realize instructors know what is happening out there.

Experience suggests that the best ways to understand the academic tasks at an institution are to discuss these factors with other professors, observe their classes, and distribute questionnaires that ask professors to describe their courses and assignments (Burrell, Tao, Simpson, & Mendez-Burreuta, 1996). Then, armed with that information, instructors can make sure they are teaching students what they need and provide practices that reflect the curriculum. To illustrate, if an instructor learns from a psychology professor that she asks numerous multiple-choice questions that require students to apply concepts to new situations, then that instructor can teach students how to locate examples and to create their own examples. Such analyses, however, must be done on a regular and recurring manner since faculty members change, texts change, and standards change.

The second prong to this recommendation is that academic assistance professionals should teach their students how to decipher their own academic tasks. Students need to learn how to define the cognitive, metacognitive, and self-regulatory processes they will have to employ to complete the exams, papers, and projects required of them in classes like geography or biology. Stated another way, the goal is to teach students to be cue seekers who understand the language and metalanguage of the college curriculum. Interestingly, research suggests that students who are oblivious to the processes involved in their tasks or the actual products they must create are the ones who usually place themselves in academic jeopardy (Hofer, 2001; Simpson & Nist, 1997).

Although there are a variety of ways academic assistance professionals can help students decipher their academic tasks in their core courses, there are two that are especially powerful. First, instructors can teach students how to interpret a syllabus and how to interact with their professors during office hours. One way to facilitate these tasks is to provide students with a list of questions to tackle and answer. For example, with the syllabus activity, students would search for answers to the following questions: (a) How many pages are you required to read in a week? (b) What types of sources will you be reading (i.e., primary, multiple)? (c) What is the overlap between the lectures and assigned readings? (d) What is the exam format (essay, short answer, objective)? and (e) What is the level of thinking emphasized? Furthermore, students can be taught to develop hypothetical essay questions based on course objectives for later study. As more institutions require that syllabi be posted on departments' homepages, it becomes easier for academic assistance professionals to plan this type of activity.

Second, instructors can teach students, using taxonomy like that created by Bloom and his colleagues (Anderson & Krathwohl, 2000; Bloom, 1956) to analyze the test questions they encounter on exams so they can determine what strategies would be most appropriate. For example, if a student determines that it's necessary to understand the interrelationships between concepts in his biology course, then to map or chart is a good choice as a study strategy. Although there are a variety of ways to teach students this type of analysis, there are three that are particularly effective. Instructors can model the process using their own exams and copies of exams that faculty members share with them. Another way to approach this analysis is to encourage students to ask their professors for sample questions before an exam so they can analyze the questions as a way to guide their thinking and studying. Finally, instructors can insist that students see their professors during their office hours so they can go over exams they have previously taken in order to note questions and patterns in their errors (i.e., I seem to be missing questions that ask me to apply concepts in this sociology course).

In sum, it is important for academic assistance professionals to delineate the academic tasks that their students are being asked to complete in courses such as chemistry and history. Then instructors should teach their students how to understand those tasks so they can make appropriate and effective choices as to how they will read and study.

Adopt Research-Based Approaches to Vocabulary Learning

According to the International Reading Association's (IRA) recent survey of reading experts, ideas about vocabulary instruction are rarely published today because literacy professionals are just not submitting these types of articles. Ironically, the IRA described vocabulary learning as a hot issue, needing far more attention than it is getting (Cassidy & Cassidy, 2004). Although we discussed the importance of vocabulary instruction in our first article, we decided to update and revisit this recommendation because of the importance of vocabulary to students' reading comprehension and because of the way it continues to be taught (Nagy & Scott, 2000; Stahl, 1999).

Many programs still use lists or textbooks that emphasize the rote-level memorization of words (Simpson & Randall, 2000). That is, students learn the definitions to words and demonstrate their mastery on multiple choice or matching exams. The problem with such an approach is that students do not understand these words at a deep level, and hence, never incorporate them into their own speaking or writing tasks (Nagy & Scott, 2000; Stahl, 1999). In other words, students take the vocabulary test, leave the classroom, and forget the words. They are doing school but not expanding their vocabularies.

What would be a more research-based approach? The literature suggests that three principles are particularly important (Blachowicz & Fisher, 2000; Nagy & Scott, 2000; Stahl, 1999). First, instructors need to place an emphasis on both additive and generative approaches to building students' vocabulary knowledge. Additive approaches focus on building vocabulary knowledge through the formal study of words that instructors typically provide to their students. In the past, such an approach meant that students studied words presented to them in a list. However, the extant literature suggests that students learn new words more effectively when they are presented and discussed from a context (Stahl, 1999). That context might be a psychology chapter, an essay, or a magazine article that the students have been assigned to read and study. Moreover, the work of Haggard (1989) and others (e.g., Harmon,

2000) suggests that students' input in the process of selecting the words to study makes the vocabulary-building activities even more productive and engaging. Generative approaches, on the other hand, emphasize the importance of creating lifelong learners of words by teaching students certain techniques to unlock the meaning of words on an independent basis. These techniques typically include how to use the dictionary, how to decipher context clues, and how to employ prefixes, roots, or suffixes to break down long words such as "psychoneuroimmunology" (Brozo & Simpson, 2003; Stahl, 1999). Because each of these generative approaches has inherent advantages and disadvantages, it is wise to keep informed of the literature. For example, studies done by McKeown (1990) and Nist and Olejnik (1995) pointed out the many difficulties students encounter as they attempt to interpret a typical dictionary entry and use that information to build their word knowledge.

Second, instructors should place an emphasis on expressive language activities (Francis & Simpson, 2003; Nagy & Scott, 2000) during their class sessions. Long before students are asked to write about the words or are tested on the words, they should be given opportunities to experiment with the targeted words in low-risk situations. These low-risk sessions where students "try out" new words should help them learn the correct pronunciation of a targeted word, the appropriate definitions that fit the context, the syntactic rules that govern the use of the words, and all the nuances and connotations connected with the words. If instructors will frontload their vocabulary instruction in this manner, students will be more likely to use the words in their own communication tasks.

Third, instructors should emphasize cumulative evaluation activities that require active processing. With cumulative evaluation, students are held accountable for the words over a period of time, not just for one exam. Although it is impossible to identify a specific time frame for all students, the research literature suggests that word ownership is reinforced when students receive multiple exposures to targeted words in multiple contexts (Blachowicz & Fisher, 2000). With active processing, students are required to understand words beyond the rote, definitional level. For example, active processing might involve students in sensing interrelationships between words or generating novel contexts for a targeted word. Unfortunately, the typical matching and multiple-choice evaluation formats in commercial materials do not encourage active processing.

To circumvent this passivity and rote level learning, academic assistance professionals can create a variety of their own evaluation and reinforcement formats (Francis & Simpson, 2003). One evaluation format that is relatively easy to create and involves students in writing and critical thinking is the paired word question format (Beck, Perfetti, & McKeown, 1982). For example, if the targeted vocabulary words for a unit included *glutton* and *obese*, the instructor could write an item similar to this one: Would a glutton be obese? Why or why not? To answer this question, students would definitely need to know the words beyond a rote definitional level, especially if they were to answer the "why" question satisfactorily.

Simply teaching students words is not enough to stimulate true vocabulary growth. Rather, instructors must be cognizant of principles important to vocabulary instruction and make sure they are incorporated into their plans and units.

Teach Students How to Read and Think about Multiple Sources

Our seventh recommendation is an acknowledgment that today's college students are routinely assigned to read and learn from a variety of texts that challenge the traditional single textbook paradigm (Pugh, Pawan, & Antommarchi, 2000; Wade & Moje, 2000). Perhaps the most challenging academic tasks college students will encounter will be the ones that require them to interpret and synthesize from a variety of primary and secondary sources, especially when those sources offer conflicting information or philosophical interpretations (Britt & Aglinskas, 2002; Stahl, Hynd, Glynn, & Carr, 1995). One example is of a history professor who asks his freshmen to read diary entries, newspaper articles, and essays so they can compare and contrast the opinions and perspectives in these sources with their textbook. Another is of a different history professor who, disgruntled with the overly simplified and biased viewpoints presented in most textbooks, has chosen to use only primary sources with his students. These tasks would be daunting for even the most seasoned consumer of either narrative or expository text. However, the students in reading and learning strategy courses are far less accustomed to reading in order to learn content-area concepts, especially first semester freshmen (Campbell, Voelkl, & Donahue, 1997; Wade & Moje, 2000).

Interestingly, most college reading or study strategy textbooks/ workbooks focus on techniques to help students deal with the single textbook as if their geography, history, and literature professors used only these materials to introduce and reinforce concepts. Therefore, if academic assistance professionals want to help students read and think about multiple sources with multiple perspectives, they will likely need to independently create these lessons and units. The first step in this endeavor is to identify interest-provoking primary sources that contain differing perspectives. Such materials organized around a thematic unit such as the environment should assist students in discerning differences across the authors, in noting omissions, and in detecting the voices of the various authors (Britt & Aglinskas, 2002; Hynd, 1999). Of course, merely providing students multiple paper and digital sources on an issue, such as the environment, will not guarantee that they will begin to think critically about what they are reading. Academic assistance professionals will need to provide modeling and guided practice for students tackling the materials from a thematic unit (Beck, McKeown, Hamilton, & Kucan, 1997).

A second way to assist students in coping with multiple sources and multiple perspectives is to teach them the processes that experts use when they read and think about complex ideas. Wineburg (1998) has researched this topic extensively and has identified three essential thinking processes that experts use when they read challenging text: corroboration, sourcing, and contextualization. The first thinking process, corroboration, involves students in comparing and contrasting texts with one another. To assist students in their corroboration, academic assistance professionals could teach their students how to create and use organizing strategies such as charts or synthesis journals (Burrell & McAlexander, 1998). The synthesis journal provides students a spatial format that helps them compare and contrast differing texts, whether oral or written. Students begin by summarizing the viewpoints and statements of authors they have read. Once students have completed this first step, they then write, in another designated part of the formatted page, their own viewpoints and ideas, as well as those of their classmates and instructor. Finally, in the center of the spatially formatted page, students are asked to create an overall generalization that summarizes and synthesizes everything they have read and discussed. Randall (1996) used a modification of the idea with a unit on the wilderness and environment and found that her struggling readers improved their abilities to paraphrase, summarize, and organize. As a result, the research papers they produced were far superior to what her students had produced previously.

The second process, sourcing, requires students to analyze the sources and to consider how the possible bias of the source might affect the document. Academic assistance professionals could help students analyze primary sources by providing them a list of questions they should ask themselves at the text and chapter level. These questions could include the following: (a) Who is the author and what are his or her qualifications? (b) Are these credentials sufficient to discuss the content presented in the source? (c) Can this information be verified by another source? (d) Is the author's motivation for writing clear to you? Additional questions similar to these can be located in the extant literature (e.g., Paul & Elder, 2003).

The third process, contextualization, asks students to situate a text in a temporal and spatial context in order to determine how time and place may have had an impact on what the writer said about the topic. For example, an author writing about Vietnam in a magazine published in the 1960s would seemingly have a different perspective from another author writing in the 1980s. Instructors could help their students contextualize what they read by encouraging them to use several simple techniques. One such simple technique is to encourage students to read the introductions or descriptions of authors in edited books or journals. We mention this simple technique knowing that many of our students overlook and skip this information, hoping to save reading time. Another effective technique would be to teach students a series of questions that they should ask themselves as they read. For example, students could be encouraged to ask themselves the following: (a) When was this article written? (b) What do I know about this time period? and (c) What did the majority of people in this time period believe about this topic? These questions, as with the sourcing questions, encourage students to read actively and critically.

Overall, students need numerous experiences with multiple sources as well as guidance in the questioning and evaluating of such sources. By modeling and teaching appropriate thinking processes, students become prepared for the twenty-first century where the single textbook paradigm is gradually being overshadowed by an intertextual academic environment drawing upon both traditional text and technology.

Use a Variety of Valid Assessment and Diagnostic Procedures

Our eighth recommendation addresses the importance of using a variety of valid procedures that will enable instructors to learn more about their students and to plan instruction accordingly. These procedures, often described as process-oriented approaches, also assist students in knowing more about their strengths and needs (Flippo & Schumm, 2000). Process-oriented procedures are identifiable by several characteristics. Most importantly, they are group-oriented, ongoing activities that seamlessly fit into instructors' lessons and units. As such, they are very similar to the Classroom Assessment Techniques described by Angelo and Cross (1991) and the classroom-embedded performance assessment described by Valencia and Wixson (2000) in that they provide instructors critical information to guide their teaching. Unlike product measures that produce grade equivalents or stanine scores, process-oriented procedures describe students in ways that facilitate instructional planning. That is, a low grade-equivalent score may inform the instructor that a student has comprehension difficulties, but a process-oriented procedure provides diagnostic details suggesting, for example, that the student may have comprehension difficulties because he has difficulties concentrating and identifying key ideas.

Another important characteristic of process-oriented procedures is that they mirror the academic tasks that students must tackle in college (Flippo & Schumm, 2000). Because these procedures focus on the cognitive, metacognitive, and self-regulatory processes involved in active learning and the beliefs and attitudes that students bring to their academic tasks at the college level, they typically have more construct validity than standardized tests. As Perry (1959) pointed out over 40 years ago, "The possession of excellent reading skills as evidenced on conventional reading tests is not a guarantee that a student knows how to read long assignments meaningfully" (p. 199).

Instructors should compile a collection of formal and informal assessment procedures rather than rely on one procedure or measure (Boylan, 2002; Flippo & Schumm, 2000). Although there is not a plethora of formal, published instruments that are process-oriented, the *LASSI* (Weinstein, Schulte, & Palmer, 2000) is certainly a worthy addition to any program. Academic assistance professionals can also gather a significant amount of data from informal measures that involve students in writing and self-report activities, whether through traditional pen and paper methods or technology enhanced formats (e.g., Blackboard). Writing activities could include autobiographical sketches that students complete at the beginning of the semester and ongoing journal entries that require students to monitor, synthesize, and reflect upon their reading and studying (Commander & Smith, 1996; El-Hindi, 2003; Quinn, 2003; Solder, 1998–1999). Another option is to use checklists or rubrics as a way to delineate students' strengths and specific areas of need. For example, checklists that focus on students' actual lecture notes or textbook annotations provide instructors considerable diagnostic information as to their abilities to note key ideas or sense the relationships between key concepts. Of course, when students analyze their own strategies or those of their classmates, they, too, learn from these process-oriented assessments.

In addition, many academic assistance professionals have historically and routinely found case studies or scenarios to be useful, especially if they are given throughout the semester (Nist & Holschuh, 2000a). At the beginning of the semester a reading instructor could ask students to solve a scenario or problem describing a typical college student. After reading and noting patterns in the students' answers, the instructor could plan lessons accordingly. For example, it is not atypical for students to recommend to Jason, a character in one of the scenarios, that he should recopy his class notes as the best way to study for an exam. Such a recommendation, of course, is counter to what research has indicated and to what most instructors emphasize in their courses. At the end of the semester the students could then revisit the same scenario, writing again their solutions but without looking back at what they wrote earlier. Students are always amazed at how much they have learned during the semester and how much they have changed in their strategic understanding of the problem.

Scenarios are also incredibly useful diagnostic activities when used in a discussion format whether in the classroom or through a computer-based system such as Blackboard. In order to engage students in thinking about the processes embedded in strategic learning, instructors could assign students to solve a scenario and come to class prepared to discuss their answers. Once the discussion ebbs, students could then write an addendum on what they learned from their classmates and hand in their papers. Instructors who read their students' solutions and online discussions are able to identify their misconceptions and the principles of strategic learning that they did not teach effectively.

The extant literature suggests that effective assessment and diagnosis will involve instructors and students in a variety of process-oriented procedures. Unlike standardized tests that generate static pieces of data, these process-oriented procedures promote dynamic classroom activities that are utilitarian.

Conduct Valid and Reliable Program Evaluation Studies

Frank Christ (1985) noted several years ago that "any activity worth doing should be evaluated" (p. 3). Hence, our ninth recommendation addresses the characteristics of effective program evaluation endeavors. Program evaluation differs from assessment activities in that the former seeks to describe the overall impact of a program or intervention, such as a required reading strategy course for at-risk freshmen or a summer elective or bridge program for incoming freshmen.

As noted by Boylan and Bonham (2003) and other individuals (e.g., O'Hear & McDonald, 1995), there is a shortage of quality programmatic research on academic assistance programs and courses. The studies that do exist have generally suffered from a series of fatal flaws (Boylan, Bliss, & Bonham, 1997; Koski & Levin, 1998; O'Hear & MacDonald, 1995). More specifically, many program evaluation studies have not been grounded in theory, have not analyzed students' academic performance using a constellation of dependent variables, and have not examined the critical questions addressing students' transfer and modification of the strategies to their own academic tasks.

According to the extant literature, valid and reliable studies have many characteristics, but we will focus on four of these. First, these studies use instruments that help answer the why questions about programs, courses, and interventions (Simpson, 2002). As noted by Boylan (2002), Weinstein (1994) and others, one of the most common why questions focuses on students' growth or change over a period of time and the factors that may have influenced that growth or change. In contrast, the what questions tend to examine products or results such as students' course grades, their retention in courses and in the institution, their scores on a standardized exam, or their grade point averages.

Second, effective program evaluation studies use a combination of theory-based qualitative and quantitative measures, not just the latter (Boylan, Bonham, White, & George, 2000; O'Hear & MacDonald, 1995). Quantitative measures (e.g., standardized reading tests, published questionnaires) have historically been favored over qualitative measures (e.g., open-ended questionnaires, focus group sessions, individual interviews) because of the much-publicized limitations of self-report data (Merriam, 1998; Pajares, 1992). What is often forgotten in these criticisms of qualitative measures is that quantitatively oriented measures are equally suspect because they can be narrow in scope, unreliable, or invalid. These particular limitations are typically present because of the ways in which quantitative instruments, such as standardized reading tests, are conceived, written, and piloted. Consequently, it makes more sense to use a combination of qualitative and quantitative instruments so the data from one can be used to triangulate and provide additional substantiation for the data gleaned from the other. Moreover, multiple sources of data enhance the internal validity and reliability of any research finding (Merriam, 1998).

Third, effective program evaluation studies should assess the perceptions of the students, the major stakeholders in this venture (Bradley, Kish, Krudwig, Williams, & Wooden, 2002; Maxwell, 1997). Students have unique insights into the academic challenges they face which academic assistance professionals often cannot fully understand. When students are asked questions about courses or delivery models, they can provide important data on what worked, and what needs to be improved and why. These types of data are particularly important to formative evaluation efforts and to the reports that must be crafted for administrators who are in charge of monies and budgets. Such questioning of students, the stakeholders, is also a task required by many accreditation agencies.

Fourth, these program evaluation studies need to be conducted over a sustained period of time. As noted by numerous researchers (e.g., Boylan, et al., 2000; Elifson, Pounds, & Stone, 1995) and professional organizations (e.g., the American Association of Higher Education, 1992), instructors and administrators should have a long-term plan for evaluating their services and programs. When studies are longitudinal and replicated over time, the internal reliability of the findings will be strengthened. Equally important is to follow the students who use academic assistance services over a period of time (Simpson, 2002). Admittedly, this is an intimidating task given the difficulty in locating former students and encouraging them to participate in a study. Randall (2002), however, was able to overcome these obstacles, conducting a noteworthy study that collected qualitative and quantitative data from 64 students who had taken a learning strategies course. At the time that Randall met with the students, they had taken three semesters of course work since their enrollment in the learning strategies course. Obviously, a longer period of time would have been ideal (i.e., 2 years later), but the data Randall collected from these students became extremely useful in a formative and summative manner for that academic assistance program.

Very few program evaluation studies have incorporated all these four characteristics, but a study by Weinstein and colleagues (Weinstein, Dierking, Husman, Roska, & Powdril, 1998) embraces, in an exemplary manner, the spirit of effective program evaluation research.

This study was grounded in self-regulation theory and was designed to collect data over a 5-year period of time. The researchers used a variety of methods and instruments to evaluate the impact of a learning to learn course at the University of Texas over a period of time. Specifically, in terms of instruments they administered the *Nelson-Denny Reading Test* (Brown, Fishco, & Hanna, 1993) and the *LASSI* (Weinstein, Schulte, & Palmer, 2000) in a pretest/posttest condition, finding that the students in the course gained significantly. They also collected data that examined the issue of far transfer, using the students' GPA and retention rate. Their findings indicated that 55% of the general student body graduated from Texas after 5 years. In contrast, 71% of the students enrolled in their course, students with lower *SAT* verbal scores and lower motivation scores on the *LASSI*, graduated after 5 years.

Given the current political climate, the need for quality program evaluation studies is becoming even more critical. Hopefully, the four characteristics we have outlined will guide administrators and instructors as they design their studies.

Understand That Neither Research nor Pedagogy Can Be Divorced from Policy

Our final recommendation focuses on the need for academic assistance professionals to understand the role that policy has had on our programs and to be proactive as additional policies are proposed and debated. Policy decisions at the federal, state, or local levels have influenced financial support for students and programs, requirements for assessment and evaluation, and mandates for academic standards and rigorous curriculums. Unlike the other nine research-based recommendations, this tenth recommendation has been forged from both experience and observations born of a long-term perspective on the field of academic assistance.

For many years policy was built on the premise that postsecondary educators would do what was best for the student and hence, for the taxpayer. However, in the past decade there has emerged from state legislators up through the federal government a form of accountability that acknowledges the value of accessibility to higher education but also focuses on achievement, retention, and fiscal responsibility. As Mark G. Yudof, Chancellor at the University of Texas, notes, "The wave has already come over the public schools, and now it's coming over higher education. Either you help to shape this accountability revolution so it's done in an intelligent way, or you're going to get run over" (Burd, 2003, p. A-19). In many states the academic assistance programs have been precariously riding the crest of this wave, and it is likely to wash over the entire field of postsecondary education in the foreseeable future. That is, the field is likely to see support for forms of access coupled with greater demands for retention and graduation, but not coupled to new allocations of resources. College reading and learning strategies programs will be adopting outcome-based programming as never before. Although standardized test driven, skills-oriented programs may be able to demonstrate a form of immediate accountability, we question whether such a pedagogical orientation will actually lead to positive outcomes related to long-term retention and completion of degree objectives.

Educators at all levels know that policy and legislation should be formulated on sound theory, informed research, and best pedagogical practices (Ruth, 2003; Valencia & Wixson, 2000). However, complicating the issue is the fact that in too many cases academic assistance professionals have been the passive recipients of policy and legislation rather than the proactive players in shaping its design and practice. As such, the field has been left with being reactive rather than focusing on long-term strategic planning, dissemination of important qualitative and quantitative research, and publicizing evaluation findings on postsecondary reading and learning instruction.

Influencing policy is not a simple process, particularly when legislators and policy makers believe that the field focuses only on postsecondary level remedial education as an offshoot of the failures in the K–12 schools. Unfortunately, academic assistance professionals have failed to address the policy concerns in two important ways. The importance of policy issues has been overlooked by professionals struggling with more immediate program issues such as scheduling and staffing courses, testing and teaching students, assessing programs, earning tenure and promotion, and participating in shared governance functions. Focusing on policy initiatives may not have always been feasible given time constraints or the reward structure in the academic system. Nevertheless, academic assistance professionals must become part of the policy arena by planning for such activities in state IRA councils and NADE chapters and by working with governmental outreach offices at institutions. The stakes are too high not to be involved.

Secondly, there is an issue of sophistication in conversing with policy makers. All too often when attempting to influence policy makers, a narrative story approach has been the main focus (e.g., "Let me tell you what is happening at our institution." or "Let me tell you about the story of Simon, one of our students."). Although such stories have the power to touch the heart, they do not demonstrate measurable and replicable findings. Individuals shaping policy and legislation, many with limited knowledge of educational research, program evaluation studies, or quality pedagogy, often define success through numerical measures such as test scores, graduation rates, and time to graduation. These quantitative measures fail to take into account the convoluted nature of the real world issues faced by developmental education students. Therefore, academic assistance personnel must be far more sophisticated in the understanding and conduct of research methodologies and equally sophisticated in the ability to explain to policymakers quality research and evaluation findings that employ varied approaches (see Duke & Mallette, 2004).

In order to tackle the demands of being informed and proactive and the need to effectively tell the story of the field, all academic assistance professionals should initiate and maintain a program of personal professional development. Never before in the history of the field have there been more opportunities to stay abreast of research, theory, and best practice through professional journals (e.g., *Journal of Developmental Education*, *Journal of College Reading and Learning*, *Learning Assistance Review*, *Research and Teaching in Developmental Education*, and *Journal of Adolescent and Adult Literacy*). In recent years, a number of scholarly texts and compendiums on the topic of college reading and learning instruction have been released (e.g., Flippo & Caverly, 2000; Maxwell, 1997; Stahl & Boylan, 2003). Academic assistance professionals also have a plethora of regional and national conferences to choose from, many with special interest group meetings (e.g., conferences sponsored by the College Reading and Learning Association, National Association of Developmental Education, National College Learning Center Association, Teaching Academic Survival Skills, and the National Center for Developmental Education). Given the challenges and external pressures faced by the field, there is little excuse not to expand our horizons and become research savvy, proactive professionals.

Conclusion

We ended "Ten Recommendations from Research for Teaching High-Risk College Students" (Stahl, Simpson, & Hayes, 1992) with the caution that the recommendations within that article did not cover all the pedagogical and professional knowledge required of a beginning academic assistance professional. We suggested that the article's content and extensive reference list provided a foundation for classroom practice and future exploration. Over a decade later, as we conclude this particular article, we are drawn back to the same conclusion. We believe that the current recommendations and references provide but a starting point for our new colleagues and a touchstone for the veterans committed to excellence in their students' strategic reading and learning. We also wish to urge our colleagues, those developmental educators who teach mathematics, ESL, and writing courses, to compile their list of research-based recommendations for the twenty-first century and submit them to professional conferences and journals such as this one.

References

Alexander, P. A. (2004). The development of expertise: The journey from acclimation to proficiency. *Educational Researcher, 32*(8), 10–14.

American Association of Higher Education. (1992). *Principles of good practice for assessing student learning.* Washington, DC: Author.

Anderson, L. W., & Krathwohl, D. R. (2000). *A taxonomy for learning, teaching, and assessing a revision of Bloom's taxonomy of educational objectives.* Boston: Allyn & Bacon.

Angelo, T. A., & Cross, K. P. (1991). *Classroom assessment techniques: A handbook for college teachers.* San Francisco: Jossey-Bass.

Beck, I., McKeown, M., Hamilton, B., & Kucan, L. (1997). *Questioning the author: An approach for enhancing students' engagement with texts.* Newark, DE: International Reading Association.

Beck, I., Perfetti, C. A., & McKeown, M. (1982). The effects of long-term vocabulary instruction on lexical access and reading comprehension. *Journal of Educational Psychology, 74*, 506–521.

Blachowicz, C. L., & Fisher, P. (2000). Vocabulary instruction. In M. Kamil, P. Mosenthal, P. D. Pearson, & R. Barr (Eds.), *Handbook of reading research, vol. III* (pp. 503–523). Mahwah, NJ: Lawrence Erlbaum.

Bloom, B. S. (1956). *Taxonomy of educational objectives, handbook I: Cognitive domain.* New York: Longmans, Green.

Bower, P., Caverly, D. C., Stahl, N., & Voge, D. J. (2003, October). *Making the transition from skills-based instruction to strategic-based instruction.* Paper presented at the annual meeting of the College Reading and Learning Association, Albuquerque, NM.

Boylan, H. R. (2002). *What works: Research-based best practices in developmental education.* Boone, NC: Continuous Quality Improvement Network and Appalachian State University National Center for Developmental Education.

Boylan, H. R., Bliss, L. B., & Bonham, B. S. (1997). Program components and their relationship to student performance. *Journal of Developmental Education, 20*(3): 2–8.

Boylan, H. R., & Bonham, B. S. (2003, October). *Criteria for program evaluation: Establishing the value of what we do.* Paper presented at the annual meeting of College Reading and Learning Association, Albuquerque, NM.

Boylan, H. R., Bonham, B. S., White, J. R., & George, A. P. (2000). Evaluation of college reading and study strategy programs. In R. Flippo and D. Caverly (Eds.), *Handbook of college reading and study strategy research* (pp. 365–401). Mahwah, NJ: Lawrence Erlbaum.

Bradley, C., Kish, K. A., Krudwig, A. M., Williams, T., & Wooden, O. S. (2002). Predicting faculty-student interaction. An analysis of new student expectations. *Journal of the Indiana University Student Personnel Association, 2*, 72–85.

Britt, M. A., & Aglinskas, D. (2002). Improving students' ability to identify and use source information. *Cognition and Instruction, 20*, 485–513.

Brown, J. L., Fishco, V. V., & Hanna, G. S. (1993). *Nelson-Denny reading test.* Itasca, IL: Riverside.

Brozo, W. G., & Simpson, M. L. (2003). *Readers, teachers, learners: Expanding literacy across the content areas* (4th ed). Upper Saddle River, NJ: Prentice-Hall.

Burd, S. (2003, July 11). Bush's next target. *The Chronicle of Higher Education, XlXI*(44), pp. A18–A20.

Burrell, K. I., & McAlexander, P. J. (1998). Ideas in practice: The synthesis journal. *Journal of Developmental Education, 22*(1), 20–22, 24, 26, 28, 30.

Burrell, K. I., Tao, L., Simpson, M. L., & Mendez-Burreuta, H. (1996). How do we know what we are preparing students for? A reality check of one university's academic literacy demands. *Research and Teaching in Developmental Education, 13*(2), 55–70.

Campbell, J. R., Voelkl, K., & Donahue, P. L. (1997). *Report in brief: NAEP 1996 trends in academic progress* (NCES Report 97986r). Washington, DC: National Center for Educational Statistics.

Campione, J. C., Shapiro, A. M., & Brown, A. L. (1995). Forms of transfer in a community of learners: Flexible learning and understanding. In A. McKeough, J. Lupart, & A. Marini (Eds.), *Teaching for transfer: Fostering generalization in learning* (pp. 35–68). Mahwah, NJ: Lawrence Erlbaum.

Cassidy, J., & Cassidy, D. (2004). What's hot, what's not for 2004. *Reading Today, 21*(3), 3.

Christ, F. (1985, July). *Managing learning assistance programs.* Symposium conducted at the Kellogg Institute for the Training and Certification of Developmental Educators, Boone, NC.

Commander, N. E., & Smith, B. D. (1996). Learning logs: A tool for cognitive monitoring. *Journal of Adolescent & Adult Literacy, 39*(6), 446–453.

Duke, N. K., & Mallette, M. H. (2004). *Literacy research methodologies.* New York: Guilford Press.

El-Hindi, A. E. (2003). Connecting reading and writing: College learners' metacognitive awareness. In N. Stahl & H. Boylan (Eds.), *Teaching developmental reading* (pp. 350–362). Boston: Bedford/St. Martin Press. (Reprinted from *Journal of Developmental Education, 21*(2), 10–12, 14, 16, & 18.)

Elifson, J. M., Pounds, M. L., & Stone, K. R. (1995). Planning for the assessment of developmental programs. *Journal of Developmental Education, 19*(1), 2–11.

Farmer, V. L., & Barham, N. A. (2001). *Selected models of developmental education in higher education.* Lanham, MD: University Press of America.

Flippo, R. F., & Caverly, D. C. (2000). *Handbook of college reading and study strategy research.* Mahwah, NJ: Lawrence Erlbaum.

Flippo, R. F., & Schumm, J. S. (2000). Reading tests. In R. Flippo and D. Caverly (Eds.), *Handbook of college reading and study strategy research* (pp. 403–472). Mahwah, NJ: Lawrence Erlbaum.

Francis, M. A., & Simpson, M. L. (2003). Using theory, our intuitions, and a research study to enhance our students' vocabulary knowledge. *Journal of Adolescent and Adult Literacy, 47*(1), 66–78.

Garner, R. (1990). *Metcognitive reading comprehension.* Mahwah, NJ: Lawrence Erlbaum.

Hadwin, A. F., Winne, P. H., Stockley, D. B., Nesbit, J. C., & Woszczyna, C. (2001). Context moderates students' self-reports about how they study. *Journal of Educational Psychology, 93*, 477–488.

Haggard, M. R. (1989). Instructional strategies for developing student interest in content area subjects. In D. Lapp, J. Flood, & N. Farnan (Eds.), *Content area reading and learning: Instructional strategies* (pp. 70–80). Englewood Cliffs, NJ: Prentice-Hall.

Harmon, J. M. (2000). Assessing and supporting independent word learning strategies of middle school students. *Journal of Adolescent and Adult Literacy, 43*(6), 518–527.

Hart, B. H. (1967). *Strategy*. London: Faber & Faber.

Hofer, B. K. (2001). Personal epistemology research: Implications for learning and teaching. *Journal of Educational Psychology Review, 13*, 353–382.

Hofer, B. K., & Pintrich, P. R. (1997). The development of epistemological theories: Beliefs about knowledge, knowing, and their relation to learning. *Review of Educational Research, 67*, 88–140.

Hofer, B. K., Yu, S. L., & Pintrich, P. R. (1998). Teaching college students to be self-regulated learners. In D. H. Shunk & B. J. Zimmerman (Eds.), *Self-regulated learning: From teaching to self-reflective practice* (pp. 57–85). New York: Guilford Press.

Hubbard, B., & Simpson, M. (2003). Developing self-regulated learners: Putting theory into practice. *Reading Research and Instruction, 42*(4), 62–89.

Hynd, C. R. (1999). Teaching students to think critically using multiple texts in history. *Journal of Adolescent and Adult Literacy, 42*(6), 428–436.

Koski, W., & Levin, N. (1998). *Replacing remediation with acceleration in higher education: Preliminary report in literature review and initial interviews.* Stanford, CA: National Center for Postsecondary Improvement.

Maxwell, M. (1997). *Improving student learning*. Clearwater, FL: H & H Publishing.

McKeown, M. G. (1990, April). *Making dictionary definitions more effective.* Paper presented at the annual meeting of the American Educational Research Association, Boston.

Merriam, S. (1998). *Qualitative research and case study applications in education*. San Francisco: Jossey-Bass.

Nagy, W. E., & Scott, J. (2000). Vocabulary processes. In M. Kamil, P. Mosenthal, P. D. Pearson, & R. Barr (Eds.), *Handbook of reading research, vol. III* (pp. 269–284). Mahwah, NJ: Lawrence Erlbaum.

Nist, S. L., & Holschuh, J. (2000a). *Active learning: Strategies for college success.* Boston: Allyn and Bacon.

Nist, S. L., & Holschuh, J. (2000b). Comprehension strategies at the college level. In R. Flippo and D. Caverly (Eds.), *Handbook of college reading and study strategy research* (pp. 75–104). Mahwah, NJ: Lawrence Erlbaum.

Nist, S. L., & Olejnik, S. (1995). The role of context and dictionary definitions in varying levels of word knowledge. *Reading Research Quarterly, 30*(2), 172–193.

Nist, S. L., & Simpson, M. L. (2000). College studying. In M. Kamil, P. Mosenthal, P. D. Pearson, & R. Barr (Eds.), *Handbook of reading research, vol. III* (pp. 645–666). Mahwah, NJ: Lawrence Erlbaum.

O'Hear, M. F., & MacDonald, R. B. (1995). A critical review of research in developmental education. *Journal of Developmental Education, 19*(2), 2–6.

Pajares, M. F. (1992). Teachers' beliefs and educational research: Cleaning up a messy construct. *Review of Educational Research, 62*, 307–332.

Paul, R., & Elder, L. (2003). Critical thinking: Teaching students how to study and learn (Part III). *Journal of Developmental Education, 26*(3), 36–37.

Perry, W. G. (1959). Students' use and misuse of reading skills. A report of the Harvard faculty. *Harvard Educational Review, 29*, 193–200.

Perry, W. G. (1970). *Forms of intellectual and ethical development in the college years.* New York: Holt, Rinehard, & Winston.

Pintrich, P., & Garcia, T. (1994). Self-regulated learning in college students: Knowledge, strategies, and motivation. In P. Pintrich, D. Brown, & C. Weinstein (Eds.), *Perspectives on student motivation, cognition, and learning: Essays in honor of W. J. McKeachie* (pp. 113–133). Hillsdale, NJ: Lawrence Erlbaum.

Pressley, M. (2000). What should comprehension instruction be the instruction of? In M. Kamil, P. Mosenthal, P. D. Pearson, & R. Barr (Eds.), *Handbook of reading research, vol. III* (pp. 545–561). Mahwah, NJ: Lawrence Erlbaum.

Pugh, S. L., Pawan, F., & Antommarchi, C. (2000). Academic literacy and the new college learner. In R. Flippo & D. Caverly (Eds.), *Handbook of college reading and study strategy research* (pp. 25–42). Mahwah, NJ: Lawrence Erlbaum.

Quinn, K. B. (2003). Teaching reading and writing as modes of learning in college: A glance at the past: A view to the future. In N. Stahl & H. Boylan (Eds.), *Teaching developmental reading* (pp. 331–349). Boston: Bedford/St. Martin's Press. (Reprinted from *Reading Research and Instruction, 34*(4), 295–314.)

Randall, S. (1996). Informative charts: A strategy for organizing students' research. *Journal of Adolescent and Adult Literacy, 39*(7), 536–542.

Randall, S. (2002). *An evaluation of an elective academic assistance course.* Unpublished doctoral dissertation, University of Georgia, Athens, GA.

Ruth, L. P. (2003). Who has the power? Policymaking in and politics in the English language arts. In J. Flood, D. Lapp, J. R. Squire, & J. M. Jensen (Eds.), *Handbook of Research on Teaching the English Language Arts* (pp. 87–113). Mahwah, NJ: Lawrence Erlbaum.

Schommer, M. (1994). Synthesizing epistemological belief research: Tentative understandings and provocative confusions. *Educational Psychology Review, 6,* 293–319.

Schommer, M., & Walker, K. (1995). Are epistemological beliefs similar across domains? *Journal of Educational Psychology, 87,* 424–432.

Schommer-Atkins, M. (2002, April). *Personal epistemology: Conflicts and consensus in an emerging area of inquiry.* Paper presented at the American Educational Research Association's Annual Meeting, New Orleans, LA.

Schunk, D. H., & Ertmer, P. A. (2000). Self-regulation and academic learning: Self-efficacy enhancing interventions. In M. Boekaerts., P. Pintrich, & M. Zeidner (Eds.), *Handbook of self-regulation* (pp. 631–649). San Diego: Academic Press.

Simpson, M. L. (2002). Program evaluation studies: Strategic learning delivery model suggestions. *Journal of Developmental Education, 26*(2), 2–10, 39.

Simpson, M. L., Hynd, C. R., Nist, S. L., & Burrell, K. (1997). College academic assistance programs and practices. *Educational Psychology Review, 9,* 39–87.

Simpson, M. L., & Nist, S. L. (1997). Perspectives on learning history: A case study. *Journal of Literacy Research, 29*(3), 363–395.

Simpson, M. L., & Nist, S. L. (2000). An update on strategic learning: It's more than textbook reading strategies. *Journal of Adolescent and Adult Literacy, 43*(6), 528–541.

Simpson, M. L., & Nist, S. L. (2002). Active reading at the college level. In C. Block & M. Pressley (Eds.), *Comprehension instruction: Research-based best practices* (365–379). New York: Guilford Press.

Simpson, M. L., & Randall, S. (2000). Vocabulary development at the college level. In R. Flippo & D. Caverly (Eds.), *Handbook of college reading and study strategy research* (pp. 43–73). Mahwah, NJ: Lawrence Erlbaum.

Solder, L. B. (1998–1999). Reflection and developmental readers: Facilitating metacognition with learning logs. *The Journal of College Literacy and Learning, 29*, 18–24.

Stahl, N. A., & Boylan, H. (2003). *Teaching developmental reading: Historical, theoretical, and practical background readings*. Boston: Bedford/St. Martin's Press.

Stahl, N. A., Simpson, M. L., & Hayes, C. G. (1992). Ten recommendations from research for teaching high-risk college students. *Journal of Developmental Education, 16*(1), 2–11.

Stahl, S. (1999). *Vocabulary development*. Cambridge, MA: Brookline Books.

Stahl, S., & Hynd, C. R. (1994, April). *Selecting historical documents: A study of student reasoning*. Paper presented at the American Educational Research Association, New Orleans, LA.

Stahl, S., Hynd, C. R., Glynn, S., & Carr, M. (1995). Beyond reading to learn: Developing content and disciplinary knowledge through texts. In P. Afflerbach, L. Baker, & D. Reinking (Eds.), *Developing engaged readers in home and school communities* (pp. 139–163). Hillsdale, NJ: Lawrence Erlbaum.

Thomas, J. W., & Rohwer, W. D. (1986). Academic studying. The role of learning strategies. *Educational Psychologist, 21*, 19–41.

Valencia, S. W., & Wixson, K. K. (2000). Policy-oriented research on literacy standards and assessment. In M. Kamil, P. Mosenthal, P. D. Pearson, & R. Barr (Eds.), *Handbook of reading research, vol. III* (pp. 609–627). Mahwah, NJ: Lawrence Erlbaum.

Wade, S., & Moje, E. (2000). The role of text in classroom learning. In M. Kamil, P. Mosenthal, P. D. Pearson, & R. Barr (Eds.), *Handbook of reading research, vol. III* (pp. 609–627). Mahwah, NJ: Lawrence Erlbaum.

Weinstein, C. E. (1994). Students at risk for academic failure: Learning to learn classes. In K. W. Prichard & R. M. Sawyer (Eds.), *Handbook of college teaching: Theory and applications* (pp. 375–385). Westport, CT: Greenwood Press.

Weinstein, C. E., Dierking, D., Husman, J., Roska, L., & Powdril, L. (1998). The impact of a course in strategic learning on the long-term retention of college students. In J. Higbee & P. Dwinell (Eds.), *Developmental education: Preparing successful students* (pp. 85–96). Columbia, SC: National Research Center for the First Year Experience and Students in Transition.

Weinstein, C. E., Husman, J., & Dierking, D. (2000). Self-regulation interventions with a focus on learning strategies. In M. Boekaerts, P. Pintrich, & M. Zeidner (Eds.), *Handbook of self-regulation* (pp. 727–747). San Diego: Academic Press.

Weinstein, C. E., Schulte, A. C., & Palmer, D. R. (2000). *The learning and study strategy inventory (LASSI)*. Clearwater, FL: H & H Publishing.

Wineburg, S. S. (1998). Reading Abraham Lincoln: An expert-expert study in the interpretation of historical texts. *Cognitive Science, 22*, 319–346.

Winne, P. H. (1997). Experimenting to bootstrap self-regulated learning. *Journal of Educational Psychology, 89*, 397–410.

Zimmerman, B. J. (2000). Attaining self-regulation: A social cognitive perspective. In M. Boekaerts, P. Pintrich, & M. Zeidner (Eds.), *Handbook of self-regulation* (pp. 13–39). San Diego: Academic Press.

Tracing the Roots of Textbook-Study Systems: An Extended Historical Perspective

Norman A. Stahl and William A. Henk

Students enrolled in study strategies classes have been instructed in how to use textbook-study systems for over a century now. A textbook-study system is a set of study strategies that have been integrated into a system designed to promote a unified approach to studying. The most widely known textbook-study system is the much emulated Survey Q3R attributed to Francis P. Robinson. "Tracing the Roots of Textbook-Study Systems: An Extended Historical Perspective," by Norman A. Stahl and William A. Henk, has achieved classic status in the field as it remains one of the few historical investigations in the field. The authors reviewed pre–World War II study strategy texts, theories underlying higher-level work skills, and the rationale for developing SQ3R.

S urveys of the curriculum and materials associated with college reading and study-skills programs consistently reveal that textbook-study systems represent a common instructional element (Bahe, 1970; Covington & Mountain, 1978; Entwistle, 1960; Fairbanks, 1974). Without question, the most widely advocated and emulated textbook-study system is SQ3R, a method attributed to Francis P. Robinson. Many historical and critical theoretical treatments of the technique mark its inception with the 1946 publication of Robinson's classic study-skills text, *Effective Study*. This assumption, however, precludes considering at least 20 years of textbook-study related history that preceded publication of the text (Kornhauser, 1924). A description of pertinent trends and events of this earlier period allows for a greater understanding of the psychological roots of SQ3R and helps explain why educators of Robinson's era were quite willing to embrace the method. And since SQ3R and its over 100 imitators enjoy regular usage (despite warnings of contemporary researchers who suggest that its rigid study regimen may stifle more flexible metacognitive learning strategies), it becomes increasingly important to include all pertinent sources of data in any prospective comprehensive assessment of the technique (refer to Stahl, 1983). For these reasons, this paper traces the evolution of SQ3R with the eventual goal of promoting more accurate critical analyses of this extremely popular method.

Influences on Robinson

While the maturing of college reading instruction in recent years is widely acknowledged, strides made prior to the 1950s in the research on reading and study skills, the publishing of instructional materials, and the development of theory go largely unnoticed. It is during this rich era between 1930 and 1945 that Robinson entered the field of college reading. In these early years of college study-skills programs, a number of pioneering studies at Ohio State University and other institutions reported the success of study-skills courses with probationary students (Behrens, 1935; Book, 1927; Ferguson, 1928; Pressey, 1928; Robinson, 1931). When Robinson joined the OSU staff in 1937, a respected how-to-study program already operated there under the direction of Sidney Pressey and Luella Cole Pressey. During this early stage of his career, Robinson was influenced by a study done by Sherburne (1938), one of the first attempts to involve both underachieving and successful students in a study-skills program. The study intrigued Robinson (1971) as it demonstrated that good and poor students alike could benefit from how-to-study training when compared to matched untrained controls.

To further test the merit of such a program, Robinson (1943) and his assistants provided study-skills instruction to soldiers from a U.S. army unit enrolled in an accelerated academic program at the university. Although these soldiers were highly intelligent and talented, assessments indicated that they did not exercise well-developed study habits. In fact, Robinson felt that past grades were obtained via native intelligence rather than by effective studying. Following training in various study skills, the troops made considerable improvement. Those completing instruction showed proportional gains in work rate (19%), comprehension (10%), notetaking (16%), and table reading (30%). Robinson inferred that students could benefit from study-skills instruction stressing higher-level work habits. The idea of nurturing higher-level work habits was not altogether new, but it began to draw the attention of educators in the early 1940s. In Robinson's case, this concept would become fully integrated with his views on college reading instruction.

Theoretical Basis for Higher-Level Work Skills

Although the formal SQ3R method evolved during the Second World War, its roots can be traced to the turn of the century. At that time, Frank and Lillian Gilbreth as well as Frederick Taylor and Henry Gantt conducted prototypical time and motion studies. These studies subsequently fostered the scientific-management approach. In short, the procedure employed task analysis, personnel assessment, pretask training, and job planning to ideally match work methods, workers, and specific tasks.

Robinson (1950) acknowledged that early work in scientific management formed the basic theoretical groundwork for SQ3R. Yet, it was ultimately Robert Seashore's work (1939) that prompted Robinson to design a higher-level study-skill system. Seashore felt the work method selected by a person (qualitative variations of reacting to a situation) was an additional variable to consider apart from traditional biological and prior training factors that influenced individual differences in human performance. Seashore suggested that a pupil might be unaware of the smaller steps of a work method because of the inclusive nature of the larger cognitive task. Moreover, to Seashore, the preliminary adoption of work methods could be discarded in favor of others, and the final work method could be refined by such processes as the overlapping of component parts and the development of "higher units." Seashore believed that work methods were important in determining individual differences in sensory, affective, intellectual, and motor activities. He warned that simply to control the amount of training for a particular task and attribute all other results to biological capacities was overlooking what is often the unknown factor, the work method. He emphasized not so much "what you are born with," as "what you do with it" (p. 126).

Drawing upon Seashore's ideas, Robinson began to design an optimum higher-level work method for textbook reading. To develop such a system, Robinson (1950) reported that

> ... the best approach to designing higher-level adjustment skills is not a descriptive analysis of what any one group of people has done — a common experimental design in psychology. Rather it is a creative use of example, related research findings, suggestions, and theory to design possible skills. The efficiency of any such skills will then have to be evaluated: these results may in turn suggest other possible refinements. (p. 235)

While Seashore's essay provides the basic theoretical foundation for most of the textbook-study systems currently in use, many textbook-study system developers are probably unaware of the relationship Seashore's or Gilbreth's work bears to their own.

Relationship of Other Early Study Systems to SQ3R's Development

While Robinson surely used principles of extant theory to design SQ3R, there is some question whether he reviewed recommendations of major study-skills texts of the era to select the most effective techniques to include in the new higher-level study method. Authors of early study-skills texts tended to provide students with lists of generally accepted, and in some cases, research-supported study skills. The research conclusions were often based on interviews of students possessing effective study habits, while, in other instances, the authors drew inferences from published research.

One of the earliest respected study-skills texts for high school and college students (Whipple, 1927) contained lists of positive study habits and skills necessary for academic success. Interestingly, the chapters on reading and textbook study recommend each of the steps later included in SQ3R. The major difference between Whipple's recommendations and those of current text-study advocates is the rather disjointed approach of the former and the packaged approach of the latter.

Kornhauser's (1924) study-skills booklet, another example from the era, provides brief introductions followed by lists of effective study rules. While rules are spread over several chapters, a consolidation of major concepts shows that all the basic tenets of SQ3R are indeed present.

Sidney Pressey and Luella Cole Pressey also greatly influenced Robinson's work at OSU. The probable nature of this influence is revealed in the study-skills booklet that Cole coauthored with Ferguson (1935). Its recommendations were also given through extended lists of efficient study rules which stressed (a) surveying the material in detail, (b) attending to graphic and textual aids, and (c) reading carefully and then reciting to assess understanding. An outlining/note-taking procedure was also advocated whereby questions are formulated from main headings. Aside from the organized package and acronym later provided by Robinson, Cole and Ferguson might largely be credited with presenting SQ3R as we know it.

In one of the first textbook-study systems, Bird (1931) recommended the use of the "Self-Recitation Study Method." As with other texts and booklets of the period, the author stressed surveying to develop gist understandings and to plan strategies for further reading. Next, the learner was to read logical divisions of text to determine main points. These main points were then used to formulate questions whose answers summarized the content. Bird felt that headings should serve as prompts for question development until the student was familiar enough with the content to pose more analytical questions. Each question would be subsequently placed in a notebook followed by corresponding answers in outline form. Later, the student would recite the answer to each question and check for accuracy. A rapid rereading of the chapter was recommended to show the relationship of parts to the whole.

Robinson's first text (1941), *Diagnostic and Remedial Techniques for Effective Study*, indicates his familiarity with Bird's study-skills method. Not only did Robinson cite Bird's text, but when one notes the striking similarities in the systems themselves and in the research rationale underlying each, the familiarity is even more apparent. Yet, short of having access to Robinson's personal notes and library, it is difficult to determine what other early study systems directly influenced him. Nevertheless, it is clear that the basic steps of SQ3R had been presented prior to World War II and that others besides Robinson were contemplating systematic textbook-study procedures. Some might even argue that Robinson only gave the field a catchy acronym for a generally accepted set of existing textbook-study techniques. Indeed, some part of SQ3R's popularity may be due to the willingness of American educators to embrace acronyms after having lived through a depression and a world war replete with governmental and military abbreviations.

Robinson's Rationale for the Development of SQ3R

In the 1941 text, Robinson included diagnostic tests and programs for remediating problems with the traditional Three Rs and with social and personal aspects of college life. Nowhere in the text is SQ3R mentioned; however, practice was recommended with several future component steps. When stating that reading comprehension was fostered by vocabulary knowledge and efficient reading rates, as well as outlining, questioning, identifying main points, adjusting pace, and reciting, Robinson provided a hint of things to come (1941, p. 227). He also recommended active reading and reviewing of the text at regular intervals. As with all revised editions of this text, Robinson presented a research base for his recommendations, content typically not included in other study-skills texts of the era.

Further research support for SQ3R came from one of Robinson's master's degree students (McCormick, 1943). This researcher measured the effectiveness of combining reading to answer questions with self-recitation as a study method. While the study was somewhat flawed, it was of value because the training procedure was essentially the precursor of SQ3R. McCormick concluded that properly motivated students could learn work-study skills if given training of sufficient duration and intensity. A major value of the McCormick thesis, beyond its direct empirical support for SQ3R, was its transformation of the construct of a higher-level work-study method (merely assumed to be effective because of research supporting the individual steps) into an integrated system that collectively prompted students' reading comprehension and rate as well as their notetaking skills.

In 1946, *Effective Study*, a much revised version of Robinson's 1941 text, was published. This text formally introduced SQ3R as a higher-level study method. As previously noted, Robinson's interpretation of scientific-management theory led him to believe that a higher-level work-study method could be devised by integrating research-driven work methods. The practical application of his thinking was the logical organization of five distinct study activities, each including between two and seven explicitly identifiable substeps, into a total system of study. The rationale presented in this text along with evidence from the initial text and McCormick's (1943) thesis formed a foundation resting on respected literature of the era. Figure 1 on page 42 illustrates the empirical base Robinson drew from as support for SQ3R.

This body of research consists of 23 published reports from respected scholarly journals of the prewar era. It provides the greatest

Figure 1. Empirical Support for Robinson's SQ3R Method (1946)

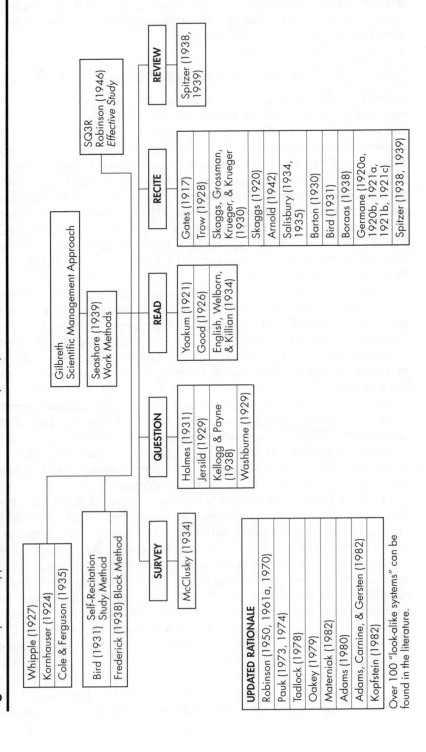

amount of support for the recitation step. This is to be expected since it involves many subroutines such as summarizing, outlining, and reciting. Less evidence is offered for the survey, question, and review steps. Interestingly, the support for active reading invokes a bit of reverse logic by noting activities considered counterproductive to the process.

Critical analyses of these studies using current standards of research quality reveal several regular faults in training issues, experimental design, statistical methodologies, and population generalizability (Graham, 1982; Stahl, 1983; Wark, 1964; Willmore, 1967). The problems identified by critics of the system should not necessarily be directed against the process which led to the product itself. After all, the overall pool of research pertaining to reading pedagogy was limited in the prewar period. Robinson and his assistants simply worked with the best available materials in the best way they knew how. And although problems existed with the initial research base, more recent theoretical papers and research reports update the construct of the system (Adams, 1980; Adams, Carnine, & Gersten, 1982; Kopfstein, 1982; Materniak, 1982; Okey, 1979; Pauk, 1973, 1974; Robinson, 1950, 1959, 1961, 1970; Tadlock, 1978).

From a historical perspective, the primary research base taken in total draws upon a credible process and promotes a subsequent product that is reasonably impressive. It is of limited significance, then, that the maturing research models and statistical processes of the latter twentieth century suggest a questioning of SQ3R's initial theoretical premises. Rather, the development of SQ3R served as a capstone for the foundation of research findings and pedagogical practices pertaining to college reading programs of the prewar era. Its popularity may then be viewed as the appropriate response by secondary and postsecondary reading specialists of the GI bill era given existing knowledge. The historical account of SQ3R demonstrates that although a strategy may seem thoroughly grounded in the finest theory and experimental research of its day, the years ahead may very well find it lacking. Simply stated, the future promises that any current construct will be evaluated against a progressively more sophisticated knowledge base. Just as SQ3R, a system predicated upon introspection and scientific management and work method theories, is apt to be questioned today from the existing theoretical base of cognitive science, so too may we expect current research-driven strategies (e.g., summarizing and mapping) to be reconsidered in light of new research or, as likely, paradigmatic shifts of the future.

References

Adams, A. (1980). The use of direct instruction to teach an independent study to skill deficient fifth grade students. *Dissertation Abstracts International, 41*, 1912A–1913A. (University Microfilms No. 90-24, 839)

Adams, A., Carnine, D., & Gersten, R. (1982). Instructional strategies for studying content area texts in the intermediate grades. *Reading Research Quar-
  terly, 18*(1), 27–55.
Arnold, H. F. (1942). The comparative effectiveness of certain study techniques
  in the field of history. *Journal of Educational Psychology, 33*, 449–457.
Babe, V. R. (1970). A content analysis of current college reading manuals. In
  G. B. Schick & M. M. May (Eds.), *Reading: Process and pedagogy*, Nineteenth
  Yearbook of the National Reading Conference (pp. 11–25). Milwaukee: Na-
  tional Reading Conference.
Barton, Jr., W. A. (1930). *Outlining as a study procedure* (Contributions to Edu-
  cation, No. 411). New York: Columbia University, Teachers College, Bureau
  of Publications.
Behrens, H. D. (1935). Effects of a how to study course. *Journal of Higher Edu-
  cation, 16*, 195–202.
Bird, C. (1931). *Effective study habits.* New York: Century.
Bird, C., & Bird, D. M. (1945). *Learning more by effective study.* New York:
  Appleton-Century.
Book, W. F. (1927). Results obtained in a special how to study course given to
  college students. *School and Society, 26*, 529–534.
Boraas, H. (1938). A comparative study of the brief, the precise and the essay
  with respect to speed of reading and ease of learning. *Journal of Educa-
  tional Psychology, 29*, 231–236.
Brown, C. W. (1941). The study habits of failing and successful students in the
  first two years of college. *Journal of Experimental Education, 9*, 205–208.
Cole, L., & Ferguson, J. M. (1935). *Student's guide to effective study* (rev. ed.).
  New York: Farrar & Rinehard.
Covington, H. C., & Mountain, L. (1978). The competencies that junior college
  chairpersons expect from their reading course graduates. In P. D. Pearson &
  J. Hansen (Eds.), *Reading: Disciplined language in process and practice*,
  Twenty-seventh Yearbook of the National Reading Conference (pp. 146–
  249). Clemson, SC: National Reading Conference.
English, H. B., Welborn, E. L., & Killian, C. D. (1934). Studies in substance
  memorization. *Journal of General Psychology, 11*, 233–260.
Entwistle, D. R. (1960). Evaluation of study skills courses. *Journal of Educational Research, 53*, 224–228.
Fairbanks, M. M. (1974). The effect of college reading improvement programs
  on academic achievement. In P. L. Nacke (Ed.), *Interaction: Research and
  practice for college-adult reading*, Twenty-third Yearbook of the National
  Reading Conference (pp. 105–114). Clemson, SC: National Reading Confer-
  ence.
Ferguson, J. M. (1928). Probation students under guidance. *Educational Re-
  view, 75*, 224–228.
Frederick, R. W. (1938). *How to study handbook.* New York: Appleton-Century.
Gates, A. I. (1917). Recitation as a factor in memorizing. In R. S. Woodworth
  (Ed.), *Archives of psychology* (No. 40, p. 114). New York: Science Press.
Germane, C. E. (1920a). The value of the controlled mental summary as a
  method of studying. *School and Society, 12*, 591–593.
Germane, C. E. (1920b). *The value of summarizing in silent reading.* Unpub-
  lished doctoral dissertation. State University of Iowa, Ames, IA.

Germane, C. E. (1921a). Outlining and summarizing compared with re-reading as methods of studying. In G. M. Whipple (Ed.). *20th Yearbook of the National Society for the Study of Education: Part II* (pp. 102–113). Bloomington, IL: Public School Publishing.

Germane, C. E. (1921b). The value of the corrected summary as compared with the re-reading of the same article. *Elementary School Journal, 21*, 461–464.

Germane, C. E. (192lc). The value of the written paragraph summary. *Journal of Educational Research, 3*, 116–123.

Good, C. V. (1926). The effect of a single reading versus two readings of a given body of material. *Journal of Educational Method, 5*, 325–329.

Graham, S. (1982). Comparing the SQ3R method with other study techniques for reading improvement. *Reading Improvement, 19*, 44–47.

Holmes, E. (1931). Reading guided by questions versus careful reading and re-reading without questions. *School Review, 39*, 361–371.

Jersild, A. T. (1929). Examination as an aid to learning. *Journal of Educational Psychology, 20*, 602–609.

Kellogg, W. N., & Payne, B. (1938). The true-false question as an aid to studying. *Journal of Educational Psychology, 29*, 581–589.

Kopfstein, R. W. (1982, April). *SQ3R doesn't work or does it?* Paper presented at the annual meeting of the Western College Reading Association, San Diego, CA. (ERIC Document Reproduction Service No. 216–327)

Kornhauser, A. W. (1924, 1937). *How to study: Suggestions for high-school and college students* (rev. ed.). Chicago: University of Chicago Press.

Materniak, G. (1982). Study skills: A practical application of information-processing theory. In A. S. Algier & K. W. Algier (Eds.), *New directions for college learning assistance: Improving reading and study skills* (No. 8, pp. 3–10). San Francisco: Jossey-Bass.

McClusky, H. Y. (1934). An experiment on the influence of preliminary skimming on reading. *Journal of Educational Psychology, 25*, 521–529.

McCormick, K. F. (1943). *The nature and training of work-study skills*. Unpublished master's thesis. Ohio State University, Columbus, OH.

Okey, L. J. (1979). Achievement with two college textbook reading methods with considerations for locus of control influences (Doctoral dissertation, West Virginia University, 1979). *Dissertation Abstracts International, 40*, 3816A. (University Microfilms No. 80-00, 202)

Pauk, W. (1973). Two essential study skills for the community college. *Reading World, 13*, 239–245.

Pauk, W. (1974). Textbook systems: Carrying a good thing too far. *Reading World, 14*, 22–24.

Pressey, L. C. (1928). The permanent effects of training methods of study on college success. *School and Society, 28*, 403–404.

Pressey, L. C., Robinson, F. P., & Horrocks, J. E. (1959). *Psychology in education*. New York: Harper.

Robinson, F. P. (1931). Can college freshmen in the lowest tenth in reading be aided scholastically? *School and Society, 34*, 843–846.

Robinson, F. P. (1941). *Diagnostic and remedial techniques for effective study*. New York: Harper.

Robinson, F. P. (1943). Study skills of soldiers in ASTP. *School and Society, 58*, 398–399.

Robinson, F. P. (1946). *Effective study.* New York: Harper.

Robinson, F. P. (1950). *Principles and procedures in student counseling.* New York: Harper & Bros.

Robinson, F. P. (1961). *Effective study* (rev. ed.). New York: Harper & Row.

Robinson, F. P. (1970). *Effective study* (4th ed.). New York: Harper & Row.

Robinson, F. P. (1971). Survey Q3R: Then and now. In D. M. Wark (Ed.), *College and Adult Reading*, Sixth Yearbook of the North Central Reading Association (pp. 248–261). St. Paul: University of Minnesota, Student Counseling Bureau.

Robinson, F. P., & Hall, P. (1941). Studies of higher-level reading abilities. *Journal of Educational Psychology, 32,* 241–252.

Salisbury, R. (1934). A study of the transfer effects of training in logical organization. *Journal of Educational Research, 28,* 241–254.

Salisbury, R. (1935). Some effects of training in outlining. *English Journal, 24,* 111–116.

Seashore, R. (1939). Work methods: An often neglected factor underlying individual differences. *Psychological Review, 46,* 123–141.

Sherburne, J. W. (1938). *Problems and outcomes of a college reading program.* Unpublished doctoral dissertation, Ohio State University, Columbus, OH.

Skaggs, E. B. (1920). The relative value of grouped and interspersed recitations. *Journal of Educational Psychology, 3,* 424–446.

Skaggs, E. B., Grossman, S., Krueger, L. O., & Krueger, W. C. F. (1930). Further studies of the reading recitation process in learning. In R. S. Woodworth (Ed.), *Archives of psychology* (No. 114, pp. 5–38). New York: Science Press.

Spitzer, H. F. (1938). *A study of retention in reading.* Unpublished doctoral dissertation, State University of Iowa, Ames, IA.

Spitzer, H. F. (1939). Studies in retention. *Journal of Educational Psychology, 30,* 641–656.

Stahl, N. A. (1983). A historical analysis of textbook-study systems. *Dissertation Abstracts International, 45,* 480A. (University Microfilms No. 84-11, 839)

Tadlock, D. F. (1978). SQ3R — Why it works, based on an information processing theory of learning. *Journal of Reading, 22,* 110–112.

Trow, W. C. (1928). Recall vs. repetition in the learning of rote and meaningful material. *American Journal of Psychology, 40,* 112–116.

Wark, D. M. (1964). Survey Q3R: System or superstition? In D. M. Wark (Ed.), *College and Adult Reading*, Third and Fourth Annual Yearbook of the North Central Reading Association (pp. 161–170). St. Paul: University of Minnesota, Student Counseling Bureau.

Washburne, J. N. (1929). The use of questions in social science material. *Journal of Educational Psychology, 20,* 321–359.

Whipple, G. M. (1927). *How to study effectively* (2nd ed.). Bloomington, IL: Public School Publishing.

Willmore, D. J. (1967). A comparison of four methods of studying a college textbook (Doctoral dissertation, University of Minnesota, 1966). *Dissertation Abstracts, 17,* 2413A. (University Microfilms No. 67-888)

Yoakum, G. A. (1921). The effect of a single reading. In G. M. Whipple (Ed.), *Twentieth Yearbook of the National Society for the Study of Education: Part II* (pp. 90–102). Bloomington, IL: Public School Publishing.

A Glossary of Developmental Education and Learning Assistance Terms

David R. Arendale

David R. Arendale wisely posits that language reflects our past, demonstrates our current practice, and guides the future. He points out that as practice advances — and one should say the same for theory and research — so must the language used to describe it. Furthermore, it can be said that without a common register, a field can never hope to advance or to gain a professional status. The glossary presented in this section provides both seasoned veterans and neophytes to the field with a linguistic and conceptual foundation that is necessary for basic communications, pedagogical transformation, programmatic evaluation, professional development, and high-impact research.

It has been 15 years since the first glossary of terms for the field of developmental education and learning assistance was published (Rubin, 1991). Much has changed with the profession in that time period. Just as the old saying states, "form follows function," it is not surprising that the language used to describe and define a field continues to reflect the changes reflected in its practice. This glossary is a heavy revision of the previous edition (Rubin, 1991). Nearly two-thirds of the terms from the first edition were revised. While only five terms were deleted, nearly 60 were added. This reflects the growth and increased sophistication of the field as well as appropriate integration of terms from related academic disciplines. Obviously, there are more extensive dictionaries for focused areas of the field, especially in reading and writing. However, only the most essential terms were included in this general purpose glossary.

Glossary Revision Process

There were four major contributing factors to this current edition of the glossary. The first is the pioneering work of the first edition of the glossary by the College Reading and Learning Association Taskforce on Professional Language (Rubin, 1991). This glossary was expanded by the coauthors of the first edition of the *NADE Self-Evaluation Guides* (Clark-Thayer, 1995). A second factor in the glossary presented here was the role of the leading organizations in the field. Draft copies of the glossary were provided to five professional associations: the Association for the Tutoring Profession, the College Reading and Learning Association, the National Association for Developmental Education (NADE), the National College Learning Center Association, and the National Tutoring Association. In addition, the draft glossary was provided to

10 national committees representing the academic disciplines within those five professional associations, the NADE Certification Board and field reviewers, and three national centers (the Center for Research in Developmental Education and Urban Literacy, the Learning Support Centers in Higher Education, and the National Center for Developmental Education). Helpful suggestions were received from individuals in these organizations. A third factor in revision of the glossary was a careful comparison with other educational dictionaries for inclusion of appropriate terms. These contributions are noted in the citations within the glossary.

The final contributing factor in improving and validating the glossary was a team of field reviewers from different types of institutions across the nation. They recommended terms for inclusion, edited current entries, and wrote new ones. As both scholars and service providers, they validated the utility of the glossary for the field today. Following are the team members: David Arendale, Dorie AuCoin, Leslie Boon, Susan Clark-Thayer, Jennifer Cole, Wilma Dulin, Irene Duranczyk, Carol Eades, Sabine Endicott, Marjorie Ginsberg, Jeanne Higbee, Gene Kerstiens, Dana Lundell, Terri Massie-Burrell, Howard Masuda, Jane McGrath, Ben Moulton, Jane Neuberger, Donald Opitz, Karen Patty-Graham, Danielle Peterson, Gladys Shaw, Karin Winnard, and Pepe Zerda.

Changes in the Glossary

As stated earlier, there has been considerable change in the glossary through the heavy revision of existing terms and the introduction of nearly 60 new ones. Building on the existing glossary, additional terms were added related to mathematics and writing. There was a major expansion of terms related to race, class, and culture since the profession is growing in its recognition of them on the learning process (Higbee, Lundell, & Duranczyk, 2003). Some of the terms are *critical literacy, critical pedagogy, diverse students, historically underrepresented students, inclusion, multicultural developmental education, multicultural education, people of color, universal design,* and *universal instructional design.* This builds on the student-centered learning approach by many educators in this field. A second expansion area for the glossary was integration of more terms from cognitive psychology such as *attribution, cognitive domain, cognitive strategies, locus of control,* and *self-efficacy.* Obviously many more terms could have been included in the glossary, but those selected were the ones which commonly appear in the literature published by the professional associations that represent the field.

The third major change in the glossary is the addition of recommended language usage for some of the most important glossary terms: *academically underprepared student, developmental student,* and *reme-*

dial student. The glossary provides an example of proper use of the glossary term in writing for a publication, for example, rather than using the term developmental students, it is suggested to instead refer to them as students with developmental issues in college algebra. This follows the admonition from the American Psychological Association in the 5th edition of their publication style manual (APA, 2001, pp. 63–65) to avoid labeling of people and to put the person first when describing a characteristic about him or her. While this may seem a subtle difference in language use, it may be more important than many in the profession understand. Many students who enroll in a remedial or developmental education course only do so in one specific discipline area (e.g., math, reading, writing). Yet, these students are commonly classified as being developmental or are described by another term previously mentioned. This leaves the impression that they have academic challenges in most academic disciplines and skills. While those within the profession may understand the nuances of the language, policy makers and the general public probably do not. This may illuminate current controversies of policy and funding that dominate the field (Arendale, 2005). Older language choices (i.e., remedial students, developmental students) can have a direct or indirect impact upon the stigma that students and developmental education programs sometimes experience and negative consequences that occur as a result (Pedlety, 2001; Schmidt et al., 2005). This issue needs to be more fully examined in a separate publication concerning language usage of these key terms.

Glossary

Words set in *italics* are defined elsewhere in the Glossary.

academic competencies. See *BASIC ACADEMIC SKILLS*.

academic preparatory academy. 1: an equivalent high school education program that contains core academic content areas that include college preparatory curriculum. **2:** services provided by commercial tutoring companies prior to or during college.

academic skills. See *BASIC ACADEMIC SKILLS*.

academically underprepared student. 1: a student assessed as having potential for college success when appropriate educational enrichment and support services are provided. **2:** a student who, while meeting college admissions requirements, is not yet fully prepared to succeed in one or more college-level courses. *Usage Rule*: Put people first followed by a descriptive phrase. *Example*:...a student academically underprepared in calculus (see APA, 2001, pp. 63–65, 69–70). Compare with *DEVELOPMENTAL STUDENT* and *REMEDIAL STUDENT*.

Accelerated Learning Groups (ALGs). Developed at the University of Southern California by Dr. Sydney Stansbury (2001) in the 1990s, ALGs are one example of a course-based learning assistance program. Compare with COOPERATIVE LEARNING and COURSE-BASED LEARNING ASSISTANCE.

accelerated learning program. College students with academic weaknesses simultaneously receive academic enrichment and support as they are enrolled in college-level courses and keep pace with other students towards degree completion. This model is based on the Accelerated Schools Program used widely in elementary and secondary schools in the United States. Support may be provided through one of several means: COURSE-BASED LEARNING ASSISTANCE, enrollment in a learning community that pairs a core curriculum content course and an appropriate developmental education course; faculty embed practice with study strategies within their college-level academic courses (Koski & Levin, 1998). Compare with COURSE-BASED LEARNING ASSISTANCE, DEVELOPMENTAL PROGRAM, and REMEDIAL PROGRAM.

access education. 1: targets HISTORICALLY UNDERREPRESENTED STUDENT POPULATIONS through a program of study to prepare them for postsecondary admission. **2:** a term used to describe programs in Europe that are comparable in some ways to U. S. DEVELOPMENTAL EDUCATION. Compare with ACADEMIC PREPARATORY ACADEMY and DEVELOPMENTAL EDUCATION.

active learning. The process of having students engage in an activity that encourages them to reflect on ideas and how they are using them (Collins & O'Brien, 2003, p. 5).

active listening. Attending to the speech, body language, facial expressions, and implied meaning of a person's communications and reciprocation of the same to the sender (Collins & O'Brien, 2003, p. 5).

adjunct instructional programs (AIP). See COURSE-BASED LEARNING ASSISTANCE.

advance organizer. 1: short introductory text or graphic material presented to students prior to a learning experience that enables them to structure the knowledge, put it in perspective, and increase receptivity to new information. **2:** draws parallels between something the reader already knows about the new material; or restates the new material at a higher level of abstraction, generalizability, and inclusiveness (Harris & Hodges, 1981).

affective domain. Attitudes, values, and emotions (Dembo, 1994).

ancillary facilities. Institutional units which exist to provide support for all units across the institution.

assistive technology. Any equipment used to increase, maintain, or improve the fundamental capacities of individuals with disabilities (Technology Related Assistance for Individuals with Disabilities Act of 1988). Compare with INSTRUCTIONAL TECHNOLOGY.

associating. 1: the process of connecting a written symbol with its meaning referent, usually a spoken word, in beginning reading.

2: the process of connecting what is presently being learned to prior knowledge or experience (Harris & Hodges, 1981).

attribution. An individual's perception of the causes of his or her own success or behavior (Dembo, 1994).

backwash. The desirable or undesirable effect a test of particular skill has on the acquisition of that skill (Kerstiens, 1990).

basic academic skills. Activities such as calculating, reading, reasoning, speaking, and writing that enable people to communicate and learn; considered to be essential to learning across the curriculum, but not always specifically taught in the regular postsecondary academic curriculum.

behavioral change. A difference in performance or attitude that is observed and documented following an intervention.

cognitive domain. Knowledge and the skills of comprehension, application, analysis, synthesis, and evaluation (Dembo, 1994).

cognitive strategies. Behaviors and thoughts that influence the learning process so that information can be retrieved more efficiently from memory (Dembo, 1994).

collaborative learning. Activities in which students work together and learn from each other. These activities may be under supervision of an instructor or other students. The focus is often on developing mastery of the academic content material. Compare with COOPERATIVE LEARNING.

college-level. The level of skill attainment, knowledge, and reasoning ability associated with/required by courses of study designed to lead to a postsecondary degree.

college-level mathematics skills. Mathematics competency for meeting expectations of the student's academic program of study required by the college. Some academic degree programs require different and higher mathematics skills than others. Compare with DEVELOPMENTAL MATHEMATICS COURSE and REMEDIAL MATHEMATICS COURSE.

college-level reader. A student who possesses the skills and strategies for comprehending college-level written materials.

college-level reading skills. 1: Skills required to decode, comprehend, analyze, and criticize information contained in college-level textbooks, supplemental texts, fiction and nonfiction books, course handouts, and examinations. Inherent in college-level reading skills are rate, flexibility, fluency, and a broad vocabulary to support comprehension of the text. This does not necessarily include knowledge of specific content-area vocabulary. **2:** Reading competency for enrollment in a rigorous college-level core curriculum course. Compare with DEVELOPMENTAL READING COURSE and REMEDIAL READING COURSE.

college-level students. Those students demonstrating possession of the necessary prerequisite skills, knowledge, and reasoning ability that suggest they are developmentally ready to pursue courses of study leading to a college degree.

college-level writing skills. 1: skills required to convey information in writing at a college-level. Inherent in this level are skills in grammar, sentence structure, organization, voice, and a broad vocabulary to demonstrate understanding and articulate meaning. **2:** Writing competency for enrollment in a college-level composition course. Compare with DEVELOPMENTAL WRITING COURSE, REMEDIAL ENGLISH COURSE, and WRITING PROCESS.

college students. Learners matriculated into a postsecondary institution.

community agencies. Publicly and privately sponsored organizations outside of institutions of higher education that can serve as resources for the institution and its students (e.g., counseling, employment agencies, and social services).

compensatory education. 1: Educational activities that remediate a previous state of discrimination. The focus is on both the individual student and an enriched learning environment to replace the previous impoverished and diminished environment in secondary education. **2:** Sometimes the term is used to describe activities and services provided through civil rights legislation for students who are eligible for participation due to past discrimination of their ethnic, social, or economic group (e.g., TRIO programs).

comprehension monitoring. The cognitive process of actively evaluating and self-regulating one's comprehension while reading (*a metacognitive skill*).

concentration. 1: ability to become absorbed in a task and continue in it despite distractions (Page & Thomas, 1980). **2:** the conscious and intensive focusing of attention on an object, task or problem (Eastridge & Price, 1969).

cooperative learning. In addition to activities in which students work together and learn from each other as in COLLABORATIVE LEARNING, they engage in activities that are more structured, planned, and purposeful. The six critical features of cooperative learning include: (1) positive interdependence among group participants; (2) individual accountability for involvement; (3) appropriate rationale and task purpose for the group; (4) structured student interactions with designated activities rather than free-form discussion; (5) instructor or expert peer facilitation; and (6) attention to development of social skills such as interpersonal communications and leadership development. Compare with COLLABORATIVE LEARNING.

course-based learning assistance (CLA). Those forms of group cooperative learning that accompany a specific course to serve as a supplement for that course. There are a variety of CLA approaches. These activities may occur outside of class or may be embedded within the course. Student participation may be voluntary or mandatory. Some CLA programs award academic credit for student participation. Examples of CLA with formal protocols for implementation include: Accelerated Learning Groups (*USC Model*), Emerging Scholars Program (UC-Berkeley Model), Peer-led Team Learning (CUNY Model), Structured Learning Assistance (Ferris State University Model), Supplemental Instruction (UMKC Model), and Video-Based Supplemental Instruction (UMKC Model). CLA can also be less formal and take the form of study cluster groups and group problem-solving sessions (Arendale, 2005). Compare with *COOPERATIVE LEARNING* and *COLLABORATIVE LEARNING*.

critical literacy. 1: Skills to critically reflect on the political and social forces that affect a community or person's life so that action can be taken to overcome barriers and improve conditions that these forces have put in place (Collins & O'Brien, 2003, p. 83). **2:** Ability to reflect on, analyze, and evaluate implications of information for practice. Compare with *LITERACY*.

critical pedagogy. An approach to teaching and learning that encourages the learners to reflect critically on issues of power and oppression in their society and on what might be done to change the current situation (Collins & O'Brien, 2003, p. 86).

critical reader. 1: One who comprehends, questions, clarifies, and analyzes in order to reach objective, reasoned judgments. **2:** Being willing and able to objectively evaluate what one reads. **3:** Reaching reasoned judgments on the basis of the evidence presented rather than accepting or rejecting information based on emotion and anecdote (J. McGrath, personal communication, September 27, 2005).

critical reading. The process of understanding, questioning, and making reasoned judgments in reading; requires evaluating ideas, recognizing assumptions, identifying relationships in form and content, reading analytically, and distinguishing fact and opinion.

cultural differences. Behavioral and attitudinal traditions based on an individual's or a group's prior and current cultural experience and socialization.

cultural literacy. 1: Awareness of facts, themes, ideas, and other information comprising the heritage of a given nation, culture, or ethnic group. **2:** The cumulative cultural knowledge that a reader brings to the current reading exercise that influences him or her when questioning, evaluating, and associating the material.

cultural sensitivity. Acting in a manner that demonstrates respect for the background of all individuals and adapting the learning environment to different learning preferences that are influenced by cultural traits.

developmental. 1: the expected sequence of learning. Any learner who is acquiring knowledge and skill is in this continuum stage of the education process. *COMMENT*: The use of the term in education has its origins in psychology, which had taken it from medicine. Development is defined as the process of growth, unfolding, and activation. Thus, expected growth is developmental. **2:** Often used in counter distinction to ACCELERATED and/or REMEDIAL learning. Use of the term at the college level recognizes there is a gap between high school skills or prior educational experience and college skills that need to be mediated for some students. Compare with ACCELERATED LEARNING PROGRAMS and REMEDIAL.

developmental course. 1: Any course organized according to the principles of cognitive and student development and designed to promote both affective and cognitive development. **2:** Any course designed to build upon existing skills to prepare students for college-level course work. Compare with REMEDIAL COURSE.

developmental education. 1: A field of practice and research within higher education with a theoretical foundation in developmental psychology and learning theory. It promotes the cognitive and affective growth of all postsecondary learners, at all levels of the learning continuum. **2:** A sensitive and responsive approach to the individual differences and special needs among learners (NADE, 1995). Compare with LEARNING ASSISTANCE, REMEDIAL EDUCATION, and MULTICULTURAL DEVELOPMENTAL EDUCATION.

developmental education program. Commonly addresses academic underpreparedness, diagnostic assessment and placement, affective barriers to learning, and development of general and discipline-specific learning strategies (NADE, 1995). Compare with ACCELERATED LEARNING PROGRAM, LEARNING ASSISTANCE PROGRAM, and REMEDIAL EDUCATION PROGRAM.

developmental educator. 1: An educational professional who works in a program designed to enhance the academic and personal growth of students who are underprepared for college-level academic tasks. **2:** An educational professional who employs the principles of cognitive and affective development in designing and delivering instruction.

developmental mathematics course. 1: Precollegiate mathematics courses that are designed to prepare students for the study of college-level mathematics, as defined by entrance requirements of the institution. Levels of developmental mathematics courses vary from basic arithmetic through any prerequisite course(s) for calculus (Duranczyk, 2004). **2:** Instruction that may contain one or more of the following topics: arithmetic operations, math symbolism, geometry and measurement, functions, discrete math algorithms, probability and statistics, and deductive proofs. **3:** Specialized mathematics instruction for students who do not meet entry into a college-level mathematics course. Compare with COLLEGE-LEVEL MATHEMATICS SKILLS and REMEDIAL MATHEMATICS COURSE.

developmental profile. Description of an individual's academic and/or cognitive competencies.

developmental reading course. 1: Instruction that builds upon students' existing reading skills and background knowledge to enable them to become proficient in processing and learning college-level reading material. **2:** College-level reading instruction that includes the reading and learning skills, and learning strategies needed to master college-level material efficiently and effectively. Compare with REMEDIAL READING COURSE and COLLEGE-LEVEL READING SKILLS.

developmental student. 1: A student assessed as having potential for college success when appropriate educational enrichment and support services are provided. **2:** A student who, while meeting college admissions requirements, is not yet fully prepared to succeed in one or more introductory college-level courses. *Usage Rule*: Put people first followed by a descriptive phrase. *Example*: ... a student with developmental issues in college algebra (see APA, 2001, pp. 63–65, 69–70). Compare with ACADEMICALLY UNDERPREPARED STUDENT and REMEDIAL STUDENT.

developmental writing course. 1: Instruction for those who have not yet mastered the basic composition skies necessary to write at the college-level. **2:** Specialized English instruction for students who do not meet entry requirements for a college-level writing course. Compare with REMEDIAL ENGLISH COURSE and COLLEGE-LEVEL WRITING SKILLS.

diagnosis. 1: The process of determining students' specific strengths and weaknesses to create a prescription for treatment (Harris & Hodges, 1981). **2:** Planning of instruction based on the evaluation of the student's needs. **3:** The classification of people or things into established categories (Harris & Hodges, 1981).

direct instruction. 1: The instructor facilitates the learning environment through presentation of content material (i.e., lecturing, explaining), demonstrations, and managing student activities (Ellis & Fouts, 1996, p. 70). **2:** Based on behavior modification principles, learning activities are sequenced and managed by the instructor to develop progressively more complex skills and knowledge. Compare with FACILITATOR and STUDENT-CENTERED LEARNING.

disability. 1: A physical or mental impairment that substantially limits one or more major life activities. **2:** A record of such impairments. **3:** Being regarded as having such impairments (Americans with Disabilities Act, 1990).

disability services. The provision of accommodations and services by the institution to enable students with a professionally diagnosed disability to perform on an equal basis with other students in academic activities and assignment.

diverse students. Students from backgrounds that differ by race, class, gender, culture, ethnicity, home language, age, disability, and sexual identity. Compare with HISTORICALLY UNDERREPRESENTED STUDENT POPULATIONS.

early exit. A student's leaving a program, course, or activity before its scheduled end. Such leave usually is based on early mastery of a skill or skills that are documented through an assessment measure.

elaboration. 1: Formation of a relationship between previously learned information and new, unfamiliar material by means of mental images or verbal extensions, such as inferences and analogies (Anderson & Armbruster, 1984). **2:** The process or result of expanding in detail or complexity a simpler object or idea. **3:** The extra processing one does that results in additional, related or redundant propositions with those serving as the memory for the material processed (Reder & Anderson, 1980).

emergency crisis management procedures. Established, step-by-step directions for dealing with extraordinary events (e.g., students in crisis, health emergencies, student discipline).

Emerging Scholars Program (ESP). Developed at the University of California-Berkeley by Dr. Uri Treisman in the 1980s. ESP is one example of a course-based learning assistance. Sometimes called the Math Workshop Model and the Treisman Model. Compare with *COOPERATIVE LEARNING* and *COURSE-BASED LEARNING ASSISTANCE*.

facilitating. Process of organizing and managing a highly participatory learning environment where learners are the primary generators of discussion, discovery, and inquiry about academic content. Compare with *MENTORING* and *TUTORING*.

facilitators. Persons who organize and manage a highly participatory learning environment in *COURSE-BASED LEARNING ASSISTANCE* programs. This role may employ students, non-student paraprofessionals, professional staff, and instructors. Compare with *COURSE-BASED LEARNING ASSISTANCE* and *TUTORS*.

first-year experience course. A class offered in the first academic term of a student's enrollment in college that explores important information and skills essential for success in both the academic and social dimensions of college life.

flexible reading. Strategies for varying reading rates based on the type of reading (e.g., skimming, scanning, studying), the purpose of reading, and the reader's familiarity with the content. Compare with *SPEED READING*.

graphic organizers. 1: A visual map, outline, graph, comparison table, or chart that identifies the major concepts and relationships of ideas in reading or lecture material. **2:** A nonlinear method for summarizing and visually representing important relationships among ideas in a text or a lecture.

higher-level thinking skills. Processing material at the cognitive levels of analysis, synthesis, or evaluation (Bloom, 1956).

historically underrepresented student populations. Student groups that have not commonly enrolled at or been successful in postsecondary educational institutions in comparison with historical trends in college enrollment and representation in the general population of the United States. Compare with DIVERSE STUDENTS and STUDENTS OF COLOR.

human development. 1: The total span of life cycle from birth to death with the notion that individuals are in a constant process of growth and change (Shafritz, Koeppe, & Soper, 1988). **2:** Changes in cognitive, affective, psychological, social, emotional, and physical domains across the human life span. May be viewed as age/stage related or on a continuum of skills and knowledge.

inclusion. Providing equal educational opportunity by co-creating learning communities in which unique needs and diverse capacities are recognized, understood, accepted, and valued. Compare with UNIVERSAL DESIGN and UNIVERSAL INSTRUCTIONAL DESIGN.

independent learners. 1: Ability to work autonomously or with others successfully. **2:** Engage in a wide range of learning tasks, apply appropriate learning strategies for the task, self-monitor comprehension level, and make adjustments in learning behaviors to meet the requirements of the learning task. Compare with INTERDEPENDENT LEARNERS and SELF-REGULATED LEARNING.

institutional educational program. An organized set of curricula and coursework designed to produce a particular result or set of results (Shafritz, Koeppe, & Soper, 1988).

instructional materials. Resources in various formats (e.g., printed, audio-visual, kinesthetic, computer-based) to be used by students or faculty members to improve academic competence for the intended learning outcome.

instructional technology. 1: A field dedicated to the theory and practice of technological design, development, use, management, and evaluation of the process for learning. **2:** Technology use in classroom environment or via the Internet to provide an intended learning experience (Collins & O'Brien, 2003, pp. 181–182). Compare with ASSISTIVE TECHNOLOGY and MEDIA SERVICES.

interacting with text. 1: Building meaning through predicting, questioning, evaluating, paraphrasing, summarizing, and analyzing. **2:** Attending for comprehension of written material.

interdependent learners. Able to work with other learners in a group due to possessing skills in interpersonal communication, analyzing learning tasks, and SELF-REGULATED LEARNING to monitor themselves and make adjustments individually and within the learning group. Compare with INDEPENDENT LEARNERS, SELF-REGULATED LEARNING, and COOPERATIVE LEARNING.

learning. Acquisition by individuals of skills, information, values, and attitudes (both intentionally and unintentionally), as well as demonstrated ability to apply or transfer to new situations.

learning assistance. Supportive activities, supplementary to the regular curriculum, that promotes the understanding, learning, and recall of new knowledge; remediation for prescribed entry and exit levels of academic proficiency; and the development of new academic and learning skills. Some activities include study skills instruction, TUTORING, COURSE-BASED LEARNING ASSISTANCE, reviews, study groups, special topic workshops, time management, exam preparation, and self-paced instruction. These services may be provided in a center that can be staffed with professionals, paraprofessionals, and/or peers. Compare with DEVELOPMENTAL EDUCATION, MULTICULTURAL DEVELOPMENTAL EDUCATION, and REMEDIAL EDUCATION.

learning assistance center. 1: A designated physical location on campus that provides an organized, multifaceted approach to offering comprehensive academic enhancement activities outside of the traditional classroom setting to the entire college community. **2:** A centralized location wherein tutorial and study skills assistance is provided most commonly. The center generally provides support to a wide array of academic disciplines. It may sometimes be focused in one academic area (e.g., mathematics, writing). **3:** A place that offers help to any student experiencing academic difficulties. Assistance is usually noncredit, individualized, and can be remedial or developmental in nature. Compare with LEARNING ASSISTANCE PROGRAM and TEACHING/LEARNING CENTER.

learning assistance program. 1: A comprehensive approach to offering instruction and activities for college students who seek skill development throughout their academic career. Areas of assistance could include skill development in critical thinking, reading, writing, study skills, and study strategies; instruction, group study, or tutoring in academic content areas; graduate and professional school exam preparation; and personal development areas such as time management. Such activities may be accessed through drop-in tutoring or study groups, independent self-paced study, workshops, or courses (Materniak & Williams, 1987). **2:** A program that enables a student to develop the attitudes and skills required for successful achievement of academic goals. Services maybe offered at the remedial, developmental, supplemental, or enhancement level. Compare with DEVELOPMENTAL EDUCATION PROGRAM, LEARNING ASSISTANCE CENTER, REMEDIAL EDUCATION PROGRAM, and TEACHING/LEARNING CENTER.

learning characteristics. The way in which an individual receives and processes new information (Shafritz, Koeppe, & Soper, 1988). Compare with LEARNING STYLE.

learning communities. A curricular approach that enrolls a common cohort of students in a restructured learning environment that builds connections among students and curriculum. There are different models for accomplishing this: linked courses, learning clusters, first-year interest groups, federated learning communities, and coordinated studies (Gabelnick et al., 1990).

learning skills. 1: Methods that permit the student to achieve understanding of desired material. **2:** Communication, organizational,
and study skills that can enhance learning.

learning style. 1: Affective and cognitive processes and preferences
governing an approach to the acquisition of knowledge by a learner.
2: A preference for a particular instructional methodology or environment. **3:** Sometimes categorized along a continuum for auditory,
kinesthetic, or visual learning modalities. Compare with *LEARNING
CHARACTERISTICS*.

literacy. 1: The ability to read. **2:** The ability to read, speak, write, and
understand the expression of a language and to perform its arithmetic and linguistic operations. **3:** Competency in a technical field,
as in computer literacy (Harris & Hodges, 1981). Compare with
CRITICAL LITERACY.

locus of control. Individual's perception of who or what is responsible
for the outcome of events and behaviors that affect his or her life
(Dembo, 1994).

long-term memory. 1: Ability to recall and use learned information
for a task after a long time period. **2:** Permanent stored information
that is capable of retrieval through association with other information (Bushy & Andrews, 1980). Compare with *SHORT-TERM MEMORY*.

lower-level thinking skills. Processing material at the cognitive levels of knowledge, comprehension, or application. *COMMENT*: These
are mental processes at the bottom half of Bloom's Taxonomy of
Educational Objectives (Bloom, 1956).

mapping. See *GRAPHIC ORGANIZER*.

media services. That unit of an educational institution that provides
consultation, media, and equipment to instructors for the purpose
of developing and utilizing supplemental materials in learning activities. Compare with *INSTRUCTIONAL TECHNOLOGY*.

mentoring. A learning or counseling relationship where an experienced person assists one less experienced to develop skills and
knowledge. This relationship often provides a learning and growth
experience for both individuals. Compare with *FACILITATING* and
TUTORING.

metacognition. 1: Reflection, understanding, and knowing how one
learns. **2:** The process of reflecting, understanding, and knowing
how a person learns. Compare with *METACOMPREHENSION*.

metacomprehension. 1: The awareness of and conscious control over
one's own understanding or lack of it. **2:** The ability to analyze and
monitor one's level of understanding or performance. Compare with
METACOGNITION.

minorities. See *DIVERSE STUDENTS* and *HISTORICALLY UNDERREPRESENTED
STUDENT POPULATIONS*.

motivation. 1: Arousing or stimulating a person through intrinsic
and extrinsic means to perform a task willingly and to complete it

with sustained enthusiasm (Eastridge & Price, 1969). **2:** Considered broadly, the process of arousing, sustaining, and regulating behaviors and thoughts. **3:** Designates the use of various devices such as the offering of rewards or an appeal to the desire to excel (Good & Thomas, 1945).

multicultural developmental education. 1: Providing inclusive academic support programs and services, and welcoming learning environments for diverse students by recognizing students' unique social identities and how they contribute to the learning process. **2:** Centralizing issues of race, class, gender, culture, ethnicity, home language, age, disability, social identities, and sexual identity to increase effectiveness of learning assistance and development programs. **3:** Embedding multiculturalism in all aspects of developmental education curricula through the selection of texts and other media and the adoption of pedagogies that respect differing perspectives and enable students to acquire and demonstrate knowledge in multiple ways (Higbee, Lundell, & Duranczyk, 2003). Compare with DEVELOPMENTAL EDUCATION, DIVERSE STUDENTS, LEARNING ASSISTANCE, MULTICULTURAL EDUCATION, and REMEDIAL EDUCATION.

multicultural education. 1: Education that recognizes and values cultural diversity, develops respect for cultural diversity, and promotes social justice and equal opportunity for all. **2:** Policies and practices that recognize, accept, and affirm human differences and similarities in gender, race, disability, class, social identities, and sexual identity (Collins & O'Brien, 2003, p. 229).

networking. Purposeful collaboration of individuals with common interests and/or roles.

orientation program. 1: A program that introduces academic and social college adjustments as well as familiarization with the institutions' facilities, programs, traditions, and services. Such programs may vary considerably between institutions in their length, scope, timing, and content (Upcraft, 1984, p. 1). **2:** A meeting or series of meetings held at the beginning of one's employment to provide information and training related to job performance, responsibilities, and logistical matters. **3:** An introductory set of activities for providing information about an institution's mission, programs, and procedures to anyone new to the institution.

outreach activity. Any effort by an educational institution to provide education, guidance, or other services to those not currently served (e.g., high school students, parents) (Shafritz, Koeppe, & Soper, 1988).

paraphrase. 1: An active strategy that requires a person to think about and understand what the author is communicating and expressing in the person's own words. **2:** A substantially different sentence structure and vocabulary than the original, often typical of a person's own writing style; a restatement of the thesis or main idea of the original (J. McGrath, personal communication, September 27, 2005). Compare with SUMMARY.

Peer-Led Team Learning (PLTL). Developed at the City University of New York in the 1990s, PLTL is one example of course-based learning assistance programs. Compare with COOPERATIVE LEARNING and COURSE-BASED LEARNING ASSISTANCE.

people of color. See HISTORICALLY UNDERREPRESENTED STUDENT POPULATIONS.

placement. The assignment of a person to an appropriate course or educational program in accordance with his/her aims, capabilities, readiness, educational background, and/or aspirations. Placement can be based on previous experiences, scores on admissions or entrance tests, or tests specifically designed for placement purposes.

power test. A test of a particular skill having no time limits.

prereading. 1: The cognitive process used by readers to gain an overview of the text and to determine how that text fits into their personal schema. **2:** A quick survey, prior to formal reading, focused on attention to the title, introductory and concluding paragraph, main divisions and subdivisions, parts set off by contrasting print, information on the author, thesis and general organization of the text, but without full comprehension (Eastridge & Price, 1969).

prewriting. Early activities in the writing process: organizing the writing topic, gathering relevant information, focusing the topic, and producing a first draft of the manuscript. Compare with WRITING PROCESS.

reading process. 1: An active, thinking process of understanding an author's ideas, connecting those ideas to what a person already knows, and then organizing all the ideas so that the person can remember and use them (J. McGrath, personal communication, September 27, 2005). **2:** The act of reading, involving primarily the recognition of printed symbols and the meaningful reaction of the reader to these symbols; such reaction may include the reader's interpretation, appraisal, and attitudinal responses as determined by his/her purposes and needs (Good & Thomas, 1945).

reading strategies. 1: techniques which facilitate the construction of meaning from text by the reader. **2:** Effective techniques for abstracting comprehension from written message. This may include such strategies as clarifying purposes for reading, identifying important aspects of the message, monitoring comprehension, and recovering from interruptions (Brown, 1981).

remedial education. 1: A process that corrects a deficit in student behaviors and/or skills. Such an approach is narrowly focused on the academic content as opposed to DEVELOPMENTAL EDUCATION, which focuses more broadly on the whole learner (Dejnozka & Kapel, 1991, pp. 478–479). **2:** Instruction designed to remove a student's deficiencies in one or more basic academic skills (i.e., math, reading, writing) to reach a level of proficiency achieved by most secondary school graduates. Additional instruction may be required, including DEVELOPMENTAL EDUCATION, for the student to be prepared for the rigor of a college-level course. **3:** Academic content taught previously in middle or secondary school as opposed to DEVELOPMENTAL EDUCATION, which focuses more often on skills and knowledge needed for college-level academic content material and skills. Compare with DEVELOPMENTAL, DEVELOPMENTAL EDUCATION, LEARNING ASSISTANCE, and MULTICULTURAL DEVELOPMENTAL EDUCATION.

remedial education program. A group of courses and/or activities to assist learners to achieve secondary school-level basic skills in their identified academic deficit areas. Compare with ACCELERATED LEARNING PROGRAM, DEVELOPMENTAL EDUCATION PROGRAM, and LEARNING ASSISTANCE PROGRAM.

remedial English course. 1: Instruction for those who have not yet mastered the basic sentence mechanics, grammar usage, and punctuation skills necessary to write at the college level. **2:** Specialized English instruction for students who do not meet entry into either a developmental or college-level writing course. Compare with DEVELOPMENTAL WRITING COURSE and COLLEGE-LEVEL WRITING SKILLS.

remedial mathematics course. 1: Instruction for those who have not yet mastered the skills necessary for competency with mathematics at the college-level. These skills may include one or more of the following: arithmetic operations, math symbolism, geometry and measurement, functions, discrete math algorithms, probability and statistics, and deductive proofs. **2:** Specialized mathematics instruction for students who do not meet entry into a developmental mathematics course. Compare with DEVELOPMENTAL MATHEMATICS COURSE and COLLEGE-LEVEL MATHEMATICS SKILLS.

remedial reading course. 1: Instruction for those who have not yet mastered the basic decoding and comprehension skills necessary to begin effectively reading college-level texts. **2:** Specialized reading instruction for students who do not meet entry or exit levels of a prescribed proficiency. Compare with DEVELOPMENTAL READING COURSE and COLLEGE-LEVEL READING.

remedial student. 1: A student assessed as having potential for college success after completing required academic improvement courses/programs due to significant underpreparation in one or more academic skill areas. **2:** A student who, as a condition of meeting provisional college admissions requirements, is not yet fully prepared to succeed in one or more introductory college-level courses. The student may have to successfully complete academic improvement courses/programs before he or she is allowed to enroll in a college-level course in the same academic area or perhaps be fully admitted to the postsecondary institution. *Usage Rule:* Put people first followed by a descriptive phrase. *Example*: . . . a student with remedial issues in fundamentals of mathematics (see APA, 2001, pp. 63–65, 69–70). Compare with ACADEMICALLY UNDERPREPARED STUDENT and DEVELOPMENTAL STUDENT.

review. Reexamination of material previously presented or studied (Good & Thomas, 1945).

scanning. Strategy that leads the reader to rapidly peruse text to find specific information (i.e., words, ideas) and to disregard any text that is not related to the focus of interest. Compare with SKIMMING.

schemata/schema. 1: The framework for organizing new information and relating it to existing knowledge that the individual brings to the learning situation. **2:** The pattern, plan, design, or system an individual is able to discern from the available information.

self-efficacy. The self-held belief of a person that he/she can successfully execute the behavior required to produce a particular behavior or outcome (Dembo, 1994).

short-term memory. Limited capacity memory of short duration which dissipates with time or is replaced by new information (Bushy & Andrews, 1980). Compare with LONG-TERM MEMORY.

self-regulated learning. Learning in which the student is actively involved in motivating himself or herself and using appropriate learning strategies (Dembo, 1994).

skill(s). 1: Behavior(s) that can be developed through instruction and practice. **2:** An activity that can be performed automatically (J. McGrath, personal communication, September 27, 2005). Compare with STRATEGY.

skimming. 1: A method of rapid reading in which the reader attempts to obtain the general idea of the passage rather than deeply reading the entire text (Eastridge & Price, 1969). **2:** A method of reading in which the reader attempts to ascertain the general meaning without attention to detail (Good & Thomas, 1945). Compare with SCANNING.

special populations. See HISTORICALLY UNDERREPRESENTED STUDENT POPULATIONS.

specialized vocabulary. 1: Words peculiar to a specific discipline, or more general words used in a particular way within a discipline. **2:** Names applied to concepts associated with a particular discipline or subject (e.g., chemical elements).

speed reading. Strategies for increasing speed while reading without interfering with comprehension. Compare with FLEXIBLE READING.

strategic learning. The selection and application by a student of strategies/procedures that are appropriate to the task.

strategy. 1: A tool or technique consciously selected to complete a task accurately and effectively (J. McGrath, personal communication, September 27, 2005). **2:** This activity is internalized and flexible, not rigid. Compare with SKILL(S).

Structured Learning Assistance (SLA). Developed at Ferris State University (MI) in the 1990s, SLA is one example of course-based learning assistance programs. Compare with COOPERATIVE LEARNING and COURSE-BASED LEARNING ASSISTANCE.

student. Learner.

student-centered learning. Students are actively engaged, have more control over the topics of study, and the means to do so. Compare with DIRECT INSTRUCTION and FACILITATORS.

study group. See COLLABORATIVE LEARNING.

study habits. A person's routine of applying study skills or approaching a study task for learning (Harris & Hodges, 1981).

study reading. 1: A process applied to the text by a student in order to learn the material. The process may include, but is not limited to, annotating the text, previewing the chapter, summarizing or outlining the main points, and paraphrasing and reciting the material. **2:** A student's usual way of getting meaning from what he or she reads. **3:** Reading for the specific purpose of absorbing and remembering information for which one will be held accountable.

study skills. Procedures to assist learners in the process of acquiring knowledge.

study strategies. Behaviors and procedures that, when thoughtfully and appropriately applied to learning tasks, improve the acquisition, understanding, and application of knowledge and skills. The learning behaviors include study skills such as time management, organizational skills, regularly planned study sessions, effective concentration, and well-developed communication skills to send and receive information in an academic setting. Compare with COGNITIVE STRATEGIES and STUDY SKILLS.

studying. Activities directed to acquiring knowledge, developing skills, and remembering what has been learned.

summarize. 1: The process of producing a condensed version of the original. **2:** Activity that begins with a paraphrase of the main ideas and details in the same order and with the same emphasis as the original. **3:** Activity used when a person needs to express the essence or gist of long narratives, such as a complete essay or book (J. McGrath, personal communication, September 27, 2005). Compare with PARAPHRASE.

Supplemental Instruction (SI). Developed at the University of the Missouri-Kansas City by Dr. Deanna Martin in the 1970s, SI is one example of course-based learning assistance programs. Unlike tutoring, which has a variety of expressions, SI has a specific set of protocols to follow. Compare with COOPERATIVE LEARNING and COURSE-BASED LEARNING ASSISTANCE.

support areas. Institutional services, other than regularly scheduled classes and labs, designed to assess and improve the academic and emotional well-being of students (Shafritz, Koeppe, & Soper, 1988).

survey. 1: (noun) An overall examination of performance, as a reading survey (Harris & Hodges, 1981). **2:** (verb) To make a comprehensive overview, as survey a textbook or chapter (Harris & Hodges, 1981).

teaching/learning center. An organized program that provides comprehensive academic enhancement activities outside of the traditional classroom setting for students and professional development services for the instructional staff. Compare with LEARNING ASSISTANCE CENTER.

teaching/learning process. A planned program for which there are expected teaching and learning outcomes.

testwiseness. The ability to correctly answer test questions on some basis other than the knowledge which the questions were designed to measure (Ferrell, 1973).

text structures/theoretical patterns. 1: Means employed by an author to develop and support the thesis or main ideas. **2:** The structure the author gives the information. Six common methods of organizational structure are examples, comparison and/or contrast, cause and effect, sequence or process, classification, and definition. In addition, the author may often combine two structures (J. McGrath, personal communication, September 27, 2005).

thinking skills. 1: The basic intellectual tools used for the acquisition, processing, organization and application of knowledge. **2:** A series of strategies for improving content mastery.

transfer. 1: Use of information gained in one domain to solve a problem encountered in a different domain. **2:** Ability to use skills and strategies acquired in a reading or study strategies class to understand the textbook and supplemental readings in a content area course (i.e., introductory core curriculum course).

tutoring. 1: One-to-one or small group facilitated learning assistance that explains, clarifies, and exemplifies a topic and ultimately promotes independent learning. **2:** Individual or small group activities designed to supplement formalized instruction that may employ a simple or complex protocol of activities. **3:** An individualized instructional technique. Compare with FACILITATING and MENTORING.

tutors. Persons who facilitate learning through the process of TUTORING. This role may employ students, nonstudent paraprofessionals, professional staff, and instructors. Compare with FACILITATORS.

universal design. 1: Spaces are planned at the outset to meet the needs of all potential users. **2:** The design of the environment is usable by all people, to the greatest extent possible, without the need for adaptation or specialized design (Higbee, 2003). Compare with INCLUSION and UNIVERSAL INSTRUCTIONAL DESIGN.

universal instructional design. Creation of an environment that is conducive to learning for all students with a lessened need for separate accommodations for a student with an academic weakness or a disability since the accommodations have been embedded into the learning situation and all students can benefit from them (Higbee, 2003). Compare with *INCLUSION* and *UNIVERSAL DESIGN*.

Video-Based Supplemental Instruction (VSI). Developed at the University of Missouri-Kansas City by Dr. Deanna Martin during the 1990s, VSI is one example of a course-based learning assistance. Compare with *COOPERATIVE LEARNING* and *COURSE-BASED LEARNING ASSISTANCE*.

visual imagery. The process, or result, of mentally picturing objects or events that are normally experienced directly (Harris & Hodges, 1981).

wait time. The period of time that an instructional staff member delays responding to a question to encourage a student response.

web-based. Information that is posted to the Internet World Wide Web.

writing process. A progression of activities that include prewriting that organizes and focuses the topic, initial drafting of ideas developed in prewriting, editing the draft text one or more times, producing a final version of the text that concludes with final proofreading, and correction of the text. Compare with *COLLEGE-LEVEL WRITING SKILLS*.

References

Americans with Disabilities Act of 1990. (1990). Pub. L. No. 101-336, § 2, 104 Stat. 328 (1991).

American Psychological Association. (2001). *Publication manual of the American Psychological Association* (5th ed.). Washington, D.C.: Author.

Anderson, T. H., & Armbruster, B. B. (1984). Studying. In P. D. Pearson (Ed.), *Handbook of reading research* (pp. 657–680). New York: Longman.

Arendale, D. (2005). Terms of endearment: Words that help define and guide developmental education. *Journal of College Reading and Learning, 35*(2), 66–82.

Bloom, B. S. (1956). *Taxonomy of education.* New York: Longman Green.

Brown, A. L. (1981). Metacognitive development and reading. In R. J. Spiro et al. (Eds.), *Theoretical issues in reading comprehension.* New York: Lawrence Erlbaum.

Bushy, C. L., & Andrews, R. C. (Eds.). (1980). *Dictionary of reading and learning disabilities.* Los Angeles: Western Psychological Services.

Clark-Thayer, S. (Ed.). (1995). *NADE self-evaluation guides: Models for assessing learning assistance/development education programs.* Clearwater, FL: H & H Publishing.

Collins, J. W., & O'Brien, W. P. (2003). *The Greenwood dictionary of education.* Westport, CT: Greenwood Press.

Dembo, M. H. (1994). *Applying educational psychology* (5th ed.). New York: Longman.

Dejnozka, E. L., & Kapel, D. E. (1991). *American educators' encyclopedia.* New York: Greenwood Press.

Duranczyk, I. M. (2004). Voices of underprepared university students: Outcomes of developmental mathematics education. (Doctoral dissertation, Grambling State University, 2002). *Dissertation Abstracts International,* 65(06), 2111B.

Eastridge, G., & Price, U. (Eds.). (1969). *Reading dictionary.* Lenoir, NC: Smith Printing Company.

Ellis, A. K., & Fouts, J. T. (1996). *Handbook of educational terms and applications.* Princeton, NJ: Eye on Education Press.

Ferrell, G. M. (1973). *The relationship of scores on a measure of test-wiseness to performance on teacher-made objective achievement examinations and on standardized ability and achievement tests, to grade-point average, and to sex for each of five high school samples.* Unpublished doctoral dissertation, University of Southern California.

Gabelnick, F., MacGregor, J., Matthew, R. S., & Smith, B. L. (1990). *Learning communities: Creating connections among students, faculty, and disciplines.* New Directions for Teaching and Learning, No. 41. San Francisco: Jossey-Bass.

Good, G. T., & Thomas, J. B. (Eds.). (1945). *Dictionary of education.* New York: McGraw-Hill.

Harris, T. L., & Hodges, R. E. (Eds.). (1981). *A dictionary of reading and related terms.* Newark, DE: International Reading Association.

Higbee, J. L. (Ed.). (2003). *Curriculum transformation and disability: Implementing universal design in higher education.* Retrieved July 30, 2007, from Center for Research on Developmental Education and Urban Literacy, College of Education and Human Development, University of Minnesota-Twin Cities. Web site: http://www.education.umn.edu/CRDEUL/publications.html

Higbee, J. L., Lundell, D. B., & Duranczyk, I. M. (Eds.). (2003). *Multiculturalism in developmental education.* Retrieved July 30, 2007, from Center for Research on Developmental Education and Urban Literacy, College of Education and Human Development, University of Minnesota-Twin Cities. Web site: http://www.education.umn.edu/CRDEUL/publications.html

Kerstiens, G. (1986, April 19). *Time-critical reading comprehension tests and developmental students.* Paper delivered at the 1986 Annual Meeting of the American Educational Research Association, San Francisco (ERIC Document Reproduction Service No. ED278700).

Kerstiens, G. (1990). A slow look at speeded reading comprehension tests. *Review of Research in Developmental Education,* 7(3), 1–6.

Koski, W. S., & Levin, H. M. (1998). *Replacing remediation with acceleration in higher education: Preliminary report on literature review and initial interviews.* Stanford, CA: National Center for Postsecondary Improvement, School of Education, Stanford University.

Materniak, G., & Williams, A. (1987). CAS standards and guidelines for learning assistance programs. *Journal of Developmental Education,* 11(1), 12–18.

National Association for Developmental Education. (1995). *Developmental education goals & definition.* Carol Stream, IL: Author. Retrieved July 24, 2005, from http://nade.net/L.%20nade_store.htm

Page, G. T., & Thomas, J. B. (Eds.). (1980). *International dictionary of education.* Cambridge, MA: Massachusetts Institute of Technology.

Pedlety, M. (2001). Stigma. In J. L. Higbee, D. B. Lundell, & I. M. Duranczyk (Eds.). *2001: A developmental odyssey.* Warrensburg, MO: National Association for Developmental Education.

Reder, L. M., & Anderson, J. R. (1980). A partial resolution of the paradox of interference: The role of integrating knowledge. *Cognitive Psychology, 12,* 447–474.

Rubin, M. (1991). A glossary of developmental education terms compiled by the CRLA Task Force on Professional Language for College Reading and Learning. *Journal of College Reading and Learning, 22*(2), 1–13.

Schmidt, J. C., Bellcourt, M. A., Xiong, K. M., Wigfield, A. M., Peterson, I. L. B., Halbert, S. D., Woodstrom, L. A., Vang, E. M., & Higbee, J. L. (2005). Sharing our experiences: General College students give voice to their perspectives of GC. In J. L. Higbee, D. B Lundell, & D. R. Arendale (Eds.). *The General College vision: Integrating intellectual growth, multicultural perspectives, and student development* (pp. 17–33). Retrieved July 30, 2007, from Center for Research on Developmental Education and Urban Literacy, College of Education and Human Development, University of Minnesota-Twin Cities. Web site: http://www.education.umn.edu/CRDEUL/publications.html

Scriven, M. (1991). *Evaluation thesaurus* (4th ed). Newbury Park, CA: Sage Publications.

Shafritz, J. M., Koeppe, R. R., & Soper, E. W. (1988). *The facts on file dictionary of education.* New York: Facts on File.

Technology Related Assistance for Individuals with Disabilities Act of 1988, P.L. 100-407.

Upcraft, M. L. (1984). *Orienting students to college.* New Directions for Student Services, No. 25. San Francisco: Jossey-Bass.

Additional Readings

Arendale, D. R. (2002). A memory sometimes ignored: The history of developmental education. *The Learning Assistance Review, 7*(1), 5–13.

Boylan, H. (2004). *What works: Research-based practices in developmental education.* Boone, NC: National Center for Developmental Education.

Boylan, H. R., & Bonham, B. S. (2007). 30 years of developmental education: A retrospective. *Journal of Developmental Education, 30*(3), 2–4.

Leedy, P. D. (1958). *A history of the origin and development of instruction in reading improvement at the college level.* Unpublished doctoral dissertation. New York University. (University Microfilms No. 59-01016).

Stahl, N. A., & Hartman, D. K. (2004). Doing historical research on literacy. In N. K. Duke & M. H. Mallette (Eds.), *Literacy research methodologies* (pp. 170–196). New York: Guilford Press.

Stahl, N. A., & King, J. R. (2009). History. In R. F. Flippo & D. C. Caverly (Eds.), *Handbook of college and study strategy research* (2nd ed., pp. 3–25). New York: Routledge.

2

Developmental Education and Learning Assistance Today

Virtually every term in the field of pedagogy brings with it a denotation, and whether immediately or over time, there will emerge a number of connotations — either positive or negative but, generally, never simply neutral — for that concept. The last sentence provides a perfect example of this point, as there is a cadre of adult educators who have taken the stance that *pedagogy* does not represent, or may even demean, the education of adults. They greatly prefer to use the more targeted term of *andragogy* when talking about curriculum and instruction for the adult population. Others will say that good pedagogy is simply good pedagogy, regardless of the student's age.

Such an example sets the stage for understanding the debates associated with a number of the descriptors used to talk about the services provided to postsecondary students seeking to demonstrate their mastery of discipline-specific, or institutional, or state, or national standards for the knowledge, skills, and dispositions expected for mastery of a subject area. For instance, what indeed is the difference between the fields of *developmental education* and *learning assistance*? What services fall within the parameters of each concept, or, maybe more to the point, which services do not fall within the parameters of each concept? Beyond that, assuming that there is a difference, which concept has a more positive connotation for students, educators, or laypeople? Of course, such terms and the associated debates originate from a myriad of historical, philosophical, regional, and political contexts and personal interactions. Perhaps in the future a combination of internal vision and external pressures will lead to a unified lexicon for an integrated profession.

One pedagogical construct that transcends all postsecondary support services — whether in classrooms, assistance centers, or tutorial programs — is the fundamental need to teach students how to be effective and efficient learners. In the best of all possible worlds all students would come to higher education with a cache of proven study strategies. Likewise, all college instructors across the disciplines would teach students to master the unique throughways, principles, and concepts that provide the foundation for a particular field.

The proponents of the college readiness movement would like to propose that the current endeavors driven by wealthy foundations, testing corporations, and well-funded policy centers should eventually lead all students to be prepared for college (or work), but history has shown us time and time again that underprepared or misprepared students will cross the thresholds of higher education regardless of the reform movement of the moment.

The proponents of professional development for college faculty members will point to the establishment of faculty development and instructional design centers across the country. Yet, as well-meaning as such efforts may be, in all too many cases the faculty members have yet to subscribe to the services, and the design of professional development courses is often modeled on the worst of public school in-service training, with one-shot, parachute-drop informational delivery sessions. Instruction in classes is likely to continue to focus on the product of the canon instead of on the processes that will allow students to master the knowledge underlying the subject or to develop positive dispositions about the subject.

If students are to have the opportunity to grow as effective, efficient, self-directed, and metacognitively aware learners, it will be the members of the developmental education, learning assistance, tutorial, supplemental instruction, FYE (First–Year Experience), student success field, united or not, under one title or not, who will be there to provide the pedagogical or andragogical support for all postsecondary students, whether they are considered prepared, underprepared, misprepared, or at-risk, in courses that are remedial, developmental, or compensatory.

The articles in this chapter build upon the historical foundations covered in the previous chapter to present an understanding of unifying constructs for the field of developmental education/learning assistance. The chapter begins with Jeanne L. Higbee's time-honored discussion on the nature of the diverse clientele found within the developmental program. The next reading in the chapter puts forth a cogent argument by Kathryn Bartle Angus and JoAnne Greenbaum that adult learners do have specific rights in the postsecondary learning environment. Then, Hunter R. Boylan builds the case that developmental education is more than a set of instructional courses as he discusses alternatives to the traditional remedial model. Finally, David R. Arendale covers cooperative learning programs that support content mastery in postsecondary classes.

Commentary: Who Is the Developmental Student?

Jeanne L. Higbee

Any discussion of courses, programs, or services designed to promote the effective delivery of strategic learning instruction must first define the scope of these programs. Higbee discusses the expanding goals of developmental education and the growing breadth of developmental programs. With such expansive parameters, the very definition of the developmental education student goes well beyond the connotations associated with remedial education.

Introduction

One of the greatest challenges of developmental education is eliminating the stigma associated with programs and services designed to enhance academic achievement. The jargon embedded in the writing of developmental education professionals exacerbates the problem. Frequently the terms "developmental" and "remedial" are used interchangeably (Casazza, 1999; Higbee, 1993) to describe courses that are often considered precollege level (Bohr, 1996), leading students, parents, faculty, administrators, government officials, and the public at large to question the appropriateness of their existence in colleges and universities throughout the United States (Hardin, 1988, 1998) and around the world (Hulme & Barlow, 1995; Lemelin, 1998; Spriggs & Gandy, 1997). Casazza (1999) states:

> An examination of the word remedial and its meaning reveals many things. It is the most common term across educational levels used to describe student weaknesses or deficiencies. It implies a "fixing" or "correction" of a deficit. For this reason, it is often associated with a medical model where a diagnosis is made, a prescription is given, and a subsequent evaluation is conducted to see if the "patient," or student, has been brought up to speed. If the evaluation shows that the student needs a little more "fixing," then perhaps another course is prescribed or, more often than not, the student is asked to refill the prescription and retake the same course. As we are only too aware, this cycle can repeat itself again and again until the student gives up, lowers expectations and simply puts in time until formal schooling is completed, or decides to drop out. (p. 4)

Developmental educators have taken steps to more clearly define their work (Boylan & Saxon, 1998; Clowes, 1982; Spann & McCrimmon, 1998). For example, during the last decade the National Association for Developmental Education (NADE, 1995), under the leadership of Gene Beckett, created its own definition and goals statement, providing the following definition:

> Developmental Education is a field of practice and research within higher education with a theoretical foundation in developmental psychology and learning theory. It promotes the cognitive and affective growth of all post-secondary learners, at all levels of the learning continuum.
>
> Developmental education is sensitive and responsive to the individual differences and special needs among learners.
>
> Developmental education programs and services commonly address academic preparedness, diagnostic assessment and placement, affective barriers to learning, and development of general and discipline-specific learning strategies. (NADE, 1995)

The goals of developmental education are stated as follows:

1. To preserve and make possible educational opportunity for each postsecondary learner.

2. To develop in each learner the skills and attitudes necessary for the attainment of academic, career, and life goals.

3. To ensure proper placement by assessing each learner's level of preparedness for college course work.

4. To maintain academic standards by enabling learners to acquire competencies needed for success in mainstream college courses.

5. To enhance the retention of students.

6. To promote the continued development and application of cognitive and affective learning theory (NADE, 1995).

Beckett (1995) observed:

> We have an identity problem. No, we have an identity crisis, and we developmental educators are greatly responsible for it. . . .
>
> There are almost as many names for developmental education departments and programs as there are colleges and universities. Is it a wonder, therefore, that people outside our field are confused?
>
> It's past time we declare "developmental education" as the precise, definitive name for our field and discipline and all it encompasses. . . . We have to let higher education know who we are and what we do. We have to resolve our identity crisis: not soon, but now. (p. 1)

Five years later, the identity crisis seems to be even greater. During the past 24 months, discussions at the Harvard Symposium (Casazza, 1999), the University of Minnesota General College's first Intentional Meeting on Future Directions in Developmental Education (Lundell & Higbee, in press), and in think tank sessions held in conjunction with NADE's 2000 annual conference in Biloxi have revisited how the profession of developmental education defines itself. Many within the field agree that developmental education has expanded in myriad directions (Commander, Stratton, Callahan, & Smith, 1996; Dwinell, Higbee, & Antenen, 1993; Farmer & Barham, 1996; Higbee, 1999; Higbee & Dwinell, 1998; Higbee, Thomas, Hayes, Glauser, & Hynd, 1998; Simpson, Hynd, Nist, & Burrell, 1997; Spriggs & Gandy, 1997; Stockwell, Ament, Butler, & Henderson, 1992; Stratton, 1998b; Wilkie, 1993; Zinn, Morris, McEnery, & Poole, 1998), and is not limited to required courses in reading, writing, and mathematics. Other programs and services that fall under the umbrella of developmental education include, but are not limited to, learning centers (Chickering & O'Connor, 1996; Culbertson & Johnson, 1994; Gamboa, Gibson, & Thomas, 1992; McDaniel, James, & Davis, 2000; Young, Adams, Davis, Haase, & Shaffer, 1996); tutorial services (Kowal, Shaw, & Wood, 1998); mentoring programs; Supplemental Instruction (Anton, Dooley, & Meadows, 1998; Arendale, 1998; Martin & Arendale, 1993; Martin, Blanc, & DeBuhr, 1983; Peled & Kim, 1995; Visor, Johnson, Schollaert, Good Mojab, & Davenport, 1995; Zaritsky, 1998); paired, linked, and adjunct courses (Blinn & Sisco, 1996; Bullock, Madden, & Harter, 1987; Byrd & Carter, 1997; Commander, Callahan, Stratton, & Smith, 1997; Commander & Smith, 1995; Dimon, 1981; Resnick, 1993; Simon, Barnett, Noble, Sweeney, & Thom, 1993; Weinstein, 1995); workshops (Bader, 1995; Higbee et al., 1998); many different types of learning communities (Carter & Silker, 1997; Cross, 1998; Dolan, 1998; Romanoff, 2000); strategic learning courses (Weinstein, Dierking, Husman, Roska, & Powdrill, 1998; Weinstein, Hanson, Powdrill, Roska, Dierking, Husman, & McCann, 1997); first-year experience programs (Deppe & Davenport, 1996; Sanford, 1998); academic counseling programs and courses (Higbee & Dwinell, 1992, 1996); retention services; elective courses (Higbee et al., 1998; Higbee, Dwinell, & Thomas, 2000); distance learning (Illingworth, 1996) and teaching on television (Hodge-Hardin, 1998; Koehler, 2000; Thomas & Higbee, 1998); critical thinking course programs and courses (Chaffee, 1992; Thomas & Higbee, 2000); workplace literacy projects (Longman, Atkinson, Miholic, & Simpson, 1999; Wall, Longman, Atkinson, & Maxcy, 1993); summer bridge programs (Stratton, 1998a); high school partnerships (Spence, Autin, & Clausen, 2000); integrated courses (Long, 1997); and broad-based developmental education curricula such as those offered within the General College at the University of Minnesota (Brothen & Wambach, in press; Ghere, in press; James

& Haselbeck, 1998; Jensen & Rush, 2000; Wambach & delMas, 1998; Wilcox & Jensen, 2000) and the General Education Program at Kean University (Best & Lees, 2000). A review of the related literature, as demonstrated above, supports the notion that developmental educators take an inclusive approach to their definition of their profession.

Given this broad interpretation of the definition and goals of developmental education, who is the developmental student? The answer includes the student who participates in Project College and Career (Illingworth & Illingworth, 1994) at the University of Alaska Fairbanks; the student who seeks assistance at the Tech Learning Center (TLC) at Muskingum Area Technical College or at the College Skills Lab at the College of Charleston; the student who enrolls in a critical thinking course at LaGuardia Community College or in "Topics in Problem Solving" at the University of Georgia; the student participating in an integrated reading, writing, and religion course at Bethune Cookman College or in an academic enhancement group at Central Michigan University; the student who meets regularly with a mentor at Indiana University Purdue University-Indianapolis; or the student who chooses to lake a logic course in the General College rather than in the College of Liberal Arts at the University of Minnesota. *Any* student at *any* postsecondary educational institution can potentially be identified as a developmental student if she or he chooses (or is required) to take advantage of one of myriad developmental education courses, programs, or services. Thus, just as we do our students and our profession a disservice by using the terms *remedial* and *developmental* interchangeably, we stigmatize our students and our programs when we imply that all developmental students are high-risk, underprepared, or academically disadvantaged. Nor can we relegate developmental education programs to specific types of institutions. Academic enrichment and retention programs are needed as much at highly selective universities as they are at two-year open-door institutions.

Most of all, we need to think before we speak. We need to take care when we represent our profession, whether orally or in writing. We must pay attention to how we describe the students we serve. And we must rethink our basic assumptions about our profession. Do we accept NADE's definition of developmental education? If so, why do we persist in applying a medical model to our work? Why, when exploring alternative labels for our profession, do we fall into the trap of using words reflecting a deficit model, terms like "assistance" and "support" that imply that students lack the means to help themselves? Why do we focus on the negative, rather than adopting terminology like "achievement," "enrichment," or "enhancement," jargon typically linked to programs for "gifted" students?

Even within the NADE definition statement, which is generally positive, stating that developmental education "promotes ... growth" and is "sensitive and responsive," there is mention of the "special needs of learners." It is truly unfortunate that in the field of education, "special" has become synonymous with "somehow deficient." Why "special" needs? Why give the impression that developmental education serves a "special" population, when the intent of the definition statement was to communicate that developmental education can enrich learning experiences among any and all postsecondary students? Even the use of the word "needs" connotes a lack of some skill, quality, or characteristic essential to achievement. The NADE definition and goals statement was an important first step, and Gene Beckett and his executive board should be commended for their foresight. However, the time has come for all professional organizations involved in the work of developmental education to reevaluate the definition statement and create a description of the field to be disseminated widely both within and outside the profession.

Semantics is important, and it is critical to the future of the profession that developmental educators articulate their mission so that it is clearly understood by practitioners, administrators, students, parents, legislators, and the public. What parent would find fault with programs aimed at enhancing academic performance? What politician would criticize retention efforts in public institutions of higher learning, given the importance of educating the citizenry to be competitive in the age of information and technology?

Who is the developmental student? More appropriate questions might be, "Is there any student who would not benefit from courses, programs, and services designed to enhance academic achievement and promote the development of the individual to his or her full potential?" or "Why place any label on the students we serve?" Of what value is the term "developmental student"? Must we "define" our students? They do not seem to have an "identity crisis." Rather than continuing to focus their efforts on the labeling, testing, and mandatory placement of a targeted, and thus stigmatized, group of students in required "basic skills" courses, developmental educators interested in defending and protecting the profession, as well as their own jobs, should embrace a broader definition of their mission and wholeheartedly accept their role in promoting "the cognitive and affective growth of all postsecondary learners, at all levels of the learning continuum" (NADE, 1995). Developmental educators must devote more than "lip service" to their definition of their profession. They must apply theory and research regarding best practices to the provision of expanded services that are responsive to all students. All students are engaged in the developmental process.

References

Anton, H. F., Dooley, J. L., & Meadows, D. C. (1998). Developmental educators as Supplemental Instruction providers: The next step. *NADE Selected Conference Papers, 4*, 6–7.

Arendale, D. (1998). Increasing efficiency and effectiveness of learning for freshman college students though Supplemental Instruction. In J. L. Higbee & P. L. Dwinell (Eds.), *Developmental education: Preparing successful college students* (pp. 185–197). Columbia, SC: National Resource Center for The First-Year Experience and Students in Transition, University of South Carolina.

Bader, C. H. (1995). Developmental studies teachers to retention specialists: Assets and liabilities. *NADE Selected Conference Papers, 1,* 1–2.

Beckett, G. (1995). President's message. *NADE Newsletter, 19*(1), 1–2.

Best, L., & Lees, B. (2000). A vision for skills development: The general education program at Kean University. *Research & Teaching in Developmental Education, 16*(2), 119–122.

Blinn, J., & Sisco, O. (1996). "Linking" developmental reading and biology. *NADE Selected Conference Papers, 2,* 8–9.

Bohr, L. (1996). College and precollege reading instruction: What are the real differences? *The Learning Assistance Review, 1*(1), 14–28.

Boylan, H. R., & Saxon, D. P. (1998). The origin, scope, and outcomes of developmental education in the 20th century. In J. L. Higbee & P. L. Dwinell (Eds.), *Developmental education: Preparing successful college students* (pp. 5–13). Columbia, SC: National Resource Center for The First-Year Experience and Students in Transition, University of South Carolina.

Brothen, T., & Wambach, C. (in press). A research based approach to developing a computer-assisted course for developmental students. In J. L. Higbee & P. L. Dwinell (Eds.), *The Many Faces of Developmental Education.* Warrensburg, MO: NADE.

Bullock, T., Madden, D., & Harter, J. (1987). Paired developmental reading and psychology courses. *Research & Teaching in Developmental Education, 3*(2), 22–29.

Byrd, E. H., & Carter, E. C. (1997). Study-reading for paired courses. *NADE Selected Conference Papers, 3,* 1–3.

Carter, J. A., & Silker, G. L. (1997). Academic enhancement groups: Transformational process for academically deficient students. *NADE Selected Conference Papers, 3,* 7–8.

Casazza, M. E. (1999). Who are we and where did we come from? *Journal of Developmental Education, 23*(1), 2–4, 6–7.

Chaffee, J. (1992). Critical thinking skills: The cornerstone of developmental education. *Journal of Developmental Education, 15*(3), 2.

Chickering, A. W., & O'Connor, J. (1996). The university learning center: A driving force for collaboration. *About Campus, 1*(4), 16–21.

Clowes, D. A. (1982). More than a definitional problem: Remedial, compensatory, and developmental education. *Journal of Developmental and Remedial Education, 4*(2), 8–10.

Commander, N. E., Callahan, C. A., Stratton, C. B., & Smith, B. D. (1997). Adjunct courses and Supplemental Instruction: A ten-step workshop. *NADE Selected Conference Papers, 3,* 14–16.

Commander, N. E., Stratton, C. B., Callahan, C. A., & Smith, B. D. (1996). A learning assistance model for expanding academic support. *Journal of Developmental Education, 20*(2), 8–16.

Commander, N. E., & Smith, B. D. (1995). Developing adjunct reading and learning courses that work. *Journal of Reading, 38*(5), 352–360.

Cross, K. P. (1998). Why learning communities? Why now? *About Campus, 3*(3), 4–11.

Culbertson, D. L., & Johnson, P. C. (1994). Winning strategies through individualized learning in the success center. *Proceedings of the 18th Annual Conference of NADE,* 3–5.

Deppe, M. J., & Davenport, F. G. (1996). Expanding the first-year experience: A report from Hamline University. *About Campus, 1*(4), 27–30.

Dimon, M. (1981). Why adjunct courses work. *Journal of College Reading and Learning, 21,* 33–40. Reprinted in M. Maxwell (Ed.) (1994), *From access to success.* Clearwater, FL: H & H.

Dolan, A. (1998, November). Welcome to the neighborhood. *The Iowa Stater, 24*(3), 3.

Dwinell, P. L., Higbee, J. L., & Antenen, W. (1993). Expanding the role of developmental education in research institutions. *Proceedings for the 17th Annual Conference of NADE,* 4.

Farmer, V. L., & Barham, W. A. (1996). Selected models of developmental education programs in postsecondary institutions. *NADE Selected Conference Papers, 2,* 10–11.

Gamboa, S., Gibson, S., & Thomas, L. (1992). Meeting diversity's challenge: The comprehensive academic support program. *Proceedings for the 16th Annual Conference of NADE,* 3–4.

Ghere, D. L. (in press). Teaching American history in a developmental education context. In J. L. Higbee & P. L. Dwinell (Eds.), *The Many Faces of Developmental Education.* Warrensburg, MO: NADE.

Hardin, C. J. (1988). Access to higher education: Who belongs? *Journal of Developmental Education, 12,* 2–6.

Hardin, C. J. (1998). Who belongs in college: A second look. In J. L. Higbee & P. L. Dwinell (Eds.), *Developmental education: Preparing successful college students* (pp. 15–24). Columbia, SC: National Resource Center for The First-Year Experience and Students in Transition, University of South Carolina.

Higbee, J. L. (1993). Developmental versus remedial: More than semantics. *Research & Teaching in Developmental Education, 9*(2), 99–105.

Higbee, J. L. (1999). New directions for developmental reading programs: Meeting diverse student needs. In J. R. Dugan, P. E. Linder, W. M. Linek, & E. G. Sturtevant (Eds.), *Advancing the World of Literacy: Moving into the 21st Century,* 21st Yearbook of the College Reading Association (pp. 172–181). Commerce, TX: College Reading Association.

Higbee, J. L., & Dwinell, P. L. (1992). The development of underprepared freshmen enrolled in a self-awareness course. *Journal of College Student Development, 33,* 26–33.

Higbee, J. L., & Dwinell, P. L. (1996). Seeking feedback to enhance developmental education counseling programs. *Research & Teaching in Developmental Education, 13*(2) 85–88.

Higbee, J. L., & Dwinell, P. L. (1998). Transitions in developmental education at the University of Georgia. In J. L. Higbee & P. L. Dwinell (Eds.), *Developmental education: Preparing successful college students* (pp. 55–61). Columbia, SC: National Resource Center for The First-Year Experience and Students in Transition, University of South Carolina.

Higbee, J. L., Dwinell, P. L., & Thomas, P. V. (2000). Beyond University 101: Elective courses to enhance retention. Manuscript submitted for publication.

Higbee, J. L., Thomas, P. V., Hayes, C. G., Glauser, A. S., & Hynd, C. R. (1998). Expanding developmental education services: Seeking faculty input. *The Learning Assistance Review, 3*(1), 20–31.

Hodge-Hardin, S. (1998). Interactive television in the classroom: A comparison of student math achievement. *NADE Selected Conference Papers, 4,* 26–27.

Hulme, T., & Barlow, A. R. (1995). A fair chance for all. *NADE Selected Conference Papers, 1,* 13–15.

Illingworth, R. D. (1996). Mining metamorphic rock: Distance delivery of developmental English classes. *NADE Selected Conference Papers, 2,* 18–19.

Illingworth, M. L., & Illingworth, R. D. (1994). Transition to college: Leveling the playing field. *Proceedings of the 18th Annual Conference of NADE,* 18–20.

James, J. P., & Haselbeck, B. (1998). The arts as a bridge to understanding identity and diversity. In P. L. Dwinell & J. L. Higbee (Eds.), *Developmental education: Meeting diverse student needs* (pp. 3–19). Morrow, GA: NADE.

Jensen, M., & Rush, B. (2000). Teaching a human anatomy and physiology course within the context of developmental education. In J. L. Higbee & P. L. Dwinell (Eds.), *The many faces of developmental education* (pp. 47–57). Warrensburg, MO: NADE.

Koehler, A. G. (2000). Teaching on television. *Research & Teaching in Developmental Education, 16*(2), 97–108.

Kowal, P., Shaw, G., & Wood, D. (1998). Certifying tutor programs: Rationale, guidelines, and models. *NADE Selected Conference Papers, 4,* 31–33.

Lemelin, R. (1998) Barriers to higher education and strategies to remove them: An international perspective. In P. L. Dwinell & J. L. Higbee (Eds.), *Developmental education: Meeting diverse student needs.* Morrow, GA: NADE.

Long, N. A. Z. (1997). Minority student success through an integrated curriculum. *NADE Selected Conference Papers, 3,* 28–29.

Longman, D., Atkinson, R., Miholic, V., & Simpson, P. (1999). Building long-range workplace literacy projects: The ABC reading apprenticeship and task analysis. In J. L. Higbee & P. L. Dwinell (Eds.), *The expanding role of developmental education.* Morrow, GA: NADE.

Lundell, D. B., & Higbee, J. L. (in press). *Proceedings of the University of Minnesota General College Intentional Meeting on Future Directions in Developmental Education.* Minneapolis, MN: Center for Research in Developmental Education and Urban Literacy, University of Minnesota.

Martin, D. C., & Arendale, D. (Eds.). (1993). *Supplemental Instruction: Improving first-year student success in high-risk courses.* Columbia, SC: National Resource Center for The Freshman Year Experience.

Martin, D. C., Blanc, R. A., & DeBuhr, L. (1983). Breaking the attrition cycle: The effects of Supplemental Instruction on undergraduate performance and attrition. *Journal of Higher Education, 54*(1), 80–89.

McDaniel, N., James, J. B., & Davis, G. (2000). The student success center at Auburn University. *About Campus, 5*(1), 25–28.

National Association for Developmental Education. (1995). *Definition and goals statement.* Carol Stream, IL: Author.

Peled, O. N., & Kim, A. C. (1995). Supplemental instruction in biology at the college level. *NADE Selected Conference Papers, 1,* 2–24.

Resnick, J. (1993). A paired reading and sociology course. In P. Malinowski (Ed.), *Perspectives in Practice in Developmental Education* (pp. 62–64). Canandaigua, NY: New York College Learning Association.

Romanoff, S. J. (2000). The learning community laboratory: A context for discovery. *Journal of College Student Development, 41*, 245–247.

Sanford, B. J. (1998). First-year experience: Easing the transition to college. *NADE Selected Conference Papers, 4*, 37–39.

Simon, J., Barnett, L., Noble, L., Sweeney, S., & Thom, H. (1993). Interdisciplinary models of pairing at three institutions. *Proceedings for the 17th Annual Conference of the National Association for Developmental Education*, 17–18.

Simpson, M. L., Hynd, C. R., Nist, S. L., & Burrell, K. I. (1997). College academic assistance programs and practices. *Educational Psychology Review, 9*(1), 39–87.

Spann, M. G., Jr., & McCrimmon, S. (1998). Remedial/developmental education: Past, present, and future. In J. L. Higbee & P. L. Dwinell (Eds.), *Developmental education: Preparing successful college students*. Columbia, SC: National Resource Center for The First-Year Experience and Students in Transition, University of South Carolina.

Spence, S. D., Autin, G., & Clausen, S. (2000). Reducing the cost of remediation: A partnership with high schools. *Research & Teaching in Developmental Education, 16*(2), 5–23.

Spriggs, L., & Gandy, C. (1997). The changing nature of learner support in English universities. *NADE Selected Conference Papers, 3*, 44–46.

Stockwell, D., Ament, R., Butler, A., & Henderson, S. (1992). Keys, access, and TLC: Diversity in academic support programs. *Proceedings for the 16th Annual Conference of NADE*, 15.

Stratton, C. B. (1998a). Bridge: Summer retention program for pre-college African American students. In P. L. Dwinell & J. L. Higbee (Eds.), *Developmental education: Meeting diverse student needs* (pp. 45–62). Morrow, GA: NADE.

Stratton, C. B. (1998b). Transitions in developmental education: Interviews with Hunter Boylan and David Arendale. In J. L. Higbee & P. L. Dwinell (Eds.), *Developmental education: Preparing successful college students* (pp. 25–36). Columbia, SC: National Resource Center for The First-Year Experience and Students in Transition, University of South Carolina.

Thomas, P. V., & Higbee, J. L. (1998). Teaching mathematics on television: Perks and Pitfalls. *Academic Exchange Quarterly, 2*(2), 29–33.

Thomas, P. V., & Higbee, J. L. (2000, April). *Student development seminars in critical thinking and problem solving*. Paper presented at the Annual Conference of the American College Personnel Association, Washington, D.C.

Visor, J. N., Johnson, J. J., Schollaert, A. M., Good Mojab, C. A., & Davenport, D. (1995). Supplemental Instruction's impact on affect: A follow-up and expansion. *NADE Selected Conference Papers, 1*, 36–37.

Wall, P., Longman, D., Atkinson, R., & Maxcy, D. (1993). Capitalizing on workplace literacy instruction for industrial construction workers: The ABC's of ABC. *Proceedings of the 17th Annual Conference of the National Association for Developmental Education*, 19–20.

Wambach, C., & delMas, R. (1998). Developmental education at a public research university. In J. L. Higbee & P. L. Dwinell (Eds.), *Developmental education: Preparing successful college students* (pp. 53–72). Columbia, SC: National Resource Center for The First-Year Experience and Students in Transition, University of South Carolina.

Weinstein, C. E., Dierking, D., Husman, J., Roska, L., & Powdrill, L. (1998). The impact of a course in strategic learning on the long-term retention of college students. In J. L. Higbee & P. L. Dwinell (Eds.), *Developmental education: Preparing successful college students* (pp. 85–96). Columbia, SC: National Resource Center for The First-Year Experience and Students in Transition, University of South Carolina.

Weinstein, C. D., Hanson, G., Powdrill, L., Roska, L., Dierking, D., Husman, J., & McCann, E. (1997). The design and evaluation of a course in strategic learning. *NADE Selected Conference Papers, 3*, 53–55.

Weinstein, G. L. (1995). Mathematics survival: A linked course. *NADE Selected Conference Papers, 1*, 38–40.

Wilcox, K. J., & Jensen, M. S. (2000). Writing to learn in anatomy and physiology. *Research & Teaching in Developmental Education, 16(2)*, 55–71.

Wilkie, C. (1993). Types and structures of developmental education programming in Pennsylvania. *Proceedings for the 17th Annual Conference of NADE*, 10–12.

Young, V., Adams, T., Davis, D., Haase, K., & Shaffer, T. (1996). New perspectives on learning and writing centers: Applying Vygotsky. *NADE Selected Conference Papers, 2*, 51–53.

Zaritsky, J. S. (1998). Supplemental Instruction: What works, what doesn't. *NADE Selected Conference Papers, 4*, 54–55.

Zinn, A., Morris, L. A., McEnery, G., & Poole, C. (1998). Moving beyond the remedial reading image. *NADE Selected Conference Papers, 4*, 57–59.

Position Statement on Rights of Adult Readers and Learners

Kathryn Bartle Angus and JoAnne Greenbaum

The College Reading and Learning Association (CRLA), with a membership of over 1,000, furnished a position statement that provides guidance for adult and postsecondary educators as they seek to improve the quality of education offered to this population. The term adult *is defined as "all students in postsecondary education, age 18 or older (traditional, nontraditional, posttraditional, reentry adults, stopouts/returning students)." Authors Kathryn Bartle Angus and JoAnne Greenbaum indicate that the position statement was developed over several years, using input from many CRLA members and then adopted by the CRLA board in 2002. Adult students' rights in the areas of quality instructors, instruction, materials, and assessment are addressed.*

Adult learners fill our college campuses and spill out onto satellite campuses and into neighborhood elementary schools for evening classes. There are more adults seeking education than at any other time in our history (National Center for Educational Statistics, 1996). Campuses strain to meet the needs of this influx of students, some of traditional age (18- to 22-year-olds) taking their next step toward mature adulthood, others, already mature adults, seeking new career opportunities or skill development. Many of these students are placed in or seek classes that help them with basic academic skills like reading comprehension and vocabulary knowledge. The National Center for Education Statistics estimates that there are 3.8 million students (30% of those in higher education) enrolled in reading and study strategy classes. Although Goal 6 of the National Education Goals Panel (1995) states that every adult American will be literate, we continue to read shocking statistics about the general lack of reading ability in the adult population. Although considerable public and scholarly attention has been given to the quality of elementary and secondary education in the United States, comparatively little has been given to the quality of postsecondary education.

The College Reading and Learning Association (CRLA) is well situated to provide a leadership role in guiding adult learning programs and teachers. The CRLA members include professionals who teach adult learners and train others to work with adults in educational settings. The CRLA has about 1,000 members in both the United States and Canada. Stated goals of the CRLA include increasing "the tools available to improve students learning" and providing "information and consultants to bodies enacting legislation directly related to college reading, learning assistance, developmental education, and tutorial services" (College Reading and Learning Association Goals, 2002). A CRLA position statement on the rights of adult readers and learners can serve as a guide to members and others in the field who want to provide the best possible education for adult students.

Statement Development

The position statement project has been under development for several years. It began with an editorial written in the CRLA California Chapter's October 1999 newsletter. In that editorial, the International Reading Association's (IRA) position statement on adolescent literacy (Moore, Bean, Birdyshaw, & Rycik, 1999) was summarized and a suggestion was posed. "Perhaps we as teachers of college reading and learning should consider our own position statement" (Angus, 1999, p. 1). The statement prompted informal discussion among CRLA members at the conference in New Orleans. It was decided that this was a project worth pursuing. A proposal was submitted to hold an institute at the 2000 conference to explore and draft an initial statement.

In Reno, a group of CRLA members met to begin the task. The group looked at the rationale for pursuing a position statement (Fabish, 2000), characteristics of adult learners (Brookfield, 1999), and current position statements from the IRA (International Reading Association, 2000; Moore et al., 1999) and the National Association for Developmental Education (NADE), (1995). It was decided that the areas of instruction, instructors, materials, and assessment would provide a framework to guide the development of a position statement. Small groups were created to focus on each area. At the end of the three-hour institute, each group presented an initial draft. In the months following the conference, the draft was sent to all group members and feedback was solicited. By employing a quasi-delphi process, a refined statement was developed.

When CRLA members convened again in Spokane, 2001, a new group met to discuss and further revise the developing document. The new version then went through the same revision process and was presented at the Developmental Education Conference in Walnut, California, January, 2001. The document that follows is the result of refinements that were made based on the feedback received at the Walnut conference and adopted by the CRLA board on November 11, 2002.

CRLA Position Statement on the Rights of Adult Readers and Learners

The term "adult" includes all students in postsecondary education, age 18 and older (traditional, nontraditional, posttraditional, reentry adults, stopouts/returning students). A distinctive characteristic of any group of adult learners is diversity; the term "adult learner" refers to a heterogeneous group of learners who are widely diverse in learning styles, motivation for learning, life transitions, life roles, learning goals, developmental tasks, prior experience, and patterns of participation in academic experience. Although adult students are an extremely diverse group, all adult readers and learners should be entitled to basic rights. These rights, described below, are presented using the following descriptors: instructors, instruction, assessment, and materials.

Adult learners have a right to instructors who:

- Engage in ongoing development and have a commitment to lifelong learning for themselves and their students
- Are knowledgeable about adult development and learning and understand the unique needs and complexities of the diverse adult learner population
- Possess expertise in their content area
- Have knowledge of learning theories, the ability to relate theory to practice, skill, and confidence in methods of presentation, modeling, and facilitating learning
- Are self-reflective, solicit feedback, and make accommodations to improve instruction
- Have a repertoire of interpersonal skills necessary to establish, maintain, and develop effective relationships (instructor/student

and student/student) and a secure, positive classroom environment that will promote active learning

- Understand their responsibilities in facilitating and guiding the learning activities of adult students while acknowledging that the adult learner retains the right and responsibility to manage his/her own life and learning, growth, discovery, and increasing skills and knowledge.

Instructors who have appropriate training and who participate in professional development are just as necessary in adult education as they are in elementary and secondary education. Continuing professional development for educators should focus on activities that enhance the educator's effectiveness. These activities should include personal growth in content knowledge, learning strategies, and educational theory. Teachers of adult learners must develop and maintain an awareness of the resources available through professional organizations, educational literature, conferences, and colleagues in their professional network. Planning professional development activities is essential because it encourages educators to take an active role in addressing their professional self-improvement (Imel, 1990).

Educators who are aware of the cognitive levels of their students can address the unique needs and challenges of these learners. This insight can result in more appropriate interactions with students, including more challenging lessons and thoughtful discussions (Frew, 1996). Adult educators should have a thorough understanding of adult intellectual development and the ability to use that understanding to design activities that foster critical thinking. Teachers must gently guide students through the levels of intellectual development to ensure lasting growth (Kloss, 1994).

Educators of adult students need to be self-reflective. Ferraro (2000) describes reflective practice in the following manner:

> The primary benefit of reflective practice for teachers is a deeper understanding of their own teaching style and ultimately, greater effectiveness as a teacher. Other specific benefits noted in current literature include the validation of a teacher's ideals, beneficial challenges to tradition, the recognition of teaching as artistry, and respect for diversity in applying theory to classroom practice . . .
>
> Research on effective teaching over the past two decades has shown that effective practice is linked to inquiry, reflection, and continuous professional growth. (p. 3)

Adult learners have a right to instruction that:

- allows them to see reading as a constructive process
- encourages reflection, critical analysis, and affective response

- includes social interaction such as collaborative and cooperative group work
- promotes interest and excitement
- is personalized to meet the needs of each learner
- is based on current theory and practice
- encourages students to become learners who are independent, autonomous, lifelong planners, and problem solvers
- integrates technology and promotes information competence

Instruction for adults should be engaging, relevant, and personalized. The central business must be about learning and not about teaching (Gardner, 2000, p. 12). Engaged readers are *motivated* to read, *strategic* in using multiple approaches, *knowledgeable in constructing* new understandings, and *socially interactive* (Guthrie, McGough, Bennet, & Rice, 1996). Adult educators need to provide instruction that is consistent with these ideas. Motivation occurs when adults see connections between their classroom experiences and their lives. The lessons they participate in need to provide relevant strategies that can be readily used in various settings.

Adult learners need to be made aware that they are active participants in constructing their own personal understandings. Chall (1996) believes that reading at the adult level is "the ability to construct knowledge on a high level of abstraction and generality and to create one's 'truth' from the 'truths' of others."

Vygotsky (1978), as well as others, has provided evidence that learning is a social activity. Instruction that incorporates social contexts (discussion and cooperative and collaborative learning activities) offers students the opportunity to learn from each other (Spencer & Angus, 2000).

"Learning is not just a cognitive process, but an affective one as well" (Taylor, 1999, p. 38). Providing opportunities that encourage critical and affective responses help students address questions about themselves as learners, specifically what they know, how they learn, and what motivates and interests them. Nell's (1988) research clearly established a correlation between reading ability and frequency. Instruction that encourages interaction with text for affective purposes is clearly important for adult readers.

Teaching and learning in the new millennium cannot ignore technology. Computers offer many benefits to adult learners, both as an instructional medium and source of content. But, the move toward computer-based technology in the classroom necessitates that educators understand theories that support sound instruction (Yaworski, 2000). Indeed, all instructional decisions should be soundly grounded in theory and current research.

Adult learners have a right to assessment that:

- Is appropriate — matching the level, purposes, and content of instruction

- Includes the student in the assessment process (e.g., self-assessment, peer review, interview, consultation)

- Occurs at frequent intervals with meaningful feedback

- Focuses on outcomes and informs instruction

- Involves multiple measures

Authentic, meaningful assessment is an integral part of any literacy program. "Literacy assessments that match knowledge of the reading process and current methods of teaching reading are needed at all levels of education" (Barksdale-Ladd, & Rose, 1997, p. 34). This type of meaningful assessment is the right of the adult learner. Instructors who work closely with adult students and use a variety of methods to measure student achievement and direct instruction are practicing informed assessment.

Wolf (1993) describes this process as follows:

> Informed assessment refers to the process that knowledgeable teachers engage in when they systematically observe and selectively document their students' performance through multiple methods, across diverse contexts, and over time as students participate in meaningful learning activities. (p. 519)

Not only are instructor assessments vital to successful adult learning, but self-assessment through metacognitive reflection is equally important. Soldner (1997) discusses the importance of metacognition, and the students' ability to reflect on the thinking strategies they use to enhance understanding and encourage cognitive development. As students engage in this self-examination they become aware of their strengths and weaknesses. Armed with this knowledge they are better equipped to accept responsibility for their learning (Porto, 2002). This self-assessment empowers adult students to gain and maintain control of their learning and thinking through increased awareness of those processes.

Adult learners have a right to materials that:

- are relevant, current, and multidisciplinary

- reflect a variety of media, genres, and cultures

- present opportunities for self-selection

Adult learners deserve materials that are appropriate for adults. The degree to which students are motivated to engage in content learning is heavily influenced by the nature of the material they encounter (Bean, 1998). Providing students with interesting and relevant materials can lead to greater engagement of students. Engaged readers are more likely to use learning strategies to see connections to prior knowledge and to construct new information (Guthrie, Alao, & Rinehart, 1997). Thus, carefully selected materials can lead to enhanced reading achievement. Additionally, selecting texts that are reflective of the cultural diversity in the classroom promotes respect and discussion among participants (Au, 1993). When students encounter materials that are connected to their culture they are more likely to feel valued as adult learners.

Offering access to a wide variety of materials that build in opportunities for choice is ideal. Allowing students to choose reading assignments that reflect their interests makes it more likely that students will become engaged and spend more time reading (Nell, 1988). Not all students enjoy reading the same subject or genre. Providing variety makes it more likely that adult students will expend the time and effort required to read and learn.

Implications and Conclusion

At the annual CRLA conference in Minneapolis, 2002, members met to continue the dialogue on the rights of adult readers and learners, and specifically to address some of the implications and potential uses of this document. Using the document as a means of informing adult learners of their rights was among the suggestions made for use at the classroom level. Supplying students with a copy of their list of rights will make them aware of what to expect from instructors and will legitimize instructional practices for students. In terms of assessment, the measures outlined in the document can be used to evaluate not only students but instructors and materials as well. Journals and portfolios were recommended as appropriate assessment tools that meet the criteria delineated in this document.

At the department level, discussion focused on how the document should serve as a guide to sound educational practice for educators of adult students and may be useful in planning postsecondary teacher training certificate programs. Departments may recommend that new and adjunct faculty refer to the document as a model when planning classroom activities and choosing materials. Further, the document could be used to create a matrix that would encourage all faculty members to examine the link between appropriate practice and existing practice in the areas addressed in the document.

Schools and departments can draw on the rights of adult readers and learners to develop or extend current mission statements and goals. Publishers of adult education texts might also find that the rights document provides guidance for development of new material. Finally, political action committees may be able to use the rights document to further political agendas that promote better quality adult education.

The membership of CRLA is dedicated to promoting quality education for adult students by ensuring that the rights of adult readers and learners are recognized and addressed. This position statement outlines these rights in the categories of appropriate materials; theory-based instruction; authentic, meaningful assessment; and knowledgeable, dedicated instructors. It is essential that teachers continue to examine and discuss the rights of their students leading to progress in adult education at many levels. Accepting responsibility to move this conversation forward will help ensure growth for students and teachers alike and quality education for all.

References

Angus, K. B. (1999, October). Adolescent literacy position statement. *CRLA California Chapter Communiqué, 7*(3).

Au, K. (1993). *Literacy instruction in multicultural settings.* New York: Harcourt Brace.

Barksdale-Ladd, M. A., & Rose, M. (1997). Qualitative assessment in developmental reading. *Journal of College Reading and Learning, 28*(1), 34–53.

Bean, T. W. (1998). Teaching literacy histories and adolescent voices: Changing content area classrooms. In D. Alvermann, D. Moore, S. Phelps, & D. Waff (Eds.), *Toward reconceptualizing adolescent literacy* (pp. 149–170). Mahwah, NJ: Lawrence Erlbaum.

Brookfield, S. D. (1999). What is college really like for adult students? *About Campus Jan.–Feb. 1999,* p. 10.

Chall, J. S. (1996). *Stages of reading development* (3rd ed.). Fort Worth: Harcourt Brace.

College Reading and Learning Association. Goals. Retrieved May 9, 2002, from http://www.crla.net/goals.htm

Fabish, J. (2000). Transacting with text: Theory and practice. *Reading Educator's Guild Newsletter, 30*(2).

Ferraro, J. (2000). Reflective practice and professional development. Washington, DC: ERIC Digest, ERIC Clearinghouse on Teaching and Teacher Education, AACTE.

Frew, A. (1996). Identifying student cognitive levels in reading responses. *Journal of Adolescent & Adult Literacy, 39*(8), 661–663.

Gardner, J. N. (2000). The changing roles of developmental educators. *Journal of College Reading and Learning, 31,* 5–18.

Guthrie, J. T., Alao, S., & Rinehart, J. M. (1997). Engagement in reading for young adolescents. *Journal of Adolescent & Adult Literacy, 40,* 438–446.

Guthrie, J. T., McGough, K., Bennett, L., & Rice, M. E. (1996). Concept-oriented reading instruction: An integrated curriculum to develop motivations and strategies for reading. In L. Baker, P. Afflerbach, & D. Reinking (Eds.), *Developing engaged readers in school and home communities* (pp. 165–190). Mahwah, NJ: Lawrence Erlbaum.

Imel, S. (1990). Managing your professional development: A guide for part-time teachers of adults. ERIC Digest (ERIC No. ED321155).

International Reading Association. (2000). Making a difference means making it different: Honoring children's rights to excellent reading instruction. Retrieved October 28, 2000, from http://www.reading.org/positions/MADMMID .html

Kloss, R. (1994). A nudge is best: Helping students through the Perry scheme of intellectual development. *College Teaching 42*(4), 151–158.

Moore, D., Bean, T., Birdyshaw, D., & Rycik, J. (1999). Adolescent literacy: A position statement. *Journal of Adolescent & Adult Literacy, 43*, 97–112.

National Association for Developmental Education. (1995). Developmental education goals and definitions. Retrieved October 28, 2000, from http:// www.umkc.edu/cad/nade/nadedocs/devgoals.htm

National Center for Educational Statistics. (1996). *Remedial education at higher education institutions in fall 1995.* [Online]. Available at http://nces.ed.gov .pub/97584.html

National Education Goals Panel. (1995). *The national education goals report: Building a nation of learners 1995.* Washington, DC: U.S. Government Printing Office.

Nell, V. (1988). *Lost in a book.* New Haven, CT: Yale University Press.

Porto, M. (2002). Implementing cooperative writing response groups and self-evaluation in South America: Struggle and survival. *Journal of Adolescent & Adult Literacy, 45*, 684–691.

Soldner, L. B. (1997). Self-assessment and the reflective reader. *Journal of College Reading and Learning, 28*, 5–11.

Spencer, B. H., & Angus, K. B. (2000). The presentation assignment: Creating learning opportunities for diverse student populations. *Journal of College Reading and Learning, 30*, 182–194.

Taylor, S. (1999). Better learning through better thinking. *Journal of College Reading and Learning, 30*, 34–45.

Vygotsky, L. S. (1978). *Mind in society: The development of higher psychological processes.* Cambridge, MA: Harvard University Press.

Wolf, K. P. (1993). From informal to informed assessment: Recognizing the role of the classroom teacher. *Journal of Reading, 36*, 518–522.

Yaworski, J. (2000). Using computer-based technology to support the college reading classroom. *Journal of College Reading and Learning, 31*, 19–41.

Exploring Alternatives to Remediation

Hunter R. Boylan

In "Exploring Alternatives to Remediation," Hunter R. Boylan addresses issues related to the cost and time investment of providing remedial courses to college students, and offers an overview of possible alternatives. Some criticisms of developmental education are examined and countered with evidence from research. Boylan also outlines current practices and then describes alternative approaches, including freshmen seminars, supplemental instruction, learning communities and collaborative learning, paired courses, critical thinking instruction, and strategic learning courses.

M any developmental educators perceive that they and their work are the subject of increasingly strident attacks by legislators and policy makers. Actually, this perception is not entirely accurate. Of the many services provided by developmental educators, only remedial courses are the target of most criticism. Developmental educators might benefit, therefore, by continuing to challenge criticisms of remedial courses while also continuing their study and exploration of alternatives to them.

In doing this it is important to note that developmental education as a whole is not under attack. Most legislators and policy makers accept and support the need for tutoring, instructional laboratories, individualized learning programs, and learning centers in colleges and universities. Although developmental education may be conceived of as a continuum of such interventions, ranging from individual basic remedial courses at one end to comprehensive learning centers at the other end, most of the criticisms are directed at the lowest end of the continuum: to remedial courses. Students, parents, administrators, faculty, and legislators regularly complain that remedial courses take too long, cost too much, and keep students from making progress toward degrees by holding them in several different levels of noncredit, remedial courses.

In response to these criticisms it should be noted that both logical and research-based arguments can be brought to bear to counter each of them. The criticisms are often based on misconceptions rather than fact. For one thing, "too long" is a relative term. According to the National Center for Education Statistics (1996) the vast majority of students complete their remedial requirements within 1 year. For the many students who are unable to succeed in college without remediation, the only alternative to an entire year's worth of effort is never completing college at all. Given this alternative, a year spent taking a few remedial courses might represent a very sound investment of student time and money. For many students, participation in remedial courses does extend their time in college by as much as a semester to a full year. For most of these students, however, it is a case of "better late than never." It is better to delay graduation than to risk never receiving a degree at all and losing access to the employment and economic opportunities resulting from a college degree (Lavin & Hyllegard, 1996).

The criticism that remedial courses represent an unreasonable proportion of public higher education expenses is simply invalid. There is little evidence that eliminating remedial courses would result in any significant savings in state allocations for higher education. A recent report from the Brookings Institute (Breneman, 1998), for instance, points out that the total national expenditure for remedial courses in a given year is less than 1% of expenditures for public higher education in the United States. The report also suggests that the benefits of remedial courses greatly outweigh this minimal cost. A follow-up to this report concludes that "remedial education draws political fire far in excess of any reasonable view of its budgetary costs" (Breneman & Haarlow, 1998, p. 20).

Another criticism of remedial courses is that many students drop out before completing them. This is a criticism with some basis in fact. A recent review of developmental education in Texas colleges and universities found some relationship between student attrition and the length of time spent in remedial courses (Boylan et al., 1996). However, such a study has not been undertaken for any other state. Nor has any national study been done on drop out rates of students who repeat remedial courses.

It does appear to be true that the greater the amount of remediation *required*, the more likely a student is to drop out (Adelman, 1998). In other words, students who are assessed as needing multiple levels of remedial courses in two or more subject areas are less likely to complete college than those who need remediation in only one area. Those who place in remedial courses in only one subject area, however, are as likely as anyone else to graduate.

Adelman (1998), notes that students who place in the lowest levels of two or more remedial courses have very weak potential for college success to begin with. This, however, is not an argument for eliminating all remedial courses, particularly since most of those who take them are eventually successful in college (McCabe & Day, 1998).

The previous discussion notwithstanding, there is at least a germ of truth to the claim that remedial courses may take too long or cost too much for some students. If a student can develop the skills essential to college success without semester-long remedial courses, then any unnecessary time spent in remedial courses is too long. Furthermore, if the student or the public has paid for any unnecessary remedial courses, then that cost is too much.

The key term here is *unnecessary*. For a great many students with weak academic backgrounds and low placement scores, the investment of time and money in remedial courses is necessary if they are to have any hope of succeeding in college. For them, immersion in a battery of remedial courses may represent the only intervention that offers a reasonable chance of success. However, for some portion of the students with low placement scores, there are other interventions available that might accomplish the objectives of remediation without requiring participation in a series of remedial courses. For such students, remediation through formal courses may really be unnecessary.

As noted at the outset, remedial courses are only one form of intervention along the continuum of interventions that comprise developmental education. Other forms of developmental education may accomplish the same purpose at a lower cost to the student and with a lesser investment of student time. This article explores alternatives to remedial courses and methods of organizing these alternatives in a manner that may reduce the amount of time required for the remediation of academic skills deficiencies. It should be noted that these alternatives are not necessarily cheaper than remedial courses and, because many of them are individualized, they may be even more labor intensive. They do, however, offer the advantage of being less time consuming for some students.

It should also be noted that these alternatives may only be applicable to a minority of the students who place into remedial courses. It is likely that the very weakest students with multiple skill deficiencies will still require the discipline of a structured course and the immersion in subject matter provided by a semester or more of remedial course work.

Nevertheless, developmental educators have a professional responsibility to ensure that participation in extensive remedial courses is required of students only when necessary. To the extent that other, less time-consuming and more efficient alternatives are available, students who might profit from these should have access to them.

Alternatives to Remedial Courses

Traditional Approaches

Traditionally, developmental education has included such activities as remedial/developmental courses, tutoring, learning laboratories, and various forms of individualized instruction. Although they have been widely criticized, remedial/developmental courses do work. Success in these courses has consistently been found to contribute to improved student academic performance as well as increased student persistence (Boylan, Bonham, Bliss, & Claxton, 1992; Cross, 1976; Donovan, 1975; Roueche & Roueche, 1993; Roueche & Snow, 1977).

Tutoring is one of the primary components of today's developmental education, and almost all colleges and universities provide some form of it (Maxwell, 1985). Furthermore, tutoring in the basic skill areas consistently has been found to contribute to student success in courses and improved retention at the institution (Boylan, Bliss, & Bonham, 1997; Donovan, 1975; Maxwell, 1985). This is particularly true when it is accompanied by strong tutor training (Boylan, Bliss, & Bonham, 1997; Casazza & Silverman, 1996).

Individualized learning laboratories and learning centers also represent traditional approaches to developmental education. When properly implemented, these approaches, too, have been demonstrated to make a positive contribution to student success (Boylan, Bliss, & Bonham, 1997; Casazza & Silverman, 1996; Cross, 1976; Maxwell, 1985).

Approaches such as those described have formed the basis of developmental education practice since the 1960s (Cross, 1976). They represent validated interventions with a history of success. They are used by developmental education practitioners because, when properly implemented, they contribute to the success of students who might not otherwise be able to succeed in college. Consequently, there is no reason to abandon them. However, the experience of the past 2 decades suggests that there are other alternatives available which, when combined with traditional developmental education, can improve the quality of practice even more, reduce the number of students taking remedial courses, and, perhaps, lead to even greater student success. At the same time, creative use of these alternatives might also reduce the amount of time students need to spend in remedial courses.

Alternative Approaches

In addition to traditional approaches, developmental educators and developmental programs currently provide a variety of more innovative alternatives. Examples of these alternatives include freshmen seminar/orientation courses (Upcraft, Gardner, & Associates, 1989), Supplemental Instruction (Martin & Arendale, 1994), paired or adjunct courses (Commander, Stratton, Callahan, & Smith, 1996), collaborative learning communities (Tinto, 1997), and critical thinking courses and programs (Chaffee, 1992).

It should, perhaps, be noted that use of the term "innovative" as applied to these alternatives is not completely accurate. Many of these interventions have been available since the 1970s and many of them are already used by developmental educators. Their use, however, has been limited in developmental programs, particularly as an alternative to remedial courses.

FRESHMAN SEMINARS. As Dwyer (1989) points out, colleges and universities have provided orientation to incoming students through most of this century. At universities, this orientation has occupied a day or two prior to the start of classes and involved students learning about their institution, its rules, regulations, procedures, and traditions. At community colleges, such orientation is generally even more limited.

As college rules and regulations became more complex, as "in loco parentis" was abandoned by institutions, and as more nontraditional students entered American colleges and universities, this "one shot" approach to orientation became increasingly ineffective (Dwyer, 1989). The freshman seminar concept, pioneered by John Gardner at the University of South Carolina in the 1970s, provided a much more comprehensive approach to the orientation of first-year college students.

Instead of lasting only a few days, the freshman seminar spans an entire academic term. Instead of concentrating on rules and traditions, the freshman seminar actually explores issues in college life, the purposes of higher education, and the requirements and expectations of college attendance through the vehicle of a regular, credit-bearing, college course conceived as an integral part of the first-year experience (Upcraft, Gardner, & Associates, 1989).

The freshman seminar has proven to be a highly effective way of integrating students into the campus culture and contributing to increased retention (Fidler & Hunter, 1989; Gardner, 1998). Because developmental students are often first-generation college students and, therefore, among the least knowledgeable of college lore, rewards, and expectations, the freshman seminar would appear to be a particularly valuable and important experience for them (Gardner). Participation in the freshman seminar would also enable developmental students to learn more about college life and the institution and obtain college credit while taking remedial courses. Although participation in the freshman seminar does not reduce the amount of time required for remediation, it does facilitate the adjustment of nontraditional students to college and contribute to their retention (Fidler & Godwin, 1994).

SUPPLEMENTAL INSTRUCTION. Supplemental Instruction, also known by its abbreviation as SI, was originally developed in the early 1970s at the University of Missouri-Kansas City by Deanna Martin (1980). It was designed to help medical school students succeed in their more difficult courses but has since been successfully applied to a variety of other groups, including developmental students (Martin & Arendale, 1998).

In Supplemental Instruction, courses in which students typically have difficulty are designated as "high-risk" courses, generally one in which 30% or more of the students enrolled obtain grades of D or F (Commander, Stratton, Callahan, & Smith, 1996). Such courses are targeted for Supplemental Instruction support. A key philosophical component of SI, therefore, is that terms such as "difficult" or "high risk" are assigned to the course rather than the students.

The support provided in SI courses consists of small-group sessions in which students who have taken the course previously serve as small-group leaders. A leader is a fellow student who attends the course, takes notes, and then meets with groups of students to discuss techniques necessary for success in the course. The student leader acts as a coach for those taking the course, offering advice and encouragement on note taking, test taking, and other study skills and strategies. This is all accomplished in small-group sessions where students may also be given oral or written quizzes or take practice tests. Another version of SI, Video-Based Supplemental Instruction or VSI, combines traditional SI activities with video tapes of lectures as a further aid in small-group sessions (Martin & Arendale, 1998).

Supplemental Instruction has been found to be particularly effective with developmental students (Blanc, DeBuhr, & Martin, 1983;

Commander, Stratton, Callahan, & Smith, 1996; Ramirez, 1997). For example, developmental students who participate in Supplemental Instruction during their early years in college are retained at far higher rates than those who do not participate (Ramirez, 1997). From this evidence, it appears likely that some of the students placed in remedial courses might be successful in regular curriculum courses supported by Supplemental Instruction.

LEARNING COMMUNITIES AND COLLABORATIVE LEARNING. Following extensive research using data from the Cooperative Institutional Research Program, Astin (1993) found that membership in one or more college communities is a critical factor in student development as well as retention. A consequence of this is that more aggressive efforts may be needed to help students develop membership in communities. The concept of learning communities at the college level is an effort to respond to this need.

At the college level, learning communities are based on the assumption that the classroom is not only a community but the only *academic community* that many students, particularly commuters and community college students, are likely to encounter in their lives. Consequently, it is important to make greater use of the classroom as a place to involve students in the academic culture. In a learning community, the classroom not only becomes a place where teaching occurs but also becomes a community in which students learn to learn.

Learning communities link courses and groups of students so that "students encounter learning as a shared rather than isolated experience" (Tinto, 1997, p. 602). Typically, a learning community is arranged by having students enroll together as a cohort in several courses linked together by a common theme. The instructors of these courses then function as a team to ensure that content in one course is related to content in the other courses and to help students make connections to that content. Students in the learning community also work collaboratively in small groups or teams to solve problems, study, or develop class projects.

Uri Treisman suggests that collaborative learning techniques are particularly important for those students who may be from nontraditional backgrounds. Results from his workshops indicate that collaborative learning contributes to greater mastery of the subject matter and higher course grades for such students (Garland, 1993). Tinto (1997) reports that the use of learning communities emphasizing collaborative learning have a positive impact on student attitudes toward learning. His research also suggests that learning communities and collaborative learning activities have a positive effect on the academic performance and persistence of developmental students (Tinto, 1998). The use of learning communities in regular curriculum courses, therefore, represents another possible alternative to remedial courses.

PAIRED COURSES.   Paired courses are, to some degree, related to collaborative learning in that a cohort of students registers for the same two courses. In the paired course model, however, one course is designed to supplement the other course. Rather than engaging students in a series of courses with a common theme, paired courses use the content of one course as a focus for the application of skills taught in another course (Commander, Stratton, Callahan, & Smith, 1996). A reading and study strategies course, for instance, might be paired with a sociology course. The instructors of the two courses would then work together to ensure that the content and rate of coverage of material are consistent between the two courses. The reading and study strategies course would use the content of the sociology course as a focus for the reading and study strategies being taught. In this way, the content of both courses becomes mutually supportive.

The use of paired courses might work well for students who read at somewhere near the level of the sociology text but who still need to develop their reading and study strategies or other academic skills. It might work well for students who require the discipline of a structured classroom setting in order to learn. Paired courses might also provide some of the benefits of a learning community by emphasizing collaboration and involvement in the learning experience.

Paired courses have been demonstrated to be a successful technique for enhancing the performance of developmental students. Developmental students participating in paired courses tend to show higher levels of performance and demonstrate greater satisfaction with their instructional experiences than similar students participating in traditional courses (Commander, Stratton, Callahan, & Smith, 1996; Wilcox, delMas, Stewart, Johnson, & Ghere, 1997).

This research suggests that, for some students, the pairing of a remedial course with a curriculum course may enhance learning. As such, thoughtful use of paired courses might reduce the amount of time spent in remediation while enabling underprepared students to earn credit in regular college courses.

CRITICAL THINKING INSTRUCTION.   The ability to think critically — to use logic, to analyze information, and to solve problems — is an essential component of success in college. Unfortunately, as Chaffee (1998) points out, students in general and developmental students in particular are rarely taught these skills. As a consequence, the inability to engage in critical thinking is a major cause for the failure of developmental students.

This problem has been addressed by developmental educators in two ways. One is the provision of a stand-alone course or workshop designed to teach critical thinking skills. The other is the integration of critical thinking skill development activities throughout an entire curriculum. Research suggests that the latter approach is the more effective of the two, particularly for the weakest students (Chaffee, 1992; Chaffee, 1998; Elder & Paul, 1994). The model used by John Chaffee at LaGuardia Community College is, perhaps, one of the best-known methods of integrating critical thinking into the curriculum. It involves teaching students to:

- solve challenging problems;
- analyze complex issues and arrive at reasoned conclusions;
- establish appropriate goals and design plans for action;
- analyze complex bodies of information and make informed decisions;
- communicate effectively through speaking, discussing, and writing; and
- critically evaluate the logic, relevance, and validity of information (Chaffee, 1997).

This is accomplished through a series of courses emphasizing these skills and linked to reading, writing, and communication content.

There is a substantial body of research indicating that the development of critical thinking skills contributes to the academic success of developmental students. Participation in programs designed to teach critical thinking skills has proven to enhance student reading and writing skills (Chaffee, 1992), improve student attitudes toward learning (Harris & Eleser, 1997), and improve student ability to do research for class assignments (St. Clair, 1994/95). An emphasis on critical thinking at the early stages of developmental students' academic careers may enable them to gain more from early remedial courses and, therefore, reduce the amount of time spent in remediation.

STRATEGIC LEARNING. Another approach to improving student learning is found in the individual learning skills courses developed by Claire Weinstein at the University of Texas at Austin (Weinstein, Dierking, Husman, Roska, & Powdrill, 1998). These courses provide students with an awareness of the systems nature of strategic learning, the range of factors which influence learning, and the impact and interaction among these factors.

Unlike many other learning skills courses or programs with focus on specific learning strategies, the strategic learning approach provides students with a basis from which to manage a variety of strategy choices and evaluate the application and effectiveness of their choices. In the Weinstein model (Weinstein, personal correspondence, December 29, 1998), students receive instruction in both the theoretical underpinnings of strategic learning and the practical application of specific learning strategies.

Weinstein's course emphasizes four main components: (a) skill, or cognitive strategies and study skills; (b) will, or motivation and self-efficacy for learning; (c) self-regulation, or time management and comprehension monitoring; and (d) academic environment, or social support and the nature of the task. Based on these main points, students learn to strategically match their selection of learning strategies to task demands and their own learning goals; identify problems and potential problems in the application of these strategies; and generate alternative learning plans based on solution-relevant factors in the context of particular problems (Weinstein, Dierking, Husman, Roska, & Powdrill, 1998).

A major benefit of strategic learning instruction is that students are able to transfer the knowledge gained to other subjects and other courses. Furthermore, these benefits appear to last throughout students' college careers. As evidence of this, Weinstein points out that those who participate in the course are retained and graduate at rates higher than those of the general student population and even those who enter the course with low placement scores are retained and graduate at a rate of 71% (Weinstein, personal correspondence, December 29, 1998). Participation in the course also has contributed to the improvement of subsequent GPA for high-risk students (Weinstein, Dierking, Husman, Roska, & Powdrill, 1998).

Certainly developmental students could benefit from this sort of training. It may not only improve their capacity to succeed more rapidly in early remedial courses but also improve their likelihood of success in the regular curriculum.

Implementing Alternative Approaches

All of the interventions discussed here, both traditional and alternative, have been and can be provided through administrative agencies organized as developmental education programs or learning assistance centers. Typically, developmental education programs are organized around a collection of courses whereas learning assistance centers are organized around a battery of support services. Frequently, these services are provided outside of either developmental programs or learning assistance centers. They are sometimes provided by counseling centers, academic departments, or student affairs programs. Often, they are not even targeted for underprepared students; instead, they are offered to students in a particular course or program, to honors students, or to any students choosing to participate. In essence, services that are frequently available to all students at an institution may be of particular benefit to developmental students.

Although many of these alternative approaches were not necessarily designed for developmental students, they have been shown to be effective for them and they have been widely adopted by developmental educators. A review of the most recent College Reading and Learning Association Conference program, for instance, indicates that 15 of 88 or 17% of concurrent sessions considered at least one of these innovative approaches. A review of the most recent program of the National Association for Developmental Education Conference indicates that 24 of 177 or 12.4% of concurrent sessions considered at least one of these approaches.

It is apparent that those who work with developmental students are well aware of alternatives to remedial courses. The problem is that they provide these alternatives randomly. Developmental educators do not offer these options nor do their students have access to them on a systematic basis. There are few, if any, institutions or programs in which:

- a variety of alternatives to remedial courses are regularly provided,

- developmental students have systematic access to them,

- assessment and advising are used to ensure that appropriate options are made available to meet the particular needs of individual students, and

- all these features are organized in a systematic manner.

It is this failure to bring to bear the resources available to assist developmental students in a manner consistent with their individual characteristics and to do this in a systematic fashion for which most developmental programs may justly be criticized. We have the means to provide alternatives to remedial courses and to do so in a manner consistent with individual student needs. We simply have not organized and delivered the alternatives systematically.

Conclusion

Obviously, the key to the success of efforts to reduce the need for remedial courses is a systematic relationship between assessment, advising, and placement activities. Such a systematic approach requires a strong advising program based on information obtained from a combination of cognitive and affective assessment. It would probably require some retraining of academic advisors and counselors and would certainly require retraining of some faculty. This systematic approach would also require greater collaboration between developmental educators and those who provide Supplemental Instruction, freshmen seminars, critical thinking courses, and other interventions representing an alternative to remedial courses. If more developmental students are to take advantage of these alternative interventions, it might also require that more personnel and financial resources be assigned to these interventions, regardless of whether they were provided by the developmental program, the learning center, or through other campus agencies.

Using the alternative intervention techniques described here, it should be possible to reduce the amount of time students spend in remedial courses. These alternatives would not only reduce the amount of time students spend in remediation, they might also reduce the number of students enrolled in remedial courses. They would, however, require more training of advisors and faculty, more collaboration among developmental educators and curriculum faculty, and, most likely, more resources than are currently assigned to developmental education.

This article has outlined a response to criticisms of remedial courses. It has described a variety of research-based alternatives to remedial courses. It has suggested that these alternatives be provided through a systematic integration of assessment, placement, and instruction designed to reduce the need for remedial courses on the campuses of American colleges and universities.

The interventions and approaches required to provide alternatives are not altogether innovative; most of them have been available for at least a decade or two. It is the systematic integration of these techniques with the assessment and advising process that represents a highly plausible alternative to traditional remedial courses. This alternative also represents, in the words of Pat Cross, a paradigm shift "Beyond education for all — Toward education for each" (Cross, 1976, p. 3).

References

Adelman, C. (1998). The kiss of death? An alternative view of college remediation. *National Crosstalk, 6*(3), 11.

Astin, A. (1993). *What matters in college?* San Francisco: Jossey-Bass.

Blanc, R. A., Debuhr, L. E., & Martin, D. C. (1983, January/February). Breaking the attrition cycle: The effect of Supplemental Instruction on undergraduate performance and attrition. *Journal of Higher Education, 54*, 80–90.

Boylan, H. R. (1980). Academic intervention in developmental education. *Journal of Developmental Education, 3*(3), 10–11.

Boylan, H., Abraham, A., Allen, B., Anderson, J., Bonham, B., Bliss, L., Morante, E., Ramirez, G., & Vadillo, M. (1996). *An evaluation of the Texas Academic Skills Program*. Austin, TX: Texas Higher Education Coordinating Board.

Boylan, H. R., Bliss, L. B., & Bonham, B. S. (1997). Program components and their relationship to student performance. *Journal of Developmental Education, 20*(3), 2–8.

Boylan, H. R., Bonham, B. S., Bliss, L. B., & Claxton, C. S. (1992, November). *The state of the art in developmental education: A report of a national study*. Paper presented at the First National Conference on Research in Developmental Education, Charlotte, NC.

Breneman, D. W. (1998). Remediation in higher education: Its extent and cost. In *Brookings papers on Education Policy 1998* (pp. 359–383). Washington, DC: The Brookings Institution.

Breneman, D. W., & Haarlow, W. N. (1998). *Remediation in higher education*. Washington, DC: The Thomas B. Fordham Foundation.

Casazza, M., & Silverman, S. L. (1996). *Learning assistance and developmental education: A guide for effective practice*. San Francisco: Jossey-Bass.

Commander, N., Stratton, C., Callahan, C., & Smith B. (1996). A learning assistance model for expanding academic support. *Journal of Developmental Education, 20*(2), 8–16.

Chaffee, J. (1992). Critical thinking skills: The cornerstone of developmental education. *Journal of Developmental Education, 15*(3), 2–8, 39.

Chaffee, J. (1997). *Thinking critically* (5th ed.). Boston: Houghton-Mifflin.

Chaffee, J. (1998, January). *Critical thinking: The cornerstone of remedial education*. Paper presented at the Conference on Replacing Remediation in Higher Education, Stanford University, Palo Alto, CA.

Cross, K. P. (1976). *Accent on learning*. San Francisco: Jossey-Bass.

Donovan, R. (1975). *Alternatives to the revolving door* (Report of FIPSE National Project II). New York: Bronx Community College.

Dwyer, J. O. (1989). A historical look at the freshmen year experience. In L. Upcraft & J. Gardner (Eds.), *The freshmen year experience* (pp. 25–39). San Francisco: Jossey-Bass.

Elder, L., & Paul, R. (1994). Critical thinking: Why we must transform our teaching. *Journal of Developmental Education, 18*(1), 34–35.

Fidler, P. P., & Hunter, M. S. (1989). How seminars enhance student success. In L. Upcraft & J. Gardner (Eds.), *The freshmen year experience* (pp. 216–237). San Francisco: Jossey-Bass.

Fidler, P. P., & Godwin, M. A. (1994). Retaining African-American students through the freshman seminar. *Journal of Developmental Education, 17*(3), 34–40.

Gardner, J. N., & Jeweler, A. J. (1992). *Your college experience. Strategies for success*. Belmont, CA: Wadsworth.

Gardner, J. (1998, November). *The changing role of developmental educators in creating and maintaining cultures of success*. Keynote address at the College Reading and Learning Association Conference, Salt Lake City, UT.

Garland, M. (1993). The mathematics workshop model: An interview with Uri Treisman. *Journal of Developmental Education, 16*(3), 14–18, 20–22.

Harris, J., & Eleser, C. (1997). Developing critical thinking: Melding two imperatives. *Journal of Developmental Education, 21*(1), 12–19.

Knopf, L. K. (1996). Remedial education: An undergraduate student profile. *American Council of Education Research Briefs, 6*(8), 1–11.

Lavin, D. E., & Hyllegard, G. (1996). *Changing the odds: Open-admissions and the life chances of the disadvantaged*. New Haven, CT: Yale University Press.

Martin, D. (1980). Learning centers in professional schools. In K. V. Lauridsen (Ed.), *New directions for college learning assistance: Examining the scope of learning centers* (pp. 69–79). San Francisco: Jossey-Bass.

Martin, D. C., & Arendale, D. R. (1994). *Supplemental instruction: Increasing achievement and retention. New directions in teaching and learning*. San Francisco: Jossey-Bass.

Martin, D. C., & Arendale, D. R. (1998, January). *Mainstreaming of developmental education: Supplemental instruction and video-based supplemental instruction*. Paper presented at the Conference on Replacing Remediation in Higher Education, Stanford University, Palo Alto, CA.

Maxwell, M. (1985). *Improving student learning skills* (2nd ed.). San Francisco: Jossey-Bass.

McCabe, R., & Day, P. (1998). *Developmental education: A twenty-first century social and economic imperative.* Mission Viejo, CA: League for Innovation in the Community College and The College Board.

National Center for Education Statistics. (1996). *The condition of education: 1996.* Washington, DC: U.S. Department of Education, Office of Educational Research and Improvement.

Ramirez, G. M. (1997). Supplemental Instruction: The long-term effect. *Journal of Developmental Education, 21*(1), 2–10.

Roueche, J., & Snow, G. (1977). *Overcoming learning problems.* San Francisco: Jossey-Bass.

Roueche, J. E., & Roueche, S. D. (1993). *Between a rock and a hard place: The at-risk student in the open door college.* Washington, DC: Community College Press.

St. Clair, L. (1994/95). Teaching students to think. Using library research and writing assignments to develop critical thinking. *Journal of College Reading and Learning, 26*(2), 65–74.

Tinto, V. (1997). Classrooms as communities: Exploring the educational character of student persistence. *Journal of Higher Education, 68*(6), 599–623.

Tinto, V. (1998, January). *Learning communities and the reconstruction of remedial education in higher education.* Paper presented at the Conference on Replacing Remediation in Higher Education, Stanford University, Palo Alto, CA.

Upcraft, M. L., Gardner, J. N., & Associates. (1989). *The freshman year experience.* San Francisco: Jossey-Bass.

Weinstein, C. E., Dierking, D., Husman, J., Roska, L., & Powdrill, L. (1998). The impact of a course in strategic learning on the long-term retention of college students. In J. Higbee & P. Dwinell (Eds.), *Developmental education: Preparing successful college students* (pp. 85–96). Columbia, SC: National Research Center for the First Year Experience and Students in Transition.

Wilcox, K. J., delMas, R. C., Stewart, B., Johnson, A. B., & Ghere, D. (1997). The "package course" experience and developmental education. *Journal of Developmental Education, 20*(3), 18–20, 22, 24, 26.

Pathways of Persistence: A Review of Postsecondary Peer Cooperative Learning Programs

David R. Arendale

This article focuses on a subset of the broader educational practice of peer collaborative learning, specifically postsecondary peer cooperative learning programs that embed study strategy practice within their activities. These practices have demonstrated higher student outcomes, including increasing student persistence toward graduation. David R. Arendale first provides clarity on the differences between the terms collaborative learning, *cooperative learning, and learning communities. He then reviews six post-secondary peer collaborative learning programs: (a) Accelerated Learning Groups, (b) Emerging Scholars Program, (c) Peer-Led Team Learning, (d) Structured Learning Assistance, (e) Supplemental Instruction, and (f) Video-Based Supplemental Instruction. The article ends with each of the learning programs placed into "Keimig's Hierarchy of Learning Improvement Programs" to assist educators in selecting programs to meet their institution's needs.*

Peer collaborative learning has been popular in education for decades. As both a pedagogy and a learning strategy, it has been frequently adopted and adapted for a wide range of academic content areas throughout education at the elementary, secondary, and postsecondary levels due to its benefits. The professional literature is filled with reports of individual professors integrating this approach into postsecondary classrooms in diverse ways. Increased attention has been placed on this practice due to claims by some programs that carefully coordinated and managed learning programs with specific protocols can increase student persistence rates toward graduation, supporting student aspirations as well as bolstering institutional revenues.

This chapter does not attempt to be inclusive of this broad field of literature concerning peer collaborative learning. Instead, it is focused intentionally on a subset of the educational practice that shares a common focus with increasing student persistence toward graduation. Rather than a meta-analysis of all published research studies, this chapter is a preliminary review and a description of six models. At the end of the chapter several suggestions are made for differentiating the models from each other and the level of institutional resources required for implementing them.

The six student peer learning programs included in this chapter meet the following characteristics: (a) must have been implemented at the postsecondary or tertiary level, (b) has a clear set of systematic procedures for its implementation at an institution, (c) has been evaluated through studies that are available for review, (d) intentionally embeds learning strategy practice along with review of the academic content material, (e) includes outcomes of both increased content knowledge and higher persistence rates, and (f) has been replicated at another institution with similar positive student outcomes. From a review of the professional literature six programs emerged: Accelerated Learning Groups (ALGs), Emerging Scholars Program (ESP), Peer-Led Team Learning (PLTL), Structured Learning Assistance (SLA), Supplemental Instruction (SI), and Video-Based Supplemental Instruction (VSI). As will be described in the following narrative, some of the programs share common history and seek to improve upon previous practices. Other programs were developed independently.

Collaborative Learning, Cooperative Learning, and Learning Communities

A review of the professional literature finds that the terms collaborative learning, cooperative learning, and learning communities are sometimes used interchangeably. Although they share similarities with one another, a more precise differentiation is needed to help explore the utility of each for its intended educational outcomes (Cooper, Robinson, & Ball, 2003). Regarding their historical development and appearance within the professional literature in the United States, collaborative learning appeared first, cooperative learning second, and learning communities last. A search of the Educational Resources Information Center (ERIC) Database (2004) found more than 8,000 entries regarding descriptive and research studies that contained one or more of the three terms indexed within their documents.

Collaborative learning refers to a wide range of formal and informal activities that include any form of peer student interaction. This is the broadest and most general of the three terms. This term describes any classroom activity by an instructor that involves student peer-to-peer involvement. Cooperative learning is more narrowly defined as a subset of collaborative learning. It often follows these principles: (a) positive interdependence established in the group through adoption of different roles that support the group's moving to complete a goal, (b) peer interaction, (c) activities structured to establish individual accountability and personal responsibility, (d) development of interpersonal and small group skills, and (e) group processing of small group activities through verification of information accuracy (Cuseo, 2002; Johnson, Johnson, Holubec, & Roy, 1984).

In contrast with collaborative and cooperative learning groups, learning communities are distinguished by their focus on interactive peer learning. Learning communities are often more focused on enhanced curricular and pedagogical outcomes. In addition to often employing some version of student interactive learning, learning communities take several approaches to modifying the classroom experience by restructuring the curriculum. Some of the ways that courses may be modified are through linked courses, learning clusters, freshman interest groups, federated learning communities, and coordinated studies (Gabelnick, MacGregor, Matthews, & Smith, 1990).

A way to understand the relationships among these three terms is through a diagram, as provided in Figure 1 on page 104. Collaborative learning is considered to be the largest construct, both due to its general definition as well as its numerical ranking as most frequently cited in professional literature (ERIC, 2004). A smaller construct lies within collaborative learning. This is cooperative learning. Although it holds to the same generalizations and goals of collaborative learning, it is much more specific in its implementation and following of specified

Figure 1. Relationships among Selected Learning Pedagogies

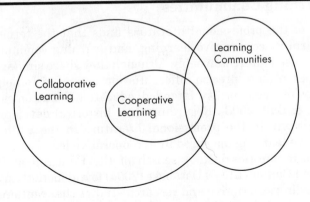

protocols for its use. A related concept to both collaborative and cooperative learning is that of learning communities. While learning communities often utilize some peer collaborative or cooperative learning activities as part of their pedagogy, they generally focus more on curricular transformation. However, it is possible to implement some aspects of learning communities without extensive use of either collaborative or cooperative learning because the focus may be more on team teaching by instructors and the integration of academic content material (e.g., a cluster course that merges the content of an introduction-to-science with an ethics course) rather than extensive use of student peer interactive learning activities.

In this chapter the focus will be on peer cooperative learning programs that embed learning strategies practice within review of the academic content material and that also meet the other selection criteria previously mentioned. This is an important topic in the field of developmental education and learning assistance in particular and for postsecondary education in general because of the need by institutions to meet the needs of a more diverse entering student body while maintaining or increasing academic rigor (Bastedo & Gumport, 2003). The institution must make systemic changes in the educational environment that will increase the academic success and persistence rates of all students to meet the expectations of stakeholders such as parents, legislators, and funding agencies. Although the number of academically underprepared students is increasing, historic delivery systems of academic development for students such as remedial and developmental courses are being reduced or eliminated by some states (Barefoot, 2003; Damashek, 1999; Parsad & Lewis, 2003). Many institutions have already adopted one or more of the six programs described in this chapter. The need for such approaches may increase due to the demands to meet the needs of access to an increasingly diverse student body without the traditional approaches offered by developmental education in the past.

Six Major Postsecondary Peer Cooperative Learning Programs

Six postsecondary peer collaborative learning programs were selected for inclusion in this chapter based on the criteria mentioned earlier in the narrative; the six are: (a) Accelerated Learning Groups (ALGs), (b) Emerging Scholars Program (ESP), (c) Peer-Led Team Learning (PLTL), (d) Structured Learning Assistance (SLA), (e) Supplemental Instruction (SI), and (f) Video-Based Supplemental Instruction (VSI). A short narrative overview of each follows with results from several research studies that have examined the impact upon student outcomes. The six programs have been divided into two groups.

The first group consists of those models that provide adjunct support through outside-of-class activities with little change by the primary course instructor. The first in this category is SI. In recent years two programs have been developed to address limitations of the SI model: ALGs and SLA. The second group of peer cooperative programs are those that share a common characteristic of a transformed classroom learning environment for all enrolled students. Major changes have been made by the primary course instructor through either integration of the peer learning model into the basic course delivery or heavy involvement by the instructor with the peer learning activities. The first of these programs is ESP, developed at approximately the same time as SI in the 1970s. In the 1990s two programs were created with similar purposes and protocols to ESP: PLTL and VSI. Most of these six programs cite in their literature reviews references concerning the other peer learning programs as it appears that each have been an incremental improvement upon previous peer learning models.

Adjunct Peer Cooperative Learning Programs to the Course

SUPPLEMENTAL INSTRUCTION (SI). The Supplemental Instruction model of academic assistance helps students in historically difficult classes master content while they develop and integrate learning and study strategies. The program was originally developed at the University of Missouri-Kansas City in 1973 and has been adopted by hundreds of institutions in the United States and abroad (Arendale, 2002). Goals of SI include: (a) improving student grades in targeted courses, (b) reducing the attrition rate within those courses, and (c) increasing graduation rates of students. All students in a targeted course are urged to attend SI sessions, and students with varying ability levels to participate. There is no stigma attached to SI because courses that have had high rates of Ds, Fs, and course withdrawals for multiple academic terms are the focus rather than attempting to identify specific students who are deemed to be high risk for failure due to predictors such as low standardized test scores or previous academic failures at the secondary or postsecondary levels. SI can be implemented in one or more courses each academic term (Martin & Arendale, 1994).

There are four key persons involved with SI. The first is the SI supervisor, a trained professional on the SI staff. The SI supervisor is responsible for identifying the targeted courses, gaining faculty support, selecting and training SI leaders, and monitoring and evaluating the program. When the historically difficult courses have been identified, the SI supervisor contacts the faculty members concerning SI for their course. The second key person for SI is the faculty member who teaches one of the identified courses. SI is only offered in courses in which the faculty member invites and supports SI. Faculty members screen SI leaders for content competency and approve selections. The third key person is the SI leader. SI leaders are students or learning center staff members who have been deemed course competent, approved by the course instructor, and trained in proactive learning and study strategies. SI leaders attend course lectures, take notes, read all assigned materials, and conduct three to five out-of-class SI sessions per week. The SI leader is the "model student," a facilitator who helps students to integrate course content with learning and study strategies. The fourth key component of the SI program is the participating students.

There have been several hundred research studies concerning SI conducted at institutions from around the world. Some of these and related information are available through Web sites maintained by the National Center for SI (Painter, 2004) and other professional organizations (Lipsky, 2004).

Doty (2003) reported on data supplied by 53 U.S. institutions between 1998 and 2003 concerning academic achievement for SI participants and nonparticipants. The data was drawn from SI reports covering 745 courses with a total enrollment of 61,868 students. SI participants were defined as those who attended one or more of the voluntary, out-of-class SI sessions sometime during the academic term. Outcomes displayed in the report included that SI participants received a D, F, or withdrew from the course at a rate between one-third and one-fourth that of nonparticipants, regardless of institutional type. In addition, mean final course grades were approximately a half letter grade higher for SI participants. These differences were statistically significant and were consistent across different types of institutions and academic content areas. The most prevalent use of SI is in the natural sciences (46%), followed by social sciences (20%), mathematics (15%), and humanities (7%).

Ogden, Thompson, Russell, and Simons (2003) assessed SI for short- and long-term impact on college academic performance and retention at Georgia State University. Data were compiled for students registered in a political science course supported by SI. Four groups were identified according to their university entry status and SI participation: traditional (regularly admitted) SI participants, conditional

(Learning Support Programs or English as a Second Language [ESL] entry status) SI participants, traditional non-SI participants, and conditional non-SI participants. All SI participants volunteered for the program and were thus self-selected. There were no statistically significant differences between SI and non-SI participants in the two comparison groups when preentry attributes were analyzed (i.e., standardized college entrance exam scores, predicted grade point average). Conditional students participating in SI had significantly higher short- and long-term outcomes compared to conditional non-SI participants. Conditional SI participants reenrolled at a higher rate than did the other three student groups included in this study. Traditional SI participants earned higher final course grades than their non-SI counterparts, though the results were not statistically significant. The ESL students were equally distributed among the four comparison groups and did not serve as a statistically significant factor in outcomes studied. The authors postulated that long-term benefits for SI would be fostered by offering the program throughout the academic course of study of students and not focused so commonly only during the first year of college.

Ashwin (2003) reported about a qualitative study on the impact of SI with an institution in the United Kingdom. More than one-third of the professional literature concerning SI has been published about programs outside the United States. Ashwin found that attendance at SI sessions was positively and significantly correlated to academic performance. This relationship was found even when prior levels of academic performance were controlled. An unusual finding of the research was that students who attended SI sessions sometimes chose not to employ rigorous study strategies, which resulted in a reduction of the quality of the learning of these students. Qualitative evidence suggested that this change in approach was in response to an increased awareness of the assessment demands of the course and that these students had chosen to devote more effort to other courses that required higher levels of rigor to pass them. It is argued that these results suggest that the outcomes and operation of the SI program were influenced by the context in which it operated.

Congos (2003) is one of the most frequently published authors concerning SI. His latest publication identified recommended policies and practices for SI programs. The document provides a means for conducting a program review with 90 recommended practices. The categories covered by the evaluation tool include: SI leader pre-semester training, SI faculty training, SI leader training during the academic term, SI session observation and feedback, in-class introduction of SI, and end-of-term evaluation.

ACCELERATED LEARNING GROUPS (ALGS). Accelerated Learning Groups were developed at the University of Southern California in Los Angeles in the early 1990s by Sydney Stansbury (2001a, 2001b) and have been adopted at several institutions. They are designed to meet the needs of students who had significant skill or knowledge deficiencies that often inhibited their effective use of other voluntary participation peer cooperative learning programs, such as SI. Stansbury noted that the college students who were least academically prepared were often the ones who never attended, or only attended one or two SI sessions at the beginning of the academic term. The reasons for their noninvolvement included both their severe cognitive deficits as well as motivational issues. This knowledge helped to prompt the need to develop another intervention for these students, which eventually resulted in creation of ALGs (Sydney Stansbury, personal communication, January 15, 2004).

ALGs combine peer-led small group learning activities, assessment, frequent feedback by a learning skills specialist, and development of an individual education plan (IEP) for each student. Students participating in ALGs are concurrently enrolled in a challenging entry-level course while they develop the necessary skills and knowledge prescribed by the IEP. The ALG students are placed into a triad with another student with similar IEP objectives and a peer leader who works intensely with the students under the supervision of a learning skills specialist. Participation in ALGs continues throughout the academic term until the learning skills specialist deems it appropriate for transition into another peer development program or individual tutoring.

Minimum requirements for implementation of ALGs include academic testing of students, staff time of a qualified learning skills specialist, academic monitoring throughout the academic term, employment of well-trained student peer leaders to facilitate the triads, faculty support for the program operating in tandem with their course, and availability of an academic enrichment program, such as SI, to continue modeling cognitive and metacognitive learning strategies with the students after they complete their work within the ALG program.

In a study with students at the University of Southern California, Stansbury (2001a) found that ALGs were especially useful for students considered academically at-risk who were enrolled in an introductory science course. A pilot study investigated whether at-risk students who participated in an ALG and SI combination demonstrated higher self-efficacy and SI attendance than those who participated in only SI. Results suggested that at-risk students were more likely to participate in 12 or more SI sessions if they attended an ALG and SI combination than if they attended only SI. In addition, the range of final grades was higher for those who attended an ALG and SI combination than for those who attended only SI.

According to ALG's creator, the development of prerequisite skills is essential for the efficacy of SI to serve academically underprepared students who may shun the very academic intervention that would be of most help to them (Stansbury 2001a, 2001b). One of the challenges for SI is that only approximately one third of students in an average class attend SI sessions. This rate of participation holds nearly the same for all groups within the class, regardless of previous levels of academic achievement as measured by standardized test scores or high school rank or grade point average (Arendale, 1997). Therefore, only one third of the students from the lowest predicted academic preparation level attend SI sessions. It was for this target population that ALGs were created.

STRUCTURED LEARNING ASSISTANCE (SLA).   Initiated in 1993 at Ferris State University (Michigan), Structured Learning Assistance workshops assist students in developing the background needed to connect to the course content and to develop and apply the learning strategies most appropriate to the content area. SLA has been recognized through several national awards and is currently supported by a three-year U.S. Department of Education grant from the Fund for the Improvement of Postsecondary Education (FIPSE). Results indicated that SLA can significantly improve student pass rates, including rates for at-risk students. Other institutions have attended training workshops hosted by Ferris State University to enable them to implement SLA. The current FIPSE grant supports four other institutions in successfully implementing the SLA model (Wolgamott, 2004).

SLA provides both an academic and an affective support system. SLA targets courses that are considered high-risk for failure, academically rigorous gateway courses for academic majors, or historically difficult upper-division courses. The SLA workshops are formally scheduled four hours weekly in the student schedule similar to an accompanying science lab. Attendance at the workshop is required of all students the first week of the course or until the first test, quiz, or other assessment is given in the class. Following this first course assessment, attendance is required only for students whose current grade in the course falls below a C. Other students may voluntarily continue to attend the SLA sessions. SLA was created, among other purposes, to address the problem of less academically prepared students who were often not attending either SI or individual tutoring sessions (Wolgamott, 2004).

SLA class professors receive regular, ongoing information about student progress, student concerns, and ways of better connecting with students. SLA sessions provide explicit instruction in learning strategies. Research studies suggest that SLA students earn higher final course grades than nonparticipants in control groups (Doyle, 1999; Kowalczyk, 2003). A faculty development component is also part of SLA, which supports higher academic achievement for students. Informal classroom assessment information is provided to participating faculty members to assist them in making modifications to classroom activities and prompt review of difficult concepts (Doyle).

Two research studies have been published externally about SLA. Doyle and Kowalczyk (1999) conducted analyses of data collected within the SLA program at Ferris State University. Data suggested the following outcomes for the SLA program: (a) higher rates of students earning C– or better in the course, (b) higher persistence rates at the institution, and (c) 73% of students attributed SLA as significant to their academic achievement.

In another study at Ferris State University, Doyle and Hooper (1997) investigated SLA during a three-year study. Results suggested that SLA can significantly improve student pass rates, even for students considered academically at-risk. In nearly 85% of the 42 courses offered with SLA support, the SLA students had higher pass rates than those of all other Ferris State students taking the same courses. This improvement was especially marked in the mathematics courses, where the average pass rate increased anywhere from 24% to 45%.

Embedded Peer Cooperative Learning Programs within the Course

EMERGING SCHOLARS PROGRAM (ESP). Developed at the University of California, Berkeley in the early 1980s, the Emerging Scholars Program is also known as the Calculus Workshop Program, the Mathematics Workshop Program, and the Treisman model after its creator, Philip Uri Treisman (1986). The ESP program has been adopted and adapted by more than 100 institutions across the United States (Born, 2001). ESP was based on qualitative research by Treisman, who investigated the difference in academic success of students of different ethnic and cultural groups. The academic success rate for African American students in math, science, and engineering graduate programs was very low in comparison to Asian students. After an extensive ethnographic study of Asian students at UC-Berkeley, Treisman designed a program that created a system based on the informal student-driven sessions created by the Asian students in challenging calculus courses. The resulting program not only was based on sound cognitive learning strategies, but was also attentive to the affective domain of learning. After successful use with students of color at many institutions, implementors of the program have found positive results for many student demographic categories (Fullilove & Treisman, 1990; Moreno, Muller, Asera, Wyatt, & Epperson, 1999).

Most ESP programs shared the following elements: (a) build a cohort community of first-year students of color that is academically oriented and a source of peer support, (b) provide the cohort with an extensive orientation to the institution and with ongoing academic advising, (c) advocate the interests of the cohort, (d) monitor their academic progress and adjustment to the environment, (e) provide the cohort with ongoing adjunct instructional sessions that promote development of cognitive and metacognitive learning strategies needed for independent learning, and (f) link high school–level and undergraduate-level affirmative action efforts (Treisman, 1986). During most ESP implementations, students commit themselves to attend two additional lab sessions weekly, each lasting two hours. At some institutions students are required to attend the sessions based on preentry test scores, and at other institutions students are encouraged to make a commitment through creation of a perception that ESP is an honors program and that it is a privilege to participate (Leapard, 2001; Mills, 1999). Following is a summary of several research studies that have been conducted concerning ESP.

Born (2001) conducted a two-year, quasi-experiment at Northwestern University to evaluate the effect of ESP on performance of historically underrepresented students (e.g., African American, Hispanic) and traditional (e.g., Caucasian, Asian) undergraduate biology students in a three-course series and to investigate motivational explanations for performance differences. Traditional students randomly assigned to the ESP workshops (n = 61) performed between one half and one standard deviation better than those assigned to the control group (n = 60; p <.05) in each quarter without spending more time studying. During the first quarter, ESP historically underrepresented students (n = 25) showed a pattern of increasing exam performance in comparison to nonparticipant students of similar ethnic background (n = 21), who showed a decreasing pattern (p <.05). Although gender differences in biology performance were studied, none were detected between those who participated in ESP and those who did not.

Fullilove and Treisman (1990) conducted an extensive study of the ESP at the University of California, Berkeley, between 1978 and 1984 with African American mathematics students. To provide comparison data, a baseline of student performance was established during the period of 1973 to 1977 before the ESP program was provided to students. The percentage of nonparticipants in ESP that earned grades of D or below ranged from 33% to 41%, depending upon the year. The ESP participants earned similar grades at a much lower rate, ranging between 3% and 7% in comparison over the time period. The percentage of nonparticipants earning grades of B− or higher ranged from 10% to 28%. The ESP participants earned much higher grades in comparison, with the percentage at B− or above ranging between 39% and 61%. The persistence and graduation rates favored the ESP participants at 65% versus 41% for the nonparticipants. The study took into account preentry attributes such as SAT scores on the verbal and mathematics subtests.

Leapard (2001) investigated affective, metacognitive, and conceptual effects of an Emerging Scholars Program on elementary teacher preparation. The study involved an elementary mathematics content course that was constructivist in nature and emphasized the tenets of the National Council of Teachers of Mathematics Standards. Qualitative measures included in the study were student interviews, mathematical autobiographies, and classroom observations. Quantitative measures consisted of surveys on metacognition and mathematics anxiety and concept maps. Data concerning affective, metacognitive, and conceptual changes was analyzed both qualitatively and quantitatively. Results indicated an increase in metacognitive skills and a decrease in mathematics anxiety. The potential effect of ESP participation upon conceptual understanding was inconclusive. However, a significant increase in the preservice teachers' level of self-confidence in teaching was noted. The ESP appeared to have a positive effect on preservice elementary teachers when considering affective and metacognitive attributes related to mathematics, but appeared to have had a neutral effect on the reconceptualization of mathematical ideas.

Mills (1999) reported an in-depth study of ESP in chemistry and physics courses at the California State Polytechnic University, Pomona. Data for the first longitudinal component of this study were obtained by tracking three groups of students during spring 1998: (a) ESP participants from historically underrepresented groups (e.g., Latino, African American, and Native American workshop students); (b) a random sample of non-ESP participants who were from the same historically underrepresented groups; and (c) a random sample of nontargeted students (e.g., Anglo and Asian) enrolled in the same classes. Data for the second component of this study, an analysis of qualitative data, were obtained by administering questionnaires, conducting interviews, and observing science students. Even after taking into account verbal and mathematics SAT scores, ESP participation was a significant predictor of first-quarter course grade for historically underrepresented students in both chemistry and physics.

VIDEO-BASED SUPPLEMENTAL INSTRUCTION (VSI). SI was developed at the University of Missouri, Kansas City, in the late 1980s and has been implemented by dozens of institutions in the United States and abroad. Video-Based Supplemental Instruction is an interactive information processing and delivery system that helps academically at-risk students master rigorous course content as they concurrently develop and refine reasoning and learning skills. Rather than requiring prerequisite enrollment in a traditional developmental course, VSI is a learning system that mainstreams the best practices of developmental education into historically difficult core curriculum courses. Research suggests the efficacy of VSI for improving academic achievement for students of diverse levels, from elementary school children studying mathematics through professional school for future doctors studying to pass the first step of their medical license examination boards. VSI is presented as a holistic alternative to traditional approaches of developmental education (Martin, Arendale, & Blanc, 1997).

VSI differs from SI in several respects. With VSI, the students enroll in a designated core curriculum course. The course professor has previously recorded all didactic presentations on videotape for use with underprepared students as well as other students who opt for this highly interactive way of learning. Instead of attending the professor's regular lecture class, students enroll in the video section of the professor's course. Students in both sections, live and videotaped, are held to the same performance standards. Specially designed facilitator and student manuals support the video sections (Martin & Blanc, 2001). Integrated within these manuals are sections that require the students to practice use of appropriate study and learning strategies with the course content material. The VSI section of the course functions much like a distance learning telecourse.

VSI participants, led by a trained facilitator, start and stop the videotaped presentation at predetermined times as well as whenever they have a question or want clarification. Professors design the video presentations to include periodic small group assignments to ensure mastery of one concept before the next is introduced. Students complete these tasks under the supervision and with the guidance of the facilitator. When the taped lecture resumes, the professor models how he or she thinks about the assigned tasks. In this way, the students have time to construct and verify their understanding as well as compare their own thinking to that of the expert (Martin & Blanc, 2001).

There are several published research studies concerning VSI. Hurley (2000) investigated several questions of the VSI program at the University of Missouri-Kansas City: (a) final grades earned by students in VSI as compared with students enrolled in a lecture-format class with the same professor; and (b) potential changes in self-efficacy, self-confidence and mastery of learning strategies of VSI participants. The major conclusions from the study were the following: (a) the VSI participants received a statistically significant higher percentage of A and B grades than a comparable group of non-VSI students in the same history class over 14 semesters, and (b) the VSI participants received a statistically significant lower rate D and F final course grades than the non-VSI participants. Interviews with VSI participants suggested that VSI was a significant factor in the acquisition of a variety of strategies that provided them with the academic tools to be successful on their history exams in that class. In addition, the VSI participants indicated that they developed a greater sense of self-efficacy in the class and greater personal confidence.

Research by Koch and Snyders (1997) is representative of the studies conducted by VSI programs outside the United States. The researchers investigated the effect of VSI on the mathematics performance of students whose matriculation marks did not enable them to be directly admitted to the Science Faculty at the University Port Elizabeth (UPE), South Africa. These students were enrolled in Ethembeni Community College in Port Elizabeth, which serves as a preparation area before admission to UPE. Fifteen students who enrolled in VSI math were matched with 14 students enrolled in a similar math course that required attendance at Supplemental Instruction (SI) sessions. Research suggests that VSI was a more useful instructional delivery system for students with a minimum level of preknowledge in mathematics. In addition, the researchers suggested the usefulness of VSI in distance learning venues where experienced and trained faculty members are unavailable to deliver live instruction.

PEER-LED TEAM LEARNING (PLTL). Peer-Led Team Learning is an innovative model in science education. PLTL was originally developed at the City University of New York (CUNY) in the mid-1990s. Support through a grant from the National Science Foundation has assisted in adoption of this model by more than 100 institutions. A Web site maintained by the national PLTL office disseminates information and research studies concerning PLTL (Dreyfus, 2004).

Student leaders guide the activities of small groups of students in weekly PLTL meetings. These meetings are included as part of the course requirements. The students work through challenging problems that are designed to be solved cooperatively. The student leaders receive extensive training before the beginning of the academic term in a wide variety of areas including how to foster student engagement with the content material and with each other. According to the program's developers, the PLTL methodology offers a number of educational opportunities: (a) the supportive format encourages questions and discussions that lead to greater conceptual understanding; (b) students learn to work in teams and to communicate more effectively which are valuable skills needed for further success in postsecondary education as well as when they enter the world of work; (c) use of standardized adjunct print curriculum materials and workbooks help to ensure higher quality learning that is more often uniformly experienced by all students at PLTL-implementing institutions; and (d) peer leaders learn teaching and group management skills (Cracolice & Deming, 2001).

A difference between the approaches of PLTL and ESP relates to curriculum development. While in ESP each course supported by the program develops its own curriculum materials, the national office for PLTL has published supplemental textbooks and workbooks that can be added to the course delivery and also serve as models for development of local curricula. In addition, PLTL offers national conferences and training workshops to support institutions with implementing the program. This latter approach allows for more efficient and effective adoption of the PLTL program and increases the quality of sessions that are facilitated by student peer leaders (Cracolice & Deming, 2001).

The following are guiding principles of PLTL: (a) the program is integral to the course through required attendance at two hours of workshop time weekly, (b) peer leaders are trained in group leadership and course content, (c) activities and materials are challenging yet accessible, (d) faculty are deeply involved in the program, (e) physical space and environments are conducive to discussion and learning, and (f) the program has strong support from the institution (Gosser, Cracolice, Kampmeier, Roth, Strozak, & Varma-Nelson, 2000; Gosser & Roth, 1998).

In addition to numerous studies provided through the national PLTL Web site, independent researchers are conducting detailed studies at their home institutions. Tien, Roth, and Kampmeier (2002) reported their study of PLTL in an undergraduate organic chemistry course. Quantitative and qualitative data were collected. PLTL participants (i.e., treatment group) were compared with students who participated in recitation sessions (control group). PLTL participants earned higher final course grades and had higher persistence rates. Analysis of interviews with PLTL participants suggested that the program helped them to learn more course material, and that they were more socially engaged, intellectually stimulated, and found the experience to be a productive use of time.

Selecting the Cooperative Learning Model for Institutional Needs

To display the relationship between the six identified peer cooperative learning programs and learning assistance programs in general, it would be helpful to compare them with Keimig's (1983) Hierarchy of Learning Improvement Programs:

> In the Hierarchy of Learning Improvement Programs, four basic program types are described and ranked, differentiated by the extent by which they are comprehensive in response to the various needs of students and institutionalized into the academic mainstream. Level 1: Isolated courses in remedial skills. Level II: Learning assistance to individual students. Level III: Provides course-related supplementary learning activities outside the class for some objectives. Level IV: Comprehensive learning system in the course. (p. 21)

Using Keimig's hierarchy it is possible to arrange the six peer cooperative programs as illustrated in Figure 2 on page 116. According to Keimig, the highest level of student outcomes occurs when a comprehensive learning system is integrated throughout the course learning experience. This requires a transformative experience by the institution due to: (a) heavy involvement of the course professor with curriculum development; (b) training, monitoring, and supervision of peer group facilitators; (c) alignment of educational objectives among all course components; (d) changes in institutional and course policies and expectations; (e) release time for professors to complete essential tasks; and (f) stable, long-term institutional funding because outside grants are difficult to obtain or maintain. ESP, PLTL, and VSI fit into this

Figure 2. Placing Peer Cooperative Learning Programs within Keimig's Hierarchy of Learning Improvement Programs

LEVELS OF INTEGRATION WITHIN THE COURSE	PEER COOPERATIVE LEARNING PROGRAMS	LIKELIHOOD OF IMPROVED STUDENT OUTCOMES
Level Four: Comprehensive learning system within the course	ESP, PLTL, and VSI	High
Level Three: Supplementary learning activities adjunct to the course	ALG, SLA, and SI	Above average
Level Two: Learning assistance to individual students, i.e., tutoring, outside of the course		Below average
Level One: Isolated separate courses in remedial skills		Low

fourth category level. Although these programs have a higher likelihood of improved student outcomes, they are also the most demanding of institutional resources and changes in the campus environment.

The next level of programs, according to Keimig, are those that are adjunct to the course and provide support for it through either voluntary or required participation. ALGs, SLA, and SI are placed into this group. The expectancy for results, based on Keimig's model, is not as high as for the level four comprehensive programs as described in the previous paragraph. But ALGs, SLA, and SI are predicted to yield higher student outcomes than either individual assistance to students such as that provided through tutoring or enrollment in remedial courses. This third category is less expensive and less labor intensive to implement, but may yield lower desired student outcomes.

Higher levels of institutionalization of peer learning programs require high levels of funding and support from administration and faculty members. This investment may pay high dividends. The future political and economic environment may be more supportive for these types of programs for supporting higher student persistence rates in comparison with traditional remedial or developmental education courses, which are under considerable pressure for curtailment as described earlier in this chapter. It is recommended that before adoption of any of the six programs, a careful review of the published literature be undertaken as well as personal communication with those successfully operating the programs.

Some of the programs, such as PLTL and SI, offer national training workshops to enable others to implement the programs. On-site observations can probably be negotiated with any of the six programs. The investment in such telephone and on-site observations will help to reveal the essential elements needed for successful implementation of the specific practice. Often these essential details are not revealed in the published literature, which tends to be more focused on statistical studies and not on the detailed implementation protocols. Based on personal experience as a former national training director for one of the six programs, I strongly recommend careful planning before attempting to implement the programs. Although the educational outcomes described in the published literature are replicable, achieving these outcomes generally requires careful implementation and constant monitoring to assure continued quality.

Further Research Issues Regarding Peer Cooperative Learning

One of the most perplexing issues facing peer cooperative learning groups is dealing with student motivation and goal orientation. Sometimes the students who could most benefit from the positive effects of peer learning are the ones least likely to participate due to fear of exposing their academic weaknesses to others or even to themselves. Most of these six programs have dealt with the issue through mandatory attendance at sessions. Although brute force does compel attendance, it does not necessarily follow that students willingly adopt the new academic behaviors and implement them in other courses when not under the dictates of program requirements. The complexity of student motivation is being carefully studied among elementary and secondary education student populations. However, this important construct is often ignored in the study of postsecondary education in general, and research regarding the provision of learning assistance at the college level is overlooked in particular.

Creating peer cooperative learning programs that provide both structure and an environment that encourages students to modify their motivations for learning will require more work by program designers. Too often students have been expected to adopt the expectations and learning conditions of the institution without direct instruction. This literature supports the notion that it is necessary for institutions to implement programs that are more attentive to individual differences among students. Much work has yet to be done.

Additional Resources

By its very nature, this chapter will be dated as soon as it is printed. Further information on these six postsecondary peer cooperative learning programs is available through the following Web site: http://www .tc.umn.edu/%7Earend011/. In addition to the interactive database, a print version of the annotated bibliography is available in the Acrobat PDF format for users to read online or to print on their computer. This print document as well as the online resource and instruction for its use are available at http://www.tc.umn.edu/~arend011/Peerbib03.pdf.

References

Arendale, D. (1997). Supplemental Instruction: Review of research concerning the effectiveness of SI from The University of Missouri-Kansas City and other institutions across the United States. In *Proceedings of the 17th and 18th Annual Institutes for Learning Assistance Professionals 1966 and 1997* (pp. 1–25). Tucson, AZ: University Learning Center, University of Arizona.

Arendale, D. (2002). History of Supplemental Instruction: Mainstreaming of developmental education. In D. B. Lundell & J. L. Higbee (Eds.), *Histories of developmental education* (pp. 15–27). Minneapolis, MN: Center for Research on Developmental Education and Urban Literacy, General College, University of Minnesota. Retrieved January 15, 2004, from http://www.gen.umn.edu/research/crdeul

Ashwin, P. W. H. (2003). Peer support: Relations between the context, process and outcomes for the students who are supported. *Instructional Science, 31*(3), 159–173.

Barefoot, B. O. (2003). *Findings from the Second National Survey of First-Year Academic Practices, 2002.* Brevard, NC: Policy Center for the First Year of College. Retrieved June 22, 2004, from http://www.brevard.edu/fyc/survey 2002/findings.htm

Bastedo, M. N., & Gumport, P. J. (2003). Access to what? Mission differentiation and academic stratification in U.S. public higher education. *Higher Education: The International Journal of Higher Education and Educational Planning, 46*, 341–359. Retrieved January 15, 2004, from, http://www .kluweronline.com/0018-1560

Born, W. K. (2001). The effect of workshop groups on achievement goals and performance in biology: An outcome evaluation. *Dissertation Abstracts International, 61*(11), 6184.

Congos, D. H. (2003). Health checklist for Supplemental Instruction (SI) programs. *The Learning Assistance Review, 8*(2), 29–45.

Cooper, J. L., Robinson, P., & Ball, D. B. (Eds.). (2003). *Small group instruction in higher education: Lessons from the past, visions of the future.* Stillwater, OK: New Forums Press.

Cracolice, M. S., & Deming, J. C. (2001). Peer-led team learning. *The Science Teacher, 68*(1), 20–24.

Cuseo, J. B. (2002). *Organizing to collaborate: A taxonomy of higher education practices for promoting interdependence within the classroom, across the campus, and beyond the college.* Stillwater, OK: New Forums Press.

Damashek, R. (1999). Reflections on the future of developmental education, Part II. *Journal of Developmental Education, 23*(2), 18–20, 22. Retrieved June 22, 2004, from http://www.ced.appstate.edu/centers/ncde/reserve%20 reading/V23-2damashek%20reflections.htm

Doty, C. (2003). *Supplemental Instruction: National data summary, 1998–2003.* Unpublished manuscript, The University of Missouri-Kansas City, The International Center for Supplemental Instruction. Retrieved June 22, 2004, from http://www.umkc.edu/cad/si/sidocs/NationalSupplementalInstruction Report 98-03.pdf

Doyle, T. (1999, Winter). Ferris State University's structured learning assistance program. *Michigan Developmental Educational Consortium Newsletter*, 4–5, 8.

Doyle, T., & Hooper, J. (1997). *Structured Learning Assistance Project. Final Report, Fall Semester 1996, Winter Semester 1997.* Unpublished manuscript, Ferris State University (OH). (ERIC Document Reproduction Service No. ED425772).

Doyle, T., & Kowalczyk, J. (1999). The Structured Learning Assistance Program model. In *Selected Conference Papers of the National Association for Developmental Education, Volume 5* (pp. 4–7). Warrensburg, MO: National Association for Developmental Education. Retrieved June 22, 2004, from http://www.umkc.edu/cad/nade/nadedocs/99conpap/tdcpap99.htm

Dreyfus, A. E. (Ed.). (2004). *Internet homepage of the Peer-Led Team Learning Program* [online]. Retrieved June 22, 2004, from http://www.pltl.org and http://www.sci.ccny.cuny.edu/~chemwksp/index.html

Educational Resources Information Center (2004). *The educator's reference desk* [online]. Retrieved June 21, 2004, from http://www.eduref.org/

Fullilove, R. E., & Treisman, P. U. (1990). Mathematics achievement among African American undergraduates at the University of California, Berkeley: An evaluation of the Mathematics Workshop Program. *Journal of Negro Education, 59*(3), 63–78.

Gabelnick, F., MacGregor, J., Matthews, R. S., & Smith, B. L. (1990). *Learning communities: Creating connections among students, faculty, and disciplines.* San Francisco: Jossey-Bass.

Gosser, D. K., Cracolice, M. S., Kampmeier, J. A., Roth, V., Strozak, V. S., & Varma-Nelson, P. (2000). *Peer-Led Team Learning: A guidebook.* Upper Saddle River, NJ: Prentice-Hall.

Gosser, D. K., & Roth, V. (1998). The workshop chemistry project: Peer-Led Team Learning. *Journal of Chemical Education, 75*(2), 185–187.

Hurley, M. A. (2000). Video-based Supplemental Instruction (VSI): An interactive delivery system that facilitates student learning [Doctoral dissertation, University of Missouri-Kansas City, 1999]. *Dissertation Abstracts International, 61*(04), 1317.

Johnson, D. W., Johnson, R. T., Holubec, E. J., & Roy, P. (1984). *Circles of learning: Cooperation in the classroom.* Washington, DC: Association for Supervision and Curriculum Development.

Keimig, R. T. (1983). *Raising academic standards: A guide to learning improvement.* ASHE-ERIC Higher Education Report No. 4. Washington, DC: Association for the Study of Higher Education.

Koch, E., & Snyders, M. (1997). *The effect of Video Supplemental Instruction on the academic performance in mathematics of disadvantaged students.* Unpublished manuscript, University of Port Elizabeth, South Africa. Available: Center for Supplemental Instruction, University of Missouri-Kansas City, 5014 Rockhill Road, SASS #210, Kansas City, MO 64110.

Kowalczyk, J. (2003). *Executive summary: Winter 2003 SLA program.* Unpublished manuscript, Ferris State University. Retrieved from June 22, 2004, from http://www.ferris.edu/htmls/colleges/university/cool/outcomes/SLAsummary/

Leapard, B. B. (2001). Affective, metacognitive, and conceptual effects of an Emerging Scholars program on elementary teacher preparation: An application of the Treisman workshop model [Doctoral dissertation, The University of Toledo, 2000]. *Dissertation Abstracts International, 61*(10), 3958.

Lipsky, S. A. (Ed.). (2004). *Internet homepage for the NADE SI Special Professional Interest Network* [online]. Retrieved June 22, 2004, from http://www.iup.edu/lec/AcadAssist/SI/SI%20Help.htm

Martin, D. C., & Arendale, D. (Eds.). (1994). *Supplemental Instruction: Increasing achievement and retention* (New Directions for Teaching and Learning No. 60). San Francisco: Jossey-Bass.

Martin, D. C., Arendale, D., & Blanc, R. A. (1997). *Mainstreaming of developmental education Supplemental Instruction and Video-based Supplemental Instruction.* Unpublished manuscript, The University of Missouri-Kansas City. Retrieved June 22, 2004, from http//www.umkc.edu/cad/si/sidocs/sivsi97.htm

Martin, D. C., & Blanc, R. (2001). Video-based Supplemental Instruction (VSI). *Journal of Developmental Education, 24*(3), 12–14, 16, 18, 45.

Mills, S. R. (1999). Academic excellence workshops in chemistry and physics (Uri Treisman) [Doctoral dissertation, The Claremont Graduate University, 1999]. *Dissertation Abstracts International, 60*(06), 1968.

Moreno, S. E., Muller, C., Asera, R., Wyatt, L., & Epperson, J. (1999). Supporting minority mathematics achievement: The Emerging Scholars Program at The University of Texas at Austin. *Journal of Women and Minorities in Science and Engineering, 5*(1), 53–66.

Ogden, P., Thompson, D., Russell, A., & Simons, C. (2003). Supplemental Instruction: Short- and long-term impact. *Journal of Developmental Education, 26*(3), 2–4, 6, 8.

Painter, S. (Ed.). (2004). *Internet homepage for the Center for Supplemental Instruction* [online]. Retrieved June 22, 2004, from http://www.umkc.edu/cad/si/

Parsad, B., & Lewis, L. (2003). *Remedial education at degree-granting postsecondary institutions in Fall 2000: Statistical analysis report.* Washington, DC: U.S. Department of Education, National Center for Education Statistics. Retrieved June 22, 2004, from http://nces.ed.gov/pubs2004/2004010.pdf

Stansbury, S. L. (2001a). Accelerated Learning Groups enhance Supplemental Instruction for at-risk students. *Journal of Developmental Education, 24*(3), 20–22, 24, 26, 28, 40.

Stansbury, S. L. (2001b). *How to turn Supplemental Instruction nonparticipants into participants.* Unpublished manuscript, University of Missouri-Kansas City. Available from the author at Sydbury@Yahoo.com

Tien, L. T., Roth, V., & Kampmeier, J. A. (2002). Implementation of a Peer-Led Team Learning instructional approach in an undergraduate organic chemistry course. *Journal of Research in Scientific Teaching, 39*, 601–632. Retrieved June 22, 2004, from http://www.chem.rochester.edu/~chem203

Treisman, P. U. (1986). A study of the mathematics performance of Black students at the University of California, Berkeley [Doctoral dissertation, University of California, Berkeley, 1985]. *Dissertation Abstracts International, 47*(05), 1641.

Wolgamott, L. (Ed.). (2004). *Internet homepage for Structured Learning Assistance* [online]. Retrieved June 22, 2004, from http://www.ferris.edu/htmls/academics/sla/

Additional Readings

Arendale, D. R. (2010). Access at the crossroads: Learning assistance in higher education [Monograph]. *ASHE Higher Education Report, 35*(6).

Arendale, D., Barrow, H., Carpenter, K., Hodges, R., McGrath, J., Newell, P., & Norton, J. (2009). Position paper: Creating a new professional association. *Journal of Developmental Education, 33*(1), 28–30, 32, 34, 35.

Boylan, H. R. (2008). How research contributes to access and opportunity around the world. *Journal of Developmental Education, 32*(1), 2–3.

The Carnegie Foundation for the Advancement of Teaching. (2008). *Strengthening pre-collegiate education in community colleges: Project summary and recommendations.* A report from Strengthening Pre-collegiate Education in Community Colleges (SPECC). Stanford, CA: The Carnegie Foundation for the Advancement of Teaching.

Collins, M. L. (2009) *Setting up success in developmental education: How state policy can help community colleges improve student outcomes.* An Achieving the Dream Policy Brief. Boston, MA: Jobs for the Future.

Paulson, E. J., & Armstrong, S. L. (2010). Postsecondary literacy: Coherence in theory, terminology, and teacher preparation. *Journal of Developmental Education, 33*(3), 2–4, 6, 8, 10–13.

Preuss, M. (2008). Developmental education literature: A proposed architecture. *Journal Developmental Education, 32*(2), 12, 14, 16, 18–22.

Truschel, J., & Reedy, D. L. (2009). National survey — What is a learning center in the 21st century? *The Learning Assistance, 14*(1), 9–22.

3

Diverse Populations in the Classroom

The learning specialist's primary goal is to instruct college students on becoming effective and efficient learners and to master and then transfer content knowledge, new competencies, and appropriate dispositions from context to context. Across the years our field has often searched for or advocated a one-size-fits-all learning system, such as Francis Robinson's Survey Q3R or Walter Pauk's Cornell System, as if it had the power of a magic bullet. Our failure was not to take into consideration the great breadth of the sociocultural backgrounds of the college population and in the pedagogical demands of the various disciplines in the postsecondary learning environment.

In other sections of this text, we examine the theory and research leading to the best strategic actions students might employ as they encounter the unique cognitive demands required to succeed in different courses across the disciplines. Indeed, it is necessary to instruct novice learners to be master learners in each field.

This chapter takes us down a somewhat different avenue. Here we examine the concept of breadth not from an academic perspective but rather from a sociocultural perspective. The allied fields of learning assistance and developmental education have always accepted the premise that the population within postsecondary education is ever-expanding and changing to accommodate students from various ethnic, religious, social, or cultural groups. Each academic or political era since 1900 has won admittance for a cadre of "new" students to the classrooms, the lecture halls, and the laboratories of our universities and colleges.

Whether classified as working-class students, returning veterans, nontraditional students, at-risk students, and so on, each group brought with them worldviews that were likely to clash with the established order of academe. Academicians in established fields had ways of knowing and understanding that were at odds with the ways of knowing and understanding that had served the new students quite well in other contexts. Yet, more often than not, the knowledge and skills brought by the new students to higher education were viewed as a deficit by the guardians of the canon rather than as troves of knowledge with their own richness, complexity, and depth that could promote student learning as well as enrich the conservatism or traditional order of the academy.

Given the multitude of student groups found on campuses in the twenty-first century, the developmental educator and academic learning specialist have unique challenges to fulfill their duties of student service and faculty support. First, there is the responsibility of assisting and training students to be successful learners in the varied disciplines that make up the postmodern academic community. Second, there is the responsibility of assisting colleagues from across the academy, who often have limited backgrounds in learning theory and pedagogy, to be effective educators for an ever-broader diversity of students.

In this chapter Ross B. MacDonald and Monica C. Bernardo examine the "dynamics of difference" as these factors play out in higher education. Successful programs and best practice solutions for serving diverse clienteles are described in the following articles concerning: African American students, by Donna McKusick and Irving Pressley McPhail; English language learners, by Kate Wilson; students with learning disabilities, by Shari Harrison; and students with attention deficit/hyperactivity disorder (ADHD), by Frances Prevatt, Abigail Reaser, Briley Proctor, and Yaacov Petscher.

Reconceptualizing Diversity in Higher Education: Borderlands Research Program

Ross B. MacDonald and Monica C. Bernardo

Whether postsecondary learning assistance services are offered through developmental education programs, learning assistance centers, orientation programs, tutorial programs, or advising programs, they reach a body of students that grows more diverse with each passing decade. Yet programs continue to operate from a group-oriented philosophical stance born out of the war on poverty and the open-door movement of the 1960s and 1970s.

Ross B. MacDonald and Monica C. Bernardo propose that professionals in learning assistance programs might better view diversity as a continually expanding awareness of the dynamics of difference in regard to social power, personal perceptions, and judgments about others. The authors go on to discuss and draw inferences about theoretical and practical foundations of the competencies brought to and demonstrated in postsecondary education by a diverse student clientele.

In this article we intend to contribute to a deeper discussion of diversity in the context of developmental education theory and practice. Our means for doing so is to discuss the theoretical and practical underpinnings of a research program identifying the competencies of multicultural students and the applications of those competencies in educational settings. From these underpinnings we offer a number of inferences. Although as yet untested, the ideas in this article are intended to challenge thinking, promote discussion, and set the stage for future articles which report on the outcomes of the research program. In other words, this is a position piece, proposing that developmental education theory and practice be enhanced by considering the unique competencies students derive from living and succeeding in multiple worlds. It also serves as an introduction to future articles reporting on the research.

We argue that an unrecognized but essential set of competencies may develop, especially among students whose identities are made problematic by social power: the presence of a dominant culture which ignores, devalues, or criticizes them because they seem somehow different. We argue further that the field could be advantaged by identifying these competencies that are derived from multicultural experiences, from existence in overlapping, multiple worlds. Thus, in addition to attending to skill development in reading, writing, math, and learning, and in addition to providing support services such as advising, tutoring, Supplemental Instruction, and so forth, the developmental education field would certainly benefit from a broadened sense of the capacities and intelligences of the students served.

The discussion has four sections. The first develops a definition of diversity based on an analogy from astrophysics and the idea that diversity might best be defined as a dynamic. The second section expands the exploration of the dynamic by considering relationships among diversity, social power, and higher education, attending particularly to the implications for the field of developmental education. The third section introduces the concept of creative adaptive strategies and briefly traces their emergence to the dynamics of diversity and social power. The fourth section introduces the "Borderlands" research program and its potential benefits to the field.

Toward a Definition of Diversity

We propose that diversity be defined as a continually expanding awareness of the dynamics of difference in regard to social power, personal perceptions, and judgments about others. It is our contention that, regardless of the context, too many discussions about diversity are superficial and limited. Further, a limited focus on that which can be more easily seen significantly undermines the ability to understand what has been ill attended: the complex dynamics around issues of diversity, the fact that all humans are participants in this dynamic, and the competencies which students develop in response to ongoing marginalization and invisibility.

Through considering those competencies, how might the mission of developmental education be redefined? What is life like for students in the margins? What skills have they developed? Additionally, how can those skills best be positioned in school curricula? Attending to these less visible parts of the universe broadens and sharpens discussions of diversity. Similarly, attending to these less visible parts of universities and colleges may well enhance the quality and effectiveness of programs and services.

We have reframed diversity as a dynamic, an ongoing and active pursuit of an ever-expanding awareness about how difference is perceived and valued. Thus we propose that our inquiry into diversity — and thus our "universe" — be continual and always expanding. We further advocate that developmental educators deliberately attend to the margins, question assumptions about what is there, seek out the abilities people derive from being marginalized, revise curricula to take advantage of these competencies, and then position those students and their competencies into the middle of a new curriculum so as to benefit all students. If the mission of developmental education is to develop students' capacities to succeed, then shouldn't a part of that be recognizing and building on strengths? Shouldn't professionals be researching and reporting on what those strengths are and putting that information to good use in colleges and universities?

Why is it important to define diversity as a dynamic? A dynamic definition moves the concept of diversity beyond its typical "head count typology" based on superficial features of skin tone, gender, and so forth. Head counts are nominal orderings, both compelling and limiting. Because they offer a static set of definitive concepts (Blumer, 1986), they support the illusion that thinking about diversity is both powerful and meaningful by virtue of simply counting the number of people in a set of ethnic or racial categories. Yet framing diversity as a definitive concept means that we "lock in" to a narrow definition of diversity based on superficial or simplistic distinctions of race or ethnicity, for example. The consequence of this kind of thinking is that individuals become data points, to be understood in terms of a set of fixed characteristics which are then used to sort them irretrievably into mutually exclusive categories. Definitive concepts of diversity delude society's institutions into believing that they have the power to define, predict, and control (Weber, 1958), while blinding its members to the less visible and more complex dynamics of difference.

In contrast to the definitive approach, Blumer's (1986) notion of a sensitizing concept can help develop deeper concepts about diversity. Definitive concepts, such as canine (dog), feline (cat), and homo sapiens (human), permit mutually exclusive sorting into well-defined categories. In contrast, sensitizing concepts, such as cool, humane, free, and diverse, require the continual pursuit of contextualized understanding based on ongoing interactions with the emerging concept, the phenomena on which it is based, and related concepts. Consider coolness, for example.

Coolness, a quality of being perceived by others as having a kind of "with-it-ness," a way of managing and playing with trends and perceptions in interesting ways, is not a firm category to which one can permanently assign any set of given behaviors. Behaviors decidedly cool in one context can be decidedly uncool in other contexts. Coolness might be better understood as a sophisticated, ongoing dynamic among people, partly consisting of continuously shifting behavioral cues and markers which in a given moment and context are somehow considered to have "attitude" in ways both recognizable and interesting. So, to understand cool, one has to engage with a variety of people, in a variety of places, in a variety of ways, over periods of time. By thinking about the concept, observing situations in which cool is an issue, working with others, and attending to all the interactions among these things, one's concept of cool is increasingly sensitized. In other words sensitizing concepts, like cool and diversity, are tools to think with.

Reframing diversity as a sensitizing concept, then reveals that the point isn't just what color or gender a person is; more important are the *dynamics* which play out in regard to people's *perceptions* of others and people's resulting *value judgments* in regard to these perceptions of difference. A key part of the dynamic of difference is that marginalization leads to invisibility.

Recent discoveries in astrophysics and the seemingly unlimited opportunities for new understanding provide an apt analogy for highlighting the quality of invisibility within the dynamic of diversity. Significant among these new discoveries are inferences as to the presence of invisible matter and invisible energy. According to recent articles in the *New York Times* (Overbye, 2003a, 2003b) and *National Geographic* (Cowan, 2003), invisible matter, long ignored by astronomers and astrophysicists, is now believed to exercise a gravitational pull essential for the formation of entities such as stars and for relationships among entities such as solar systems and galaxies. Invisible energy, also once ignored but now thought to roughly comprise an estimated 75% of the energy in the universe, is believed to exercise forces so powerful as to compel the continuing expansion of the universe.

Prior to the emergence of these insights, scientists had relied almost exclusively on what they could see — visible light and its properties — to explain the universe and its workings. However, increasingly compelling evidence that there is energy outside the visible light spectrum provides a powerful reminder that the absence of an individual's ability to detect something too often leads to the assumption that there is simply nothing there. Similarly, the realization that nontraditional students possess competencies outside the vision of traditional research should not be subject to the false assumption that there is simply nothing there. Like so-called invisible light and invisible matter, these students are very much a part of this universe, representing little understood forms of energy which could expand us all.

What are the implications of the dynamics of difference for developmental education students and programs? We first recognize that developmental education students are more likely to be minorities and thus subject to superficial judgments which push them to the margins and render them less visible. This combination of marginalization and invisibility is often described as "otherness" and derives from the exercise of social power (hooks, 1990, 2003). Otherness refers to processes of marginalization in which those with more social power make inclusion/exclusion decisions about others or are unable or unwilling to even acknowledge them (hooks, 1990). In these decisions, perceived differences in experiences, capacities, appearances, preferences, and/or behaviors are devalued because the nature of those differences is unfamiliar or misunderstood.

For developmental education students, therefore, inclusion/exclusion decisions determine reductions or increases in access to the privileges and services a college or university automatically offers to those in the mainstream, such as access to courses or presumptions of certain kinds of competence. Further, these misguided decisions about capacities result in lost opportunities to position students' heretofore invisible skills in ways advantageous to the central purposes of a university: open-ended inquiry, new and integrated learning, personal and social empowerment, and high levels of collegiality (Astin, 1991; Giroux, 1992, 1997; Giroux & Giroux, 2004; Hytche, 1992; Wilson, 1992).

Just as astrophysicists have tended to study the best and brightest — the most visible light, that light which is physically closest to where they stand, so have those in the university tended to see those who are most similar to them in skills and talents as the best and brightest. Who has not heard an administrator in higher education speak of the "best and brightest" without at least some twinge of doubt as to the administrator's capacity to recognize all of the energy and capacity in his or her "universe?" Yet in both the universe and the university, there is much to be learned from the unseen. A critical step is to recognize the limitations of one's vision: In the case of astrophysics, the limitations of telescopes and mathematical models, and in the case of developmental education, the limitations of identifying intelligence and capacity based only on historical criteria of the majority culture. In the same way that scientists now see tremendous energy in formerly invisible areas of space, so might educational researchers see and better understand the "invisible" competencies derived from student's experiences living in multiple worlds by simply directing attention there.

Diversity and Empowerment in Higher Education

Once developmental educators recognize that there is much which has been invisible, then the inquiry into what might actually be there is opened. To empower society around diversity, the inquiry into those skills which have been invisible to date must be begun. Once discovered, the next step is to ask how to use that knowledge to revise programs and reposition students.

Currently, too many developmental education programs may be contributing to the very inequities they propose to address. Considering placement practices, it seems likely that developmental education students are positioned in terms of presumed deficits in their preparation, and mainstream students are positioned too often in terms of their presumed capacities. So, compared to their mainstream peers, developmental education students may face a double disadvantage: The presumption that they are deficient in visible skills and the failure of educators and society to recognize and build on skills they do have but are invisible. Ironically, capacities derived from coping with multiple "worlds" often remain unrecognized. The term "multiple worlds" refers to the different sociocultural contexts which many minority students daily experience. Consider, for example, a student who at home and in her immediate community is immersed in Mexican culture, speaking exclusively Spanish, and then moments later is at school interacting with other students from a variety of backgrounds in a school where English is the spoken language and American culture is dominant. Isn't she well prepared, if only by her experiences, to answer the recurring call from employers, communities, and business groups for people accomplished in multiperspective, open-ended inquiry, for people who can work effectively in teams while effectively encouraging and conscientiously attending to diverse voices?

Marginalization

Indeed, a number of researchers, theorists, and practitioners have argued that marginalized student populations possess talents ironically developed because of their marginalization (Astin, 1991; Bowen & Bok, 1998; Delpit, 1995; Freire, 1970; Giroux & Giroux, 2004; hooks, 1990,

2003). Yet if identified and positioned well, the expression of those talents could benefit us all. One would expect that higher education in the United States, almost universally regarded as serving the democratic ideal, would be well practiced in understanding and positioning a diversity of talents. Although the intention is clearly there, in practice, the dynamic surrounding diversity has to do with a presumption of deficiency and a subsequent channeling into support programs. So the dynamic first regards nontraditional students as somehow different than other students, next presumes that they are somehow deficient, and then takes action to undo the deficiencies they are presumed to have. Under the process of mainstreaming, then, once students are labeled as deficient, the irony is that the system then intervenes to undo its own process of marginalizing.

Compounding the problem, developmental education programs are often marginalized by the same institutional dynamic. Therefore, not only are developmental education students too often positioned on the margins, so are those programs that serve them. Yet one can build capacities in students without communicating to them that they are somehow deficient if the focus is on understanding the competencies they have already developed (Astin, 1991). Astin's research has consistently shown that students' leadership and citizenship skills increase sharply as a result of multicultural coursework and cocurricular activities. This suggests that multicultural experience, infinitely richer and more intense than living abroad for a year, can give rise to the development of valuable competency sets.

A broad view of — and deep experience with — diversity also develops higher ethical practices (Clarke, 1996). Clarke links the presence of multiple identities with the development of citizenship. Emphasizing the importance of ethical action, Clarke advocates a "deep citizenship," which requires a profound understanding of what he calls multiplicity. Multiplicity refers to the presence of multiple identities, multiple contexts, multiple experiences, and multiple standpoints. Clarke's description of multiplicity applies to a great number of developmental education students. According to Clarke, the experience of multiplicity particularly readies people to develop high ethical standards in the practice of citizenship. Ethical citizenship, therefore, requires negotiating multiple and sometimes conflicting standpoints internally as well as an understanding of the consequences of decisions as they radiate outwards across multiple contexts.

Thus, agreement with Astin (1991) that providing multicultural experiences as part of an undergraduate curriculum builds students' capacities, and acceptance of Clarke's (1996) contention that ethical civic action results from deep experiences with diversity leads to the conclusion that students with lifelong multicultural experiences would possess significant skill sets which have been less visible to us. Bowen and Bok (1998) make just this case in their landmark book, *The Shape of the River*, investigating the consequences for society of affirmative action admissions in higher education. According to their data, affirmatively admitted students in both public and private universities are much more likely to engage in community service activities both during and long after their college careers. If we presume that affirmatively admitted students are more likely to represent marginalized populations than their regularly admitted peers, then Bowen and Bok's results suggest that marginalization plus education is related to the development of higher levels of civic and social responsibility. Therefore, taken in aggregate, the work of Giroux (1992, 1997, 2001), Astin, Bowen and Bok, and Clarke suggest to us that a significant portion of developmental education students possess considerable capacities, residing just below the visual surface which developmental educators have not prepared themselves to fully expand.

Social Power

Because marginalization is a product of the exercise of social power, understanding the nature and workings of social power is a critical component of any continually expanding awareness of the dynamics of diversity. Lisa Delpit (1995), Paolo Freire (1970), Henry Giroux (1995, 2001), Ira Shor (Shor, 1992; Shor & Freire, 1987), and others make just this case when they argue for "an education for liberation" in tune with the needs of students. Fundamental to this approach is an attempt to deeply understand the dynamics of social power as it marginalizes and oppresses those near the fringes of a given society or context. In carrying out this approach, teachers are responsible for helping students see linkages between their personal experiences and broader social and political issues of relevance to them. Seeing these links helps marginalized students develop voice and identity. When voice and identity are expressed and directed to these social issues such as minimum-wage workers' ability to support themselves, it moves marginalized students closer to the social and political center by revealing their connections. In other words, issue-based inquiry taps into the skills which marginalization develops — like making one's voice heard from the bottom of the heap — and then pulls those skills and the students who possess them closer to the middle of our efforts, advantaging all participants.

The nature of these skills and their significance to this inquiry become even more profound upon considering the force of social power within the dynamics of diversity. Lisa Delpit (1995) advocates that students need to learn how to make sense of their own experiences and voice their learning. Delpit first advocates that power issues critically influence the dynamics of diversity. In particular, Delpit's work suggests that an important capacity possessed by developmental education students, when compared to their mainstream peers, may be a deeper understanding of the presence of social power and how it operates. A social structure that oppresses group members is more visible to them than one that is supportive. Delpit argues that students need to be accurately informed of the existence of a power structure in society if they are to enter into and succeed in the mainstream. She asserts that those with less power in almost any context are more likely to be judged as different and therefore deficient as compared to those with more social power. Yet individuals with less social power may actually understand power and power dynamics better than those who hold more power. It is easier to identify oppression than privilege.

Key to any in-depth discussion of diversity is this fundamental irony about social power and self-awareness, according to Delpit (1995). Those with *more power*, whether in educational settings or in the larger society, are frequently *less aware* of or less willing to acknowledge that power. Correspondingly, those with *less power* are frequently *more aware* of its existence and likely have greater understanding of how it is used.

It follows that those with less power need to be positioned so as to help others learn about power and diversity. Therefore those less aware of power (and who ironically are likely to have more of it) need to be able to listen to and accept the experiences of those in the margins. There is much to be learned in these "invisible spaces" of colleges and universities. Further, positioning those with less power more in the middle of the curriculum communicates to them the same message the more mainstream students already receive: that they have skills and capacities which, if expressed, would actually help them gain access and be accepted in the institution. Engaging in these practices might give greater depth of meaning to the oft-used phrase, "honoring the experiences of others."

Understanding the workings of social power is important for two reasons. First the exercise of social power fuels the dynamic of diversity. Diversity is such an issue in our society in large part because of inequities deriving from the exercise of social power. In short, social power marginalizes difference. Second, the awareness that some deeply understand social power because of their experiences serves as one enticing example of what might be a broad set of capacities ironically derived from being judged as different.

Diversity, Creative Adaptive Strategies, and Higher Education

Bell hooks (1990, 2000, 2003) discusses in detail additional capacities which are developed while confronting the dynamics of social power. She describes how the exercise of social power can marginalize individuals, disassociating them from the mainstream. The result is a quality of "otherness," which in turn produces considerable stress. At the same time, this stress can stimulate considerable creative energy. Hooks advocates that this energy be directed to inventing "spaces of radical openness . . . a new location from which to articulate our sense of the world." This we infer from applying hooks' premise to the thesis of this article, these creative adaptations in these "new locations" reveal previously invisible strategy sets. These sets derive from and are directed to managing the complexities of multiple identities in the face of a power structure which can neither see the marginalizing processes nor the creative strategies people develop as a response to them.

Gloria Anzaldua (1987) provides creative and vivid descriptions of her personal experiences in the margins, the stress which accompanies them, and the creative adaptive strategies that emerge. She is cited here as one of many writers publishing personal accounts of marginalization and struggle (hooks, 2000; Liu, 1999; Moraga & Anzaldua, 1984). She represents her simultaneous identities as Navajo, Mexican, mixed race, lesbian, and female as a borderlands, a place where all her identities are present and expressive. Anzaldua (1987) describes her life in the borderlands in verse form, alternating between English and Spanish.

> To live in the Borderlands means you
> are neither hispana india negra española
> ni gabacha, eres mestiza,[1] half-breed
> caught in the cross fire between camps
> while carrying all five races on your back . . .
>
> To survive the Borderlands
> you must live sin fronteras[2]
> Be a crossroads. (p. 216)

Similarly, in a class assignment, a first-year student in a major western university describes her personal borderlands and contrasts it with the mainstream as follows:

> Most Americans are used to a certain way of life. They do not know about assimilation because they already belong. For many immigrants, or sons and daughters of immigrants, fitting into American culture becomes a difficult task. As a young girl, I was taught that maintaining my culture was one of the most important things that I could possibly do. My Mexican traditions, celebrations, and beliefs are part of what make me who I am. However, there is another culture to which I belong and that is the American culture.

In this passage, the student identifies her multiple identities, Mexican and American, as potentially problematic, and at the same time, she recognizes that she belongs to both cultures. Her resolution demon-

[1]Hispanic, Indian, black, Spanish, nor foreigner, you are mixed race.
[2]Without borders

strates one example of the kinds of strategies under discussion in this article. In this case, the acceptance of simultaneous, seemingly contradicting truths about her identity are not mutually exclusive. Instead of having to choose between being Mexican or American, she recognizes that both identities are within her and further recognizes that she can attend to the immediate context for signals as to which should be more present. This strategy seems to be a creative adaptation in response to the anxiety that emerges from creating legitimacy for all her identities, a way to move towards a more balanced and harmonious understanding of self. Clearly the student and Anzaldua express considerable creative energy in describing their lives in multiple worlds and their continuous crossing of boundaries.

The experiences and ideas of hooks (1990, 2000, 2003), Anzaldua (1987), and the student vividly support the contention that when identity and integrity are threatened by the exercise of social power, creative responses are forged. Considering the experiences of hooks, Anzaldua, and the student cited previously in combination leads to the inference that there may be some commonality in the capacities for coping with the maintenance of complex identities across multiple contexts, independent of the particulars of each situation. In other words, Anzaldua and the student may share common learning despite the more superficial differences in their respective experiences. The dynamic of diversity may have enough consistency such that one's creative adaptive strategies may be the same or similar as others. Neither Anzaldua nor the student cited an intent to represent the experiences and perspectives of others. However, taken together, these "cultural crossings," their effects on people, and the creative responses they stimulate have the potential to continuously expand the understanding of diversity — if it is placed in a common field of vision.

This sense of diversity recognizes the simultaneous presence of multiple identities within every individual, sometimes rendered more prominent and more problematic against the foreground of the more monocultural expectations of the dominant population. Perhaps because all people are individuals and not prototypes, each individual lives to varying degrees in a personal borderland, a place where all identities are present but some are unseen; where creative responses to marginalization and otherness are developed and expressed; and where skills and capacities are being developed, practiced, and refined, again unseen by many. If all participants could develop and tap into these skills, the process could greatly expand the content and value of the experience of higher education.

According to Sandra Harding (1996), for example, the university needs to rearrange its existing disciplinary resources to produce new kinds of disciplinary practices. Harding calls for a new kind of creative thinking: a "knowledge collage." She defines the knowledge collage as an *epistemological borderland* that "values the distinctive understanding of nature that different cultures have resources to generate." She promotes learning "when to use one science as a reliable guide and when to use another; what to value in modern sciences and what to value in other knowledge systems . . . this is an epistemology seeking the most useful collage, rather than one perfect representation of the world" (Harding, 1996). In effect Harding is describing the simultaneous presence of multiple worlds but in the context of *ways of knowing* rather than *ways of being*.

The creative space in which such a way of knowing occurs can be likened to a borderlands. Considering Anzaldua, one can see that the borderlands is a metaphor, representing the social, intellectual, and emotional dynamics of multiple identities, made problematic by the overbearing presence of monocultural expectations which dominate American society. For Harding, the borderlands is also a metaphor referring to the social, intellectual, and emotional dynamics of multiple ways of knowing, made problematic by overbearing "monodisciplinary" ways of knowing which dominate school curriculum. The borderlands metaphor, therefore, provides an important tool to think with as developmental educators consider more deeply the concept of diversity and the curricular and pedagogic implications which follow.

Mapping Diversity's Landscape: The Borderlands Research Program

What do we mean by the borderlands? We offer the following discussion as a catalyst to additional inquiry. The following definition is meant to describe the borderlands concept at a level of abstraction applicable to either multicultural experience or multidisciplinary inquiry. This level of abstraction places each academic discipline as a culture and therefore considers the university as an entity in pursuit of a multicultural identity. The approach also shows how students' creative adaptive strategies for life in the borderlands particularly lend themselves to multidisciplinary inquiry.

The borderlands metaphor draws on geography as an expression of the mind, terrain as the map of that mind, and political boundaries between countries as social boundaries between peoples and ways of knowing. Any intersection of these boundaries, whether between cultures or disciplines, is a borderland. Therefore the borderlands refers to that figurative place where issues of who one is (identity) and the principles to which one aspires (integrity) are made complex by the simultaneous presence of more than one way of being and knowing (culture). Formation and maintenance of identity and integrity must account for the multiple cultures of which one is a member. Expressing that membership in culture and exercising integrity is citizenship of which education is a part. Borderlands issues are made problematic as privilege and resources (social power) are inequitably distributed.

However, when one *is* aware of being in such a figurative place (borderlands consciousness) and one is attempting to maintain or define identity while keeping integrity, it is likely that there is some level of personal, intellectual, and emotional uncertainty (anxiety). This in turn creates a need to lessen that anxiety in order to feel comfortable with self and with one's place in the world. What emerges are creative adaptive strategies, frameworks for living and thinking (borderlands competencies), which account for multiple identities, multiple citizenships, and multiple cultures. These competencies shape thinking and behavior in complex and sophisticated ways. How can developmental educators create very inclusive and thus expanding places of belonging for those in the borderlands, not only in an institutional setting but in their consciousness?

Current Research

We are developing a research program which explores answers to this question. Reframing diversity as a dynamic of difference informed each step of a research process using grounded theory methodology (Charmaz, 2000; Glaser & Strauss, 1968; Strauss & Corbin, 1998). First, we could account for the uniqueness of individual experience in regards to diversity while building greater understanding about the underlying dynamics which are present across experiences. In our research this meant we could gather and analyze student's individual stories and identify recurring themes. Second, we could explore relationships among themes while using each to better understand the others. In our research this meant that we could hypothesize relationships among themes in pursuit of explanatory power. Third, we could apply concepts and frameworks in a variety of contexts for a variety of purposes. In our research that meant applying concepts related to diversity to understand the nature of multicultural experiences, multidisciplinary inquiry, and the role of developmental education.

We currently are analyzing data, to be reported in future articles, which suggests that nontraditional students, students who live in the borderlands, possess a set of learned competencies which are too often invisible or devalued because they derive from experiences of otherness, an experience largely invisible and thus discredited by those who don't share it. We are engaged in mapping this creative terrain with an initial focus on borderlands competencies: sets of creative adaptive strategies which emerge from lifelong multicultural experiences in the margins of society. We are finding that, ironically, the very forces making identity problematic for people with multicultural identities also develops in them potentially powerful skills for critical inquiry. These are the same skills that society expects higher education to promote and teach! These abilities include, for example, capacities for exploring issues for which there aren't known answers, working deeply with multiple perspectives, incorporating a variety of disciplines as appropriate, recognizing the complexity of issues and people affected by those issues, and understanding that the nature of the answers one develops is a truth to some degree limited by the frameworks from which one operates. As the passages from Anzaldua and the first-year student demonstrate, for example, deep questioning regarding identity and societal values can be a way of life to individuals in the borderlands. Critical thinking experts (Elder & Paul, 2003) also advocate the importance of questioning: "To learn well is to question well" (p. 36).

Conclusion

The creative responses and the ability to consciously employ them which are found in the borderlands would seem to be of particular importance to developmental education. After all, society rightfully expects that colleges and universities produce graduates with the ingenuity and creativity to address complex contemporary issues (Homer-Dixon, 2000; Kellogg Commission, 1999, 2001). Therefore, an essential part of the mission of developmental education is to advantage marginalized students drawing on these competencies and then inform curricular design and practices throughout the university. We advocate that developmental students' experiences in the borderlands and the competencies they develop in response should inform the processes and practices of higher education. In this way, those of us in developmental education can help create colleges and universities which develop the talents of diversity — and develop a diversity of talents — much needed in a world too full of monocultural thinking and too often expressing the importance of self at the expense of others, producing tragic misunderstandings, distrusts, hatreds, gross inequities, and dehumanization.

Perhaps a better understanding of the dynamic struggles in the borderlands may reveal inspiration and practical guidance for addressing the ongoing struggle for identity, belonging, and expression of self which fundamentally define human experience. The ability to peer into the universe and understand more deeply the complex dynamics of all its elements and forces which may be realized by this process is of benefit to all. It offers a new opportunity to recognize and develop borderlands competencies and to better understand how to use them to improve the lives and learning of all and is worth pursuing, especially for the benefit of often marginalized developmental education students.

References

Anzaldua, G. (1987). La conciencia de la mestiza. Towards a new consciousness. In G. Anzaldua (Ed.), *Borderlands = la frontera: the new mestiza* (pp. 99–123). St. Paul, MN: Consortium Book Sales & Distributors.

Astin, A. W. (1991). *Assessment for excellence: The philosophy and practice of assessment and evaluation in higher education.* New York: MacMillan Publishing Company.

Blumer, H. (1986). *Symbolic interactionism: Perspective and method.* Berkeley, CA: University of California Press.

Bowen, W. G., & Bok, D. (1998). *The shape of the river: Long term consequences of considering race in college and university admissions.* Princeton, NJ: Princeton University Press.

Charmaz, K. (2000). Grounded theory: Objectivist and constructivist methods. In N. K. Denzin & Y. S. Lincoln (Eds.), *Handbook of qualitative research* (2nd ed.). Thousand Oaks, CA: Sage Publications.

Clarke, P. B. (1996). *Deep citizenship.* London, England: Pluto Press.

Cowan, R. (2003, February). Galaxy hunters: The search for cosmic dawn. *National Geographic*, 2–29.

Delpit, L. (1995). *Other people's children: Cultural conflict in the classroom.* New York: The New Press.

Elder, L., & Paul, R. (2003). Critical thinking: Teaching students how to study and learn (part IV). *Journal of Developmental Education, 27*(1), 36–37.

Freire, P. (1970). *Pedagogy of the oppressed.* New York: Continuum.

Giroux, H. A. (1992). *Border crossings: Cultural workers and the politics of education.* New York: Routledge.

Giroux, H. A. (1997). *Pedagogy and politics of hope: Theory, culture, and schooling: A critical reader.* Boulder, CO: Westview Press.

Giroux, H. A. (2001). *Theory and resistance in education: Towards a pedagogy for the opposition* (revised and expanded ed.). Westport, CT: Greenwood Publishing.

Giroux, H. A., & Giroux, S. S. (2004). *Take back higher education: Race, youth, and the crisis of democracy in the post-civil rights era.* New York: Palgrave Macmillan.

Glaser, B. G., & Strauss, A. L. (1968). *The discovery of grounded theory: Strategies for qualitative research.* Chicago, IL: Aldine.

Harding, S. (1996). Science is "good to think with": Thinking science, thinking society. *Social Text 46/47, 14*(1&2), 15–26.

Homer-Dixon, T. (2000). *The ingenuity gap.* New York: Random House.

hooks, b. (1990). *Yearning: Race, gender, and cultural politics.* Boston, MA: South End Press.

hooks, b. (2000). *Where we stand: Class matters.* New York: Routledge.

hooks, b. (2003). *Teaching community: A pedagogy of hope.* New York: Routledge.

Hytche, W. P. (1992). Educating a culturally diverse professional work force for the agricultural, food, and natural resource system. In *Agriculture and the undergraduate: Proceedings* (pp. 86–94). Sponsored by the Agricultural Research Council. Washington, DC: National Academy Press.

Kellogg Commission. (1998, May). *Returning to our roots: Student access* (2nd Report). Washington, DC: National Association of State Universities and Land Grant Colleges. Retrieved July 26, 2005, from http://hasulgc.org/Kellogg/Kellogg

Kellogg Commission. (1999, February). *Returning to our roots: The engaged institution* (3rd Report). Washington, DC: National Association of State Universities and Land Grant Colleges. Retrieved July 26, 2005, from http://hasulgc.org/Kellogg/Kellogg

Kellogg Commission. (2000, January). *Returning to our roots: Towards a coherent campus culture* (5th Report). Washington, DC: National Association of State Universities and Land Grant Colleges. Retrieved July 26, 2005, from http://hasulgc.org/Kellogg/Kellogg

Kellogg Commission. (2001, January). *Returning to our roots: Executive summaries of the reports of the Kellogg Commission on the future of state and land-grant universities.* Washington, DC: National Association of State Universities and Land Grant Colleges. Retrieved July 26, 2005, from http://hasulgc.org/Kellogg/Kellogg

Liu, E. (1999). *The accidental Asian.* New York: Random House.

Moraga, C., & Anzaldua, G. (Eds.). (1984). *This bridge called my back, writings by radical woman of color.* New York: Kitchen Table/Women of Color Press.

Overbye, D. (2003a, February 12). Cosmos sits for early portrait, gives up secrets. *New York Times*, p. A1.

Overbye, D. (2003b, February 18). Scientist at work: Adam Reis. His prey: Dark energy in the cosmic abyss. *New York Times*, p. F1.

Shor, I., & Freire, P. (1987). *A pedagogy for liberation: Dialogues on transforming education.* Boston, MA: Bergin & Garvey Publishers.

Shor, I. (1992). *Empowering education: Critical teaching for social change.* Chicago, IL: University of Chicago Press.

Strauss, A. L., & Corbin, J. M. (1998). *Basis of qualitative research: Techniques and procedures for developing grounded theory.* Thousand Oaks, CA: Sage.

Weber, M. (1958). *From Max Weber: Essays in sociology.* Oxford, England: Oxford University Press.

Wilson, E. P. (1992). Striving toward cultural diversity. In *Agriculture and the undergraduate: Proceedings* (pp. 165–172). Sponsored by the Agricultural Research Council. Washington, DC: National Academy Press.

Walking the Talk: Using Learning-Centered Strategies to Close Performance Gaps

Donna McKusick and Irving Pressley McPhail

Donna McKusick and Irving Pressley McPhail postulate that for the diverse students to be able to succeed in higher education, institutions must do more than talk *about multiculturalism. Rather, each institution must adopt a learning paradigm that posits all students can learn and all learners can connect with knowledge to construct meaning. Hence, faculty and staff at postsecondary institutions must understand and promote cognitive learning preferences that often differ according to a learner's culture.*

The authors discuss how a learning-centered community college has adopted a set of practices to close the achievement gap between African American and Caucasian students through five strategies: (a) providing professional development to faculty and staff, (b) delivering responsive, culturally-mediated instruction, (c) utilizing culturally attuned methods for academic preparation, (d) customizing student support services, and (e) implementing a hospitable institutional climate.

A quiet revolution has been going on in colleges across the country. Institutions of higher education are shifting their focus from the institution to the learner. According to Barr and Tagg (1995), "Subtly but profoundly we are shifting to a new paradigm: A college is an institution that exists to produce learning. This shift changes everything" (p. 13). The learning paradigm distinguishes itself from the instructional paradigm in a number of ways that are important to serving the needs of diverse learners (Barr & Tagg, 1995). The essential nature of knowledge and the learning process are challenged in the learning paradigm. Whereas, in the instructional paradigm, knowledge is viewed as an absolute entity outside of the life of the learner, in the learning paradigm, knowledge is shaped by, constructed from, and connected to each learner's background. In the learning paradigm, learning is a process in which knowledge is "nested" and connected rather than accumulated and stored. In the learning paradigm, learning environments are cooperative and collaborative, rather than individualistic and competitive. Finally, and most important, in the learning paradigm, talent and ability are abundant in all individuals. To quote Smilkstein (2002), "We're born to learn!"

The Learning College and At-Risk Students of Color

The tenets of the learning paradigm have an important relationship to the future of developmental students in the United States, who are becoming more culturally and ethnically diverse every day. In the beginning of the 1990s, about a third of developmental students were minorities (specifically African American and Hispanics), with the largest group as African Americans (Boylan, Bonham, Claxton, & Bliss, 1992). According to a recent study of developmental education by McCabe (2000), 20% of African American students enrolled in community colleges have *seriously* deficient skills; that is, they are placed in developmental reading, writing, *and* math, and assigned to a lower-level remedial course in at least one area. Only 5% of White students, however, come to community colleges with seriously deficient skills.

According to the U.S. Bureau of the Census (2001), in the next 50 years, minority populations including African Americans, Hispanics, American Indians, and Asians will increase as the White population decreases. African American and Hispanic students are more likely to be underserved by secondary and postsecondary institutions than are White students (McCabe, 2000). The Education Trust (2001), a nonprofit agency concerned with improving the education of populations who have been historically disenfranchised in the American school system, reports that by 12th grade, African American and Hispanic students in the American public school system are about four years behind other people on the National Assessment of Education Progress (NAEP). Gaps in performance between African American students and

White students continue into postsecondary institutions (Harvey, 2002). The Education Trust's research shows that African Americans obtain college degrees at only half the rate of White students. The reasons for these gaps are many. Low expectations, lack of standards, lack of accountability, poor teaching, communication problems, and failure to address the specific learning styles of culturally and ethnically diverse students all appear to be major factors in perpetuating the performance gap between these students and White students (Education Trust, 2001; McPhail & McPhail, 1999).

To insure success for these students, institutions must do more than talk about multiculturalism. The learning paradigm asserts not only that all students can learn, but also that it is the institution's responsibility to help all learners connect with knowledge to construct meaning. In order to do this, the institution must better understand the cognitive learning preferences of all learners, which may differ according to culture (Hollins, 1996; Hoover, 1982; Irvine & York, 2001; McPhail & McPhail, 1999; Shade, Kelly, & Oberg, 1997). These differences may involve communication style, social interaction style, response style, or linguistic style (Shade et al., 1997) and may be represented by a difference in views about individualism, concepts of time, ideas about social hierarchies, and orientation to change (Education Research Service, 2003). For example, many African American learners prefer to (a) process knowledge within its context rather than in isolated parts; (b) use inferential reasoning rather than deductive or inductive reasoning; (c) perceive approximate quantities rather than exact quantities; (d) learn about people rather than things; (e) use active learning activities that incorporate freedom of movement; (f) learn in collaborative, social situations, and (g) learn visually and kinesthetically (Education Research Service, 2003; McPhail & McPhail, 1999; Shade et al., 1997). Learning preferences such as these can be used to create learning environments that produce success for all learners.

Applying the Principles

LearningFirst

How do institutions apply the principles of the learning-centered paradigm to performance gaps? The Community College of Baltimore County (CCBC), named as one of 12 Vanguard Learning Colleges by the League for Innovation in the Community College, has named its strategic plan LearningFirst. This plan is characterized by an articulated belief system that the institution: (a) makes learning its central focus, (b) makes students active partners in the learning process, (c) creates holistic environments that support student learning, (d) ensures that every member of the college community is a learner, (e) focuses on learning outcomes to assess student learning and success, and (f) assumes final responsibility for producing student learning.

In everyday practice, these beliefs mean that CCBC applies two questions to every institutional decision: "Does it improve learning?" and "How do we know?" (O'Banion, 1997). Answers to these questions are determined at all levels through institutional research, learning outcomes assessment, and classroom assessment.

Defining the Gaps at CCBC

In exploring the learning outcomes of developmental students in 2001, CCBC uncovered unacceptable gaps in performance between African American and White students for course pass rates, retention rates, graduation rates, and transfer rates. In general, at the course level, the differences in pass rates between White Students and African American students were largest for students taking developmental courses, ranging from approximately 10% to 20%, depending on the developmental discipline and level. This is significant because a disproportionate number of African American students enroll in developmental courses. Although only 25% of the students at CCBC are African American, 40% of the students enrolled in developmental courses are African American.

At the 100 course level, a 12% gap existed between the pass rates of African American and White students; at the 200 course level, a 7% gap existed. Gaps of 3% (part-time) and 4% (full-time) occurred between African American and White students' fall semester to spring semester retention rates; gaps of 4% (part-time) and 8% (full-time) occurred with fall to fall retention rates. Four-year graduation rates showed a gap of 10%, and four-year transfer rates revealed a gap of 14%.

Taking Action

The LearningFirst philosophy of CCBC asserts that until *all* learners are successful, the institution has not yet made good on the promise of access and opportunity. To make this promise a reality, the institution began to address performance gaps in two intersecting populations of "at promise" students, its African American students and its developmental students. It also assumed an important institutional stance early on, consistent with the learning paradigm: rather than seek to "fix" its students, the institution would work by itself and in tandem with the elementary-secondary (K–12) system to "fix" itself so that it could better serve the needs of its learners. After conducting a review of best practices, the institution constructed a vision statement and a mission statement for its Closing the Gap Initiative.

Vision statement. CCBC produces improved and expanded learning out-comes that reflect no difference in achievement between African American and White learners. (CCBC Catalogue, 2002–2004)

Mission Statement. CCBC offers, through all segments of its institution, an organizational culture, a responsive methodology of instruction, and an array of student services that address the needs of all learners, with particular attention to those students who have been historically disen-franchised in the American education system. CCBC actively promotes a responsive and diverse organizational culture by attracting, retaining, and supporting a faculty, staff, and student community that reflects the diversity of the region it serves. CCBC further responds in its various learning environments by providing students with learning experiences that embrace the cultural backgrounds of all students. CCBC maintains high expectations of all learners and assists them with an array of aca-demic and personal support services such as developmental education, tutoring, mentoring, and advising to ensure success. CCBC also works actively with K–12 schools to promote academic readiness of high school students. Finally, in keeping with its role as a learning college, CCBC is outcomes driven in all efforts to close the achievement gap among groups of diverse learners and to promote continuous institutional improvement. (CCBC Catalogue, 2002–2004)

Furthermore, CCBC established strategies that would focus on five areas: professional development, instruction, academic preparation, student services, and institutional culture. All of these interrelated areas have direct bearing on the success of diverse developmental students.

Learning-Centered Strategies for Closing the Gaps

Professional Development

Effective professional development is the first tool that institutions can use to build a coalition for change (Boylan, Bonham, & Bliss, 1993; Boylan, Saxon, White, & Erwin, 1994). At the minimum, all learners, regardless of level, need faculty and staff who have adequate expe-rience, subject-matter expertise, and classroom effectiveness (Haycock, 2003). In addition, however, institutions need to provide opportunities for faculty and staff to grow in their understanding of the effects of race and culture on teaching and learning. This staff development includes workshops on racial identity (Tatum, 1997), faculty mentoring and training in pedagogical techniques to address the varied learning styles of a diverse student body, and instruction in revamping the curriculum so that it is relevant to a multicultural society (Banks, Cookson, Gay, Hawley, Irvine, Nieto, Schofield, & Stephen, 2001). In particular, fac-ulty can be trained in the techniques of culturally mediated instruc-tion (Hollins, 1996) and in what Banks and Banks (1995) have named "equity pedagogy," "teaching strategies and classroom environments that help students from diverse racial, ethnic, and cultural groups attain the knowledge, skills, and attitudes needed to function effectively within, and help create and perpetuate, a just, humane, and democratic society" (p. 152). More is said about culturally mediated instruction later in this chapter.

APPLYING PROFESSIONAL DEVELOPMENT STRATEGIES. In accordance with its belief that every member of the college community is a learner, in the summer of 2002 CCBC held a Symposium on Closing the Gap. The purpose of this event, which was voluntarily attended by 350 faculty and staff, was (a) to create a sense of urgency in participants by presenting institutional data on performance gaps, and (b) to begin to create a guiding coalition for institutional transformation. These two techniques are necessary for getting institutional change started (Kotter, 1996). Powerful and effective speakers challenged the myth that socioeconomic reasons were accountable for the gap (Education Trust, 2001). Faculty were praised for their ability to produce change in the classroom, were exposed to new pedagogies such as culturally mediated instruction (Hollins, 1996), and were challenged to adapt their instruction to better meet the needs of all learners. At the end of the symposium, faculty and staff who attended were invited to submit "powerful ideas" they obtained from the day. Below is a sampling of the numerous responses.

From a reading professor: "From the talk, I would like to use more visual graphic organizers to teach strategies for handling the different reading tasks involved in discipline specific textbooks." From a literacy instructor:

I was extremely impressed with the presentation on voluntary and involuntary minorities and the phenomenon of "cultural inversion." For me, it provided the missing factor in the whole discussion of the "learning gap." I see now how crucial this concept is to any remedy for solving this intractable problem.

From a biology professor:

One powerful idea I derived from the day is that students are looking for instructors that are willing to "connect," meaning, without being too pushy or too personal, instructors should help their students to succeed or help to find the reason(s) for lack of success.

Since the original symposium, the institution has continued to hold conferences, workshops, and departmental discussions about addressing the needs of diverse learners. New faculty members participate in a year-long learning community in which they discuss instructional approaches that are effective for all learners.

Instruction

Because increased learning is the ultimate goal of the learning college, and because the student-teacher relationship is fundamental to learning, what happens in the classroom is at the heart of closing the gap. Learning facilitators need a caring attitude and an ability to communicate with all learners (Gonsalves, 2002), regardless of diverse sociolinguistic communication patterns (Delpit & Dowdy, 2002). The ability to further connect with learners can be enhanced by an understanding of brain-based learning (Smilkstein, 2002), a theory which suggests that to construct new learning, new ideas must be linked to prior learning and exercised through practice. To build curricula around this learning model necessitates an understanding of the many varying worldviews and prior cultural background knowledge brought to the classroom by diverse learners. The curriculum should be transformed to reflect the histories and perspectives of all people (Banks et al., 2001), and should be adapted to make learning relevant to the lives of all learners through contextualization and application to everyday life (Hoover, 1982; McPhail & Morris, 1986; Moses, 2002; Schoenfeld, 2002). Classroom assessment practices that help the instructor gauge student response lead to instructional modification (Cross & Steadman, 1996). The result, culturally mediated instruction, can be used to address the learning styles and backgrounds of all learners (Hollins, 1996; Hoover, McPhail, & Ginyard, 1992; McPhail & McPhail, 1999) This fine tuning of instruction to make it responsive and relevant to lives of learners is most effective in a small class environment (Roach, 2001). High expectations, expressed explicitly to all students, coupled with institutional accountability, guarantee that instruction is on track (Education Trust, 2001; Hrabowski, 2002).

APPLYING INSTRUCTIONAL STRATEGIES. CCBC faculty have been involved in study groups to learn how to facilitate learning in a culturally mediated manner. The following list summarizes specific research-based techniques instructors have been using to relate better to diverse learners:

1. Make a personal connection with each student.

2. Communicate high expectations to each student, and assure students that you believe they can meet these expectations.

3. Listen "through the dialect" to better hear what the student is really saying.

4. Explain to students that dialects, regionalisms, and speech patterns reflect cultures and are not inherently right or wrong. Explain directly to students that although no language pattern is

better, Standard American English may be necessary to succeed in this country.

5. Do more visual presentation in class; present a more visual overview of the content by using more graphic organizers.

6. Use works that represent many cultures and belief systems.

7. Use a number of pedagogies — some direct instruction, some individual work, some group work, and lots of active learning opportunities to address the cultural learning needs of all students.

8. Be more intentional in the makeup of small groups, putting together students of different cultural backgrounds.

9. Create zones for safe discussion of racial issues in each class.

10. Monitor daily what is working with students through classroom assessment and adjust activities to benefit students who appear not to be "getting it" from the "planned" activities.

Academic Preparation

Reaching back to feeder high schools to provide assessment and early intervention helps boast students' skills before they enroll in college (McCabe, 2000). Research has also provided postsecondary institutions with many best practices that can be used in the developmental classroom to hone the basic skills of underprepared students from historically underrepresented populations. In general, the use of mastery learning provided within a highly structured learning environment is recommended because of its effectiveness with all developmental learners (Boylan & Saxon, 1999). Students who are academically underprepared should be provided with many instructional delivery choices that address their particular cultural learning styles. An active, contextualized, small group methodology that characterizes culturally mediated instruction is particularly beneficial for African American learners (Hollins, 1996; Hoover, McPhail, & Ginyard, 1992). Developmental learning communities provide opportunities for students to contextualize learning with topics related to diversity (Boylan & Saxon, 1999; Hollins, 1996; Hoover et al., 1992; Moses, 2002; Stahl, Simpson, & Hayes, 1992; Tinto, 1997).

LANGUAGE SKILLS. The principles of culturally mediated instruction can be easily applied to meet the specific needs of underprepared students. One valuable method that addresses the cultural learning style of African American students is the Nairobi Method (Hoover et al., 1992). This method of literacy instruction originated in 1969 at a community-oriented independent African American college in California called the School of Wisdom and Knowledge, and has been used in a variety of settings including developmental programs. The approach uses the background of learners to provide a platform from which students can grow and learn. As opposed to many developmental programs that are individualized, this program recognizes the preference of many African American learners for group learning by promoting active, collaborative, and participatory instruction. For example, vocabulary building activities include practicing word patterns with partners, using corrected dictation with partners, and group paraphrasing. A semi-foreign language approach is used in reading instruction because many diverse learners bring with them a dialect or another language in addition to Standard American English. Knowledge of English orthography and structural analysis is used to build vocabulary, while daily controlled composition on generative themes is used to improve writing.

MATH SKILLS.   The work of Robert Moses (2002) provides an example of how to culturally mediate instruction in basic math. Linking issues of math and science literacy to the ongoing struggle for citizenship and equality for African Americans, Moses initiated the Algebra Project in McComb County, Mississippi, in 1982. The project taught algebra, a crucial stepping-stone to college level math, to middle school students. Moses' instructional model begins with a physical trip, even if it is just walking students around the block. Next, students are asked to create a pictorial representation or construct a model, which includes important features of the event. This starts the process of abstraction. Then, students are asked to use intuitive language about the event, by speaking and writing in their own language. Later, students are trained to use structured language or a common language about the features of the trip. In doing so, four mathematical concepts of the trips are introduced: start, finish, direction, and distance. Finally, the students invent symbols to represent these ideas. These symbols are then manipulated to solve meaningful mathematical problems. Moses' approach takes advantage of meaningful situations, students' own language patterns, and visual representation to help learners connect with mathematics.

APPLYING STRATEGIES THAT IMPROVE ACADEMIC PREPARATION.   In accordance with the LearningFirst principle of making students active learners in the learning process, at CCBC developmental students can participate in special sections that use culturally mediated instruction. Some of these sections use the framework of a learning community to provide a contextual basis for instruction by combining a developmental reading or writing course and a general education course, such as African American History, Introduction to American Pluralism, Health 101, and Psychology 101. Under normal circumstances, developmental reading and writing are prerequisites for most general education courses, but in the developmental learning communities, developmental students are permitted to enroll in a general education course because they receive extra support. In these communities, the reading or writing instructor uses materials from the textbook of the general education course to teach developmental skills to the students. Students are easily engaged in the learning of the developmental skills because they are using these skills to actively construct meaning in the general education course.

In the learning communities, because students attend several courses together, they are able to bond with each other and use their relationships to benefit their learning. Collaborative activities abound in the communities, providing opportunities for students to connect with each other and to learn cross-culturally from one another. "Border crossings," or opportunities for students to explore another culture, and "safe-zones" for discussions of sensitive racial content provide opportunities for students to establish social trust (Steele, 1999; Tatum, 2000).

One element that makes the program unique is the addition of a Master Learner to each learning community. Master Learners are faculty or counselors who are not experts in the discipline that is being taught in the general education course. After being trained, these individuals spend the semester with the students in the general education course and act as models by attending class regularly, taking notes, completing assignments and tests, and writing papers. In addition, once a week the Master Learners run a required seminar for the students; these seminars provide guidance in the skills and behaviors needed to be successful in the course.

Learning outcomes assessments have determined the communities to be a powerful contributor to student retention. The fall to spring retention rate of students in the learning communities is 77%, as compared to the college's average of 66%. The fall to fall rate is 60%, as compared to the college's average of 42%. Grades of students in the learning communities are also routinely higher than grades of other CCBC students in the same courses. These statistics may represent the motivation level of the students who enroll in learning communities. Most important, however, is that the 12% pass rate gap between White students and African American students in all 101 level courses has been reduced to 5% in the learning communities. Assuming that African American and White motivation for enrolling in the learning communities is the same, this reduction in the pass rate gap represents true progress.

Several factors contribute to the general effectiveness of the developmental learning communities. First, the developmental students are working with authentic texts and are motivated to succeed in the developmental course because it will help them with the general education course. Second, the Master Learner is able to provide the instructors with feedback on whether instruction is adequately connecting with the learners. Third, the Master Learner gets to observe another instructor and to learn from that individual's teaching techniques. Fourth, Master Learners discover materials that they can incorporate into courses in their disciplines. For example, a career/technology instructor was able to incorporate more diversity content in his courses after he was a Master Learner in a pluralism course.

Student Support

A host of specific student support services documented as best practices are used in serving at-risk students of color. To determine which services students most need, affective variables such as motivation, attitude, metacognition, and study skills should be assessed along with basic skills (Archer, 2002). Students need opportunities to build academic skills through tutoring, which is enhanced through cross-cultural tutor training (MacDonald, 1994). In addition, Freshmen Year Experience Programs (Fidler & Godwin, 1994), Summer Bridge Programs (Kulik, Kulik, & Schwalb, 1983), and Orientation Programs (Hackett, 2002) provide students with a community, an orientation to higher education, and a structured learning environment critical for learners who may be the first generation in their families to attend college. Peer counseling (Brown, 1991) and mentoring (Carriuolo, 2001) help students connect with each other and with the institution. Inclusion of family members in campus programs supports students by providing parents with base knowledge about higher education (Fries-Britt, 2002) and by helping the institution learn more about students' backgrounds. Finally, supplemental financial aid programs provide financial access to college for many students who otherwise would not have been able to attend college.

APPLYING STUDENT SUPPORT STRATEGIES.   In accordance with the LearningFirst belief that institutions must create holistic environments that support student learning, CCBC has supported its instructional efforts with a host of student supports geared directly to meeting the needs of diverse learners. All developmental reading students are required to enroll in a student success orientation course, Achieving Academic Success (SDEV 101), where an inventory of affective skills in attitude, motivation, learning styles, and study skills is taken and where strategies to meet affective needs are taught. Students in this course develop individualized learning plans, which are web-stored, to guide their progress through the following semesters. Student Success Centers on all campuses provide tutoring and computer-aided instruction by paraprofessional and peer tutors, who are trained in cross-cultural communication. A summer bridge program called the Pre-College Institute enables students to complete developmental courses in a few intensive weeks while introducing them to the campus. Finally, a peer mentoring program matches students who have high grade point averages and recommendations from faculty with African American developmental students. These pairs meet regularly to help the mentees navigate through the new world of higher education.

Institutional Culture

These instructional and student support efforts to close performance gaps produce a culture that celebrates diversity and expects high levels of learning of all students. Affirming identity, building community, and cultivating leadership are mechanisms an institution can use in all of its interactions with learners to transform its culture to one that celebrates high levels of success for all learners (Tatum, 2000). Hiring faculty and staff who culturally represent the institution's learners promotes affiliations between students and faculty, an important retention strategy. Identity affirmation is enhanced through the establishment of cultural centers, clubs, programs, and activities that make obvious the institution's commitment to students of all races and cultures. Special programs that foster and celebrate the high achievements of students of color encourage enrollment of academically accelerated students of color who can provide examples and mentorships for underprepared students (Fries-Britt, 2002; Hrabowski, 2002). Through the creation of "safe-zones," faculty, staff, and students are encouraged to "border cross" into other cultural experiences (Tatum, 2000) and to discuss sensitive cultural issues, in order to develop social trust (Banks et al., 2001; Steele, 1999). Institutional climate audits can help an institution know how successful it has been in transforming culture.

APPLYING STRATEGIES TO IMPROVE INSTITUTIONAL CULTURE. In the final analysis, an institutional culture that supports high levels of learning for all students is the ultimate trait of the learning college. At CCBC, all steps to become more learning-centered have included strategies that address institutional culture. CCBC has created an atmosphere for faculty in which pedagogy is discussed at college, department, and division meetings. A safe-zone for professionals to discuss the role of culture in learning has been established through a college-wide electronic discussion board and campus-based discussion groups. Closing the gap is a consideration in all college plans and garners the attention of everyone through its own strategic plan. Safe-zone discussions for students occur in courses across the curriculum, in learning communities, in mentoring sessions, and at campus Multicultural Centers. Special events that feature prominent African American intellectuals and artists speaking on topics such as the hip-hop culture or African geography occur weekly. Student trips to historically African American colleges and universities provide a message to students that CCBC expects them to graduate and transfer on to receive a four-year degree.

Conclusion

Although CCBC has always been welcoming to students of all cultures, it has only recently begun its intentional 10-year journey to close the performance gap between African American learners and White learners. As a Vanguard Learning College, CCBC has discovered that the principles and strategies of the learning revolution provide a perfect framework for colleges to "walk the talk." The principles behind the specific strategies that CCBC is using to close the gap between African American learners and White learners can be used for any performance gap, because they focus on the learner rather than the institution. These include (a) professional development to help learning facilitators better understand the learning needs of diverse students; (b) rethinking instructional delivery systems to include positive representations of the cultural heritage of underserved populations in the curriculum, and informing students about the brain's natural learning process; (c) reaching back to address the academic preparation of students by using culturally appropriate pedagogies; (d) providing students with customized supports that meet the specific needs of diverse learners; and (e) creating an institutional culture that places the highest value on the success of all learners. Through continued assessment of learning outcomes, the compass that helps steer the direction of a learning-centered institution, CCBC will be able to monitor its own progress and make adjustments along the way. Finally, we hope that the determination to "walk the talk" will generate the type of discussion and action planning that will lead to improved practice and documented learning outcomes for all learners.

References

Archer, L. (2002). *A study of institutional responses to community college students with serious deficiencies in reading skills.* Unpublished doctoral dissertation, Morgan State University, Baltimore, MD.

Banks, C., & Banks, J. (1995). Equity pedagogy: An essential component of multicultural education. *Theory into practice* (a publication of the College of Education, Ohio State University), *34*, 152–158.

Banks, J., Cookson, P., Gay, G., Hawley, W., Irvine, J., Nieto, S., Schofield, J., & Stephen, W. (2001). Diversity within unity: Essential principles for teaching and learning in a multicultural society. *Phi Delta Kappan, 83*, 196–202.

Barr, R., & Tagg, J. (1995). From teaching to learning: A new paradigm for undergraduate education. *Change, 27*(6), 13–25.

Boylan, H., Bonham, B., & Bliss, L. (1993). The performance of minority students in developmental education. *Research in Developmental Education, 10*(2), 1–4.

Boylan, H., Bonham, B., Claxton, C., & Bliss, L. (1992, November). *The state of the art in developmental education.* Paper presented at the First National Conference on Research in Developmental Education, Charlotte, NC.

Boylan, H., & Saxon, D. (1999). *What works in remediation: Lessons from 30 years of research.* Unpublished research prepared by The National Center for Developmental Education for The League for Innovation in the Community College. Available at http://www.ncde.appstate.edu/reserve

Boylan, H., Saxon, D., White, J., & Erwin, A. (1994) Retaining minority students through developmental education. *Research in Developmental Education, 11*(3), 1–4.

Brown, C. (1991). Increasing minority access to college: Seven efforts for success. *NASPA Journal, 28*, 224–230.

Carriuolo, N. (2001). Helping low-income and minority students succeed in college: An interview with Blenda Wilson. *Journal of Developmental Education, 25*(1), 26–28.

Community College of Baltimore County (2002–2004). *Catalogue.* Baltimore, MD: Author.

Cross, P. K., & Steadman, M. H. (1996). *Classroom research.* San Francisco: Jossey-Bass.

Delpit, L., & Dowdy, J. (Eds.). (2002). *The skin that we speak: Thoughts on language and culture in the classroom.* New York: The New Press.

Educational Research Service. (2003). *What we know about: Culture and learning.* Arlington, VA: Author.

Education Trust, Inc. (Spring, 2001). New frontiers for a new century: A national overview. *Thinking K–16, 5*(2). Available at www.edtrust.org

Fidler, P., & Godwin, M. (1994). Retaining African-American students through the Freshman seminar. *Journal of Developmental Education, 17*(3), 34–36, 38, 40.

Fries-Britt, S. (2002). High-achieving Black collegians. *About Campus, 7*(3), 2–8.

Gonsalves, L. M. (2002). Making connections: Addressing the pitfalls of White faculty/Black male student communication. *Journal of the Conference on College Composition and Communication, 53*, 435–465.

Hackett, T. (2002). Survival strategies for African-American women in community colleges. *Learning Abstracts, 5*(11), 1–3. Available at http://www.league.org/publication/abstracts/learning/lelabs1102.htm

Harvey, W. (2002). *Minorities in higher education 2000–2001, 18th annual status report.* Washington, DC: American Council on Education.

Haycock, K. (2003). Toward a fair distribution of teacher talent. *Educational Leadership, 60*(4), 11–15.

Hollins, E. (1996). *Culture in school learning: Revealing the deep meaning.* Mahwah, NJ: Lawrence Erlbaum.

Hoover, M. R. (1982). A culturally appropriate approach to teaching basic (and other) critical communication skills to Black college students. *Negro Educational Review, 33*, 14–27.

Hoover, M. R., McPhail, I. P., & Ginyard, L. (1992). Literacy for miseducated Black adults: The Nairobi method, a culturally appropriate approach. In A. M. Scales & J. E. Burley (Eds.), *Perspectives: From adult literacy to continuing education* (pp. 212–218). Dubuque, IA: William C. Brown.

Hrabowki, F. (2002). Postsecondary minority achievement: How to raise performance and close the achievement gap. *The College Board Review, 195*, 40–47.

Irvine, J. J., & York, D. E. (2001). Learning styles and culturally diverse students: A literature review. In J. A. Banks (Ed.), *Handbook of research on multicultural education* (pp. 484–497). San Francisco: Jossey-Bass.

Kotter, J. P. (1996). *Leading change.* Boston, MA: Harvard Business School Press.

Kulik, G-L., Kulik, J., & Schwalb, B. (1983). College programs for high-risk and disadvantaged students: A meta-analysis of findings. *Review of Educational Research, 53,* 397–414.

MacDonald, R. (1994). *The master tutor.* Williamsville, NY: Cambridge Stratford Lt.

McCabe, R. H. (2000). *No one to waste.* Washington, DC: Community College Press, American Association of Community Colleges.

McPhail, I. P., & McPhail, C. (1999, September). Transforming classroom practice for African-American learners: Implications for the learning paradigm. *Removing vestiges: research-based strategies to promote instruction.* Washington, DC: American Association for Community Colleges.

McPhail, I. P., & Morris, P. L. (1986). A new look at reading/communication arts in the inner-city junior high school. *Reading Improvement, 23,* 49–60.

Moses, R. (2002). *Radical equations: Math literacy and civil rights.* Boston, MA: Beacon.

O'Banion, T. (1997). *A learning college for the 21st century.* Phoenix, AZ: Oryx Press.

Roach, R. (2001). In the academic and think tank world, pondering achievement-gap remedies takes center stage. *Black Issues in Higher Education, 18*(1) 26–27.

Schoenfeld, A. (2002). Making mathematics work for all children: Issues of standards, testing, and equity. *Educational Researcher, 31*(1), 13–25.

Shade, B., Kelly, C., & Oberg, M. (1997). *Creating culturally responsive classrooms.* Washington, DC: American Psychological Association.

Smilkstein, R. (2002). *We're born to learn.* Thousand Oaks, CA: Corwin.

Stahl, N. A., Simpson, M. E., & Hayes, C. G. (1992). Ten recommendations from research for teaching high-risk college students. *Journal of Developmental Education, 16*(1), 2–4, 6, 8, 10.

Steele, C. (1999). Thin ice: "Stereotype threat" and Black college students. *The Atlantic Monthly, 284*(2), 44–47, 50–54.

Tatum, B. (1997). *Why are all the Black kids sitting together in the cafeteria and other conversations about race.* New York: Basic Books.

Tatum, B. (2000). The ABC approach to creating climates of engagement on diverse campuses. *Liberal Education, 86*(4), 22–30.

Tinto, V. (1997). Classrooms as communities: Exploring the educational character of student persistence. *Journal of Higher Education, 68*(6), 599–623.

U.S. Bureau of the Census (2001). Census Data. Washington, DC: Public Information Office.

Note-Taking in the Academic Writing Process of Non-Native Speaker Students: Is It Important as a Process or a Product?

Kate Wilson

Research on note-taking has for several decades investigated whether the encoding hypothesis (product of note-taking) is responsible for the positive effects of the strategy. While the body of research is extensive, Kate Wilson points out that research on the habits of note-taking with non-native speakers (NNS), particularly with regard to academic writing, is wanting. Wilson queries, "Is note-taking a valuable process in terms of facilitating learning from texts for NNS students as well as providing a tangible product from which they can write their essays?" This article provides a comprehensive review of the literature, as well as a report on a qualitative investigation of six non-native speakers, as they move through an authentic writing task.

In teaching academic skills, I have sometimes found that non-native speaker (NNS) students may be resistant to the idea of note-taking as part of the reading-writing process in preparing assignments. Native speakers have generally been trained to take notes from sources during their high school or even primary school education, but students from other cultural backgrounds may not have had experience writing assignments or research papers, let alone taking notes as part of this process. For many NNS, the challenge of writing academic assignments in a foreign language is immense, and to be asked to take notes can be perceived as just an added burden. "What's the point of taking notes?" they say. "It's not efficient!"

To find some good answers to my students' questions, I decided to investigate the function of note-taking in the assignment or paper preparation process of non-native speakers. Is note-taking significant for its process function; in other words, does it enhance and facilitate learning from text? Or is it important for its product function, that is providing the student with prompts for the actual writing process?

What Does the Literature Tell Us about Note-Taking?

Note-taking in the second-language writing process is not a well-researched area, perhaps because of the traditional divide in the English as a Second Language (ESL) curriculum between reading and writing (see Blanton, 1994). Particularly the product-process distinction does not seem to have been explored. However, studies of note-taking in classes have investigated the product-process function of notes. Kiewra (1985) found that students who took notes in class were better able to recall the main points than non-note-takers, suggesting that note-taking as a process facilitated learning. However, those who were able to review the notes performed even better. In this case, the notes as a product served as a useful external means of storing information.

White (1996) made a somewhat similar distinction in her investigation of the role of note-taking in language learning. She felt it was important to distinguish between overt note-taking behaviors and the underlying cognitive processes which are "inaccessible to observation but central to learning" (p. 91). She commented that behaviors like underlining, listing, and copying are "traces of cognition," in that they give a tangible indication of the students' internal cognitive processing.

The literature on reading and note-taking contains both prescriptive texts and empirical research. The prescriptive texts of the past 50 or 60 years have offered a range of note-taking formulae. Most of these methods have encouraged students to pick out the main ideas of the text; to reflect, question, or comment on the material; or sometimes to transpose the information into graphic or diagrammatic form. Perhaps the most famous of these methods include the various versions of Robinson's (1946) Survey-Question-Read-Recite-Review (SQ3R) in which the second "R," recitation, has sometimes been interpreted to mean noting down the main points of the text. Bird's "Inductive Outline Procedure" was an even earlier reading and note-taking method; the main points were summarized on the left side of the page and students added their comments on the particular and overall significance of these points in two columns on the right side (as cited in King & Eilers, 1996). More recently, Pauk (as cited in King & Eilers) proposed "the Cornell Method" in which the text is summarized in point form on the right, keywords are jotted down in a narrow column on the left, and an overall summary is noted down at the bottom of each page of notes. Various forms of concept mapping and other graphic organizers also became fashionable during the 1960s and 1970s, popularized in particular by Buzan (1976). In postmodern times, an emphasis on dialogic reflection has led to the concept of the double-entry journal (Hughes, Kooy, & Kanevsky, 1997) in which students write their summary notes on the left and their reflections in the right-hand column.

Empirical research has set about showing the effectiveness of various note-taking methods in promoting learning from texts. For example, Fischer and Mandl (1984) taught college students to use note-taking strategies such as highlighting, margin notes, and text reconstruction and found that both high-level and low-level students improved their performance on recall tests. McCagg and Dansereau (1991) developed a complex system of knowledge mapping which involved picking out key ideas and showing the links between them. Recall protocols and multiple choice comprehension answers showed that students benefited from this procedure.

Working specifically with non-native speakers at an Egyptian university, Amer (1994) taught one group of students to use underlining, a second group to use knowledge mapping and a control group to use conventional ESL reading techniques focusing on vocabulary and structures. In comprehension and free recall tests, both note-taking groups performed better than the control group; however, the knowledge mapping group outperformed the underlining group in free recall. This finding supports the argument that more complex cognitive processing, such as transforming written to visual information, aids comprehension and recall.

Not all studies of note-taking have shown such positive results, however. For example, Sarig (1987) in her qualitative study of 10 Hebrew-speaking students found that self-monitoring and clarification-and-simplification strategies tended to promote comprehension more than "technical aids." In particular she pointed out that highlighting was associated with poor comprehension if students picked out lower-order propositions.

Summarizing, another form of note-taking, has also been shown to have dubious benefits in terms of learning from text if it is used inappropriately. For example, Armbruster and Anderson (as cited in Gagne, 1985) taught a treatment group to use summarizing techniques. On a recall test, the results of the treatment group were mixed. Armbruster and Anderson theorized that it is not sufficient to teach students to use an observable behavior (a note-taking technique) without stressing the underlying cognitive processes. Similarly, Hidi and Anderson (1986) found that the "copy-delete" summarizing technique led to poor performance on subsequent recall tests. They also found that some students tended to personalize the summary too much — picking out what was important to them rather than the most significant propositions in terms of the text.

Another recent study (Beeson, 1996) found that writing after reading contributed more effectively to synthesis of knowledge than note-taking. Beeson divided 111 college nursing students into 3 groups: one group read a given text and took notes; one group read without any pen-to-paper activity; and a third group was asked to read and then write a short essay about the texts. The note-taking group was found to have the best recall of facts in a subsequent test. However, the reading-only group and the essay writing group were both more able to synthesize the readings later into an essay. This is a significant study because the synthesizing task attempted to assess how well students could apply the knowledge they had gained from the texts. In contrast, most earlier studies had merely tested the quantity of students' learning from text through comprehension tests or recall protocols which typically count the number of macro- or micro-propositions recalled by the subjects. However, the study does not differentiate between note-taking techniques unlike the more recent study by Lahtinen, Lonka, and Lindblom-Ylänne (1997).

Lahtinen et al. (1997) used an authentic academic test, the entrance exam to a medical school, to investigate the qualitative outcome of students' spontaneous note-taking behavior. In this test, the 502 candidates were asked to read two texts before writing three short essay questions on the same topic. The students were unlikely to have had prior knowledge of this topic. Before writing, the texts and the students' notes were removed. As this was an authentic test situation, the students were free to choose their own note-taking techniques. The researchers analyzed the students' techniques into the following categories: no notes, underlining only, verbatim notes, summarizing, and/or concept-mapping. They related these to the students' performance and found that students who used no notes wrote the poorest quality essays. The best essays were written by students who used generative note-taking techniques such as summarizing and concept-mapping rather than merely underlining or verbatim notes. The authors concluded that "constructive mental activity is facilitated by study strategies aiming at transforming knowledge into a coherent whole through generative processing" (p. 15). Unfortunately, this claim is too sweeping, as the generative note-taking strategies may have been selected by students who were already more inclined to write analytically. Nevertheless, this study does suggest that there is a relationship between generative note-taking and good essay writing.

To summarize, the literature overall shows that note-taking, particularly what Lahtinen et al. (1997) term "generative" note-taking, can have beneficial effects on students' ability to recall and use information from texts. However, previous studies have not investigated the function of note-taking in the context of the academic assignment writing process. Lahtinen et al. removed the texts before students could write, whereas in an assignment-writing situation, students would continue to have access to textbooks, photocopied journal articles, and printouts from the Internet. Moreover, students in real life have access to computers as well as pen-and-paper. In these circumstances, what note-taking strategies do NNS students employ and how do these strategies relate to the quality of their essays?

A Qualitative Study of NNS Students' Note-Taking Strategies

In order to explore NNS students' note-taking strategies in depth, I conducted a qualitative study with a small number of students and investigated in detail how these students traveled through an authentic essay writing process.

I invited NNS students from a second-year Humanities unit to participate in the study and six students volunteered: Annie, Toni, Jim,

Mei Wen, Chu Li, and Emma. Coincidentally, all these students came from Chinese backgrounds (PRC, Taiwan, and Hongkong). They had been in Australia between 3 and 9 years and were all in their early twenties. Five of the students were female and only one was a migrant to Australia. All of the students, except one, had passed a first year university writing course for non-native speakers.

The students were about to write a 3,000-word essay worth 20% of their mark for the semester. They were told to use at least five sources, including journal articles as well as the recommended textbooks.

In order to obtain data that were as full, rich, and reliable as possible, I used three sources. First, I asked the students to keep all their notes, computer printouts, essay drafts, final drafts, and the lecturer's comments. Second, I asked them to tape-record an introspective protocol of their thoughts as they were taking notes. Third, I interviewed each student before and immediately after they prepared their essays.

Note-Taking as a Process

The students in the study all used some form of note-taking from the source texts in their assignment writing process. The first stage of note-taking for most of the students was highlighting or underlining sections of text — usually the keywords. One student (Chu Li) also sprinkled her text with translation equivalents in Chinese. Jim and Toni added a few margin notes. Several students used page stickers to mark particularly useful parts of the texts. Annie, Jim, and Toni also started to write point-form, or outline, notes from the various texts.

At a fairly early stage, all six students decided upon an overall structure for their essays and started to keep notes under the headings they had identified. Annie was the most systematic note-taker: she kept separate pages for each main section of her essay and used different colored pens to identify the different texts she had used. She used outline notes, summarizing key points in brief phrases. Jim followed a similar procedure but wrote relatively few notes, which included more wordings from the text than rephrasing. Toni was ebullient in her note-taking! She took copious outline notes, drew up charts, developed concept maps, and took notes of her notes.

The other three students relied almost entirely on verbatim copying in their notes. In some cases they did this by hand, but generally their "note-taking" consisted of copying chunks of texts — sometimes several paragraphs in length — from the textbooks on to their computers. As Mei Wen said, "I give that a heading and then I copy all this stuff."

Their mechanism for selecting suitable passages was often to identify keywords which fitted their essay outline rather than picking out macro- or micro-propositions.

A. **INFORMATION PROCESSING.** From the perspective of cognitivists such as Ausubel (1960), Anderson (1985), or Chamot and O'Malley (1994), the note-taking techniques described above were means by which the students were able to process the information from the texts. In particular, note-taking was useful in relating the readings to the task, and in organizing the material under task-based headings which in turn enabled the students to synthesize material from different texts.

Note-taking also helped students to understand the material. Even verbatim copying appeared to be useful in this regard to some extent. Mei Wen, for example, said that copying pieces of text was useful "to give my mind more balance and . . . to give your mind more understand what it's all about." As Lee Wing On (1996) points out, learning by repetition does not preclude a "deep approach" to learning. He cites these words of the Confucian scholar, Zhu Xi: "Learning is reciting. If we recite it then think it over, think it over then recite it, naturally it'll become meaningful to us" (p. 36).

Unfortunately, this understanding-by-repetition technique was not always successful. As Mei Wen said:

> If I don't understand it, I probably won't write it, but maybe I will . . . Well, I think that every time I write something down I want to try to understand it . . . Probably it won't be important but it gives me idea.

Jim, on other hand, used note-taking as a way of monitoring his understanding of the texts: "In jotting down the notes, everything I took down I sure I understand. If I don't understand I don't put it in my notes." Other students commented on the use of note-taking to help them memorize the information in the source texts.

While the note-taking process appeared to help the students with the practical task of selecting and organizing information, the important aspect of note-taking in terms of cognition was not *what* the students did but *how* they did it. For example, the activity of copying verbatim was helpful not because of the sheer repetition but because of the underlying thinking processes used by the students in attempting to make sense of the information. In other words, the important aspect of "learning by reciting" is not the repetition but the cognitive activity which accompanies it. To further expand on Zhu Xi's quote (as cited in Lee, 1996): "Learning is reciting . . . if we recite it but do not think it over, we still won't appreciate its meaning" (p. 26).

B. **DIALOGIC INTERACTION.** The note-taking process can also be analyzed in terms of the students' dialogue with the texts. According to Bakhtin (1994),[1] for meaning to exist, at least two voices must interact: those of the speaker and the listener. Vygotsky (1978, 1987) describes learning as both an intermental and intramental process; in other words dialogue takes place between writer and reader (intermental activity), but also inside the reader's own mind (intramental activity). This dialogic view of learning contrasts with the information processing approach of cognitive psychologists such as Ausubel (e.g., 1960, 1968) in which knowledge is transmitted from the source and assimilated by the reader, rather than being reconstructed or transformed.

From a dialogic point of view, then, the essay writing process entails reading and transforming the ideas of the source texts in order for the student to write in his/her own voice. Note-taking can be a manifestation of this dialogue between student and text. Most of the NNS students in this study participated only as listeners in this process, however. They assumed the role of "mute outsiders" (Penrose & Geisler, 1994), rather than becoming active participants in constructing meaning. This role is particularly clear in the verbatim copying technique, in which students shuffled around bits of disconnected texts rather than attempting to construct meaning.

However, other students were more active in their note-taking. Annie, for instance, in summarizing and using outline notes, was making something of an attempt to transform the texts. Although Annie's own voice was not strongly evident in her notes, she was attempting to understand by what Bakhtin (1994) calls "laying down a set of answering words" (p. 77).

Jim was yet more active. In Jim's notes, we hear *his* voice, as well as the voice of the texts. For example, Jim added question marks, comments, and brief summaries in the margins of his texts as well as underscoring pieces of text. In contrast to the verbatim note-takers, Jim clearly distinguished his own comments or summaries from the pieces of text that he copied by using quotation marks. Jim used other techniques to gain a voice in the content area besides pen-to-paper note-taking. He discussed the texts with his friends, framing examples of his own to test out the theories presented in the texts, comparing case studies in the journal articles with his previous experience (however limited), and asking whether these theories would be practical in the cultural context of his home country. Nevertheless, Jim remained a deferential participant in the discourse community. For example:

Kate: Are there things that the textbook says that you don't agree with?

Jim: At this stage I don't have enough knowledge to criticize. I like to think about it. But I don't have enough knowledge to criticize . . . I may do something like comparison or contrast, but not criticize.

The most vociferous student was Toni. In her notes, her own voice dominates. She used no verbatim quotes: her T-charts and concept maps, although stimulated by the text, were constructed from her own head. In the recorded protocol, she talked with enthusiasm of the ideas she had developed. This extract from the interview illustrates her use of intramental dialogue:

> Those are the things you discuss with yourself . . . [You] speak to your
> brain about what you are going to do and probably that step will help you
> lay down what you want to do in your essay in your own ideas, talking . . .
> You do some time overworking in your brain.

The data give a picture, then, of how the note-taking process can be
used by students to enhance their dialogue with the texts. Again, however, it is not so much *what* students do in note-taking as *how* they do
it. The dialogic analysis of students' note-taking demonstrates how important is the role assumed by the student in terms of the discourse
community: outsider or participant; attentive listener or confident gen-
erator of ideas.

Note-Taking as a Product

Next, I would like to discuss how the students in this study used their
notes as a product from which to write their essays.

A. THE CUT-AND-PASTE TECHNIQUE. The three verbatim copiers used
their word-processed notes as a first draft for their essays. They used
the cut-and-paste technique to assemble the final draft from their
copied chunks of text and sometimes paraphrased sections of these
"notes." They added introductions and conclusions and sometimes topic
sentences in their own words. They included citations at judicious
intervals. The end result in each case was an essay which read well
and fitted the requisite features of the essay genre, including reasonably academic grammar and academic expression. All these essays
received a pass grade, and it was plain from the lecturer's comments
that she could not detect the copying that had taken place, although
more than 50% of the texts, sometimes several paragraphs long, were
plagiarized.

This essay writing technique has been observed in NNSs by other
researchers including Currie (1998), Leki (1995), and Adamson (1993).
While the approach is a successful coping strategy, and several authors
recently have called for academics to reexamine the concept of plagiarism (Pennycook, 1996; Scollon, 1995; Wilson, 1998), it is questionable
how much students benefit from writing in this way. The verbatim-
copiers in this study found the essay writing process time-consuming,
unrewarding, and painful. For example, Mei Wen said:

> When you write essay, since you write down some of the words are not
> your own and unless you write you wouldn't remember it . . . After one or
> two week I'll probably forget everything.

She explained that the most important thing for her was "to get it
down and finish it off."

As Chu Li complained:

> My assignments is too many and the time is not enough to think in my own words . . . I think I put a lot of time into my study but not efficiency. Probably I spend many hour to study, but thing I really need to learn is not much. I always need to spend a lot of time to read a lot.

Chu Li, in fact, submitted her essay without understanding much of what she had "written." She claimed that the most useful part of her essay-preparation process had been my explanation, as study adviser, of the meaning of some of the passages she had copied into her text.

B. THE BACK-TO-THE-TEXTBOOK TECHNIQUE. Surprisingly, Annie, who had been so thorough in preparing outline notes, abandoned them when it came to writing. She explained that she had not included sufficient "phrases and wordings" from the texts to support her writing. So although she followed the structure she had used in her note-taking, she was forced to refer back to the texts for the language she wanted to use. She intended to rephrase much of what she had written, but in the end she ran out of time. The result was that about 90% of the language she used in her essay was plagiarized. Unlike the verbatim copiers, however, Annie was able to synthesize pieces from many different texts (she had used 15 sources as opposed to the average of 3 used by the verbatim copiers). The note-taking process had allowed her to organize and structure the information, even though the end product was not very useful as a prompt for her writing. Her essay received a credit minus.[2]

C. THE FREE-FLIGHT TECHNIQUE. Toni, unlike any of the other students, used neither the texts nor her notes when it came to writing. For her, the note-taking process had been so constructive that she was able to write without recourse to any prompts. She was so familiar with the structure and content of her notes that she did not need to refer to them. She said:

> Normally, I do all the notes and then when I start to write, I tend to write and not to go back to the textbooks. Just put the textbooks away. Before I start to write I organize my notes again: my introduction, the content and then I feel like writing the introduction and write, write, write.

Toni likened the essay writing process to an international flight. You have to do lots of preparation, but once you get on board, you just sit back and enjoy it. And enjoy it she did! Toni was excited by the new ideas she had formed, and deeply satisfied by both the learning process and the essay she had written. Her grade, however, was a disappointment: credit minus. There were two reasons for this. First of all, Toni's essay contained few references to the source texts. Ironically, this suggested plagiarism to the lecturer. Secondly, the level of grammar errors was appalling (five times as many errors as Annie). At times it was difficult to understand the point she was making. From a dialogic point of view, Toni's voice was not balanced with the voices of the source texts. Instead of listening and responding, Toni's voice took over the essay — not an appropriate role for an undergraduate. Instead of expressing the intermental dialogue between texts and reader, her essay was an expression of her intramental dialogue.

D. THE NOTES-AS-A PROMPT TECHNIQUE.   Only Jim used his notes as a prompt for writing his essay. Although he had to refer back to the textbooks at times, Jim's notes contained sufficient wordings from the texts to allow him to write efficiently. Instead of agonizing for days as Chu Li had done, Jim spent only four or five days and enjoyed the process as well. He said:

> I didn't worry about this essay. It took me four or five days. I had been thinking about this essay for a week and then I start writing and I just keep writing, writing . . . In the night you just keep writing until you cannot stand and then you go to sleep.

Jim's essay contained almost 40% wordings from the texts, but well synthesized into a coherent argument. Unfortunately he shied away from making a forceful conclusion, where it would have been appropriate for him to express his point of view more clearly and this lowered his final grade to a credit rather than a distinction.

To sum up, the students' notes were useful to them as a structure on which to base their essays. However, they were most useful to the students in actually writing their essays if they contained wordings from the text which could be used to support their academic expression. Such wordings, as in Jim's case, could be sentences or even phrases, rather than whole paragraphs.

Conclusions

The data indicate, then, that for the NNS students in this study, note-taking served both a process function, in facilitating learning from text, and a product function in providing a skeleton outline and some of the flesh for the essay itself.

Observing the students in this study made one thing very clear: it was not the physical behavior of note-taking that enabled students to interact with the texts. More important were the underlying cognitive strategies which the students used and the way in which they positioned themselves in the discourse community. For example, like the verbatim note-takers, Jim also copied sections of text into his notes. However, while he did so, Jim was making comparisons and contrasts, relating the theories to his prior knowledge, evaluating the texts and self-monitoring his own comprehension.

In dialogic terms, the verbatim note-takers were outsiders to the discourse community. In contrast, the more successful note-takers positioned themselves as participants in the discourse community, although striking the right balance between listening to the voices of the source texts and speaking in their own voices was a major difficulty for these students.

It was also apparent from this study that NNS students rely heavily on wordings from the texts to support their writing. The only student who used her own words (Toni) ended up being penalized for the poor quality of her expression. Thus if notes are to be useful to NNS students as a product that can support their essay writing, they must be rich in wordings from the texts. This suggests that, rather than censuring students for plagiarism and burdening them with the notion of "putting it into your own words," we should be encouraging them to increase their academic language base by using more (but using more wisely) the language of the source texts. This is a challenging notion that I have discussed in more detail in Wilson (1998).

The findings of this qualitative study depend on a specific group of students, a specific task, and the assessment criteria of a specific university lecturer. However, three conclusions can be drawn which may be more widely applicable:

1. Effective note-taking behavior in academic writing depends on underlying cognitive strategies.

2. Note-takers need to position themselves as participants in the discourse community — both listening attentively and responding in their own voice.

3. The product of note-taking for NNSs is more helpful if their notes contain wordings from the source texts.

However, my students' original question remains unanswered: is note-taking efficient? While the more successful note-takers in this study certainly enjoyed and benefited from the essay writing process more than the verbatim copiers, it is not clear whether indeed it would have been more "efficient" for the students in the latter group to change their note-taking style. Perhaps verbatim copying was more suited to these students' attitudes to study; it certainly allowed them to complete the assignment successfully and obtain a pass.

In the interview, Chu Li said miserably:

> . . . some textbook is just so hard for me I couldn't read it. I will ask myself to read it but every time I need to check the vocabulary. I will sit for many hours like that reading but after a few days I just don't want to do that.

Would teaching note-taking strategies to such a student allow her to break through the fetters of virtual academic illiteracy, or would it just add an extra burden to her load?

As Hidi and Anderson (1986) point out, it is not enough to teach note-taking formats. Students like Chu Li need to be encouraged as well to adopt a much deeper approach to study (Biggs, 1991; Ramsden, 1988) in order to engage in more interactive cognitive strategies. Above all, they need to be encouraged to see themselves as valued members of the discourse community, and to develop an intrinsic interest in the content area.

If students like Chu Li can be welcomed into a community of scholars and encouraged to participate rather than remaining marginalized; and if students like Toni can be helped to understand their roles as attentive listeners as well as confident contributors, then they will be able to benefit from note-taking in the academic writing process both as product and as process.

Notes

1. For a clear explanation and synthesis of Vygotsky and Bakhtin, I recommend Wertsch (1991).
2. In Australian universities, assignments are graded Pass, Credit, Distinction, or High Distinction. Only the very best assignments, usually in the 80th and 90th percentile, are graded D or HD respectively; a Credit is often around the 70th to 80th percentile, so a Credit Minus is reasonable.

References

Adamson, H. D. (1993). *Academic competence. Theory and classroom practice: Preparing ESL students for the content courses.* New York: Longman.

Amer, A. A. (1994). The effect of knowledge-map and underlining training on the reading comprehension of scientific texts. *English for Specific Purposes 13*(1), 35–45.

Anderson, J. R. (1985). *Cognitive psychology and its implications.* New York: W. H. Freeman.

Ausubel, D. (1960). The use of advance organizers in the learning and retention of meaningful verbal material. *Journal of Educational Psychology, 51,* 58–88.

Ausubel, D. (1968). *Educational psychology: A cognitive view.* New York: Holt, Rinehart and Winston.

Bakhtin, M. M. (1994). The dialogic imagination: Four essays. In P. Morris (Ed.), *The Bakhtin reader.* London: Edward Arnold.

Beeson, S. A. (1996). The effect of reading on college nursing students' factual knowledge and synthesis of knowledge. *Journal of Nursing Education 45*(6), 258–263.

Biggs, J. B. (Ed.). (1991). *Teaching for learning: The view from cognitive psychology.* Melbourne: ACER.

Blanton, L. L. (1994). Discourse, artefacts and the Ozarks: Understanding academic literacy. *Journal of Second Language Learning 3*(1), 1–17.

Buzan, T. (1976). *Use both sides of your brain.* New York: Dutton.

Chamot, A., & O'Malley, J. M. (1994). *The CALLA handbook: Implementing the cognitive academic language learning approach.* Reading, MA: Addison Wesley.

Currie, P. (1998). Staying out of trouble: Apparent plagiarism and academic survival. *Journal of Second Language Writing 7*(1), 1–18.

Fischer, P. M., & Mandl, H. (1984). Learner, text variables and the control of text comprehension and recall. In H. Mandl, N. Stein, & T. Trabasso (Eds.), *Learning and comprehension of text.* Hillsdale, NJ: Lawrence Erlbaum.

Gagne, E. (1985). *The cognitive psychology of school learning.* Boston: Little, Brown and Co.

Hidi, S., & Anderson, V. (1986). Producing written summaries: task demands, cognitive operations and implications for instruction. *Review of Educational Research 56*, 473–493.

Hughes, H. W., Kooy, M., & Kanevsky, L. (1997). Dialogic reflection and journaling. *The Clearing House 70*(4), 187–190.

Kiewra, K. A.(1985). Investigating note-taking and review: The research and its implications. *Educational Psychology 20*(1), 23–32.

King, J. R., & Eilers, U. (1996). Postsecondary reading strategies rediscovered. *Journal of Adolescent and Adult Literacy 39*(5), 368–379.

Lahtinen, V., Lonka, K., & Lindblom-Ylänne, S. (1997) Spontaneous study strategies and the quality of knowledge construction. *British Journal of Educational Psychology 67*, 13–24.

Lee Wing On. (1996). The cultural context for Asian learners. In D. A. Watkins & J. B. Biggs (Eds.), *The Chinese learner: Cultural, psychological, and contextual influences.* Hong Kong and Melbourne: Comparative Education Research Centre and Australian Council for Educational Research.

Leki, I. (1995). Coping strategies of ESL students in writing tasks across the curriculum. *TESOL Quarterly 29*(2), 235–259.

McCagg, E. C., & Dansereau, D. E (1991). A convergent paradigm for examining knowledge mapping as a learner strategy. *Journal of Educational Research 84*(6), 317–324.

O'Malley, J. M., & Chamot, A. U. (1990). *Learning strategies in second language acquisition.* New York: Cambridge University Press.

Pennycook, A. (1996). Borrowing others' words: Text, ownership, memory, and plagiarism. *TESOL Quarterly 30*(2), 201–230.

Penrose, A., & Geisler, C. (1994). Writing without authority. *College Composition and Communication 45*(4), 505–520.

Ramsden, P. (1988). Studying learning: Improving teaching. In P. Ramsden (Ed.), *Improving learning: New perspectives.* London: Kogan Page.

Robinson, F. P. (1946). *Effective study.* New York: Harper.

Sarig, G. (1987). High level reading in the first and in the foreign language: Some comparative process data. In J. Devine, P. L. Carrell, & D. E. Eskey (Eds.), *Research in reading English as a second language.* New York: Cambridge University Press.

Scollon, R. (1995) Plagiarism and ideology: Identity in intercultural discourse. *Language and Society 24*(1), 1–28.

Vygotsky, L. S. (1978). *Mind in society: The development of higher psychological processes.* Eds. M. Cole, V. John-Steiner, S. Scribner, & E. Souberman. Cambridge, MA: Harvard University Press.

Vygotsky, L. S. (1987). *Thinking and speech.* Ed. and Trans. N. Minick. New York: Plenum Press.

Wertsch, J. (1991). *Voices of the mind.* Cambridge, MA: Harvard University Press.

White, C. (1996). Note-taking strategies and traces of cognition in language learning. *RELC Journal 27*(1), 89–102.

Wilson, K. (1998). Plagiarism in the interdiscourse of international students. In the Proceedings of the Higher Education Research and Development Society of Australia Conference in Adelaide, South Australia, 8–11 July 1997.

Creating a Successful Learning Environment for Postsecondary Students with Learning Disabilities: Policy and Practice

Shari Harrison

As the basis for this article, Shari Harrison raises two important questions that should be considered by all postsecondary learning strategy specialists. First, Harrison asks, "Does my current pedagogical approach meet the learning needs of the students in my classroom?" And second, "How can I effectively create a responsive and diverse lifelong learning environment for all students, and especially those with learning disabilities, in my classroom?"

Harrison goes on to propose answers to her questions throughout the article as she (a) defines learning disabilities (LD) and discusses the prevalence of LD students in postsecondary education along with the legal mandates about serving them, (b) explores the challenges to learning faced by such individuals, and (c) provides a rationale and guideline for using learning strategies and student-centered instruction with LD students.

As postsecondary enrollment increases and diversifies, colleges and universities are focusing attention on providing accessible, responsive, and diverse opportunities for lifelong learning. However, creating an accessible and responsive environment for all students, and especially those students with learning disabilities, isn't as simple as it may first appear. Ultimately, it is a reflective process that requires instructors to question their pedagogical approach and beliefs by asking themselves: "Does my current pedagogical approach meet the learning needs of the students in my classroom? How can I effectively create a responsive and diverse lifelong learning environment for all students, and especially those with learning disabilities, in my classroom?" One answer to these questions is to use learning strategies in conjunction with student-centered instruction to encourage and enable students with learning disabilities, and indeed, all students, to become successful lifelong learners. The aim of this article, then, is to explore policies and practices that support the creation of a successful learning environment for postsecondary students with learning disabilities. I will: (1) define learning disabilities in general and explore the prevalence of learning disabled students in postsecondary institutions; (2) outline the learning challenges that learning disabled students face and discuss the legal mandate for accommodating students with learning disabilities; (3) outline the pedagogical rationale for using learning strategies and student-centered instruction; and finally, (4) explore the use of learning strategies and student-centered instruction as effective postsecondary instructional techniques for all learners.

Defining Learning Disabilities

The quest for a definitive definition of learning disabilities is an ongoing one and the current definition has evolved over time. Both the Learning Disabilities Association of Canada and the American National Joint Committee on Learning Disabilities have adopted parallel, comprehensive definitions of learning disabilities. In short, these definitions of learning disabilities tell educators that people with learning disabilities are intellectually capable individuals who have varying degrees of difficulty within a range of academic areas, such as listening, speaking, reasoning, reading, writing, and mathematical skills, as a result of impairments affecting one or more processes related to learning; these individuals may also experience difficulty with organizational skills, social perception, social interaction, and perspective taking (Learning Disabilities Association of Canada, 2002; National Joint Committee on Learning Disabilities, 1990). Especially significant for postsecondary educators is the fact that learning disabilities are a "persisting problem, a lifelong condition that evolves throughout the developmental continuum" (Gerber, 1998, p. 1). Children with learning disabilities become adults with learning disabilities, adults who continue to have varying degrees of difficulty in receiving and/or expressing information (Sills, 1995) and likewise, continue to display weaknesses in reading, writing, and math (Hock, Deshler, & Schumaker, 1993) throughout their postsecondary academic careers.

The Prevalence of Learning Disabled Students in Postsecondary Institutions

People with learning disabilities represent the largest segment of the disability population and the number of postsecondary students with learning disabilities is on the rise (Kerka, 2000; Vogel, 1998). Estimates of the numbers of people affected by learning disabilities range from 5–20% of the population (Kerka, 2000), and Lauffer (2000) reports that in 1994, "students with learning disabilities accounted for 32 percent of postsecondary students with disabilities" (p. 41). Gerber and Reiff (1998) also remind educators that the numbers of adults with learning disabilities may even be greater due to the "unresolved question yet persistent belief that one half" of all adults with low literacy skills in fact have learning disabilities (as cited in Kerka, 2000, pp. 1–2).

Two factors affect the documented numbers of students with learning disabilities in postsecondary institutions. First, not all students with learning disabilities identify themselves as learning disabled, for reasons including "the social stigma, the loss of esteem by professors, and the fear that future employers will have access to their record" (Lauffer, 2000, p. 42). Second, many may not know that they have a learning disability, as not all students with learning disabilities have been assessed and diagnosed prior to university entry (Kovach & Wilgosh, 1999). It is important, therefore, for instructors to be aware that the student who has chosen to identify may not be the only one in the classroom with a learning disability (Lauffer, 2000) and others may be silently struggling with the course material without institutional support services.

The Challenges Faced by Students with Learning Disabilities in Postsecondary Institutions

The transition to postsecondary education is difficult for many students with learning disabilities and educators cannot assume these students will meet the academic and social demands of the postsecondary classroom (Hock et al., 1993). Ellis (1993) argues that in addition to mastering the content information, students must also be self-regulated learners; they need to be "strategic problem solvers who proactively analyze tasks, reflect on their prior experiences and knowledge, set goals, select and employ appropriate strategies for solving the problems and monitor the effectiveness of their problem-solving behaviours" (p. 359). However, many students with learning disabilities lack effective task approach strategies (Butler, 1995). Typically they do not understand their disability, lack the skills to be self-regulated learners, and have not had learning strategies instruction to allow skill generalization across contexts (Kovach & Wilgosh, 1999). In addition, students with learning disabilities continue to have difficulty in academic skills that were not mastered during the school-age years (Gerber, 1998) and they are often overwhelmed, disorganized, and frustrated in learning situations (Vaidya, 1999).

Vogel (1998) identified the areas of greatest difficulty experienced by students with learning disabilities in a college setting:

- concentrating in a noisy environment (72%);

- reading comprehension, reading fast, spelling, learning the rules of grammar, and working math word problems (62%);

- learning a foreign language, learning the rules of punctuation and capitalization, taking essay exams, writing compositions, recognizing misspelled words, and reading in front of a group (52–55%) (as cited in Vogel, 1998, p. 14).

Significantly, a majority of the skills identified as challenging by students with learning disabilities are language based. Merritt and Calcutta (1998) argue that language skills are the embedded curriculum in postsecondary classrooms that students must master in order to achieve success in higher education (as cited in Olivier, Hecker, Klucken & Westby, 2000). Thus, although individuals with learning disabilities have varying strengths and weaknesses, they almost certainly will struggle with the oral and/or written language expectations of a postsecondary classroom.

Adults with learning disabilities may also grapple with low self-efficacy beliefs, low self-esteem, and a poor self-concept. Bandura (1986) defines self-efficacy as the beliefs we hold about our capabilities to achieve certain goals and states that human behavior is most affected by our judgment of these capabilities (as cited in Stipek, 1998). The beliefs that adults with learning disabilities hold about themselves and their ability to succeed in school then become vital forces in their ultimate success or failure. However, because many adults with learning disabilities have had particularly painful experiences during their school-age years, they often continue to feel dumb, stupid, and incompetent in postsecondary classrooms. Low self-efficacy beliefs combined with a poor self-concept can leave students with learning disabilities viewing themselves as incapable or as losers; "in essence, they feel that if they get something right, they are lucky, and if they get it wrong, then they are dumb" (Gerber, 1998, p. 3).

Students with learning disabilities not only bring with them low expectations for success based on their past experiences, but these experiences also form the foundation for their future learning in postsecondary classrooms (Stipek, 1998). As Knowles (1973) states, "to a child, experience is something that happens to him; to an adult, his experience is who he is" (as cited in Krupp, 1982). Adults with learning disabilities who have had negative educational experiences in the past bring those expectations to the postsecondary classroom, and this psychological aspect of learning disabled students makes the creation of a positive learning environment and successful experiences all the more important.

The Mandate for Accommodating Students with Learning Disabilities

The legal mandate for accommodating students with learning disabilities arises out of human and civil rights legislation. In Canada, the foundation for accommodation is laid by Section 15 (1) of the Canadian Charter of Rights and Freedoms, which states that:

> ... every individual is equal before and under the law and has the equal
> right to equal protection and equal benefit of the law without discrimina-
> tion and, in particular, without discrimination based on race, national or
> ethnic origin, colour, religion, sex, age or mental or physical disability
> (Constitution Act, 1982).

This section of the Charter of Rights and Freedoms protects the
rights of students with learning disabilities to attend postsecondary
institutions, guaranteeing them legal protection from discrimination
based on their learning disability, and is further strengthened by
human rights laws enacted by individual provinces. Likewise, Section
504 of the Rehabilitation Act of 1973 prohibits discrimination against
persons with disabilities in the United States, stating that:

> ... no otherwise qualified individual with a disability in the United
> States ... shall solely by reason of his or her disability, be excluded from
> the participation in, be denied the benefits of, or be subjected to discrimi-
> nation under any program or activity receiving federal financial assis-
> tance (as cited in U.S. Department of Education, Office for Civil Rights,
> 1998, p. 1).

Furthermore, the Americans with Disabilities Act of 1990 (ADA)
strengthens this policy by prohibiting state and local governments
from discrimination against persons with disabilities (U.S. Department
of Education, Office for Civil Rights, 1998). Together, these laws mandate equal access to postsecondary education programs and services
and reasonable accommodations for people with learning disabilities
(National Joint Commission on Learning Disabilities, 1999). Thus, postsecondary institutions across North America are legally obligated by
federal, and provincial law in Canada, to admit learning disabled students into their programs without discrimination and to make appropriate adjustments in order to provide effective services and reasonable
accommodations to students with disabilities.

While these laws secure the right of equal access to postsecondary
institutions for persons with disabilities, they also outline the responsibilities of both the student requesting accommodation and the institutions to make accommodations. Both the Rehabilitation Act of 1973
and the ADA (1990) require postsecondary institutions to supply appropriate educational auxiliary aids and services to students with a
disability in order to provide that individual with an equal opportunity
to participate. It is important to note, though, that the student is obligated to identify the need of support and give adequate notice of the
need. The postsecondary institution also has the right to ask the student to provide documentation from a physician or psychologist of the
disability prior to the implementation of any accommodations. Once
this documentation is received, the institution will undertake to make
feasible and appropriate accommodations for the student (U.S. Department of Education Office for Civil Rights, 1998).

However, due to the fact that many students with learning disabilities do not self-disclose, and that many students have undiagnosed learning disabilities which often remain undiagnosed, accommodation may be sought infrequently in a small institution. Yet, students with learning disabilities continue to enroll in and attempt to struggle through postsecondary classes. As a result, it is important for instructors to adopt pedagogical practices, such as the use of learning strategies and student centered instruction, which see accommodation as "an attitude that allows for the full expression of human talent" (Yuker, 1988, as cited in Lauffer, 2000, p. 36) and set the foundation for building an accessible and responsive learning environment for all students.

Pedagogical Rationale for Using Cognitive and Metacognitive Learning Strategies

As the number of diagnosed and undiagnosed students with learning disabilities entering postsecondary institutions rises, so too must the instructor's pedagogical awareness. In the past, the paradigm for postsecondary education has mistaken a means for an end, making provision of instruction the primary purpose of college faculty (Howell, 2001); however, the traditional postsecondary "sage on the stage" instructional approach presents a significant barrier to students with learning disabilities. Imagine a student who has difficulty concentrating in a noisy environment, processes information slowly, has difficulty identifying key ideas in a lecture, and writes slowly and it becomes readily apparent why students with learning disabilities struggle in a postsecondary environment. A shift to a more learner-centered approach, one that focuses on effective learning strategies and teaching techniques, would help to create an environment that encourages and supports lifelong learning for all students.

According to the American Psychological Association's (1993) Presidential Task Force on Psychology in Education, learner-centered instruction is based on the following principles: Learning is an active process of creating meaning based on personal experience and existing knowledge; it is affected by personal interests, motivation, goals, expectations, and both positive and negative beliefs; relevant, authentic, and challenging tasks stimulate learning; strategies for "thinking about thinking" help students to think creatively and critically; learning is social; individuals develop in unique ways; and, individuals learn at different rates in different ways (Paris & Ayres, 1994). For optimum learning to occur then, it is important for instructors to make pedagogical choices which are informed by an understanding of the differences students bring to the classroom. One choice is to consider students' learning styles, described by Dunn and Dunn (1993) as "the way in which each person begins to concentrate on, process, internalize, and remember new and difficult academic information or skills" (as cited in Stevenson & Dunn, 2001, p. 1). Some research has found that using learning style-based instruction in a traditional classroom improves the performance of students with disabilities (Braio, Dunn, Beasley, Quinn, & Buchanan, 1997; Brunner & Majewski, 1990). Thus, by using and integrating such pedagogical knowledge and understanding, instructors can begin to focus on the experience of learning from the student's perspective. The philosophy of valuing the learner's experience of learning is intertwined with the phenomenological approach to curriculum theory, an approach which focuses on individual perceptions and experiences of education and learning (Kincheloe, Slattery, & Steinberg, 2000; Marton, Hounsell, & Entwistle, 1984; Pinar, Reynolds, Slattery, & Taubman, 2000). The phenomenological approach looks at the experience of learning and students' perceptions of teaching and assessment and how those perceptions influence their learning (Kincheloe et al., 2000). This learner-centered focus then informs teaching practice and provides practical rationales and conceptual connections for integrating instructional activities, assessment, and self-reflection.

Adult students with learning disabilities bring a diverse range of life experiences to the classroom. Knowles (1980), in defining andragogy as the "the art and science of helping adults learn" (p. 43), suggests that adult learners have a need to be self-directing; they bring the rich resource of life experience to the classroom which can form the foundation of experiential learning in the classroom; they are motivated to learn when they have a need to learn something that is relevant to their current situation; and they tend to have a perspective of immediacy of application toward most of their learning. To adults, education is a process of improving their ability to cope with life problems they face now. Thus, they tend to approach education from a problem-centered or performance-centered frame of mind (Knowles, 1980). Additionally, Knowles suggests that individual differences between learners increases with age and experience. Adopting an instructional style, which takes into account the characteristics of adults as learners and likewise considers how individuals learn most effectively can begin the paradigm shift toward a more responsive and accommodating learning environment for all postsecondary students, and most particularly those with learning disabilities.

Effective Instruction for Postsecondary Students with Learning Disabilities

For students with learning disabilities, effective instruction is a "critical element in the accessibility of learning environments" (Shaw, Scott, & McGuire, 2001, p. 1). Student achievement and effective instruction go hand in hand; in order for students with learning disabilities to be academically successful, they must experience learning as a "reflective activity which enables the learner to draw upon previous experience to understand and evaluate the present so as to shape future action and formulate new knowledge" (Abbott, 1994, as cited in Watkins, Carnell,

Lodge, Wagner, & Whalley, 2000, p. 91). The effective instructor sees learning as an active process of relating new meaning to existing meaning, which involves making connections between past, present, and future learning (Watkins et al., 2000).

Instructors undertaking this paradigm shift toward learner-centered instruction may be concerned about maintaining assessment standards. Rather than being lowered, standards must be applied equitably in a way that does not adversely affect students with learning disabilities (Spillane, 1990, as cited in Lauffer, 2000). Traditionally, instructors have required students to demonstrate understanding in a limited and prescribed fashion, with little consideration for a student's learning needs or abilities. For example, in a humanities course, students may be asked to analyze and synthesize events, concepts, or themes in essay format — or perhaps two essays and a timed essay exam for a final. But assessing subject knowledge only through the filter of writing ability may severely disadvantage a student with learning disabilities. A promising approach for adapting instruction for diverse learning needs is Universal Design for Learning or UDL (Meyer & Rose, 2000; Pisha & Coyne, 2001). It follows the tenets of the principle of universal design in architecture to integrate adaptations into curriculum, instruction, and assessment. In the humanities course example, an instructor can offer a choice of assessment products, such as a poster, a PowerPoint presentation, or a traditional essay, yet retain analysis and synthesis as the focus for assessment. The instructor can equitably assess each student's skill and also maintain assessment standards.

Successful classroom performance requires that students understand the cognitive and linguistic demands both of the academic content and the rules for social behavior (Olivier et al., 2000) and using learning strategies is one way to achieve this required understanding. A strategy can be defined as an "individual's approach to a task and includes how a person thinks and acts when planning, executing, and evaluating performance on a task and its outcomes" (Lenz, 1989 as cited in Lenz, 1992, p. 206). According to this definition, a strategy includes both cognitive (what goes on in a person's head) and behavioral (what the student actually does) elements that guide student performance on and evaluation of the task. The strategy also incorporates the reflective process of making the connection between effort and results (Lenz, 1992). Strategies can be classified as cognitive or metacognitive. Cognitive strategies are learning strategies, those learner behaviors which influence the processing and manipulation of information; while metacognitive strategies are self-regulatory strategies, used when planning, monitoring, and evaluating learning (Vaidya, 1999; Wong, 1993).

Strategy instruction is particularly important for students with learning disabilities in postsecondary classrooms, many of whom do not think efficiently or effectively and need support to become purposeful, effective, and independent learners (Vaidya, 1999). As Weber

(1982) points out "they need . . . to be taught first, that there are strategies and, secondly, that they must use them" (pp. 97–98). The use of strategy instruction has been shown to be effective in promoting skills such as reading comprehension, listening comprehension, note-taking, memory for content, essay writing, and effective test taking. All of these skills are required in textbook-based approaches to content area instruction commonly found in postsecondary education (Scruggs & Mastropieri, 1993). Therefore, strategy instruction should be encouraged in college (Brinckerhoff, Shaw, & McGuire, 1996). In addition, if strategies are taught in conjunction with content, students can see relationships between content elements and learning processes (Deshler & Schumaker, 1993). For strategy instruction to be successful, however, students must be explicitly informed of what strategies are being taught, when to appropriately use them, and why strategy use can facilitate learning success (Ellis, 1993). Instructors need to purposefully integrate learning strategies into teaching, thus presenting a framework that will assist students in remembering and recalling concepts and likewise, providing models which students can incorporate into their own learning. The research on practice suggests a number of ways that instructors can integrate learning strategies into teaching to support all students and in particular, those with learning disabilities.

The starting point for creating an accessible and responsive learning environment for all students is the course outline. To help individuals with learning disabilities, course outlines should be detailed and include the topic of each class, readings for those classes, and specific reminders and dates for assignments and examinations (Crux, 1991). Designing a clear and simple course outline in a table format can make the information more accessible to all students.

In planning instruction, the postsecondary instructor should consider activities-based or hands-on approaches which take into account the learning strengths of students with learning disabilities, as these approaches emphasize active manipulation of concrete phenomena and de-emphasize language and literacy requirements (Scruggs & Mastropieri, 1993). Activities-based and hands-on approaches can take many forms, including role playing, building and manipulating a model, creating a computer simulation, or performing an experiment. Thus, through active engagement and involvement in the learning, the learner becomes aware of the processes used during learning, evaluates the effectiveness of his or her own learning strategies, and sets personal goals for future growth (Jochum & Curran, 1998).

Advance organizers can orient students to a new learning task before the lesson begins. An organizer can focus attention and organize student thinking by facilitating the recall of prior knowledge. According to Lenz (1983, 1987, as cited in Schmidt & Harriman, 1998, pp. 291–292), advance organizers can perform the following functions: state the concepts to be learned, provide relevant background information or establish the relevance of the content, list topics and subtopics to be covered, preview the order of presentation for new information, explain task requirements, introduce relevant vocabulary, and introduce the goals or outcomes for the lesson. Advance organizers can take many forms, such as an oral introduction to the lesson, written questions at the beginning of a chapter in a text, or a graphic organizer (e.g., Venn diagram, sequence chart, or web). Instructors can integrate advance organizers into their teaching and, through their use, train students to listen for information presented in the advance organizers; advance organizers then become an internally mediated strategy, one used and implemented by the student to meet the demands of the academic task.

Because language (both oral and written) and listening skills present the most difficulty for the majority of students with learning disabilities (Vogel, 1998), these are areas where students benefit most from strategy instruction. In fact, Larson and McKinley (1995) argue that it is vital to teach listening skills explicitly, as this is the skill most used by college students, yet it is the least taught (as cited in Olivier et al., 2000).

Many students with learning disabilities also struggle with the language skills of proficient reading which are essential for success in the postsecondary classroom. There are a number of reading strategies designed to help learners read with more accuracy and acquire more meaning that can easily be integrated with active learning techniques and included in postsecondary classrooms. One teaching and learning technique that combines reading strategies with active learning is literature circles. Literature circles are small, temporary discussion groups for which each participant reads a predetermined portion of text and also prepares to take a specific responsibility or role in the upcoming group discussion. The circles meet regularly and discussion roles rotate each session. Research with middle school students has shown that students feel using literature circles in the classroom gives them tools for success and increases their understanding of the text (Blum, Lipsett, & Yocom, 2002; Katz & Kuby, 1997). Above all, literature circles allow each participant to talk about what and how meanings are achieved in written materials, discussions that are important to the development of those cognitive and interpretive skills, which are basic to being literate.

Writing strategies are also vitally important to the success of learning disabled students in the postsecondary classroom, since most course grading schemes focus heavily on a student's performance on written tasks such as essays and exams. An instructor can facilitate the writing process before the students even begin writing by giving clear and explicit instructions (Sills, 1995). Often students will not understand what various direction words — such as analyze, compare, criticize, define, discuss, evaluate, prove, and summarize — actually mean in terms of completing the assignment. Providing a concise explanation of what the students are being asked to do is the surest way to promote their success in doing it. For example, instead of just asking the students to criticize a theory or incident, instruct them to "give your judgment of both good points and limitations and provide evidence for each." Writing strategies successful with younger students with learning disabilities may apply to the college classroom. Schmidt and Harriman (1998) is a useful source of such strategies, such as SCORE A for writing research papers.

Peer writing workshops facilitate the writing process for all students, but especially those with learning disabilities. Such social learning experiences promote group construction of knowledge, and allow students to observe each other's models of successful learning and encourage emulation (Stage, Muller, Kinzie, & Simmons, 1998). Lauffer (2000) notes that conferencing, with both the instructor and peers, improves learning disabled students' understanding and use of strategies. Peer writing workshops can be used as teaching and learning opportunities throughout the writing process and can be as short as ten minutes or as long as the entire class period. Not only have instructors found peer writing groups beneficial to student achievement, Miller (n.d.) reports that on course feedback forms "about 99% of students identify writing workshops as the single classroom activity most useful to them in their progress as writers" (p. 9).

Summary

As instructors and institutions grapple with the challenge of creating educational environments that will foster lifelong learning and also prepare students, including those with learning disabilities, to meet the new and ever-varying demands of life and work in the twenty-first century, they must reevaluate traditional instructional procedures. Students' abilities to confront real-world challenges — to understand their work in relation to others, to build on their strengths, to see new possibilities and challenges in their work — all depend on their capacity to step back from their work and consider it carefully, drawing new insights and ideas about themselves as learners (Zessoules & Gardner, 1991). Instructors need to shift their focus away from merely providing instruction, and instead concentrate on facilitating learning by meeting the needs of the individual learner in their classroom. Implicit in the use of learning strategies and learner-centered instruction is this desire to empower students as learners, both within and beyond the classroom environment; thus, embedding effective learning strategies in instruction and using student-centered instruction methods will indeed create an accessible, responsive and diverse learning environment, one which enables and empowers all students and "creates a desire for continued growth and supplies the means for making the desire [achievable]" (Dewey, 1916, p. 53).

References

Blum, H. T., Lipsett, L. R., & Yocom, D. J. (March/April 2002). Literature circles: A tool for self-determination in one middle school inclusive classroom. *Remedial and Special Education, 23*(2), 99–108.

Braio, A., Dunn, R., Beasley, M. T., Quinn, P., & Buchanan, K. (1997). Incremental implementation of learning-style strategies among urban low achievers. *Journal of Educational Research, 91*, 15–25.

Brinckerhoff, L., Shaw, S., & McGuire, J. (1996). Promoting access, accommodations, and independence for college students with learning disabilities. In J. R. Patton & E. A. Polloway (Eds.), *Learning disabilities: The challenges of adulthood* (pp. 71–92). Austin, TX: Pro-Ed Inc.

Brunner, C. E., & Majewski, W. S. (October 1990). Mildly handicapped students can succeed with learning styles. *Educational Leadership, 48*(02), 21–3.

Butler, D. (1995). Promoting strategic learning by postsecondary students with learning disabilities. *Journal of Learning Disabilities, 28*(3), 170–190.

Canadian Charter of Rights and Freedoms, Part I of the Constitution Act, 1982, being Schedule B of the *Canada Act 1982* (U.K.), 1982, c.11. Retrieved February 5, 2002, from http://www.laurentia.com/ccrf/ccrf.html

Crux, S. (1991). *Learning strategies for adults*. Toronto, Ontario, Canada: Wall & Emerson.

Deshler, D., & Schumaker, J. (1993). Strategy mastery by at-risk students: Not a simple matter. *The Elementary School Journal, 94*(2), 153–167.

Dewey, J. (1916). *Democracy and education*. New York: The Free Press.

Ellis, E. (1993). Integrative strategy instruction: A potential model for teaching content area subjects to adolescents with learning disabilities. *Journal of Learning Disabilities, 26*(6), 358–383, 398.

Gerber, P. (1998). Characteristics of adults with specific learning disabilities. In B. K. Lenz, N. A. Sturomski, & M. A. Corley (Eds.), *Serving adults with learning disabilities: Implications for effective practice* (n.p.) Washington, DC: U.S. Department of Education. Retrieved January 25, 2002, from LD Online website, http://ldonline.org

Hock, M., Deshler, D., & Schumaker, J. (1993). Learning strategy instruction for at-risk and learning-disabled adults. *Preventing School Failure, 38*(1), pp. 1–11. Retrieved January 15, 2002, from EBSCO Database, http://www.nlc.bc.ca/library/indexes.html

Howell, C. (2001). Facilitating responsibility for learning in adult community college students. *ERIC Digests*. Retrieved January 16, 2002, from ERIC Digests online database, http://www.ed.gov/databases/ERIC_digests/index/ (Identifier EDD00036).

Jochum, J., & Curran, C. (1998). Creating individual education portfolios in written language. *Reading & Writing Quarterly, 14*(3), pp. 1–19. Retrieved March 2, 2001, from EBSCO database, http://www.nlc.bc.ca/library/indexes.html

Katz, C. A., & Kuby, S. A. (1997). Trapped in a month of Mondays. *Journal of Adolescent & Adult Literacy, 41*(2), 1–6. Retrieved July 5, 2002, from EBSCO Database, http://www.nlc.bc.ca/library/indexes.html

Kerka, S. (2000). Adults with learning disabilities. *ERIC Digests*. Retrieved January 25, 2002, from ERIC Digests online database, http://www.ed.gov/databases/ERIC_digests/index/ (Identifier ED414434).

Kincheloe, J., Slattery, P., & Steinberg, S. (2000). *Contextualizing teaching.* New York: Addison-Wesley.

Knowles, M. (1980). *The modern practice of adult education: From pedagogy to andragogy.* Englewood Cliffs, NJ: Cambridge Adult Education.

Kovach, K., & Wilgosh, L. R. (1999). Learning and study strategies, and performance anxiety in postsecondary students with learning disabilities: A preliminary study. *Developmental Disabilities Bulletin, 27*(1), 47–57.

Krupp, J. (1982). *The adult learner: A unique entity.* Manchester, CT: Adult Development and Learning.

Lauffer, K. (2000). Accommodating students with specific writing disabilities. *Journalism & Mass Communication Educator* (Winter), 29–46.

Learning Disabilities Association of Canada. (2002, January). *National definition of learning disabilities.* Retrieved February 3, 2002, from http://www.ldac-taac.ca/english/defined.htm

Lenz, B. K. (1992). Self-managed strategy systems for children and youth. *School Psychology Review 21*(2), 1–19. Retrieved January 15, 2002, from EBSCO Database, http://www.nlc.bc.ca/library/indexes.html

Marton, F., Hounsell, D., & Entwistle, N. (1984). *The experience of learning.* Edinburgh: Scottish Academic Press.

Meyer, A., & Rose, D. H. (November 2000). Universal design for individual differences. *Educational Leadership, 58*(3), 39–43.

Miller, H. (n.d.) *Making peer writing workshops work in writing-intensive courses.* Retrieved June 8, 2001, from University of Minnesota, College of Liberal Arts, Center for Interdisciplinary Studies of Writing Web site, http://cisw.cla.umn.edu/was_makingpeerwritingworkshopswork.html

National Joint Committee on Learning Disabilities. (1990). *Collective perspectives on issues affecting learning disabilities.* Austin, TX: Pro-Ed Publications.

National Joint Committee on Learning Disabilities. (1999, January). Learning disabilities: Issues in higher education. *ASHA Desk Reference,* 1999 Edition. Retrieved October 25, 2002, from http://www.ldonline.org/njcld/higher_ed.html

Olivier, C., Hecker, L., Klucken, J., & Westby, C. (2000). Language: The embedded curriculum in postsecondary education. *Topics in Language Disorders, 21*(1), 15–29.

Paris, S., & Ayres, L. (1994). *Becoming reflective students and teachers with portfolios and authentic assessment.* Washington, DC: American Psychological Association.

Pinar, W., Reynolds, W., Slattery, P., & Taubmann, P. (2000). *Understanding curriculum.* New York: Peter Lang.

Pisha, B., & Coyne, P. (July/Aug 2001). Smart from the start. *Remedial and Special Education, 22*(4), 1–10. Retrieved November 4, 2002, from EBSCO Database, http://www.nlc.bc.ca/library/indexes.html

Schmidt, M., & Harriman, N. (1998). *Teaching strategies for inclusive classrooms: Schools, students, strategies, and success.* Fort Worth, TX: Harcourt Brace College Publishers.

Scruggs, T. E., & Mastropieri, M. A. (1993). Special education for the twenty-first century: Integrating learning strategies and thinking skills. *Journal of Learning Disabilities, 26*(6), 392–398.

Shaw, S., Scott, S., & McGuire, J. (2001). Teaching college students with learning disabilities. *ERIC EC Digests.* Retrieved January 12, 2002, from ERIC EC Digests online database, http://ericec.org/digests (Identifier E618).

Sills, C. (1995). Success for learning disabled writers across the curriculum. *College Teaching, 43*(2), 1–10. Retrieved January 15, 2002, from EBSCO Database, http://www.nlc.bc.ca/library/indexes.html

Stage, F., Muller, P., Kinzie, J., & Simmons, A. (1998). Creating learning centered classrooms. What does learning theory have to say? *ERIC Digests.* Retrieved February 28, 2001, from Eric Digests online database, http://www .ed.gov/databases/ERIC_digests/index/ (Identifier ED422777).

Stevenson, J., & Dunn, R. (December 2001). Knowledge management and learning styles: Prescriptions for future teachers. *College Student Journal, 35*(4), 1–6. Retrieved November 14, 2002, from EBSCO Database, http:// www.nlc.bc.ca/library/indexes.html

Stipek, D. (1998). *Motivation to learn: From theory to practice* (2nd ed). Boston, MA: Allyn and Bacon.

U.S. Department of Education, Office for Civil Rights. (September 1998). *Auxiliary aids and services for postsecondary students with disabilities.* Washington, DC: Author. Retrieved November 2, 2002, from http://www.ed.gov/ offices/OCR/docs/auxaids.html

Vaidya, S. (1999). Metacognitive learning strategies for students with learning disabilities. *Education, 120*(1), 186–189, 81.

Vogel, S. (1998). Adults with learning disabilities. In S. Vogel & S. Reder (Eds.), *Learning disabilities, literacy and adult education* (pp. 5–28). Baltimore, MD: Paul H. Brookes.

Watkins, C., Carnell, E., Lodge, C., Wagner, P., & Whalley, C. (2001). *Learning about learning: Resources for supporting effective learning.* New York: Routledge.

Weber, K. (1982). *The teacher is the key.* Milton Keynes: Open University Press.

Wong, B. Y. L. (1993). Pursuing and elusive goal: Molding strategic teachers and learners. *Journal of Learning Disabilities, 26*(6), 354–357.

Zessoules, R., & Gardner, H. (1991). Authentic assessment: Beyond the buzzword and into the classroom (pp. 47–71). In V. Perrone (Ed.), *Expanding student assessment.* Alexandria, VA: Association for Supervision and Curriculum Development.

The Learning/Study Strategies of College Students with ADHD

Frances Prevatt, Abigail Reaser, Briley Proctor, and Yaacov Petscher

Using the Learning and Study Strategies Inventory (LASSI) as a means of comparison, Frances Prevatt, Abigail Reaser, Briley Proctor, and Yaacov Petscher report that college students with attention-deficit/hyperactivity disorder (ADHD) and those with learning disabilities (LD) differ from each other and from their non-ADHD and -LD counterparts. Based on the results, the researchers conclude that the needs and interventions required for all three groups of students are unique. The researchers also suggest that LASSI may not be a useful tool for predicting academic achievement for college students with ADHD. Interventions for working with students with ADHD are given.

I t is well known that students of all ages with ADHD are at risk for academic achievement problems and school failure, and are less likely to complete a postsecondary education (Barkley, 2006; Faraone, Biederman, Lehman et al., 1993; Gaub & Carlson, 1997). However, it does not appear that students with ADHD lack the intellectual ability to learn, as students with ADHD are often found to be of average to above-average intelligence (Barkley, 1994). While these students seem capable of learning, their hyperactivity, impulsivity, and/or inattention make concentration difficult and may negatively affect their performance (Fowler, 1994).

High levels of academic aptitude, efficient study skills, and positive attitudes are important components of academic performance for both students with disabilities and those without (Larose & Roy, 1991). It is well documented that children with ADHD tend to perform poorly compared to their non-ADHD peers in terms of planning, attention, cognitive processing, and self-control (Frazer, Belzner, & Conte, 1992). Most of the research on the components necessary for academics success has focused on school-age children, not college students and adults with ADHD. One of the few studies of college students diagnosed with ADHD found that this group of students exhibits difficulties with study skills, note-taking, summarizing, outlining, and test-taking (Zwart & Kallemeyn, 2001). Other documented problems that contributed to academic failure included negative attributional style (internal, stable, and global causes) and internal restlessness (Weyandt et al., 2003). Wallace, Winsler, and NeSmith (1999), found that college students with ADHD demonstrated motivational impairments characterized by a preference for easy work, less enjoyment of learning, less persistence, and a greater reliance on external than on internal standards to judge their performance.

While many publications offer practical advice to help students with ADHD succeed in college (Brinckerhoff, McGuire, & Shaw, 2002; Nadeau, 1995; Parker & Benedict, 2002; Quinn, 2001), only a small number of studies have conducted empirical investigations of the academic difficulties faced by these students. In particular, there remains a lack of research on the study strategies of this population. One measure that is commonly used with college students is the Learning and Study Strategies Inventory (LASSI; Weinstein & Palmer, 2002). This measure has been translated into over 30 languages and is estimated to be in use by half of all colleges in the United States (Murray, 1998).

It is important for researchers to investigate the learning and study strategies used by students with ADHD so that college service providers can help these students achieve optimal academic success at the postsecondary level. Although it is predicted that students diagnosed with ADHD will look more similar to students diagnosed with learning disabilities (LD) than to a non-disability comparison group, students with ADHD and LD are too often lumped together, and significant differences between them have not been adequately identified. Adequate remediation at the college level is contingent upon understanding the specific learning strategies of these two at-risk groups and differentiating treatment needs.

This article summarizes the findings of our earlier published study on this subject (Reaser, Prevatt, Petscher, & Proctor, 2007). Our aims were to determine:

1. How do the learning strategies and study strategies of students with ADHD compare to those of students with learning disabilities and normal controls?

2. What relative weaknesses are evident within the ADHD group?

3. Are learning and study strategies predictive of academic success (e.g., GPA) in all three groups (students with ADHD, students with LD, and normal controls)?

The College Students

The learning and study strategies of a sample of college students diagnosed with ADHD were compared to two other samples: college students diagnosed with a learning disability (LD) and college students without LD or ADHD. We studied 150 undergraduate students from a large public university in the southeastern United States, with 50 students in each of the ADHD, LD, and non-disability (ND) groups. The sample was 60% female. Ethnicity was 54% white, 33% African American, 9% Hispanic, 1% Asian, 1% multiracial, and 2.3% unreported. Students with ADHD and learning disabilities were self-referred to a campus academic assessment center; they had all encountered academic difficulties and school failure, which led them to seek testing. The ND students were solicited from general education classes.

Our Measures

All participants were administered the Learning and Study Strategies Inventory, 2nd edition (LASSI; Weinstein & Palmer, 2002). The LASSI is a self-report of college student learning and study strategies. It contains 10, 8-item scales that measure Anxiety, Attitude, Concentration, Information Processing, Motivation, Self-Testing, Selecting Main Ideas, Study Aids, Time Management, and Test Strategies. LASSI raw scores were converted to a standard T-score ($M = 50$; $SD = 10$) using the population M and SD across all three groups.

Our Findings

Significant group differences were found for all 10 subscales. Subsequent pair-wise differences were noted between ADHD and ND groups, with subjects in the ND group scoring in a more positive direction on the following subscales: Anxiety, Motivation, Concentration, Information Processing, Self-Testing, Selecting Main Ideas, Test Strategies, and Time Management. Additionally, there were significant differences between ADHD and LD groups, with subjects in the LD group scoring in a more positive direction on the following subscales: Concentration, Selecting Main Ideas, Study Aids, Test Strategies, and Time Management.

Testing subscale strengths and weaknesses for the ADHD population required computing grand mean scores for each subscale, excluding the tested subscale from each analysis. The mean score of each subscale was then compared to the grand mean score of the sample. A positive significant mean difference indicated a strength, while a negative significant mean difference indicated a weakness. Weaknesses were observed for Concentration, Test Strategies, and Selecting Main Ideas. Strengths were found for Attitude, Information Processing, and Study Aids; however, the effect sizes for all these comparisons were in the small range. The remaining four subscales had nonsignificant differences in the comparative analysis.

We then studied the relationship of these LASSI scales to grade point average (GPA) for each group. There was a positive, significant effect of motivation for both the ND and ADHD groups, and a positive, significant effect for anxiety for the LD group. In the ND and LD groups, the LASSI subscales accounted for a significant amount of variance in the prediction of GPA. However, for the ADHD group, this relationship was nonsignificant. Detailed analyses can be found in earlier complete article by Reaser et al. (2007).

Our Conclusions and Recommendations

In summary, there were four areas where the ADHD group reported lower scores than *both* the ND and LD group: Time Management, Concentration, Selecting Main Ideas, and Test Strategies. These areas include characteristics and behaviors that will significantly impact college performance. Time management requires that students create realistic schedules, take into account good and bad times of day and difficulty level of their subjects, and take responsibility for their daily activities. This may be especially difficult for college students with ADHD. Many students have come to rely on parents and teachers in high school who have taken over this function for them. Parents of children with ADHD often report that they monitor many aspects of their child's life, providing structure, discipline, rewards, and consequences necessary to keep their child on track. When these students are on their own at college, they may have little to no experience in managing these functions for themselves. At the clinic where the authors work, it is common to interview students with ADHD who have small yellow "sticky notes" pasted on themselves as reminders, where appointment books are rare, alarm clocks are unused, and long-term schedules or plans are a foreign concept. A standard intervention is to teach these students how to effectively create and use schedules and planners.

Concentration allows college students to selectively direct their attention to school-related tasks and to maintain their focus when thoughts or activities provide distraction. Students in this study reported that their "mind wandered," that they didn't listen carefully, and that they were unable to refocus once they began thinking about something else. Students with ADHD should be encouraged to sit in the front of the classroom, use note-taking to help increase concentration, take frequent breaks to avoid fatigue, and reward themselves for attainment of small goals.

The LASSI scale for Selecting Main Ideas measures the student's ability to separate the important from the unimportant details. Deficits in this skill area lead students to study voluminous amounts of unimportant information, become overwhelmed by the information, and, consequently, retain very little. Students with ADHD may report that they spend a great deal of time studying, often more than other students, yet they frequently run out of time and find themselves inadequately prepared for tests. Similarly, the scale for Test Strategies measures the student's ability to understand and prepare for different types of tests (multiple choice, short answer, essay), as well as utilize different strategies, depending on whether memorization or recall is required. Again, poor skills in this area lead students to waste time as they attempt too much, too late, too haphazardly. Interventions targeting these study areas should include very specific skills, such as note-taking, underlining important points, creating outlines and summaries, identifying potential test questions, and reviewing test answers.

There were four areas where the ADHD group reported lower scores than the ND group, but *not* lower scores than the LD group: Motivation, Anxiety, Information Processing, and Self-Testing. Maxwell (1981) suggested that differences in motivation between normal students and developmentally challenged students may lie in the fact that normal students are motivated *intrinsically*, while developmentally challenged students (e.g., ADHD and LD students) often enter higher education as a means to a better job or self-improvement, and this *extrinsic* motivation is often not sufficient to help them succeed. Similar to time management, students with ADHD are accustomed to parents or teachers providing motivation. Many parents of high school students have developed daily or weekly behavior management plans, with rewards (cell phone, car, allowance) dependent on regular study time and completion of school assignments. However, college life is not as conducive to these external monitors. Interventions at the college level should help students with ADHD internalize their motivation for academic behaviors. Generally, this first requires establishing their *external* goals (e.g., I will study for 15 minutes and then watch my favorite TV show; I will attend class every day this week and then go to the football game on Saturday). Next, a transition can be made to more *intermediate* goals (e.g., if I study hard and get a good grade in this class, I will have the GPA to qualify for the Business school). Finally, the transition can be made to more *internal* motivations (e.g., I'm going to choose to write my paper on a topic I find challenging and interesting, and I'm really beginning to enjoy understanding the concepts involved in writing a business plan). This type of work can be done through the process of ADHD coaching (Swartz, Prevatt, & Proctor, 2005).

Students with ADHD engage in anxiety that may well be a reciprocal process with long-standing roots. Early on, these students experienced school failure consistent with their symptoms of hyperactivity, impulsiveness, and inattention. Task-irrelevant responses affected their information processing abilities, thus hindering encoding, storage, and retrieval of information. Subsequent failures created internalized self-referents, leading to beliefs that failure was likely. Anxiety ensued in an escalating, self-perpetuating cycle. Specific recommendations for test anxiety in ADHD students should include interventions utilizing a cognitive-behavioral approach, such as systematic desensitization and relaxation (Hembree, 1988).

The two final areas where the students with ADHD and LD performed less effectively than the ND students were Information Processing and Self-Testing. These skills include the ability to create relationships between what one is learning and what one already knows, to put things into one's own words, to frequently review notes, and to make up one's own test questions. Practical interventions would be to help students with ADHD to better process the information they take in from lectures, reading, and studying. For example, students can be encouraged to create analogies based on information they learn, relate new material to material with which they are already familiar, and develop practical examples from their own experiences that seem to them to relate to concepts presented in their readings or class notes.

Students with ADHD were found to perform similarly to ND students in the area of study aids. The Study Aids subscale includes utilization strategies such as Web sites, learning centers, study partners, review sessions, and instructors. Again, students with ADHD report knowledge of strategies, while not always following through on the approach due to their motivation and concentration difficulties. The final area where students with ADHD were no different from the ND group was the Attitudes subscale. This suggests that students with ADHD do not have a particular difficulty with being interested in school, liking their classes, or finding college worthwhile. Although their motivation to attend to specific tasks may be poor, their attitude in general is positive. In the clinic where this study took place, counselors commonly report that the students with ADHD are quite positive about their abilities, often to the point of being unrealistic. A useful intervention can be ongoing discussions and monitoring of the specific behaviors needed to accomplish goals.

Relative strengths and weakness were found in the ADHD group: relative strengths were attitudes, information processing, and study aids, while relative weaknesses were test strategies, selecting main ideas, and concentration. Previous work has suggested that college students who seek help for their disabilities may be overwhelmed by the sheer numbers of recommendations received (Prevatt, Johnson, Allison, & Proctor, 2005). This can be especially problematic for students with ADHD, who have difficulties attending to more than one central issue or idea at a time. The ipsative analyses suggest areas of priority and may indicate starting with interventions in the specific areas of weakness outlined here. However, given the small effect sizes for these analyses, these results may not be as noteworthy as the group comparisons. Also, it will be important to determine specific strengths and weaknesses for individual students, and help them to utilize their strengths to create ways of coping with their difficulties.

For the students with ADHD, grades could not be reliably predicted with the LASSI subscales. Other work utilizing the LASSI suggests that this measure may not work as well in students with lower academic ability (Prevatt, Petscher, Proctor, Hurst, & Adams, 2006). Further work is needed to better understand variables affecting the ADHD population that may make standard measures of learning and study strategies less useful. If measures such as the LASSI are not useful in predicting the mainstay of college achievement (GPA), then other measures need to be developed that can help us to screen and develop preventive intervention programs for these students.

Overall, the present study provides valuable information documenting the learning and study styles of students with ADHD. The current study shows clear differences between students with ADHD and a comparison group without disabilities. This study also elucidates commonalities and differences between students with ADHD and LD. It is important to differentiate ADHD students from students with learning disabilities and not automatically provide standard interventions across the board. Finally, it is important to prioritize those areas in which the students with ADHD are most likely to experience difficulties.

References

Barkley, R. A. (2006). *Attention deficit hyperactivity disorder: A handbook for diagnosis and treatment* (3rd ed.). New York: Guilford.

Barkley, R. A. (1994). It's not just an attention disorder. *Attention!, 1*(2), 22–27.

Brinckerhoff, L. C., McGuire, J. M., & Shaw, S. F. (2002). *Postsecondary education and transition for students with learning disabilities* (2nd ed.). Austin, TX: Pro-Ed.

Faraone, S. V., Biederman, J., Lehman, B. K. et al. (1993). Intellectual performance and school failure in children with attention deficit hyperactivity disorder and in their siblings. *Journal of Abnormal Psychology, 102*(4), 616–623.

Fowler, M. (1994). Attention-deficit/hyperactivity disorder. NICHCY Briefing Paper. Revised Edition. Monmouth, NJ: Mary Fowler.

Frazer, C., Belzner, R., & Conte, R. (1992). Attention deficit hyperactivity disorder and self-control. *School Psychology International, 13*, 339–345.

Gaub, M., & Carlson, C. (1997). Behavioral characteristics of DSM-IV ADHD subtypes in a school-based population. *Journal of Abnormal Child Psychology, 25*(2), 103–111.

Hembree, R. (1988). Correlated causes, effects, and treatment of test anxiety. *Review of Educational Research, 58*, 47–77.

Larose, S., & Roy, R. (1991). The role of prior academic performance and nonacademic attributes in the prediction of the success of high-risk college students. *Journal of College Student Development, 32*, 171–177.

Maxwell, M. (1981). *Improving student learning skills.* San Francisco: Jossey-Bass.

Murray, D. E. (1998). An agenda for literacy for adult second language learners. *Prospect, 13*(3), 42–50.

Nadeau, K. (1995). Diagnosis and assessment of ADD in postsecondary students. *Journal of Postsecondary Education and Disability, 11*(2–3), 3–15.

Parker, D. R., & Benedict, K. B. (2002). Assessment and intervention: Promoting successful transitions for college students with ADHD. *Assessment for Effective Intervention, 27*(3), 3–24.

Prevatt, F., Johnson, L. E., Allison, K., & Proctor, B. E. (2005). Perceived usefulness of recommendations given to college students evaluated for learning disability. *Journal of Postsecondary Education and Disability, 18*, 71–79.

Prevatt, F., Petscher, Y., Proctor, B., Hurst, A., & Adams, K. (2006). The revised learning and study strategies inventory (LASSI): An evaluation of competing models. *Educational and Psychological Measurement, 66*, 448–458.

Quinn, P. O. (2001). *ADD and the college student: A guide for high school and college students with Attention Deficit Disorder* (Rev. ed.). Washington, DC: American Psychological Association Press.

Reaser, A., Prevatt, F., Petscher, Y., & Proctor, B. (2007). The learning and study strategies of college students with ADHD. *Psychology in the Schools, 44*(6), 1–12.

Swartz, S. L., Prevatt, F., & Proctor, B. E. (2005). A coaching intervention for college students with Attention Deficit/Hyperactivity Disorder. *Psychology in the Schools, 6*, 647–656.

Wallace, B. A., Winsler, A., & NeSmith, P. (1999). *Factors associated with success for college students with ADHD: Are standard accommodations helping?*

Paper presented at the annual meeting of the American Educational Research Association (Montreal, Quebec, Canada, April 19–23, 1999).

Weinstein, C. E., & Palmer, D. R. (2002). *Learning and Study Strategies Inventory (LASSI): Users manual* (2nd ed.). Clearwater, FL: H & H.

Weyandt, L. L., Iwaszuk, W., Fulton, K., Ollerton, M., Beatty, N., Fouts, H., Schepman, S., & Greenlaw, C. (2003). The Internal Restlessness Scale: Performance of college students with and without ADHD. *Journal of Learning Disabilities, 36*(4), 382–389.

Zwart, L. M., & Kallemeyn, L. M. (2001). Peer-based coaching for college students with ADHD and learning disabilities. *Journal of Postsecondary Education and Disability, 15*(1),1–15.

Additional Readings

Abbate-Vaughn, J. (2009). Addressing diversity. In R. F. Flippo & D. C. Caverly (Eds.), *Handbook of college reading and study strategy research* (2nd ed., pp. 289–313). New York: Routledge.

Banks, J. (2005). African American college students' perceptions of their high school literacy preparation. *Journal of College Reading and Learning, 35*(2), 22–37.

Boylan, H. R., Sutton, E. M., & Anderson, J. A. (2003). Diversity as a resource in developmental education. *Journal of Developmental Education, 27*(1), 12–17.

Boyle, J. R. (2001). Enhancing the note-taking skills of students with mild disabilities. *Intervention in School and Clinic, 36*(4), 221–224.

Bruch, P. L., Jehangir, R. R., Jacobs, W. R., & Ghere, D. L. (2004). Enabling access: Toward multicultural developmental curricula. *Journal of Developmental Education, 27*(3), 12–19, 41.

Casazza, M. E., & Bauer, L. (2006). *Access, opportunity, and success.* Westport, CT: Praeger.

Cross, K. P. (1971). *Beyond the open door: New students to higher education.* San Francisco: Jossey-Bass.

Gonzalez, N., Moll, L. C., & Amanti, C. (2005). *Funds of knowledge: Theorizing practices in households and classrooms.* Mahwah, NJ: Lawrence Erlbaum.

Harrison, S. (2003). Creating a successful learning environment for postsecondary students with learning disabilities: Policy and practice. *Journal of College Reading and Learning, 33*(2), 131–145.

Heinman, T., & Precel, K. (2003). Students with learning disabilities in higher education: Academic strategies profile. *Journal of Learning Disabilities, 36*(3), 248–258.

Higbee, J. L. (2009). Student diversity. In R. F. Flippo & D. C. Caverly (Eds.), *Handbook of college reading and study strategy research* (2nd ed., pp. 67–94), New York: Routledge.

Higbee, J. L., Lundell, D. B., & Duranczyk, I. M. (2003). *Multiculturalism in developmental education.* Minneapolis: Center for Research on Developmental Education and Urban Literacy, General College, University of Minnesota.

Hinckley, J., & Alden, P. (2005). Women with attentional issues: Success in college learning. *Journal of Developmental Education, 29*(1), 10–17, 27.

Lincoln, F., & Rademacher, B. (2006). Learning styles of ESL students in community colleges. *Community College Journal of Research & Practice, 30*(5–6), 485–500.

Price, G., & Skinner, J. (2007). *Support for learning differences in higher education: The essential practitioners' manual*. Staffordshire, UK: Trenthan Books.

Rose, M. (1989). *Lives on the boundary*. New York: Penguin.

Simoncelli, A., & Hinson, J. M. (2008). College students' with learning disabilities personal reactions to online learning. *Journal of College Reading and Learning, 38*(2), 49–62.

4

Students' Beliefs about Study Strategies

Imagine a student who has just received a grade of B on a history exam. What can you predict about how receiving such a grade will affect this student? "It depends" is probably the answer. Would an "A" student who typically toils over the material for weeks at a time be disappointed and even begin to experience a lack of confidence in his abilities as he prepares for the next history exam? How would the typical "C" student respond to receiving a B grade? More than likely, this student might experience an increased confidence in his future abilities.

Educational psychologists have coined the term *self-efficacy* — one's beliefs about one's capabilities to produce designated levels of performance. Students' beliefs about how they might perform in a particular course or even in an entire field of study can be determined from their past academic experiences in similar courses or from a particular grade while enrolled in a course. Particularly, failures can quickly undermine a student's sense of efficacy. If students believe their outcomes don't match their efforts, they may find little incentive to put forth future effort and implement good study behaviors in difficult courses even if they actually have the capacity to do well. As noted, students' beliefs can change quickly as a result of new experiences. Changing beliefs can often lead to changing behaviors.

One of the early pioneers in teaching students the rituals of college studying was Francis P. Robinson, author of the 1946 textbook *Effective Studying* and the creator of the Survey Q3R method of studying. Robinson claimed his own how-to-study course was useful to all students, since all had inefficiencies, but "brighter" students benefited most.

Some research still supports Robinson's claim that brighter students tend to benefit most from these courses. So how do educators effectively help all students enrolled in these courses to become more masterful at learning? Many of these courses are now designed for high-risk populations of students entering college, those on academic probation, or first-generation students with little understanding of the demands of college work. Educators teaching these courses must recognize the important motivational consequences that students' beliefs have on academic behaviors and achievement. While the attempt is honorable to provide students with a useful list of study skills and strategies, the real goal is to help students understand their resistance to changing the way they think about themselves and their approach to studying. Without doing so, helping students translate study skills and strategies into action may be futile.

Research studies — many of which are included within this book — have found positive results for courses that emphasize both the theoretical underpinning of learning strategies and the transfer of strategies. Including curriculum that provides insights and reflection on students' beliefs can add powerful ammunition to helping students transfer the knowledge learned in an academic success course.

This chapter covers a number of constructs to foster our understanding of students' beliefs. Myron H. Dembo and Helena Praks Seli's article focuses on self-regulation theory with a unique self-management component. The researchers ask students to explain their resistance to change and learn that students believe they can't change, don't want to change, don't know what to change, or don't know how to change. By developing a self-management project, Dembo and Seli experienced positive results helping students adopt new study behaviors. Sherrie L. Nist and Jodi Patrick Holschuh delve into research on students' epistemological beliefs, a focus on students' perceptions about what knowledge is and where knowledge comes from. The authors believe that the most obvious influence these beliefs have on learning is on students' selection of study and test preparation strategies. For example, students who define learning as memorizing are going to select low-level learning strategies such as memorizing. The authors provide five suggestions for "nudging" students' epistemological beliefs. Barry J. Zimmerman rounds out the chapter with a discussion on self-regulation as a way for students to compensate for their individual learning differences. He defines the essential qualities of academic self-regulation, describes the structure and function of the self-regulatory process, and gives an overview of methods for guiding students to learn on their own.

Students' Resistance to Change in Learning Strategies Courses

Myron H. Dembo and Helena Praks Seli

Instructors are commonly frustrated by the fact that many of their students will not transfer the strategies they were taught to their own academic tasks. The question then becomes: Why? In this article Myron H. Dembo and Helena Praks Seli tackle this question of students' resistance to strategic change. First, they discuss self-regulation theory and a framework that addresses problems that occur during the change process (e.g., "I can't change" or "I don't want to change"). The authors offer an outline for assisting anxious students in accepting a change in their behaviors and approaches. The outline contains four essential processes: self-observation and evaluation; goal setting and strategic planning; strategy-implementation and monitoring; and strategic-outcome monitoring. In order to test the effectiveness of these four processes and phases, Dembo and Seli tested them via two self-report studies with their own students. They discuss these studies and offer suggestions for future research.

Colleges provide considerable support services to help students improve their learning. These programs include learning to learn courses, Supplemental Instruction, required programs for underprepared students, and integrated reading/writing courses (see Simpson, Hynd, Nist, & Burrell, 1997, for a comprehensive review of these programs). In 2000–2001, more than three-quarters (75.1%) of institutions of higher learning offered at least one remedial reading, writing, or mathematics course. More specifically, 80.4% of 2-year, 81.7% of public, and 67.9% of private 4-year institutions provided remedial courses (National Center for Education Statistics, 2002).

In addition to remedial courses, Supplemental Instruction and learning to learn courses play an important role in providing academic assistance to undergraduate students. Supplemental Instruction uses collaborative learning strategies in high-risk courses in which students participate in regularly scheduled, out of class, peer-facilitated study sessions. These sessions allow students an opportunity to discuss and review course information (Martin, Lorton, Blanc, & Evans, 1977). Learning to learn courses (e.g., Dembo & Jakubowski, 1999; Hofer, Yu, & Pintrich, 1998) teach students a variety of learning strategies to help them become more self-regulated learners. More specifically, students learn strategies to improve their time management, acquire higher-level content knowledge, manage their environment, develop critical thinking skills, and pursue extra help outside of class when needed. These courses are different from the more traditional study skill courses because they are based on learning theory, whereas study skill courses often are atheoretical (Pintrich, McKeachie, & Lin, 1987).

Unfortunately, there is limited systematic research on the effectiveness of many academic assistance programs (see Simpson, Hynd, Nist, & Burrell, 1997). There appear to be three interrelated problems that need the attention of administrators, researchers, and instructors of academic support programs. The first problem is that many students fail to seek help. Students, particularly those at the lower academic achievement levels, do not readily participate in academic support services unless they are required (Friedlander, 1980; Karabenick & Knapp, 1988, Rosen, 1983). For example, Karabenick and Knapp (1988) have found a curvilinear relationship between help seeking and academic need. Their findings show that the rate of help seeking increased from low to moderate need, maximizing in the B– to C+ grade range, and then decreased with high need levels. Karabenick and Knapp (1988) ask: "Why is the rate of help seeking so low among students who are performing poorly, who have undoubtedly experienced repeated academic failure, and who could most benefit from assistance?" (p. 408).

A second problem is that students who enroll in academic support programs often fail to attend sessions or classes on a regular basis. For example, although research evidence indicates that Supplemental Instruction has been successful in helping students achieve higher grades than comparable groups of students who do not enroll in the program (Arendale, 1994), administrators report that attendance at weekly study groups is a problem (Rettinger & Palmer, 1996; Sydney Stansbury, personal communication, June 10, 2002).

A third problem is that students who do enroll in academic support programs often fail to benefit from such programs or courses because they do not change their academic behavior. In a review of the effects of study skills courses in higher education institutions, Hattie, Biggs, and Purdie (1996) have reported the following:

> It is very difficult to change the study skills that students have acquired, usually over many years of study . . . older students are more resistant to change. . . . Although most programs in which the thrust is study skills use by university students, the effects on study skills are minimal.
> (p. 126)

Educational researchers have ignored motivation as an explanation of why students fail to change their learning and study strategies (Nist & Simpson, 1993).

The purpose of this paper is to provide insights into why students have difficulty changing their academic behavior despite being enrolled in a course of study to prepare them for the demands of college. We shall use the term "learning strategies courses" to refer to all programs and courses that intend to change students' learning and study strategies. Our intent is not to identify every possible reason for failure to change but to identify some of the major factors that can account for why students have difficulty changing their academic behavior. We conclude the paper with some suggestions for assisting instructors in the change process.

Conceptual Framework

In this paper, we draw upon the work of Zimmerman and his colleagues (Zimmerman, 1998, 2000; Zimmerman, Bonner, & Kovach, 1996; Zimmerman & Risemberg, 1997) and Prochaska and Prochaska (1999). Zimmerman focuses on self-regulation as a process in becoming a more successful learner, whereas Prochaska and Prochaska provide insight into the difficulties related to changing one's behavior.

Self-Regulation

As students transition from high school to college, they need to learn how to take greater personal control of their learning, which often includes changing aspects of their academic behavior. Researchers have found that the more successful the students are in implementing strategies that lead to personal control of their learning, the more likely they are to be successful learners (Zimmerman & Martinez-Pons, 1990; Zimmerman & Risemberg, 1997).

Zimmerman refers to the ability to take control of one's learning, including changing aspects of one's behavior, as self-regulation or self-regulatory learning. Self-regulatory learners establish optimum conditions for learning and remove obstacles that interfere with their learning. For example, self-regulatory learners establish goals and an action plan for how they will prepare for exams, carefully monitor their understanding of the material when studying, use a variety of learning strategies and ask for help when needed, take breaks to renew their concentration, and change their learning environment if it is distracting. An important consequence of self-regulatory behavior is that students who self-regulate find a way to learn. It does not matter if the instructor is a poor lecturer, the textbook is confusing, the test is difficult, the room is noisy, or if multiple exams are scheduled for the same week; self-regulatory learners find a way to excel. Researchers have demonstrated that self-regulation can be taught and that it can enhance academic achievement and a sense of self-confidence or efficacy (Zimmerman, 1998, 2000; Zimmerman & Risemberg, 1997).

Problems in the Change Process

Zimmerman (1998) makes the distinction between skillful self-regulators and naive self-regulators. Unlike skillful self-regulators, naive self-regulators often have no goals or plans on how to succeed, possess little self-confidence or efficacy, don't want to master the material in class but just get by, demonstrate disinterest in class, avoid self-evaluation, and in general, are nonadaptive in identifying problems and changing their academic behaviors. These are the types of students that frustrate instructors in courses and programs that provide academic support services to help learners succeed in college.

Prochaska and Prochaska (1999) suggest four reasons why individuals have difficulty changing their behaviors: (a) they believe they can't change, (b) they don't want to change, (c) they don't know what to change, or (d) they don't know how to change. Previously, this framework has been used to understand why people do not change health-related behaviors, such as alcohol abuse, obesity, and smoking (Prochaska & DiClemente, 1983; Prochaska, DiClemente, & Norcross, 1992). We will apply this framework to the academic setting.

I Can't Change

> Ralph has been getting Cs in his college courses. Though the learning strategies course has taught him several effective strategies, Ralph believes that he lacks the strength and willpower to change the inadequate study habits he has acquired over the 12 years of previous schooling. In addition, he believes that the instructor dislikes him and will not grade him fairly. When he reluctantly attempts to apply a new set of skills to prepare for exams, he gives up easily when he cannot predict exam questions and returns to his old, ineffective study habits from high school. He seems anxious, demoralized and having lost hope about ever doing well on exams.

Ralph demonstrates many behaviors that cause students to believe that they can't change. First, he studies in the same way as he did in high school without having to think about his study strategies. Prochaska and Prochaska (1999) point out that people can't change aspects of themselves that are not conscious. Studies in psychology (e.g., Bargh & Chartrand, 1999; Wegner & Wheatley, 1999) indicate that certain behaviors have become automated (i.e., nonconscious, unintentional) from years of repeated and consistent practice. When it comes to automated behaviors, individuals have difficulty being aware when engaging in them and explaining how and why they do certain things. For example, it would be difficult for most people to explain how they bowl or hit a baseball or even how they learn certain material for an exam (e.g., how far in advance of an exam they study, whether they play music in the background while studying or not, whether or not they highlight while they read material, etc.). Without realizing it, many students have probably automated their study habits through their repeated use during the 12 years of schooling prior to college. Changing such automated behaviors requires considerable commitment, effort, and time, leading some students to conclude that they lack the willpower and inner strength and therefore cannot change. It is not uncommon for students enrolled in a learning strategies course to report that they can't learn the new system since their old methods, though ineffective, are automated to the point whereby they function in a nonconscious, effortless way. What makes matters worse is that when students are under pressure, such as preparing for an important midterm exam, they often resort back to their existing automated skills even when they know that these skills are not as useful or effective as the new skills they have learned or practiced. The combination of the ease with which automated skills function, the effort that it takes to change this type of skill, and their tendency to reassert themselves when students most need to shift to new skills causes some students to believe that they simply cannot change their existing inefficient academic habits.

Second, when Ralph does identify an automated study habit, such as how he prepares for exams, he gives up easily in the face of difficulty as he attempts to change. Researchers have identified a motivational variable called self-efficacy that helps to explain his behavior. Self-efficacy refers to the evaluation students have about their abilities or skills to successfully complete a task (Bandura, 1982). The key question that determines self-efficacy is: "Am I capable of succeeding at this task?" Educational researchers have found that efficacy beliefs are important predictors of student motivation and self-regulated behaviors (see Pajares, 1996; Schunk, 1989; Zimmerman, 1995, 2000) for a comprehensive discussion of self-efficacy and academic motivation and achievement). Specifically, students with low self-efficacy are less likely than their high-efficacy counterparts to choose difficult tasks, they expend less effort, persist for shorter periods of time, use less deep processing skills, do not ask for help when they need it, and experience fear and anxiety regarding academic tasks. Educational researchers have found that when students have low self-efficacy, they are not likely to learn new, more effective skills, and they are more likely to give up easily when they encounter difficulties practicing the new skills. Since effective study strategies, such as those taught in learning strategies courses, require the use of deeper processing skills such as planning, checking, and monitoring one's work, students with a low sense of self-efficacy may not engage in them. They are likely to experience self-doubts, show resignation and apathy, and believe that they cannot change.

Ralph also believes that the instructor doesn't like him and will not grade him fairly. Researchers (e.g., Weiner, 1986) have demonstrated that the attributions students make about events influence their beliefs that they can't change. An attribution is an individual's perception of the causes of his or her success or failure. When an event occurs, especially with a negative or unexpected outcome, individuals can interpret it in different ways. Consider three college students of equal ability or aptitude in the same class who just received a "C" on an exam.

The first student, like Ralph, is very upset because he believes that the instructor is biased against him and does not grade fairly. He decides that there is not much he can do to obtain a high grade in the course. The second student determines that the grade reflects the amount of time he spent on the task and decides that he needs to work harder in the future. The third student believes that she doesn't have the aptitude to succeed in the class and plans to reduce future effort on exams.

Why did the three students of equal aptitude interpret their experiences so differently? One explanation is that the three students made different attributions about their performances on the term papers. Two of the students made stable attributions for the outcome. That is, they blamed factors that are fixed and over which they have no control, such as their aptitude and the grader's bias. The third student made an unstable attribution by believing that inadequate effort spent on the specific task caused the low grade. According to attribution theory (Weiner, 1986), many students believe that they are born with stable and uncontrollable innate ability or aptitude but that the effort they spend on specific situations can be controlled by the individual and is thus unstable. Attribution researchers believe that how students perceive the causes of their prior successes and failures is the most important factor determining how they will approach a particular task and how long they will persist at it. Therefore, when students see effort as the cause for failure (i.e., an unstable and controllable factor), they are likely to try harder in future situations, persist on difficult tasks, and seek assistance from their instructor. However, when students make stable and uncontrollable attributions for failure (e.g., aptitude or the instructor's bias), they expect the same negative consequences in the future. These students are less likely to seek the help they need, use effective learning strategies, and, ultimately, believe that they can't change.

I Don't Want to Change

Although Laura is enrolled in the mandatory learning strategies course based on her high school GPA, she believes that she does not need to change her study habits. After all, she got admitted to college! She believes that her study strategies are as good as the ones discussed in the course. In addition, she sees learning and using new study strategies as taking up time when all she wants to do is to get through the courses with good enough grades.

Some students, like Laura, are not convinced they need to change their academic behavior. These students often raise questions, publicly or privately: "Why do I need to change?" "I graduated from high school," or "I was accepted to this college." It is not until the first midterm exams that some students realize that many of the learning and study strategies used in high school are insufficient for academic success in college. Although many students realize they need to improve, they tend to stick with familiar strategies, even though they are not achieving the best results. Some students report to us that it takes too much effort and time to learn new methods of learning. They simply are not motivated to change.

In contrast to a low sense of self-efficacy, students who do not want to change often display an unrealistically high sense of self-efficacy or overconfidence (Clark, 1991) because of the relative success of their high school experience. In reality, many of these students have experienced a teacher-controlled academic environment (i.e., the instructor tells one what to learn, how to learn, and when to learn) with a focus on lower-level learning (i.e., studying factual material — who, what, when, and where). As a result, they lack the skills needed for the college level, such as critical thinking. Overconfident students lack the ability to judge the academic situation as different from high school and hold on to the faulty belief that they have the necessary study strategies when new ones in fact are needed. These students demonstrate displeasure when faced with a requirement to take a learning strategies course since it conflicts with their perception of the level of skills they possess for academic studies. It is common for overconfident students to not take responsibility for their failures and instead blame the tests and instructors, justifying their desire of not wanting to change.

Another reason for students not wanting to change their academic behavior may lie in their reason for achieving or goal orientation. In our description of Laura, her goal was just to get through her courses with good-enough grades. Educational researchers have determined that students have different reasons for achieving in different courses (see Midgley, 2002; Pintrich, 2000). A student with a mastery goal is oriented toward learning as much as possible in a course for the purpose of self-improvement, irrespective of the performance of others. A student with a performance goal focuses on social comparison and competition, with the main purpose of outperforming others, or, on the other hand, just "getting through the course" and not mastering its content. Though a performance goal orientation has been related to higher grades than a mastery goal orientation, students who endorse performance goals demonstrate less interest and curiosity in the subject matter than those with a mastery orientation (Harackiewicz, Barron, Tauger, Carter, & Elliot, 2000). Therefore, adopting a performance orientation may cause students to lower their value for a learning strategies course, resulting in disinterest and an unwillingness to acquire and practice self-regulated learning skills. A performance orientation, coupled with overconfidence, may lead students to not want to change.

I Don't Know What to Change

Felicia has a difficult time identifying what is preventing her from attaining her academic goal of getting a B average in her courses. She is not sure whether it is her poor use of time, study methods, or test preparation that is causing her to get Cs. Her problem is that she does not know where to begin to bring about change.

Felicia is having trouble with observing and evaluating her own performance which, according to research in self-regulation (Zimmerman, Bonner, & Kovach, 1996), is a key component in determining what to change. For example, elite athletes observe their performances by viewing videotapes. After a short period of time, they are able to modify their performances from the feedback they obtain by viewing their own physical movements. Dance studios place handrails next to mirrors to enable dancers to self-observe as they practice their routines, and musicians learn to listen to their playing in order to critique their own performances (Glaser, 1996). Since they are able to effectively monitor themselves both during and immediately after a task, experts are able to make very detailed changes that optimize their performance.

Similarly, self-observation and evaluation are important contributors to the success of college students (Zimmerman & Paulsen, 1995). For example, students need to be able to monitor their learning strategy use and evaluate whether they correctly matched different learning strategies to the complexity of different tasks. Specifically, students need to learn that tasks that require simple recognition and recall can be learned by using rehearsal strategies, but tasks that require analysis and synthesis may require elaboration and organization strategies (Weinstein & Mayer, 1986). If students cannot self-observe and evaluate the effectiveness of their behavior, they are likely to not know what to change in order to become more successful.

I Don't Know How to Change

Mark knows that he needs to change the way he takes lecture notes but is having trouble applying the learning strategies in his calculus class. The note-taking strategy be learned from his learning strategies course seemed to work well for the history lectures, but calculus presents a different challenge.

Even though learning strategies courses teach skills that are intended to bring about change in one's academic behavior, students like Mark, in reality, may not know how to change. This may be due to two factors: The students may not have had adequate practice with the strategy in the learning to learn course to use it on their own, and the students may not know how to transfer the strategies from the learning to learn course to other courses. In order for learning strategies to become fully implemented across different courses, students need both numerous and diverse opportunities to practice them. Researchers estimate that it takes thousands of hours of practice to become an expert in any field (Ericsson & Charness, 1994). Even if one doesn't expect a given learner to attain the level of expertise identified in the literature, it is not difficult to understand the limitations of a single assignment or two to learn a given behavior. Our belief is that many learners are not benefiting from learning strategies courses because they are not given the level of practice that is necessary to produce change in academic behavior (Hofer, Yu, & Pintrich, 1998). Clearly, an introduction to a strategy with limited practice in only certain types of courses is not sufficient to adequately learn and apply the strategy. Though the students may be exposed to potentially effective strategies, they, in reality, may not know how to change.

Implications

There are likely many approaches to help students change their academic behavior. As instructors in a learning to learn course, we have been using a self-management study assignment, consisting of four interrelated processes, to help students develop self-regulatory skills and, at the same time, deal with the reasons why they often resist change as identified in this paper (see Zimmerman, Bonner, & Kovach, 1996 for a discussion of the model and Dembo, 2004 for a detailed explanation of how students complete self-studies using the model to change their behavior). Students conduct this study as the final paper for our learning strategies course.

The following is an outline for developing a strategic plan for students who identify anxiety as a major academic problem. Similar outlines are available for improving time management and exam preparation, managing motivation, as well as other academic problems (Dembo, 2004). Concrete examples of steps that can be accomplished at each stage follow the outline.

Four Processes Defined

1. Self-observation and evaluation. How does anxiety influence my academic and/or personal life? Do I need to change the way I deal with anxiety? If yes, what problem(s) do I encounter? What are the symptoms of my problem(s), that is, when, where, and how often does my problem occur? What factors (e.g., beliefs, perceptions, feelings, physiological responses, and/or behaviors) contribute to this problem? What do I need to change to reduce or eliminate my problem?

2. Goal setting and strategic planning. What are my goals? What strategies will I implement to reduce my anxiety? When will I use these strategies? How will I record my progress?

3. Strategy-implementation and monitoring. What strategies did I use to reduce my anxiety? When did I use these strategies? What method(s) did I use to record my progress (e.g., documents, charts, logs, tally sheets, checklists, and/or recordings)? When did I use these methods? How and when did I monitor my progress to determine if my anxiety-reducing strategies were working? What changes, if any, did I make along the way?

4. Strategic-outcome monitoring. Did I attain the goal(s) I set for myself? Has the reduction in my anxiety improved my academic performance and/or personal life? What strategies were the most and least effective? What changes, if any, do I need to make in the future?

Four Processes Applied

The first of the four processes in self-regulation is *self-observation and evaluation* as students become aware and assess their previous and current academic behavior. Students identify, observe and evaluate an academic problem by using a variety of formal and informal diagnostic instruments such as the Learning and Study Strategies Inventory (LASSI; Weinstein, Schulte, & Palmer, 1987), writings from their weekly journals, and checklists from self-assessment exercises that are provided in the course literature. For example, in order to determine one's level of anxiety, the LASSI includes a subscale specifically for anxiety, indicating where students score in relation to other college students taking the assessment. In addition, students can assess the nature of their self-talk and identify where, why, and how they engage in negative self-talk by recording it in a thought journal. The journal includes such data as the date of occurrence, the settings, and the nature of the negative self-talk. The information allows students to analyze the conditions affecting their behavior. Also, students can assess their level of anxiety by examining whether they have panicky thoughts or worries that frustrate their efforts to concentrate, whether they rush through test questions so quickly that they misinterpret directions or fail to notice important information, and whether they experience physiological symptoms, such as muscle tightness and abdominal distress. In addition to identifying their problem, we ask students to reflect about its history (i.e., When did they start being anxious about school performance? Did it happen in middle school or high school?) and ask the students to diagnose the problem (i.e., What are the reasons for their perceived anxiety? Is it unrealistic parental expectations? Is it painful experience with failure in previous schooling?).

After students better understand their previous and current behavior in a given area, they are able to engage in *goal setting and strategic planning*. This step begins with the students determining their intermediate and long-term goals. An example goal for students who have identified anxiety as an academic problem could be reducing negative self-talk and feeling more confident, and as a result, obtaining a B average for the current semester and improving performance on exams in the long term. Students should plan on using specific strategies, identified in course literature, to deal with their problem area. For example, students whose goal is to reduce their anxiety may plan to engage in positive self-talk by assuring themselves that they can successfully accomplish each task they face every day for one week. They may also plan to counter each instance of negative self-talk with a positive one to increase confidence. Additionally, they may use relaxation techniques, such as abdominal breathing and muscle relaxation (McKay, Davis, & Fanning, 1997) to reduce their anxiety and stress. It is important at this stage in the study that the students determine specific documentation methods to keep track of strategy use. For example, students can plan to record self-talk in a thought journal and relaxation techniques by marking each time they practice them onto a weekly calendar.

Following goal setting and strategic planning, the *strategy-implementation and monitoring* occurs as students try to execute the strategy and monitor its effectiveness. Students attempt to answer the question: Am I reaching my goals through the strategies I created? Most importantly, the students are required to use documentation to support the answer to this question. At this point in the process, students with high anxiety should be able to provide evidence of their attempted behavior change. According to the plan, they should record the nature of their negative self-talk as well as the content of the countering positive self-talk in a thought journal. Also, the students' weekly calendar should indicate each time they practiced a certain relaxation technique.

In the final stage, *strategic-outcome monitoring*, students must look at their performance and answer the following questions: Did I attain each of the goals I set for myself? How do I know? The students need to review every document, chart, journal, tally sheet, and/or checklist they used throughout the self-study and describe what each piece of evidence tells them about how successful they were at reducing their anxiety. The students should also assess their academic performance: Did they attain a B average for the current semester? Of specific importance at this stage is determining which strategies were the most and least effective in helping them reduce this problem. This information helps determine whether there are any changes they need to make to improve their academic performance in the future.

An important aspect of this project is that each student determines his or her own self-study, and, as a result, appears to be less defensive about changing his or her behavior. Most importantly, students are required to identify and practice the learning strategies most relevant to deal with their own academic problems.

Zimmerman, Bonner, and Kovach (1996) believe that one of the major advantages of using this self-regulatory process is that it can improve not only the students' learning, but it can enhance their perception of self-confidence and control over the learning process. By learning to self-observe one's current learning and study behavior and by determining for oneself what methods are effective and ineffective, students can begin replacing ineffective methods with better ones and can become more aware of the improved effectiveness of these new strategies.

Evaluative Data

In order to assess the effectiveness of the learning to learn course overall and the self-management study, specifically, we conducted two self-report surveys during the Fall 2003 semester. The first survey was administered after two-thirds of the course was completed. It asked the students to identify whether they had or had not changed their academic behavior at that point in the course. Additionally, we asked students who did not change their behavior to identify one of the four reasons discussed in this paper as the reason for their lack of change. The following is the informal assessment we used:

> The purpose of this course is to help you make any necessary changes in your academic learning and motivation to become a more successful student. Check one of the following as it relates to you:
>
> ___ 1. I identified some behaviors that I needed to change and made attempts to change my behavior.
>
> Explain how you have changed.
>
> ___ 2. Basically, I didn't change my behavior very much. For the most part, I presently use the same strategies that I used in high school.
>
> Explain how you are able to change or why you can't seem to change. If you didn't change, identify which one of the following explanations most closely pertains to you and explain why.
>
> ___ 1. I can't change.
>
> ___ 2. I don't want to change.
>
> ___ 3. I don't know how to change.
>
> ___ 4. I don't know what to change.

We found that of the 169 students enrolled in the course, 49 students (29%) indicated that they had not changed their behavior. Of the 49 students who had not changed, 33 (67%) indicated that they did not want to change, 3 (6%) stated that they could not change, 9 (18%) said that they did not know how to change, and 4 (8%) expressed that they did not know what to change.

The following demographic information may be helpful in understanding why 33 of the 169 students indicated that they did not want to change. The entering SAT scores for all freshmen at the university during Fall 2003 were 1341. Students who were required to take our learning-to-learn course had an average SAT score of 1050, with the student athletes averaging 1000. Our conversations with many of the 33 students indicated that they believed they could be successful in college without taking our course, and they were probably correct. However, the scores on some of the students' Learning and Study Skills Inventory, their high school grade-point averages, as well as their academic progress during their first semester indicated they needed help in improving their learning and study strategies. Thus, it appears that the students in our learning to learn course do not comprise a homogenous subgroup but rather fall under several categories when it comes to reasons for lack of change.

Two options are offered as a final paper for the course: One is to conduct the self-management study as described in this paper; the other is to conduct a career assessment study wherein the students are required to conduct interviews with a professional in their field of interest and an academic advisor, as well as to assess the appropriateness of their current coursework in relationship to their long-term career goals. Of the 49 students who, according to the first survey, had not changed, 19 students (39%) conducted the self-management study as opposed to the career assessment study. In order to assess the effectiveness of the four-process self-management study, we conducted a survey that included two questions specifically targeting the area of changing one's behavior. Those questions were: (1) Before doing the self-management study, to what degree did you believe you could change the specific aspect of your behavior? (2) To what degree did the self-management study help you change your behavior? The students responded on a 1 (very little) to 5 (very much) Likert scale. For the sample of 19 students, we found a significant difference between the means of the first ($M = 2.74$) and second question ($M = 3.42$), t (18) $= -2.387$, $p < .05$. This difference indicated that the self-management study contributed significantly to the students' ability to change their behavior. However, one must be cautious in interpreting this finding. It may be that the students in this subgroup who selected the self-management project were more amenable to changing their behavior as compared to the subgroup who selected the career assessment paper. Nevertheless, a group of students who stated that they had not changed their behavior during the course provided evidence that the project helped them change their behavior.

Additionally, the students' open-ended comments validated each of the four stages in the study as important in bringing about behavior change. For example, self-monitoring and evaluation was reported as valuable since it helped the students to actually "see the amount of distractions in . . . everyday life." Another student stated, "The most effective part of the study was identifying the root of my problem because once I knew where the problem stemmed from I was able to know what strategies to use to fix it." Goal setting and strategic planning were effective since setting a goal, for one student, "forced ... [her] to stick to it" and, for another student, "it [setting a goal] made me sit down and think about my problem rather than just accept it." Comments about strategic implementation and monitoring highlighted the importance of documenting one's progress. As one student indicated, "I am in a constant battle with my self-talk so keeping track of it with a thought journal helped me see how and when I think negatively." Another student mentioned that using specific strategies, such as planning one's use of time for two weeks in trying to combat procrastination, gave her a sense that she can actually do something about her problem. In addition, strategic monitoring highlighted "the consequences of ... procrastination" for one student. The overall impact of the assigned paper is summed up by a statement from a student who in the first survey indicated that he did not want to change his academic behavior. According to him, the most effective part of the self-management study was "just the fact that ... [he] was forced to initiate a plan and implement it for this paper — otherwise, little action would have been taken."

Future Research

Although the literature explaining the characteristics and processes of academic self-regulation has grown extensively in recent years, research still reveals little about why certain students are more likely or willing than others to change their learning and study skills and become more self-regulated learners. Hofer, Yu, and Pintrich (1998) point out this problem: "There is a clear need for more process-oriented studies, which will probably involve more qualitative and ethnographic observations and interviews of students as they are enrolled in a learning-to-learn course as well as when they leave it" (p. 81). More specifically, they point out that there is little research on how different entry beliefs and strategies constrain or facilitate the learning of self-regulatory strategies.

We concur with Hofer, Yu, and Pintrich (1998) and believe that we need to include qualitative assessments in our evaluation designs. Recently, Spradling and Dembo (2002) completed such an evaluation whereby they interviewed four students each week during a 14-week semester. The study provided interesting insights into the students' perceptions of their behavior. One of the emergent themes in the investigation was the dichotomy between knowing what to do and actually doing it. The students indicated that self-motivation was a determining factor in the amount of behavioral change in the course. It will be important to conduct further qualitative investigations to better understand what motivational factors inhibit students from changing ineffective behaviors.

Conclusions

This study has identified a number of reasons why students have difficulty changing their behavior and linked these reasons with major learning and motivational variables and processes: automaticity of behavior, level of self-efficacy (both too low and too high), nature of attributions, type of goal orientation, problems in self-observation and evaluation, negative self-talk, and problems in the transfer of learning. It is clear that these problems are related to what has been called the skill and the will: the knowledge or strategies regarding how to learn (the skills) and the motivational processes that support or impede learning (the will). Problems related to automaticity of behavior and the transfer of strategies from one course to another are related to issues in learning, whereas the level of self-efficacy; nature of attributions; type of goal orientation; and problems of self-observation, evaluation, and negative self-talk relate to motivation. If educators only focus on one dimension — skill or will — it is unlikely that they will be able to help students change their academic behavior.

We also provided an outline and specific examples for what we believe to be an effective way of facilitating behavior change: the four-process self-management study assignment. Our data demonstrate that this approach has benefited even students who up to the last one-third of the course indicated that they had not changed their behavior despite their participation in the learning-to-learn course.

In summary, educators must be prepared to teach students who are not eager to benefit from their instruction. When faced with resistance to change, developing strategies for teaching students how to change becomes imperative. This change strategy involves more than providing information about how to learn, such as note-taking and exam preparation strategies; it involves helping students use this information so they can learn to control their own behavior and actually benefit from the knowledge of the strategies. For this reason, instructors can best help students by teaching self-regulatory skills through projects such as the self-management assignment described in this paper in courses that provide academic support services to students. In addition, it is important to understand the reasons why students resist change to ensure that these issues can be appropriately addressed in learning strategy courses.

References

Arendale, D. (1994). Supplemental Instruction: Increasing achievement and retention. In D. Martin & D. Arendale (Eds.), *New directions for teaching and learning: No. 60. Supplemental Instruction: Increasing achievement and retention* (pp. 11–21). San Francisco: Jossey-Bass.

Bandura, A. (1982). Self-efficacy mechanism in human agency. *American Psychologist, 37*, 122–147.

Bargh, J. A., and Chartrand, T. L. (1999). The unbearable automaticity of being. *American Psychologist, 54*, 462–479.

Clark, R. E. (1991). Ten cognitive science principles for human performance technologies. In H. Stolovich & E. Keeps (Eds.), *Handbook of human performance technology*. New York: Macmillan.

Dembo, M. H. (2004). *Motivation and learning strategies for college success: A self-management approach* (2nd ed.). Mahwah, NJ: Lawrence Erlbaum.

Dembo, M. H., & Jakubowski, T. G. (1999, April). *Outcomes of a learning to learn course: Implications for future research*. Paper presented at the meeting of the American Educational Research Association, Montreal, Quebec.

Ericsson, A. K., & Charness, N. (1994). Expert performance: Its structure and acquisition. *American Psychologist, 49*, 725–747.

Friedlander, J. (1980). Are college support programs and services reaching high-risk students? *Journal of College Student Personnel, 212*, 23–28.

Glaser, R. (1996). Changing the agency for learning: Acquiring expert performance. In K. Ericsson (Ed.), *The road to excellence: The acquisition of expert performance in the arts and sciences, sports and games*. Mahwah, NJ: Lawrence Erlbaum.

Harackiewicz, J. M., Barron, K. E., Tauger, J. M., Carter, S. M., & Elliot, A. J. (2000). Short-term and long-term consequences of achievement goals: Predicting interest and performance over time. *Journal of Educational Psychology, 92*, 316–330.

Hattie, J., Biggs, J., & Purdie, N. (1996). Effects of learning skills interventions on student learning: A meta-analysis. *Review of Educational Research, 66*, 99–136.

Hofer, B., Yu, S. L., & Pintrich, P. R. (1998). Teaching college students to be self-regulated learners. In D. H. Schunk & B. J. Zimmerman (Eds.), *Self-regulated learning: From teaching to self-reflective practice* (pp. 57–85). New York: Guilford Press.

Karabenick, S. A., & Knapp, J. R. (1988). Help-seeking and the need for academic assistance. *Journal of Educational Psychology, 80*, 406–408.

Martin, D. C., Lorton, M., Blanc, R. A., & Evans, C. (1977). *The learning center: A comprehensive model for colleges and universities* (Report No. CS004505). Kansas City, MO: University of Missouri. (ERIC Document Reproduction No. ED 162 294)

McKay, M., Davis, M., & Fanning, P. (1997). *Thoughts and feeling: Taking control of your moods and your life*. Oakland, CA: New Harbinger Publications.

Midgley, C. (Ed.) (2002). *Goals, goal structures, and patterns of adaptive learning*. Mahwah, NJ: Lawrence Erlbaum.

National Center for Education Statistics. (2002). *Percent of degree-granting institutions offering remedial services, by type and control of institution: 1987–88 to 2000–01*. Washington, DC: Author. Retrieved June 5, 2003, from http://nces.ed.gov/pubs2002/digest2001/tables/dt313.asp

Nist, S. L., & Simpson, M. L. (1993). Why strategies fail: Students' and researchers' perceptions. In C. K. Kinzer & D. Leu (Eds.), *Multidimensional aspects of literacy research, theory, and practice. Forty-Third Yearbook of the National Reading Association* (pp. 287–295). Charleston, SC: NRA.

Pajares, F. (1996). Self-efficacy beliefs in academic settings. *Review of Educational Research, 66*, 543–578.

Pintrich, P. (2000). An achievement goal theory perspective on issues in motivation terminology, theory, and research. *Contemporary Educational Psychology, 25*, 92–104.

Pintrich, P. R., McKeachie, W. J., & Lin, Y. G. (1987). Teaching a course in learning to learn. *Teaching of Psychology, 14*, 81–86.

Prochaska, J. O., & DiClemente, C. C. (1983). Stages and processes of self-change in smoking: Toward an integrative model of change. *Journal of Consulting and Clinical Psychology, 5*, 390–405.

Prochaska, J. O., DiClemente, C. C., & Norcross, J. C. (1992). In search of how people change. Applications to addictive behaviors. *American Psychologist, 47*, 1102–1114.

Prochaska, J. O., & Prochaska, J. M. (1999). Why don't continents move? Why don't people change? *Journal of Psychotherapy integration, 9*(1), 83–102.

Rettinger, D. L., & Palmer, T. M. (1996). Lessons learned from using Supplemental Instruction: Adapting instructional models for practical applications. *Research and Teaching in Developmental Education, 13*(1), 57–68.

Rosen, S. (1983). Perceived inadequacy and help-seeking. In B. M. DePaulo, A. Nadler, & J. D. Fisher (Series Eds.), *New Directions in helping: No. 2. Help seeking* (pp. 73–107). New York: Academic Press.

Schunk, D. H. (1989). Self-efficacy and achievement behaviors. *Educational Psychology Review, 1*, 173–208.

Simpson, M. L., Hynd, C. R., Nist, S. L., & Burrell, K. I. (1997). College academic assistance programs and practices. *Educational Psychology Review, 9*, 39–87.

Spradling, P., & Dembo, M. H. (2002, April). *Personal change in a learning strategies course.* Paper presented at the annual meting of the American Educational Research Association, New Orleans, LA.

Wegner, D. M., & Wheatley, T. (1999). Apparent mental causation: Sources of the experience of will. *American Psychologist, 54*, 480–492.

Weiner, B. (1986). *An attributional theory of motivation and emotion.* New York: Springer-Verlag.

Weinstein, C. F., & Mayer, R. F. (1986). The teaching of learning strategies. In M. C. Wittrock (Ed.), *Handbook of research on teaching* (3rd ed., pp. 315–327). New York: Macmillan.

Weinstein, C. E., Schulte, A. C., & Palmer, D. R. (1987). *LASSI: Learning and study strategies inventory.* Clearwater, FL: H&H Publishing.

Zimmerman, B. J. (1995). Self-efficacy and educational development. In A. Bandura (Ed.), *Self-efficacy in changing societies* (pp. 202–231). New York: Cambridge University Press.

Zimmerman, B. J. (1998). Developing self-fulfilling cycles of academic regulation: An analysis of exemplary instructional models. In D. H. Schunk & B. J. Zimmerman (Eds.), *Self-regulated learning: From teaching to self-reflective practice* (pp. 1–19). New York: Guilford Press.

Zimmerman, B. J. (2000). Attaining self-regulation: A social cognitive perspective. In M. Boekarts, P. R. Pintrich, & M. Zeidner (Eds.), *Handbook of self-regulation* (pp. 13–39). San Diego: Academic Press.

Zimmerman, B. J., Bonner, S., & Kovach, R. (1996). *Developing self-regulated learners: Beyond achievement to self-efficacy.* Washington, DC: American Psychological Association.

Zimmerman, B. J., & Martinez-Pons, M. (1990). Student differences in self-regulatory learning: Relating grade, sex, and giftedness to self-efficacy and strategy use. *Journal of Educational Psychology, 82,* 284–290.

Zimmerman, B. J., & Paulsen, A. S. (1995). Self-monitoring during collegiate studying: An invaluable tool for academic self-regulation. *New Directions for Teaching and Learning, 63,* 13–27.

Zimmerman, B. J., & Risemberg, R. (1997). Self-regulatory dimensions of academic learning and motivation. In G. D. Phye (Ed.), *Handbook of academic learning: Construction of knowledge* (pp. 105–125). San Diego: Academic Press.

Practical Applications of the Research on Epistemological Beliefs

Sherrie L. Nist and Jodi Patrick Holschuh

The research on epistemological beliefs focuses on students' perceptions of knowledge, especially the origins of knowledge and what constitutes knowledge and learning. According to researchers such as William G. Perry (1999) and Marlene Schommer (1990), students' beliefs influence, in part, the cognitive and metacognitive processes they choose to employ during their independent learning tasks. In this article, Sherrie L. Nist and Jodi Patrick Holschuh summarize the theories and research studies concerning epistemological beliefs, outlining in detail Schommer's work that suggests that students' beliefs consist of five independent, nonhierarchical, non-developmental dimensions: certain knowledge, simple knowledge, omniscient authority, quick learning, and innate ability. The authors describe how they use these theories about epistemological beliefs in their learning strategy courses and how they "nudge" their students' naive beliefs to more mature ones that are associated with successful independent learning.

Theories of epistemological beliefs focus on individuals' perceptions about what knowledge is and where knowledge comes from. These beliefs are part of, and may in fact direct, the cognitive processes involved in learning (Kitchener & King, 1990; Perry, 1999; Schommer, 1990). Research stemming from these theories offers varied explanations as to how beliefs relate to student learning and academic success.

Although the results of this research are equivocal at best, they do offer several general insights into the impact of beliefs on learning. First, some research focuses on the relationship between beliefs and monitoring. Some researchers (e.g., Ryan, 1984) found that epistemological beliefs influence how students monitor the acquisition of knowledge. Students who were classified as dualists reported trying to recall facts from the text, but those classified as relativists reported trying to paraphrase and summarize the text in their own words. However, when Glenberg and Epstein (1987) used Ryan's scale to examine learning in science courses, they found no significant relationship between episte-mological beliefs and students' ability to accurately monitor their com-prehension of scientific text. Second, research has focused on the issue of domain and beliefs. Some researchers found differences in beliefs depending on domain or discipline (Palmer & Marra, 2004; Schommer-Aikins, Duell, & Barker, 2003). For example, Palmer and Marra (2004) found differences in the epistemological beliefs of engineering and science students across the disciplines of the sciences and the humani-ties. However, Buel, Alexander, and Murphy (2002) found evidence of domain-generality in undergraduates' epistemological beliefs. Third, research has examined the relationship between task and beliefs. Simpson and Nist's (1997) research on how students learn and study history found that in order to be successful, students either had to have beliefs about history that were similar to their professor's or have a clear understanding of course task.

Other research indicates that epistemological beliefs might affect the depth to which individuals learn (Schommer, 1990, 1993; Schreiber & Shinn, 2003). There is evidence that students with naive epistemic assumptions tend to endorse surface-level strategies while students with sophisticated epistemological beliefs tend to endorse deep-level strategies (Holschuh, 1998; Schommer, 1990; Schreiber & Shinn, 2003). Thus, epistemological beliefs may function as a benchmark against which individuals compare comprehension and learning to the task de-mands, which, in turn, would influence students' strategy selection and use (Hofer & Pintrich, 1997; Ryan, 1984). For example, when encoun-tering complex tasks, individuals holding naive epistemological beliefs, may not understand the necessity of choosing deep-level processing strategies. In fact, individuals with naive beliefs may not be able to discriminate between surface- and deep-level strategies. Such students may choose to make flash cards to study for an exam and would believe they were well-prepared when they memorized all of the facts or bold-faced terms. In addition, given an exam where the professor expects students to synthesize ideas or to analyze information, students with naive beliefs would be unprepared for the task and would have no idea where the questions were coming from because they do not match their conception about what knowledge is and where knowledge comes from.

One of the leading researchers in the area of epistemological be-liefs and how they influence studying and learning is Marlene Schom-mer (now Schommer-Aikins). Her work has had a considerable influence on our approach to introducing students to the role of beliefs in the classroom. Schommer (1990) conceptualized an individual's episte-mological beliefs as consisting of five independent, nonhierarchical, nondevelopmental dimensions: certain knowledge, simple knowledge, omniscient authority, quick learning, and innate ability. Each of the five dimensions is viewed as a continuum beginning at a naive perspective and moving toward a mature perspective.

The first dimension, certain knowledge, deals with the extent to which a person sees knowledge as fixed (set) or changeable. The belief that knowledge is absolute is readily apparent and common in first-year students. Such students believe that there are no shades of gray — things are black or white, true or false, right or wrong. Students who are absolute learners have a particularly difficult time in courses where they are expected to evaluate theories or where there is no one decisive explanation for something. They want the professor to give them an answer. In addition, they may not be open to exploring or, in some cases, even being exposed to alternative explanations of the world, especially when it has to do with religious or political beliefs (Schommer, 1990).

The second dimension, simple knowledge, is the extent to which a person sees knowledge as a group of individual facts or as concepts that are related to each other (Schommer, 1990). For example, two students who are studying for their chemistry exam can take very different approaches. One student believes that knowledge is a series of unrelated facts, so he tries to memorize all of the formulas and key terms to prepare for the exam. The other student believes that knowledge consists of interrelated ideas, so she tries to understand the chemical processes and their underlying theories when she studies for the exam. The first student does not even attempt to link ideas together because his beliefs are such that he actively attempts to keep each concept discrete (Schommer, 1990).

The third dimension, omniscient authority, is the extent to which students believe that knowledge is external and is transmitted to individuals from an outside authority such as a teacher or a parent, or is internal and comes from within the individual (Schommer, 1990). A good number of first-year students hold the belief that their professors own the key to their learning rather than believing that learning ultimately should be a shared experience. This belief manifests itself in a number of ways, from being intimidated by professors to students believing that it is their professors who are responsible for their learning. We call this the "empty vessel syndrome" because these students regard themselves as passive participants in the learning process. Such students believe that it is the professor's role to dispense all of the important information and the student's role to simply absorb it. Thus, if students struggle in the course or perform poorly on exams, they can always say that the professor wasn't a good teacher, didn't care about students, or made up tricky exams. Unfortunately, students holding a belief in omniscient authority tend not to take credit for their failures or their successes. If they hold the belief that the professor is in charge of their learning, when they experience success, they are likely to say that it was because they had a good professor, an easy test, or just plain luck — not that they worked hard and studied appropriately.

The fourth component, quick learning, deals with beliefs about the speed of learning. Some college students believe that learning happens quickly or not at all, while others believe that learning happens gradually. This belief probably arises because in previous learning experiences, students have been given tasks that required little time to complete. In addition, many students believe that if learning is going to happen it is going to happen immediately or not at all rather than viewing the learning process as something that is gradual. Students who believe in quick learning find it difficult to stick with a task or to try a different approach when their first doesn't work. Their attitude is "If I can't learn this quickly, I can't learn it at all" (Schommer, 1990).

The fifth and final component, innate ability, deals with beliefs about the control of learning (Schommer, 1990). Some students believe that the ability to learn is fixed at birth while others believe that people can learn how to learn. For example, if students have always struggled with math they may believe that they "just can't do math," no matter how hard they work at it. Students who hold this belief will not make much effort to learn because they believe that their success in math is related to their lack of ability. Students like this are much less likely to seek out help when they don't understand something. They are also more apt to give up. Although most students are stronger in some subjects than others, students who believe that they cannot learn a specific discipline show poor persistence and often will avoid enrolling in those courses until they absolutely have to.

What strikes us as interesting about the research on epistemological beliefs is that to our knowledge, none of the researchers has shared his or her results with students. Although Baxter Magolda (1992) shared general findings with students, she did not disclose individual scores to each student. It may be that by informing students about their own beliefs, educators may be able to help students move towards more mature epistemological perspectives. Intuitively, it seems that providing such diagnostics would bring objective beliefs into awareness, perhaps even directing motivational effort towards intentionally developing subjective beliefs and strategic learning approaches. In other words, it may be that if students know what is possible, they may rise to the challenge.

Because epistemological beliefs seem to have such a great impact on student thinking and learning, we routinely include it in our textbooks and in the curriculum of our Learning to Learn courses. These courses already address affective issues such as motivation, attitude, and stress management so discussing beliefs seems a natural addition.

The Instruction

As with much of our teaching, the first thing we try to do is create awareness in our students by having them take a brief assessment of epistemological beliefs. Students read a scenario, which describes how Chris, a college student, approaches studying and learning in biology course (Holschuh, 1998). The Epistemological Scenario is used to help students think about their own epistemological beliefs within the context of an introductory science classroom. Previous research has indicated that scenarios help students focus on a particular topic (Grossman, 1994). Research using scenarios as a means of assessment has also found that individuals are more willing to share their own views after reading a scenario, because the cases provide a focus for their views (Echiejile, 1994; Grossman, 1994). Following reading, students respond to 15 Likert-type items that ask them to what extent they agree with Chris's approaches.

The next step is to have students read about beliefs and how they impact college learning. They read the chapter on this topic from their textbook (Nist & Holschuh, 2000). Then the class engages in a discussion about each of the five dimensions of epistemological beliefs (Schommer, 1990), focusing on the implications and impact on classroom learning. In this discussion we are careful to present many examples tied to research to help make this abstract theory more concrete for students. For example, when discussing the role of speed of learning we talk about Schoenfeld's (1985) research, which found that most mathematics problems students encounter before they enter college can be solved in under two minutes. In a college setting, students enrolled in calculus might get frustrated or give up when unable to complete a problem within that timeframe. Students may be unaware that they held this arbitrary time as a standard (and probably have some conceptions about how long it should take to write a paper, read a textbook chapter, take an essay exam, or other academic tasks that are also based on K–12 educational experiences) for solving mathematics problems. Once students become aware that they might simply be giving up too soon, they may make an attempt to spend more time on calculus before becoming frustrated. This is just one of the many examples we discuss with students. In addition to teaching through examples, we ask students to examine their score on the assessment and write a reflection about what it means for them as college learners. As we present new strategies we discuss how an individual's beliefs affects the perceived benefit of the strategy.

Some preliminary research has suggested that providing instruction to undergraduates about epistemological beliefs increases their awareness of their own beliefs and how those beliefs affect everyday decision-making and classroom learning (Holschuh, Hubbard, Francis, & Randall, 2000). In response to open-ended interview questions, students said that learning about the concept of epistemological beliefs and considering their current beliefs helped them think about learning differently. Additionally, students reported that thinking about their relationship to knowledge helped them make better strategic learning decisions.

One of the most obvious influences that beliefs have on learning is students' selection of study and test preparation strategies. Students who define learning as memorizing are going to select strategies that lead to memorizing, regardless of the task. A large number of first-year students fall into this category for two reasons. First, for many college freshmen, memorizing is what they have had to do for 12 years of schooling. That's what the task has been and the majority of college-bound high school students easily meet this challenge. They have earned top-notch grades in high school and perhaps even have scored well on the SAT or ACT. But when students get to college, most professors expect students to think on higher levels. They are expected to apply, to synthesize, and to analyze; yet they continue to use the strategies that made them successful memorizers. Second, few students receive any formal, extended instruction on how to be an efficient and effective learner. For some reason, learning how to learn has been kept a secret from them. Thus, when they enter the college classroom, students may not bring with them the strategies to do anything but memorize.

Five Suggestions for "Nudging" Students' Epistemological Beliefs

There are many ways that we can "nudge" students' beliefs to move closer to the mature rather than the naive side of the scale. In addition to talking to students about their own beliefs, structuring class assignments to reflect mature beliefs can be very effective. We offer five suggestions.

First, one of the most informative assignments we have used is to ask our students to define our content. Students write responses to the following questions: What is learning? What is studying? How do learning and studying differ? How do people typically go about learning? How the students respond to these questions tell us volumes about their beliefs about learning. For example, when students say that learning is "absorbing information from teachers," we know that they probably hold a belief in omniscient authority. We use student responses as a jumping board for discussion about learning and studying issues throughout the semester.

Second, we teach students strategies that promote higher-level thinking and then give them complex problems to solve. For example, after we teach students strategies for reducing, organizing, and elaborating on information, we give them a piece of text with the conclusion missing. At first, students are likely to try to oversimplify the issue. We ask students to write their own conclusion and discuss all possible solutions with a small group (this can help them see that there is often more than one answer to a problem).

Third, we teach students how to monitor their learning. One approach we take to help students monitor is to remind students that not all learning happens quickly. We talk about our experiences as learners and have students share their own experiences where they have spent a lot of time learning (for example, playing an instrument or pursuing a hobby). We also find it helpful to discuss the notion that even their college professors are spending a good deal of time learning new things.

Fourth, we help students recognize the importance of understanding the academic task demands in each of their classes. As with solving complex problems, students tend to oversimplify the tasks in their classes. For example, for science classes we discuss the importance of understanding each concept as it is taught because the concepts build on each other. If students don't understand something early on, it may impact future understanding. This may be obvious to us, but it is often news to students.

Fifth, we talk with students about the support available on campus. This can include seeking out tutoring, coming to office hours, forming study groups, attending review sessions (if available), and using old exams for studying. Students with naive beliefs tend not to utilize the supports available to them. We believe that the more they hear about the options for support, the more they will consider them in times of need.

Although there are no definitive answers about the extent to which epistemological beliefs influence how students study and learn, from our experiences, we believe that creating awareness and providing students with appropriate assignments can nudge their beliefs in the right direction. We have seen students who believe knowledge is simple or quickly rethink these stances and take measures to change their approaches to learning and studying. Still, additional research is needed to connect the role of epistemological beliefs to actual classroom learning and experience.

References

Baxter Magolda, M. B. (1992). *Knowing and reasoning in college: Gender-related patterns in students' intellectual development.* San Francisco: Jossey-Bass.

Buel, M. M., Alexander, P. A., & Murphy, P. K. (2002). Beliefs about schooled knowledge: Domain specific or domain general? *Contemporary Educational Psychology, 27,* 415–440.

Echiejile, I. (1994). Training as an instrument of change: The effectiveness of case studies. *Training and Management Development Methods, 8,* 609–620.

Glenberg, A. M., & Epstein, W. (1987). Inexpert calibration of comprehension. *Memory and Cognition, 10,* 597–602.

Grossman, R. W. (1994). Encouraging critical thinking using the case study method and cooperative learning techniques. *Journal on Excellence in College Teaching, 5,* 7–20.

Hofer, B. K., & Pintrich, P. R. (1997). The development of epistemological theories: Beliefs about knowledge and knowing and their relation to learning. *Review of Educational Research, 67,* 88–140.

Holschuh, J. P. (1998). Assessing epistemological beliefs in biology: Measurement concerns and the relation to academic performance. Unpublished doctoral dissertation: University of Georgia, Athens.

Holschuh, J. P., Hubbard, B., Francis, M., & Randall, S. (2000, December). Epistemological beliefs development in a learning-to-learn course: A study of epistemic nudging. Paper presented at the annual meeting of the National Reading Conference, Scottsdale, AZ.

Kitchener, K. S., & King, P. M. (1990). The reflective judgment model: Ten years of research. In M. L. Commons, J. D. Sinnot, F. A. Richards, & C. Armon (Eds.), *Adult development: Vol. 2. Models and methods in the study of adolescent and adult thought* (pp. 63–78). New York: Praeger.

Nist, S. L., & Holschuh, J. P. (2000). *Active learning: Strategies for college success.* Needham Heights, MA: Allyn & Bacon.

Palmer, B., & Marra, R. M. (2004). College student epistemological perspectives across knowledge domains: A proposed grounded theory. *Higher Education, 47,* 311–336.

Perry, W. G., Jr. (1999). *Forms of intellectual and ethical development in the college years: A scheme.* San Francisco: Jossey-Bass. (Original work published 1970. New York: Holt, Rinehart, & Winston.)

Ryan, M. P. (1984). Monitoring text comprehension: Individual differences in epistemological standards. *Journal of Educational Psychology, 76,* 248–258.

Schoenfeld, A. H. (1985). *Mathematical problem solving.* Orlando, FL: Academic Press.

Schommer, M. (1990). Effects of beliefs about the nature of knowledge on comprehension. *Journal of Educational Psychology, 82,* 498–504.

Schommer, M. (1993). Comparisons of beliefs about the nature of knowledge and learning among post-secondary students. *Research in Higher Education, 34,* 355–370.

Schommer-Aikins, M., Duell, O. K., & Barker, S. (2003). Epistemological beliefs across domains using Biglan's classification of academic disciplines. *Research in Higher Education, 44,* 347–367.

Schreiber, J. B., & Shinn, D. (2003). Epistemological beliefs of community college students and their learning processes. *Community College Journal of Research and Practice, 27,* 699–710.

Simpson, M. L., & Nist, S. L. (1997). Perspectives on learning history: A case study. *Journal of Literacy Research, 29,* 363–395.

Becoming a Self-Regulated Learner: An Overview

Barry J. Zimmerman

Self-regulation researchers have assisted many study strategy instructors in understanding how their students develop and regulate their thinking processes in order to become successful, independent learners. Barry J. Zimmerman developed one of the more prevalent theories of self-regulated learning, taking the position that individual differences in learning can be attributed to students' lack or possession of self-regulation. That is, successful students are those individuals who possess the self-awareness and strategic knowledge necessary to assist them with complex tasks. In this article Zimmerman provides a brief history of the field before he defines the essential qualities involved in academic self-regulation. He then describes the structure and functions of the three recursive phases involved in his model of self-regulation: forethought, performance, and self-reflection. After explaining this model in detail, he offers instructors suggestions on how to teach students to become self-regulated learners.

In an era of constant distractions in the form of portable phones, CD players, computers, and televisions for even young children, it is hardly surprising to discover that many students have not learned to self-regulate their academic studying very well. Consider the case of Tracy, a high school student who is infatuated with MTV.

An important midterm math exam is two weeks away, and she has begun to study while listening to popular music "to relax her." Tracy has not set any study goals for herself — instead she simply tells herself to do as well as she can on the test. She uses no specific learning strategies for condensing and memorizing important material and does not plan out her study time, so she ends up cramming for a few hours before the test. She has only vague self-evaluative standards and cannot gauge her academic preparation accurately. Tracy attributes her learning difficulties to an inherent lack of mathematical ability and is very defensive about her poor study methods. However, she does not ask for help from others because she is afraid of "looking stupid," or seek out supplementary materials from the library because she "already has too much to learn." She finds studying to be anxiety-provoking, has little self-confidence in achieving success, and sees little intrinsic value in acquiring mathematical skill.

Self-regulation researchers have sought to understand students like Tracy and to provide help in developing key processes that she lacks, such as goal setting, time management, learning strategies, self-evaluation, self-attributions, seeking help or information, and important self-motivational beliefs, such as self-efficacy and intrinsic task interest.

In recent years, there have been exciting discoveries regarding the nature, origins, and development of how students regulate their own learning processes (Zimmerman & Schunk, 2001). Although these studies have clearly revealed how self-regulatory processes lead to success in school, few teachers currently prepare students to learn on their own. In this article, I discuss students' self-regulation as a way to compensate for their individual differences in learning, define the essential qualities of academic self-regulation, describe the structure and function of self-regulatory processes, and, finally, give an overview of methods for guiding students to learn on their own.

Changing Conceptions of Individual Differences

Since the beginning of public schooling in the United States, educators have wrestled with the presence of substantial differences in individual students' backgrounds and modes of learning. Some students grasped important concepts easily and seemed highly motivated to study, whereas others struggled to understand and retain information and often seemed disinterested. In the nineteenth century, learning was viewed as a formal discipline, and a student's failure to learn was widely attributed to personal limitations in intelligence or diligence. Students were expected to overcome their individual limitations in order to profit from the curriculum of the school. Conceptions of self-regulatory development at the time were limited to acquiring desirable personal habits, such as proper diction and handwriting.

At the dawn of the twentieth century, psychology emerged as a science, and the topic of individual differences in educational functioning attracted widespread interest. Diverse reformers, such as John Dewey, E. L. Thorndike, Maria Montessori, and the progressive educators, suggested various ways to alter the curriculum to accommodate students' individual differences, such as grouping of students homogeneously according to age or ability, introducing perceptual-motor learning tasks, and broadening course work to include training in practical skills. Later reformers matched instructional treatments to students' aptitude or attitude scores on standardized tests (Cronbach, 1957). Despite these notable efforts, critics charged that the curriculum of American schools remained too narrow and inflexible to accommodate the psychological needs of all students. Many psychologists and educators discussed the adverse effects of a rigid curriculum on students' self-images (ASCD Yearbook, 1962).

During the late 1970s and early 1980s, a new perspective on students' individual differences began to emerge from research on metacognition and social cognition. *Metacognition* is defined as the awareness of and knowledge about one's own thinking. Students' deficiencies in learning were attributed to a lack of metacognitive awareness of personal limitations and an inability to compensate. *Social cognitive* researchers were interested in social influences on children's development of self-regulation, and they studied issues such as the effects of teacher modeling and instruction on students' goal setting and self-monitoring (Schunk, 1989; Zimmerman, 1989). Students were asked to set particular types of goals for themselves, such as completing a certain number of math homework problems, and to self-record their effectiveness in achieving these goals. Students who set specific and proximal goals for themselves displayed superior achievement and perceptions of personal efficacy. Interestingly, simply asking students to self-record some aspect of their learning, such as the completion of assignments, often led to "spontaneous" improvements in functioning (Shapiro, 1984). These effects, termed *reactivity* in the scientific literature, implied that students' metacognitive (i.e., self) awareness of particular aspects of their functioning could enhance their self-control. Of course, self-awareness is often insufficient when a learner lacks fundamental skills, but it can produce a readiness that is essential for personal change (Zimmerman, 2001).

These and related results led researchers to attribute individual differences in learning to students' lack of self-regulation. This perspective focused instead on what *students* needed to know about themselves in order to manage their limitations during efforts to learn, such as a dyslexic student's knowing to use a particular strategy to read. Although teachers also need to know a student's strengths and limitations in learning, their goal should be to empower their students to become self-aware of these differences. If a student fails to understand some aspect of a lesson in class, *he* or *she* must possess the self-awareness and strategic knowledge to take corrective action. Even if it were possible for teachers to accommodate every student's limitation at any point during the school day, their assistance could undermine the most important aspect of this learning — a student's development of a capability to self-regulate.

Defining Self-Regulated Learning in Process Terms

Self-regulation is not a mental ability or an academic performance skill; rather it is the self-directive process by which learners transform their mental abilities into academic skills. Learning is viewed as an activity that students do for themselves in a *proactive* way rather than as a covert event that happens to them in reaction to teaching. Self-regulation refers to self-generated thoughts, feelings, and behaviors that are oriented to attaining goals (Zimmerman, 2000). These learners are proactive in their efforts to learn because they are aware of their strengths and limitations and because they are guided by personally set goals and task-related strategies, such as using an arithmetic addition strategy to check the accuracy of solutions to subtraction problems. These learners monitor their behavior in terms of their goals and self-reflect on their increasing effectiveness. This enhances their self-satisfaction and motivation to continue to improve their methods of learning. Because of their superior motivation and adaptive learning methods, self-regulated students are not only more likely to succeed academically but to view their futures optimistically.

Self-regulation is important because a major function of education is the development of lifelong learning skills. After graduation from high school or college, young adults must learn many important skills informally. For example, in business settings, they are often expected to learn a new position, such as selling a product, by observing proficient others and by practicing on their own. Those who develop high levels of skill position themselves for bonuses, early promotion, or more attractive jobs. In self-employment settings, both young and old must constantly self-refine their skills in order to survive. Their capability to self-regulate is especially challenged when they undertake long-term creative projects, such as works of art, literary texts, or inventions. In recreational settings, learners spend much personally regulated time learning diverse skills for self-entertainment, ranging from hobbies to sports.

Although the relationship of self-reliance to success in life has been widely recognized, most students struggle to attain self-discipline in their methods of study today as they did a century ago. What does contemporary research tell us about this desirable but elusive personal quality? First, self-regulation of learning involves more than detailed knowledge of a skill; it involves the self-awareness, self-motivation, and behavioral skill to implement that knowledge appropriately. For example, there is evidence (Cleary & Zimmerman, 2000) that experts differ from nonexperts in their application of knowledge at crucial times during learning performances, such as correcting specific deficiencies in technique.

Second, contemporary research tells us that self-regulation of learning is not a single personal trait that individual students either possess or lack. Instead, it involves the selective use of specific processes that must be personally adapted to each learning task. The component skills include: (a) setting specific proximal *goals* for oneself, (b) adopting powerful *strategies* for attaining the goals, (c) *monitoring* one's performance selectively for signs of progress, (d) *restructuring* one's physical and social context to make it compatible with one's goals, (e) managing one's *time use* efficiently, (f) *self-evaluating* one's methods, (g) *attributing* causation to results, and (h) *adapting* future methods. A student's level of learning has been found to vary based on the presence or absence of these key self-regulatory processes (Schunk & Zimmerman, 1994; 1998).

Third, contemporary research reveals that the self-motivated quality of self-regulated learners depends on several underlying beliefs, including perceived efficacy and intrinsic interest. Historically, educators have focused on social encouragement and extrinsic "bells and whistles" to try to elevate students' level of motivation. Unfortunately, self-directed studying or practicing was often derided as inherently boring, repetitive, and mind-numbing with catchy phrases such as "Drill and kill." However, interviews with experts reveal a very different picture of these experiences (Ericsson & Charness, 1994). Experts spend approximately four hours each day in study and practice and find these activities highly motivating. They vary their methods of study and practice in order to discover new strategies for self-improvement. With such diverse skills as chess, sports, and music, the quantity of an individual's studying and practicing is a strong predictor of his or her level of expertise. There is also evidence that the quality of practicing and studying episodes is highly predictive of a learner's level of skill (Zimmerman & Kitsantas, 1997; 1999).

However, few beginners in a new discipline immediately derive powerful self-motivational benefits, and they may easily lose interest if they are not socially encouraged and guided, as most music teachers will readily attest (McPherson & Zimmerman, in press). Fortunately, the motivation of novices can be greatly enhanced when and if they use high-quality self-regulatory processes, such as close self-monitoring. Students who have the capabilities to detect subtle progress in learning will increase their levels of self-satisfaction and their beliefs in their personal efficacy to perform at a high level of skill (Schunk, 1983). Clearly, their motivation does not stem from the task itself, but rather from their use of self-regulatory processes, such as self-monitoring, and the effects of these processes on their self-beliefs.

Structure and Function of Self-Regulatory Processes

This brings us to the essential question: How does a student's use of specific learning processes, level of self-awareness, and motivational beliefs combine to produce self-regulated learners? Social learning psychologists view the structure of self-regulatory processes in terms of three cyclical phases. The forethought phase refers to processes and beliefs that occur *before* efforts to learn; the performance phase refers to processes that occur *during* behavioral implementation, and self-reflection refers to processes that occur *after* each learning effort. The processes that have been studied in each phase to date are shown in Figure 1, and the function of each process will be described next (Zimmerman, 2000).

Forethought Phase

There are two major classes of forethought phase processes: task analysis and self-motivation. Task analysis involves *goal setting* and *strategic planning*. There is considerable evidence of increased academic success by learners who set specific proximal goals for themselves, such as memorizing a word list for a spelling test, and by learners who plan to use spelling strategies, such as segmenting words into syllables.

Figure 1. Phases and Subprocesses of Self-Regulation

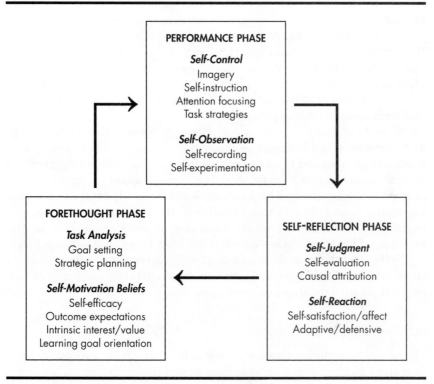

Source: From B. J. Zimmerman and M. Campillo (in press), "Motivating Self-Regulated Problem Solvers." In J. E. Davidson and Robert Sternberg (Eds.), *The Nature of Problem Solving*. New York: Cambridge UP. Adapted with permission.

Self-motivation stems from students' beliefs about learning, such as *self-efficacy* beliefs about having the personal capability to learn and *outcome expectations* about personal consequences of learning (Bandura, 1997). For example, students who feel self-efficacious about learning to divide fractions and expect to use this knowledge to pass a college entrance exam are more motivated to learn in a self-regulated fashion. *Intrinsic interest* refers to the students' valuing of the task skill for its own merits, and *learning goal orientation* refers to valuing the process of learning for its own merits. Students who find the subject matter of history, for example, interesting and enjoy increasing their mastery of it are more motivated to learn in a self-regulated fashion.

Performance Phase

Performance phase processes fall into two major classes: self-control and self-observation. Self-control refers to the deployment of specific methods or strategies that were selected during the forethought phase. Among the key types of self-control methods that have been studied to date are the use of *imagery*, *self-instruction*, *attention focusing*, and *task strategies*. For example, in learning the Spanish word *pan* for "bread," an English-speaking girl could form an image of a bread pan or self-instruct using the phrase "bread pan." She could also locate her place of study away from distracting noises so she could control her attention better. For a task-strategy, she could group the Spanish word *pan* with associated words for foods.

Self-observation refers to self-recording personal events or self-experimentation to find out the cause of these events. For example, students are often asked to *self-record* their time use to make them aware of how much time they spend studying. A boy may notice that when he studied alone, he finished his homework more quickly than when studying with a friend. To test this hypothesis, the boy could conduct a *self-experiment* in which he studied parallel lessons alone and in the presence of his friend to see whether his friend was an asset or a liability. Self-monitoring, a covert form of self-observation, refers to one's cognitive tracking of personal functioning, such as the frequency of failing to capitalize words when writing an essay.

Self-Reflection Phase

There are two major classes of self-reflection phase processes: self-judgment and self-reaction. One form of self-judgment, *self-evaluation*, refers to comparisons of self-observed performances against some standard, such as one's prior performance, another person's performance, or an absolute standard of performance. Another form of self-judgment involves *causal attribution*, which refers to beliefs about the cause of one's errors or successes, such as a score on a mathematics test. Attributing a poor score to limitations in fixed ability can be very damaging motivationally because it implies that efforts to improve on a future test will not be effective. In contrast, attributing a poor math score to controllable processes, such as the use of the wrong solution strategy, will sustain motivation because it implies that a different strategy may lead to success.

One form of self-reaction involves feelings of *self-satisfaction* and positive *affect* regarding one's performance. Increases in self-satisfaction enhance motivation, whereas decreases in self-satisfaction undermine further efforts to learn (Schunk, 2001). Self-reactions also take the form of adaptive/defensive responses. *Defensive* reactions refer to efforts to protect one's self-image by withdrawing or avoiding opportunities to learn and perform, such as dropping a course or being absent for a test. In contrast, *adaptive* reactions refer to adjustments designed to increase the effectiveness of one's method of learning, such as discarding or modifying an ineffective learning strategy.

This view of self-regulation is cyclical in that self-reflections from prior efforts to learn affect subsequent forethought processes (e.g., self-dissatisfaction will lead to lower levels of self-efficacy and diminished effort during subsequent learning) (Zimmerman & Bandura, 1994). In support of this cyclical view of self-regulation, high correlations were found among learners' use of forethought, performance, and self-reflection phase processes (Zimmerman & Kitsantas, 1999). For example, students who set specific proximal goals are more likely to self-observe their performance in these areas, more likely to achieve in the target area, and will display higher levels of self-efficacy than students who do not set goals (Bandura & Schunk, 1981). Other studies have revealed that experts display significantly higher levels of self-regulatory processes during practice efforts than novices (Cleary & Zimmerman, 2000).

The self-regulation profile of novices is very distinct from that of experts. Novices fail to engage in high-quality forethought and instead attempt to self-regulate their learning reactively. That is, they fail to set specific goals or to self-monitor systematically, and as a result, they tend to rely on comparisons with the performance of others to judge their learning effectiveness. Because typically other learners are also progressing, their performance represents a constantly increasing criterion of success that is very difficult to surpass. Furthermore, learners who make comparative self-evaluations are prompted to attribute causation to ability deficiencies (which are also normative in nature), and this will produce lower personal satisfaction and prompt defensive reactions. In contrast, the self-regulation profile of experts reveals they display high levels of self-motivation and set hierarchical goals for themselves with process goals leading to outcome goals in succession, such as dividing a formal essay into an introduction, a body, and a conclusion. Experts plan learning efforts using powerful strategies and self-observe their effects, such as a visual organizer for filling in key information (Zimmerman & Risemberg, 1997). They self-evaluate their performance against their personal goals rather than other learners' performance, and they make strategy (or method) attributions instead of ability attributions. This leads to greater personal satisfaction with their learning progress and further efforts to improve their performance. Together these self-reactions enhance various self-motivational beliefs of experts, such as self-efficacy, outcome expectations, learning goal orientation, and intrinsic interest.

Knowing the differences in the structure and function of self-regulatory processes between experts and novices has enabled researchers to formulate intervention programs in schools for children who display lower levels of self-regulatory development (Schunk & Zimmerman, 1998).

Teaching Students to Become Self-Regulated Learners

Research on the quality and quantity of students' use of self-regulatory processes has revealed high correlations with academic achievement track placement as well as with performance on standardized test scores (Zimmerman & Martinez-Pons, 1986). There is also evidence that students' use of self-regulatory processes is distinctive from but correlated with general measures of ability, such as verbal ability (Zimmerman & Bandura, 1994). Although many self-regulatory processes, such as goal setting and self-monitoring, are generally covert, teachers are aware of many overt manifestations of these processes, such as students' self-awareness of the quality of their work and preparedness in class (Zimmerman & Martinez-Pons, 1988). Recent research shows that self-regulatory processes are teachable and can lead to increases in students' motivation and achievement (Schunk & Zimmerman, 1998).

Although research findings strongly support the importance of students' use of self-regulatory processes, few teachers effectively prepare students to learn on their own (Zimmerman, Bonner, & Kovach, 1996). Students are seldom given choices regarding academic tasks to pursue, methods for carrying out complex assignments, or study partners. Few teachers encourage students to establish specific goals for their academic work or teach explicit study strategies. Also, students are rarely asked to self-evaluate their work or estimate their competence on new tasks. Teachers seldom assess students' beliefs about learning, such as self-efficacy perceptions or causal attributions, in order to identify cognitive or motivational difficulties before they become problematic.

Contrary to a commonly held belief, self-regulated learning is not asocial in nature and origin. Each self-regulatory process or belief, such as goal setting, strategy use, and self-evaluation, can be learned from instruction and modeling by parents, teachers, coaches, and peers. In fact, self-regulated students seek out help from others to improve their learning. What defines them as "self-regulated" is not their reliance on socially isolated methods of learning, but rather their personal initiative, perseverance, and adoptive skill. Self-regulated students focus on how they activate, alter, and sustain specific learning practices in social as well as solitary contexts. In an era when these essential qualities for lifelong learning are distressingly absent in many students, teaching self-regulated learning processes is especially relevant.

References

ASCD Yearbook. (1962). *Perceiving behaving becoming.* Washington DC: Association for Supervision and Curriculum Development.

Bandura, A. (1997). *Self-efficacy: The exercise of control.* New York: W. H. Freeman.

Bandura, A., & Schunk, D. H. (1981). Cultivating competence, self-efficacy, and intrinsic interest through proximal self-motivation. *Journal of Personality and Social Psychology, 41*, 586–598.

Cleary, T., & Zimmerman, B. J. (2000). Self-regulation differences during athletic practice by experts, nonexperts, and novices. *Journal of Applied Sport Psychology, 13*, 61–82.

Cronbach, L. J. (1957). The two disciplines of scientific psychology. *American Psychologist, 12*, 671–684.

Ericsson, A. K., & Charness, N. (1994). Expert performance: Its structure and acquisition. *American Psychologist, 49*, 725–747.

McPherson, G. E., & Zimmerman, B. J. (in press). Self-regulation of musical learning: A social cognitive perspective. In R. Colwell (Ed.), *Second handbook on music teaching and learning.* New York: Oxford University Press.

Schunk, D. H. (1983). Progress self-monitoring: Effects on children's self-efficacy and achievement. *Journal of Experimental Education, 51*, 89–93.

Schunk, D. H. (1989). Social cognitive theory and self-regulated learning. In B. J. Zimmerman & D. H. Schunk (Eds.), *Self-regulated learning and academic achievement: Theory, research, and practice* (pp. 83–110). New York: Springer-Verlag.

Schunk, D. H. (2001). Social cognitive theory and self-regulated learning. In B. J. Zimmerman & D. H. Schunk (Eds.), *Self-regulated learning and academic achievement: Theoretical perspectives* (2nd ed., pp. 125–152). Mahwah, NJ: Lawrence Erlbaum.

Schunk, D. H., & Zimmerman, B. J. (Eds.). (1994). *Self-regulation of learning and performance: Issues and educational applications.* Hillsdale, NJ: Lawrence Erlbaum.

Schunk, D. H., & Zimmerman, B. J. (Eds.). (1998). *Self-regulated learning: From teaching to self-reflective practice.* New York: Guilford Press.

Shapiro, E. S. (1984). Self-monitoring procedures. In T. H. Ollendick & M. Hersen (Eds.), *Child behavior assessment: Principles and procedures* (pp. 148–165). New York: Pergamon.

Zimmerman, B. J. (1989). A social cognitive view of self-regulated academic learning. *Journal of Educational Psychology, 81*, 329–339.

Zimmerman, B. J. (2000). Attainment of self-regulation: A social cognitive perspective. In M. Boekaerts, P. R. Pintrich, & M. Zeidner (Eds.), *Handbook of self-regulation* (pp. 13–39). San Diego, CA: Academic Press.

Zimmerman, B. J. (2001). Theories of self-regulated learning and academic achievement: An overview and analysis. In B. J. Zimmerman & D. H. Schunk (Eds.), *Self-regulated learning and academic achievement: Theoretical perspectives* (2nd ed., pp. 1–37). Mahwah, NJ: Lawrence Erlbaum.

Zimmerman, B. J., & Bandura, A. (1994). Impact of self-regulatory influences on writing course attainment. *American Educational Research Journal, 31*, 845–862.

Zimmerman, B. J., Bonner, S., & Kovach, R. (1996). *Developing self-regulated learners: Beyond achievement to self-efficacy.* Washington, DC: American Psychological Association.

Zimmerman, B. J., & Campillo, M. (in press). Motivating self-regulated problem solvers. In J. E. Davidson & R. Sternberg (Eds.), *The nature of problem solving.* New York: Cambridge University Press.

Zimmerman, B. J., & Kitsantas, A. (1997). Developmental phases in self-regulation: Shifting from process to outcome goals. *Journal of Educational Psychology, 89*, 29–36.

Zimmerman, B. J., & Kitsantas, A. (1999). Acquiring writing revision skill: Shifting from process to outcome self-regulatory goals. *Journal of Educational Psychology, 91*, 1–10.

Zimmerman, B. J., & Martinez-Pons, M. (1986). Development of a structured interview for assessing students' use of self-regulated learning strategies. *American Educational Research Journal, 23*, 614–628.

Zimmerman, B. J., & Martinez-Pons, M. (1988). Construct validation of a strategy model of student self-regulated learning. *Journal of Educational Psychology, 80*, 284–290.

Zimmerman, B. J., & Risemberg, R. (1997). Becoming a self-regulated writer: A social cognitive perspective. *Contemporary Educational Psychology, 22*, 73–101.

Zimmerman, B. J., & Schunk, D. H. (Eds.). (2001). *Self-regulated learning and academic achievement: Theoretical perspectives* (2nd ed.). Mahwah, NJ: Lawrence Erlbaum.

Additional Readings

Horne, W. R. (2000). How students spend their time. *The Learning Assistance Review, 5*(2), 22–33.

Kachgal, M. M., Hansen, L. S., & Nutter, K. J. (Fall 2001). Academic procrastination prevention/intervention: Strategies and recommendations. *Journal of Developmental Education, 25*(1), 14–24.

Mar, M. (1999). The role of a developmental framework in teaching learning strategies. *Journal of College Reading and Learning, 29*(2), 136–148.

Moore, R. (2006). Do high school behaviors set up developmental education students for failure? *The Learning Assistance Review, 11*(2), 19–32.

Moore, R., & Jensen, M. (2005). What factors predict the academic success of developmental education students? *The Learning Assistance Review, 10*(1), 25–40.

Nelson, R. (1998). Using a student performance framework to analyze success and failure. *Journal of College Reading and Learning, 29*(1), 82–89.

Newman, R. S. (2002). How self-regulated learners cope with academic difficulty: The role of adaptive help seeking. *Theory into Practice, 41*(2), 132–142.

Peverly, S. T., Graham, M., Shaw, R., & Brobst, K. E. (2003). College adults are not good at self-regulation: A study on the relationship of self-regulation, note taking, and test taking. *Journal of Educational Psychology, 95*, 335–346.

Van Blerkom, D. L., Van Blerkom, M. L., & Bertsch, S. (2006). Study strategies and generative learning: What works? *Journal of College Reading and Learning, 37*(1), 7–18.

Yaworski, J., Weber, R., & Ibrahim, N. (2000). What makes students succeed or fail? The voices of developmental college students. *Journal of College Reading and Learning, 30*(2), 195–221.

Young, D., & Ley, K. (2005). Developmental college student self-regulation: Results from two measures. *Journal of College Reading and Learning, 36*(1), 60–80.

5

Theory, Research, and Best Practices

Although articles detailing a particular theory may not be as compelling as articles written by practitioners who share a lesson or activity, it is important to remember that everything we do in our classroom emanates from the paradigms we adhere to regarding teaching and learning. Theory provides us with the underpinnings and rationales for all our actions, whether making a decision about our assessment procedures, selecting programs, assigning texts, leading classroom activities, or collecting evaluation data. These theories, of course, also ensure that our programs are coherent rather than fragmented.

Fortunately, the cognitive revolution in the second half of the twentieth century has provided reading professionals with substantive theories about strategic learning that seem tailor-made for college students. Although these theories may have differing names (e.g., self-regulation, strategic learning), there is agreement among all of them on the importance of teaching students a variety of essential cognitive and metacognitive processes. These theories, in turn, have provided the framework for many of the studies conducted during the past 30 years. These theory-based studies have investigated the efficacy of programs and approaches used with college students enrolled in required or elective reading courses. The ultimate goal of these studies is to translate and describe for the practitioner what is pedagogically sound and useful. Many developmental educators have aptly labeled these pedagogically sound ideas as "best practices."

Of course, that is the ideal relationship between theory, research, and best practices. Although many studies and articles have slighted or circumvented this ideal, the articles in this chapter have not, and that is why they were chosen for inclusion. The chapter begins with an article by Paul R. Pintrich, who focuses on metacognitive awareness, one important aspect of self-regulated learning. Pintrich defines three types of metacognition and then outlines the implications for learning, teaching, and assessing. Taking a slightly different perspective, Myron H. Dembo and Keith Howard debunk many of the myths concerning learning styles and the importance of matching instruction to a student's modality preference. In their article they examine whether learning style instruments are valid and reliable and whether students actually benefit from such instruction. Melinda S. Burchard and Peter Swerdzewski describe a study they conducted on a learning strategy course designed for college students with learning disabilities. The students enrolled in their theory-based course learned a variety of strategies and completed a pre- and posttest instrument focusing on metacognition. Using a model of self-regulated learning, Michele L. Simpson and Leslie Rush investigate the impact of teaching students strategies in SI-type courses attached to biology, history, and chemistry. In addition to collecting data on the students' final course grades, Simpson and Rush examine whether students changed in terms of their epistemological beliefs and strategy employment and whether they applied the strategies to other academic disciplines. In "The Effectiveness of Strategic Reading Instruction for College Developmental Readers," David C. Caverly, Sheila A. Nicholson, and Richard Radcliffe consider the short- and long-term effects of teaching college students a research-based heuristic titled PLAN. Among other findings, the authors determine that the combination of PLAN with instruction in metacognition assisted students in strategy transfer. In his comprehensive article, Kenneth A. Kiewra focuses on techniques that will assist students in mastering lecture material. He explains his theory-based heuristic titled NORM, outlines teaching suggestions, and reviews research on a variety of issues related to note-taking (e.g., the use of skeletal notes, lecture cues, matrices). In the final article, Russ Hodges, De Sellers, and Carol W. Dochen trace the evolution of a traditional study skills course to a learning framework course that integrates theory, research, and best practice. In addition to providing a useful matrix summarizing possible delivery models, the authors detail the four components of their learning framework model and share research studies that have examined the effects of such a model on students' academic performance and retention.

The Role of Metacognitive Knowledge in Learning, Teaching, and Assessing

Paul R. Pintrich

Of the four knowledge categories — factual, conceptual, procedural, and metacognitive — the latter one is perhaps the most important to study-strategy instructors and college students. That is, if students are not meta-cognitively aware, they probably will not succeed in college. In this article Pintrich defines metacognition and explains the three types of metacognitive knowledge: strategic, knowledge about cognitive tasks, and self-knowledge. He then discusses the implications of metacognitive knowledge for students' learning and for teachers' methods of instruction and assessment. Pintrich builds a strong case for the importance of explicit and embedded strategy instruction and for informal and ongoing assessment of students that he labels "assessment conversations."

As Krathwohl . . . states, the revised Taxonomy contains four general knowledge categories: Factual, Conceptual, Procedural, and Metacognitive. While the first three categories were included in the original Taxonomy, the Metacognitive Knowledge category was added. The purpose of this article is to discuss the Metacognitive Knowledge category and its implications for learning, teaching, and assessing in the classroom.

Metacognitive knowledge involves knowledge about cognition in general, as well as awareness of and knowledge about one's own cognition. One of the hallmarks of psychological and educational theory and research on learning since the original Taxonomy was published is the emphasis on helping students become more knowledgeable of and responsible for their own cognition and thinking. This change cuts across all the different theoretical approaches to learning and development — from neo-Piagetian models, to cognitive science and information processing models, to Vygotskian and cultural or situated learning models. Regardless of their theoretical perspective, researchers agree that with development students become more aware of their own thinking as well as more knowledgeable about cognition in general. Furthermore, as they act on this awareness they tend to learn better (Bransford, Brown, & Cocking, 1999). The labels for this general developmental trend vary from theory to theory, but they include the development of metacognitive knowledge, metacognitive awareness, self-awareness, self-reflection, and self-regulation.

Although there are many definitions and models of metacognition, an important distinction is one between (a) knowledge of cognition and (b) the processes involving the monitoring, control, and regulation of cognition (e.g., Bransford et al., 1999; Brown, Bransford, Ferrara, &

Campione, 1983; Flavell, 1979; Paris & Winograd, 1990; Pintrich, Wolters, & Baxter, 2000; Schneider & Pressley, 1997). This basic distinction between metacognitive knowledge and metacognitive control or self-regulatory processes parallels the two dimensions in our Taxonomy Table.

Metacognitive knowledge includes knowledge of general strategies that might be used for different tasks, knowledge of the conditions under which these strategies might be used, knowledge of the extent to which the strategies are effective, and knowledge of self (Flavell, 1979; Pintrich et al., 2000; Schneider & Pressley, 1997). For example, learners can know about different strategies for reading a textbook as well as strategies to monitor and check their comprehension as they read. Learners also activate relevant knowledge about their own strengths and weaknesses pertaining to the task as well as their motivation for completing the task. Suppose learners realize they already know a fair amount about the topic of a chapter in a textbook (which they may perceive as a strength), and that they are interested in this topic (which may enhance their motivation). This realization could lead them to change their approach to the task, such as adjusting their reading approach or rate. Finally, learners also can activate the relevant situational or conditional knowledge for solving a problem in a certain context (e.g., in this classroom; on this type of test; in this type of real-life situation, etc.). They may know, for example, that multiple-choice tests require only recognition of the correct answers, not actual recall of the information, as required in essay tests. This type of metacognitive knowledge might influence how they subsequently prepare for an examination.

In contrast, metacognitive control and self-regulatory processes are cognitive processes that learners use to monitor, control, and regulate their cognition and learning. As such, they fit under the six cognitive process categories and specific cognitive processes in the revised Taxonomy. The metacognitive and self-regulatory processes are well represented in tasks such as checking, planning, and generating. Accordingly, on the Knowledge dimension, Metacognitive Knowledge categories refer only to knowledge of cognitive strategies, not the actual use of those strategies.

Three Types of Metacognitive Knowledge

In Flavell's (1979) classic article on metacognition, he suggested that metacognition included knowledge of strategy, task, and person variables. We represented this general framework in our categories by including students' knowledge of general strategies for learning and thinking (Da — Strategic knowledge) and their knowledge of cognitive tasks as well as when and why to use these different strategies (Db — Knowledge about cognitive tasks, including appropriate contextual and conditional knowledge). Finally, we included knowledge about the self (the person variable) in relation to both cognitive and motivational components of performance (Dc — Self-knowledge).

Strategic Knowledge

Strategic knowledge is knowledge of general strategies for learning, thinking, and problem solving. These strategies are applicable across all or most academic disciplines or subject matter domains in contrast to more specific strategies from the disciplines or domains. Consequently, these strategies can be used across a large number of different tasks and domains, rather than being most useful for one particular type of task in one specific subject area (e.g., solving a quadratic equation in mathematics, applying Ohm's law in science).

Strategic knowledge includes knowledge of the various strategies students might use to memorize material, to extract meaning from text, and to comprehend what they hear in classrooms or what they read in books and other course materials. Although there are a large number of different learning strategies, they can be grouped into three general categories: rehearsal, elaboration, and organizational (Weinstein & Mayer, 1986). Rehearsal strategies refer to the strategy of repeating words or terms to be remembered over and over to oneself, generally not the most effective strategy for learning more complex cognitive processes. In contrast, elaboration strategies include various mnemonics for memory tasks, as well strategies such as summarizing, paraphrasing, and selecting main ideas from texts. These elaboration strategies result in deeper processing of the material to be learned and result in better comprehension and learning than do rehearsal strategies. Finally, organizational strategies include various forms of outlining, concept mapping, and note taking, where the student makes connections between and among content elements. Like elaboration strategies, these organizational strategies usually result in better comprehension and learning than rehearsal strategies.

In addition to these general learning strategies, students can have knowledge of various metacognitive strategies that will be useful to them in planning, monitoring, and regulating their learning and thinking. These strategies include ways individuals plan their cognition (e.g., set subgoals), monitor their cognition (e.g., ask themselves questions as they read a piece of text; check their answer to a math problem), and regulate their cognition (e.g., reread something they don't understand; go back and "repair" their calculating mistake in a math problem). Again, in this category we refer to students' knowledge of these various strategies, not their actual use.

Finally, there are a number of general strategies for problem solving and thinking. These strategies represent the various heuristics individuals can use to solve problems, particularly ill-defined problems where there is no definitive algorithmic solution. In the problem-solving area they can include the knowledge of means-ends analysis as well as knowledge of working backward from the desired goal state. In terms of thinking, there are a number of general strategies for deductive and inductive thinking, such as evaluating the validity of different logical statements, avoiding circularity in arguments, making appropriate inferences from different sources of data, and drawing on appropriate samples to make inferences.

Knowledge about Cognitive Tasks

In addition to knowledge about various strategies, individuals also accumulate knowledge about different cognitive tasks. Knowledge of tasks includes knowledge that different tasks can be more or less difficult and may require different cognitive strategies. A recall task is more difficult than a recognition task, for example, because in the recall task, the individual must actively search memory and retrieve the relevant information; while in the recognition task, the emphasis is on discriminating among alternatives and selecting the appropriate answer.

As students develop their knowledge of different learning and thinking strategies and their use, this knowledge reflects the "what" and "how" of the different strategies. However, this knowledge may not be enough for expertise in learning. Students also must develop some knowledge about the "when" and "why" of using these strategies appropriately (Paris, Lipson, & Wixson, 1983). Because not all strategies are appropriate for all situations, the learner must develop some knowledge of the different conditions and tasks where the different strategies are used most appropriately.

If one thinks of strategies as cognitive "tools" that help learners construct their understanding, then just as the carpenter uses a variety of different tools for all the tasks that go into building a house, the learner must use different tools for different cognitive tasks. Of course one tool, such as a hammer, can be used in different ways for different tasks, but this is not necessarily the most adaptive use of the hammer — particularly if there are other tools that are better suited to the task. In the same way, specific learning and thinking strategies are better suited to different tasks. For example, if one confronts a novel problem that is ill-defined, then general problem-solving heuristics may be very useful. In contrast, if one confronts a physics problem regarding the second law of thermodynamics, more specific procedural knowledge, not general metacognitive knowledge, will be much more useful and adaptive for this task. An important aspect of learning about strategies is the knowledge of when and why to use them appropriately.

Another important aspect of conditional knowledge concerns the local situational and general social, conventional, and cultural norms for the use of different strategies. For example, a teacher may encourage the use of certain strategies for reading. A student who knows the teacher's strategic preferences is better able to adapt to the demands of this teacher's classroom. In the same manner, different cultures may have norms for the use of different strategies and ways of thinking about problems. Again, knowing these norms can help students adapt to the demands of the culture in terms of solving the problem.

Self-Knowledge

Along with knowledge of different strategies and knowledge of cognitive tasks, Flavell (1979) proposed that self-knowledge was an important component of metacognition. Self-knowledge includes knowledge of one's strengths and weaknesses. For example, a student who knows that he or she generally does better on multiple-choice tests than on essay tests has some metacognitive self-knowledge about his or her test-taking ability. This knowledge may be useful to the student as he or she studies for the two different types of tests. One of the hallmarks of experts is that they know when they don't know something and have to rely on some general strategies for finding the appropriate information. This self-awareness of the breadth and depth of one's own knowledge base is an important aspect of self-knowledge. Finally, individuals need to be aware of the different types of strategies they are likely to rely on in different situations. An awareness that one overrelies on a particular strategy when there may be other more adaptive strategies for the task could lead to the possibility of a change in strategy use.

In addition to general self-knowledge, individuals also have beliefs about their motivation. These include judgments of their capability to perform a task (self-efficacy), their goals for completing a task (learning or just getting a good grade), and the interest and value the task has for them (high interest and high value versus low interest and low value). Although these motivational beliefs are usually not considered in cognitive models, there is a fairly substantial body of literature emerging that shows important links between students' motivational beliefs and their cognition and learning (Pintrich & Schrauben, 1992; Pintrich & Schunk, 2002; Snow, Corno, & Jackson, 1996). It seems important that just as students need to develop self-knowledge and self-awareness about their knowledge and cognition, they also need to develop self-knowledge and self-awareness about their motivation.

Although self-knowledge itself can be an important aspect of metacognitive knowledge, it is important to underscore the idea that *accuracy* of self-knowledge seems to be most crucial for learning. That is, we are not advocating that teachers try to boost students' self-esteem (a completely different construct from self-knowledge) by providing students with positive, but false, inaccurate, and misleading feedback about their strengths and weaknesses. It is much more important to have accurate perceptions and judgments of one's knowledge base and expertise than to have inflated and inaccurate self-knowledge (Pintrich & Schunk, 2002). If students do not realize they do not know some aspect of factual, conceptual, or procedural knowledge, it is unlikely they will make any effort to acquire or construct new knowledge. Accordingly, we stress the need for teachers to help students make accurate assessments of their self-knowledge, not inflate their self-esteem.

Implications for Learning, Teaching, and Assessing

Metacognitive knowledge can play an important role in student learning and, by implication, in the ways students are taught and assessed in the classroom (Bransford et al., 1999). First, as previously noted, metacognitive knowledge of strategies and tasks, as well as self-knowledge, is linked to how students will learn and perform in the classroom. Students who know about the different kinds of strategies for learning, thinking, and problem solving will be more likely to use them. After all, if students do not know of a strategy, they will not be able to use it. Students who do know about different strategies for memory tasks, for example, are more likely to use them to recall relevant information. Similarly, students who know about different learning strategies are more likely to use them when studying. And, students who know about general strategies for thinking and problem solving are more likely to use them when confronting different classroom tasks (Bransford et al., 1999; Schneider & Pressley, 1997; Weinstein & Mayer, 1986). Metacognitive knowledge of all these different strategies enables students to perform better and learn more.

In addition, metacognitive knowledge of all these different strategies seems to be related to the transfer of learning; that is, the ability to use knowledge gained in one setting or situation in another (Bransford et al., 1999). Students are often confronted with new tasks that require knowledge and skills they have not yet learned. In this case, they cannot rely solely on their specific prior knowledge or skills to help them on the new task. When experts find themselves in this situation, they are likely to use more general strategies to help them think about or solve the problem. In the same manner, students, who by definition lack expertise in many areas, need to know about different general strategies for learning and thinking in order to use general strategies for new or challenging tasks.

Finally, in terms of learning, self-knowledge can be either an important facilitator or a constraint. Students who know their own strengths and weaknesses can adjust their own cognition and thinking to be more adaptive to diverse tasks and, thus, facilitate learning. If, for example, a student realizes that she does not know very much about a particular topic, she might pay more attention to the topic while reading and use different strategies to make sure she understands the topic being studied. In the same manner, if a student is aware that she has difficulties on certain tests (e.g., mathematics versus history tests), then she can prepare for an upcoming mathematics test in an appropriate manner. Students who lack knowledge of their own strengths and weaknesses will be less likely to adapt to different situations and regulate their own learning in them. For example, if a student reads a text and thinks he understands it, but in reality does not, then he will be less likely to go back and reread or review the text to make sure it is understood. Similarly, a student who believes he understands the material thoroughly will not study for an upcoming test to the same extent as a student who knows he does not understand the material. A student who believes he understands the material when he does not will not do well on the test of that material because he did not study as well as the student who had an accurate perception of his lack of knowledge. Accordingly, lack of self-knowledge can be a constraint on learning.

There are several implications of the relationships among metacognitive knowledge, learning, teaching, and assessing. In terms of instruction, there is a need to teach for metacognitive knowledge *explicitly*. Teachers may do this in some lessons, but in many cases the instruction is more *implicit*. Simply stated, many teachers assume that some students will be able to acquire metacognitive knowledge on their own, while others lack the ability to do so. Of course, some students do acquire metacognitive knowledge through experience and with age, but many more students fail to do so. In our work with college students (see Hofer, Yu, & Pintrich, 1998; Pintrich, McKeachie, & Lin, 1987), we are continually surprised at the number of students who come to college having very little metacognitive knowledge; knowledge about different strategies, different cognitive tasks, and, particularly, accurate knowledge about themselves. Given the fact that students who go on to college are more likely to be better students in general suggests that there is a need to explicitly teach metacognitive knowledge in K–12 settings.

Having said this, it is not our expectation that teachers would teach for metacognitive knowledge in separate courses or separate units, although this can certainly be done (see Hofer et al., 1998; Pintrich et al., 1987). It is more important that metacognitive knowledge is embedded within the usual content-driven lessons in different subject areas. General strategies for thinking and problem solving can be taught in the context of English, mathematics, science, social studies, art, music, and physical education courses. Science teachers, for example, can teach general scientific methods and procedures, but learning will likely be more effective when it is tied to specific science content, not taught in the abstract. Of course, in some skill areas, such as reading or writing, the teaching of metacognitive knowledge about different general strategies for reading comprehension or writing is both acceptable and desirable.

The key is that teachers plan to include some goals for teaching metacognitive knowledge in their regular unit planning, and then actually try to teach and assess for the use of this type of knowledge as they teach other content knowledge. One of the most important aspects of teaching for metacognitive knowledge is the explicit labeling of it for students. For example, during a lesson, the teacher can note occasions when metacognitive knowledge comes up, such as in a reading group discussion of the different strategies students use to read a section of a story. This explicit labeling and discussion helps students connect the strategies (and their names/labels) to other knowledge they may already have about strategies and reading. In addition, making the discussion of metacognitive knowledge part of the everyday discourse of the classroom helps foster a language for students to talk about their own cognition and learning. The shared language and discourse about cognition and learning among peers and between students and teacher helps students become more aware of their own metacognitive knowledge as well as their own strategies for learning and thinking. As they hear and see how their classmates approach a task, they can compare their own strategies with their classmates' and make judgments about the relative utility of different strategies. This type of discourse and discussion helps makes cognition and learning more explicit and less opaque to students, rather than being something that happens mysteriously or that some students "get" and learn and others struggle and don't learn.

In addition to the development of a classroom discourse around metacognitive knowledge, another important instructional strategy is the modeling of strategies, accompanied by an explanation of them. For example, as the teacher is solving a problem for the class, he might talk aloud about his own cognitive processes as he works through the problem. This provides a model for students, showing them how they use strategies in solving real problems. In addition, the teacher also might discuss why he is using this particular strategy for this specific problem, thereby also engaging students in issues concerning the conditional knowledge that governs when and why to use different strategies. As experts in their field, teachers have all kinds of implicit knowledge about strategies and when and why they are appropriate to use; however, students often lack the means to gain access to this knowledge. If the knowledge is never shared through discussion, modeling, or explicit instruction, it is difficult for students to learn.

In terms of implications for assessment, the inclusion of metacognitive knowledge in the revised Taxonomy is not meant to generate the development of separate sections of standardized or formal classroom tests on metacognitive knowledge. Metacognitive knowledge is important in terms of how it is used by students to facilitate their own learning. In this sense, it is more likely that any assessment of metacognitive knowledge by teachers will be informal rather than formal. For example, if teachers are teaching and discussing metacognitive knowledge as part of their normal classroom discourse, they will need to talk to their students about metacognitive knowledge and, perhaps more important, actually listen to the students as they talk about their own cognition and learning. As a result of these conversations, teachers will become aware of the general level of metacognitive knowledge in their classrooms and will be able to judge fairly quickly the level and depth of students' metacognitive knowledge. In many respects, this is no different from what teachers do to assess the level of content knowledge their students bring to their classrooms. They start a discussion, ask some questions, listen to the answers, and talk with the students. Based on this discourse, they can quickly estimate the depth of students' prior knowledge. This type of informal assessment can be used to calibrate the instruction to help students gain both content knowledge (whether it be factual, conceptual, or procedural) and metacognitive knowledge.

From these informal "assessment conversations," teachers also may be able to make inferences about the level of metacognitive knowledge of individual students. Just as there is variance in the content knowledge that students bring to the classroom, it is likely there will be a wide distribution of metacognitive knowledge in a class of 20 to 30 students. This information about individual students can be used to adapt instruction to individual differences. Teachers can talk to students individually or in small groups to estimate levels of metacognitive knowledge. Finally, more formal questionnaires and interview procedures can be used to assess students' metacognitive knowledge concerning their learning strategies as well as their knowledge about different tasks and contexts (see Baker & Cerro, 2000; Pintrich et al., 2000).

As mentioned previously, an important component of metacognitive knowledge is self-knowledge. In terms of assessment, a focus on self-knowledge implies that students should have the opportunity to assess their own strengths and weaknesses. Although this will occasionally happen in larger, public groups, it is important for motivational reasons that self-assessment is more private, occurring between one teacher and one student (see Pintrich & Schunk, 2002). In this way, students are able to meet individually with their teachers to discuss their perceptions of their own strengths and weaknesses, and teachers can provide them with feedback about these perceptions. Portfolio assessment sometimes offers students the opportunity to reflect on their work as represented in the portfolio and this certainly provides self-assessment information to them. As students have more opportunities to reflect on their own learning, they will develop more self-knowledge that can be helpful to them.

Conclusion

In summary, metacognitive knowledge is a new category of knowledge in the revised Taxonomy. However, given its important role in learning, it is a welcome and much-needed addition. Although there are different kinds of metacognitive knowledge, three general types are of particular importance. Strategic knowledge refers to knowledge of strategies for learning and thinking. Knowledge of tasks and their contexts represents knowledge about different types of cognitive tasks as well as classroom and cultural norms. Finally, self-knowledge is a critically important component of metacognitive knowledge. Because metacognitive knowledge in general is positively linked to student learning, explicitly teaching metacognitive knowledge to facilitate its development is needed. As the revised Taxonomy emphasizes, the need to align objectives, instruction, and assessment requires us to consider the role that metacognitive knowledge plays in the classroom.

References

Baker, L., & Cerro, L. (2000). Assessing metacognition in children and adults. In G. Schraw & J. Impara (Eds.), *Issues in the measurement of metacognition* (pp. 99–145). Lincoln, NE: Buros Institute of Mental Measurements.

Bransford, J., Brown, A., & Cocking, R. (1999). *How people learn: Brain, mind, experience, and school.* Washington, DC: National Academy Press.

Brown, A., Bransford, J., Ferrara, R., & Campione, J. (1983). Learning, remembering, and understanding. In P. H. Mussen (Series Ed.) & J. Flavell & E. Markman (Vol. Eds.), *Handbook of child psychology: Vol. 3. Cognitive development* (4th ed., pp. 77–166). New York: John Wiley & Sons.

Flavell, J. (1979). Metacognition and cognitive monitoring: A new area of cognitive-developmental inquiry. *American Psychologist, 34,* 906–911.

Hofer, B., Yu, S., & Pintrich, P. R. (1998). Teaching college students to be self-regulating learners. In D. H. Schunk & B. J. Zimmerman (Eds.), *Self-regulated learning: From teaching to self-reflective practice* (pp. 57–85). New York: Guilford Press.

Paris, S., Lipson, M., & Wixson, K. (1983). Becoming a strategic reader. *Contemporary Educational Psychology, 8,* 293–316.

Paris, S., & Winograd, P. (1990). How metacognition can promote academic learning and instruction. In B. F. Jones & L. Idol (Eds.), *Dimensions of thinking and cognitive instruction* (pp. 15–51). Hillsdale, NJ: Lawrence Erlbaum.

Pintrich, P. R., McKeachie, W. J., & Lin, Y. (1987). Teaching a course in learning to learn. *Teaching of Psychology, 14,* 81–86.

Pintrich, P. R., & Schrauben, B. (1992). Students' motivational beliefs and their cognitive engagement in classroom tasks. In D. Schunk & J. Meece (Eds.), *Student perceptions in the classroom: Causes and consequences* (pp. 149–183). Hillsdale, NJ: Lawrence Erlbaum.

Pintrich, P. R., & Schunk, D. H. (2002). *Motivation in education: Theory, research, and applications.* Upper Saddle River, NJ: Merrill Prentice-Hall.

Pintrich, P. R., Wolters, C., & Baxter, G. (2000). Assessing metacognition and self-regulated learning. In G. Schraw & J. Impara (Eds.), *Issues in the mea-*

surement of metacognition (pp. 43–97). Lincoln, NE: Buros Institute of Mental Measurements.

Schneider, W., & Pressley, M. (1997). *Memory development between two and twenty.* Mahwah, NJ: Lawrence Erlbaum.

Snow, R., Corno, L., & Jackson, D. (1996). Individual differences in affective and cognitive functions. In D. Berliner & R. Calfee (Eds.), *Handbook of Educational Psychology* (pp. 243–310). New York: Macmillan.

Weinstein, C. E., & Mayer, R. (1986). The teaching of learning strategies. In M. C. Wittrock (Ed.), *Handbook of research on teaching* (pp. 315–327). New York: Macmillan.

Advice about the Use of Learning Styles: A Major Myth in Education

Myron H. Dembo and Keith Howard

The use of learning styles has been advocated by many professionals as a way of enhancing students' learning effectiveness, especially if a match is forged between the instructor's teaching style and the student's preferred learning mode. In this article Myron H. Dembo and Keith Howard examine many of the "unsubstantiated claims made by authors of learning style instruments and by instructors" and question the format, reliability, and validity of learning style instruments. They cite numerous research reviews that have challenged the efficacy of learning styles, especially in terms of improving students' concentration, memory, self-confidence, and grades. Rather than rely on learning styles, the authors urge instructors to adopt a "best practices" approach to developmental education.

The authors' idea for this paper stems from John Stossel's (2006) book, *Myths, Lies, and Downright Stupidity.* Stossel is a consumer advocate and *20/20* anchor who has spent his career challenging consumer myths. As we talked about some of the ideas in his book we thought about common educational myths, and learning styles quickly appeared at the top of our list.

Although the use of learning styles has been challenged for years (see Curry, 1990; Doyle & Rutherford, 1984; Gutierrez & Rogoff, 2003; Kampwirth & Bates, 1980; Snider, 1990; Stahl, 1999), it seems as though the issues raised by these papers have had little impact on the continuing use of learning style instruction in education. In fact, there is a whole industry that has developed around learning styles that includes books, tapes, and consultants promoting its use in education.

Our goal in this paper is not to conduct another extensive review of literature in the area, but to initiate a dialogue among educators who continue to make assertions about the usefulness of identifying students' learning styles with little or no research support. We will discuss the status of learning style instruction and the unsubstantiated claims made by authors of learning style instruments and by instructors. Many of our comments are influenced by two recent comprehensive reviews of learning styles (Coffield et al., 2004a, 2004b).

To begin, let's look at the advice given by a sample of authors who have written professional development and study skills textbooks about the use and benefits of learning styles. We only quote a few textbooks, but could have quoted dozens of textbooks. These statements represent the type of advice given by authors about learning styles and, in part, have been adopted by many instructors of study skills courses.

Nolting (2002) states, "Research has shown that students who understand their learning styles can improve their learning effectiveness in and outside of the classroom" (p. 46). Later in his book he also says, "Try to find an instructor who matches your learning style" (p. 57).

Van Blerkom (2006) advises students:

Understanding how you learn best can also improve your concentration. When you're working in your preferred learning mode, you probably find that you are better able to concentrate on your study tasks. Approaching a task from your preferred style results in a better fit or match — studying feels right. (p. 14)

Jenkins (2005) tells students that "If you discover that your learning style and the instructor's model of teaching clash, speak with your instructor about it" (p. 91). He goes further to suggest

If you are a left-brain (linear) learner, become an active listener in class. Lectures tend to provide information in the way that most linear learners prefer. If you are a right brain (global) learner, read any assigned material before attending a lecture or ask your instructors for a summary of what they will discuss in the next class. (p. 96)

Finally, Coman and Heavers (1998) make numerous claims about the benefits of learning style instruction:

If you approach studies using your preferred learning style(s), you should be able to study for the same amount of time (or less), remember more, get better grades, raise your level of self-confidence, and reduce your anxiety as you tackle classroom life. (p. 9)

Based on the advice of such authors, instructors typically either use learning style instruments identified in the literature or sometimes develop their own instruments for students to assess their learning styles. This latter practice is especially used in identifying modality preferences related to visual, auditory, or kinesthetic learners (e.g.,

Coman & Heavers, 1998; Jenkins, 2005). For example, Sprenger (2003) tells her readers that students have a preference for a dominant sensory pathway and "...*always* learn best if they begin with that strength" (p. 33).

Based on the advice given by these writers, a number of key questions need to be explored:

1. Are learning style instruments valid and reliable?

2. Do students benefit when the type of instruction matches their preferred learning style?

3. More specifically, is there evidence that understanding one's learning style improves concentration, memory, self-confidence, and reduces anxiety, and leads to better grades?

Unsubstantiated Claims

Having alluded to the far-reaching claims that many textbooks attribute to the use of learning styles, we now turn a critical eye to the foundation upon which such claims are built. Any usefulness that might be derived from applying learning styles must be substantiated by valid and reliable instruments, as well as by evidence that, when used as prescribed, learning styles can affect learning outcomes.

Validity

Before tackling the question of whether or not instruments used to measure learning styles have validity, one must recognize that there are several dimensions to "validity" that researchers and statisticians concern themselves with. At the surface level, researchers are concerned with whether a test appears to be measuring what it purports to measure. Referred to as "face validity," this is an assessment based on a common-sense judgment of what appears to be valid to an untrained observer, but it is not a technical or statistical assessment. It is this dimension of validity that enables many supporters of learning styles to attract unquestioned acceptance for their respective models because it appeals to the intuitive sense of what "feels right."

However, critics of this blind faith approach argue that there are other dimensions to validity that ought to be considered when assessing whether a particular learning styles instrument is a truly valid evaluator of what it purports to measure. If a learning styles model has construct validity, meaning the instrument measures the construct (e.g., learning style, intelligence, motivation) it purports or claims to measure, it should not be influenced by other unrelated factors. Learning styles instruments are driven by forced-choice questionnaires that attempt to categorize respondents into one style or another. Stahl (1999) criticizes forced-choice learning styles inventories because for some of the questions, "people seem to make the same choices. Nearly everybody would prefer a demonstration in a science class to an uninterrupted lecture. This does not mean that such individuals have a visual style, but that good science teaching involves demonstrations" (p. 3). A choice of demonstration over uninterrupted lecture, on its face, can be interpreted as an indicator of a visual learner. However, if most respondents choose the same answer, then it does not really measure anything in particular except, perhaps, the ability to read the question. Furthermore, the question has little value in discerning possible distinctive characteristics of the learner.

What may be worse than not measuring anything in particular is measuring something completely different from what one intends to measure. Stahl (1999) again cites learning style inventory questions that probe for students' difficulty remembering rules about sounding out words, or whether they mix up letters when attempting to write words. Poor or struggling readers will likely respond in the affirmative for both questions, but this is likely the result of their lack of reading proficiency rather than a learning style. Do these questions probe learning style or reading ability?

Coffield et al. (2004a) identified 71 different models of learning styles. The different theoretical perspectives behind the models result in instruments that attempt to measure different attributes, traits, characteristics, and/or preferences. With so many theoretical perspectives and instruments it becomes nonsensical to try to discuss the construct validity of "learning styles" in general, as construct validity would need to be assessed based on the theory and instrument for each of the models. The question as to whether the measure agrees with its underlying theory is going to be different for each model because each is based on its own theoretical framework.

Reliability

If, given a particular model, one were able to satisfy all questions as to validity, the second major hurdle to determining its usefulness is establishing whether the measurement instrument is reliable — that is, will it consistently produce the same or similar results when reapplied over time? Of the 13 major models subjected to full review by Coffield et al. (2004b), 10 were identified as having problems or questions related to reliability. In addition, the different perspectives as to the fixed or variable nature of the construct used will clearly influence views as to the expected reliability of any instrument devised to measure it. If the theory underpinning a model suggests that the style may change over time and in different situations, one would hardly expect that the instrument used to measure it would produce consistent results when reapplied over time. This reasoning led Coffield and his colleagues to conclude that

> Some of the best known and widely used instruments have such serious weaknesses (e.g., low reliability, poor validity, and negligible impact on pedagogy) that we recommend that their use in research and practice should be discontinued. On the other hand other approaches emerged from our rigorous evaluations with fewer defects and, with certain reservations we suggest that they deserve to be researched further. (p. 55)

Application

The third and perhaps the most important hurdle to establishing the usefulness of learning styles is identifying empirical support for positive pedagogical impact on learning as a result of applying learning styles research. Just how learning styles research should be used to bring about these results is the subject of some debate. Should we attempt to match students' learning styles to pedagogical approaches that are user-friendly to those students? Or should we attempt to make learners more rounded in their ability to learn from an array of methods designed to tap different styles?

The idea of matching styles has a long history of empirical research. One critique of learning styles identified five different reviews on matching learning styles, spanning 14 years and examining over 90 studies (Stahl, 1999), and it failed to find empirical evidence that matching learning styles improves learning. One of those reviews (Arter & Jenkins, 1979) examined 14 studies and concluded that the use of remedial prescriptions based on differential patterns of ability strengths and weaknesses (so called Differential Diagnosis–Prescriptive Teaching) is an approach that cannot be justified, stating that "Children do not appear to profit from current applications of Differential Diagnosis–Prescriptive Teaching" (p. 517). They further stated, ". . . it is not surprising that DD-PT has not improved academic achievement, since most ability assessment devices have inadequate reliability and suspect validity" (p. 549). Coffield et al. (2004a) conclude that the evidence for matching is ". . . equivocal at best, and deeply contradictory at worst" (p. 40). Their view on deliberate mismatching does not offer much promise either, as they write, "deliberate mismatching has the status of an intuitively appealing argument which awaits empirical verification or refutation" (p. 42). With such a long and storied history of different approaches, one would expect that if matching learning styles could produce measurable and consistent improvements in learning we would have ample evidence to this effect. Nevertheless, textbooks and entrenched proponents continue to trumpet the virtues of various forms of learning styles-based approaches, seemingly unconcerned with the unimpressive track record that such approaches possess.

Clark (1982) reported that students often say they enjoy most those methods from which they learn the least, perhaps because they underestimate the amount of effort needed for success. That is, low-ability students prefer more permissive methods of instruction (e.g., independent study or small-group activities) because students can maintain a low profile that makes their failure less visible. However, these students need more direction and attention to achieve success in academic tasks. High-ability students on the other hand, like structured methods (e.g., lecture-recitation sessions), which they believe will help them learn more efficiently. However, the research indicates that students with high ability actually learn more from permissive methods, which allow them more independence in using their abilities.

Although this research is limited to structured and permissive environments and to students with high and low ability, it does suggest that an instructor should consider whether it is always advantageous to match student preferences and instructional environment — not only because the preferences may not lead to improved academic achievement but also because students simply may not benefit from certain instructional approaches whether they like them or not.

Although there does not appear to be much support for matching learning styles with instruction, no one can argue with the fact that instructors need to be more sensitive to the individual differences of students in the classroom and may be more successful if they try different teaching methods with different students. However, teachers must be aware of the danger of incorrectly categorizing any group of students according to a specific learning style.

The bottom line is that there is no consistent evidence that matching instruction to students' learning styles improves concentration, memory, self-confidence, grades, or reduces anxiety. An instructor may argue that he or she has found such studies. The problem is that most of these investigations are poorly designed. Coffield et al. (2004a) state,

> Our review shows that, above all, the research field of learning styles needs independent, critical longitudinal and large-scale studies to test the claims for pedagogy made by the test developers. The investigators need to be independent — that is, without any commitments to a particular approach — so that they can test, for instance, the magnitude of the impact made by the innovation, how long the purported gains last, and employ a research design which controls for the Hawthorne effect. (pp. 62–63)

What is the appeal of learning styles? First, many authors promise instructors a simple solution for solving educational problems related to improving academic achievement, motivation, and attitudes. Second, authors provide a reasonable explanation for why students do not achieve as well as they could. Instructors respond well to examining their own teaching and learning styles, which may lead to greater sensitivity to students whose learning styles are different. Third, a learning style approach focuses more on how students learn or fail to learn, and less on understanding how subject matter should be taught. Finally, for some learning style advocates, there is no special category of students who cannot learn. The problem is simply that instructors have not learned that their teaching styles are not appropriate for a small percentage of students (Coffield et al., 2004a).

In summary, the answers to the three questions at the beginning of this paper indicate that learning style instruments have not been shown to be valid and reliable, there is no benefit to matching instruction to preferred learning style, and there is no evidence that understanding one's learning style improves learning and its related outcomes. This conclusion is based on the lack of well-designed investigations by researchers who are not committed to any particular framework, and replicated in numerous educational settings.

As a result, the assertions made by textbook authors quoted early in the paper are based on fiction and not fact. How can we maintain our professional status by neglecting important research findings regarding learning styles and continue to make unsubstantiated claims about its impact? We urge instructors to reconsider their instructional practices, especially the advice they give students about learning styles, and base their practices on sound research.

If a focus on learning styles doesn't work, what does? Educational research supports the teaching of learning strategies (e.g., Dembo, 2004; Dembo & Junge, 2005; Nist & Hogrebe, 1987; Simpson & Nist, 2000); systematically designed instruction that contains scaffolding features (e.g., Merrill, 2002); and tailoring instruction for different levels of prior knowledge (Clarke et al., 2005; Spires & Donley, 1998; Thompson & Zamboanga, 2004). The *best practices* approach to instruction can help students become more successful learners.

References

Arter, J. A., & Jenkins, J. R. V. (1979). Differential diagnosis-prescriptive teaching: A critical appraisal. *Review of Educational Research, 49*, 517–555.

Clark, R. E. (1982). Antagonism between achievement and enjoyment in ATI studies. *Educational Psychologist, 17*, 92–101.

Clarke, T., Ayres, R, & Sweller, J. (2005). The impact of sequencing and prior knowledge on learning mathematics through spreadsheet applications. *Educational Technology Research and Development, 53*(3), 15–24.

Coffield, F., Moseley, D., Hall, E., & Ecclestone, K. (2004a). *Should we be using learning styles?* Retrieved June 7, 2006, from the London: Learning and Skills Research Centre: http://www.LSRC.ac.uk.

Coffield, F., Moseley, D., Hall, E., & Ecclestone, K. (2004b). *Learning styles and pedagogy in post-16 learning: A systematic and critical review.* Retrieved June 6, 2006, from the London: Learning and Skills Research Centre: http://www.LSRC.ac.uk.

Coman, M. J., & Heavers, K. L. (1998). *How to improve your study skills* (2nd ed.). Lincolnwood, IL: NTC Publishing.

Curry, L. (1990). A critique of research on learning styles. *Educational Leadership, 48*(2), 50–52, 54–56.

Dembo, M. (2004). *Motivation and learning strategies for college success: A self-management approach* (2nd ed.). Mahwah, NJ: Lawrence Erlbaum.

Dembo, M., & Junge, L. G. (2005). Learning strategies. In H. F. O'Neil (Ed.), *What works in distance learning: Guidelines* (pp. 41–63). Greenwich, CT: Information Age Publishing.

Doyle, W., & Rutherford, B. (1984). Classroom research on matching learning and teaching styles. *Theory Into Practice, 23*, 20–25.

Gutierrez, K. D., & Rogoff, B. (2003). Cultural ways of learning: Individual styles or repertoires of practice. *Educational Researcher, 32*, 19–25.

Jenkins, C. (2005). *Skills for success: Developing effective study strategies.* Belmont, CA: Wadsworth/Thompson Learning.

Kampwirth, T. J., & Bates, M. (1980). Modality preference and teaching methods: A review of the research. *Academic Therapy, 15*, 597–605.

Merrill, M. D. (2002). First principles of instruction. *Educational Technology Research and Development, 50*(3), 43–59.

Nist, S., & Hogrebe, M. (1987). The role of underlining and annotating in remembering textual information. *Reading Research and Instruction, 27*(1), 12–25.

Nolting, P. D. (2002). *Winning at math: Your guide to learning mathematics through successful study skills* (4th ed.). Bradenton, FL: Academic Success Press.

Simpson, M., & Nist, S. (2000). An update on strategic learning: It's more than textbook reading strategies. *Journal of Adolescent and Adult Literacy, 43*, 528–542.

Snider, V. (1990). What we know about learning styles for research in special education. *Educational Leadership, 48*(2), 53.

Spires, H. A., & Donley, J. (1998). Prior knowledge activation: Inducing engagement with informational texts. *Journal of Educational Psychology, 90*(2), 249–260.

Sprenger, M. (2003). *Differentiation through learning styles and memory.* Thousand Oaks, CA: Corwin Press.

Stahl, S. A. (1999). Different strokes for different folks? A critique of learning styles. *American Educator, 23*(3), 27–31.

Stossel, J. (2006). *Myths, lies, and downright stupidity.* New York: Hyperion.

Thompson, R. A., & Zamboanga, B. L. (2004). Academic aptitude and prior knowledge as predictors of student achievement in introduction to psychology. *Journal of Educational Psychology, 96*(4), 778–784.

Van Blerkom, D. L. (2006). *College study skills: Becoming a strategic learner* (5th ed.). Boston: Thompson Higher Education.

Learning Effectiveness of a Strategic Learning Course

Melinda S. Burchard and Peter Swerdzewski

Melinda S. Burchard and Peter Swerdzewski investigate the effectiveness of a three-credit strategies course designed for college students with learning disabilities. During their study, the authors were particularly interested in whether the students' metacognition improved and whether those gains were similar to students who participated in the course but were not identified as having learning disabilities. The 78 undergraduates who participated in the study were enrolled in four different sections of the course. They were taught theory-based strategies and participated in a variety of activities and assignments requiring them to apply what they had learned. Using a pretest-to-posttest design, the authors administered the Metacognitive Awareness Inventory (MAI; Schraw & Dennison, 1994) at the beginning and end of the semester. For the students with learning disabilities, the results indicated statistically significant gains that had meaningful effect sizes. These gains were similar to the gains of the students without disabilities.

Educators attempt to empower learners with self-awareness and strategies for areas of need, which consequently lead to learners' increased reliance on strategic approaches to the process of learning. Learning strategies include procedures for note-taking, reading textbooks or articles, organizing thoughts prior to writing, managing time, test-taking and many other skill areas. Learning strategies are not tricks or shortcuts; instead, strategic learning focuses on matching specific approaches, processes, or strategies to the individual's learning needs. Most learning strategies also involve metacognitive processing, which involves intentionally thinking about one's learning strengths or needs and actively applying a strategy to regulate some aspect of one's learning. Educational researchers advocated that postsecondary learners should actively employ individualized strategies that meet the learner's personal learning preferences, strengths, weaknesses, and even disabilities (Davidson & Sternberg, 1998; Gamache, 2002; Hacker, 1998; Minskoff & Allsopp, 2003). Importantly, postsecondary students who approached learning with higher metacognitive awareness or self-regulation showed greater academic performance (Davidson & Sternberg, 1998; Highley, 1995; Ruban, McCoach, McGuire, & Reis, 2003; Schraw & Dennison, 1994; Sungar, 2007; White & Kitchen, 1991; Wolters, 1997). Furthermore, research has consistently provided evidence for the effectiveness of various learning strategies for postsecondary learners, especially in increasing self-regulation (Minskoff, Minskoff, & Allsopp, 2001; Peterson, Lavelle, & Guarino, 2006; Van Blerkom, D. L., Van Blerkom, M. L., & Bertsch, 2006).

The value of learning strategies in improving performance outcomes, such as grades or specific curriculum-based measures, is established by the previous research. Furthermore, existing research demonstrated the connection between learning strategies and metacognition.
This study goes one step further to explore the challenges of creating
effective interventions that increase students' metacognitive self-
awareness and consequently lead to students' successful independent
implementation of learning strategies in their academic careers. Specifically, this study investigates whether a learning strategies course
could improve metacognitive regulation beyond gains made through
typical maturation, with special interest in gains made by students
with disabilities.

Previous Research

The review of the literature discussed below describes studies that
focus both on the importance of learning strategies and the outcomes of
various learning strategy interventions employed at the postsecondary
level. Additionally, the literature that informs the current study deals
with the impact that metacognition has on postsecondary learning.
Further studies investigate the effectiveness of specific learning strategies or strategy programs for postsecondary students with learning
disabilities.

Importance of Learning Strategies

Content knowledge requires mastery of facts and reasoning in a specific field or topic. The process of learning itself reaches beyond content
knowledge to encompass the way a student learns with ever-increasing
effectiveness. The improvement of learning, not just content knowledge, is an important outcome of postsecondary education. Various researchers connected the successful employment of strategic learning
to aspects of metacognitive awareness and/or regulation (Braten &
Stomso, 2005; Carnell, 2007; Dahlin, 1999; Garner, 1990; Hanley, 1995;
Sungar, 2007; Wolters, 1997). For example, a student who was more
aware of his or her learning strengths and weaknesses demonstrated
greater readiness to employ strategies related to these strengths and
weaknesses. Numerous universities such as Louisiana State, Stanford
University, and Muskingum College have implemented programs or
courses to teach learning strategies (Louisiana State, 2006; Muskingum, 2007; Stanford University, 2007). Various data supported implementation of learning strategies to assist in meeting the complex
learning requirements inherent in postsecondary education (Ryan &
Glenn, 2004; White & Kitchens, 1991). Furthermore, freshmen who participated in a learning strategies seminar during their first semester
as opposed to participating in a socialization style seminar or no semi-

nar at all had higher retention rates into their second semester of college (Ryan & Glenn, 2004). Moreover, in the same study, it was found that learning strategies training improved performance measures for freshmen regardless of prior ability. These scholars present a strong body of evidence supportive of learning strategy interventions for post-secondary learners primarily for performance outcomes. Additionally, this body of evidence showed that metacognitive awareness and regulation are connected to learning strategies use.

Outcomes of Implementing Various Learning Strategies Interventions

The successful implementation of learning strategies into one's academic pursuits is predicated on learning and using specific techniques. Some of the key components of successful metacognitive training include modeling, active student participation and self-monitoring (Allsopp, Minskoff, & Bolt, 2005; Deshler & Shumaker, 1986; Swanson, 1989; Trainin & Swanson, 2005; Vogel & Adelman, 1992; Zimmerman, 1989). Furthermore, students who implemented metacognitive processing demonstrated superior knowledge acquisition and stronger self-efficacy (Ford, Smith, Weissbein, Gully, & Salas, 1998).

Previous research implemented a required course for at-risk students focusing primarily upon regulatory strategies with some coverage of motivational theories. A study of this course found intercorrelations among metacognition, student organization and elaboration, but with limited statistical significance (Highley, 1995). Garcia and Pintrich (1991) studied postsecondary learning within one semester and demonstrated relationships between personal and behavior influences, such as motivation and metacognitive characteristics and performance, but there were no interventions in that particular study. Zimmerman, Bandura and Martinez-Pons (1992) investigated causal relationships between various constructs, including self-regulated learning on final grades. That study demonstrated a significant causal link between "self-efficacy for self-regulated learning, efficacy for academic achievement, and academic attainment." In that study, self-regulatory factors accounted for 26% of the variance in performance outcomes.

Development of Metacognition

Metacognition, the act of monitoring and evaluating one's learning, and implementing intentional strategies to regulate learning beneficially impact learning by increasing either effectiveness, efficiency or both (Pintrich, 2002; Schraw & Dennison, 1994). Researchers have differentiated two important aspects of metacognition: the awareness of learning and regulation of metacognition (Pintrich, 2002; Schraw & Dennison, 1994). The *awareness of learning*, also termed metacognitive awareness, includes three components: (a) declarative knowledge: awareness of strengths, weaknesses and resources; (b) procedural knowledge: knowing steps to various strategies; and (c) conditional knowledge: knowing when and why to use those strategies. Metacognitive regulation is comprised of five components: (a) planning; (b) information management, involving how one organizes new information; (c) monitoring, the act of checking for understanding or strategy effectiveness during a learning event; (d) debugging, "fixing" those learning behaviors which are not working; and (e) evaluation, checking for understanding or effectiveness after a learning event (Nietfeld, Cao, & Osborne, 2005; Schraw & Dennison, 1994; Schraw & Moshman, 1995).

Metacognitive strategies include intentional strategic approaches to learning such as monitoring one's attention, reading specific styles of text, taking lecture notes, and thinking critically. Studies show that metacognitive awareness may be an important component in metacognitive regulation. Researchers have shown strong connections between declarative knowledge (such as knowing specific weaknesses in organizing one's writing) and conditional knowledge (such as when and why to use a specific writing strategy) and successful implementation of regulation strategies (Kuhn, Garcia-Mila, Zohar, & Anderson, 1995; Vermunt, 1998). One key finding is that learning strategies or metacognitive training programs are most effective when instructors encourage students to practice the strategies with college course content and reinforce the benefit of this practicing, in part because sufficient practice tends toward the development of new habits (Kuhn et al., 1995; Van Blerkom & Van Blerkom, 2004). Most importantly, students do demonstrate improvements in academic achievement with participation in learning strategies training (Butler, 1995; Minskoff et al., 2001; Tuckman, 2003). Thus, research shows metacognitive learning approaches are beneficial to postsecondary learners for performance outcomes such as specific skills, grades, or retention.

Developing metacognitive awareness may involve student exploration of other contributing factors in learning. A positive relationship has been demonstrated between self-regulation and college students' readiness to change. Consequently, we should expect one student who is already actively seeking a new reading comprehension strategy to demonstrate greater effectiveness in self-regulated reading than a peer who is only just beginning to be aware that he needs a new approach to reading. Thus, students' exploration of their own readiness to change is an important component in programs designed to develop self-regulation (Jakubowski & Dembo, 2004).

Evidence of Strategy Effectiveness for Students
with Learning Disabilities

Importantly, researchers have provided substantial evidence for the connection between successful strategy use and academic success for postsecondary students with learning disabilities (McGuire, Hall, & Litt, 1991; Minskoff et al., 2001; Ruban et al., 2003). McGuire et al. established a hierarchy of transition needs for students with learning disabilities in which study strategies ranked first (including time management, organization and test-taking strategies); specific training in written expression ranked second in need. Swanson (1989) established principles for instruction to promote strategy development. Swanson's work clearly connected high-quality strategy programs to metacognitive aspects such as procedural and conditional knowledge and self-regulatory monitoring. Specifically, college students with learning disabilities who exhibited high strategy use were successful in compensating for their disabilities (Butler, 1995; Minskoff et al., 2001; Trainin & Swanson, 2005). In a study by Barga (1996), students with learning disabilities reported that their colleges did not typically meet their academic support needs, and Barga thus challenged college instructors to develop skills to teach a variety of learning strategies and self-management techniques for a continuum of learners while challenging students to become more self-determined in finding learning supports. Vogel and Adelman (1992) suggested that the learning strategy support programs developed specifically for postsecondary students with learning disabilities may benefit additional populations of students, such as athletes or students from lower socioeconomic backgrounds. With increasing numbers of students with disabilities pursuing postsecondary education, this evidence is compelling for the specific value of learning strategies for the academic success of postsecondary students with disabilities.

Training students in specific learning strategies can positively influence common postsecondary outcomes including retention, students' grades in specific courses, or students' overall GPAs. Metacognitive regulation is an important indicator of postsecondary student learning and contributes to student success. Importantly, researchers have found evidence that training in specific strategies has a positive impact on the development of specific components of metacognitive regulation. The importance of learning strategies to student success is clear, yet the mechanism with which students can effectively learn these strategies is not. For example, one significant gap in the literature is whether course-based training in several specific learning strategies can lead to significant gains in metacognitive regulation. Moreover, it is as yet unknown if the impact of such training differs between populations of students with and without disabilities.

Despite the established relationships between metacognition and various desirable learning outcomes, research demonstrated that explicit training is necessary to influence the metacognition of learners (Allsopp et al., 2005; Nietfeld et al., 2005). A study of postsecondary learning strategies by Allsopp et al. resulted in the establishment of a learning strategies program for students with disabilities. Initially, this program offered one-on-one lessons and accountability by a graduate student trained in learning strategies as a free service to students with learning disabilities or ADHD. In response to increasing demand, a special educator specializing in learning strategies was hired as full-time faculty, offering expanded opportunity for an increasing number of students to participate. This postsecondary learning strategies program then further expanded to offer a strategic learning course open to any student at the university. Sanford (1966) asserted, "There is nothing quite so practical as good theory and nothing so good for theory-making as direct involvement with practice" (p. ix). Heeding this perspective, instructors designing this course integrated educational theory with practical learning strategies. The program upon which the course had been based emphasized primarily regulation, with limited attention to personal awareness and no learning theories instruction to the participants. Thus, integration of learning theory with training in learning strategies was a new approach. While there is correlational evidence connecting metacognition with learning strategies, and evidence of effectiveness of strategies courses, there is limited empirical data in the literature demonstrating that such a course could positively affect the metacognitive skills of targeted populations, particularly students with disabilities. Specifically, this study seeks to determine if postsecondary students with disabilities will benefit from learning strategies instruction in a course format. If so, we furthermore seek to determine how the growth in metacognition experienced by students with learning disabilities compares to the growth experienced by students who are not learning disabled. This study answers the following questions:

1. For students who participate in the course, are posttest scores on the two aspects of metacognition significantly higher than students' pretest scores? In other words, can students' metacognitive awareness and regulation improve through instruction?

2. Do students with disabilities gain similarly on the two aspects of metacognition due to participation in the course, compared to students who participated in the course but did not identify themselves as having disabilities?

3. Do students who complete the strategic learning course score higher on the regulation aspect of metacognition compared to students from the general student population?

4. Are students who self-select to take this course different in metacognitive regulation compared to students from the general student population?

Method

Students and Setting

Students who participate in this course are from a mid-size mid-Atlantic four-year university that offers student-focused services and strong teaching. Nearly 90% of the 17,393 students at the university are undergraduates. The average combined reading and math SAT score of incoming freshmen is 1,140. The four-year graduation rate for undergraduate students is 67%, and 80% graduate within six years. Males comprise 38.5% of the student population. The student population is 83.71% White. A total of 78 undergraduates participated in the Strategic Learning class over the first four semesters. Each semester, an average of 20 students complete the course (see Table 1 on page 258 for details by semester). Most participants were in their freshman or sophomore year and, given the traditional nature of the university, were between 18 and 20 years old (three course participants were non-traditional adult degree seeking students). Sixty-two percent of the course participants were female, and 44% had documented learning disabilities. This course is credit-bearing but voluntary for all participants. Course participants tend to learn about the course through targeted marketing efforts that focus on freshmen advisors, the university's athletic student services office, the university's office for students with disabilities, a high demand scholarship program, and through an academic support program for students on academic probation.

The effectiveness of the course is evaluated for the specific sample of students with disabilities. For the purpose of this study, a student with a disability is defined as a student who is formally registered with the institution's Office of Disability Services with a qualifying disability. Forty-four percent of course participants registered with a mild cognitive disability at the Office of Disability Services. In order to register with the Office of Disability Services, the student must present current comprehensive documentation meeting guidelines based upon the DSM-IV criteria for the applicable disabilities. The disabilities of course participants were varied; most students in the course reported a qualifying learning disability (i.e., dysgraphia, dyslexia, or reading comprehension disabilities), Attention Deficit Hyperactivity Disorder, depression, or anxiety. One student with a mild hearing loss and related language impairments also completed the course.

Procedure

The strategic learning class, a 16-week, three-credit academic course, covers prominent learning theories; students' personal assessment of their learning styles, strengths and weaknesses; and practical application of strategy and theory. Learning theories include academic goal orientation, goal setting, change theory, multicultural perspectives, memory and forgetting, multiple intelligences and metacognition. Students are required to relate the theories to personal experience or perspective through written reflection, class discussion, and projects. Theory instruction is balanced with practical strategies. For example, after learning several strategies and principals of mnemonics, students work in small groups based upon their other courses to invent mnemonic strategies to meet specific needs, such as reasoning through scenario test questions. Students are challenged to then try their invented strategies and report back to the class. Additionally, there is evidence that students learn to use the strategies taught in the course because of an application-based assignment that requires students to demonstrate employment of one specific strategy in other coursework outside the learning strategies class. For example, students may show notes taken in a psychology course using a note-taking strategy or the use of a planner that demonstrates the student broke down long-term assignments into manageable steps.

Strategies include note-taking, task analysis, time management, complex thinking, planning for writing, use of assistive technology for writing, editing tools and resources, techniques for reading textbooks and articles, research approaches, memory-improvement skills, test-taking strategies, and others. Instruction emphasizes strategies that followed a system of connections with theory or prior experience, explanation, modeling, guided practice, and opportunity for independent practice (Minskoff & Allsopp, 2003). Assignments stress the application of theory as well as specific strategies to personal learning, especially in coursework for other classes. For example, the first paper in the course requires students to reflect on results from various learning assessment tools and examples from academic experiences. The assessment tools completed by students address learning styles (measured by the Index of Learning Styles; Felder & Silverman, 1988), academic goal orientation (measured by the Achievement Goal Questionnaire; Finney, Pieper, & Barron, 2004), metacognitive awareness and regulation (measured by the Metacognitive Awareness Inventory; Schraw & Dennison, 1994), and multiple intelligences (as measured by a multiple intelligences inventory; Gardner, 1993).

The consistent approach of the course is to require students to intentionally apply strategies to personal learning. For example, one class assignment requires students to further expand personal awareness through participation in any two activities from a list of career and academic exploration activities, ranging from taking a career assessment inventory to participation in a career exploration workshop. In a creative research project, training for the project includes research, reading and writing strategies. Grading then reinforces demonstration of those specific strategies. Points are earned on each test for visible evidence of memory or test-taking strategies employed *during the course of the test*, such as jotting down a mnemonic strategy in the margin of the test or by circling key words such as "except" in a test item.

The final project in the class requires students to create a resource notebook that includes five sections: (a) reflection on personal learning strengths, weaknesses, and changes over time; (b) career and academic exploration and the connection between such exploration and specific strategies; (c) academic goals written in measurable terms with specific strategies delineated to meet them; (d) a collection of specific strategies that were found personally useful in current or future courses; and (e) resources from various campus, community, or on-line learning supports.

While a bulk of the course is consistent from semester to semester, the instructor ensures flexibility to address specific student areas of need. For example, when a majority of students identify planning as a need, additional emphasis is given to explicit training in time management and organizational strategies. When more students find monitoring strategies to be a need, the instructor gives more emphasis to explicit training and modeling of monitoring strategies in every lesson. Early in the course, students learn to write measurable goals addressing identified areas of weakness, some of which are then addressed during the current semester. Reflection on achievement of those goals is included in the final project.

Using four self-report tools, each student in the strategic learning course assessed personal learning styles, learning preferences, and learning strengths and weaknesses. The learning assessments in the course set the stage for early evaluation of personal learning and personal application of learning theories. The Metacognitive Awareness Inventory (MAI; Schraw & Dennison, 1994) was administered at both the beginning and end of the semester. Students used this specific tool to identify both strengths and target areas for improvement over the course of the semester with regard to metacognitive skills (a major component to the course curriculum). In the thirteenth week of the course, students reassessed their awareness and regulation of learning by again completing the MAI and then reflecting on changes from the beginning of the semester to the end of the semester.

For the purposes of this study, the independent variables analyzed include course participation and disability status. The dependent variables for the first three research questions are scores on an assessment of metacognitive awareness and regulation. A simple t-test was conducted to test the fourth research question and compare for differences between the students who took the course and those who did not.

Instrumentation

The assessment tool used to assess metacognitive awareness and regulation was the Metacognitive Awareness Inventory, the MAI. This tool is a 52-item self-report measure designed to assess metacognition in adults (including the collegiate population) using two subscales: (1) Knowledge of Cognition (referred to as the "Awareness" subscale; 17 items) and (2) Regulation of Cognition (referred to as the "Regulation" subscale; 35 items). Students rate each item on a five-point Likert-type scale from "always false" to "always true." Schraw and Dennison (1994) found acceptable psychometric properties for the instrument: reliability (Cronbach's coefficient alpha) was consistently greater than .90 and evidence supported a two-factor scoring solution. For the purpose of this study, the instrument subscales were analyzed separately.

Results

Research Question 1: For students who participate in the course, are posttest scores on the awareness and regulation aspects of metacognition significantly higher than students' pretest scores?

The gains of each specific semester cohort were compared. A statistical test to compare the slopes from pretest to posttest for the four semesters found that there were no statistically significant differences among the slopes of the four semesters on either Awareness ($F(3,74) = 2.34, p = .080, \eta_p^2 = .09$) or Regulation ($F(3,74) = 1.63, p = .189, \eta_p^2 = .06$). The lack of a statistically significant difference across the four semesters in which the class was offered indicates that combining the data across all four semesters is permissible.

Pretest and posttest scores on the Awareness subscale of the MAI were subsequently examined to see if students' scores significantly increased during the Strategic Learning course. A repeated-measures ANOVA was used to test the null hypothesis that students' increase from pretest to posttest was significantly different than zero. There was both a statistically significant increase from pretest to posttest ($F(1, 77) = 76.33, p < .001$) and a practically significant increase from pretest to posttest ($\eta^2 = .50$), indicating that students' metacognitive awareness scores did increase from pretest to posttest (see Figure 1 and Table 1).

The Regulation subscale of the MAI was next examined to determine if students increased significantly in their scores from pretest to posttest. A repeated-measures ANOVA was again used to test the null hypothesis that students' increase from pretest to posttest was significantly different than zero. There was both a statistically significant increase from pretest to posttest ($F(1, 77) = 35.16, p < .001$) and a practically significant increase from pretest to posttest ($\eta^2 = .31$), indicating that students' metacognitive regulation scores did increase from pretest to posttest (see Figure 2 and Table 1).

Research Question 2: Do students with disabilities gain similarly on the awareness and regulation aspects of metacognition due to participation in the course compared to students who participated in the course but did not identify themselves as having disabilities?

Figure 1. Awareness Pretest to Posttest Gains Made by the Last Four Cohorts

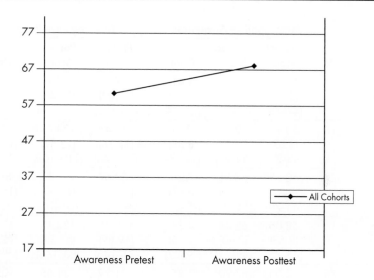

Figure 2. Regulation Pretest to Posttest Gains Made by the Last Four Cohorts

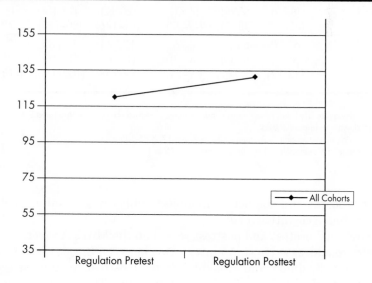

MAI responses were analyzed using a repeated measures mixed ANOVA to test the null hypothesis that postsecondary students with disabilities increased their scores on each of the subscales of the instrument from pretest to posttest, similar to students without cognitive disabilities. The within-subjects effect was the students' pretest/

Table 1. Pretest and Posttest Scores on Both MAI Subscales[a]

Cohort	N	Metacognitive Awareness[b]			Metacognitive Regulation[c]		
		Pretest Score	Posttest Score	Gain	Pretest Score	Posttest Score	Gain
Fall 05	17	61.82 (8.68) (47–76)	70.24 (6.69) (53–79)	8.41 (7.91) (–3–29)	127.12 (17.04) (89–158)	133.94 (16.46) (99–156)	6.82 (14.72) (–11–40)
Spring 06	18	58.94 (8.03) (43–74)	70.22 (7.53) (52–81)	11.28 (8.34) (–5–26)	117.44 (17.34) (77–146)	134.78 (13.87) (110–160)	17.33 (17.38) (–13–53)
Fall 06	27	60.85 (9.89) (44–79)	68.11 (7.40) (56–81)	7.26 (6.91) (–9–23)	124.67 (17.51) (89–164)	133.15 (16.50) (101–161)	8.48 (16.28) (–22–49)
Spring 07	16	58.06 (8.58) (42–70)	62.44 (7.60) (48–72)	4.38 (8.16) (–9–27)	113.75 (19.89) (71–146)	124.13 (17.32) (80–146)	10.38 (12.51) (–6–43)
All Cohorts	78	60.05 (8.90) (42–79)	67.90 (7.76) (48–81)	7.85 (7.93) (–9–29)	121.29 (18.28) (71–146)	131.85 (16.28) (80–161)	10.55 (15.72) (–22–53)
Not Disabled	44	59.70 (8.79) (42–79)	67.61 (7.99) (48–81)	7.91 (7.71) (–9–27)	119.64 (20.12) (71–146)	130.68 (17.18) (80–161)	11.05 (16.58) (–22–53)
Disabled	34	60.50 (9.17) (43–77)	68.26 (7.56) (52–80)	7.76 (8.33) (–9–29)	123.44 (15.61) (89–158)	133.35 (15.16) (103–156)	9.91 (14.74) (–13–45)

[a]Standard deviations are listed below score in parentheses; observed score ranges are listed below standard deviations in parentheses
[b]Possible range of Metacognitive Awareness Scores from 17 to 85
[c]Possible range of Metacognitive Regulation scores from 35 to 175

posttest scores and the between-subjects effect was whether or not a student had a cognitive disability.

Students' pretest and posttest scores on the MAI's Awareness subscale were addressed first. An interaction between the status of having a cognitive disability and students' pretest/posttest Awareness scores was not found ($F(1, 76) = .01, p = .937, \eta^2 = .00$). This finding indicates that disability status did not explain a significant amount of variance in pretest/posttest gains on the Awareness subscale. In other words, students with disabilities gained similarly to students without disabilities on the Metacognitive Awareness subscale of the MAI. Disaggregating students by whether or not they have a disability does not provide explanatory utility in explaining pretest/posttest scores, thus a more parsimonious model in which Awareness pretest and posttest scores are evaluated without disability status as a between-subjects predictor is more appropriate. In the absence of a statistically significant difference between students with and without disabilities, the results demonstrate that students with and without disabilities made similar gains on Metacognitive Awareness.

Similar results were found for the model in which students' scores on the MAI Regulation subscale were examined by cognitive disability status. As with the Awareness subscale, an interaction between whether or not a student had a cognitive disability and students' pretest/posttest Regulation scores was not found ($F(1, 76) = .10, p = .754, \eta^2 = .00$). This indicates that disability status did not explain a significant amount of variance in pretest/posttest gains on the Regulation subscale. In other words, students in the course with disabilities gained similarly to students without disabilities in the course on the Metacognitive Regulation subscale of the MAI. Disaggregating students by disability status did not provide additional predictive utility in explaining pretest/posttest scores; thus, a more parsimonious model in which Regulation pretest and posttest scores are evaluated without disability status as a between-subjects predictor would be more appropriate. This study demonstrates that students' disability status did not interact with gains made in Metacognitive Regulation.

Research Question 3: Do students who complete the strategic learning course score higher on the regulation aspects of metacognition compared to students from the general student population?

A purpose of the strategic learning course is to increase course participants' knowledge and skills related to adaptive metacognitive behavior. One would thus hypothesize that students who complete the strategic learning course would score higher on the MAI than students who do not take the course. For the purpose of this research question, researchers examined only scores for the Regulation subscale, as these items address positive behaviors that one would observe in a general population of students who have not completed a study skills or learning strategies-type course. In other words, comparing Awareness scores of students who participated in the course to students who did not participate in the course is not appropriate because the awareness dimension of metacognition includes specific knowledge not commonly encountered by members of the general student population. Students were sampled from the university population ($N = 1463$) to complete the Regulation subscale under standardized, proctored conditions at two points in time: once when the students were freshmen and again 18 months later when the students were sophomores. Scores from the general student population were not obtained during the same time frame as scores from the strategic learning course participants (the elapsed time between pretest and posttest for the learning course participants was approximately 13 weeks); accordingly, inferences should be made with caution.

Posttest scores on the Regulation subscale for students who participated in the strategic learning course ($N = 78$) were compared to scores for students from the general population who completed the same subscale ($N = 1463$) using a repeated measures mixed ANOVA (see Figure 3 and Table 2). Due to the unequal sample sizes, Type III Sums of Squares were employed and F-max was evaluated at a permissible level (i.e., an F-max value less than 3.0 is permissible for a standard mixed ANOVA) for the variances of all applicable comparisons, providing evidence that no adjustments were necessary to conduct the analysis. Students who were in the strategic learning class experienced larger gains over the 13-week period compared to students in the general population over an 18-month period (i.e., an interaction was present) $F(1,1539) = 28.74$, $p < .001$, $\eta^2 = .02$. In other words, strategic learning course participants gained on the Regulation subscale at a greater rate than would be expected due to simple maturation over the first two years of college (see Figure 3 and Table 2), thereby lending evidence to the worth of the strategic learning course.

Figure 3. Regulation Pretest to Posttest Gains Made by the Last Four Cohorts

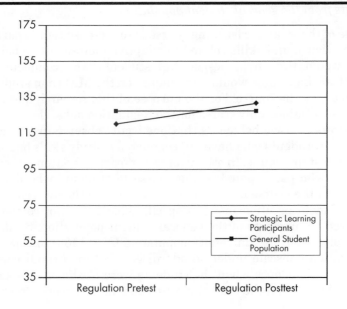

Table 2. Descriptive Statistics for Regulation Subscale: Participants versus General Student Population

| Cohort | N | Metacognitive Regulation | | | | | |
		Pretest Score	Pretest SD	Pretest CI	Posttest Score	Posttest SD	Posttest CI
Learning Strategies Participants	78	121.29	18.28	117.23 to 125.35	113.85	16.28	128.24 to 135.46
General Student Population*	1463	126.14	15.221	125.36 to 126.92	127.57	17.327	126.68 to 128.461

*Time between the pretest and posttest for the general student population is 18 months.

It is important to stress that the interval between pretest and posttest measures taken for course participants was one semester only, while the interval between pretest and posttest measures for the general student population was just over three semesters. The results of this specific question are important in demonstrating that students who participate in a course with a metacognitive approach to teaching learning strategies do show gains in metacognitive regulation which are significantly greater than peers who do not participate in such a course. The difference in intervals between pretesting and posttesting raises additional questions for future study, such as the longitudinal benefits of metacognitive regulation after course participation.

Research Question 4: Are students who self-select to take this course different in metacognitive regulation compared to students from the general student population?

It is important to note that the results from an additional analysis reveal that the average *pretest* score for students who participated in the strategic learning course was statistically and practically significantly *lower* than the score on the Regulation subscale obtained from the general population ($t(809) = 2.418, p = .016, d = .288$; see Figure 3 and Table 2). In other words, students who participated in the strategic learning course *started* with Regulation scores significantly lower (.288 pooled standard deviations lower) than the general student population, and *completed the course* with Regulation scores significantly higher than those of the general student population. Importantly, the much lower starting rate at which course participants used strategies to regulate learning gives additional evidence that the strategic learning course provides students with a powerful and beneficial learning experience. Given the lower starting scores of their students on metacognitive regulation, instructors might be satisfied to help students achieve regulation at levels similar to their peers, yet these course participants reached post course levels of regulation significantly higher than peers who did not take the course.

Implications

Results of this study indicate that students enrolled in a postsecondary course combining learning theory with practical application of learning strategies show significant gains in both metacognitive awareness and regulation. Students who took the course made regulation gains significantly greater than the general student population. Most significantly, students with disabilities demonstrated metacognitive gains in both awareness and regulation similar to gains made by students without disabilities. In this case, an intervention had positive results for both students with and without disabilities, demonstrating a good model for postsecondary intervention for students in at-risk groups regardless of disability status. Whereas many skills taught at universities are specific to various fields, students who increase their metacognitive skills gain a critical *foundational* skill set not often taught in postsecondary education. Students with greater metacognitive skills are potentially more adept at higher-level processing, implying greater academic success.

While many universities have implemented programs or courses to promote use of learning strategies, none has thus far reported a course integrating theory with practical strategies. For students who experience academic challenges, we recommend course-based support with the integration of theory and practical learning strategies within the context of the course. Future research should investigate effectiveness of a similar instructional approach with different populations or in a different context. Future research should also explore longitudinal gains in metacognition and impact on grades for students who take such courses compared to students who do not. Studies that vary the theory and strategy content related to specific areas of gain (e.g., varying emphasis on specific theories or strategies such as goal setting or information management across different semesters) may gain valuable insight into components of this approach which are most effective in improving student learning. Indeed, such research could be extended to explore the structure of knowledge for all postsecondary learners who experience academic challenges.

References

Allsopp, D. H., Minskoff, E. H., & Bolt, L. (2005). Individualized course-specific strategy instruction for college students with learning disabilities and ADHD: Lessons learned from a model demonstration project. *Learning Disabilities Research and Practice, 20,* 103–118.

Barga, N. K. (1996). Students with learning disabilities in education: Managing a disability. *Journal of Learning Disabilities, 29*(4), 413–421.

Braten, I., & Stomso, H. I. (2005). The relationship between epistemological beliefs, implicit theories of intelligence, and self-regulated learning among Norwegian postsecondary students. *British Journal of Educational Psychology, 75*(4), 539–565.

Butler, D. L. (1995). Promoting strategic learning by postsecondary students with learning disabilities. *Journal of Learning Disabilities, 2*(3), 170–190.

Carnell, E. (2007). Conceptions of effective teaching in higher education: Extending the boundaries. *Teaching in Higher Education, 12*(1), 25–40.

Dahlin, B. (1999). Ways of coming to understand: Metacognitive awareness among first-year university students. *Scandinavian Journal of Educational Research 43*(2), 191–208.

Davidson, J. E., & Sternberg, R. J. (1998). How metacognition helps problem solving. In D. J. Hacker, J. Dunlosky, & A. C. Graesser (Eds.), *Metacognition in Educational Theory and Practice.* New Jersey: Lawrence Erlbaum.

Deshler, D. D., & Shumaker, J. B. (1986). Learning strategies: An instructional alternative for low-achieving adolescents. *Exceptional Children, 52*(6), 583–590.

Felder, R. M., & Silverman, L. K. (1988). Learning and teaching styles in engineering education. *Engineering Education, 78*(7), 674–681.

Finney, S. J., Pieper, S. L., & Barron, K. E. (2004). Examining the psychometric properties of the achievement goal questionnaire in a general academic context. *Educational and Psychological Measurement, 64*(2), 365–382.

Ford, J. K., Smith, E. M., Weissbein, D. A., Gully, S. M., & Salas, E. (1998). Relationships of goal orientation, metacognitive activity, and practice strategies with learning outcomes and transfer. *Journal of Applied Psychology, 83*(2), 218–233.

Gamache, P. (2002). University students as creators of personal knowledge: An alternative epistemological view. *Teaching in Higher Education, 7*(3), 277–294.

Garcia, T., & Pintrich, P. R. (1991). Student motivation and self-regulated learning: A LISREL model. Paper presented at the American Educational Research Association Convention, Chicago, IL.

Gardner, H. (1993). *Multiple intelligences: The Theory in Practice.* New York: Basic Books.

Garner, R. (1990). When children and adults do not use learning strategies: Toward a theory of settings. *Review of Educational Research, 60*(4), 517–529.

Hacker, D. J., (1998). Definitions and empirical foundations. In J. Dunlosky, & A. C. Graesser (Eds.), *Metacognition in Educational Theory and Practice.* New Jersey: Lawrence Erlbaum.

Hanley, G. L. (1995). Teaching critical thinking: Focusing on metacognitive skills and problem solving. *Teaching of Psychology, 22*(1), 68–72.

Highley, D. C. (1995). *The effects of a "learning to learn" course on at risk students' motivation, self-regulated learning processes and academic achievement.* Unpublished doctoral dissertation, University of Southern California, Los Angeles.

Jakubowski, T. G., & Dembo, M. G. (2004). The relationship of self-efficacy, identity style, and stage of change with academic self-regulation. *Journal of College Reading and Learning, 35*, 7–24.

Kuhn, D., Garcia-Mila, M., Zohar, A., & Anderson, C. (1995). Strategies of knowledge acquisition. *Monographs of the Society for Research in Child Development, 60*(4), 1–128.

Louisiana State University. (2006). *Center for Academic Success.* Retrieved November 20, 2006, from: http://appl003.lsu.edu/slas/cas.nsf/index

McGuire, J. M., Hall, D., & Litt, V. (1991). A field-based study of the direct service needs of college students with learning disabilities. *Journal of College Student Development, 32*(2), 101–108.

Minskoff, E. H., & Allsopp, D. (2003). *Academic Success Strategies for Adolescents with Learning Disabilities & ADHD.* Baltimore: Paul H. Brooks.

Minskoff, E. H., Minskoff, J. G., & Allsopp, D. (2001). A systematic model for curriculum-based assessment and intervention for postsecondary students with mild disabilities (Final report). Unpublished manuscript, James Madison University.

Muskingum College. (2007). *Center for Advancement and Learning.* Retrieved October 26, 2007, from: http://www.muskingum.edu/%7Ecal/

Nietfeld, J. L., Cao, L., & Osborne, J. W. (2005). Metacognitive monitoring accuracy and student performance in the postsecondary classroom. *Journal of Experimental Education, 74*(1), 7–28.

Peterson, R., Lavelle, E., & Guarino, A. J. (2006). The relationship between college students' executive functioning and study strategies. *Journal of College Reading and Learning, 36*, 59–67.

Pintrich, P. R. (2002). The role of metacognitive knowledge in learning, teaching, and assessing. *Theory into Practice, 41*(4), 219–226.

Ruban, L. M., McCoach, D. B., McGuire, J. M., & Reis, S. M. (2003). The differential impact of academic self-regulatory methods on academic achievement among university students with and without learning disabilities. *Journal of Learning Disabilities, 36*(33), 268–284.

Ryan, M. P., & Glenn, P. A. (2004). What do first-year students need most: Learning strategies instruction or academic socialization? *Journal of College Reading and Learning, 34*, 4–28.

Sanford, N. (1966). *Self & society: Social change and individual development.* New York: Atherton Press.

Schraw, G., & Dennison, R. S. (1994). Assessing Metacognitive Awareness. *Contemporary Educational Psychology, 19*(4), 460–475.

Schraw, G., & Moshman, D. (1995). Metacognitive theories. *Educational Psychology Review, 7*(4), 351–371.

Stanford University. (2007). *Center for Teaching and Learning.* Retrieved October 26, 2007, from: http://ctl.stanford.edu/

Sungar, S. (2007). Contribution of motivational beliefs and metacognition to students' performance under consequential and nonconsequential test conditions. *Educational Research and Evaluation, 13*(2), 127–142.

Swanson, H. L. (1989). Strategy instruction: Overview of principles and procedures for effective use. *Learning Disability Quarterly, 12*(1), 3–14.

Trainin, G., & Swanson, H. L. (2005). Cognition, metacognition, and achievement of college students with learning disabilities. *Learning Disability Quarterly 28*, 261–272.

Tuckman, B. W. (2003). The effect of learning and motivation strategies training on college students' achievement. *Journal of College Student Development, 44*(3), 430–437.

Van Blerkom, D. L., Van Blerkom, M. L., & Bertsch, S. (2006). Study strategies and generative learning: What works? *Journal of College Reading and Learning, 37*, 7–18.

Van Blerkom, M. L., & Van Blerkom, D. L. (2004). Self-monitoring strategies used by developmental and non-developmental college students. *Journal of College Reading and Learning, 34*, 45–60.

Vermunt, J. D. (1998). The regulation of constructive learning processes. *British Journal of Educational Psychology, 68*(2), 149–171.

Vogel, S. A., & Adelman, P. B. (1992). The success of college students with learning disabilities: Factors related to educational attainment. *Journal of Learning Disabilities, 25*(7), 430–441.

White, W. F., & Kitchen, S. (1991). Teaching metacognitive awareness to entering college students with developmental lag. *College Student Journal, 25*(4), 521–523.

Wolters, C. A. (1997). Issues in self-regulated learning: Metacognition, conditional knowledge and the regulation of motivation. *Dissertation Abstracts International, 57*(11-A), 4651. (UMI No. 1997-95009-078)

Zimmerman, B. J. (1989). A social cognitive view of self-regulated academic learning. *Journal of Educational Psychology, 81*(3), 329–339.

Zimmerman, B. J., Bandura, A., & Martinez-Pons, M. (1992). Self-motivation for academic attainment: The role of self-efficacy beliefs and personal goal setting. *American Educational Research Journal, 29*(3), 663–676.

College Students' Beliefs, Strategy Employment, Transfer, and Academic Performance: An Examination across Three Academic Disciplines

Michele L. Simpson and Leslie Rush

To help students with the rigors of the first year of college, many postsecondary institutions offer some form of academic assistance. Coauthors Michele L. Simpson and Leslie Rush describe a program evaluation study that aims to determine if students change in their personal beliefs about an academic discipline and if they change in the strategic behavior they employ. The authors are also interested in examining whether students are transferring study strategies learned in a one-hour strategic learning course to their other courses. Using three assessment instruments, the study investigates differences across three high-risk courses — biology, chemistry, and history.

Most models of self-regulated learning (SRL) describe successful students as those who hold mature beliefs about learning, have a repertoire of cognitive and metacognitive processes, and can correctly interpret their tasks (Pressley, 2000; Zimmerman, 2000). Although self-regulated learning is particularly important at the college level, we know from the extant research that many students are not prepared for approaching the rigors of college (Nist & Simpson, 2000). In order to help students with these demands, many postsecondary institutions offer some form of academic assistance. Generally, these academic assistance efforts have used either generic study skills approaches or integrated approaches that embed instruction across the academic disciplines (Hofer, Yu, & Pintrich, 1999). The integrated approach reflects SRL theory and is represented in two different models: learning to learn courses (e.g., Weinstein, 1994) or adjunct study strategy courses (e.g., Warkentin, Stallworth-Clark, & Nolen, 1999). This study focused on the latter.

Adjunct study strategy courses (ASSC) are elective courses that are linked to high-risk core courses (e.g., chemistry). Rather than teaching generic strategies, the ASSC instructor does a task analysis of the targeted course and then teaches the cognitive, metacognitive, and self-regulatory processes essential to students' academic success. Although the ASSC model is not a recent innovation and is somewhat similar to some other academic assistance models (i.e., paired courses, supplemental instruction), very few experimental or programmatic evaluation studies have appeared in the literature (Boylan, 1997; Simpson, Hynd, Nist, & Burrell, 1997). The studies that do exist in this area have typically focused on quantitative measures (e.g., standardized test scores) or single indicators of success (e.g., students' course grades or retention), overlooking qualitative measures and possible differences across the academic disciplines (Alexander & Jetton, 2000). Moreover, except for the work of Warkentin and his colleagues (1999), most of the studies have been atheoretical or have failed to make explicit the theoretical base for the academic assistance model being examined (O'Hear & McDonald, 1995; Weinstein, Husman, & Dierking, 2000).

We wanted to build upon the work by Warkentin et al. (1999) and to address some of the apparent gaps in the extant program evaluation studies that have examined models similar to ASSC. That is, we wanted to experiment with a variety of qualitative measures rather than rely solely on quantitative measures such as course grades. We also agreed with other researchers that it would be important to examine students' beliefs about learning and their transfer of strategies to other academic tasks (Alexander & Jetton, 2000; Hofer et al., 1999). Finally, using the recommendations of other researchers (e.g., Maxwell, 1997), we deemed it important to access the viewpoints of the students, important stakeholders at any institution.

Thus, the four general purposes of this program evaluation study were: (a) to determine if students changed in their personal beliefs about an academic discipline and if they changed in the strategic behaviors they employed; (b) to examine whether students were transferring the strategies to their other courses; (c) to describe the participants' academic performance and their personal viewpoints on this performance; and (d) to investigate the usefulness of students' beliefs and strategies in relationship to their academic performance. As we addressed these questions, we looked at differences across three academic disciplines — biology, chemistry, and history.

Methodology

The Context and Participants

This program evaluation study took place at a large southeastern university. We chose three different high-risk core courses — biology, chemistry, and history — for the ASSC. These three courses were selected because they required students to think critically (e.g., create generalizations, sense interrelationships across concepts) and to demonstrate their understanding on demanding exams. With the permission of the professors teaching these core courses, three different one-hour elective courses (i.e., ASSC) were then created and opened to any interested student. The courses met once a week for the entire semester and were taught by doctoral students in either biology, chemistry, or history. These three doctoral students had taken a two-hour course in learning theory and classroom management that the first author had taught the semester prior to the study. In addition, the first author met on a weekly basis with the doctoral students (i.e., the ASSC leaders) and observed them three times during the semester in order to make sure that the activities and strategies introduced in the ASSC reflected SRL theory and were task-appropriate to their academic discipline.

Although the exact strategies varied across the academic disciplines, all three ASSC leaders taught the participants how to think about the specific academic discipline, how to interpret academic tasks, and how to employ a variety of learning strategies and processes. These strategies focused on how to (a) read textbook assignments, (b) solve problems, (c) take effective notes from labs, lectures, and discussions, (d) prepare for objective and essay examinations, (e) plan and set goals, and (f) review and rehearse. In addition, the ASSC leaders involved the participants in an evaluation and self-reflection activity after each of the exams in the targeted core course. These activities enabled the participants to identify the strategies that seemed to work for them (e.g., concept cards in biology) and to construct credible reasons for their performance on each exam (e.g., I received a "C" on the exam because I waited until the last minute to study.).

The subject pool consisted of 252 students who chose to enroll in the ASSC. All of the 252 participants finished the ASSC, but because of absences on the days that we collected data, the total number in the study was reduced to 176 participants for whom we had complete data. Of these 176 participants, 95% were freshmen or sophomores and 5% were juniors. The average SATV for these participants was 510, an average similar to the university's average (i.e., 525). The ASSC leaders evaluated the students on their attendance and participation during class. Consequently, any technique or strategy the students chose to employ for their reading or studying was done in a completely voluntary manner.

Data Sources and Analysis

In order to answer the program evaluation questions, we created three different instruments. In addition, we collected from the professors the participants' final course grades in the targeted classes (i.e., biology, chemistry, and history). The first two instruments, the Getting Acquainted Activity and the Learning Strategy Inventory, were developed and piloted with similar students during the previous semesters. We established the content validity of both instruments using a panel of experts (i.e., doctoral students in each academic discipline and in reading education).

The Getting Acquainted Activity (GAA) — designed to measure students' personal beliefs about reading, studying, and learning in a specific academic discipline — consisted of three open-ended questions: (a) What do you believe is important to understand and learn in _____?; (b) What do you believe to be critical characteristics of successful students in _____?; (c) How will you study and prepare for exams in _____?. The three different versions of the GAA (i.e., biology, chemistry, history) were scored using each of the rubrics that had been created by experts representing each of the three academic disciplines. Each question was worth 5 points, making a total of 15 points possible. To illustrate, for the History GAA an exemplary answer worth 5 points to the first question had to contain at least two of the following responses: (a) trends and changes over time, (b) causes/effects, (c) the significance of events or certain individuals, or (d) themes and patterns. In order to insure reliability in evaluating the students' answers on the GAA, we both read and scored their answers independently. The initial inter-rater reliability or percentage of agreement for this scoring was 88%. We then met and resolved any differences so that there was 100% agreement on the GAA scoring.

The Learning Strategies Inventory (LSI) was designed to measure students' self-reported processes and behaviors in five areas considered important to self-regulated learning: planning, monitoring, text processing, rehearsing, and reviewing (Zimmerman, 2000). The 5-point Likert scale contained 40 questions, 8 per area, for a total of 200 points. One half of the questions contained statements describing desirable behaviors, and the other half were items describing counterproductive or ineffective behaviors. For example, the following question, a text-processing question, describes a positive behavior: "Before I read a chapter, I often skim it to see how it is organized and what I already know about the topic." The following question, another text-processing question, describes a negative behavior: "In order to understand and remember what I read, I reread my assignments several times."

The third instrument, the Adjunct Study Seminar Evaluation Form (ASSEF), was created in order to measure students' viewpoints on the usefulness of ASSC and to determine if they had transferred any of the targeted strategies to their other courses. The ASSEF contained three open-ended questions: (a) Would you recommend ASSC to a friend? Why or why not? (b) Do you think ASSC influenced your performance in this class? Why or why not? (c) Will the information that you learned in ASSC change the way in which you study in your other classes? Why or why not? The first author did a content analysis of the participants' responses to these three questions and grouped their answers into observable patterns.

The participants completed the GAA and LSI at the beginning and end of the semester; they completed the ASSEF on the last day of class. After scoring the GAA and LSI, t-tests were conducted to measure the participants' gain scores on the two instruments. In order to address the question of differences across the academic disciplines, separate ANOVAs were conducted. Correlational analyses were used to investigate the relationship between students' course grades, their beliefs, and strategic behaviors.

Findings and Discussion

This program evaluation study was designed to address four general questions. The findings are discussed below.

Changes in Beliefs and Strategic Behaviors

The first program evaluation question focused on whether the students made any changes in their beliefs about an academic discipline or in the strategic behaviors they reported to employ as they studied. The paired samples test indicated that there were significant differences between the students' scores on the GAA pretests and posttests, t (176) = 19.933, $p < .001$. For the LSI, paired sample tests revealed significant differences between the students' pretest and posttest scores, $t(176) = 8.524, p < .001$.

We were also interested in whether there would be any differences across the three academic disciplines. On the GAA posttest, the analysis of variance indicated that there were significant differences $[F(3,173) = 3.82, p = .023, d = .032]$, between the academic disciplines. Post hoc multiple comparisons indicated that the students in the history ASSC scored significantly higher on the GAA ($p = .046$) than the students in the biology or chemistry ASSC. In terms of the LSI, the analysis indicated that there were no significant differences across the academic disciplines $[F(3,173) = .441, p = .644]$.

These findings suggested that the participants made significant changes in their beliefs about the academic discipline targeted by the ASSC. Given that the ASSC leaders focused on these beliefs by routinely discussing how authorities in their academic discipline think about their content, these findings made sense. Across the disciplines, the history students scored higher than the other participants on the GAA posttest and made the most gains. Previous studies have determined that college students possess numerous misconceptions about history, believing it to be a series of facts and dates (e.g., Hynd, 1999; Simpson & Nist, 1997). The history students' low scores on the pre-GAA (5 points out of a possible 15) would certainly support these previous studies. Had the ASSC students not modified their beliefs about history, they would not have survived this course with academic tasks requiring them to synthesize multiple sources, create generalizations, and answer thought-provoking essay questions.

As indicated on the LSI, the participants also made significant changes in their reported processes and behaviors. These results support the work of previous researchers who have also provided students intensive, recursive instruction and who have incorporated activities that encouraged students to set goals, reflect, and evaluate their performance (Hofer & Pintrich, 1997; Weinstein et al., 2000). The difference between those studies and this one is the fact that the strategy instruction in this study was embedded in a specific academic discipline and taught by an authority in that discipline.

Strategy Transfer

Using the ASSEF, a self-report instrument, we addressed the second research question that focused on whether students were applying the strategies learned in the ASSC to their other core courses (e.g., political science, sociology). We were aware of the possible limitations to self-report data (Garner, 1988; Pajares, 1992). However, we reasoned that the self-report data collected in this situation might be less contaminated given that the ASSC students viewed the ASSEF as an opportunity to share their opinions in a low-stakes situation. That is, the participants knew their course grade had no relationship to what they reported on the ASSEF.

The content analyses of the participants' responses on the ASSEF indicated that 72% of the students said that they were applying the strategies to their other courses. These courses represented a wide variety of core courses that undergraduates must take during their first two years at the university (e.g., psychology, sociology, and geography). The responses across the academic disciplines were as follows: strategy transfer in biology, 65% of the students; strategy transfer in chemistry, 62% of the students; and strategy transfer in history, 78% of the students. Given that the students were not required to transfer the strategies taught in ASSC to their other core courses, this finding was quite interesting.

When asked what strategies they were transferring to their other courses, the students replied in a variety of ways (e.g., textbook annotation, concept cards, question prediction), but the most predominant response was that they were using the techniques for planning and distributing their study time. The importance of planning and time distribution, important self-regulatory processes, held true across the three academic disciplines and did not vary significantly. In previous studies these self-regulatory processes have been found to be related to students' performance on a variety of academic tasks (Britton & Tesser, 1991; Light, 2001).

Academic Performance

In order to determine the potential impact of the ASSC, the third question examined the participants' grades in the targeted core course (i.e., biology, chemistry, and history). The average final course grade for the ASSC students was 84% or a "B"; no significant differences occurred across the academic disciplines. Less than 7% of the ASSC students received a course grade lower than a "C." As a reference point, over twice as many (17%) of the non-ASSC students received a course grade lower than a "C." Although such trends were encouraging, the use of the quasi-experimental design in this program evaluation study and the use of volunteers (i.e., the role of motivation) must be acknowledged as substantive limitations.

In order to deal with some of these limitations, we triangulated the quantitative findings with descriptive data obtained from the participants. When we asked the participants on the ASSEF whether they believed the ASSC had made an impact on their course grades, 80% of them replied "Yes," 10% said "Somewhat," and 10% said "No." In addition, when asked on the ASSEF whether they would recommend the adjunct seminar concept to their friends, 85% of the participants said, "Yes."

Thus, both the quantitative and self-report data suggested that the ASSC had an impact on the participants' academic performance. The anecdotal evidence collected by the ASSC leaders revealed that many of the students made jumps in their exam scores from "D's" to "B's" once they incorporated one or more of the targeted strategies into their study routine. Concrete improvements such as these are often the necessary stimulus for influencing permanent changes in students' beliefs and behaviors.

Beliefs, Strategic Behaviors, and Academic Performance

The fourth question investigated the usefulness of students' beliefs and strategic behaviors by correlating their posttest scores on the GAA and LSI to their final grades in the targeted core courses. Overall, the correlation between the participants' scores on the GAA and their final course grades was significant ($r = .135, p < .05$). Across the academic disciplines, the correlations were as follows: biology ($r = .212, p\ .120$); chemistry ($r = .034, p = .735$); and history ($r = .317, p < .01$). The overall correlation between the participants' scores on the LSI and their courses grades was also significant ($r = .233, p < .001$). When we analyzed this relationship across the academic disciplines, the correlations were: biology ($r = .180, p = .215$); chemistry ($r = .227, p < .05$); and history ($r = .322, p < .01$).

These findings suggested that there were significant, albeit small, relationships between students' beliefs, their strategic behaviors, and their course grades. Although previous program evaluation studies have not addressed the issue of students' beliefs, they have found significant relationships between students' strategies and their course grades (Pintrich, Smith, Garcia, & McKeachie, 1993; Stallworth-Clark, Nolen, & Warkentin, 1999). When we examined this question across the academic disciplines, we discovered that the only significant and moderately sized correlations occurred for the participants in the history ASSC. Given that this history course was extremely demanding and required students to synthesize and recall information for several essay exams, it might be that students had to know more than just content if they were to succeed.

Implications

The findings from this program evaluation study have implications for academic assistance professionals interested in program evaluation and instructional improvement. Specifically, there are four implications that should be noted. Most importantly, the qualitative and quantitative measures used in this theory-driven study provide a model to others seeking ways to justify their courses to administrators demanding accountability (Boylan, 1997; Breneman & Haarlow, 1999). Although students' course grades or retention are important factors in any program, we should be cautious in judging a program's success solely on one or two product-based measures. For example, there are so many reasons for the grade point averages students earn (e.g., course load, type of classes selected) that a mere number cannot reveal all the nuances involved in students' growth and self-regulated learning. This study attempted to unravel some of those nuances and to generate a variety of qualitative data that would both triangulate the quantitative data and would provide additional support for the trends emerging from the qualitative data. Perhaps most noteworthy of these trends was the finding that the history students profited the most from ASSC. This finding was reaffirmed through the combined use of the qualitative measures (i.e., LSI, GAA, and ASSEF) and the quantitative measures (i.e., students' final course grade in history) and through the complementary use of a variety of data analyses methods (e.g., use of rubrics, content analysis, ANOVAs, correlations).

Second, this study tackled the extremely important issue of students' transfer of strategies and processes to academic tasks beyond the targeted instruction. As noted by researchers such as Zimmerman (2000) and Pressley (2000), transfer is the touchstone of any program evaluation or instructional intervention, but it is an issue routinely ignored. The issue of strategy transfer has probably been ignored because it is extremely difficult to measure whether or not students are transferring targeted strategies and processes to other academic tasks. Most academic assistance professionals do not have the time to shadow their students or conduct numerous case studies. Open-ended questionnaires, such as the ASSEF and GAA, allow academic assistance professionals an efficient tool that will help address the questions about students' strategy use and transfer. Moreover, a carefully written open-ended questionnaire can circumvent the limitations of checklists that prompt students to answer in a particular way (e.g., Do you annotate your textbooks?) and Likert-type scales that encourage students to answer to the middle and not in the extremes (Pajares, 1992).

Third, the findings from this study reiterated the importance of students' beliefs about learning and their beliefs about what constitutes excellence in a specific academic discipline. Interestingly, the students in the history ASSC were the ones who experienced the most growth or change in their beliefs about learning, and they were the ones who profited the most from the instruction. This trend in the study reiterates the powerful influence that students' beliefs about learning have on their academic performance. That is, it seems that students' belief systems act as filters for how they interpret tasks, how they interact with text, and ultimately, the strategies and processes they choose to employ (Simpson & Nist, 1997). If students perceive learning as simple, quick, and easy, they certainly will not see a need to embrace alternative strategies that appear to be time-consuming and far more complex and cognitively demanding. We all should remember this when we are attempting to change the way in which college freshmen read and study.

Finally, this study also examined students' growth across three academic disciplines. Given that the history ASSC students made the most improvement in this study, we would recommend that academic assistance professionals include in their future program evaluation efforts an examination of the differential effects that an intervention can have on students' performance across a variety of academic disciplines. Academic assistance professionals who are not involved in program evaluation studies could certainly capitalize on this finding by making sure that they are aware of the academic tasks students are being required to complete in their core courses. With that information, they then can develop lessons and activities to teach their students a repertoire of strategies and processes in order to survive their first two years of college.

Program evaluation studies can be formidable tasks, but they also can provide us the necessary data to justify our delivery models to administrators demanding accountability and the necessary information to improve our courses and delivery models. This study accomplished both.

References

Alexander, P. A., & Jetton, T. L. (2000). Learning from text: A multidimensional and developmental perspective. In M. L. Kamil, P. B. Mosenthal, P. D. Pearson, & R. Barr (Eds.), *Handbook of reading research*, Volume III (pp. 285–310). Mahwah, NJ: Lawrence Erlbaum.

Boylan, H. R. (1997). Criteria for program evaluation in developmental education. *Research in Developmental Education, 12*, 1–4.

Breneman, D. W., & Haarlow, W. N. (April, 1999). Establishing the real value of remedial education. *Chronicle of Higher Education*, XIV (31), pp. B6–B7.

Britton, B. K., & Tesser, A. (1991). Effects of time-management practices on college grades. *Journal of Educational Psychology, 83*, 405–410.

Garner, R. (1988). *Metacognition and reading instruction.* Norwood, NJ: Ablex.

Hofer, B., & Pintrich, P. R. (1997). The development of epistemological theories: Beliefs about knowledge and knowing and their relation to learning. *Review of Educational Research, 67*, 88–140.

Hofer, B., Yu, S. L., & Pintrich, P. R. (1999). Teaching college students to be self-regulated learners. In B. Zimmerman & D. H. Schunk (Eds.), *Self-regulated learning and academic achievement: Theory, research, and practice* (pp. 57–85). New York: Springer-Verlag.

Hynd, C. R. (1999). Teaching students to think critically using multiple texts in history. *Journal of Adolescent and Adult Literacy, 42*, 428–436.

Light, R. J. (2001). *Making the most of college: Students speak their minds.* Cambridge, MA: Harvard University Press.

Maxwell, M. (1997). *Improving student learning.* Clearwater, FL: H & H Publishing.

Nist, S. L., & Simpson, M. L. (2000). College studying. In M. L. Kamil, P. B. Mosenthal, P. D. Pearson, & R. Barr (Eds.), *Handbook of reading research*, Volume III (pp. 645–666). Mahwah, NJ: Lawrence Erlbaum.

O'Hear, M. F., & McDonald, R. B. (1995). A critical review of research in developmental education: Part I. *Journal of Developmental Education, 19,* 2–6.

Pajares, M. F. (1992). Teachers' beliefs and educational research: Cleaning up a messy construct. *Review of Educational Research, 62,* 307–322.

Pintrich, P. R., Smith, D. F., Garcia, T., & McKeachie, W. J. (1993). Reliability and predictive validity of the motivated strategies for learning questionnaire (MSLQ). *Educational and Psychological Measurement, 53,* 801–813.

Pressley, M. (2000). What should comprehension instruction be the instruction of? In M. L. Kamil, P. B. Mosenthal, P. D. Pearson, & R. Barr (Eds.), *Handbook of reading research*, Volume III (pp. 545–561). Mahwah, NJ: Lawrence Erlbaum.

Simpson, M. L., Hynd, C. R., Nist, S. L., & Burrell, K. (1997). College academic assistance programs and practices. *Educational Psychology Review, 9,* 39–87.

Simpson, M. L., & Nist, S. L. (1997). Perspectives on learning history: A case study. *Journal of Literacy Research, 29,* 363–395.

Stallworth-Clark, R., Nolen, M. T., & Warkentin, R. (1999, April). *College students' strategy engagement and transfer: Two case studies in the social sciences.* Paper presented at the annual meeting of the American Educational Research Association, Montreal.

Warkentin, R., Stallworth-Clark, R., & Nolen, M. (1999, April). *Course features that influence self-directed study practices in a college history course: Linking strategy instruction to authentic content and context.* Paper presented at the annual meeting of the American Educational Research Association, Montreal.

Weinstein, C. E. (1994). Students at risk for academic failure: Learning to learn classes. In K. W. Prichard & R. M. Sawyer (Eds.), *Handbook of college teaching: Theory and applications* (pp. 375–385). Westport, CT: Greenwood Press.

Weinstein, C. E., Husman, J., & Dierking, D. R. (2000). Self-regulation interventions with a focus on learning strategies. In M. Boekaerts, P. R. Pintrich, & M. Zeidner (Eds.), *Handbook of self-regulation* (pp. 727–747). San Diego: Academic Press.

Zimmerman, B. J. (2000). Attaining self-regulation: A social cognitive perspective. In M. Boekaerts, P. R. Pintrich, & M. Zeidner (Eds.), *Handbook of self-regulation* (pp. 13–39). San Diego: Academic Press.

The Effectiveness of Strategic Reading Instruction for College Developmental Readers

David C. Caverly, Sheila A. Nicholson,
and Richard Radcliffe

Can a reading approach help developmental readers not only learn strategic reading skills but also transfer those skills to their core content area classes? David C. Caverly, Sheila A. Nicholson, and Richard Radcliffe find that short-term effects show significant pretest–posttest growth in cognitive, metacognitive, and affective areas, while long-term effects show transfer of the increased reading skill to a future core curriculum reading-intensive history course. The success of the reading program may lie in the coupling of the new reading technique PLAN (Predict, Locate, Add, Note) with instruction in a metacognitive approach to reading that includes teaching students to use their awareness of task, performance, self, and strategy before, during, and after reading.

S uccess in college depends to a considerable degree upon students' ability to engage in strategic reading of extensive academic or informational text. Simpson and Nist (2000) reported that 85% of college learning requires careful reading. Extensive reading is also needed, as lower-division students often must understand 150 to 200 pages per week to meet sophisticated reading tasks in writing research papers and preparing for tests at both the university (Burrell, Tao, Simpson, & Mendez-Berrueta, 1997) and community college level (Colarusso, 2000).

In 2000, 35.2% of all undergraduate students receiving financial aid (i.e., 5.8 million) were enrolled in developmental reading courses (Horn, Peter, & Rooney, 2002) and 11% of first-time, first-year college students nationwide (i.e., over 843,000 students) received some form of developmental reading instruction (Parsad & Lewis, 2003). Such students have difficulty discerning important from unimportant information; selecting, organizing, and interpreting across multiple texts; accessing a repertoire of effective reading strategies; managing executive control over underlying cognitive, metacognitive, and affective processes that are the foundation of these strategies; believing in their ability to control their success; and being motivated to read actively (Alexander & Murphy, 1999; Pressley, Yokoi, Van Meter, Van Etten, & Freebern, 1997; Simpson & Nist, 1997). In addition, their goals for reading may not match their instructors' goals, especially given the competing demands of work, families, social events, personal problems, and other courses (Barnett, 1996).

Unfortunately, research on students who enter college with reading problems has pointed to their lack of success, even after compensatory reading instruction. Bohr (1994) found low correlations between participation in developmental reading courses and grades in challenging college courses. Similarly, after following 2.45 million students from the high school class of 1982, Adelman (1996) found a negative correlation between amount of reading remediation and college graduation. In reviewing traditional, mandatory college remedial reading instruction, Maxwell (1997) found that students felt stigmatized and resentful. Maxwell also noted weaknesses in the remediation, such as skills taught in isolation and unrelated to college task demands, faculty untrained in teaching reading to adults, and lack of course or program evaluation.

Fortunately, research on cognitive, metacognitive, and affective processes has clarified the strategic nature of effective, skillful reading (Alexander & Jetton, 2000) and shown that it is fostered through quality instruction (Pressley, 2002). Models for teaching students to meet the demands of college reading include stand-alone developmental reading courses, linked courses, and learning center support. Researchers have called for studies of the effectiveness of these models that consider the theoretical foundation, that assess with multiple measures, and that evaluate the ability of students to transfer strategic reading skills to subsequent, authentic college tasks (Boylan, Bonham, White, & George, 2000; Simpson, 2002). Following those recommendations, we systematically evaluated the effectiveness of one model of developmental reading instruction, a stand-alone course on strategic reading. We looked at how the instruction aligned with current theory and research on strategic reading; assessed students along cognitive, metacognitive, and affective dimensions; and investigated whether students transferred strategic reading skills to future semesters — specifically, to a reading-intensive core academic course and to performance on a standardized reading test.

Background

In describing the nature of college strategic reading, a number of researchers have concluded that although a reading strategy may meet a reading task demand, no single strategy meets every task demand that students face (Anderson & Armbruster, 1984; Caverly, Orlando, & Mullen, 2000; Nist & Simpson, 2000). Researchers have begun to explore how these effective reading strategies can be adapted to meet the variety of task demands of academic literacy and also to determine how to develop student belief structures for using such strategies (Simpson & Nist, 2000).

Strategic Reading Processes

Strategic reading has been defined through several reviews of the research. Pressley and Afflerbach (1995) concluded that strategic readers use a finite set of cognitive and metacognitive processes including prediction, imaging, interpretation, comprehension monitoring, and summarization. Alexander and Jetton (2000) concurred, arguing that strategic, academic reading is procedural, purposeful, effortful, willful, essential, and facilitative. Nist and Simpson (2000) concluded that for college students, specific cognitive and metacognitive processes have been validated by research (e.g., question generation, text summarization, student-generated elaborations, and organizing strategies like mapping).

Simpson and Nist (2002) found that strategic college readers identified the professor's beliefs for learning in the course, orchestrated reading tactics to fit those beliefs, and adapted that orchestration as needed. Zimmerman (2002) added that college readers become self-regulated learners through three phases. First, students analyze tasks, set goals, strategically plan, and motivate themselves to value learning. Next, they monitor and adjust their strategies. Finally, they judge their success or failure against some standard, attribute that success or failure to their own actions, and develop a positive affect that increases motivation to be self-regulated in the future. They also reflect on the effectiveness of their strategic application, attributing success or failure to it rather than to difficult material, hard instructors, or bad luck.

Teaching Strategic Reading

Teaching students to be strategic readers requires quality instruction and a substantial amount of time for learning (Nist & Simpson, 1990). Such instruction uses more-considerate text while students are novices in strategic reading and moves to less-considerate text as students develop strategic reading expertise (Alexander & Jetton, 2000). It begins with explicit instruction as a teacher models strategic reading through think-alouds, then employs guided practice where students apply strategies in authentic texts by constructing an understanding of what was modeled. Further, it requires independent practice, where students apply strategies in a variety of authentic situations, preferably embedded within a content course (Duffy, 2002). Students need to learn to be self-efficacious (Zimmerman, 2002) as they take on the responsibility for their own learning. Teaching all of this within a specific context or domain helps to develop conditional knowledge (Hattie, Biggs, & Purdie, 1996). Multiple assessments inform instruction and document growth in these cognitive, metacognitive, and affective processes as well as short- and long-term transfer (Simpson, 2002).

Instructional Effectiveness

Research on the effectiveness of this instruction at the college level is typically limited to the semester of instruction and assessed by only one or two measures. For example, in a stand-alone course, El-Hindi (1996) taught students to identify a purpose for reading, activate prior knowledge, make predictions about the text before reading; to self-question and monitor comprehension during reading; and to evaluate understanding and relate the text to prior knowledge after reading. She reported significant growth for the semester on a questionnaire assessing metacognition. Similarly, Doughty (1990) taught strategic reading as metacognitive awareness through discussion, charts for self-monitoring, critical reading through pictures, and memory devices and found pre-post program improvement for reading, according to student self-reports and standardized reading test scores. While students in both studies improved, transfer of these tactics beyond the intervention was not investigated.

Inconsistent results are reported for strategic reading taught as an algorithm, or a set of tactics connected into a step-by-step procedure, not taught for adaptation to changing contexts (Alexander & Jetton, 2000). In reviewing the research on a well-known strategic reading algorithm, SQ3R (Survey, Question, Read, Recite, and Review; Robinson, 1970), Caverly and Orlando (1991) found evidence of improvement on broad measures of success, such as semester grade point average (GPA), but little evidence that this success was due to strategic reading. Similarly, Donley and Spires (1999) found that few students reported using another algorithm for strategic reading, PROR (Preread-Read-Organize-Review) during the semester following instruction. While students seem to be able to learn these algorithms and use them during the semester taught, there is little evidence that students indeed become more strategic readers in future college classes.

Some success has been found for teaching strategic reading as a heuristic — that is, as broad cognitive processes that can contribute to success when adapted to fit a variety of contexts (Alexander & Jetton, 2000). For example, Nist and Simpson (1990) taught a heuristic called PLAE (Preplan, List, Activate, and Evaluate) to developmental readers over four weeks and compared their performance to a comparable group of developmental readers who learned study skills. All students read and studied four college textbook chapters. Students who applied and adapted PLAE scored significantly higher on the teacher-made chapter tests than did the control group. Similarly, Caverly, Mandeville, and Nicholson (1995) taught a strategic reading heuristic called PLAN (Predict, Locate, Add, and Note) using college textbook chapters from classes in which students were enrolled as well as from classes in which they were not. Students in a stand-alone reading course who applied and then adapted PLAN scored higher on a standardized reading test and had greater retention over four semesters compared to developmental readers who chose not to take the reading course. However, this study did not report data or account for the many variables that can explain retention. Finally, Maloney (2003) taught strategic reading as a heuristic to students placed in a stand-alone reading course after failing a standardized reading test. She taught students to preview, annotate, self-question, and summarize authentic, college-level, narrative texts, from a critical literacy perspective. Nearly all of the students passed the standardized reading test on a subsequent retake, but there was no assessment of long-term transfer.

However, factors other than developmental reading instruction may account for student gains, an issue raised by Stallworth-Clark, Scott, and Nist (1996). They found that for a stand-alone developmental reading course, student performance on three dependent variables (developmental course grade, standardized reading test, and GPA in a reading-intensive course taken the next semester) was explained by cognitive aptitude (i.e., SAT Verbal and high school GPA), not by the strategic reading instruction. They also looked at the developmental instructional approach (basic skills, strategy training, strategy training with skills, or whole language) and found that instructional approach impacted the developmental course grade, but did not predict student performance in a college, core-curriculum course.

Stand-alone vs. linked courses. Strategic reading instruction also has been examined when taught as a course linked to a challenging, core-academic course. For example, Simpson and Rush (2003) linked strategic reading instruction to three reading-intensive courses (biology, chemistry, and history). Students who completed a linked course earned higher grades than those who completed the course without linked support. Significant positive correlations were found between students' beliefs about reading and learning and their performance in one of the three courses (history), but not in the other two. However, this sample might be considered strong developmental reading students, as their mean SAT Verbal score ($M = 510$) was comparable to scores of all freshmen ($M = 525$).

In a comparison of linked and stand-alone courses, Stallworth-Clark, Nolen, Warkentin, and Scott (2000) examined total grade points and depth of engagement in strategic reading for three groups of students in a freshman level psychology course. One group ($N = 22$) enrolled in a stand-alone, developmental reading course in a semester before the psychology course, though no description of the content of the reading course was given. Another group ($N = 22$) learned strategic reading in a course linked to the psychology course. A control group ($N = 184$) of nondevelopmental students took the psychology course without taking a strategic reading course. Results showed significantly higher self-efficacy and systematic studying in the linked course compared to the stand-alone course, suggesting benefits for linked courses. Also, both the stand-alone and the linked course performed as well as the control group on the total grade points for the course supporting the benefits of either intervention. Yet, small sample sizes limit their findings.

Cox, Friesner, and Khayum (2003) compared the performance of students in a linked course with credit and grades to those enrolled in a stand-alone course without credit or grades. Students identified as weak in reading ability according to the standardized Degrees of Reading Power Test (DRP) were placed into one of three developmental courses: those who scored below 66 on the DRP were required to enroll in a stand-alone, noncredit, pass-fail reading course; those who scored 67–71 on the DRP had a choice to enroll in a credit, graded reading course, either stand-alone or linked with an Economics course (linked course). The researchers found a positive, significant relationship between successful reading course completion and long-term success (over four academic years) as measured by credit-hour completion, cumulative GPA, and grades in math and English composition, core-curriculum courses. Unfortunately, they provided no description of the reading instruction interventions.

They also claimed those who completed the credit, graded reading courses with an A grade performed better than those who completed the noncredit, nongraded reading course. However, those with lowest DRP scores were placed into the noncredit course while the stronger readers had the option to enroll in the credit, graded course or the linked course. This sampling error makes untenable the conclusion that credit reading courses were better than noncredit courses.

Despite the problems typical of research on developmental instructional interventions (O'Hear & MacDonald, 1995), studies show that college students can learn strategic reading tactics, but the evidence of transfer beyond the intervention semester is inconsistent. For the strongest developmental students, linked courses have led to stronger beliefs about learning, self-efficacy, and study management, and to improved performance in reading intensive courses. However, little research has differentiated the performance of weaker developmental readers, who score significantly lower than their peers on more than one reading assessment.

We saw a need for systematic research on the effectiveness of strategic reading taught to weaker developmental readers in a stand-alone course, research that assessed with cognitive, metacognitive, and affective measures and examined the transfer of these strategies over several semesters in reading-intensive courses. The two investigations presented here report the effectiveness of strategic reading instruction by documenting student performance using multiple assessments as well as short- and long-term transfer. Specifically, we sought answers to two research questions.

Research question 1. Does strategic reading instruction in a stand-alone course contribute to reading performance among developmental college readers as measured by their (a) comprehension on a college reading task, (b) performance on a standardized reading test, (c) report of metacognitive awareness of strategies they choose to employ,

(d) report of self-efficacy in reading, and (e) report of beliefs in strategic reading during the semester following instruction?

Research question 2. When compared to a control group, does this strategic reading performance for developmental college readers transfer beyond one semester as measured by their (a) performance on a standardized reading test and (b) grades in a reading-intensive college course?

Context of the Studies

The two investigations reported here examined the performance of developmental reading students at a large, state university in the Southwest over four academic years from fall semester 2000 through spring semester 2004. Since 1989, the university has offered a three-hour, institutional credit-only, developmental reading course for students who failed the reading subtest of the state-mandated basic skills test (TASP–Texas Academic Skills Program, now the THEA–Texas Higher Education Assessment; National Evaluation Systems, 2003). Students are required by state law to demonstrate reading competency by remaining in developmental reading until they pass the TASP reading subtest (TASP-Rdg), earn a credit grade in a developmental reading course, or earn an A or B grade in a "reading-intensive" course such as American History (on this campus HIST 1310). The university designated these courses as required, core curriculum course with an intensive reading load, where reading is necessary to succeed. During the time of this study, students were not allowed to enroll in more than 60 credits until the reading requirement was met (this has since been changed). Students who also failed writing or math subtests of this test were allowed to enroll in developmental writing or math classes and delay enrollment in the reading course, thus creating a natural control group.

From a population of all freshmen students who enrolled in the university over the four academic years (N = 7661), a subpopulation (N = 289) was selected of those who failed the TASP-Rdg subtest and enrolled only as first semester freshmen during the fall semester (i.e., they did not transfer credits from another college, but started their college career at this university during the fall semester). To avoid confounding study results, transfer students and students who opted to delay developmental reading instruction were not included.

Study One

Participants

Sample 1 (see Table 1) comprised all students who enrolled in a developmental reading course during fall semester 2002 (N = 36). These "true"

Table 1. Standardized Reading Scores for Study One

	TASP-R			SATV			ACTE		
	N	M	SD	N	M	SD	N	M	SD
Sample One	33	202.3	28.4	27	400.3	70.8	17	15.6	3.6
University (02)	1004	257**	18	2638	516.0**	73.0	1375	21.0**	4.0

**p < .000

Table 2. Sample One Demographics

	Gender (%)		Ethnicity (%)					
	M	F	Anglo	African Amer.	Hisp.	Asian	Amer. Indian	Inter- national
Sample One	50.0	50.0	47.0	28.0	19.0	3.0	0.0	3.0
University	57.0	43.0	72.0	5.0	18.0	2.0	1.0	2.0

developmental reading students were defined by having failed the TASP-Rdg subtest (i.e., as having scored less than 230/300), and also by having scored less than 500 on the SAT Verbal [SATV] subtest or less than 20 on the ACT English [ACTE] subtest.

Table 1 shows that students in Sample One performed significantly lower than the university freshmen population as a whole, confirming their designation as "true" developmental reading students.

Table 2 reveals that the demographics of Sample One were decidedly more diverse than the university as a whole. This diversity is typical of developmental education populations in general, particularly for those receiving financial aid (Horn et al., 2002).

To investigate whether students could learn strategic reading, a single group, pretest, posttest study design was implemented in a stand-alone reading course during the fall 2002.

Study One Materials

The instruction utilized authentic instructional materials, chapters from college textbooks required in the core-curriculum courses that all students must eventually pass. These chapters were selected to meet instructional purposes by being considerate, less-than considerate, and inconsiderate (Alexander & Jetton, 2000). For example, when teaching students to recognize text structure, specific chapters were selected with explicit structure (i.e., considerate), less-than explicit structure (i.e., less-than considerate), and implicit structure (i.e., inconsiderate). To address some limitations of Donley and Spires (1999) or Stallworth et al. (2000), we used considerate and less-than considerate text for modeling and guided practice during strategic reading instruction, but during independent practice, students applied strategic reading to textbook chapters for other courses in which they were enrolled.

Study One Assessment

To broadly evaluate growth in strategic reading (Simpson, 2002), we used multiple assessments in the form of cognitive, metacognitive, and affective measures administered during the developmental reading course as pretest and final test. (For this study, a control group was untenable, as the assessments were aligned to the course instruction.)

Cognitive measures. Two measures assessed students' ability to read strategically. The first was utilized to address Research Subquestion 1.1: *Was there significant growth in reading performance on a teacher-made Comprehension test from the beginning to the end of the semester?* We developed a Comprehension test for a 10-page chapter (4,298 words) from an online college textbook on ecology (Moyle, 2003), with permission from the author (P. B. Moyle, personal communication, September 16, 2002). The same test over the same chapter with the same instructions and grading protocol was administered 14 weeks later, at the end of the semester, as a final test in the course. On both testing dates students were told to study the chapter outside of class, using whatever reading strategies they believed appropriate. Each Comprehension test counted 5% of the final course grade. Before taking each test, students turned in their notes and the assigned chapter.

The Comprehension test consisted of 12 multiple-choice questions (four each of literal, interpretive, and application) that accounted for 60% of the score and one short-essay question that counted for 40% of the score. The short-essay was scored using a rubric that assessed students' discussion of the predominate text structure (10 points), the three major concepts presented in the text (15 points), and the supporting details (15 points). To limit examiner bias, a colleague and a doctoral student scored the answers without input from the course instructor. This Comprehension test provided an assessment of students' performance on a typical college-level, reading task — to study a chapter and prepare for a test over classroom material.

The second cognitive assessment of students' ability to read strategically was utilized to address Research Subquestion 1.2: *Was there significant growth in reading performance on a standardized test (TASP-Rdg) from before the course to a subsequent semester?* Students' performance on the TASP-Rdg subtest prior to taking the developmental reading course was compared to their retesting scores after the course ended. The reading subtest of the TASP consisted of seven passages of 300–750 words, similar to sections of college textbooks, with six multiple-choice questions for each passage. These questions measured students' ability to determine meanings of words and phrases; understand main ideas and supporting details; identify a writer's purpose, point of view, and intended meaning; analyze relationships among ideas; evaluate with critical reasoning skills; and apply study skills.

Metacognitive measure. A measure of students' metacognitive awareness was utilized to address Research Subquestion 1.3: *Was there significant growth in metacognitive awareness of strategic reading strategies from the beginning to the end of the semester?* To assess students' developing metacognitive knowledge of strategic reading, we created a checklist (hereafter Checklist). The Checklist of 30 effective reading strategy statements represented categories identified by Weinstein and Mayer (1985), including basic and complex rehearsal, elaboration, organization, and monitoring study reading strategies. Of the 30 strategies, 27 were considered effective strategic reading tactics (e.g., "I quizzed myself by thinking up and answering questions") while three were considered ineffective tactics (e.g., "I skipped parts I didn't understand"). The Checklist followed the Comprehension test in the pre- and postassessments. Students were told to mark the strategies they used in preparing for the Comprehension test, either "Yes, I used it," or "No, I didn't use it." Checklist items were scored with one point for each effective strategy and zero points for each ineffective strategy, generating a possible total score of 27 points.

Affective measure. A measure of students' sense of self-efficacy after strategic reading instruction was utilized to address Research Subquestion 1.4: *Was there significant growth in self-efficacy scores from the beginning to the end of the semester?* To identify students' self-efficacy in their ability to strategically read, we adapted a survey (hereafter Survey) of 10 items from Scholz, Gutierrez-Dona, Sud, and Schwarzer (2002) into a 25-item scale. Additional items were added to measure students' perceptions about their attribution and persistence with a difficult task such as the Comprehension test. The final Survey consisted of 23 items considered positive (e.g., "I made a special effort to learn new things") and two considered negative (e.g., "I met with success because I was lucky"). Students rated each item on a four-point Likert scale (i.e., "Not at all true," "Hardly true," "Moderately true," or "Exactly true").

Transfer measure. Lastly, an assessment of students' beliefs was utilized to address Research Subquestion 1.5: *Does belief in a strategic reading process transfer to the academic semester after the course?* An interview protocol (hereafter Interview) assessed students' perceptions of strategies and the need for strategic reading. A group of 18 students from Sample One was contacted during the middle of spring semester 2003, after their fall 2002 enrollment in the developmental reading course. Students were selected through stratified random sampling by their level of participation and performance in the developmental reading course: high, average, and low performing. A doctoral student with strong communication skills conducted telephone interviews. She asked students to tell what they considered to be the most important concepts learned in the course, to discuss the PLAN strategy, whether they used strategic reading during the spring semester, and if so, how and what effects they attributed to it.

Study One Procedures

On the second class meeting, students were assigned a less-than considerate chapter from the college-level text to take home to study. They were asked to return the third class meeting to take multiple assessments of their understanding of this chapter. After completing the Comprehension test, they responded to the Checklist and to the Survey. Students' scores on these assessments were returned during the fourth class period and discussed.

The semester-long instruction in strategic reading began with the fifth class period. First, students were taught tactics for being metacognitively aware before, during, and after reading (Wade & Reynolds, 1989): *task awareness* (what do the professor and/or course expect), *performance awareness* (how capable were they for meeting these tasks), *self-awareness* (how much they believed they controlled their reading performance; i.e., self-efficacy), and *strategy awareness* (what reading strategies they used that were effective and efficient and for which task demands). Next, students were taught tactics for activating prior knowledge when reading informational text. They were taught tactics to recognize ordination and relational macrostructures within informational text. Next, they were taught various rehearsal tactics for improving remembering of what was read. Then, students were taught to orchestrate all these tactics into a reading heuristic strategy called PLAN (Caverly et al., 1995). (For an explanation of PLAN, see Appendix.) By midterm, after students demonstrated the ability to orchestrate PLAN within a variety of considerate and inconsiderate texts, instruction shifted to adapting the strategy to critical reading for both expository and narrative texts.

Instruction in the PLAN strategy was explicit and direct (Duffy, 2002). It began with instructor modeling of strategic reading within authentic, considerate text selected from textbooks in use in core-curriculum courses. Modeling included think-alouds that demonstrated comprehending and metacognitive behaviors. Next, in small groups, students completed guided practice using the tactics in less-considerate and inconsiderate college-level texts, pausing frequently to discuss procedures, effectiveness, difficulties, and adaptations. Concurrent with instruction, practice, and discussion throughout the semester, students kept a weekly electronic journal in which they reflected upon applications, adaptations, and effects of PLAN towards the development of self-efficacy (Zimmerman, 2002). After demonstrating competence in the strategy through guided practice, students were required as independent practice to apply the strategy to reading assignments in their other college courses. This requirement provided opportunities for students to transfer cognitive and metacognitive knowledge to a variety of different contexts and domains (Hattie et al., 1996). In a linked course, strategies are applied to one course and its task demands. In this study, however, students were asked to apply strategies to task demands both in courses in which they were not enrolled (but would be) as well as courses in which they were currently enrolled. They were required to describe both in writing and in class discussions the reading task demands of these courses and the effectiveness of their application of strategic reading in these different environments. The assessments were given again at the end of the course.

Study One Results

To assess whether developmental students were able to become strategic readers, we explored the effectiveness of the instruction using the PLAN heuristic as measured by multiple assessments, including a reading comprehension test, a standardized reading test, a checklist of effective reading strategies, a survey of self-efficacy, and interviews during the following semester.

   Research subquestion 1.1: Reading comprehension test. Students were asked to read and study a college textbook chapter both at the beginning and the end of the semester. Results of a paired samples t-test measure indicated significant improvement from the Comprehension pretest ($M = 41.2, SD = 12.55, N = 35$) to the posttest ($M = 50.3$, $SD = 10.25$, N $= 35$); $t (31) = 3.67, p < .001$. This result suggested that the instruction improved students' reading performance on a teacher-made comprehension test. This finding was consistent with Nist and Simpson (1990) and reviews of the effectiveness of explicit strategy instruction. One problem with this assessment is the level of practical significance. If a score of 70 is considered passing, these students would still fail this classroom test. A second problem is the small number of questions. While typical of a classroom quiz, the assessment was not typical of larger tests in freshmen courses.

   Research subquestion 1.2: Standardized reading test. Students' scores on retaking the TASP-Rdg subtest were calculated for this Sample One. Results of a paired samples t-test measure showed significant improvement on the TASP-Rdg subtest from the test taken before the developmental reading course ($M = 201.3, SD = 27.05, N = 33$) and the best score on the test taken after the developmental reading course (M = 252.0, SD = 18.18, N = 28); t (31) = 8.31, p < .0001. This finding supports previous research with college students (Caverly et al., 1995; Maloney, 2003) where strategic reading instruction has been found to improve performance on a standardized reading test. This course met its goal of teaching students strategic reading sufficiently to improve their performance on this TASP-Rdg subtest. Still, without a control group, it is unknown how many of these students would have passed this test without instruction. This issue is addressed in Research Subquestion 2.1 for Study Two. Passing the standardized reading test was a high-stakes goal for these students, yet those who pass the test might still perform poorly on classroom-based tests (as found in Research Subquestion 1.1), or fail college courses.

Research subquestion 1.3: Metacognitive measure. Students were asked to report the strategic reading tactics they used in preparation for the Comprehension test. Results of a paired samples t-test showed significant improvement on the Checklist from pretest (M = 15.36, SD = 3.80, N = 33) to posttest (M = 20.73, SD = 4.00, N = 33); t (32) = 8.83, p < .001. This result suggested students' metacognitive awareness of effective strategic reading tactics improved after strategic reading instruction. This finding was consistent with El-Hindi (1996) where specific strategy instruction before, during, and after reading improved metacognitive awareness. It seemed students improved in their awareness of which strategic reading tactics were more effective. The improvement on the Comprehension test and the TASP-Rdg subtest suggests that these students not only were aware of strategic reading, but also knew what strategies were more effective, and they reported using them in these reading tasks.

Research subquestion 1.4: Self-efficacy measure. Students were asked to assess their attribution of success to internal or external factors on a self-efficacy survey. Results of a paired samples t-test measure indicated no significant improvement on this survey from pretest (M = 3.07, SD = 0.26, N = 31) to posttest (M = 3.16, SD = 0.32, N = 31; t (30) = 1.42, p = .166. The strategic reading instruction did not seem to improve students' self-efficacy beliefs about where to attribute success when reading. While students were asked to reflect in a weekly, electronic journal on their applications of their strategic reading behaviors to other course task demands, this seemed insufficient to change their self-efficacy beliefs. Seeing greater self-efficacy change, might entail more discussion about the effectiveness of these strategies (Simpson & Nist, 1997) or the use of a linked course, where the effectiveness of strategic reading would be more immediate and explicit (Simpson & Rush, 2003; Stallworth-Clark et al., 2000).

Research subquestion 1.5: Transfer. To assess the transfer of students' use of strategic reading to the semester following instruction, interviews were conducted during spring 2004 of 18 of the 36 students who had enrolled in the developmental reading course the previous fall semester. All but one student reported that reading comprehension strategies were the most important concepts learned. They described in general terms how they learned to understand better, break ideas down and remember them, how to recognize the main idea, and specifically how to orchestrate their reading. One student shared, "I wasn't a good reader before that class. For me it's important because finally I can understand the reading." Another explained that "Before I took that class I was just reading and trying to memorize the information. After I took that class I learned I can reduce unnecessary reading. I was able to organize my studies." These statements suggest a beginning understanding of strategic reading.

In response to specific questions about reading strategically, four students reported using the PLAN strategy during the semester in which they were enrolled in the course, 11 of 18 students reported using the strategy during the following semester, and three students reported not using it at all. When the 15 students were asked to explain how they had employed PLAN, they described how they had adapted it to differing task demands. For example, one student said, "I've used the PLAN because I think it's one of the best ways to organize yourself right before an exam because it helps you get more details and things instead of just getting information that really doesn't matter. . . ."

Students were also asked to explain what benefits derived from using the PLAN strategy. While six students stated they perceived no benefit, 12 students claimed that PLAN helped them improve their grades, their performance on the TASP-Rdg subtest, and in studying and testing in general. Interestingly, several students saw additional benefits such as "Like now I can actually sit down and read"; "I don't always do it, but I know what I need to do to get on track. I know different strategies. I'm more aware"; and "I actually started reading newspapers." From these data, we concluded that students were beginning to employ self-regulation when strategically reading. These belief statements are consistent with those of Simpson and Rush (2003) where, following instruction, students were more aware of what strategies they should employ to be successful under specific situations.

Study Two

To answer Research Question 2, whether strategic reading skills transferred to authentic college tasks, a quasi-experimental design was used to compare the performance of developmental students who had been taught strategic reading and those who had not. Study Two, Sample Two (see Table 3) was comprised of all first-semester students enrolled at this university from fall 2000 to fall 2002 who were selected through a stratified random sampling by low TASP-Rdg, SATV, and ACTE performance. Sample Two was divided into two groups: (a) those who passed the developmental reading course (treatment group); and (b) those who did not take the reading course over these three academic years (control group).

Table 3 shows that the treatment and control groups were comparable in ability as measured by TASP-Rdg subtest scores, SATV, or ACTE. This confirms the designation of those in the control group as comparable to the treatment group. It also removes the confounding effect of existing cognitive or reading ability found in previous research (Cox et al., 2003; Simpson & Rush, 2003; Stallworth-Clark et al., 1996).

Table 3 also shows that students in Sample Two performed significantly lower than the university freshmen population as a whole, confirming their designation as "true" developmental reading students along several measures. Table 4 reveals that the demographics of the treatment and control groups were decidedly more diverse than the university as a whole. This diversity is typical of developmental education populations in general. The tables suggest these two groups were comparable and, indeed, composed of true, developmental students.

Table 3. Standardized Reading Scores for Study Two

	TASP-R			SATV			ACTE		
	N	M	SD	N	M	SD	N	M	SD
Treatment	51	207.5	17.8	48	413.1	51.4	25	17.5*	2.4
Control	78	210.9*	13.8	63	413.3*	53.1	59	17.2	3.2
University	1197	257.3**	17.0	2554	517.3**	72.3	1387	21.0**	4.0

*not significant, **$p < .000$

Table 4. Sample Two Demographics

	Gender (%)		Ethnicity (%)					
	M	F	Anglo	African Amer.	Hisp.	Asian	Amer. Indian	International
Treatment	47.1	52.9	52.9	17.6	23.5	3.9	0.0	2.0
Control	37.4	62.6	61.7	7.8	27.0	2.6	0.9	0.0
University	56.0	44.0	71.9	5.1	18.4	2.0	0.6	1.9

Study Two Materials

The developmental course materials were used in this as well the first study. All students in this study used the required materials for the reading-intensive course (HIST 1310), which ranged from course textbooks, course handouts, materials on reserve, and Web pages.

Study Two Assessments and Procedures

The first assessment for Research Question Two was subsequent performance on the standardized reading test (TASP-Rdg). It addressed Research Subquestion 2.1: *Did students who were taught to use strategic reading outperform students who were not taught strategic reading on a subsequent retaking of a standardized reading test?*

Research Subquestion 2.2 asked: *Did students who were taught to use strategic reading outperform students who were not taught strategic reading as shown by the grade in a reading-intensive course?* To address this question, we collected grades for three entering freshmen classes (fall 2000, 2001, and 2002) from the fall semester 2000 through the spring semester 2004 for six courses defined by this university as reading-intensive. These were two courses in American history, one introductory course in psychology, two introductory courses in political science, and one sophomore level English literature course. One of the courses, History 1310, was selected as the most appropriate of the reading-intensive courses to use as a dependent variable. To select this course, we computed mean grades for the subpopulation of students who failed the TASP-Rdg subtest and who took these reading-intensive courses at the university ($N = 242$). A confounding variable was courses transferred from a community college or another university, for which reading task demands were unknown. Therefore, grades in transferred courses were dropped from the analysis. Mean grades can be found in Table 5.

Table 5. Performance in Reading-Intensive Courses

	N	M	SD	z	DFW%
POSI 2320	32	2.19	0.99	11.47*	n.a.
ENG LIT	39	2.18	1.12	13.22*	28.6
HIST 1320	39	2.05	1.05	12.89*	22.0
POSI 2310	44	1.86	1.02	14.55*	n.a.
PSY 1300	32	1.81	1.30	11.57*	14.2
HIST 1310	56	1.34	1.15		39.2

*$p < .0000$

The average grade in HIST 1310 was the lowest grade, suggesting it was the most difficult course. Results (Meyers, personal communication, May 11, 2004) from internal studies of percentages in freshmen level courses of D, F, and W grades (DFW%) showed that HIST 1310 has a much higher DFW% rate (39.2%) when compared to the other freshmen level courses, also confirming its difficulty. Because DFW% rates were not available for POSI 2310 or POSI 2320, we interviewed the department chair of Political Science, who stated that although reading was required in these courses, it accounted for a small part of the examinations compared to lecture and other instruction (Mihalkanin, personal communication, May 13, 2004). Finally, a Mann-Whitney U test of significance showed students' grades in HIST 1310 were significantly lower than all the other reading-intensive courses. Therefore, the final grade in History 1310 was selected as the dependent variable for Research Question Two.

Study Two Results

Research question 2.1: Transfer on standardized reading test performance. To determine whether strategic reading improved performance on a subsequent retaking of a standardized reading test when compared to a control group, we followed students' performance from the fall semester 2000, through spring semester 2004. Results of a paired samples t-test measure indicated significantly greater improvement on a subsequent retaking of the TASP-Rdg subtest for the treatment group ($M = 252.61, SD = 16.10, N = 56$) than for the control group ($M = 242.47, SD = 22.77, N = 43$); t (72) = 2.51, p = .014. This supports findings of Research Subquestion 1.2 as well as previous research (Caverly et al., 1995; Maloney, 2003) in which students who enrolled in a developmental reading course who learned strategic reading performed better on subsequent retaking of standardized tests.

Research question 2.2: Transfer to a reading-intensive course. A second question explored whether strategic reading improved transfer to reading-intensive courses when compared to a control group. Students' performance was followed from the fall semester 2000 through spring semester 2004 in one reading-intensive course, HIST 1310.

Using a nonparametric Mann-Whitney U test statistic, we compared grades in HIST 1310 for the treatment group ($M = 1.97, SD = 0.72, N = 30$) against the grades in HIST 1310 for the control group ($M = 1.34, SD = 1.15, N = 56$). A significantly higher grade for the treatment group occurred ($U = 579.5$, $z = 2.46$, Asymptotic Significance = .014). Because of the ordinal nature of the HIST 1310 grade data, nonparametric Spearman rho correlation as a measure of association (i.e., effect) was calculated between the median rank of the treatment group and the median rank of the control group. The Spearman rho correlation coefficient ($r = 0.09$, $N = 121$) was a low positive effect (Cohen, 1988). Developmental students who were explicitly taught strategic reading outperformed developmental students who were not taught it. This finding of long-term transfer for a stand-alone course was consistent with others (Cox et al., 2003; Simpson & Rush, 2003; Stallworth-Clark et al., 2000) who found such transfer for linked courses.

Discussion

The two investigations reported here looked at the effectiveness of strategic reading instruction in a stand-alone course for true developmental students, defined as having scored significantly lower than their peers on more than one reading assessment. Instruction over one semester resulted in significant growth in their scores on a standardized reading test, in an assessment of their metacognitive awareness of effective strategic reading tactics, and in their report of beliefs in strategic reading. There was small but significant gain in reading performance as measured by a teacher-made comprehension test of a college textbook chapter but no gain on a self-efficacy scale. In other words, students learned a strategic reading strategy called PLAN and became strategic readers as assessed by four out of five measures.

This strategic reading instruction in a stand-alone course had a significant long-term transfer effect according to two measures, a standardized reading test and the grade in a subsequent reading-intensive college core course. Specifically, students enrolled in the reading course scored significantly higher on a standardized reading test compared to a control group of developmental readers who did not take the course. For students enrolled in the strategic reading course, there was a small, but significant effect size for grade in a subsequent reading-intensive history course, when compared to a control group, even after several semesters. This finding suggests a need for stronger or sustained intervention to garner a more robust effect. It is consistent with Cox et al. (2003), who found transfer of developmental reading measured as course grade in English composition and basic math. Such results are vital, not only for keeping developmental readers in college, but also for supporting the continuation of programs in light of criticism of college developmental reading instruction (Adelman, 1996; Maxwell, 1997).

Our two studies were conducted in a single university, which restricts generalizability. Moreover, selective admission criteria resulted in a smaller population of true developmental reading students. Still, similar strategic reading courses have been successfully taught to true developmental readers, though little evaluative or empirical research has emerged (Bower, Caverly, Stahl, & Voge, 2003). Future studies should differentiate true developmental readers from those so defined by a single assessment.

Research in linking a developmental reading course with a reading-intensive course has shown some success for teaching students strategic reading, self-efficacy, and the benefits of both (Simpson & Nist, 1997; Simpson & Rush, 2003; Stallworth-Clark et al., 2000). Still, little transfer of strategic reading has been found to other courses beyond the linked course, though there is some evidence of transfer for study strategies (Hattie et al., 1996). Improving self-efficacy and transfer of strategic reading in developmental readers calls for a strengthening of teaching and an attention to transfer of strategies. For example, pairing a stand-alone, strategic-reading course to a reading-intensive core course can provide guided practice. Subsequent support for transfer to other reading-intensive courses is needed to build independence.

The final course grade in reading-intensive courses still might not be the best measure of strategic reading transfer, although it is a more precise measure than semester GPA or retention. Many factors can enter into the computation of a final course grade (such as attendance, extra-credit work, or group projects) that require little strategic reading. Future studies should identify dependent variables that more precisely assess transfer, such as performance on specific classroom tests or tasks in subsequent semesters, and that are valid and reliable measures of knowledge developed primarily through reading.

College reading can be a daunting task. Not only must students read successfully and extensively, but also they must monitor their success, change strategies to meet varying learning demands, and attribute success to their strategic approaches to reading rather than to chance or external factors (Simpson & Nist, 2002; Zimmerman & Paulsen, 1995). We have been able to teach strategic reading to developmental students as documented by cognitive, metacognitive, affective, and self-report assessments. We also have been able to document transfer beyond one semester to performance on a standardized reading test and to a reading-intensive core course. Students seem to have learned PLAN. More importantly, the assessments suggest these students have begun to develop a plan for reading strategically.

Appendix

P or Predict step

Students were taught to predict the content and text structures of assigned readings by previewing titles, introductions, subtitles, boldfaced and italicized words, visual aids such as pictures and graphs, and summaries. As students predicted, they were also taught to create a concept map of ideas from this preview. They were taught to judge the task demands of the text and to compare it to the task demands of the professor.

L or Locate step

Students were taught to consider their prior knowledge of the mapped ideas by placing check marks next to known and question marks next to unknown information.

A or Add step

Students were taught to engage in close reading as they confirmed their prior knowledge and answered their questions about unknown information. They were taught to add new branches to their map where there were question marks as well as to confirm where there were check marks adding new information if incorrect.

N or Note step

After reading, students were taught to consider what they now knew and how well it satisfied the task demands assessed before reading. If they perceived the task required the recall information, students learned to review their maps using the graphic organizer to help them remember. If they perceived the task required them to reconstruct information, students learned to rebuild their maps to represent the macrostructure of the author's argument and to review this new structure in preparation for a variety of assessments.

References

Adelman, C. (1996, October 4). Point of view: The truth about remedial work: It's more complex than windy rhetoric and simple solutions suggest. *Chronicle of Higher Education*, p. A36.

Alexander, P. A., & Jetton, T. L. (2000). Learning from text: A multidimensional and developmental perspective. In M. Kamil, P. Mosenthal, P. D. Pearson, & R. Barr (Eds.), *Handbook of reading research* (Vol. 3, pp. 285–310). Mahwah, NJ: Lawrence Erlbaum.

Alexander, P. A., & Murphy, P. K. (1999). Learner profiles: Valuing individual differences within classroom communities. In P. L. Ackerman, P. C. Kyllonen, & P. D. Roberts (Eds.), *Learning and individual differences Processes, traits, and content determinants* (pp. 412–432). Washington, DC: American Psychological Association.

Anderson, T. H., & Armbruster, B. B. (1984). Studying. In P. D. Pearson (Ed.), *Handbook of reading research* (pp. 657–680). New York: Longman.

Barnett, J. (1996, April). *Self-regulation of reading strategies in a college course.* Paper presented at the annual meeting of the American Educational Research Association, New York.

Bohr, L. (1994). College classes that attract and generate good readers. *Journal of College Reading and Learning, 26*(2), 30–44.

Bower, P., Caverly, D. C., Stahl, N., & Voge, D. J. (2003, October). *Making the transition from skills-based reading instruction to strategy-based instruction;*

Parts 1 and 2. Paper presented at the annual meeting of the College Reading and Learning Association, Albuquerque, NM.

Boylan, H. R., Bonham, B. S., White, J. R., & George, A. P. (2000). Evaluation of college reading and study strategy programs. In R. F. Flippo & D. C. Caverly (Eds.), *Handbook of college reading and study strategy research* (pp. 365–402). Mahwah, NJ: Lawrence Erlbaum.

Burrell, K. I., Tao, L., Simpson, M. L., & Mendez-Berrueta, H. (1997). How do we know what we are preparing students for? A reality check of one university's academic literacy demands. *Research & Teaching in Developmental Education, 13*, 15–70.

Caverly, D. C., Mandeville, T. P., & Nicholson, S. A. (1995). PLAN: A study-reading strategy for informational text. *Journal of Adolescent & Adult Literacy, 39*(3), 190–199.

Caverly, D. C., & Orlando, V. P. (1991). Textbook study strategies. In R. F. Flippo & D. C. Caverly (Eds.), *Teaching reading and study strategies at the college level* (pp. 86–165). Newark, DE: International Reading Association.

Caverly, D. C., Orlando, V. P., & Mullen, J. L. (2000). Textbook study strategies. In R. F. Flippo & D. C. Caverly (Eds.), *Handbook of college reading and study strategy research* (pp. 105–147). Mahwah, NJ: Lawrence Erlbaum.

Cohen, J. (1988). *Statistical power analysis for the behavioral sciences.* Mahwah, NJ: Lawrence Erlbaum.

Colarusso, K. (2000). *Using a faculty survey of college-level reading and writing requirements to revise developmental reading and writing objectives. Kellogg Institute final report, practicum 1999.* (ERIC Document Reproduction Service No. ED448823)

Cox, S. R., Friesner, D. L., & Khayum, J. (2003). Do reading skills courses help underprepared readers achieve academic success in college? *Journal of College Reading and Learning, 33*, 170–196.

Donley, J., & Spires, H. A. (1999). Effects of instructional context on academic performance and self-regulated learning in underprepared college students. *Research & Teaching in Developmental Education, 16*, 23–32.

Doughty, I. D. (1990). *Improving reading comprehension of underprepared college students.* Unpublished master's thesis, Nova University, Miami, FL.

Duffy, G. G. (2002). The case for direct explanation of strategies. In C. C. Block & M. Pressley (Eds.), *Comprehension instruction: Research-based best practices* (pp. 28–41). New York: Guilford Press.

El-Hindi, A. E. (1996). Enhancing metacognitive awareness of college learners. *Reading Horizons, 36*(3), 214–230.

Hattie, J., Biggs, J., & Purdie, N. (1996). Effects of learning skills interventions on student learning: A meta-analysis. *Review of Educational Research, 66*, 99–126.

Horn, L., Peter, K., & Rooney, K. (2002). *Profile of undergraduates in U.S. postsecondary institutions: 1999–2000* (A. G. Malizio, Project Officer) [Statistical Analysis Report NCES 2002-168]. Retrieved June 1, 2004, from U.S. Department of Education, National Center for Education Statistics World Wide Web Electronic Catalog: http://nces.ed.gov/pubsearch

Maloney, W. H. (2003). Connecting the texts of their lives to academic literacy: Creating success for at-risk first-year college students. *Journal of Adolescent & Adult Literacy, 46*, 664–673.

Maxwell, M. (1997). *The dismal state of required developmental reading programs. Roots, causes and solutions.* (ERIC Document Reproduction Service No. ED415501)

Moyle, P. B. (Ed.). (2003). Biodiversity and biogeography. In *Essays in wildlife conservation: A reader for WFC 10, Wildlife Conservation and Ecology* (chap. 3). Retrieved October 8, 2003, from http://www.meer.org/chap3.htm

National Evaluation Systems. (2003). *THEA: Texas Higher Education Assessment.* Retrieved June 1, 2004, from http://www.thea.nesinc.com/

Nist, S. L., & Simpson, M. L. (1990). The effect of PLAE upon students' test performance and metacognitive awareness. In J. E. Readence & R. S. Baldwin (Eds.), *39th Yearbook of the National Reading Conference: Literacy theory and research: Analyses from multiple paradigms* (pp. 321–328). Chicago: National Reading Conference.

Nist, S. L., & Simpson, M. L. (2000). College studying. In M. Kamil, P. Mosenthal, P. D. Pearson, & R. Barr (Eds.), *Handbook of reading research* (Vol. 3, pp. 645–666). Mahwah, NJ: Lawrence Erlbaum.

O'Hear, M. F., & MacDonald, R. B. (1995). A critical review of research in developmental education: Part I. *Journal of Developmental Education, 19*(2), 2–6.

Parsad, B., & Lewis, L. (2003). *Remedial education at degree-granting postsecondary institutions in fall 2000* (B. Greene, Project Officer) [Statistical Analysis Report NCES 2004-010]. Retrieved December 26, 2003, from U.S. Department of Education, National Center for Education Statistics World Wide Web Electronic Catalog: http://nces.ed.gov/pubsearch

Pressley, M. (2002). Comprehension strategies instruction: A turn-of-the-century report. In C. C. Block & M. Pressley (Eds.), *Comprehension instruction: Research-based best practices* (pp. 11–27). New York: Guilford Press.

Pressley, M., & Afflerbach, P. (1995). *Verbal protocols of reading: The nature of constructively responsive reading.* Hillsdale, NJ: Lawrence Erlbaum.

Pressley, M., Yokoi, L., Van Meter, P., Van Etten, S., & Freebern, G. (1997). Some of the reasons preparing for exams is so hard: What can be done to make it easier. *Educational Psychology Review, 9,* 1–38.

Robinson, F. P. (1970). *Effective study* (4th ed). New York: Harper & Row.

Scholz, U., Gutierrez-Dona, B., Sud, S., & Schwarzer, R. (2002). Is perceived self-efficacy a universal construct? Psychometric findings from 25 countries. *European Journal of Psychological Assessment, 18*(3), 242–251.

Simpson, M. L. (2002). Program evaluation studies: Strategic learning delivery model suggestions. *Journal of Developmental Education, 26*(2), 2–4, 6, 8, 10, 39.

Simpson, M. L., & Nist, S. L. (1997). Perspectives on learning history: A case study. *Journal of Literacy Research, 29*(3), 363–395.

Simpson, M. L., & Nist, S. L. (2000). An update on strategic learning: It's more than textbook reading strategies. *Journal of Adolescent & Adult Literacy, 43*(6), 528–541.

Simpson, M. L., & Nist, S. L. (2002). Encouraging active reading at the college level. In C. C. Block & M. Pressley (Eds.), *Comprehension instruction: Research-based best practices* (pp. 365–381). New York: Guilford Press.

Simpson, M. L., & Rush, L. (2003). College students' beliefs, strategy employment, transfer, and academic performance: An examination across three academic disciplines. *Journal of College Reading and Learning, 33,* 146–156.

Stallworth-Clark, R., Nolen, M. T., Warkentin, R., & Scott, J. S. (2000, April). *College students' academic performance: The interaction of strategy engagement, content, and context.* Paper presented at the annual meeting of the American Educational Research Association, New Orleans, LA.

Stallworth-Clark, R., Scott, J. S., & Nist, S. L. (1996, April). *The teaching-learning process and postsecondary at-risk reading students: Cognitive, metacognitive, affective, and instructional variables explaining academic performance.* Paper presented at the annual meeting of the American Educational Research Association, New York.

Wade, S. E., & Reynolds, R. E. (1989). Developing metacognitive awareness. *Journal of Reading, 33*(1), 6–15.

Weinstein, C. E., & Mayer, R. E. (1985). The teaching of learning strategies. In M. C. Wittrock (Ed.), *Handbook of research on teaching* (pp. 315–327). New York: Macmillan.

Zimmerman, B. J. (2002). Becoming a self-regulated learner: An overview. *Theory into Practice, 41*(2), 64–70.

Zimmerman, B. J., & Paulsen, A. S. (1995). Self-monitoring during collegiate studying: An invaluable tool for academic self-regulation. *New Directions for Teaching and Learning, 63*, 13–27.

How Classroom Teachers Can Help Students Learn and Teach Them How to Learn

Kenneth A. Kiewra

Different from reading instruction, a collection of study strategies called NORM (Note taking, Organizing, Relating, Monitoring) helps ineffective students improve their ability to learn. Kenneth A. Kiewra's NORM strategies are learning and study methods that college instructors can teach their students by embedding the lessons in a content-based lecture. Kiewra's main assertion is that instructors will promote good strategy use by teaching subject matter in ways compatible with his favored NORM study system.

You would think that college students are expert learners; after all, they have completed 12 years of school and have chosen to extend their academic path. In reality, many college students are deficient learners who employ weak strategies in the classroom and while studying (Gubbels, 1999; Kiewra, 1991; Pressley, Yokoi, Van Meter, Van Etten, & Freebern, 1997).

I teach a college-level study skills course and have seen students' learning deficits firsthand. The first day of class, for example, I assess students' learning potential by presenting a lecture, providing an opportunity for students to review their lecture notes, and then testing them. What I observe are students recording sketchy notes, creating outlines, and studying noted ideas by rehearsing them one idea at a time. Employing these ineffective strategies (Craik & Watkins, 1973; Kiewra, DuBois, Christian, McShane, Meyerhoffer, & Roskelley, 1991) naturally leads to poor test performance.

Why are many students ineffective learners? It could be that students are rarely instructed *how* to learn. Strategy instruction is rarely incorporated into the curriculum (Applebee, 1984; Durkin, 1979). Durkin, for example, viewed more than 7,000 minutes of reading and social studies instruction and did not observe a single incidence of strategy instruction. Educators, it seems, teach content such as math and science, but fail to teach students *how* to learn such content. Reflect on your own education: Did anyone teach you how to record notes and study for exams? Probably not. Yet students are expected to know how to learn.

Fortunately, students can learn how to learn when taught strategies in the context of study stills courses. Study skills, or "Learning to Learn" (Gall, Gall, Jacobsen, & Bullock, 1990; Simpson, Hynd, Nist, & Burrell, 1997) courses, like the one I teach, often include units on motivation and time management, note taking, text learning, studying, and test taking (Kiewra & DuBois, 1998). Completing a study skills course, though, is not the only way to learn how to learn. Ideally, instructors can teach students how to learn by embedding strategy instruction within their subject matter courses (Pressley & Woloshyn, 1995). While teaching psychology or history, for example, instructors can also teach students strategies for text learning, lecture note taking, or studying for exams.

Good strategy instructors must know two things: (a) which strategies are effective and (b) how to teach them by embedding strategy instruction into content teaching. The latter — how to embed strategy instruction — is not too complicated. Strategy instructors should (a) *introduce* the strategy by modeling it and describing it, (b) *sell* the strategy by telling why it works, (c) *generalize* the strategy by telling where else it is useful, and (d) *perfect* the strategy by providing practice opportunities (Pressley & Woloshyn, 1995). As for the matter of which strategies are effective, this article focuses on strategies appropriate for four crucial learning components: Note taking, Organizing, Relating, and Monitoring. Together, the first letters of these four learning components spell "NORM." As you will see, these four learning components are hardly the norm for most college students who were never taught how to learn. This article addresses each NORM component by describing students' typical practices and specific strategies that should be employed. Examples of how instructors might embed strategy instruction into content teaching are also provided. The article's purpose, then, is to improve teaching so students achieve more and, ultimately, learn how to learn.

Note Taking

Lecture learning is prominent in college classrooms. Armbruster (2000) reported that college students usually spend about 80% of class time listening to lectures. Indeed, the lecture method remains "the 'sacred cow' among most college ... instructors" (Carrier, Williams, & Dalagard, 1988, p. 223). If lecturing is the instructor's sacred cow, then lecture note taking is the students' "pet calf" (Titsworth & Kiewra, 2001). Ninety-nine percent of college students record lecture notes (Palmatier & Bennett, 1974), and 94% of American students believe that note taking is a valued and important activity (Dunkel & Davy, 1989).

Students are right to record notes and value note taking. There is strong evidence that recording lecture notes leads to higher achievement than not recording notes, whether the notes are reviewed or not (Kiewra, 1985a). Moreover, higher quantities of note taking are associated with higher achievement (and vice versa) (Kiewra & Benton, 1988; Kiewra & Fletcher, 1984; Titsworth & Kiewra, 2001). More specifically, students have about a 50% chance of recalling noted information on a test, but only about a 15% chance of recalling nonnoted information (Aiken, Thomas, & Shennum, 1975).

The problem is that students typically record incomplete notes — usually 20–40% of the important lecture ideas (e.g., Kiewra, 1985b; O'Donnell & Dansereau, 1993). Students must record more notes and instructors should take steps to increase lecture note-taking.

Providing the Instructor's Notes

One obvious strategy for increasing the quantity of notes available to students is for instructors to provide a detailed set of notes to review. Research shows that students who listen to a lecture and later review instructor-provided notes outperform students who record and review their own notes (see Kiewra, 1985c). One study went so far as to show that reviewing the instructor's notes is so effective, it can compensate for missing the lecture (Kiewra, 1985d). I certainly do not advocate that students miss class. I do advocate that instructors, if so inclined, provide students with detailed notes and explain the benefits of reviewing them. Of course, many instructors are too busy to generate complete notes or simply believe that note taking is the students' responsibility (Kiewra, 1984). For these instructors, there is, perhaps, a middle ground — providing skeletal note-taking devices.

Providing Skeletal Notes

Skeletal notes contain the lecture's main ideas interspersed with spaces for note-taking. Skeletal notes provide the lecture's organization in advance and, if ample space is provided (Hartley, 1976), invite complete note taking. In one study, skeletal note takers recorded 56% of the lecture ideas, whereas conventional note takers recorded only 38% (Kiewra, DuBois et al., 1991).

Providing Lecture Cues

Another strategy for increasing note taking is providing lecture cues. Cues signaling important ideas can be written on the chalkboard (Locke, 1977), on transparencies (Baker & Lombardi, 1985), or presented orally (Maddox & Hoole, 1975; Scerbo, Warm, Dember, & Grasha, 1992). In all of these studies, note taking or achievement or both were raised when importance cues were presented. Consider, for example, that Locke (1977) found that students record about 80% of information written on the chalk board — a huge jump in note taking beyond the roughly 30% of lecture points students normally record without assistance.

Instructors can also boost note taking by providing organizational cues that signal the lecture's main topics and common categories. Titsworth and Kiewra (2001) inserted organizational cues signaling the lecture's four topics (the names of four communication theories) and five common categories pertaining to each topic (e.g., definition, application, and context) throughout the lecture and at the start. Students receiving the brief lecture cues (e.g., "Now I'll address the context for personal communication theory") recorded 54% of the lecture's organizational points compared to 15% for those hearing an uncued lecture. Students hearing the cued lecture also recorded 64% of the lecture details, whereas uncued students recorded only 29% of the lecture details. This study shows that organizational cues can drastically boost organizational points and related details in notes.

Re-presenting the Lecture

A fourth strategy for increasing note taking is re-presenting the lecture (Kiewra, Mayer, Christensen, Kim, & Risch, 1991). College students recorded notes while watching a videotaped lecture presented one, two, or three times. Students viewing the lecture twice (53%) or three times (60%) recorded more notes than those viewing the lecture one time (38%). Given these findings, I recommend that instructors and students make audio- or videotaped copies of lectures for students to replay so they can add to their notes each time they do so.

Reconstructing Lecture Notes

A fifth strategy for increasing the number of lecture notes for review is "reconstruction." Following the lecture, students should review their notes in hopes that their recorded notes prompt them to reconstruct and add missing lecture points (Rickards & Friedman, 1978).

Several informal studies I have conducted with my study skills classes show that reconstruction alone boosts the percentage of noted lecture points from about 30% to 50%. Students reconstructing notes with a partner boost the number of noted lecture points even higher. This greater increase is probably the result of note sharing and collaborative reconstruction. Whatever the reason, students' individual or joint attempts to embellish notes following the lecture seem worthwhile.

In summary, instructors can help students compile more complete notes by providing (a) detailed notes, (b) skeletal note-taking devices, (c) lecture cues, (d) audio- or videotaped copies of the lecture for re-presentation, or (e) opportunities to reconstruct missed lecture points at the conclusion of lectures. These instructional strategies, although immediately helpful, may not result in students' acquiring strategies they can use in future settings. The narrative below is an example of how an instructor might promote note taking and simultaneously teach a note-taking strategy. Notice that the four components of strategy instruction mentioned in the introduction are present.

"Class, I noticed that many of you recorded incomplete notes when I lectured last week about schedules of reinforcement. Here is a set of complete notes that I created from that lecture to model good note taking. I numbered each lecture point that I recorded and you can see there were 90 key points. Quickly examine your notes from that lecture, and count how many of these 90 points you have. (Introduce strategy)

"I'm not surprised that most of you have just 20 to 40 of these lecture points in your notes. Research shows that most students record only about 30% of the important lecture ideas. This is too bad because research also shows that the more notes students record the better they perform on tests. Let me tell you now about a strategy you can use to increase note taking. I call it the reconstruction strategy and it works like this: Soon after a lecture, reread your notes and try to recall or reconstruct lecture information missing from your notes. When you do, add the 'new' information to your notes. It really works. I've had students try it in my study skills class and they report that they double the number of lecture points in notes — especially when they use the reconstruction strategy with a partner. (Introduce and sell strategy)

"Let's have everyone practice the reconstruction strategy now in pairs by working through your notes from today. In a while, we'll see how much more complete your notes are. (Perfect strategy)

"The reconstruction strategy, of course, is useful for any psychology lecture or for lectures in any subject area. Try using it in your other classes." (Generalize strategy)

Organizing

Once students record notes, what should they do with them to best learn the material and prepare for tests? Some study skills books recommend that students first organize their notes in outline form (e.g., Ferrett, 2000), and many students apparently take that suggestion to heart (Van Meter, Yokoi, & Pressley, 1994). The purpose of outlining is to readily see how information is organized into topics, categories, and associated details.

Using Matrix Notes

A great deal of research, however, has confirmed that organizing comparative information into a matrix results in greater learning than organizing it into an outline (see Kiewra, 1994; Robinson & Kiewra, 1995). Figure 1 is an outline containing information about four wildcats. Notice it contains four topics (tiger, lion, cheetah, and bobcat), five categories common to all topics (call, weight, life span, habitat, and social behavior), and details pertaining to the intersection of topics and categories (e.g., the tiger's call is a roar). The outline presents this information in a linear, top-to-bottom, structure. Figure 2 is a matrix representing the same information. Notice that topics appear on top, categories down the left margin, and details within the matrix cells. The matrix's two-dimensional structure is superior because it localizes

Figure 1. Wildcat Outline

WILDCATS

I. Tiger
  A. Call
    1. Roar
  B. Weight
    1. 450 pounds
  C. Life span
    1. 25 years
  D. Habitat
    1. Jungle
  E. Social behavior
    1. Solitary

II. Lion
  A. Call
    1. Roar
  B. Weight
    1. 400 pounds
  C. Life span
    1. 25 years
  D. Habitat
    1. Plains
  E. Social behavior
    1. Groups

III. Cheetah
  A. Call
    1. Purr
  B. Weight
    1. 125 pounds
  C. Life span
    1. 8 years
  D. Habitat
    1. Plains
  E. Social behavior
    1. Groups

IV. Bobcat
  A. Call
    1. Purr
  B. Weight
    1. 30 pounds
  C. Life span
    1. 6 years
  D. Habitat
    1. Forest
  E. Social behavior
    1. Solitary

Figure 2. Wildcat Matrix

WILDCATS	Tiger	Lion	Cheetah	Bobcat
Call	Roar	Roar	Purr	Purr
Weight	450	400	125	30
Life span	25	25	8	6
Habitat	Jungle	Plains	Plains	Forest
Social behavior	Solitary	Groups	Groups	Solitary

(Kauffman & Kiewra, 1999; Kiewra, Kauffman, Robinson, DuBois, & Staley, 1999) related information better than the outline. For example, if asked which wildcat has the shortest life span, a student studying the outline would have to locate the details pertaining to each wildcat's life span from the four distinct sections of the outline, hold each fact in memory, then compare the life spans to devise a response (Robinson & Skinner, 1996). In contrast, the matrix localizes the four life spans in a single matrix row, making them easier to compare. Consider another example involving information pertaining to two categories: weight and life span. Students studying the outline are likely to overlook the relationship between wildcats' weight and life span. This information must be gathered and synthesized from eight different and separated lines within the outline. In contrast, this same information is localized along adjacent matrix rows, making it easy to see that heavier cats live longer than lighter-weight cats.

As was true with note taking in general, instructors can help students obtain matrix notes for review by providing completed matrix notes (Kauffman & Kiewra, 1999; Kiewra et al., 1999) or by providing matrix frameworks for note taking (Kiewra, Dubois, et al., 1991). Instructors can also train students to construct matrices and other representations (Connelly, DuBois, & Staley, 1998; DuBois, Staley, Guzy, & DiNardo, 1995; Kiewra, 1994; Kiewra & DuBois, 1998).

An instructor can use matrices while teaching and embed matrix strategy training, as well. While teaching about the solar system, for example, an instructor can provide a matrix framework (containing topics and categories but no details) or a completed matrix like that shown in Figure 3. Presenting the matrix is, of course, the springboard for teaching the matrix strategy as briefly exemplified below.

Figure 3. Solar System Matrix

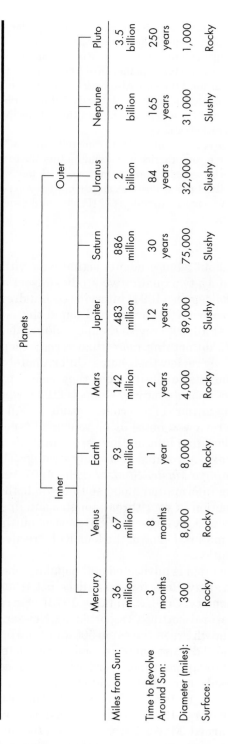

		Inner					Outer		
	Mercury	Venus	Earth	Mars	Jupiter	Saturn	Uranus	Neptune	Pluto
Miles from Sun:	36 million	67 million	93 million	142 million	483 million	886 million	2 billion	3 billion	3.5 billion
Time to Revolve Around Sun:	3 months	8 months	1 year	2 years	12 years	30 years	84 years	165 years	250 years
Diameter (miles):	300	8,000	8,000	4,000	89,000	75,000	32,000	31,000	1,000
Surface:	Rocky	Rocky	Rocky	Rocky	Slushy	Slushy	Slushy	Slushy	Rocky

"Class, I'm providing you with a matrix about the solar system. The matrix strategy is a good one. It localizes or groups information in a way so you can easily spot relationships. Notice in the matrix how easy it is to see that the greater the distance planets are from the sun, the greater their time to revolve around the sun. Also notice that inner planets are smaller and rockier than outer planets (with the exception of Pluto). Notice how difficult it is to spot these relationships in the outline I've also provided. (Introduce and sell strategy)

"Matrices are easy to construct. Let me tell you how I constructed this one. . . . Let's have you practice by extending this one to include new information about orbit speed and rotation time. . . . Before we stop, let's think of some other situations where we can use matrices in science, such as when comparing parts of an atom. . . ." (Perfect and generalize strategy)

Relating

Little is known about what students actually do with notes following lectures. Fortunately, two qualitative studies reveal a partial answer. Van Meter and colleagues (1994) interviewed hundreds of college students about their review behaviors and found that some students do not review notes at all; 29% revise them by adding, deleting, or reorganizing notes; 12% do nothing more than recopy them verbatim; and 47% report that they review their notes. Unfortunately, the researchers did not press students to clarify what they meant by "review." Some clarification comes from a study by Gubbels (1999) who investigated in depth the study behaviors of five college students. All five students reported that they reviewed notes using rehearsal-type strategies, such as repeating or rewriting information verbatim.

Rehearsal is also advocated as a study strategy. The popular study skills text, *Becoming a Master Student* (Ellis, 1997) recommends reciting and repeating information aloud so that you both hear it and "get the physical sensation in your throat, tongue, and lips." A leading cognitive psychology text (Anderson, 1985) reports on the PQ4R Method for learning text material. One of the four Rs is "recite," which involves repeating information.

Although rehearsal is advocated and popular, rehearsal is actually a weak study strategy. Rote rehearsal does not transfer information into long-term memory (Craik & Watkins, 1973). One remarkable study of memory in natural settings (reported by Neisser, 1982) even described a professor who read the same 500-word prayer aloud each day for 25 years and still did not know the prayer completely from memory. He required over 100 promptings in order to recall it correctly.

If not rehearsal, then what should students do with their lecture notes or other review materials? According to Mayer (1984, 1996) and others (e.g., Sternberg, 1985), students must relate or connect the material to be learned. Mayer advocated two types of connections: internal connections and external connections. Figure 4 shows the two types of connections. The broken lines represent the internal connec-

Figure 4. Diagram Showing Internal and External Connections

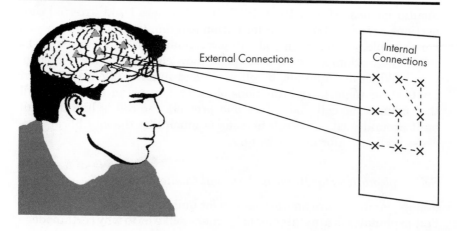

tions made within the material studied (the Xs). For example, a student acquiring the facts that white rhinos eat grass, have square lips, and live in grasslands might connect these three facts by saying: "It makes sense that an animal in the grasslands eats grass because grass is plentiful. It makes sense that it has square lips that are useful for scooping mouthfuls of grass." Figure 4's solid lines show the external connections made between the material studied (Xs) and past knowledge (the triangles). For instance, a student might relate new information about white rhinos to past knowledge about cows, which also eat grass, have square lips, and live in grasslands.

Matrices for Building Internal Connections

Matrices aid in building internal connections. As already mentioned, matrices localize related information, making it faster and easier to build connections among ideas. Robinson and Skinner (1996) had students search informationally equivalent texts, outlines, and matrices to answer relational questions such as "which animal is the largest?" Relationships were found more quickly when students searched a matrix compared to a text or outline.

Studying matrix notes also led to higher achievement on relational test items than studying an informationally equivalent text or outline following a lecture about wildcats (Kauffman & Kiewra, 1999). Two types of relational questions were used: local relations that involved relationships among wildcats relevant to one category such as call (e.g., Which two cats purr?), and global relations that involved relationships among wildcats relevant to two categories such as call and weight (e.g., "What is the relationship between call and weight?"). Students studying matrix notes outperformed the other groups on both relational item types.

Mental Models for Building External Connections

Mental models (Mayer, 1989, 1996) help learners build external connections as they relate new information to a familiar analogous model. For example, when learning about how a pump works, a learner might relate the workings of a pump to past knowledge about how a syringe works. When learning about cell parts and functions, learners might relate these to parts and functions of a city. For instance, the cell wall that defines the cell's boundary and protects the cell is like the wall built around a city. The cell nucleus is much like the city library because both are information centers.

Self-Explanations for Building External Connections

Self-explanations are another means for building external connections. Self-explanations are statements learners make as to why certain ideas are so. For instance, given the facts that tigers knock their prey over and cheetahs run their prey down, I ask myself why that is so. I may then use my past knowledge that tigers are large and cheetahs are fast to generate the self-explanations that these wildcats exploit their greatest strengths to capture prey.

Self-explanations have empirical support. For example, Bielaczyc, Pirolli, and Brown (1991) taught college students to generate self-explanations that linked facts and examples about LISP computer programming. Students trained in self-explanations outperformed students using memorization and recall techniques with respect to learning and applying LISP programming techniques. Pressley and his colleagues (1997) sometimes refer to self-explanations as "elaborative interrogation." They contend that students should habitually ask themselves "why" questions about new material to increase understanding. A series of studies by King (1989, 1991, 1992) and reported by Armbruster (2000) reveal the value of why-type questions. College and high school students taught to generate and answer why-type questions as a review strategy following lectures outperformed untrained students who reviewed in their normal fashion.

Instructors can easily embed strategy training for relating information in their courses. Below are excerpts of what an instructor might say while teaching students about the characteristics of fish and concurrently teaching a relation strategy.

> "The text points out that the catfish has a mottled appearance and lives at the bottom, while the albacore has a light-colored belly and lives at the surface. You might be able to simply memorize this information, but you might also forget it or reverse it because it seems rather arbitrary. Let me teach you a strategy for relating information that makes learning more meaningful and memorable. (Sell strategy)
>
> "I call this the self-explanation strategy. What I do is raise the question "why?" and then use my past knowledge to seek a logical explanation.

In this case, I wonder why these fish have the appearance they do and how it might relate to their habitat. I know from past experiences that many animals such as deer and polar bears blend into their surroundings so they won't be easily seen by predators or prey. Perhaps, the catfish's dark upper side makes it hard to see from above because its dark upper side blends into a lake's dark bottom. Similarly, the albacore's light-colored belly makes it hard to be seen by other fish below because it blends well with the light-colored surface. (Introduce strategy)

"Now try using this strategy to explain the relationships between the crappie and croaker's appearance and habitat. . . ." (Generalize and perfect strategy)

Monitoring

Ideally, students should know whether they are prepared for exams. According to Pressley and colleagues (1997), most students do not adequately monitor their understanding before exams and are, therefore, unaware that they do not know all they need to know. Pressley and colleagues (1990a, 1990b) had college students read short passages and report the main ideas after reading. Students also reported how confident they were in their responses. Results showed that readers were almost as confident in their incorrect responses as their correct ones. Thus, they were unable to accurately monitor their understanding.

It seems that students sometimes do not even try to monitor their understanding. Bransford and Nitsch (1978) gave students the short passage below and asked them to rate its comprehensibility:

> The man was worried. His car came to a halt and he was all alone. It was dark and cold. The man took off his overcoat, rolled down the window, and got out of the car as quickly as possible. Then he used all his strength to move as fast as he could. He was relieved when he finally saw the lights of the city, even though they were far away.

All agreed the passage made sense. Students were then asked questions such as "Why did the man take off his overcoat if it was cold outside?" "Why did he roll down this window?" Only after pondering these teacher-delivered questions did students recognize that they did not understand the passage (which was actually about a submerged car).

Self-testing

The problem is that many students do not know that they don't know the material until they are tested. Of course, then it is too late. An excellent strategy to improve self-monitoring is self-testing (Davey & McBride, 1986; Meichenbaum, 1977). Students should test themselves so thoroughly prior to an exam that there is nothing the instructor can ask them that they haven't already asked themselves. Instructors can facilitate self-testing by providing students with previous tests or practice tests as study devices (Pressley et al., 1997). Or, they can do what I do in my study skills class and assign students to generate practice tests. In the context of this assignment, I teach students the self-testing strategy as follows:

> "Class, you are going to be tested next week on our motivation unit. Raise your hand if you think you know this material well. Almost all of you believe you know it well. Let's find out. Take this brief practice test now. . . . Hmm, results indicate that the average score was 64%. Now how well do you think you know this information? Most of you thought you knew this information but only realized you did not when I tested you. Had this been a real test, most of you would have failed. Let me teach you a great strategy: self-testing. (Sell strategy)
>
> "You should generate and answer test questions when you study. In fact you should do this cooperatively with others (O'Donnell & Dansereau, 1993) so you have more and different questions to assess your knowledge. (Introduce strategy)
>
> "Let's practice together generating more potential test questions for our upcoming exam and exams in your other classes." (Generalize and perfect strategy)

Conclusion

The strategies for Note taking, Organizing, Relating, and Monitoring recommended in this article are, unfortunately, not the "NORM" for most students who record brief lecture notes, and then review notes by constructing outlines, rehearsing details, and failing to monitor their test readiness. Good instructors, though, can promote good strategy use by teaching their subject matter in ways compatible with the favored NORM strategies presented in this article. For example, you can provide note-taking frameworks, lecture cues, and re-present lectures to boost lecture note taking; provide matrices to aid organization and build relationships among presented ideas; connect newly presented ideas to familiar models to build relationships between new and past knowledge; and supply practice tests to increase self-monitoring for test readiness.

Instructors who do these things — who present information effectively — are good instructors, but they can and should do more. Recall the old adage "If you give a man a fish, you feed him for a day, but if you teach him *how* to fish, you feed him for a lifetime." Instructors who present information so effectively that students are compelled to learn in effective ways are good "fish givers." They give students the means to learn what is being taught right now. What more can instructors do? Be fishing teachers (Kiewra et al., 2001). As you teach in ways that help students learn, teach students how to do these things (e.g., develop matrices and build models) on their own. Embed the teaching of learning strategies in content instruction so that the fishing pole is gradually transferred from your hands to students' hands, thereby helping them learn now and for a lifetime.

References

Aiken, E. G., Thomas, G. S., & Shennum, W. A. (1975). Memory for a lecture: Effects of notes, lecture rate and informational density. *Journal of Educational Psychology, 67*, 439–444.

Anderson, J. R. (1985). *Cognitive psychology and its implications.* New York: W. H. Freeman.

Applebee, A. N. (1984). *Contexts for learning to write.* Norwood, NJ: Ablex.

Armbruster, B. B. (2000). Taking notes from lectures. In R. F. Flippo & D. C. Caverly (Eds.), *Handbook of college reading and study strategy research* (pp. 175–199). Mahwah, NJ: Lawrence Erlbaum.

Baker, L., & Lombardi, B. R. (1985). Students' lecture notes and their relation to test performance. *Teaching of Psychology, 12*, 28–32.

Bielaczyc, K., Pirolli, P., & Brown, A. L. (1991, March). *The effects of training in explanation strategies on the acquisition of programming skills.* Paper presented at the annual meeting of the American Educational Research Association, Chicago.

Bransford, J. D., & Nitsch, K. E. (1978). Coming to understand things we could not previously understand. In J. F. Kavanagh & W. Strange (Eds.). *Speech and language in the laboratory, school, and clinic* (pp. 267–307). Cambridge. MA: MIT Press.

Carrier, C. A., Williams, M. D., & Dalgaard, B. R. (1988). College students' perceptions of note taking and their relationship to selected learner characteristics and course achievement. *Research in Higher Education, 28*, 223–239.

Connelly, K., DuBois, N. F., & Staley, R. (1998, April). *Structured interview study of the long-term effects of a college study skills course: Traces and self-report measures.* Paper presented at the annual meeting of the American Educational Research Association, San Diego.

Craik, F. I. M., & Watkins, M. J. (1973). The role of rehearsal in short-term memory. *Journal of Verbal Learning and Verbal Behavior, 12*, 599–607.

Davey, B., & McBride, S. (1986). Generating self-questioning after reading: A comprehension assist for elementary students. *Journal of Educational Research, 80*(1), 43–46.

DuBois, N. F., Staley, R., Guzy, L., & DiNardo, P. (1995, April). *Durable effects of a study skills course on academic achievement.* Paper presented at the annual meeting of the American Educational Research Association, San Francisco.

Dunkel, P., & Davy, S. (1989). The heuristic of lecture note taking: Perceptions of American and international students regarding the value and practice of note taking. *English for Specific Purposes, 8*, 33–50.

Durkin, D. (1979). What classroom observations reveal about reading comprehension instruction. *Reading Research Quarterly, 14*, 481–538.

Ellis, D. (1997). *Becoming a master student.* St. Charles, IL: Houghton Mifflin.

Ferrett, S. K. (2000). *Peak performance: Success in college and beyond.* Columbus, OH: McGraw-Hill.

Gall, M. D., Gall, J. P., Jacobsen, D. R., & Bullock, T. L. (1990). *Tools for learning: A guide to teaching study skills.* Alexandria, VA: Association for Supervision and Curriculum Development.

Gubbels, P. S. (1999). *College student studying: A collected case study.* Unpublished doctoral dissertation. University of Nebraska-Lincoln.

Hartley, J. (1976). Lecture handouts and student note taking. *Programmed Learning and Educational Technology, 13*, 58–64.

Kauffman, D. F., & Kiewra, K. A. (1999, April). *Indexing, extraction, and localization effects for learning from matrices, text and outlines.* Paper presented at the annual meeting of the American Educational Research Association, Montreal, Canada.

Kiewra, K. A. (1984). Acquiring effective note-taking skills: An alternative to professional note taking. *Journal of Reading, 27,* 299–302.

Kiewra, K. A. (1985a). Investigating note taking and review: A depth of processing alternative. *Educational Psychologist, 20,* 20–32.

Kiewra, K. A. (1985b). Students' note-taking behaviors and the efficacy of providing the instructor's notes for review. *Contemporary Educational Psychology, 10,* 378–386.

Kiewra, K. A. (1985c). Providing the instructor's notes: An effective addition to student notetaking. *Educational Psychologist, 20,* 33–39.

Kiewra, K. A. (1985d). Learning from a lecture: An investigation of note taking, review, and attendance at a lecture. *Human Learning, 4,* 73–77.

Kiewra, K. A. (1991). Aids to lecture learning. *Educational Psychologist, 26,* 37–54.

Kiewra, K. A. (1994). The matrix representation system: Orientation, research, theory and application. In J. Smart (Ed.), *Higher education: Handbook of theory and research* (pp. 331–373). New York: Agathon.

Kiewra, K. A., & Benton, S. L. (1988). The relationship between information-processing ability and note taking. *Contemporary Educational Psychology, 13,* 33–44.

Kiewra, K. A., & DuBois, N. F. (1998). *Learning to learn: Making the transition from student to lifelong learner.* Needham Heights, MA: Allyn and Bacon.

Kiewra, K. A., DuBois, N. F., Christian, D., McShane, A., Meyerhoffer, M., & Roskelley, D. (1991). Note-taking functions and techniques. *Journal of Educational Psychology, 83,* 240–245.

Kiewra, K. A., & Fletcher, H. J. (1984). The relationship between levels of note taking and achievement. *Human Learning, 3,* 273–280.

Kiewra, K. A., Hart, K., Scoular, J., Stephen, M., Sterup, G., & Tyler, B. (2001). Fishgiver or fishing teacher? The lure of strategy instruction. *The Teaching Professor, 15,* 5–6.

Kiewra, K. A., Kauffman, D. F., Robinson, D., DuBois, N., & Staley, R. K. (1999). Supplementing floundering text with adjunct displays. *Journal of Instructional Science, 27,* 373–401.

Kiewra, K. A., Mayer, R. E., Christensen, M., Kim, S., & Risch, N. (1991). Effects of repetition on recall and note taking: Strategies for learning from lectures. *Journal of Educational Psychology, 83,* 120–123.

King, A. (1989). Effects of self-questioning training on college students' comprehension of lectures. *Contemporary Educational Psychology, 14,* 366–381.

King, A. (1991). Improving lecture comprehension: Effects of a metacognitive strategy. *Applied Cognitive Psychology, 5,* 331–346.

King, A. (1992). Comparison of self-questioning, summarizing, and note taking–review as strategies for learning from lectures. *American Educational Research Journal, 29,* 303–323.

Locke, E. A. (1977). An empirical study of lecture note taking among college students. *Journal of Educational Research, 77,* 93–99.

Maddox, H., & Hoole, E. (1975). Performance decrement in the lecture. *Educational Review, 28,* 17–30.

Mayer, R. E. (1984). Aids to text comprehension. *Educational Psychologist, 19,* 30–42.

Mayer, R. E. (1989). Models for understanding. *Review of Educational Research, 59,* 43–64.

Mayer, R. E. (1996). Learning strategies for making sense out of expository text: The SOI model for funding three cognitive processes in knowledge construction. *Educational Psychology Review, 8,* 357–372.

Meichenbaum, D. (1977). *Cognitive behavior modification.* New York: Plenum.

Neisser, U. (1982). Professor Sanford's morning prayer. In U. Neisser (Ed.), *Memory observed.* San Francisco: W. H. Freeman.

O'Donnell, A., & Dansereau, D. F. (1993). Learning from lectures: Effects of co-operative review. *Journal of Experimental Education, 61,* 116–125.

Palmatier, R. A., & Bennett, J. M. (1974). Note-taking habits of college students. *Journal of Reading, 18,* 215–218.

Pressley, M., Ghatala, E. S., Woloshyn, V., & Pirie, J. (1990a). Being really, really certain you know the main idea doesn't mean you do. *Yearbook National Reading Conference, 39,* 249–256.

Pressley, M., Ghatala, E. S., Woloshyn, V., & Pirie, J. (1990b). Sometimes adults miss the main ideas in text and do not realize it: Confidence in responses to short-answer and multiple-choice comprehension items. *Reading Research Quarterly, 25,* 232–249.

Pressley, M., & Woloshyn, V. (1995). *Cognitive strategy instruction that really improves children's academic performance.* Cambridge, MA: Brookline Books.

Pressley, M., Yokoi, L., Van Meter, P., Van Etten, S., & Freebern, G. (1997). Some of the reasons why preparing for exams is so hard: What can be done to make it easier? *Educational Psychology Review, 9,* 1–38.

Rickards, J. P., & Friedman, F. (1978). The encoding versus the external storage hypothesis in note taking. *Contemporary Educational Psychology, 3,* 136–143.

Robinson, D., & Kiewra, K. A. (1995). Visual argument: Graphic organizers are superior to outlines in improving learning from text. *Journal of Educational Psychology, 87,* 455–467.

Robinson, D. H., & Skinner, C. H. (1996). Why graphic organizers facilitate search processes: Fewer words or computationally effective indexing? *Contemporary Educational Psychology, 21,* 161–180.

Scerbo, M. W., Warm, J. S., Dember, W. N., & Grasha, A. F. (1992). The role of time and cuing in a college lecture. *Contemporary Educational Psychology, 17,* 312–328.

Simpson, M. L., Hynd, C. R., Nist, S. L., & Burrell, K. I. (1997). College academic assistance programs and practices. *Educational Psychology Review, 9,* 39–87.

Sternberg, R. J. (1985). *Beyond IQ: A triarchic theory of human intelligence.* Cambridge, England: Cambridge University Press.

Titsworth, S., & Kiewra, K. A. (2001). *Organizational lecture cues and student note taking as facilitators of student learning.* Unpublished manuscript.

Van Meter, P., Yokoi, L., & Pressley, M. (1994). College students' theory of note taking derived from their perceptions of note taking. *Journal of Educational Psychology, 86,* 323–338.

Implementing a Learning Framework Course

Russ Hodges, De Sellers, and Carol W. Dochen

Learning framework courses represent the most recent manifestation of American higher education's efforts to help undergraduate students become academically successful. These courses integrate theory and practice from an array of educational and psychological theories, and the courses are increasingly successful in helping students achieve academic goals and persist to graduation. In "Implementing a Learning Framework Course," Russ Hodges, De Sellers, and Carol W. Dochen describe the evolution of such a course developed at a four-year, regional, public, postsecondary institution, from its beginnings as a traditional study skills course in 1973 through its current status using a four component model: self-assessment, self-regulation, cognitive theories and strategies, and self-change. A "matrix of academic success courses" is also included, which provides an overview of various academic success courses currently being offered at postsecondary institutions.

S tudy skills and college reading courses have shared a common history in American higher education as the birth of this field began with a reading improvement experiment designed for college students in 1894 (Stahl, Hynd, & Henk, 1986). Colleges have formally focused on teaching students the rituals of college study since the 1920s (Maxwell, 1997), and through most of the century, study skills content was an integral part of remedial reading courses or was taught separately in remedial study skills courses or as noncredit minicourses. However, the pedagogy of simply teaching students specific skills such as a note taking, reading, or time management systems began to erode in the late 1970s and was replaced by numerous academic support classes with such titles as Orientation, Learning Strategies, Effective Learning, Creative Learning, Freshman Seminar, and Strategic Learning. Confusion exists in understanding the purpose and determining the academic rigor of these various academic success course models. Researchers have attempted to differentiate academic success courses by assessing syllabi and textbooks and surveying faculty members involved in teaching these courses across the country. Cole, Babcock, Goetz, and Weinstein (1997) created a matrix to classify academic success courses. The matrix begins with those courses that focus on lower-level skills and topics, such as a one-credit hour orientation course that provides students with an overview of their postsecondary institution, and ends with a three-credit hour learning framework course steeped in cognitive theory and learning strategies. These learning framework courses have the avowed purpose of teaching students to become independent learners.

A synopsis of each course type follows; however, Figure 1 provides a more extensive overview. Orientation courses provide students with a comprehensive overview of university resources and facilities. Navigation courses teach students how and when to use a variety of university resources and facilities. Academic and Personal Development courses facilitate students' transition from high school into the university environment by focusing on adjustment to college. Academic Skills courses help students develop good academic habits and study skills. Learning to Learn courses facilitate students' abilities to understand and retain course material as well as provide instruction in study skills. Some courses integrate low-level theory into their content. Critical Thinking courses promote the evaluation of independent thought and decision-making processes. Learning Framework courses foster students' abilities to monitor and regulate their own learning through the development of a perspective about themselves as learners. Theories from cognitive and behavioral psychology are deeply rooted into the course curriculum (Cole et al., 1997).

Definition of a Learning Framework Course

The hallmark of a learning framework course is the presentation of theoretical models as the curricular core (Cole et al., 1997). Although such courses do teach study skills and learning strategies as applications, those skills are taught at a sophisticated, reflective, individualized level — a level characteristic of collegiate learning. In contrast, study skills courses teach students specific and simplified study techniques and methods where the focus is on the acquisition of the skill, not the comprehension of why and how human learning can be enhanced. Study skills topics include instruction in time management, notetaking, textbook study methods, strategies for preparing and taking examinations, and strategies in memory and concentration. Other topics include units on research paper writing, career planning, adapting to academic regulations, and improving personal and social adjustment to college (Maxwell, 1997).

By comparison, learning framework courses teach students the process of collegiate learning (i.e., cognitive skills); the focus is on the comprehension of human learning based on current theories. Students then develop individualistic learning strategies based on their knowledge of these theoretical underpinnings. Learning framework courses integrate cognitive psychology theory with learning strategies in order that students will understand the reasons for engaging in specific study behaviors and how to adapt to differing circumstances. For instance, information processing models help students understand the elaborate set of internal or cognitive processes involved in the acquisition and organization of knowledge. Learning framework courses have strong academic content with a solid foundation in research and theory.

Figure 1. Matrix of Academic Success Courses

COURSE TYPE & TYPICAL CREDITS	DEFINITION	SAMPLE TOPICS	STUDY METHODS TAUGHT
Orientation (Where/What) 1 credit	Overview of resources and services	Student services on campus, financial aid, library tours	Where to study on campus
Navigation (How) 1–3 credits	How and when to use a variety of resources and facilities	How and when to meet with an advisor/faculty member. How to fill out financial aid forms.	Developing time management plans and goals for studying
Academic & Personal Development (Transition) 1–3 credits	Facilitates students' transition into college; focus on adjustment issues	Homesickness, roommates, career development, independence, stress management	Differences between studying in high school and college, stress management, independence
Academic Skills (Study Skills) 3 credits	Helps students develop academic skills and habits related to locating and recording information	Time management, listening to lectures, note taking, study groups, test taking	How to take notes or tips for studying effectively in groups
Learning to Learn (Learning Strategies) 3 credits	Courses which facilitate students' abilities to understand and retain material	Mnemonics, SQ3R, concept mapping, annotating texts, learning styles	Development of learning strategies for use during individual and group study
Critical Thinking (Independent Thinking) 3 credits	Promote the evaluation of and independent thought	Evaluation, organization, recognizing errors in thinking, application of problem solving, debate	Information about studying might focus on the development of critical thinking strategies such as evaluating evidence
Learning Framework (Theoretical Perspective of Knowledge Acquisition) 3 credits	Fosters students' abilities to monitor and regulate their own learning through an understanding of themselves as learners	Self-regulated learning, strategic learning, information processing, methods of inquiry	Student's ability to independently create an environment conducive to learning using a repertoire of appropriate learning and monitoring strategies

Note: From "An In-depth Look at Academic Success Courses," by R. P. Cole, C. Babcock, E. T. Goetz, and C. E. Weinstein, 1997. Paper presented at the meeting of the College Reading and Learning Association, Sacramento, CA. Adapted with permission from the authors.

One example of a learning framework course has been offered since 1977 at the University of Texas at Austin (UT-Austin). Claire Ellen Weinstein, co-author of the *Learning and Study Strategies Inventory* (Weinstein, Palmer, & Schulte, 1987), has led the field in developing a learning framework course. Weinstein's course was recently cited as one of five innovative alternative approaches to developmental education (Boylan, 1999). The course, titled "Educational Psychology: Individual Learning Skills (EDP 310)," is a three-credit hour undergraduate course taken for a grade. It is not required for any degree program and is considered a free elective. EDP 310 targets students who enter the university under special circumstances or who experience academic difficulty after reentry. Instructors are advanced graduate students in educational psychology who receive extensive, continuous training. The course content is driven by Weinstein's Model of Strategic Learning, a model inspired by systems theory and Gestalt psychology (Weinstein, Dierking, Husman, Roska, & Powdrill, 1998). The model emphasizes how students learn in specific academic environments and is presented as a series of four major components: skill, will, self-regulation, and the academic environment.

Weinstein attributes much of her inspiration in developing the strategic learning model to the earlier work by Wilbert J. McKeachie, from the University of Michigan, and his research on strategic teaching (Weinstein, 1994). McKeachie and his colleagues have developed a four-credit hour introductory cognitive psychology course titled "Learning to Learn." The goal of the course is to help students develop efficient learning strategies and become life-long learners (Pintrich, McKeachie, & Lin, 1987). Learning to Learn, first taught in 1982, provides instruction in theory and research in cognitive psychology and in the application of learning strategies for studying. Topics covered include learning for lectures, texts, and discussions; memory models and strategies; motivation; writing skills; test-taking strategies; problem solving; and self-management. Research on the effectiveness of Learning to Learn found significant changes in students' self-reports of learning strategies and small changes in students' grade point averages (Pintrich et al., 1987).

A third learning framework course, "Educational Psychology 1350: Effective Learning (EDP 1350)" of Southwest Texas State University (SWT), represents a classic evolution from a traditional study skills course to a fully integrated learning framework course. The remainder of this chapter will review its history, current curriculum, student population, and retention outcomes. A final section will comment on the new statewide funding policies in Texas for learning framework courses.

Evolution of a Model Learning Framework Course

In 1973, SWT hired an educational specialist to create a psychology course to enhance students' academic success. This traditional study skills course had both a classroom and a laboratory experience. As EDP 1350 migrated from the traditional format to a learning framework course over the next 30 years, the laboratory component of the course evolved into a multifaceted learning assistance center, which is funded by state appropriations and student fees. The center provides free individual, group, and online peer tutoring for most freshman and sophomore courses, with the greatest demand in mathematics, accounting, English, and the natural sciences. The center also provides Supplemental Instruction (SI) and study skills workshops. The center's holistic philosophy trains tutors to instruct students in learning and study strategies in addition to content skills. The director of the course also coordinated the early development of the learning center's program, and many tutors from the center have served as undergraduate facilitators for the course. Students needing more instruction in learning skills and strategies often have been referred to the course by the tutors. The synergy of the simultaneous development of two coordinated programs energized the creativity of each one.

The course was first offered in the psychology department, and the early curriculum was similar to that of many college reading and study skills courses originating in the early 1970s. The focus was on improving students' reading comprehension, vocabulary, note-taking, time management, and test-taking skills. At the end of the semester, the students evaluated their accomplishments and goals in a written self-evaluation. The course used projects and papers as the basis for grading, and much class time was devoted to practice exercises. Theory was rarely a topic. In the years that followed, the wide diversity of faculty members, many with extensive backgrounds in psychology and education, transformed the course into an applied learning and behavior management skills course that offers students both current learning theory and research applications. Some of the hallmark changes included: content tests as 30 to 50% of the grade, strict attendance and late paper policies, and cognitive behavior modification theory and practice. Grading standards increasingly became congruent with the normal undergraduate grading standards in the liberal arts and the social sciences. At the annual curriculum conferences, faculty agonized over the array of required subjects as new topics were added and old topics discarded.

An important dichotomy emerged. Theories crept into the curriculum: first, those stressing cognitive behavior modification, then cognitive and moral development in adults, and finally information processing. A concurrent development was the faculty's conviction that the course must be a realistic laboratory experience; that is, students must be accountable for their academic behaviors. Thus, attendance and time-liness of assignments were rewarded. Syllabi were especially specific in the required behavioral demands on students. Faculty extensively used behavioral counseling techniques to help students accept the re-sponsibility for their actions and modify their academic behaviors, if necessary.

Currently, EDP 1350 is offered through the department of Edu-cational Administration and Psychological Services within the College of Education at SWT. The course enrolls approximately 500 to 600 students throughout the academic year. Class enrollment is limited to 30 students per section. Usually 10 sections are offered each fall and spring semester, and one or two sections are offered each summer term. What has evolved over almost a 30-year period is a four-part curriculum model for the course, which consists of self-assessment, self-regulation, cognitive theories and strategies, and self-change. The curriculum enables students to develop effective learning skills and strategies that offer maximal opportunities for them to transfer and apply learning skills and strategies across many academic courses and programs. The model integrates theory and practice throughout the course. Every element of the course — readings, lectures, discus-sions, directed group activities, assignments, projects, and tests — il-lustrates a carefully planned sequence that leads students toward a thoughtful, self-sufficient mode of academic behaviors.

Self-assessment, the first unit of the course, helps students formu-late a clear portrait of themselves as learners by having them complete self-assessment inventories and then use the data from each to deepen understanding of their learning strengths and weaknesses. Weinstein's *Learning and Study Strategies Inventory* (Weinstein et al., 1987) as-sists students in assessing their preferred learning strategies. Kolb's *Learning Styles Inventory* (Kolb, 1999), based on his theory of experi-ential learning, introduces students to the concept of differing learn-ing preferences. The *Myers-Briggs Type Indicator Form M* (Briggs & Myers, 1998) illustrates how personality type directly influences val-ues, decisions, communication, and learning preferences. The introduc-tion of multiple intelligence theory (Gardner, 1993) allows students to develop a more comprehensive view of their own abilities. Students also evaluate their own skills in reading, writing, critical thinking, and mathematics.

Self-regulation, the second part of the course, is a way of approach-ing academic tasks through experience and self-reflection. Students develop a greater awareness of their own behavior, motivation, and academic learning. Students come to understand self-regulation (Pin-trich, 1995) by setting achievement goals, using self-monitoring tech-niques, investigating their motivation, and using principles of self-discipline and time planning. Motivation theories introduced in the course include Maslow's (1970) Theory of Motivation and Weiner's

(1986) Attribution Theory. Students also study Perry's (1968) theory on how intellectual and moral values develop and the implications such development has on how adults study and learn. Two particularly important concepts are self-discipline (Peck, 1978) and self-esteem (Branden, 1994), especially the deliberate development of self-efficacy (Bandura, 1993).

Cognitive theory and strategies are the focus of the third section of the course. An information-processing model of adult college learning (Gagné, Yekovich, & Yekovich, 1993) is the primary theoretical basis of this section, but the curriculum also stresses related theoretical concepts. Helping students transfer successful strategies of learning across academic programs by using techniques appropriate for different types of academic pursuits is the primary goal of this unit, so students learn techniques to memorize information at a surface level and then process information at deeper levels using elaborative techniques such as maps and networks.

The fourth part, self-change, presents a model of cognitive behavior modification and maintenance (Martin & Poland, 1980). Students design a project based on research and theory, present that research and design in a scholarly format, attempt the project for several weeks, and evaluate the results. During the research phase of the project, students learn to conduct research using different library database computer programs, and they become familiar with Internet resources. Operant and classical conditioning, reinforcement theory, positive self-talk, and collaborative partnerships are the focus of this section as students learn techniques to modify academic behaviors.

Throughout the course, faculty members use various techniques to evaluate students' progress. Papers, journals, projects, and tests comprise the normal structure. Tests, both traditional in-class objective and essay as well as take-home essay, comprise 60 to 75% of the grading criteria. Attendance and paper submission policies remain strict. Some students withdraw from the course because they are surprised by the academic rigor of the course, and they are unwilling to put forth the necessary effort. About 75% of students who complete the course earn a passing grade of a C or better. A perennial problem is the lack of suitable textbooks, although a few study skill books have begun to incorporate theory. Another problem is the lack of adequate graduate and in-service education possibilities. There are few graduate-level programs in developmental education. Most faculty members who teach learning framework courses come from related disciplines and have to dedicate themselves to independent study of the material to be taught.

Student Population

SWT is a regional comprehensive institution of higher education offering undergraduate and masters level instruction, as well as one doctoral program. Student enrollment is approximately 21,000. Several categories of undergraduate students register for EDP 1350. The first group includes students who are not experiencing academic problems but simply want to improve their grades or learning skills. Many of these students are first-semester freshmen who hear about the course at summer orientation or are referred by students who have been in school for several semesters. Former students refer approximately 25% of students who take the course.

The second group are students who enter the university under regular admission procedures but experience academic difficulties at some point in their program. Typically, university officials refer students to the course as a condition of a special agreement they have made with students who have been suspended or are on academic appeal. Some of these students are required to take the course while others are strongly encouraged by their advisors, departmental chairs, or deans.

The third group is composed of a select group of conditionally admitted students who fail to meet regular admission requirements at the institution. These students are in the top three-quarters of their high school classes, but their test scores do not quite meet the general admission requirements. Students are granted conditional admission based on a consideration of high school courses taken and grades earned, the academic rigor of the senior year experience, specific rank in class, and English and mathematics scores on the Scholastic Aptitude Test (SAT) or American College Test (ACT). A select group of these students are required to take the course.

Marketing efforts for EDP 1350 have been extremely deliberate. The coordinator meets regularly with the academic deans or advisors, the admissions office staff, orientation advisors, athletic advisors, and other key university personnel. At the end of the fall term, the vice president for academic affairs sends a letter to selected freshmen who have been placed on probation. In that letter, he recommends that the student consider enrolling in EDP 1350 for the following term.

Instructors and Facilitators

A full-time tenured faculty member with a doctorate in developmental education coordinates the EDP 1350 program. Instructors are faculty members with degrees in educational psychology, developmental education, counseling, and reading. On occasion, part-time faculty members teach the course as well as advanced graduate students. New instructors receive close supervision and training from the coordinator and the more experienced instructors. Members of the faculty meet throughout the semester for continuous training and professional development. Faculty members participate in professional development through state and national organizations such as the National Association for Developmental Education (NADE), the College Reading and Learning Association (CRLA), and their local chapters.

Former students of EDP 1350 receive invitations to co-teach the class collaboratively with instructors. Although student facilitators, as they are called, may perform clerical duties, the focus of their work is to foster student learning. The role of the facilitator depends on the facilitator's talents and ambitions and the instructor's teaching style. Ideally, facilitators share the teaching activities. Facilitators ask questions and turn the class into a question and answer mode; give alternate explanations of the material (from a student's viewpoint); articulate a student's perspective on information; provide individual attention and feedback before, during, and after class; help supervise small group work and discussion; provide appropriate role models of active student learning; give encouragement; and change the climate of the classroom. EDP 1350 facilitators are unpaid volunteers (Hodges, Sellers, & White, 1994/95).

Research on Learning Framework Courses

Both SWT and UT-Austin have studied the effects of their learning framework courses on students' subsequent academic performance and retention. In a descriptive study conducted at UT-Austin, researchers (Weinstein, Roska, Hanson, & Van Mater Stone, 1997) found that freshmen who completed EDP 310 during the Fall 1990 and Spring 1991 semesters were retained for one year at higher rates than freshmen who did not take the course. The researchers also reported that students who completed the course earned higher first-year cumulative grade point averages (GPAs), failed fewer hours, and passed more courses. Freshmen with low SAT verbal and quantitative scores who enrolled in EDP 310 because they were predicted to be "at-risk" academically actually achieved higher GPAs and one-year retention rates than students not enrolled in the course.

A longitudinal study of EDP 1350 students at SWT produced several statistically significant results with regard to academic success and persistence. The study, conducted on first-semester freshmen enrolled in the course in 1991, revealed that both regularly admitted and conditionally admitted students who completed the course had significantly higher first-year GPAs, first-year retention rates, and six-year graduation rates than first-semester freshmen not enrolled in EDP 1350 (see Table 1).

The first two columns of data represent all entering freshmen, including those admitted conditionally. Although learning frameworks courses are not exclusively designed for at-risk populations, the researchers found that the conditionally admitted freshmen who completed EDP 1350 had first-year retention rates and six-year graduation rates that compared favorably to those of the freshman population in general.

Table 1. T-test for Differences between Freshmen and Freshmen Enrolled in EDP 1350, Fall 1991

	First-Semester Freshmen		Conditionally Admitted Freshmen	
	Freshmen Enrolled in EDP 1350	All Other Freshmen	Conditionally Admitted Freshmen Enrolled in EDP 1350	All Other Conditionally Admitted Freshmen
Mean Cumulative GPA, 1st Semester	2.40* 87	2.09* 2914	2.18* 34	1.74* 879
Mean Cumulative GPA, 2nd Semester	2.35* 85	2.20* 2382	2.16* 33	1.83* 698
Mean Cumulative GPA, 3rd Semester	2.38 81	2.42 1694	2.24 31	2.10 469
One-Year Retention (Students enrolled for Fall 1992)	93.10%* 81	58.13%* 1694	91.17%* 31	53.35%* 469
Mean SAT Verbal	389.00 70	403.88 2275	353.21 28	352.37 678
Mean SAT Quantitative	441.57 70	448.39 2275	402.86 28	389.84 678
Students Graduating in 6 Years	65.52%* 57	32.49%* 951	76.47%* 26	26.16%* 231

Note. Italicized numbers represent cell sizes
Independent t-tests *p < .05

Current Status of Learning Framework Courses in Texas

In October 1999, after years of debate, the Texas Higher Education Coordinating Board (THECB) authorized formula funding of up to three semester credit hours for what were described as "Learning Framework" courses designed to improve students' understanding of the learning process and their ability to succeed in college. Four-year postsecondary institutions had offered such courses for many years, but prior to October 1999, all collegiate courses that focused primarily on the improvement of students' individual learning skills were classified as "developmental" and, consequently, were not eligible for formula funding. According to the THECB's recent decision, to receive formula funding learning framework courses must focus on (a) research and theory in the psychology of learning, cognition, and motivation; (b) factors that impact learning; and (c) application of learning strategies (Texas Higher Education Coordinating Board, 1999). SWT and UT-Austin are the two institutions currently offering a course that meets the new criteria. Faculty and administrators from both institutions were instrumental in shaping the new statewide policy.

Implications

Learning framework courses merit funding and traditional academic status; these courses are developmental in nature, not remedial, and also have a strong academic content based in cognitive psychology research and theory. Research data support that learning framework courses aid retention, success, and graduation of undergraduate students. Much needs to be done to disseminate this information to the various constituencies of higher education: students, faculty, staff, administrators, trustees, legislators, and publishers. As developmental educators continue to investigate and promote learning framework courses, more students will succeed academically.

References

Bandura, A. (1993). Perceived self-efficacy in cognitive development and functioning. *Educational Psychologist, 28*, 117–148.

Boylan, H. R. (1999). Exploring alternatives to remediation. *Journal of Developmental Education, 22*(3), 2–4, 6, 8, 10.

Branden, N. (1994). *The six pillars of self-esteem.* New York: Bantam.

Briggs, K. C., & Myers, I. B. (1998). *Myers-Briggs Type Indicator.* Palo Alto, CA: Consulting Psychologists.

Cole, R. P., Babcock, C., Goetz, E. T., & Weinstein, C. E. (1997, October). *An in-depth look at academic success courses.* Paper presented at the meeting of the College Reading and Learning Association, Sacramento, CA.

Gagné, E. D., Yekovich, C. W., & Yekovich, F. R. (1993). *Cognitive psychology of school learning* (2nd ed.). New York: HarperCollins.

Gardner, H. (1993). *Multiple intelligences: The theory in practice.* New York: HarperCollins.

Hodges, R. B., Sellers, D. E., & White, W. G. (1994–95). Peer teaching: The use of facilitators in college classes. *Journal of College Reading and Learning, 26*(2), 23–29.

Kolb, D. A. (1999). *Learning Style Inventory* (Version 3). Boston: Hay/McBer.

Martin, R. A., & Poland, E. Y. (1980). *Learning to change.* New York: McGraw-Hill.

Maslow, A. H. (1970). *Motivation and personality* (2nd ed.). New York: Harper & Row.

Maxwell, M. (1997). *Improving student learning skills.* Clearwater, FL: H & H.

Peck, M. S. (1978). *The road less traveled.* New York: Simon & Schuster.

Perry, W. G., Jr. (1968). *Forms of intellectual and ethical development in the college years.* New York: Holt, Rinehart and Winston.

Pintrich, P. (1995). Understanding self-regulated learning. In P. Pintrich (Ed.), *Understanding self-regulated learning* (pp. 3–12). San Francisco: Jossey-Bass.

Pintrich, P. R, McKeachie, W. J., & Lin, Y. (1987). Teaching a course in learning to learn. *Teaching of Psychology, 14*(2), 81–85.

Stahl, N. A., Hynd, C. R., & Henk, W. A. (1986). Avenues for chronicling and researching the history of college reading and study skills instruction. *Journal of Reading, 29,* 334–341.

Texas Higher Education Coordinating Board. (1999). Consideration of board policy on funding of courses designed to improve students' understanding of the learning process and their ability to succeed in college. *Texas Higher Education Coordinating Board Quarterly Meeting, October 28, 1999* (Agenda Item 5G). Austin, TX: Texas Higher Education Coordinating Board.

Weiner, B. (1986). *An attribution theory of motivation and emotion.* New York: Academic Press.

Weinstein, C. E. (1994). Strategic learning/strategic teaching: Flip sides of a coin. In P. R. Pintrich, D. R. Brown, & C. E. Weinstein (Eds.), *Student motivation, cognition, and learning* (pp. 257–273). Hillsdale, NJ: Lawrence Erlbaum.

Weinstein, C. E., Dierking, D., Husman, J., Roska, L., & Powdrill, L. (1998). The impact of a course in strategic learning on the long-term retention of college students. In J. L. Higbee & P. L. Dwinell (Eds.), *Developmental education: Preparing successful college students* (pp. 85–96). Columbia, SC: National Resource Center for The First-Year Experience and Students in Transition.

Weinstein, C. E., Palmer, D. R., & Schulte, A. C. (1987). *Learning and study strategy inventory.* Clearwater, FL: H & H.

Weinstein, C. E., Roska, L. A., Hanson, G. R, & Van Mater Stone, G. (1997, March). *EDP 310: A course in strategic learning.* Paper presented Courses for Academic Success Symposium at the Annual Meeting of the American Educational Research Association, Chicago, IL.

Additional Readings

Harper, C., & de Jong, E. (2004). Misconceptions about teaching English-language learners. *Journal of Adolescent and Adult Literacy, 48*(2), 152–162.

Hofer, B. (2001). Personal epistemology research: Implications for learning and teaching. *Educational Psychology Review, 13*(4), 353–383.

Holschuh, J. P., & Aultman, L. P. (2009). Comprehension development. In R. A. Flippo and D. C. Caverly (Eds.), *Handbook of College Reading and Study Strategy Research* (pp. 121–144). New York: Routledge.

Nesbit, J. C., & Adescope, O. O. (2006). Learning with concept and knowledge maps: A meta-analysis. *Review of Educational Research, 76*(3), 413–448.

Paris, S. G., & Paris, A. H. (2001). Classroom applications of research on self-regulated learning. *Educational Psychologist, 36*(2), 89–101.

Simpson, M. L., & Nist, S. L. (2000). An update on strategic learning: It's more than textbook reading strategies. *Journal of Adolescent and Adult Literacy, 43*(6), 528–541.

Taraban, R., Rynearson, K., & Kerr, M. S. (2004). Analytic and pragmatic factors in college students' metacognitive reading strategies. *Reading Psychology, 25,* 67–81.

CHAPTER

6

Assessment and Evaluation

Assessment and evaluation are integral parts of the instructional cycle, providing teachers and administrators with important evidence about their students' strengths, needs, and achievement. The instruments and techniques used should be theory-based, reliable, valid, and authentic, representing the tasks students must tackle. Moreover, it is important that instructors use multiple data sources across multiple contexts rather than just one instrument or one measurement. Experts remind us that effective assessment techniques involve our students so they become equal partners and consumers of the collected information (Stiggins, 2005). When students are provided these opportunities, they internalize processes essential to their academic achievement and independent learning. The six articles selected for this chapter reflect these principles of effective assessment and evaluation.

The chapter begins with an article by Noel Entwistle and Velda McCune analyzing several different study strategy inventories, including the Learning and Study Strategies Inventory (LASSI) by Claire Ellen Weinstein and her colleagues. Carol Boston's brief article provides an excellent introduction to the concept of formative assessment. Formative assessment is based on the principle that classroom assessment can support, stimulate, and verify students' learning in a seamless fashion. Kouider Mokhtari and Ravi Sheorey explain the development of an instrument, the Survey of Reading Strategies, that measures ESL students' reading strategies. The authors describe the reliability and validity indices of the SORS instrument and outline some instructional implications. In "The Learning Portfolio: A Valuable Tool for Increasing Metacognitive Awareness," Nannette Evans Commander and Marie Valeri-Gold capitalize on the notion of formative assessment with their explanation of the learning portfolio. The authors use their version of the learning portfolio and note an increase in their at-risk students' confidence, reflection, and metacognition. Mary P. Deming's article provides a rationale for using learning logs as a means of linking assessment to instruction, an important aspect of authentic assessment. Instructors will find her specific teaching suggestions extremely useful. The chapter ends with an article on program evaluation by Michele L. Simpson. In this article Simpson urges developmental educators to undertake more theory-based program evaluation studies that use a variety of dependent variables and address important but overlooked issues such as strategy transfer. She concludes with seven specific suggestions for those individuals planning to conduct program evaluation studies at their institution.

References

Stiggins, R. J. (2005). *Student-involved assessment for learning.* Upper Saddle River, NJ: Pearson.

The Conceptual Bases of Study Strategy Inventories

Noel Entwistle and Velda McCune

In the late sixties Brown and Holtzman developed one of the first study strategy inventories that defined effective study habits in terms of work methods, delay avoidance, teacher approval, and educational acceptance. Since then, researchers have developed and fine-tuned a variety of other inventories that have gained popularity as a means of student assessment and evaluation (e.g., the LASSI authored by Weinstein, Schulte, and Palmer in 1987). In this article Entwistle and McCune describe these other inventories, providing a historical and conceptual analysis for each. They also offer an insightful comparison of the various inventories and outline issues they believe need to be addressed.

There has recently been an upsurge in interest in describing and measuring the study strategies of students in higher education. This development can be attributed, in part, to the increasing requirements on universities to justify public funding by demonstrating effectiveness and efficiency in their teaching. Moreover, convincing empirical evidence is increasingly being sought to inform policy decisions, some of which relate to the training and certification of teachers in higher and further education (see, for example, Dearing Committee, 1997).

Research into student learning initially built up evidence about the relationships of motivation and study methods with academic performance (Biggs, 1970, 1976; Brown & Holtzman, 1966; Entwistle & Entwistle, 1970; Entwistle & Wilson, 1977; Schmeck, Ribich, & Ramanaiah, 1977). Subsequently, the link between teaching methods and study strategies has been demonstrated, indicating the indirect influences that faculty members have on students' study behavior. University teachers not only affect academic performance directly by their methods of presenting information and ideas, they also have an often unrecognized impact on the ways in which students study (Biggs, 1999; Prosser & Trigwell, 1999; Ramsden, 1992). It is also clear that the effects of teaching go well beyond the influence of the teacher to include other features of the whole teaching-learning environment, particularly assessment procedures (Biggs, 1999; Entwistle, 1998, 2000).

The recognition of this web of influences has been paralleled by the development of a variety of self-report questionnaires designed to assess differences in how students learn and study. Although these instruments use similar formats and psychometric principles (Likert scales), they were developed for rather different purposes, derived from contrasting theoretical perspectives, and labeled in differing ways. As a result, other researchers or university teachers may find it difficult to determine which instrument best suits their purposes. This article seeks to clarify the conceptual bases of some of the most frequently used and best-documented inventories. Those selected were three from the United States (developed by Schmeck, Weinstein, & Pintrich), and three from other countries (Biggs — Australia, Entwistle — Britain, and Vermunt — Netherlands), together with a new version currently being developed.

This conceptual analysis starts with the historical origins of attempts to measure study methods and strategies and leads to a consideration of four of the earlier inventories. Each instrument is examined in detail using evidence from content analyses of items, factor structures and correlation analyses, along with a consideration of the research aims and theoretical perspectives that informed its design. Then, we look at more recent developments, including a description of the other three inventories, which introduce additional aspects of studying to provide a more complete description. Comparisons among scales from all the inventories are set out in tabular form (Table 1 on p. 332) to allow the conceptual bases of the different instruments to be more fully considered. In some cases there is also empirical data to support the equivalence of the subscales and scales; these findings are discussed later in this paper.

Developing Inventory Measures of Study Strategies, Learning Processes, and Motivation

The measurement of study methods became possible only after techniques of attitude measurement had been established in the 1930s and more elaborate statistical procedures had been developed (see Fishbein, 1967). Research at that time stressed the importance of the student's own effort and application in determining levels of academic achievement. The responsibility for high attainment was seen as the student's alone, with effort explained in terms of the student's motivation, and application shown through study habits. It was also believed that generally effective study methods could be described. In the United States, these ways of studying were defined by Brown and Holtzman (1966) through one of the first inventories in this field. It contained four subscales: work methods (effective study procedures); delay avoidance (promptness in completing work); teacher approval (favorable opinions about teachers); and educational acceptance (approval of educational objectives).

One of the first British instruments also described generalized "good" study methods but added "academic motivation" (Entwistle & Entwistle, 1970), derived from a competitive and self-confident form of "achievement motivation" (Atkinson & Feather, 1966). Study methods were also found to be related to personality, indicating that students with differing personality and motivation were likely to study in contrasting ways (Entwistle, Thompson, & Wilson, 1974). Even in this early research, the complexity of interrelationships affecting different ways of studying was becoming clear. Extroverts generally had "worse" study methods than introverts, and yet extroverts who had high motivation achieved as much as introverts with the same level of motivation. And anxiety worked in different ways too. Fear of failure was linked to conscientious study methods, high motivation, and high academic performance, and yet anxiety could also be debilitating or associated with ineffective studying, leading to poor grades (Entwistle & Wilson, 1977; Wankowski, 1973).

Biggs (1970), too, had recognized the importance of personality and motivation within studying and had developed an inventory that also drew ideas from the emerging literature in cognitive information-processing psychology. Information enters the memory system through the senses; the model then suggested a series of processing systems activated through "arousal" (such as interest or anxiety). Information is taken into short-term or working memory and coded so as to make links with prior knowledge within a long-term memory store (Broadbent, 1966). A development of this basic model suggested different levels of processing, distinguishing a surface level, involving "repetition of analyses already carried out," from a deep level using "a greater degree of semantic or cognitive analysis" (Craik & Lockhart, 1972, pp. 675–676). Around the same time, a similar distinction was made within educational psychology between *rote learning* and *meaningful learning* (Ausubel, 1968), and their distinct memory processes.

Within an early form of Biggs' inventory, test anxiety and academic motivation were scales describing differing forms of arousal. The distinct learning processes were labeled as "fact-rote" and "meaningful learning." This inventory was developed further into 10 subscales that included differing forms of motivation and study strategies within three main domains (Biggs, 1976, 1979). *Utilizing* described studying directed toward obtaining the necessary grades, unquestioning acceptance of the knowledge presented, and anxiety about course work and assessment. *Internalizing* indicated intrinsic interest in the course content, matched by a determination to understand, and an openness to alternative interpretations and values. Finally, *achieving* focused mainly on study skills linked to the need for achievement (Biggs, 1987).

About the same time, Marton and Säljö (1976) introduced the distinction between deep and surface *approaches to learning* and Pask (1976) identified holist and serialist *learning strategies*. Both concepts came from naturalistic experiments in which students were required to learn complex material under controlled conditions. In Marton and Säljö's study, students were asked to read an academic article and to be ready to answer questions on it afterwards. These instructions left the specific demands of the task somewhat ambiguous. The students' descriptions of how they went about studying suggested differences in what was initially described as "levels of processing," with an acknowledged link to Craik and Lockhart. However, the deep learning process was found to be associated with an intention — to understand — while surface learning was accompanied by an intention to reproduce. The coexistence of intention and process suggested that the categories might better be described as "approaches to learning" (Marton & Säljö, 1997) and implied differing ways of interpreting the requirements of the task as it was presented within a specific learning context.

Pask (1976, 1988) also set a learning task for students, but required the students to *understand* the material and be able to explain that understanding to the researcher. In effect, students were being forced to learn deeply, and yet he found that students still tackled the task in distinctly different ways. Again a dichotomy could be discerned, with some students seeing the task in a broad context and in personal terms; they also tended to be impulsive in reaching conclusions (holist strategy). Other students were more comfortable with a step-by-step and impersonal strategy, focusing on the particular task and using the evidence critically and cautiously (serialist). Where students adopted one or other strategy fairly consistently, Pask saw this as a learning style or preferred learning process (comprehension learning — holist; operation learning — serialist). Extremes of either strategy led to learning pathologies and incomplete understanding.

In the light of these alternative conceptualizations of student learning, Entwistle recast his earlier inventory on the basis of interviews that focused on the everyday experience of studying (Entwistle, Hanley, & Hounsell, 1979). Deep and surface approaches were apparent across differing tasks, suggesting that these approaches had developed into relatively consistent study habits. Yet, students also indicated that their approaches varied, depending on the course and the lecturer. In everyday contexts, assessment strongly affects studying, and so an additional category was introduced, namely a *strategic* approach *to studying* (as opposed to learning). The items for the new inventory were derived partly from interview transcripts and partly from the defining features of the categories that Marton and Pask had identified. Factor analyses of the subscales of this new instrument — the *Approaches to Studying Inventory* (*ASI*) (Entwistle & Ramsden, 1983) produced three main factors that brought together three distinctive sets of intentions, motives, and processes of learning and studying. These combinations of subscale scores were described as *orientations to studying*, covering very similar dimensions to those identified by Biggs (see Table 1 on p. 332).

The *reproducing orientation* indicated the use of a surface approach, with an emphasis on rote memorizing, and a narrow syllabus-bound attitude, associated with both extrinsic motivation and fear of failure. In contrast, *meaning orientation* indicated an intention to understand for oneself — comprehension learning, relating ideas, and using evidence being all motivated by interest in the ideas presented. The *achieving orientation* involved a strategic approach (being aware of study requirements and making sure they were achieved), linked positively to achievement motivation and negatively to disorganized studying. The final and less well defined orientation — *nonacademic* — indicated negative attitudes to studying and was associated with both of Pask's learning pathologies — improvidence and globetrotting.

Biggs (1987) subsequently adopted Marton's terminology in describing his revised inventory — the *Study Processes Questionnaire* (*SPQ*) — in which deep, surface, and achieving factors were each subdivided into a motive and an accompanying strategy (see Table 1). This structure is conceptually similar to that of ASI and the relationship has been confirmed empirically in a recent study (Wilson, Smart, & Watson, 1996). Biggs argued that the link between motive and strategy in his inventory are not just empirical, but also forms of "psycho-logic"

in describing how people construe their role in a situation, and in deciding to do something about it. If, in a learning situation, one decides that a pass is sufficient, then it seems to make best sense to rote learn only those facts and details which are judged (or guessed) as most likely to be tested. If one is interested in a particular subject, then it makes sense to find out as much as possible about it, and work out what it all means, regardless of any testing which might ensue. (Biggs, 1987, p. 11)

Table 1. Comparison of Scales from Inventories Measuring Study Strategies

ASI	SPQ	ILP-R	LASSI
Meaning orientation	**Deep approach**		
Deep approach (intention)			
Relating ideas	Deep strategy	Deep semantic	Information processing
Comprehension learning		Elab. self-actualization Elaborative episodic	
Use of evidence		Deep critical thinking Self-effic. critical thinking	
			Selecting main ideas
Intrinsic motivation	Deep motive	Motivation — interest	
Reproducing orientation	**Surface approach**		
Surface approach	Surface strategy	Literal memorization Self-effic. fact retention Self-effic. organization	
Syllabus boundness			
Operation learning		Agentic serial Agentic analytic	
Extrinsic motivation	Surface motive		
Fear of failure		Self-esteem	Anxiety
Achieving orientation	**Achieving approach**		
(-ve Disorganized studying)	Achieving strategy	Methodical study	Time management
Strategic approach			
			Concentration Study aids Self-testing Test-strategies
Achievement motivation	Achieving motive	Motivation — effort	Motivation
Nonacademic orientation			
Negative attitudes			Attitude
Improvidence			
Globetrotting			
Self-rating of performance		Self-efficacy (all three scales) Self-assertion Motivation — responsibility	

Table 1. (continued)

ILS	MSLQ	ALSI
Meaning directed		**Deep approach**
		Intention to understand
Relating and structuring	Elaboration	Relating ideas
Critical processing	Critical thinking	Use of evidence
Concrete processing		
	Organization	
Personally interested	Intrinsic goal orientation	
orientation	Task value	**Monitoring studying**
Self-regulation	Self-regulation	Monitoring study effectiveness
Construction of knowledge		Monitoring understanding
model		Monitoring generic skills
Reproduction directed		**Surface approach**
Memorizing and rehearsal	Rehearsal	Memorizing without
		understanding
		Unthinking acceptance
		Fragmented knowledge
Analyzing		
Certificate oriented		
Self-test oriented		
	Test anxiety	
External regulation		
Intake of knowledge model		
		Organized studying
	Time/study environment	Time management
		Study organization
		Effort management
		Concentration
Self-regulation	Self-regulation	
	Effort regulation	Effort
	Extrinsic goal orientation	
Undirected		
Ambivalent		
Lack of regulation		Unreflective studying
		(with surface)
Stimulating education model		
Cooperating learning model	Peer learning/help seeking	
Application directed		
Concrete processing		
Certificate oriented		
Vocation oriented		
Use of knowledge mental		
model		
	Self-efficacy	
	Control beliefs about learning	

This "psycho-logic" could be extended to the strategic or achieving approach, by suggesting that, if you really want to do well, you need to know what "counts" in getting high marks and then work hard and systematically to meet those requirements. In spite of this logical association between motive and strategy, subsequent research has queried the empirical consistency and strength of the connection (for example, Richardson, 2000). Nevertheless, the most recent, short form of the inventory still retains the motive/strategy distinction, although now just on two scales — deep and surface (Biggs, Kember, & Leung, 2001).

The combination of ideas derived from cognitive psychology and educational research, which is reflected in the work described so far, was a more general trend (Biggs, 1993). Building on the earlier work, researchers in the United States had also combined measurements of study methods with ideas about learning processes coming from cognitive psychology. Schmeck et al. (1977) reported the development of their *Inventory of Learning Processes* (*ILP*), which contained items "generated by applying information processing theory (e.g., Craik & Tulving, 1975) to analyze the activities that can be employed in academic studying" (Schmeck, Geisler-Brenstein, & Cercy, 1991, p. 344). By the mid-1970s, the main information processing dimensions distinguished between *deep* and *elaborative* processing. In Schmeck's inventory, these emerged as distinct factors, along with *fact retention* (which was seen as a judgment of self-efficacy) and *methodical studying*. Drawing on the ideas on student learning embodied in the *SPQ* and *ASI* and extending the notion of self-efficacy into the broader area of academic self-concept, a revised inventory was produced (*ILP-R*; Schmeck et al., 1991). Four main domains were established through factor analysis — academic self-concept (in various forms), reflective processing (both deep and elaborative), "agentic" or conforming serial-reiterative processing, and methodical study. Since then, the scales have been revised again to produce the set of scales shown in Table 1 on the previous page (Geisler-Brenstein & Schmeck, 1996), where the elements of motivation and self-efficacy have been disaggregated further, and additional social and emotional aspects have been included. It proved difficult to establish convincing parallels with other inventories for some of the scales within the most recent *ILP-R* on the basis of the evidence currently available; one scale (conventional attitudes) was omitted from Table 1 through a lack of equivalence to other inventory scales.

The main purpose of the previous inventories was to describe the different ways in which students went about their academic work. In contrast, Weinstein and her colleagues (Weinstein, 1982; Weinstein, Schulte, & Palmer, 1987; Weinstein & Meyer, 1991) linked inventory development directly to a program of training in study skills. Their *Learning and Study Strategies Inventory* (*LASSI*) incorporated a wide range of the study strategies typically found in training schemes, supplemented by the developing ideas about learning processes. They distinguished rehearsal, elaboration, and organizational learning strategies, which parallel the three main domains identified by Biggs and Entwistle. While the majority of *LASSI* subscales shown in Table 1 describe aspects of study methods, two of them cover the areas of information processing (elaborative and relational), and an undifferentiated form of academic motivation.

So far, only the descriptive similarities of the inventories have been mentioned, but there is also empirical evidence of conceptual overlap between some of the scales. Both Entwistle and Waterston (1988) and Speth and Brown (1988) compared *ASI* with *ILP*. Cano-Garcia and Justicia-Justicia (1994) included both of these inventories, and also *LASSI*, in their analysis, which produced three main factors. Based on loadings above 0.45, the first factor described methodical studying (*ILP*) along with time management, concentration, and positive attitudes (all *LASSI*); it correlated negatively with disorganized study methods (*ASI*). The second factor combined positive loadings on surface approach (*ASI*), anxiety (*LASSI*), fear of failure (*ASI*), and improvidence (*ASI*), with negative loadings on deep processing (*ILP*) and test strategies (*LASSI*). The final factor was defined by information processing (*LASSI*), relating ideas (*ASI*), and elaborative processing (*ILP*), and was supported by deep approach and use of evidence (both *ASI*).

These empirical findings, in combination with conceptual considerations and a detailed analysis of individual items, informed the mapping of the inventories presented in Table 1 in which subscales that are broadly equivalent in conceptual terms are placed in the same row. Where scale names exist for a particular questionnaire, these have also been included (in bold type). This table draws attention to the overlap between the inventories, and also brings out more clearly several recurring study strategies. The common elements found in all four instruments are the two distinctive types of learning process (deep/reflective/elaborative vs. surface/serial-reiterative/rehearsal), each with associated intentions and motives. The third aspect of studying describes methodical, well-organized studying linked to effort and achievement motivation.

Recent Advances in Conceptualization

The earlier inventories had often been used to predict future academic performance and so emphasized the relative stability of study strategies, but approaches to studying are substantially affected by students' perceptions of their teaching-learning environments. Students can also adapt their ways of tackling academic work to circumstances, and more recent inventories have thus emphasized self-conscious reflection on studying, drawing on the ideas of *metacognition* and *self-regulation*. In education, "metacognition" has been used to encompass beliefs and knowledge about learning, as well as monitoring, regulating, and reflecting on learning (Entwistle, 1997; McKeachie, 1990; Vermunt, 1996, 1998). The term "self-regulation" overlaps with this grouping, also referring to students monitoring and regulating their learning (Garcia, 1996; Schunk & Zimmerman, 1994; Vermunt, 1996, 1998; Vermunt & van Rijswijk, 1988; Zimmerman, 1989). Conceptualizations of deep and strategic approaches in the earlier inventories implicitly included certain aspects of these ideas; "time management," for example, can be seen as a form of self-regulation. The newer inventories, however, made these dimensions explicit and emphasized their value in encouraging reflection on study processes. This new approach can be seen most clearly in Vermunt's (1998) *Inventory of Learning Styles (ILS)* and the *Motivated Strategies for Learning Questionnaire (MSLQ)* developed by Pintrich and his colleagues (1991).

MSLQ was developed from a theoretical model that brought together an information processing view of cognition with a social-cognitive perspective on motivation (Pintrich, Smith, Garcia, & McKeachie, 1993; Pintrich & Garcia, 1993, 1994). It was derived from an extensive body of literature, including much of the research already described, and particularly the distinction made by Weinstein and Mayer (1986) between rehearsal, elaboration, and organizational strategies (Pintrich & Garcia, 1991). Development of the *MSLQ* began in the early 1980s with a range of self-report instruments designed to evaluate the effectiveness of a "learning to learn" course, and continued subsequently through psychometric analyses and by investigating predictive relationships with grades (Pintrich et al., 1993). Besides being a research and emulation tool, *MSLQ* has been used by both students and faculty to enhance student learning (Pintrich & Garcia, 1994).

The motivational scales in *MSLQ* describe three main constructs — expectancy, value, and affect. Expectancy refers to students' beliefs about whether they can perform a task and is operationalized in terms of scales describing "self-efficacy" and "control beliefs about learning" (Pintrich et al., 1993). From Table 1 on page 332, it can be seen that the closest parallels with these scales are those of the "self-efficacy" and "personal responsibility" scales from the *ILP-R*. The value component within *MSLQ* indicates why students engage in particular academic tasks, and is covered partly by contrasting intrinsic and extrinsic "goal orientation" and partly by "talk value." This latter scale explores the extent to which students find a particular task interesting, useful, and important. The only scale related to "affect" in *MSLQ* is "test anxiety," which maps on to similar scales in other inventories (Pintrich et al., 1993).

MSLQ contains a number of learning strategies scales, several of which map on to deep, meaningful learning processes. The "rehearsal" scale from *MSLQ* also has parallels in several other inventories, but its explicit and detailed metacognitive and self-regulation elements are distinctive. The "effort regulation" scale from the *MSLQ* overlaps with items from *LASSI*, and relates to the theme of volition, which is emerging as an issue in the higher education literature. Volition can be seen as students' ability to maintain the effort needed to achieve their goals, even in the face of adversity (Wolters, 1998). The work of Volet (1997) considered disengagement versus preoccupation, indicating how well students are able to put study problems into perspective and carry on working. Initiative versus hesitation was also addressed, in terms of students' ability to initiate study activity without external pressure. Volet also measured the amount of effort students intended to put into the course, and their ability to persist with their studies, which suggested that "surface" intentions are not necessarily associated with minimal effort, nor are "deep" intentions always associated with greater effort.

The *Inventory of Learning Styles* has also been used partly as a research tool, and partly to allow students to reflect on, and develop, their ways of learning. The term "style" is used here rather in the same sense that "orientation to studying" was used earlier — to indicate a grouping of interrelated scales. It is seen in terms of relatively stable, but not unchangeable, ways in which students learn . . . *not* . . . as an unchangeable personality attribute, but as the result of the temporal interplay between personal and contextual influences" (Vermunt, 1996, p. 25, 29). The initial set of items was derived from analyses of student interviews, together with an examination of existing inventories (particularly those developed by Janssen, 1996) and the more general literature on student learning. The groupings of inventory items were refined through psychometric analyses and, in conjunction with qualitative analyses of the interview transcripts, four "learning styles" were identified (Vermunt, 1996, 1998; Vermunt & van Rijswijk, 1988) (see Table 2 on p. 338). This led to a model of studying in which conceptions or mental models of learning, along with learning orientations, influenced study regulation strategies, which in turn affected processing strategies.

Vermunt uses the term *mental model* to describe how students think about the nature of learning. Perry (1970) was the first to describe a developmental trend in students' *epistemological beliefs*, distinguishing between dualist and relativist thinking. Säljö (1979) introduced a similarly broad construct describing differences in adults' conceptions of learning in terms of a hierarchy of five categories, with learning seen as a quantitative increase in knowledge at the simplest level, leading to an interpretative process aimed at understanding reality as its highest category. Vermunt describes similar categories, seeing learning in terms of the "intake of knowledge," the "use of knowledge," and the "construction of knowledge." The other two mental models describe a dependence on "stimulating education" and "cooperative learning," which is associated with "intake of knowledge" rather than "construction of knowledge." Subsequent work on conceptions of learning has suggested additional categories, including a higher level — "changing as a person" (Marton, Dall'Alba, & Beaty, 1993; Van Rossum & Schenk, 1984) and additional qualitative variants intended to take account of cultural variations, such as "learning as a duty" (Meyer, 2000a).

Table 2. Four Distinctive Learning Styles
(based on Vermunt, 1996, 1998)

Constructs at differing levels of analysis	Meaning directed	Reproduction directed	Application directed	Undirected
Mental model	Construction of knowledge	Intake of knowledge	Use of knowledge	Relying on teachers or other students
Learning orientation	Personal orientation	Certificate and self-test orientations	Vocational orientation	Ambivalent
Regulation of learning	Mostly self-regulation	Mostly external regulation	Both external and internal regulation	Lack of regulation
Cognitive processes	Deep processing	Stepwise processing	Concrete processing	Processing not identified
Affective processes	Intrinsic interest	Fear of forgetting	Practical interest	Low self-esteem and expectation of failure

In related work, Beaty identified contrasting *learning orientations*, which capture differences in students' reasons for taking courses and are categorized in terms of their orientations (vocational, academic, personal, social) and the type of interest shown (intrinsic or extrinsic) (Beaty, Gibbs, & Morgan, 1997). Vermunt incorporated five learning orientations in the *ILS* to explore students' aims and goals in relation to higher education: The "certificate directed" orientation describes a focus on passing examinations or earning credits, whereas the "vocational orientation" involves a focus on the professional application of the content studied. The "personally interested orientation" is similar to scales describing interest or intrinsic orientations in other inventories. The "self-test directed orientation" describes students' testing or proving their capabilities, while the "ambivalent orientation" indicates students' doubts about both the value of their courses and their ability to cope with the work.

Vermunt also included three aspects of regulation in his inventory — "self-regulation," "external regulation," and "lack of regulation." The processing strategies were similar to the process components of the *ASI*, with "relating and structuring" along with "critical processing" being equivalent to deep, and "analyzing" with "memorizing and rehearsal" being surface. But he also included "concrete processing," not found in other inventories but linked with vocational orientation.

Principal component analyses suggested four groups of subscales within the *ILS* (Vermunt, 1998). The first component linked self-regulation combined with deep and concrete processing to a mental model of constructing knowledge. It also incorporated orientations that indicated personal interest in the subject matter, rather than in obtaining certificates. The second component was essentially the reverse of this with loadings on the surface processing scales and external regulation, associated with being certificate-oriented and seeing learning as the intake of knowledge. The remaining components accounted for much less variance. One linked a model of learning as depending on stimulating education and cooperative learning to an ambivalent orientation and a lack of regulation; the other was defined mainly by learning as the use of knowledge and a vocational orientation, together with smaller loadings on concrete processing and being certificate-oriented.

Emerging Conceptualizations

It is apparent in all of this research that the development of succeeding generations of inventories has built on the earlier ones. This evolution process is illustrated here by developments in the *ASI*. That instrument incorporated motivation and study methods from an earlier inventory, but was designed mainly to explore the interrelationships between the approaches to learning described by Marton and the learning styles introduced by Pask. Since then, it has been revised to suit the purposes of successive projects, and so exists in several versions which have steadily refined the conceptualization of the original scales and added new scales to keep up with more recent research. Some of these versions appear only in research reports, while others, such as *RASI* (Tait & Entwistle, 1996) and *ASSIST* (Tait, Entwistle, & McCune, 1998), have been described in more accessible forms. The term "orientation" used to describe the factors in the *ASI* was replaced by "approach" as the latter term was being increasingly used in higher education. The most recent inventory — *Approaches to Learning and Studying Inventory (ALSI)* — is currently being developed for a project designed to investigate how specific changes in the teaching-learning environment affect students' approaches to studying. The *ALSI* forms part of two more extensive questionnaires, the *Learning and Study Questionnaire (LSQ)* and the *Experiences of Teaching and Learning Questionnaire (ETLQ)*. The component elements of the *ALSI* are shown in Table 1 on page 332; details of its development can be found on the project web site — http://www.ed.ac.uk/etl/publications.html.

ALSI contains five scales. *Deep approach* is defined explicitly by a combination of intention and process, with items covering "intention to understand," together with the associated thinking processes of "relating ideas" and "use of evidence" that parallel Pask's holist and serialist strategies. "Relating ideas" was broadened to include aspects of constructivist thinking (Phillips, 2000) and an additional scale — *monitoring studying* — was created by combining items describing "monitoring understanding," "monitoring generic skills" and "monitoring study effectiveness." This scale is empirically related to deep approach, but is conceptually distinct, describing metacognitive aspects of learning. In the *surface* domain, the items describe four aspects — "unreflective studying," "unthinking acceptance," "memorizing without understanding" (Meyer, 2000b), and "fragmented knowledge" (Meyer, 1991). The achieving orientation within *ASI* was subsequently labeled "strategic approach" (Tait et al., 1998), but successive changes in the inventory have gradually lost the strategic element in this domain. It is now covered by two scales, one indicating *organized studying* (including time management), and the other describing *effort management* (including concentration).

Within item factor analyses, the majority of items load on only one of the three main domains, but a few do show overlap with another factor in conceptually understandable ways. Some interconnection between domains should not be seen as a weakness; rather it is an inevitability of the seamlessness of human behavior that we are seeking to simplify by creating analytic categories. Looking at the patterns of loadings emerging across the three main factors has helped to see how the underlying processes work together to create effective studying (see Janssen, 1996).

Concluding Discussion

This analysis has concentrated on six distinct inventories widely used in higher education to measure study strategies and associated constructs. The development of inventories in the United States, compared with Europe and Australia, followed rather different tracts in the early stages. The *ILP* and *MSLQ* both had strong roots in the mainstream psychological literature, and the *MSLQ* has kept quite close to those origins by defining many tightly focused concepts that retain their psychological meaning and nomenclature. Although the *SPQ* and the *ASI* both acknowledged links to the psychological literature, they were guided strongly by conceptualizations drawn from educational research. Both these inventories, along with the *ILS*, also grouped subscales into broader composites derived from factor analyses, and having distinctive meanings. As the instruments have been developed further, the distinction between American and non-American conceptualizations has diminished (Biggs, 1993), with the *ILS*, for example, having several aspects in common with the *MSLQ*, and the most recent version of the *ASI* (*ALSI*) including elements of both metacognition (monitoring studying) and self-regulation (effort management).

One of the main problems in reading this literature on study strategies for the first time is the different meanings given to the same term, and the existence of different terms apparently covering the same aspect of studying. For example, Entwistle and Ramsden (1983) used the term *orientation to studying* — meaning, reproducing, achieving, and nonacademic — to describe the four factors that emerged from the *ASI*. The term "orientation" implied sufficient breadth to include intention and process, but also remained narrower than either "epistemological beliefs" or "conceptions of learning." Vermunt uses the term, still at a general level, to describe what Beaty, Gibbs, and Morgan (1997) referred to as "learning orientations" or contrasting ways of valuing vocational, academic, personal, and social goals in higher education.

The term *approach to learning* was seen by Marton and Säljö (1976) as a specific reaction to the content of the task and the context within which it was experienced. It has, however, also been used to indicate a more consistent or "typical" way of studying across contexts with similar demands (as in *ALSI*). The term *style* has also been given different meanings. Pask (1976, 1988) used it to suggest not just relative consistency over time and context, but also a *preference* in choosing between contrasting learning processes, Messick (1994), in particular, has argued that *style* brings together aspects of personality and ability, and that contrasting poles exist which represent alternative, but equally effective, learning processes: Vermunt, however, uses the term "style" to indicate the collection of related subscales within his inventory.

Researchers' conceptualizations depend on their previous academic training and experience, which lead initially to a particular choice of terminology, and subsequently to the defence of their own conceptual scheme, once it has been buttressed by extensive work and publication. It then becomes extremely difficult to change terminology, or even to bring in additional dimensions, which may threaten the "purity" or elegant simplicity of the original conception. Yet, without some compromise between the competing descriptions and theoretical positions, future researchers will be forced into choices between inventories without necessarily understanding the reasons for the differences. Ideally, we would need factor analyses of the whole set of inventories to provide empirical evidence of what are the main dimensions through which to describe student learning and studying. The total number of items would make any such analysis impracticable, so we are forced to rely mainly on descriptive similarity or face validity through the detailed analysis of the items within the inventories considered here.

Table 1, on page 332, drew on that analysis to suggest that the three main factors, repeatedly found in the separate analyses, are variants of the same underlying dimensions. The close similarity between *ASI* (or *ALSI*) and *SPQ* is already accepted. While there is less equivalence of subscales between those and the *ILP-R*, the three main dimensions remain essentially equivalent; the main difference lies in an extensive exploration of differing forms of self-efficacy and esteem which merge into the affective area. *LASSI* concentrates on the aspects of studying that are "coachable" through workshops, but the inventory also contains subscales covering distinct types of information processing that have a descriptive similarity to factors found in other inventories. *ILS* emphasizes study regulation but the two most prominent factors — meaning directed and reproducing directed — map directly on to deep and surface respectively, using items at different levels of analysis. It has no explicit motivational items, nor does it cover effort or study organization, and so the achieving dimension is lacking. However, the "application-directed" style represents a potentially valuable addition to the lexicon and conceptualization of study strategies by suggesting a more practical way of thinking, linked to the vocational and certificate orientations. Finally, *MSLQ* concentrates predominantly on the positive "deep" and "self-regulation" aspects of studying, with just two elements that might be seen as in the "surface" domain. It does, however, draw attention to components of motivation and self-regulation to indicate how these more specific aspects affect studying. However, perhaps the most important addition in this inventory (and *ILS*) is the more explicit recognition of collaboration within studying. Most of the inventories describe studying essentially as a solitary activity affecting the individual. In higher education today, collaboration of various forms is being given greater prominence, and this should now be reflected in the descriptions of study strategies.

Looking through all the inventories there is a surprising lack of emphasis on emotion in learning. The positive forms are implicit in some of the scales describing academic interests and motivation, but only a negative form — anxiety or fear of failure — has been developed explicitly. Again, current work in educational psychology (see, for example, Boekaerts, Pintrich, & Zeidner, 2000), has begun to trace the interplay between cognition and emotion in relation to self-regulation, and that might be a way of extending inventories in the future. However, much as the wealth of interesting but closely interrelated aspects of studying tempt scale constructors to cover them all, parsimony urges caution both theoretically and practically. The longer the inventory, the less care students take in completing it, and the less likely are staff to use it. In the British context, the maximum acceptable length is generally around 75 items, while 50 items is more manageable, taking about 15 minutes to complete and producing little loss in reliability for three or four main scales.

There are continuing debates in the literature about how dimensions are really needed. Richardson (2000), in his extensive review of the psychometric properties and usage of study strategy inventories, sees no advantage in including the achieving/strategic dimension. To other researchers, the overlap between deep and strategic suggests a single scale of effective studying, while "surface" and "nonacademic" can also be seen as simply the negative ends of "deep" and "strategic." However, this analysis of six distinct inventories leaves the strong impression that at least three dimensions are required to cover the main elements of variance found in studying. Conceptually, the "deep" approach, with its emphasis on learning processes to develop understanding, can be clearly distinguished from the self-regulation of study strategies allied to effort and concentration. Of course, the combination of these is bound to enhance the quality of learning outcomes, and so empirical relationships are to be expected. While there are negative correlations between factors describing deep and surface approaches, these are typically quite low, and there are distinct learning processes associated with each approach. A possible fourth dimension, mentioned in discussing the *ILS*, centres on vocational orientation and concrete processing, perhaps distinguishing the practical from the theoretical, and this grouping of scales could prove to be a valuable way of describing differences in study strategies in professional courses in higher education.

Finally, the validity of any inventory describing study strategies depends on relative consistency in ways of studying. Inventories have been used to predict future academic performance, and so have anticipated relative stability over substantial time intervals. But they have also been used to detect changes attributable to a particular approach to teaching, thus accepting the influence of the teaching-learning environment on the processes of learning and studying. Study strategies must thus be somewhat consistent, but also affected by the specific situation or context. Pervin (2001) reached a similar conclusion from his extensive research on personality.

> Over the years, I have become increasingly impressed with the contextualization of behavior and the idiosyncratic nature of individual perceptions of situations. I have been struck with the importance of cultural differences and taken seriously the suggestions . . . that meaning is all-important . . . and that meaning is highly idiosyncratic. . . . At the same time, . . . I believe that regularities can be found . . . — (that) a science of personality may need to be based on principles of person-system functioning . . . (Moreover,) the person has a construct system, providing some stability (i.e. structure), but the system also is dynamic in that different constructs apply to different situations and become more or less important in different contexts. (pp. 313–315).

Learning and studying has surely to be considered in similarly complex terms, with study strategy inventories making a contribution to the investigation of the principles and general construct systems relating to person–environment functioning. At the same time, the limitations of this methodology have to be accepted, and alternative approaches to research used to capture change and individuality more fully.

References

Atkinson, J. W., & Feather, N. T. (1966). *A theory of achievement motivation*. New York: John Wiley & Sons.

Ausubel, D. P. (1968). *Educational psychology: A cognitive view*. New York: Holt, Rinehart and Winston.

Beaty, L., Gibbs, G., & Morgan, A. (1997). Learning orientations and study contracts. In F. Marton, D. J. Hounsell, & N. J. Entwistle (Eds.), *The experience of learning* (2nd ed., pp. 72–88). Edinburgh, UK: Scottish Academic Press.

Biggs, J. B. (1970). Faculty pattern in study behavior. *Aust. J. Psychol., 22,* 161–174.

Biggs, J. B. (1976). Dimensions of study behaviour: Another look at a.t.i. *Br. J. Educ. Psychol., 46,* 68–80.

Biggs, J. B. (1979). Individual differences in study processes and the quality of learning outcomes. *Higher Educ., 8,* 381–394.

Biggs, J. B. (1987). *Student approaches to learning and studying.* Melbourne, Australia: Australian Council for Educational Research.

Biggs, J. B. (1993). What do inventories of students' learning processes really measure? A theoretical review and clarification. *Br. J. Educ. Psychol., 63,* 3–19.

Biggs, J. B. (1999). *Teaching for quality learning at university.* Buckingham, UK: Open University Press.

Biggs, J. B., Kember, D., & Leung, D. Y. P. (2001). The Revised Two-Factor Study Process Questionnaire: R-SPQ-2F. *Br. J. Educ. Psychol, 71,* 133–149.

Boekaerts, M., Pintrich, P., & Zeidner, M. (Eds.) (2000). *Handbook of self-regulation.* San Diego, CA: Academic Press.

Broadbent, D. E. (1966). The well-ordered mind. *Am. Educ. Res. J., 3,* 281–295.

Brown, W. F., & Holtzman, W. H. (1966). *Manual of the survey of study habits and attitudes.* New York: Psychological Corporation.

Cano-Garcia, F. C., & Justicia-Justicia, F. J. (1994). Learning strategies, styles, and approaches: An analysis of their interrelationships. *Higher Educ., 27,* 239–260.

Craik, F. I. M., & Lockhart, R. S. (1972). Levels of processing: A framework for memory research. *J. Verbal Learn. Verbal Behav., 11,* 671–684.

Craik, F. I. M., & Tulving, E. (1975). Depth of processing and the retention of words in episodic memory. *J. Exp. Psychol. (Gen), 104,* 268–294.

Dearing Committee. (1997). *Higher education in the learning society.* London: National Committee of Inquiry into Higher Education (also HMSO).

Entwistle, N. J. (1997). Metacognitive and strategic awareness of learning processes and understanding. Paper presented at the 7th EARLI conference, Athens, Greece.

Entwistle, N. J. (1998). Improving teaching through research on student learning. In J. J. F. Forest (Ed.), *University teaching: International perspectives* (pp. 73–112). New York: Garland.

Entwistle, N. J. (2000). Approaches to studying and levels of understanding: The influences of teaching and assessment. In J. C. Smart (Ed.), *Higher education: Handbook of theory and research* (Vol. XV, pp. 156–218). New York: Agathon.

Entwistle, N. J., & Entwistle, D. M. (1970). The relationships between personality, study methods, and academic performance. *Br. J. Educ. Psychol., 40,* 132–141.

Entwistle, N. J., Hanley, M., & Hounsell, D. J. (1979). Identifying distinctive approaches to studying. *Higher Educ., 8,* 365–380.

Entwistle, N. J., & Ramsden, P. (1983). *Understanding student learning.* London: Croom Helm.

Entwistle, N. J., Thompson, J. B., & Wilson, J. D. (1974). Motivation and study methods. *Higher Educ., 3,* 379–396.

Entwistle, N. J., & Waterston, S. (1988). Approaches to learning and levels of processing: A comparison of inventories derived from contrasting theoretical bases. *Br. J. Educ. Psychol, 58,* 258–265.

Entwistle, N. J., & Wilson, J. D. (1977). *Degrees of excellence: The academic achievement game.* London: Hodder and Stoughton.

Fishbein, M. (1967). *Readings in attitude theory and measurement.* New York: John Wiley & Sons.

Garcia, T. (1996). Self-regulation: An introduction. *Learn. Individ. Differences, 8,* 161–163.

Geisler-Brenstein, E., & Schmeck, R. (1996). The revised inventory of learning processes: A multifaceted perspective on individual differences in learning. In M. Birenbaum & F. Dochy (Eds.), *Alternatives in assessment of achievements, learning processes, and prior knowledge.* Norwell, MA: Kluwer Academics.

Janssen, P. J. (1996). Studaxology: The expertise students need to be effective in higher education. *Higher Educ., 31,* 117–141.

Marton, F., Dall'Alba, G., & Beaty, E. (1993). Conceptions of learning. *Int. J. Educ. Res., 19,* 277–300.

Marton, F., & Säljö, R. (1976). On qualitative differences in learning: I. Outcome and process. *Br. J. Educ. Psychol., 46,* 4–11.

Marton, F., & Säljö, R. (1997). Approaches to learning. In F. Marton, D. J. Hounsell, & N. J. Entwistle (Eds.), *The experience of learning* (2nd ed., pp. 39–58). Edinburgh, UK: Scottish Academic Press.

McKeachie, W. J. (1990). Research on college teaching: The historical background. *J. Educ. Psychol, 82,* 189–200.

Messick, S. (1994). The matter of style: Manifestations of personality in cognition, learning, and teaching. *Educ. Psychol., 21,* 121–136.

Meyer, J. H. F. (1991). Study orchestration: The manifestation, interpretation, and consequences of contextualized approaches to studying. *Higher Educ., 22,* 297–316.

Meyer, J. H. F. (2000a). An overview of the development and application of the Reflections on Learning Inventory (RoLI). Paper presented at the invitational RoLI Symposium, Imperial College, London, July 25.

Meyer, J. H. F. (2000b). Variation in contrasting forms of "memorising" and associated observables. *Br. J. Educ. Psychol., 70,* 163–176.

Pask, G. (1976). Styles and strategies of learning. *Br. J. Educ. Psychol., 46,* 128–148.

Pask, G. (1988). Learning strategies, teaching strategies, and conceptual or learning style. In R. Schmeck (Ed.), *Learning strategies and learning styles* (pp. 83–100). New York: Plenum.

Perry, W. G. (1970). *Forms of intellectual and ethical development in the college years: A scheme.* New York: Holt, Rinehart and Winston.

Pervin, L. A. (2001). Persons in context: Defining the issues, units, and processes. In J. M. Collis & S. Messick (Eds.), *Intelligence and personality: Bridging the gap in theory and measurement* (pp. 307–317). Mahwah, NJ: Lawrence Erlbaum.

Phillips, D. C. (Ed.). (2000). *Constructivism in education.* Chicago: National Society for the Study of Education.

Pintrich, P. R., & Garcia, T. (1991). Student goal orientation and self-regulation in the college classroom. In M. L. Maehr & R. R. Pintrich (Eds.), *Advances in motivation and achievement: Vol. 7. Goals and self-regulatory processes* (pp. 371–402). Greenwich, CT: JAI.

Pintrich, R. R., & Garcia, T. (1993). Intra-individual differences in students' motivation and self-regulated learning. *Ger. J. Educ. Psychol., 7*, 99–107.

Pintrich, P. R., & Garcia, T. (1994). Self-regulated learning in college students: Knowledge, strategies, and motivation. In P. R. Pintrich, D. R. Brown, & C. E. Weinstein (Eds.), *Student motivation, cognition, and learning* (pp. 113–134). Hillsdale, NJ: Lawrence Erlbaum.

Pintrich, P. R., Smith, D. A. F., Garcia, T., & McKeachie, W. J. (1991). *A manual for the use of the Motivated Strategies for Learning Questionnaire (MSLQ).* Ann Arbor, MI: National Center for Research to Improve Postsecondary Teaching and Learning.

Pintrich, P. R., Smith, D. A. F., Garcia, T., & McKeachie, W. J. (1993). Reliability and predictive validity of the Motivated Strategies for Learning Questionnaire (MSLQ). *Educ. Psychol. Meas., 53*, 801–813.

Prosser, M., & Trigwell, K. (1999). *Understanding learning and teaching: The experience of higher education.* Buckingham, UK: SRHE/Open University Press.

Ramsden, P. (1992). *Learning to teach in higher education.* London: Kogan Page.

Richardson, J. T. E. (2000). *Researching student learning: Approaches to studying in campus-based and distance education.* Buckingham, UK: SRHE/Open University Press.

Säljö, R. (1979). *Learning in the learner's perspective: I. Some common-sense conceptions* (Report 76), University of Gothenburg, Department of Education, Gothenburg, Sweden.

Schmeck, R., Geisler-Brenstein, E., & Cercy, S. P. (1991). Self-concept and learning: The revised inventory of learning processes. *Educ. Psychol., 11*, 343–362.

Schmeck, R., Ribich, F., & Ramanaiah, N. (1977). The development of a self-report inventory for assessing individual differences in learning processes. *Appl. Psychol. Meas., 1*, 413–431.

Schunk, D. H., & Zimmerman, B. J. (Eds.). (1994). *Self-regulation of learning and performance: Issues and educational applications.* Hillsdale, NJ: Lawrence Erlbaum.

Speth, C., & Brown, R. (1988). Study approaches, processes, and strategies: Are three perspectives better than one? *Br. J. Educ. Psychol., 58*, 247–257.

Tait, H., & Entwistle, N. J. (1996). Identifying students at risk through ineffective study strategies. *Higher Educ., 31*, 97–116.

Tait, H., Entwistle, N. J., & McCune, V. (1998). ASSIST: A reconceptualisation of the approaches to studying inventory. In C. Rust (Ed.), *Improving student learning: Improving students as learners.* Oxford, UK: Oxford Centre for Staff and Learning Development.

Van Rossum, E. J., & Schenk, S. (1984). The relationship between learning conception, study strategy, and learning outcome. *Br. J. Educ. Psychol., 54*, 73–83.

Vermunt, J. D. (1996). Metacognitive, cognitive, and affective aspects of learning styles and strategies: A phenomenographic analysis. *Higher Educ., 31*, 25–50.

Vermunt, J. D. (1998). The regulation of constructive learning processes. *Br. J. Educ. Psychol., 68*, 149–171.

Vermunt, J. D., & van Rijswijk, F. A. W. M. (1988). Analysis and development of students' skill in self-regulated learning. *Higher Educ., 17*, 647–682.

Volet, S. E. (1997). Cognitive and affective variables in academic learning: The significance of direction and effort in students' goals. *Learn. Instr., 7*, 235–254.

Wankowski, J. A. (1973). *Temperament, motivation and academic achievement.* Birmingham, UK: Birmingham University Educational Survey.

Weinstein, C. E. (1982). Training students to use elaboration learning strategies. *Contemp. Educ. Psychol., 7,* 301–311.

Weinstein, C. E., & Mayer, R. (1986). The teaching of learning strategies. In M. C. Wittrock (Ed.), *Handbook of research on teaching* (3rd ed., pp. 315–327). New York: Macmillan.

Weinstein, C. E., & Meyer, D. K. (1991). Cognitive learning strategies and college teaching. In *New directions of teaching and learning, no. 45.* San Francisco: Jossey-Bass.

Weinstein, C. E., Schulte, A., & Palmer, D. (1987). Learning and study strategies inventory (LASSI). Clearwater, FL: H. and H.

Wilson, K. L., Smart, R. M., & Watson, R. J. (1996). Gender differences in approaches to learning in first-year psychology students. *Br. J. Educ. Psychol., 66,* 59–71.

Wolters, C. A. (1998). Self-regulated learning and college students' regulation of motivation. *J. Educ. Psychol., 90,* 224–235.

Zimmerman, B. J. (1989). Models of self-regulated learning and academic achievement. In B. J. Zimmerman & D. H. Schunk (Eds.), *Self-regulated learning and academic achievement: Theory, research, and practice* (pp. 1–26). New York: Springer-Verlag.

The Concept of Formative Assessment

Carol Boston

One of the best ways to assess students' mastery of study strategies is to capitalize on the data that emerges from a classroom teaching environment. Some savvy instructors have labeled this type of assessment as "diagnostic teaching" while others, such as Carol Boston, refer to it as formative assessment. Regardless of the terminology used, classroom assessments are extremely valuable to instructors because they promote and validate students' learning. In this article Boston explains the purposes and advantages of formative assessment, provides concrete examples, and outlines resources for future professional reading on the topic.

While many educators are highly focused on state tests, it is important to consider that over the course of a year, teachers can build in many opportunities to assess how students are learning and then use this information to make beneficial changes in instruction. This diagnostic use of assessment to provide feedback to teachers and students over the course of instruction is called formative assessment. It stands in contrast to summative assessment, which generally takes place after a period of instruction and requires making a judgment about the learning that has occurred (e.g., by grading or scoring a test or paper). This article addresses the benefits of formative assessment and provides examples and resources to support its implementation.

Purpose and Benefits of Formative Assessment

Black and Wiliam (1998b) define assessment broadly to include all activities that teachers and students undertake to get information that can be used diagnostically to alter teaching and learning. Under this definition, assessment encompasses teacher observation, classroom discussion, and analysis of student work, including homework and tests. Assessments become formative when the information is used to adapt teaching and learning to meet student needs.

When teachers know how students are progressing and where they are having trouble, they can use this information to make necessary instructional adjustments, such as reteaching, trying alternative instructional approaches, or offering more opportunities for practice. These activities can lead to improved student success.

Black and Wiliam (1998a) conducted an extensive research review of 250 journal articles and book chapters winnowed from a much larger pool to determine whether formative assessment raises academic standards in the classroom. They concluded that efforts to strengthen formative assessment produce significant learning gains as measured by comparing the average improvements in the test scores of the students involved in the innovation with the range of scores found for typical groups of students on the same tests. Effect sizes ranged between .4 and .7, with formative assessment apparently helping low-achieving students, including students with learning disabilities, even more than it helped other students (Black & Wiliam, 1998b).

Feedback given as part of formative assessment helps learners become aware of any gaps that exist between their desired goal and their current knowledge, understanding, or skill and guides them through actions necessary to obtain the goal (Ramaprasad, 1983; Sadler, 1989). The most helpful type of feedback on tests and homework provides specific comments about errors and specific suggestions for improvement and encourages students to focus their attention thoughtfully on the task rather than on simply getting the right answer (Bangert-Drowns, Kulick, & Morgan, 1991; Elawar & Corno, 1985). This type of feedback may be particularly helpful to lower achieving students because it emphasizes that students can improve as a result of effort rather than be doomed to low achievement due to some presumed lack of innate ability. Formative assessment helps support the expectation that all children can learn to high levels and counteracts the cycle in which students attribute poor performance to lack of ability and therefore become discouraged and unwilling to invest in further learning (Ames, 1992; Vispoel & Austin, 1995).

While feedback generally originates from a teacher, learners can also play an important role in formative assessment through self-evaluation. Two experimental research studies have shown that students who understand the learning objectives and assessment criteria and have opportunities to reflect on their work show greater improvement than those who do not (Fontana & Fernandes, 1994; Frederiksen & White, 1997). Students with learning disabilities who are taught to use self-monitoring strategies related to their understanding of reading and writing tasks also show performance gains (McCurdy & Shapiro, 1992; Sawyer, Graham, & Harris, 1992).

Examples of Formative Assessment

Since the goal of formative assessment is to gain an understanding of what students know (and don't know) in order to make responsive changes in teaching and learning, techniques such as teacher observation and classroom discussion have an important place alongside analysis of tests and homework.

Black and Wiliam (1998b) encourage teachers to use questioning and classroom discussion as an opportunity to increase their students' knowledge and improve understanding. They caution, however, that teachers need to make sure to ask thoughtful, reflective questions rather than simple, factual ones and then give students adequate time to respond. In order to involve everyone, they suggest strategies such as the following:

- Invite students to discuss their thinking about a question or topic in pairs or small groups, then ask a representative to share the thinking with the larger group (sometimes called think-pair-share).

- Present several possible answers to a question, then ask students to vote on them.

- Ask all students to write down an answer, then read a selected few out loud.

Teachers might also assess students' understanding in the following ways:

- Have students write their understanding of vocabulary or concepts before and after instruction.

- Ask students to summarize the main ideas they've taken away from a lecture, discussion, or assigned reading.

- Have students complete a few problems or questions at the end of instruction and check answers.

- Interview students individually or in groups about their thinking as they solve problems.

- Assign brief, in-class writing assignments (e.g., "Why is this person or event representative of this time period in history?")

(The November/December 1997 issue of *Clearinghouse* magazine is devoted to practical ideas for formative assessment. See especially Mullin and Hill for ideas for history classes, McIntosh for mathematics, Childers and Lowry for science, and Bonwell for higher education.)

In addition to these classroom techniques, tests and homework can be used formatively if teachers analyze where students are in their learning and provide specific, focused feedback regarding performance and ways to improve it. Black and Wiliam (1998b) make the following recommendations:

- Frequent short tests are better than infrequent long ones.

- New learning should be tested within about a week of first exposure.

- Be mindful of the quality of test items and work with other teachers and outside sources to collect good ones.

Portfolios, or collections of student work, may also be used formatively if students and teachers annotate the entries and observe growth over time and practice (Duschl & Gitomer, 1997).

Resources for Teachers Interested in Formative Assessment

Formative assessment is tightly linked with instructional practices. Teachers need to consider how their classroom activities, assignments, and tests supports learning aims and allow students to communicate what they know, then use this information to improve teaching and learning. Two practitioner-oriented books that offer many helpful ideas about, and examples of, classroom assessments are *A Practical Guide to Alternative Assessment* (Herman, Aschbacher, & Winters, 1992) and *Classroom Assessment Techniques: A Handbook for College Teachers* (Angelo & Cross, 1993).

The Northwest Regional Educational Laboratory has put large sections of its helpful training kit, *Improving Classroom Assessment: A Toolkit for Professional Developers* online at http://www.nwrel.org/assessment/toolkit98.asp. The readings, overheads, exercises, and handouts could help groups of teachers think through assessment issues in their schools. The Assessment Training Institute provides some free newsletter and journal articles about classroom assessment on its Web site (http://www.assessmentinst.com/) as well as publications, videos, and training sessions for a fee. A recent issue of the *Maryland Classroom* newsletter from the Maryland State Department of Education features a lead article on effective feedback in the classroom with example responses from an assignment involving persuasive text (http://www.msde.state.md.us/Maryland%20Classroom/2002_05.pdf).

The National Research Council (2001) has produced a useful, accessible book on classroom assessment in science that contains many interesting vignettes about how teachers can adjust their teaching based on their observations, questioning, and analysis of student work. While the anecdotes are specific to K–12 science teaching, the chapters about the documented value of formative assessment on classroom achievement, as well as what it requires in terms of teacher development and how classroom assessment relates to summative assessment such as state tests, have broad applicability. See http://www.nap.edu/catalog/9847.html for a browsable version of *Classroom Assessment and the National Science Education Standards.*

Training and professional development in the area of classroom assessment are essential in order to provide individual teachers with the time and support necessary to make changes. Teachers need time to reflect upon their assessment practices and benefit from observing and consulting with other teachers about effective practices and about changes they would like to make (NRC, 2001). Black and Wiliam (1998b) recommend setting up local groups of schools — elementary and secondary; urban, suburban, and rural — to tackle formative assessment at the school level while collaborating with other local schools. They anticipate that challenges will be different in different subject areas and suggest that external evaluators could help teachers with their work and collect evidence of effectiveness. They also point to potential conflicts between state assessments and classroom assessments, where the external tests can shape what goes on in the classroom in a negative way if the emphasis is on drill and test preparation versus teachers' best judgment about learning.

Teachers generally need to undertake or participate in some summative assessment as a basis for reporting grades or meeting accountability standards. However, the task of summative assessment for external purposes remains quite different from the task of formative assessment to monitor and improve progress. While state tests provide a snapshot of a student's performance on a given day under test conditions, formative assessment allows teachers to monitor and guide students' performance over time in multiple problem-solving situations. Future research might examine how teachers deal with the relationship between their formative and summative roles, how teachers' classroom assessments relate to external test results, and how external test results can be made more helpful in terms of improving student performance.

References

Ames, C. (1992). Classrooms: Goals, structures, and student motivation. *Journal of Educational Psychology, 84*(3): 261–271.

Angelo, T. A., & Cross, K. P. (1993). *Classroom assessment techniques: A handbook for college teachers* (2nd ed.). San Francisco: Jossey-Bass.

Bangert-Drowns, R. L., Kulick, J. A., & Morgan, M. T. (1991). The instructional effect of feedback in test-like events. *Review of Educational Research, 61*(2): 213–238.

Black, P., & Wiliam, D. (1998a). Assessment and classroom learning. *Assessment in Education, 5*(1): 7–74.

Black, P., & Wiliam, D. (1998b). Inside the black box: Raising standards through classroom assessment. *Phi Delta Kappan, 80*(2): 139–148. (Available online: http://www.pdkintl.org/kappan/kbla9810.htm.)

Bonwell, C. C. (1997). Using active learning as assessment in the postsecondary classroom. *Clearing House, 71*(2): 73–76.

Childers, P., & Lowery, M. (1997). Engaging students through formative assessment in science. *Clearing House, 71*(2): 97–102.

Duschl, R. D., & Gitomer, D. H. (1997). Strategies and challenges to change the focus of assessment and instruction in science classrooms. *Educational Assessment, 4*(1): 37–73.

Elawar, M. C., & Corno, L. (1985). A factorial experiment in teachers' written feedback on student homework: Changing teacher behaviour a little rather than a lot. *Journal of Educational Psychology, 77*(2): 162–173.

Fontana, D., & Fernandes, M. (1994). Improvements in mathematics performance as a consequence of self-assessment in Portuguese primary school pupils. *British Journal of Educational Psychology, 64*(3): 407–417.

Frederiksen, J. R., & White, B. J. (1997). Reflective assessment of students' research within an inquiry-based middle school science curriculum. Paper presented at the annual meeting of the American Educational Research Association, Chicago, IL.

Herman, J. L., Aschbacher, P. R., & Winters, L. (1992). *A practical guide to alternative assessment.* Alexandria, VA: Association for Supervision and Curriculum Development.

McCurdy, B. L., & Shapiro, E. S. (1992). A comparison of teacher monitoring, peer monitoring, and self-monitoring with curriculum-based measurement in reading among students with learning disabilities. *Journal of Special Education, 26*(2): 162–180.

McIntosh, M. E. (1997). Formative assessment in mathematics. *Clearing House, 71*(2): 92–97.

Mullin, J., & Hill, W. (1997). The evaluator as evaluated: The role of formative assessment in history class. *Clearing House, 71*(2): 88–92.

National Research Council (2001). *Classroom assessment and the national science education standards*, edited by J. M. Atkin, P. Black, & J. Coffey. Washington, DC: National Academy Press. (Browse online at: http://www.nap.edu/catalog/9847.html.)

Ramaprasad, A. (1983). On the definition of feedback. *Behavioral Science, 28*(1): 4–13.

Sadler, D. R. (1989). Formative assessment and the design of instructional systems. *Instructional Science, 18*(2): 119–144.

Sawyer, R. J., Graham, S., & Harris, K. R. (1992). Direct teaching, strategy instruction, and strategy instruction with explicit self-regulation: Effects on the composition skills and self-efficacy of students with learning disabilities. *Journal of Educational Psychology, 84*(3): 340–352.

Vispoel, W. P., & Austin, J. R. (1995). Success and failure in junior high school: A critical incident approach to understanding students' attributional beliefs. *American Educational Research Journal, 32*(2): 377–412.

Measuring ESL Students' Awareness of Reading Strategies

Kouider Mokhtari and Ravi Sheorey

Taking the position that existing assessment tools do not reflect some of the strategies that are unique to ESL students, Mokhtari and Sheorey describe in this article the Survey of Reading Strategies, *an instrument designed for adolescent and adult ESL learners. SORS measures via a Likert scale the type and frequency of reading strategies that ESL students perceive they use while reading academic materials. The SORS has been field-tested and has demonstrated reliability and validity as a measure of ESL students' metacognition and reading strategies. Citing recent research, the authors discuss the development and rationale for SORS and outline procedures for administering and scoring. In addition, they provide practical suggestions on how instructors and students can use the data gleaned from this assessment instrument.*

I n this article, we describe an instrument, *Survey of Reading Strategies* (SORS), which is intended to measure adolescent and adult English as a Second Language (ESL) students' metacognitive awareness and perceived use of reading strategies (broadly defined here as mental plans, techniques, and actions taken while reading academic or school-related materials). We further suggest ways of using the instrument as a means of increasing learner awareness of reading strategies, which has been shown to help students improve reading comprehension skills.

The development of SORS is our attempt to assist developmental education teachers in helping their ESL students increase metacognitive awareness and become thoughtful, constructively responsive, and strategic readers while reading academic materials — one of the major reasons for their learning of English. Three compelling reasons have motivated us to develop the SORS: First, there is strong research support for the positive relationship between students' metacognitive awareness of reading processes and their ability to read and excel academically (e.g., Alderson, 1984; Carrell, 1991; Clarke, 1979; Cziko, 1978). Second, although there are several instruments aimed at assessing native speakers' metacognitive awareness of reading processes (see Mokhtari & Reichard, 2002, for a brief review of these instruments), we could not find any published instruments that are specifically designed to assess ESL students' metacognitive awareness and perceived use of reading strategies while reading for academic purposes. Third, we have found that, even though there is some agreement among researchers that a number of reading strategies are transferable from one language to another (c.f., Alderson, 1984; Carrell, 1991), the existing instruments do not take into account some of the strategies that are unique to students who are literate in more than one language such as translating from English into one's native language or using both languages when reading to maximize understanding. Consequently, such instruments may not be appropriate for an ESL population. Finally, given the recent and projected increases in cultural and linguistic diversity in schools, colleges, and university classrooms (August & Hakuta, 1997), instructors will be in need of adequate tools for assessing skills and teaching students how to read academic materials efficiently and effectively.

Instruments such as SORS should fit within a comprehensive reading assessment for ESL learners at the institution. It should effectively complement many of the traditionally used standard reading assessment tests, such as the Nelson Denney (Brown & Brown, 1993), which simply do not assess students' awareness and control of comprehension processes while reading. SORS is presented as a simple, yet effective tool for enabling students to develop a better awareness of their reading strategies, for helping teachers assess such awareness, and for assisting students in becoming constructively responsive readers.

The development of the SORS was initially inspired by the review and use of another instrument, Metacognitive Awareness of Reading Strategies Inventory (MARSI), which was developed by Mokhtari and Reichard (2002) as a measure of students' metacognitive awareness of reading strategies. Because MARSI was originally designed for students who are native English speakers, it was inappropriate for use with non-native speakers, which led us to adapt it so that it could be used appropriately for an ESL population. The development of SORS was further inspired by our own experiences teaching language and literacy skills to college-level ESL students.

Such experiences are highlighted by a series of observations concerning the mental processes some ESL students go through and the actions they take when reading for academic purposes. Auerbach and Paxton (1997) provide the following illustration of such processes:

> I used to believe that I have to know all the words in the English readings in order to understand the readings. Therefore, I read in English with the dictionary beside me all the time. I read English readings only for homework before I came to this reading class. I never read any English readings because I wanted to read them. I read them because they were my homework. I like to read in my first language, but I just could not read in English with the same feeling as I read in Chinese. The belief that I have to know all the words in order to understand the reading made me lose interest — Li. (p. 237)

What Li says is probably not atypical of the beliefs held by many students about reading in a second language. The statement reveals some of the conscious and unconscious thought processes students such as Li go through when reading in a second language. These processes shed light on the struggles as well as the successes of second language readers and provide essential information not only for understanding how they construct meaning from text but also how they can become thoughtful, strategic readers. For example, Li appears to make sense of what she reads and what strategies she deploys in order to overcome reading difficulties and to facilitate reading comprehension.

Li's statements are consistent with the findings from research studies which have focused on the reading process and the ways in which students respond to reading and learning to read in both the first and the second language. Research in reading has revealed that there is a direct relationship between ESL students' reading strategies and their conceptions of literacy (Auerbach & Paxton, 1997). For example, readers like Li, who are in the beginning stages of developing their reading skills in a second language (L2), "feel they have to know all the words in a text in order to understand it, rely heavily on the dictionary, are unable to transfer productive L1 [native language] strategies or positive feelings about reading, spend long hours laboring over sentence-by-sentence translation, and attribute their difficulties to a lack of English proficiency" (p. 238). Similar findings have been reported for L1 readers by Garner and Alexander (1989): "Younger and poorer readers often rely on a single criterion for textual understanding: Understanding of individual words" (p. 145).

Second-language reading research has also shown that reading difficulties are closely associated with L2 readers' level of proficiency in the target language. Alderson (1984) points out that "proficiency in a foreign language may be more closely associated with foreign-language reading ability [than reading ability in the native language]" (p. 20). Alderson does not, of course, imply that high proficiency in the second language equals higher level reading skills. Rather, as Cziko (1978) suggests, once second language learners reach higher levels of overall competence in the target language, there is concurrent improvement in their reading ability in that language. In addition, there is evidence that good L2 readers can compensate for a lack of English proficiency by increasing awareness of reading strategies and learning how to use these strategies while reading to enhance comprehension (Carrell, Pharis, & Liberto, 1989).

In recent years, considerable attention has been paid to understanding what proficient, skilled readers typically do while reading (in both L1 and L2), including identifying the types of strategies they use, how they use them, and under what conditions they use those strategies (e.g., Block, 1992; Jimenez, Garcia, & Pearson, 1996; Kern, 1989; Kletzien, 1991; Paris, Lipson, & Wixon, 1983; Pressley, Beard El-Dinary, & Brown, 1992; Song, 1998; Zhicheng, 1992). Insights from these research studies have been helpful for both L1 and L2 teachers in assisting their students to become strategic readers. Auerbach and Paxton

(1997) and Carrell et al. (1989) consider metacognitive awareness or metacognitive control — that is, planning and consciously executing appropriate actions to achieve a particular goal — to be a critical element of proficient, strategic reading.

Auerbach and Paxton (1997), in fact, designed an ESL course aimed specifically at applying L2 reading research findings in the classroom with readers like Li and letting them discover the effects of new reading strategies on comprehension performance. The authors reported that the results of this type of intervention, in which a combination of direct and indirect strategy instruction was used, were generally positive. Students were able not only to increase their metacognitive awareness and regulation of their reading strategies but also to increase their level of engagement in reading English texts. As for reading in L1, Pressley and Afflerbach (1995), after examining 38 research studies on native English speakers' reading, proposed that proficient readers who are strategic and "constructively responsive" take specific and conscious steps while at the same time orchestrating their cognitive and affective resources to ensure maximum comprehension. It is this awareness that distinguishes the skilled from unskilled readers.

As Paris and Jacobs (1984) also point out, "skilled readers often engage in deliberate activities that require planful thinking, flexible strategies, and periodic self-monitoring ... [whereas] novice readers often seem oblivious to these strategies and the need to use them" (p. 2083). The purpose of this paper is to describe the development of the Survey of Reading Strategies (SORS), an instrument designed to measure adolescent and adult ESL students' metacognitive awareness and perceived use of reading strategies while reading academic materials such as textbooks.

Instrument

Development of SORS

The Survey of Reading Strategies is based on the Metacognitive Awareness of Reading Strategies Inventory (MARSI), originally developed by Mokhtari and Reichard (2002) as a tool for measuring native English speaking students' awareness and perceived use of reading strategies while reading academic or school-related materials. MARSI was validated using a large native speaker population ($N = 825$) representing students with reading abilities ranging from middle school to college. The internal consistency reliability coefficients (as determined by Cronbach's alpha) for its three subscales, which were based on the results of a series of factor analyses, were as follows: Global Reading Strategies (.92), Problem Solving Strategies (.79), and Support Strategies (.87). The reliability for the overall scale was .93, indicating a reasonably dependable measure of students' metacognitive awareness of reading strategies. A complete description of MARSI, including its psychometric properties as well as its theoretical and research foundations, can be found in Mokhtari and Reichard (2002).

The major impetus for using MARSI to develop SORS was to enable it to be used with adolescent and adult students for whom English is a second or foreign language. To accomplish this objective, we made three basic, yet important, revisions: First, we refined the wording of several items to make them easily comprehensible to ESL students. Second, consistent with relevant research about reading strategies used across languages (c.f., Jimenez, Garcia, & Pearson, 1996), we added two key strategies clearly *not* used by L1 readers but often invoked by L2 learners ("translating from one language to another" and "thinking in the native and target language while reading"). Finally, we removed two items (namely "summarizing information read" and "discussing what one reads with others") which do not specifically constitute reading strategies as conceived in the current research literature on metacognition and reading comprehension. Following the aforementioned revisions, we field-tested the revised instrument on a population of ESL students studying at two universities in the United States and found consistent results relative to the instrument's reliability (internal reliability = .89 or better), indicating a reasonable degree of consistency in measuring awareness and perceived use of reading strategies among non-native students of English (see Sheorey & Mokhtari, 2001, for details).

Description of the Instrument

The SORS, like MARSI, is intended to measure the type and frequency of reading strategies that adolescent and adult ESL students perceive they use while reading academic materials in English (such as textbooks, journal articles, class notes, etc.). The SORS consists of 30 items, each of which uses a 5-point Likert scale ranging from 1 ("I never or almost never do this") to 5 ("I always or almost always do this"). Students are asked to read each statement and circle the number that applies to them, indicating the frequency with which they use the reading strategy implied in the statement. Thus the higher the number, the more frequent the use of the strategy concerned. A short background questionnaire, which can be administered along with the SORS statements, can include items requesting information about their age, gender, and self-rated ability in reading English; students can also be asked to self-rate their proficiency in English as well as to estimate the overall score they might have obtained on a standardized test like the Test of English as a Foreign Language (TOEFL). The SORS measures three broad categories of reading strategies: namely, global reading strategies, cognitive strategies, and support strategies. These categories (or subscales) were based on MARSI's factor analyses and theoretical considerations. A brief description of each SORS category and the number of items within each category are given below:

- Global Reading Strategies (GLOB) are those intentional, carefully planned techniques by which learners monitor or manage their reading, such as having a purpose in mind, previewing the text as to its length and organization, or using typographical aids and tables and figures (13 items).

- Problem Solving Strategies (PROB) are the actions and procedures that readers use while working directly with the text. These are localized, focused techniques used when problems develop in understanding textual information; examples include adjusting one's speed of reading when the material becomes difficult or easy, guessing the meaning of unknown words, and rereading the text to improve comprehension (8 items).

- Support Strategies (SUP) are basic support mechanisms intended to aid the reader in comprehending the text such as using a dictionary, taking notes, underlining, or highlighting textual information (9 items).

Procedures for Administering and Scoring SORS

The Survey of Reading Strategies (see Appendix) is fairly easy to read and administer (Flesch Reading Ease = 34.7; Flesch-Kincaid Grade Level Equivalent = 4.5–6.0) and can be administered individually or to groups of ESL students. We suggest that the SORS be administered after removing strategy category identifications (that is, GLOB, PROB, and SUP) as it may confuse the students. The total administration time is estimated to be approximately 10 to 12 minutes, depending on the students' overall language and reading ability. After explaining the purpose of the inventory, teachers should direct students to read each statement and indicate how often they use the strategy described in that statement, using the 5-point Likert scale provided after each statement. It is important to remind the students that their responses are to refer only to the strategies they use when reading school-related materials, not leisure materials such as newspapers or magazines. They should also be encouraged to respond honestly to each statement in the inventory and to ask questions about any aspect of the inventory they do not understand.

Scoring SORS is quite easy and can be done by the students themselves. Students simply transfer the scores obtained for each strategy to the scoring sheet, which accompanies the instrument. After the individual scores are recorded, they should be added up in each column to obtain a total score for the entire instrument as well as for each strategy subscale (i.e., Global, Problem Solving, and Support Strategies).

These scores can then be interpreted using the interpretation key provided. Three levels of reading strategy usage are identified along the lines suggested by Oxford and Burry-Stock (1995) for general learning strategy usage: High (mean of 3.5 or higher), moderate (mean of 2.5 to 3.4), and low (mean of 2.4 or lower). These usage levels provide a convenient standard that can be used for interpreting the score averages obtained by students. The scores obtained should be interpreted using the high, moderate, and low usage designations included on the scoring sheet that accompanies the instrument (contact the *JDE* or authors for a copy of the scoring sheet).

As a general rule, the overall score average indicates how often students believe they use the strategies in the instrument when reading academic materials. The averages for each subscale in the inventory show the mean frequency with which students use a given category of strategies when reading academic materials. This information will serve as a useful means of raising learner awareness of their reading processes when reading. For instance, a very low score on any of these strategy groups or subscales indicates that there may be some strategies in these categories that they might want to learn about and consider using when reading.

Implications: Using SORS to Improve Strategy Instruction to L2 Readers

The SORS provides a convenient tool for assisting teachers in addressing the academic reading needs of adolescent and adult ESL students. The information derived from the instrument can be helpful to students increasing their awareness of reading strategies while reading, improving their understanding of the reading process, and enhancing confidence in their own reading ability. This information can also be helpful to teachers in helping their students learn to become "constructively responsive" and thoughtful readers. Ideas about how to help students develop awareness and use reading strategies have been offered by a number of L1 and L2 reading researchers.

In a recent study aimed at examining the differences in metacognitive awareness and perceived strategy use among ESL ($n = 152$) and U.S. ($n = 150$) college students, Sheorey and Mokhtari (2001) found that students' reading ability was related to their awareness and use of reading strategies while reading. In both student groups, low-ability readers reported a lower level of awareness and strategy use when reading academic materials than did high-ability readers.

These findings are consistent with prior research which has shown that awareness — and use — of reading strategies are positively related to superior reading comprehension and successful learning among native English speakers (Alexander & Jetton, 2000; Pressley, 2000). Such findings would seem to indicate that low-ability readers are not prepared to read academic reading materials such as textbooks and, further, tend not to possess the necessary reading strategies and skills for efficient comprehension. In our experiences in teaching developmental reading to college students, we consistently find that students who lack metacognitive awareness and control of reading strategies often have difficulties coping with academic reading materials such as textbooks. They tend to expend more time and energy struggling with individual words than on constructing meaning from the text — a condition which often results in a slow, labored, and choppy reading style that strains their attention and interest.

Strategy instruction can help all students, especially struggling ones, become more active readers and thinkers. Paris and Winograd (1990, pp. 31–41) make several excellent suggestions for reading strategy instruction, which can be used for all readers, and particularly the struggling ones. For example, when teaching a particular reading strategy, such as setting purpose for reading or adjusting reading rate, they recommend using the following steps: (a) describe what the strategy is, (b) explain why the strategy should be learned and use, and (c) provide examples of the circumstances under which the strategy should be used. Constructing the meaning of unfamiliar words from the context (rather than relying constantly on a dictionary), for example, is one of several strategies that can be easily taught through this type of direct explanation approach; in turn, such instruction can provide a useful way of increasing students' metacognitive awareness and use of reading strategies when coping with academic reading tasks.

It is important for all readers, whether native or non-native, to be aware of some of the key strategies proficient readers use before reading (e.g., thinking about what one knows about a subject, knowing the purpose for which they read), during reading (e.g., concentrating well while reading, monitoring one's comprehension), and after reading (e.g., understanding how pieces of information fit together, evaluating what one reads). Teachers can play a key role in increasing students' awareness of such strategies and in helping them become "constructively responsive" readers (Pressley & Afflerbach, 1995). According to Ciborowski (1999, p. 46), the success of strategy instruction depends to a large degree on three important criteria including (a) the commitment teachers make to arm themselves with a set of strategies that have shown promise with all readers, particularly the struggling ones; (b) how well instructors can model their own strategic thinking while reading; and (c) how well they can convince their students that such strategies are useful in improving reading comprehension.

Mere awareness of certain reading strategies does not always translate into actual use of the strategies concerned. Nonetheless, it is important for metacognitive reading strategies instruction to be integrated within the overall reading curriculum so as to enhance students' metacognition about reading. Such instruction can help promote an increased awareness of what is involved in reading and the development of thoughtful and constructively responsive reading. Teaching students to become strategic, thoughtful, and constructively responsive readers can be a powerful way to promote skillful academic reading, which will, in turn, enhance academic achievement. However, our own teaching experiences have taught us that strategy instruction takes time to teach. Ciborowski (1999) states that strategy instruction requires careful reflection on the teachers' part about "how to teach: why, when, and in what problems or circumstances to use a strategy. It involves frequent modeling, and reteaching specific strategies when necessary" (p. 46). Ideally, effective strategy instruction should take place frequently; employ small cooperative groups; and use a variety of reading materials such as textbooks, trade books, and newspapers.

Limitations in Using SORS

Using SORS with ESL students has a few limitations and reading teachers should be aware of them. First, SORS should be used to supplement, not to supplant, existing assessment measures of students' reading comprehension. Instructors should consider SORS as only one source of information about students' reading abilities that must be analyzed in conjunction with other measures of reading ability. Such caution is consistent with prior research on reading strategies, which has shown that there is a need for triangulation (with qualitative methodology such as observation and in-depth interviews) of data in order to get complete and reliable results (Merriam, 1998). Additionally, because SORS is a self-report measure, one cannot tell with absolute certainty from the instrument alone whether students actually engage in the strategies they report using. Identifying certain strategies through an inventory such as SORS may indicate that the students know about or are aware of those strategies. However, mere awareness of strategies is not sufficient; rather, teacher judgment and common sense are clearly required to validate the discrepancy between students' beliefs about using the strategies and actual practice. Teachers should carefully scrutinize the responses to SORS statements and interpret them in light of their own experiences with their students before making instructional decisions. Finally, strategy instruction may require more work on the part of teachers, but the benefits for all students — especially for those who find reading difficult — would make the extra effort worthwhile.

Concluding Remarks

Reading research on the relationship between reading ability and reading strategy awareness and use among readers of English as a second language (e.g., Carrell, 1991; Kern, 1989; Sheorey & Mokhtari, 2001;

Song, 1998) has revealed that good readers are typically able to reflect on and monitor their cognitive processes while reading. They are not only aware of which strategies to use, but they also tend to be better at regulating the use of such strategies while reading. In other words, they know which strategies to use and how to use them to ensure success in reading comprehension. Consequently, it would be helpful for second language readers, whether or not they are proficient in the target language, to be aware of the strategies proficient reading requires. Instruments like the SORS can be useful in helping students discover their strategic strengths and weaknesses. Developmental reading educators can use such an instrument as a valuable tool for increasing students' awareness of reading strategies to help them become "constructively responsive" readers (Pressley & Afflerbach, 1995). As teachers strive to create the conditions under which their students can learn to become thoughtful and strategic readers, they will need to help their students develop the ability to read academic materials efficiently and thereby enhance their overall academic achievement in school and college.

Appendix: Survey of Reading Strategies (SORS)

The purpose of this survey is to collect information about the various techniques you use when you read **academic materials in English** (e.g., reading textbooks for homework or examinations, reading journal articles, etc.).

All the items below refer to your reading of **college-related academic** materials (**such as textbooks**, *not* newspapers or magazines). Each statement is followed by five numbers, 1, 2, 3, 4, and 5, and each number means the following:

"1" means that "I **never or almost never** do this."
"2" means that "I do this **only occasionally**."
"3" means that "I **sometimes** do this." (About **50%** of the time.)
"4" means that "I **usually** do this."
"5" means that "I **always or almost always** do this."

After reading each statement, *circle the number* (1, 2, 3, 4, or 5) which applies to you. Note that there are **no right or wrong responses** to any of the items on this survey.

Category	Statement	Never				Always
GLOB	1. I have a purpose in mind when I read.	1	2	3	4	5
SUP	2. I take notes while reading to help me understand what I read.	1	2	3	4	5

GLOB   3. I think about what I know to help me understand what I read.   1 2 3 4 5

GLOB   4. I take an overall view of the text to see what it is about before reading it.   1 2 3 4 5

SUP   5. When text becomes difficult, I read aloud to help me understand what I read.   1 2 3 4 5

GLOB   6. I think about whether the content of the text fits my reading purpose.   1 2 3 4 5

PROB   7. I read slowly and carefully to make sure I understand what I am reading.   1 2 3 4 5

GLOB   8. I review the text first by noting its characteristics like length and organization.   1 2 3 4 5

PROB   9. I try to get back on track when I lose concentration.   1 2 3 4 5

SUP   10. I underline or circle information in the text to help me remember it.   1 2 3 4 5

PROB   11. I adjust my reading speed according to what I am reading.   1 2 3 4 5

GLOB   12. When reading, I decide what to read closely and what to ignore.   1 2 3 4 5

SUP   13. I use reference materials (e.g., a dictionary) to help me understand what I read.   1 2 3 4 5

PROB   14. When text becomes difficult, I pay closer attention to what I am reading.   1 2 3 4 5

GLOB   15. I use tables, figures, and pictures in text to increase my understanding.   1 2 3 4 5

PROB   16. I stop from time to time and think about what I am reading.   1 2 3 4 5

GLOB   17. I use context clues to help me better understand what I am reading.   1 2 3 4 5

SUP   18. I paraphrase (restate ideas in my own words) to better understand what I read.   1 2 3 4 5

PROB   19. I try to picture or visualize information to help remember what I read.   1 2 3 4 5

GLOB   20. I use typographical features like bold face and italics to identify key information.   1 2 3 4 5

GLOB   21. I critically analyze and evaluate the information presented in the text.   1 2 3 4 5

SUP   22. I go back and forth in the text to find relationships among ideas in it.   1 2 3 4 5

GLOB	23.	I check my understanding when I come across new information.	1 2 3 4 5
GLOB	24.	I try to guess what the content of the text is about when I read.	1 2 3 4 5
PROB	25.	When text becomes difficult, I re-read it to increase my understanding.	1 2 3 4 5
SUP	26.	I ask myself questions I like to have answered in the text.	1 2 3 4 5
GLOB	27.	I check to see if my guesses about the text are right or wrong.	1 2 3 4 5
PROB	28.	When I read, I guess the meaning of unknown words or phrases.	1 2 3 4 5
SUP	29.	When reading, I translate from English into my native language.	1 2 3 4 5
SUP	30.	When reading, I think about information in both English and my mother tongue.	1 2 3 4 5

References

Alderson, J. (1984). Reading in a foreign language: A reading problem or a language problem? In J. Alderson, and A. Uruhart (Eds.), *Reading in a foreign language* (pp. 1–24). New York: Longman.

Alexander, P. A., & Jetton, T. L. (2000). Learning from text: A multidimensional and developmental perspective. In M. Kamil, P. Mosenthal, P. D. Pearson, & R. Barr (Eds.), *Handbook of reading research* (Vol. III, pp. 285–310). Mahwah, NJ: Lawrence Erlbaum.

Auerbach, E., & Paxton, D. (1997). "It's not the English thing": Bringing reading research into the ESL classroom. *TESOL Quarterly, 31*, 237–261.

August, D., & Hakuta, K. (1997). *Improving schooling for language-minority children: A research agenda.* Washington, DC: National Academy Press.

Block, E. (1992). See how they read: Comprehension monitoring of L1 and L2 readers. *TESOL Quarterly, 26*, 319–343.

Brown, F., & Brown, H. (1993). *Nelson Denney Reading Test.* Chicago, IL: Riverside Publishing.

Carrell, P. (1991). Second language reading: Reading ability or language proficiency? *Applied Linguistics, 12*, 159–179.

Carrell, P., Pharis, B., & Liberto, J. (1989). Metacognitive strategy training for ESL reading. *TESOL Quarterly, 23*, 647–678.

Clarke, M. (1979). Reading in Spanish and English. *Language Learning, 29*, 201–215.

Ciborowski, J. (1999). *Textbooks and the students who can't read them: A guide to teaching content.* West Rutland, VT: Brookline Books.

Cziko, G. (1978). Differences in first and second language reading: The use of syntactic, semantic, and discourse constraints. *Canadian Modern Language Review, 34*, 473–489.

Garner, R., & Alexander, P. (1989). Metacognition: Answered and unanswered questions. *Educational Psychologist, 24*(2), 143–158.

Jimenez, R., Garcia, G., & Pearson, P. (1996). The reading strategies of bilingual Latina/o students who are successful English readers: Opportunities and obstacles. *Reading Research Quarterly, 31*, 90–112.

Kern, R. (1989). Second language reading strategy instruction: Its effects on comprehension and word inference ability. *Modern Language Journal, 73*, 135–146.

Kletzien, S. (1991). Strategy use by good and poor comprehenders reading expository text of differing levels. *Reading Research Quarterly, 25*, 67–86.

Merriam, S. B. (1998). *Qualitative research and case study applications in education.* San Francisco, CA: Jossey-Bass.

Mokhtari, K., & Reichard, C. (2002). Assessing students' metacognitive awareness of reading strategies inventory. *Journal of Educational Psychology, 94*, 249–259.

Oxford, R., & Burry-Stock, J. (1995). Assessing the use of language learning strategies worldwide with the ESL/EFL version of the strategy inventory for language learning SILL. *System, 23*, 1–23.

Paris, S., & Jacobs, J. (1984). The benefits of informed instruction for children's reading awareness and comprehension skills. *Child Development, 55*, 2083–2093.

Paris, S., Lipson, M., & Wixon, K. (1983). Becoming a strategic reader. *Contemporary Educational Psychology, 8*, 293–316.

Paris, S., & Winograd, P. (1990). How metacognition can promote academic learning and instruction. In B. Jones & L. Idol (Eds.), *Dimensions of Thinking and Cognitive Instruction* (pp. 15–51). Mahwah, NJ: Lawrence Erlbaum.

Pressley, M. (2000). What should comprehension instruction be the instruction of? In M. Kamil, P. Mosenthal, P. D. Pearson, & R. Barr (Eds.), *Handbook of reading research* (Vol. III, pp. 545–561). Mahwah, NJ: Lawrence Erlbaum.

Pressley, M., & Afflerbach, P. (1995). *Verbal protocols of reading: The nature of constructively responsive reading.* Mahwah, NJ: Lawrence Erlbaum.

Pressley, M., Beard El-Dinary, P., & Brown, R. (1992). Skilled and not-so-skilled reading: Good information processing or not-so-good processing. In M. Pressley, K. Harris, & J. Guthrie (Eds.), *Promoting academic competence and literacy in school* (pp. 91–127). San Diego, CA: Academic Press.

Sheorey, R., & Mokhtari, K. (2001). Differences in the metacognitive awareness of reading strategies among native and nonnative readers. *System, 29*(4), 431–449.

Song, M. (1998). Teaching reading strategies in an ongoing EFL university reading classroom. *Asian Journal of English Language Teaching, 8*, 41–54.

Zhicheng, A. (1992, November). *The effects of teaching reading strategies on improving reading comprehension for ESL learners.* Paper presented at the Annual meeting of Mid-South Educational Research Association, Knoxville, TN. (ERIC Document Reproduction Service No. ED 356 643)

The Learning Portfolio: A Valuable Tool for Increasing Metacognitive Awareness

Nannette Evans Commander and Marie Valeri-Gold

Portfolios have been touted as vehicles for engaging students in their learning and for enhancing their metacognitive awareness, but they are also valuable assessment tools for both the instructor and the student. In this article, Nannette Evans Commander and Marie Valeri-Gold describe how they used portfolios with at-risk students in a learning strategies course, providing examples of what students included in their portfolios and explaining how they used the data from the portfolios. In addition, the authors outline the benefits of the portfolio (e.g., increased confidence, reflection, metacognition) by sharing their students' testimonials about the experience.

Portfolios are not a new concept. Artists and writers have used portfolios for years. In the field of education, portfolios have been adapted to virtually any subject area and grade level. Ample research literature attests to the positive impact of portfolios on teachers and students from kindergarten level through college (Askham, 1997; Cambridge, 1996; Mullin, 1998; Tillema & Smith, 2000). Definitions vary but portfolios usually involve examples of student work that tell the story of achievement or growth. For example, Wolf and Siu-Runyan (1996) define portfolios as:

> A portfolio is a selective collection of student work and records of progress gathered across diverse contexts over time, framed by reflection and enriched through collaboration, that has as its aim the advancement of student learning. (p. 31)

Many educators are drawn to portfolio use because of the promise it offers for engaging students in the learning process and for improved assessment. Some attributes of portfolios are that they (a) capture the intellectual substance and learning situation in ways that other methods of evaluation cannot; (b) encourage students to take a role in the documentation, observation, and review of learning; (c) are a powerful tool for improvement; and (d) create a culture of professionalism about learning (Cambridge, 1996). Arter, Spandel, and Culham (1995) remind us that the two basic reasons for doing portfolios are instruction and assessment. For instructional purposes, the process involved in assembling a portfolio fosters "student self-reflection, critical thinking, responsibility for learning, and content area skills and knowledge" (p. 1). For assessment purposes, some reasons offered for the collection of student work over time include the possibility for a more in-depth look at what students know and can do and the opportunity to base assessment on more "authentic" work.

It was with these positive qualities in mind that a portfolio system designated the "Learning Portfolio" was designed as part of the curriculum of a study strategies course for at-risk students in a major urban university. This three-credit hour course, entitled, "Survival Skills for College," is a central component of a retention effort for students between 15 and 60 hours whose cumulative grade point average (gpa) is below a 2.0. Of the students enrolled in this course during Spring semester 2001 ($n = 995$), 55% were female ($n = 551$) and 45% were male ($n = 44$), 32% were white ($n = 320$), 50% were black ($n = 500$), and 18% were Asian/Asian American, Hispanic, Native American or other, and 49% ($n = 484$) entered the university as freshmen. Although students receive a letter grade that is computed into their earned gpa, the course, which in some instances may be required, does not apply toward graduation. Instructional modules include study skills (time management, note taking, test taking, reading-comprehension, memory); student identity (values, cultural identity, student campus identity, cultural integration and personal growth); health and wellness (stress, nutrition, anxiety, managing feelings); communication (oral and written, financial aid, civility, harassment, discrimination); relationships (verbal and nonverbal listening, assertiveness); and confidence building (multiple intelligences, sense of self, locus of control). Instructors meet with students one-on-one at the beginning, middle, and end of the semester to focus on personal, social, and academic needs and to review progress.

Research indicates that many college students would benefit from direct instruction in the skills that are often offered in such study strategies courses. Weinstein (1996; 1993) argues that students would benefit from adopting characteristics of expert learners with learning-to-learn strategies that enhance metacognition. In fact, research suggests that metacognitive awareness of both reading and writing skills can be enhanced through direct instruction (El-Hindi, 1996). Thus, efforts to enhance metacognition or one's ability to think about thinking and to regulate thinking processes are worthwhile. To this end, instructors of "Survival Skills for College" use the Learning Portfolio as a tool for increasing students' metacognitive awareness. Students engage in the process of compiling documents that reflect their efforts to improve and monitor their academic success throughout the semester. Since the majority of students are enrolled concurrently in credit-bearing, content area courses, strategy transfer is encouraged as students document in their portfolio how they are practicing and applying academic skills. Further, students are asked to select one particular content area course to identify as their "target course." The Learning Portfolio is presented as a method of demonstrating efforts for effective and successful learning in this particular course. Although emphasis is placed on the target course, documentation in the portfolio of application of learning skills in other courses is welcomed.

Contents of the Learning Portfolio

According to Busboom (1991), a "literacy-based portfolio" contains material that fits into the four major areas of attitudinal awareness, process, product, and evaluation and feedback. The area of attitudinal awareness includes any materials that address the students' feelings toward school and academics. Examples are reading inventories, surveys, questionnaires, observations, study skills inventories, and so forth. The process area includes materials addressing reactions to academic tasks, such as literature logs in which students record their readings and react to what they have read. The product area documents the students' strengths and skills in need of improvement. Examples are work samples of edited and revised drafts, reports, projects, and so forth. Finally, the area of evaluation and feedback includes any materials that document growth. For instance, standardized and nonstandardized tests, comments from instructors, and reviews of work by peers represent documentation in the area of evaluation and feedback.

The Learning Portfolio is designed as a literacy-based portfolio in that it contains documents in the four areas outlined by Busboom (1991). Students receive general directions for creating their Learning Portfolio (see Appendix A on p. 373) at the individual conference at the beginning of the semester. Students are also asked to submit a formal Action Plan in writing, signed by both the student and instructor, that focuses on improving academic progress with concrete measurable goals and specific dates for accomplishment of these goals. In collaboration with the instructor, students monitor the plan and make appropriate changes when necessary and then evaluate the success or failure of the plan in terms of their goals. Students are informed that the portfolio requires a three-ring binder notebook with a table of contents and dividers or tabs for different sections. Creativity regarding the cover of the notebook or the dividers is strongly encouraged. It is suggested that students include at a minimum the following sections in their portfolio: Personal, Note Taking, Test Taking, Learning Styles, Writing, and Reading.

One strength of the Learning Portfolio is that it focuses students' attention on attitudinal awareness. When students compile different materials that document personal feelings toward academics, it heightens their awareness of how their attitude might be affecting academic outcomes. Objective instruments, such as *The Study Attitudes and Motivation Survey* (Michael, Michael, & Zimmerman, 1985) and the *Strong Interest Inventory* (Harmon, Hansen, Borgen, & Hammer, 1994) have been distributed during class time in the Survival Skills for College course for this purpose of increasing attitude awareness.

Likewise, objective documentation of materials representing learning as a process encourages students' engagement in learning and assessment of their own progress. For this purpose, journal writing is required of students in order to focus attention on the skills of self-assessment and metacognitive awareness. Presented as a Monitoring

Journal to be included in the Learning Portfolio, specific directions are provided to structure responses with weekly prompts for each journal entry (see Appendix B on p. 374).

Requirements of the student's selected "target course" as well as materials from other content area courses, such as essays, research papers, or projects, readily provide the product materials. Grades on tests, teacher comments on papers, or peer reviews of work are examples in the area of evaluation and feedback.

Example Learning Portfolio

A Learning Portfolio from a typical student in the Survival Skills for College class contained the following documents representing Busboom's (1991) four areas of a "literacy-based portfolio":

Attitudinal Awareness

- *Study Attitudes and Methods Survey* (Michael et al., 1985)
- *Strong Interest Inventory* (Harmon et al., 1994)
- Autobiographical Essay on "Who Am I?"
- Learning Style Inventory

Process

- Monitoring Journal

Product

- Examples of Different Methods of Note Taking (Cornell, Note Cards, Mapping, etc.)
- Writing Samples

Evaluation and Feedback

- Peer review of writing samples
- Teacher comments on essays
- Tests from content area course

Evaluating the Learning Portfolio

Instructors periodically collect the portfolios to provide feedback on the Learning Portfolio on an informal basis. At the end of the semester the Learning Portfolio is formally reviewed during a conference with the student and instructor. Students are required to include an essay titled "That Was Then, This Is Now!" at the front of the portfolio that guides the reader through the documents. Directions for the essay follow:

This essay will be a guide for the reader of your Learning Portfolio. The overall theme of the essay is the growth you have experienced as a learner supported by the materials you have selected to include as documentation. Your essay should address, but not be limited to, the following questions:

1. What is your vision of a successful learner? Do you feel that you have accomplished your goals this semester? Refer to your action plan and address the extent to which you have fulfilled the criteria established at the beginning of the semester (please attach the action plan to the essay). If you did not reach your goals, explain why not and what actions you intend to take in the future.

2. How have you gained more control and sophistication about your learning? Answer this question for each section of the Learning Portfolio: tests, note taking, learning style, writing, and reading. For each area of growth, provide some information on "then and now." What have you done differently this semester as far as your approach to learning?

3. Finally, do you feel creating a Learning Portfolio was a worthwhile experience? Why or why not? A portfolio is a record of learning that focuses on your work and your reflections or metacognition regarding that work. Did the portfolio encourage reflection on learning? Describe how you monitor your learning "then and now."

An evaluation form (see Appendix C on p. 376) given to students as they begin work on their portfolios structures feedback in terms of content and style of the essay. Relevance, number, and quality of supporting documents are reviewed as well as appearance and overall creativity. Typically, students can earn a total of 100 points for the portfolio, which represents one-fifth of their course grade.

Benefits to Students

Each activity of the Learning Portfolio provides an important opportunity for self-assessment. Reviewing work samples, projects, academic skill building, and progress while sharing personal responses to school work all represent self-assessment of products and processes of learning. Such assessment opportunities foster benefits to students such as increased reflection, evaluation of one's work, and feelings of ownership and responsibility for learning (Paris & Paris, 2001). Although there is a surprisingly small number of empirical investigations on how these types of activities are related to self-assessment, a study by van Kraayenoord and Paris (1991) indicated that students are able to assess their own work and provide cognitive and affective evaluations according to particular features that influence learning. Further, the results of this study indicated that the ability to assess one's work is linked to the ability to evaluate literacy strategies.

The Learning Portfolio is a structured method for developing this important skill of self-assessment. In essays and journals, students provided comments that indicated that the creation of the portfolio increased awareness of learning. While anecdotal evidence, many of these comments had clear themes of the positive effects of self-assessment of learning. Students' comments also reinforced the concept that what is really important is not the Learning Portfolio itself as much as what students learn by creating it. In other words, the Learning Portfolio is a means to an end, not the end itself.

Portfolio excerpts reveal that increased awareness of learning is evident in a variety of forms. In a sample of responses ($n = 28$) to the question, "Do you feel creating a Learning Portfolio was a worthwhile experience? Why or why not? 39% ($n = 11$) of the students wrote that creating the Learning Portfolio increased their confidence. Examples of these responses follow:

> Overall I feel the idea of a portfolio is a good concept. It is a form of hindsight that can help people see how far they've come. A portfolio can either show areas of improvement or show areas where improvement is needed. It allows people to see their accomplishments and how far they've come. Creating the portfolio as the semester progressed helped me see my improvements more clearly.

> Overall my confidence level has come up. I doubt myself less and I'm fully aware that I'm in total control of my success. This attitude has affected my personal life also. I find myself glowing and happier. It has been a long, long time since I felt this way.

> My first thought on a portfolio was "Why?" I thought that it was too much work for the class and that I should just turn in my work and be done with it. Then I realized that I was making an easy situation difficult. I like to see what progress that I have made. Also it will be nice to have something to reflect on when I am out of this class and more importantly when I graduate. The Learning Portfolio made me realize that I have come further than I thought. Previously I was measuring my academic success by how quickly I was completing my degree. With the portfolio I learned to see the little steps and the progress I am making. It allows me to see that what I thought was a little progress is not so little after all.

In the same sample of responses ($n = 28$) to the question, "Do you feel creating a Learning Portfolio was a worthwhile experience? Why or why not?" 50% ($n = 14$) of the students described the benefits of reflecting on learning. Examples of these responses follow:

> Through the various lectures, activities, and assignments we had in this course, I feel that having a portfolio helped me substantially. Through organizing the information, I was able to reflect back on anything I was having trouble on. Not to mention the portfolio itself holds a great amount of significance to me because it carries information that helped me improve and become a successful learner. Looking back I see that I was a student that lacked learning skills, but after the information that was shared with me in my portfolio, I can truly say I became a successful student.

> The Learning Portfolio gave me a chance to reflect on the semester. I can see where I've changed, where I haven't, and where I still need improvement. After the semester is over I know that I'll continue to use everything that I've learned throughout the rest of my college life and maybe even into my career. I learned that if I just sit down and actually monitor my learning I can see where I need the help and improve on it. I know now that I will succeed in whatever I put my heart into.

In addition to increased confidence and engagement in reflection, written comments from 11 students (47%) in this same sample indicate that creating a Learning Portfolio fostered monitoring of the learning process. Examples of these responses follow:

> The Learning Portfolio required a lot of time, thinking, and work. Yes, this portfolio gave me an overview of what I have learned and done this semester, but actually doing it added to the stress and pile up of work that comes with the end of the semester. Even though I felt the pressure of putting this portfolio together it did push me to monitor my learning, which is something that I did not do before.

> Creating the Learning Portfolio was a big help to see all the work I have done this semester come together and see the big picture of what kind of student I am, so this was a very worthwhile project. The portfolio helped me to see my strengths and weaknesses and what I really need to work on to become a successful student. I will monitor my learning from now on by putting together my own portfolio every semester to see how I am coming along.

Excerpts also reveal that 21% of the students ($n = 6$) believe the Learning Portfolio resulted in an awareness of the academic benefits of organizational skills. Examples of these responses follow:

> I feel that having to do a Learning Portfolio is a good idea. I feel that each class should require each student to do one. This is the first time that I have had to do a portfolio and I love it. It helps me to gather all the work that I have done, and it gives me a sense of encouragement. This has encouraged me to keep a portfolio of all my work in the future for future classes. Before I began this portfolio, my work was scattered everywhere. I would constantly have to look through my book bag. I would have to look through my notebooks and I would even have to look through my trunk. Since we started this portfolio, it is easier for me to reference my work. This is an idea that I plan to continue with, not only with my school assignments but also with personal information.

> The Learning Portfolio is a great way to show how well you learn as time goes by. I have learned many things with this portfolio. While I made a portfolio for this class I also made one for another class and put what I learned from this class into it. I was reaching for an A in that class. My portfolio was nice and neat and I received an A in the class thanks to the first portfolio I had to make.

Conclusion

Psychologist Lauren Resnick comments that "What we assess is what we value. We get what we assess, and if we don't assess it, we don't get it" (cited in Wiggins, 1990). This statement is being applied to the connection between what teachers assess and what students learn. These same principles may apply to what students assess and what they learn. The Learning Portfolio is a method for students to participate in self-assessment of what they have learned about learning. For at-risk students, creating Learning Portfolios results in increased metacognitive awareness, a crucial element for successful academic achievement.

Appendix A: Directions for the Learning Portfolio

Description

The Learning Portfolio is an opportunity for you to collect your academic work in a way that reflects your academic development and accomplishments. As you are collecting various documents, think of your portfolio as a work in progress with movable pages and changing content. This will be a record of your skills, knowledge, and attitude toward your academics. You may want to consider the portfolio as a learning tool that provides an opportunity to maintain a comprehensive record of your work. Each student will select a content area course to focus on, and the Learning Portfolio will document progress made in this "target" course.

One problem with today's culture is the lack of time taken for reflection. Great leaders make the time to reflect on accomplishments and set benchmarks for success. Use the Portfolio to reflect on your accomplishments and to set benchmarks for success in the academic arena. Remember, however, that success often requires a willingness to grow and change, and the Learning Portfolio serves as a means to measure and record your growth and change.

Materials

The Portfolio will require a three-ring binder notebook and dividers or tabs for different sections.

Sections

Sections will include, but not be limited to Personal Information (this area may include photos and a record of previous achievements), Monitoring Journal, Learning Style, Time Management, Note Taking, Test Taking, Writing, and Reading.

Appendix B: Monitoring Journal

Weekly Prompts:

1. *Monitoring Others' Behaviors.* Carefully observe the behaviors of students in your target class. What surprises you? What did you expect? Take notes on what you see. What behaviors do you feel will foster success, and what behaviors will hinder success? Describe several students.

2. *Monitoring Note Taking.* Reflect on your ability to take notes both in your target class and from the text for your target class. Within your discussion include an evaluation of changes you have made in your method of note taking, your progress, problems that you have encountered, and solutions that work and do not work for you. How are you organizing your notes to show levels of significance? How are you indicating possible test questions? Are you able to understand your notes when you review them? Are you editing your notes? When you study your notes, are you using the recall column and reciting the information out loud?

3. *Monitoring Use of Resources.* We have talked at length about the various resources available on campus to help students succeed academically. Select one of these resources (professor's office hours, tutorial lab, writing center, study groups, etc.) and seek learning assistance. Describe what happened. What did you ask? What did you learn? How would you evaluate the benefits? Describe other students who were also there. Will you go again? Why or why not?

4. *Monitoring Test Taking.* Select one test from your target class and answer the following questions:
   A. Which part of the exam was the easiest for you? Why?
   B. Which part of the exam was the most difficult? Why?
   C. Which of the following activities did you complete prior to the exam?
      1) All required reading assignments
      2) Preparation and review of reading notes
      3) Review of lecture notes
      4) Self-testing of materials to be covered by the exam
      5) Prediction of possible questions by you prior to the exam
      6) Study with friends
   D. Which of the above did you find most helpful in preparing for this exam?
   E. How much time (in hours) did you spend preparing for the exam?
   F. Did you feel prepared when you walked into the exam? Why or why not?

     G. What changes might you make in the way you study for the next exam in this course?

5. *Monitoring Your Academic Behavior.* Portray the part of you that may be preventing you from being an "A" student. Write a two-page script to portray yourself in a situation that exemplifies what you feel are nonproductive behaviors, bad habits, and/or poor choices. Through your script let us see the part of you that needs change. Be entertaining and informative.

6. *Monitoring Collaborative Learning.* Throughout this course you have been encouraged to collaborate with fellow students. You have probably experienced collaborative learning by small groups in class or you may have collaborated independently with another student. On the basis of your experiences, what insights have you gained from collaborative learning? What factors do you feel are essential for successful collaborative learning? When does it click for you? Why is collaborative learning sometimes unsuccessful? How do you think you will use collaborative learning in the future?

7. *Monitoring Your Writing.* You have most likely been assigned many various writing tasks in your academic courses. Please discuss anything you would like to regarding your experiences with the writing process. Some questions you might consider are:
    A. Is the process of writing a positive or negative experience for you? Give reasons for your answer.
    B. Describe how you approach a writing task, and what strategies you have found to be helpful.
    C. Have you ever experienced writer's block, and if so, how did you overcome it?
    D. How often do you revise papers and how often do you get help with the process of revising?
    E. What advice would you give other students on writing?

8. *Monitoring Your Learning Style.* What is your learning style? Write about how you learn best based on the information provided by the *Meyers-Briggs Type Indicator* and the exercises in your text on learning style. Some questions to consider are:
    A. Identify your learning style and describe what the inventory revealed about you.
    B. Explain how you learn best and why. Then explain the circumstances that may make learning difficult for you and why that is the case.
    C. Describe how your learning style complements and conflicts with your instructors' style of teaching. Explain the strategies you use when your learning style conflicts with your instructor's teaching style.
    D. How can you adapt your learning style for different types of courses?

9. *Monitoring Your Reading.* What specific strategies do you use when reading a textbook? How do these strategies help you to comprehend the material? Are you systematic in your approach to understanding text? Reflect on your comprehension level while using the SQ3R (Survey, Question, Read, Recite, and Review) or SOAR (Survey, Organize, Anticipate Test Questions, and Recite) methods for textbook reading.

10. *Monitoring This Course.* What have you learned in this course that was the most helpful? Why? What have you learned in this course that has been least helpful? Was the Monitoring Journal beneficial to you? Why or why not? If you were the instructor of a course to help students succeed academically what would be the main topic you would focus on? How would you design the course? What suggestions do you have that might make this course more effective for future students?

Appendix C: Portfolio Evaluation

Student's Name _____

Maximum Score = 100 points

Required Essay (30 points)

- Content: Clarity of growth areas, actions taken to facilitate growth, and outcomes   excellent   good   fair   poor
- Style: Overall quality of writing   excellent   good   fair   poor

Supporting Documents (50 points)

- Relevance of supporting documents to growth areas   excellent   good   fair   poor
- Number of supporting documents included   excellent   good   fair   poor
- Quality of supporting documents   excellent   good   fair   poor

Additional (20 points)

- Appearance of portfolio   excellent   good   fair   poor
- Overall creativity   excellent   good   fair   poor

Total number of points: _____   Percentage: _____   Letter grade: _____

Comments:

References

Askham, P. (1997). An instrumental response to the instrumental student: Assessment for learning. *Studies in Educational Evaluation, 23*(4), 299–317.

Arter, J. A., Spandel, M. A., & Culham, R. (1995). *Portfolios for assessment and instruction.* (ERIC Document Reproduction Service No. ED 388 890)

Busboom, J. (1991, February). *Evaluation: Portfolio documentation of student literacy learnings.* Paper presented at the National Reading Conference, Tucson, AZ.

Cambridge, B. L. (1996). The paradigm shifts: Examining quality of teaching through assessment of student learning. *Innovative Higher Education, 40*(4), 287–297.

El-Hindi, A. (1996). Enhancing metacognitive awareness of college learners. *Reading Horizons, 36*(3), 214–230.

Harmon, L. W., Hansen, J. C., Borgen, F. H., & Hammer, A. L. (1994). *Strong interest inventory: Applications and technical guide.* Stanford, CA: Consulting Psychologists Press.

Michael, W. B., Michael, J. J., & Zimmerman, W. S. (1985). *Study attitudes and methods survey.* San Diego, CA: Educational & Industrial Testing Service.

Mullin, J. A. (1998). Portfolios: Purposeful collections of student work. *New Directions for Teaching and Learning, 74,* 79–87.

Paris, S. G., & Paris, A. H. (2001). Classroom applications of research on self-regulated learning. *Educational Psychologist, 36*(2), 89–101.

Tillema, H. H., & Smith, K. (2000). Learning from portfolios: Differential use of feedback in portfolio. *Studies in Educational Evaluation, 26*(3), 193–210.

van Kraayenoord, C. E., & Paris, S. G. (1997). Children's self-appraisal of their work samples and academic progress. *Elementary School Journal, 97,* 523–537.

Weinstein, C. E. (1996). Learning to learn: An essential skill for the 21st century. *Educational Record, 66*(4), 49–52.

Weinstein, C. E. (1993). Broadening our conception of general education: The self-regulated learner. *New Directions for Community Colleges, 21*(1), 31–39.

Wiggins, G. (1990, June). *The truth may set you free, but the test may keep you imprisoned: Toward assessment worthy of the liberal arts.* Paper presented at the Fifth AAHE Conference on Assessment in Higher Education, Washington, DC.

Wolf, K., & Siu-Runyan, Y. (1996). Portfolio purposes and possibilities. *Journal of Adolescent & Adult Literacy, 40*(1), 30–37.

Learning Logs: A Vehicle for Student Learning and Reflective Teaching

Mary P. Deming

Learning logs, like portfolios, are an excellent vehicle for authentic assessment because they encourage students to reflect on and self-evaluate their learning and progress. They also allow instructors to link assessment to instruction in a seamless fashion throughout the semester. Mary P. Deming explains in her article how she uses learning logs with her students, provides examples of possible prompts, and shares some of her students' responses. In addition, she outlines advantages to using the logs and offers suggestions on how to overcome possible difficulties in their implementation.

Introduction

Recently, I reflected on the configuration of my college reading/writing classes, looking for more innovative ways to improve teaching and, consequently, to increase students' learning. In particular, I searched for methods that would encourage students to read and write college-level materials more effectively, respond more meaningfully and analytically to what they read, and monitor and measure their reading and writing processes. At the same time, I searched for a method of evaluation to help gauge the effectiveness of my instruction in a timely manner. I did not want to learn at the end of the academic term that students did not understand what I was teaching or that they had not mastered the material necessary to pass the course.

One technique I explored and have found worthwhile is the use of learning logs based on focused, varied prompts. My eventual experimentation with learning logs has allowed students to describe their personal situations, name their fears, and share their questions and doubts. Each log entry provided a variety of insights for me as well. In particular, from reading students' learning logs, I have learned a great deal about what it is like to participate in a varsity college sport, nurse a critically ill baby, grieve the early death of a parent, practice newly discovered oratory skills, work at a fast-food restaurant, and take pictures of professional models. I have also experienced life as a fraternity brother, a single mother, and a nontraditional student returning to college. I have witnessed friendships develop in the classroom and blossom through the learning logs, with students encouraging and complimenting each other. Most important, I have seen growth in my students, both academically and personally, and I have witnessed their satisfaction with this growth in their learning log responses.

Authentic Assessment and Learning Logs

I teach in a university department that until recently offered a two-course, noncredit writing sequence designed to prepare students for their freshman composition classes. Students were required to enroll in one or both of these courses based on their high school grade point averages (GPAs), their Scholastic Aptitude Verbal Test scores (SAT), and their university placement test scores. I often taught the first-level writing course, one in which students begin with narrative writing and eventually move on to exposition. In this class, students work on writing fluency, composing multiple drafts, and revising and editing their papers. Student-teacher conferences are an important part of the course, and collaborative work helps students to write for a real audience. In addition, this class utilizes a literature-based approach, having students read from a thematically arranged text (Gold & Deming, 1994) that represents a wide breadth of selections and authors. After students' initial introduction to the writing process, academic writing, and the parts of an essay, they read thematic chapters in the text and write weekly essays related to the particular chapter.

Recently, I experimented with learning logs with this first-level, basic writing class. A learning log is defined as a type of journal in which students respond to specific aspects of their learning, unlike a personal journal where they write primarily about their feelings and personal reflections (Commander & Smith, 1996). Wilson (1989) sees the benefits of logs, in particular reading logs, as a place where students can admit their confusion, ask questions, make connections, read with attention, identify with characters and authors, revise readings, and question. Furthermore, in her research on reading logs, Wilson (1989) notes that

> Students who keep reading logs do on their own what their teachers have urged them, in vain, to do. They ask questions, make predictions, form opinions, read the text to find evidence to support their opinions, and notice the subtleties of a writer's craft. (p. 68)

I decided to use learning logs to help students meet three goals I had set for the course:

1. Students should understand the literary selections that we read for discussion and writing.

2. Students should understand the basic composition principles presented.

3. Students should learn to monitor their reading and writing processes in order to regulate and improve each.

In addition, I wanted to employ learning logs to help me meet a goal I had set for myself — to improve my instruction by carefully reviewing and reflecting on the information provided by the learning logs. In particular, I wanted to utilize them to link assessment with instruction. Rhodes and Shanklin (1993) advise teachers to use assessment "to discover the power of your teaching. To learn more about the development of reading and writing. To sharpen the quality of your observations and your confidence in them" (p. 5). Consequently, I hoped that reading students' comments in their learning logs would help me become a more reflective teacher, one who monitors students' responses, responds to students as individuals, and evaluates the effectiveness of instruction. As Hillocks (1995) suggests, a reflective teacher maintains "a basic posture of inquiry in teaching, regarding actions as hypotheses to be assessed" (p. 30). Furthermore, reflective teaching can lead to research based on classroom practice and can produce a reexamination of theory.

Description of Learning Log Activities

I asked students to respond to ten learning log prompts, with at least one learning log prompt assigned weekly. Sample prompts asked students to reflect on their understanding of the readings and class instruction, discuss their implementation of writing strategies, and analyze their experiences with various aspects of composition. Most learning log responses were written outside of class with responses ranging between one and two pages long depending on the topic.

Some instructors evaluate learning logs based on the number of pages, while others prefer a credit or no credit score for each entry. Still other instructors measure the quality of the response in terms of insight and evidence of growth (Fulwiler, 1980). In this class, learning log responses received a score ranging from 0 to 10, with 10 as the maximum score (Commander & Smith, 1996), and learning logs were worth 5% of the students' final grade. I gave the students a Learning Log Assignment Description Sheet, similar to the one employed by Commander and Smith (1996), that provided an overview of the types of assignments, the purpose for using learning logs, grading procedures, format requirements, and a model of an effective learning log assignment.

Learning log responses were collected once a week. I responded to the students' comments in writing and returned the responses to them. For my own records, I kept a running account of students' comments, while I looked for trends concerning students' understanding of what they were reading, their comprehension and use of various reading and writing strategies, and their ability to monitor their reading and writing processes. I looked for trends in the class in general, trends developing over time, and differences between students' responses. This information was used to monitor and adjust instruction.

Sample Learning Log Prompts

Sample Learning Log Prompt #1 asked students to reflect on the literary selections they had read for homework in order to aid them in their understanding of the text: *1. What was your favorite literary selection in Chapter 3, "Our Feelings and the Feelings of Others"? Tell why you liked it in a paragraph or two. 2. What was your least favorite literary selection in Chapter 3? Tell why you disliked it. 3. What literary selection was the most difficult for you? Discuss why it was difficult.*

Responses from Learning Log #1 provided an arena for students to consider carefully the literature they were reading and to share the experiences, both positive and negative, they were having in this process. Consequently, such responses became a place to begin to link systematic assessment with instruction. An analysis of the responses indicated that the students' favorite literary selection for that week was "Shame," a short autobiographical piece by Dick Gregory (as cited in Gold & Deming, 1994, pp. 48–52). Not surprisingly, students reported they liked it because it was easy to follow and understand, they could identify with the characters and the story, and it was a touching, meaningful selection. Interestingly, students identified primarily with Gregory's experience of "shame" as a student, but they failed to mention Gregory's "shaming" of another person at the end of the story. These responses reminded me of the importance of choosing literature with which students can identify, understand, and relate.

Students' least favorite piece was less clear-cut, as students mentioned three different works. Common reasons for disliking a work included that it brought back too many unhappy memories, they could not identify with the story, they disliked the topic, or they could not understand the structure. Finally, the most difficult reading for most students was the poem "The Death of the Hired Man," by Robert Frost (as cited in Gold & Deming, 1994, pp. 67–74). Students had difficulty following the story line, so I developed a short minilesson on the poem, using a reader's-theater technique. As a result, all of us garnered a clearer understanding of the work.

Sample Learning Log Prompt #2, also designed to help students monitor their understanding and their comprehension, combined a technique often used in response to literature assignments (Probst, 1984) with a technique recommended by Writing Across the Curriculum (WAC) experts (Hynds, 1994; Wills, 1993; Young, 1996). This prompt asked students to respond in letter form to the selections that they had read: *Write a letter to a classmate responding to the literary selections you have read for homework. Tell which were your favorite and your least favorite readings. Explain why. If you have any questions about the readings, pose them to your classmate. Exchange papers with your classmate. Respond to your classmate's papers.*

As with Learning Log #1, students liked a particular essay or short story because it was easy to follow and understand, they could identify with the story or the characters, or it touched them in some way. Many students liked both the coach and the moral presented in the essay "A Winner's Secret," by John Feinstein (as cited in Gold & Deming, 1994, pp. 232–237), the story of Duke University's varsity basketball coach, Mike Krzyzewski.

Students' letters to each other produced interesting dialogues. One male student wrote to his partner, a female volleyball player; "I already knew of Coach K. I like a story that talks about how someone goes through a hard time to achieve his goals." The female volleyball player responded, "I really liked your letter. I strongly agree with you. Basketball is one of my interests and I love sports. We have the same interests." Another male student identified with "A Winner's Secret" as well and wrote to his partner, "My father and I are big Duke fans. It tells a good lesson . . . the best way to success is by failing. You learn how to use failure." The student who read and responded to his letter agreed with this theme:

> I definitely can relate to the fact that the best way to success is by failure. I can't relate to it in the sports' aspect, but I can in life. I think you picked out the important lesson in the essays we read.

Again, students in their letters demonstrated the importance of their personally identifying with a literary text. One student referred to a different essay studied later in the term, "He Rocked, I Reeled," by Tama Janowitz (as cited in Gold & Deming, 1994, pp. 166–168), an essay describing the qualities of a good teacher. This student wrote:

> My favorite was "He Rocked, I Reeled." I can relate to it. I once took a chemistry class in high school, and at first I hated it. But when my chemistry teacher taught the class, I began to like chemistry. She is so dedicated to science. . . . Because of her enthusiasm, it inspired me to learn chemistry more.

The letter format of Learning Log #2 was quite exciting and revealing. With a particular audience in mind — one of their classmates — students assumed similar roles. First, most of them adopted the role of a casual friend using an informal letter format beginning with a "Dear . . ." salutation, followed by a sentence or two inquiring about their fellow student's well-being ("I hope you are doing well"). After establishing a friendly context, most students assumed the role of confident literary critics describing their favorite and least favorite reading selections and offering reasons why. Some students referred to interests they shared. For example, one student offered another a compliment:

I liked the same stories that you liked. . . . In reading the education assignments, it reminded me of you. I know that you want to be a teacher, and I think that you would be the type of teacher that would teach the lesson plus another message that would be behind the object lesson. I hope that all of your children in your class get to know you the way that I have. You are a caring person and a well-rounded individual. I think that you would be a good teacher because you have showed us that you are an excellent student.

This letter format might be used earlier and more frequently, since it allowed students to picture and relate to their audience, encouraged them to find and remain faithful to their writing voices, and most importantly, validated their opinions as readers and peers.

The next learning log prompt, **Sample Learning Log Prompt #3**, was designed to help students begin to monitor their reading and writing processes during the first two weeks of class: *1. Reflect on what we have discussed and read in this class so far. Summarize what you have learned about writing so far. 2. Reflect on what we have discussed and read in this class so far, including writing our first drafts for Essay #1. List and discuss any questions you need answered or any problems with which you might need help. Let me know what is unclear to you at this point.*

Some students commented about the literature components of the course, stating they were learning more about the different literary styles of writers. Other students summarized the readings, as Anderson (1992) had warned, and a few students mentioned their favorite authors. However, most comments were related to the writing process — its relationship to reading and the parts of an essay. For two students, the first two weeks of the class were a review. Perhaps more students felt that way as well. The use of a "Quick Take" (Barry, 1996) or a "K-W-L" activity (Ogle, 1986) would have prevented some students from sitting through material they already knew. Assessing students' prior knowledge before teaching a lesson is a much more valuable use of students' time and attention.

Students were also encouraged to ask questions or to make comments about the class, and many did. Some students requested that I review various aspects of grammar, such as run-ons and fragments. Others asked for help with writing thesis statements and expanding their body paragraphs. A few students shared fears: "The writing process is not working for me"; "I am having trouble absorbing the passage"; and "I'm not as good of a writer as I thought I was."

As a result of students' comments, particularly the last student's poignant admission, I strove harder to point out their successes and to work more diligently to prepare them for the demands of a new form of writing, academic discourse. In order to encourage students to continue to feel free enough to ask questions, they needed answers immediately and expected their suggestions for the class to be taken seriously.

Sample Learning Log Prompt #4 is an example of an assignment designed to evaluate students' understanding and use of the composition principles taught in the course and their ability to monitor their own writing processes: *You have now received Essay #1 back, graded with some comments. How do you feel about your grade? What strategies did you use effectively in this first essay? What areas do you need to strengthen? What steps will you take to improve in these areas? What questions do you have for your instructor related to her comments or topics that you want explained in class?*

As with all the learning log prompts, students were encouraged to ask questions. Seven students declared disappointment with their grades. One student wrote, "I am still making the same mistakes I made in high school, still frustrated." Yet, a few students were happily surprised with their good grades. Still other students noted the difference between writing in high school and writing in college. A few students addressed the need to be aware of their audience: "I realized that all teachers have different expectations. I am used to getting higher grades"; and "My professor liked my second solution about setting up a special address for the homeless. I know what my professor is looking for."

Despite their disappointment with their grades, most students astutely noted the areas they had to improve: grammar, spelling, writing thesis statements, and paragraph development. In recalling the strategies they used in writing their first essays, students mentioned utilizing various types of prewriting and organizational strategies (brainstorming, mapping, and outlining), using various kinds of introductions and conclusions ("I started off broadly. . . ."), writing thesis statements, and trying a variety of words and sentence structures. In examining their areas for improvement, students mentioned many of the same strategies, plus their need to add more details to their body paragraphs and to allow more time for proofreading. Clearly, students were recognizing and monitoring their writing processes and striving to improve them. Some students asked me to give them more time to complete their first drafts and group reviewing of essays, to find out the schedule of the lab tutors, to allow them to select their own topics, and to explain my grading procedures for essays. Three students asked me to meet with them individually to clarify my assignments and expectations. One student's comment, "Are you grading too critically for our level?" made me reflect once again about my expectations concerning the quality of beginning students' writing. Consequently, we had a class discussion on this topic, differentiating between evaluating effort versus evaluating product in a writing class.

Since many of the students evidenced pervasive difficulties with various aspects of grammar, in particular sentence structure, I decided to review some of these elements in class. To make sure that we shared the same grammar vocabulary, I assigned a "Quick Take," **Sample**

Learning Log Prompt #5, to determine what students already understood about certain grammatical terms: *1. Please define as thoroughly as possible the following terms. You may offer an example, in a sentence, instead of a definition. Do not look up any of these terms. I am using this "Quick Take" to determine what I need to teach in these areas.*

1. Subject
2. Verb
3. Object or complement
4. Phrase
5. Independent clause
6. Dependent clause
7. Fragment

8. Run-on sentence
9. Comma splice
10. Simple sentence
11. Compound sentence
12. Compound-complex sentence
13. Ways to vary sentences

Sample Learning Log #5 was designed to assess, in a hierarchical way, students' knowledge of and understanding of certain grammatical terms. Students' responses fell into three categories. The least knowledgeable group of students knew only the meaning of certain grammatical words, like "subject," verb," and "object." The middle group not only knew those words, but also could define or give examples of certain types of clauses and sentence structure errors, like run-on sentences, fragments, and comma splices. The most knowledgeable group knew the meaning of basic grammatical words, types of clauses, and some types of sentences. However, no one in the class knew all types of sentences or the ways to ensure sentence variety. Based on the results of this learning log, I adjusted my plan of instruction. First, I recommended privately to the members of the least knowledgeable group that they visit our learning lab to review rudimentary grammatical knowledge. In class, students reviewed various types of clauses and sentence errors, but the major portion of the instruction dealt with sentence types and other ways to vary sentences in an essay. This learning log exercise helped diagnose students' strengths and areas for improvement, and as a result, I learned to teach primarily to the majority — the middle group.

The final example, **Learning Log Prompt #6**, asked students to evaluate the use of learning logs in their college composition class throughout the term: *Please take some time to review and assess the value of using learning logs this quarter in this composition class. BE HONEST! In particular, consider how this assessment tool has helped you (or not helped you) to understand the literary selections that we have read and the basic composition principles presented in the course. In addition, assess whether or not the learning logs have assisted you in* *monitoring your reading and writing processes, and note whether or not I have adjusted instruction based on your learning log comments. Finally, please comment on the logistics of using learning logs in the class including the length of the entries, the types of entries, the number of the entries, and their value in relation to the course grade. Feel free to include any other issues.*

Responses from Sample Learning Log #6 were mostly positive, although only a few students reported that writing learning logs significantly improved their understanding of the selections in the text.

- "This assessment tool did a decent job making sure I understood what I read . . . by making me report what I read on paper."

- "I admit that they were time consuming, but they were very helpful. They helped me to understand the reading selections because it made me think about them more because I had to write about them. . . . I learned how to look into things more closely and see and understand things that were not told to me."

- "The learning logs haven't really helped me understand the selections better but it has helped my improvement on monitoring my reading and writing process. The best thing about the learning logs are that they let the teacher know what students do and don't know."

Students also reported that they liked writing learning logs because they were something different and gave them an opportunity to communicate with their instructor.

- "Teachers don't usually want to know about how a student might feel about the class."

- "They gave us a chance to express our thoughts on the readings and gave you a chance to see how we felt about certain things and also from the reading the logs, you would know whether or not we did the readings."

- "For one, class was adjusted so that we read fewer selections so that we could concentrate better and to learn the importance of each and also I remember I had asked about extra credit and you didn't exactly give us extra credit, but you let us do two revisions. . . . I felt that when you were asked if we could have a little more time for our first drafts that you gave us that extra time."

Students also made recommendations for future learning log assignments, requesting more feedback so that the learning logs became more "interactive." Other suggestions included more variety in assignments, less emphasis on length of responses, and flexibility in assigning grade values, in particular, allowing learning logs to count more than just 5% of their final grade. By counting the learning logs only 5% as compared to the 85% value I assigned to the formal essays of the class, I had been giving my students a mixed message about what I value. I could identify with Fulwiler (1989) when he confessed to the same imbalance: "While I believed that I valued — and therefore emphasized — the *process* of learning, my assignments suggested that I really valued the *product* of learning — the demonstrations of skills and knowledge in the formal papers and examinations" (p. 151).

Advice to Teachers

Anderson (1992) notes that many of the journal responses he has encountered are primarily summaries of what students read rather than careful analysis, synthesis, or reflection. Some of my students' responses reflected this phenomenon. When asked what was their favorite literary selection, some students said they liked a particular selection and then, as evidence for this preference, summarized it. This problem can be addressed by providing models of reflective responses. Model responses might include a debatable thesis statement, major reasons or points, and evidence from the text supporting the author's main points. In addition, students might be asked if they identified with a particular setting, character, or event. If so, they could compare their experience with those in the text. Both these exercises move students from literal analysis of a text to a deeper, more analytical one.

Anderson also mentions a lack of growth in some students' reading and writing processes over time. Rather than viewing this situation as a problem or a weakness in a student, this type of response can be seen as a red flag encouraging teachers to modify their teaching methods and curriculum to challenge students, so they will try to improve their abilities and performance. Perhaps it is not the students who are evidencing a lack of growth, but rather the assignments that are not challenging the students. I suggest, not only offering a variety of learning log prompts, but also assigning prompts that create a hierarchy of skills — each one increasing in difficulty. For example, prompts about literature might move from the personal response, "Who is your favorite character?" to the more difficult analytical prompts, "Compare two characters in the story," or "Compare a character in this story with a character in another literary work" (Probst, 1984).

A personal fear I had about this project was that the amount of information might be overwhelming. However, foremost was my goal to analyze and monitor all my students' comprehension. An interesting idea might involve studying in depth two or three students' learning log responses over time to describe their understanding of what they have read, their reading and writing processes, and their cognitive monitoring of these processes. With such an in-depth analysis of a few students, instructors could create what Alderman, Klein, Seeley, and Sanders (1993) call "Portraits of Learners" (p. 49).

Another of my original worries about using learning logs was that I wouldn't know how to organize the learning log topics, but this dilemma worked itself out by using three topics paralleling the three goals that I had set for the class. Specifically, students were asked to evaluate the literature they were reading, demonstrate their understanding of writing principles they were learning, and monitor the reading and writing processes they were practicing. Also, some learning log topics result from what students revealed in earlier learning log responses. If students had questions, I learned to answer them immediately and to sympathize with their concerns. If nothing else, I learned how well my students were doing; when students did not understand an assignment, I was able to reteach it. I slowed the pace of the class if necessary and gave more time for certain topics and projects. Assuredly, learning logs help teachers notice problems while they occur, not after. Most importantly, learning logs allow instructors to monitor and to change their instruction. Hence, instructors can use learning logs to determine students' prior knowledge or lack of knowledge of an assignment. Additionally, using learning logs frequently and responding to entries immediately is critical.

Teachers might experiment with a variety of learning log types and topics. For example, instructors can ask students to examine the effectiveness of a particular assignment, or, encourage students to engage in metacognitive activities such as analyzing their writing processes. In particular, students could be requested to describe their proofreading processes. They could be questioned, "Do you read for errors in general and/or read for particular errors? Are there any special proofreading techniques that you can recommend?" A colleague suggests using a learning log prompt early in an academic term in order to learn more about students. She asks her at-risk high school students, "What are you serious about?" (E. Lewis, personal communication, February 5, 1997).

End-of-the-term evaluation prompts might query students, "What was your favorite reading this quarter? Describe why you liked it." Or, "What was your favorite activity this quarter? Describe why you liked it. What was your least favorite activity this quarter? Tell why." Or, "If you were the instructor in this class, what topics, assignments, readings, and activities would you continue to teach, which would you add, and which would you drop?" (Commander & Smith, 1996, p. 448).

Reflecting on Using Learning Logs

Although I used learning logs in a literature-based basic writing class, I believe they have a value in all literacy classrooms and in learning centers for students, teachers, and tutors. Learning logs are valuable for a number of reasons. First, learning logs allow students to discover writing as a "mode of learning" (Emig, 1977, p. 1). Through writing, students can discover what they know about a subject, what they still need to know about a subject, and to share their feelings about it. Learning logs also provide students practice with a variety of writing assignments, not just those related to an academic essay. Through these assignments, students can explore the various functions of language, in particular the "expressive" function and can learn to write for different audiences (Britton, Burgess, Martin, McLeod, & Rosen, 1975). Martin, D'Arcy, Newton, and Parker (1994) write:

> The expressive is basic. Expressive speech is how we communicate with each other most of the time and expressive writing, being the form of writing nearest to speech, is crucial for trying out and coming to terms with new ideas. Because it is the kind of writing in which we most fully reveal ourselves to our reader — in a trusting relationship — it is instrumental in setting up a dialogue between writer and reader from which both can learn. (p. 43)

Learning logs also help students to monitor their reading and writing processes and to reflect on their understanding of the literary selections and the other academic texts they read. Soldner (1998) notes many college students are not even aware of their own literacy processes and consequently have little control over them. "Students lack the necessary metacognitive awareness necessary to monitor, direct, and regulate their learning of text. They are inexperienced with comprehension monitoring and this lack of ability becomes apparent when developmental learners attempt to tackle college textbook material" (1998). Teachers can use responses in learning logs to determine some of the reasons students like or dislike a particular reading, to note if students monitor their reading habits and processes, and consequently, to adjust instruction if students have difficulty with particular selections.

Finally, learning logs can open up a private place for communication between teachers and students and between students and peers. Using learning logs helped me to know my students better and fostered a type of intimacy and deeper level of communication. One student, for example, whom I praised for her absolute honesty early in her learning logs eventually felt comfortable enough to describe in an essay, a more public forum, a major "turning point" in her life — a time when she was arrested for a minor infraction and subsequently experienced personal troubles. In her final learning log, she wrote "The only reason I liked writing Learning Logs in this composition class was because it gave me a chance to be honest with my professor . . . I was glad to see that she adjusted her instruction. . . . The teacher of the class can make all of the difference on whether I enjoy the course or not . . ."

Another student demonstrated growth in his reading and writing strategies. It is revealing to compare his early learning log response, "I find it hard to believe that these essays will help me . . ." with his end-of-the-term response, "This quarter I learned that I do not know as much as I thought I did about writing. I had to learn new strategies for composing essays . . . I feel I have improved greatly as a writer . . . I am ready to go on."

In conclusion, learning logs, in unique and intimate ways, assist teachers to monitor their students' reading and writing processes, assess their students' understandings of texts and strategies, and reveal their students' particular needs and interests. As a result, reflective teachers continue to monitor and adjust their own instructional beliefs, strategies, and materials.

References

Alderman, M. K., Klein, R., Seeley, S. K., & Sanders, M. (1993). Metacognitive self-portraits: Preservice teachers as learners. *Reading Research and Instruction, 32,* 38–54.

Anderson, J. (1992). Journal writing: The promise and the reality. *Journal of Reading, 36,* 304–309.

Barry, L. (1996, March). *One hundred and one ways to use writing in class to improve students: Thinking about your subject matter.* Paper presented at the College Conference on Composition and Communication Annual Conference, Milwaukee, WI.

Britton, J., Burgess, T., Martin, N., McLeod, A., & Rosen, H. (1975). *The development of writing abilities (11–18).* London: Macmillan.

Commander, N. E., & Smith, B. D. (1996). Learning logs: A tool for cognitive monitoring. *Journal of Adolescent and Adult Literacy, 39,* 446–453.

Emig, J. (1977). Writing as a mode of learning. *College Composition and Communication, 28,* 122–128.

Fulwiler, T. (1980). Journals across the disciplines. *English Journal 69*(9), 14–19.

Fulwiler, T. (1989). Responding to student journals. In C. M. Anion (Ed.), *Writing and response: Theory, practice, and research.* Urbana, IL: NCTE.

Gold, M. V., & Deming, M. P. (1994). *Making connections through reading and writing.* Belmont, CA: Wadsworth.

Hillocks, G. (1995). *Teaching writing as reflective practice.* New York: Teachers College Press.

Hynds, S. (1994). *Making connections: Language and learning in the classroom.* Norwood, MA: Christopher-Gordon, Inc.

Martin, N., D'Arcy, P., Newton, B., & Parker, R. (1994). The development of writing abilities. In C. Baseman & D. Russell (Eds.), *Landmark essays on writing across the curriculum* (pp. 33–49). Davis, CA: Hermagoras.

Ogle, D. M. (1986). K-W-L: A teaching model that develops active reading of expository text. *The Reading Teacher, 39,* 564–570.

Probst, R. E. (1984). *Adolescent literature: Response and analysis.* Columbus: Charles E. Merrill.

Rhodes, S. K., & Shanklin, N. L. (1993). *Windows into literacy: Assessing learners K–8.* Portsmouth, NH: Heinemann.

Soldner, L. (1998, May). *Using learning logs to help developmental readers in content area courses.* Paper presented at the 43rd Annual International Reading Association Conference College Literacy and Learning Group, Orlando, FL.

Wills, H. (1993). *Writing is learning. Strategies for math, science, social studies, and language arts.* Bloomington, IN: EDINFO Press.

Wilson, N. (1989). Learning from confusion: Questions and change in reading logs. *English Journal, 78*(7), 62–68.

Young, A. (1996, January). *Writing across the curriculum.* Paper presented at the College Conference on Composition and Communication Winter Workshop, Clearwater, FL.

Program Evaluation Studies: Strategic Learning Delivery Model Suggestions

Michele L. Simpson

Although strategic learning delivery models such as study strategy courses or paired courses are essential in assisting college freshmen with their challenging academic tasks, very few program evaluation studies have been conducted on their efficacy. In order to encourage educators to evaluate their strategic models, Michele L. Simpson, in this award-winning article from the Journal of Developmental Education *(Winter 2002), shares seven suggestions that have been drawn from personal experiences and actual research studies. These suggestions focus on important questions that should be asked, instruments that might be used, possible data analyses methods, and tips for collecting data and writing reports.*

B ecause the academic tasks vary so dramatically from high school to college, many entering freshmen have difficulties during the first year of college (Martin & Arendale, 1994; Nist & Simpson, 2000). According to the extant literature, one reason for these difficulties can be traced to the fact that many college freshmen tend to be passive learners rather than active, strategic learners (Alexander & Jetton, 2000; Hofer, Yu, & Pintrich, 1999). In order to assist college students with these higher-level thinking tasks, many colleges have established academic assistance programs that offer generic learning strategy courses as well as content-embedded models such as paired or linked courses (Warkentin, Stallworth-Clark, & Nolen, 1999). Although these academic assistance programs are not recent innovations, only a few evaluation studies of such have appeared in the literature (Weinstein, Husman, & Dierking, 2000). The lack of quality programmatic research is not surprising given that Boylan, Bliss, and Bonham (1997) have found in a survey that approximately 25% of the four-year institutions complete ongoing and systematic evaluation of their academic assistance programs. Much of the program evaluation research that does exist has often been "cursory" (Maxwell, 1997) and has overlooked important issues. More specifically, three criticisms have been leveled against the studies on strategic learning delivery models.

The first criticism of the studies on strategic learning delivery models is that researchers have typically failed to make explicit the theoretical grounding of their studies (O'Hear & MacDonald, 1995). In particular, there seems to be a mismatch between the theory underpinning a program and the questions and instruments used to evaluate that program. Without a consistent theoretical grounding to a program such as a learning strategy course or a paired course, it becomes extremely difficult to gather valid and useful information. The second criticism is that many studies have not examined students' academic performance using a constellation of dependent variables (Gebelt, Parilis, Kramer, & Wilson, 1996). Rather than posing a variety of questions and employing a battery of instruments that provide a more comprehensive picture of students, many studies seem to focus on one variable and one measure (Boylan, Bonham, White, & George, 2000). The third criticism is that many program evaluation studies have overlooked the critical questions addressing students' transfer and modification of strategies to their own academic tasks (Simpson, Hynd, Nist, & Burrell, 1997). That is, students who complete a learning strategy or paired course should have acquired the declarative, procedural, and conditional strategy knowledge necessary to become active learners across the academic disciplines (Hofer et al., 1999; McKeough, Lupart, & Marini, 1995). Admittedly, transfer is difficult to measure and to ensure, but in-depth studies using qualitative measures should be attempted if we really believe that the transfer of learning is the ultimate aim of teaching (McKeough et al., p. vii).

These criticisms of the literature were particularly important to me because I have been coordinating the Adjunct Study Strategy Seminar, an experimental program that was a modification of the paired course model. In that capacity I have spent a considerable amount of time determining what questions I wanted answered about the program, designing instruments to address those questions, collecting and analyzing data, and writing reports. Rather than share the mounds of data I have collected over a period of eight semesters, I would rather focus on what I have learned from conducting research on the Adjunct Study Strategy Seminar Program. Hence, this article will share seven suggestions, using the experiences and data from my studies to illustrate each point. Such an approach is somewhat unconventional in that a typical journal article describes in depth one program evaluation effort. However, my overall goal is slightly different in that I hope to assist individuals in thinking about their own institutions and how they might evaluate their own strategic learning delivery models (i.e., a learning strategy course or paired course). Before I discuss these seven suggestions, I will share some background information about the Adjunct Study Strategy Seminar (ASSC).

Background Information

In order to address the needs at our university, I modified the paired or linked course in several ways. At our university the adjunct study strategy courses (ASSC) are one-hour elective courses that are paired or linked to high-risk core courses such as biology, chemistry, history, and anthropology. With the permission of the professors teaching these core courses, ASSC is attached to their courses and opened to any interested student. Most of the students who choose to enroll in an ASSC are first- or second-semester freshmen and are representative of the student body. The ASSC meet once a week for the entire semester and are taught by doctoral students who are knowledgeable in the content of the targeted core course. That is, a botany doctoral student might teach the ASSC biology course, or a chemistry doctoral student might teach the ASSC chemistry course. These doctoral students or ASSC leaders volunteer to participate in the ASSC program because they want teaching experience before they graduate. In order to prepare the ASSC leaders for their responsibilities, they take a two-hour course in learning theory and classroom management that I teach one semester prior to their teaching. In addition, I meet on a weekly basis with the ASSC leaders and observe them three times during the semester in order to make sure that the strategies introduced in ASSC are task-appropriate for the content area and that the students are engaged and participating in the activities.

Although the exact subject matter of each ASSC varies across the content areas, all ASSC leaders teach their students how to think about the specific content, how to interpret academic tasks, and how to employ a variety of learning strategies. These strategies focus on how to (a) read textbook assignments; (b) solve problems; (c) take effective class notes from labs, lectures, and discussions; (d) prepare for objective and essay examinations; (e) plan and set goals; and (f) review and rehearse. In addition, all ASSC leaders involve the students in an evaluation and self-reflection activity after each of the exams in the targeted course.

The ASSC program has been in existence for four years. Throughout these four years and eight different semesters I have conducted a variety of qualitative and quantitative studies as a way to improve the instruction and as a way to substantiate its viability to administrators (e.g., vice-presidents) who were in charge of funding. Many of these studies were descriptive or quasi-experimental in nature and had no cohort groups because "traditional experimental designs are less appropriate than other designs for evaluating reading programs" (Boylan et al., 2000, p. 387). A few of these studies were experimental and used more traditional methods of data analysis (e.g., ANOVAS, correlations). However, for all of the studies I conducted I made sure that I posed a variety of research questions and employed a constellation of dependent variables (e.g., students' performance, students' choice of strategies, students' satisfaction with the program). The instruments I used in the studies varied, but always had been piloted for reliability and examined for validity. In the next section I share what I have learned from these endeavors in the form of seven suggestions.

Seven Suggestions for Conducting Program Evaluation Studies

These seven suggestions are relevant to academic assistance professionals involved in delivery models such as learning strategy courses or paired courses. I begin with more theoretical suggestions and end with more pragmatic ones.

Suggestion 1: Seek Instruments That Help Answer the "Why" Questions

Academic assistance professionals should seek out a variety of qualitative and quantitative instruments in order to address the "why" questions about our programs, courses, and interventions. As noted by researchers such as Pressley (2000) and Zimmerman (2000), the why questions are extremely important because they focus on students' cognitive and metacognitive processes, their beliefs, and their strategic behaviors. When we ask why questions it permits us to tease out the reasons for students' growth and changes or the lack thereof. In contrast, the "what" questions tend to examine products or results such as students' grade point average, their performance in a course, or their retention at the university (Casazza & Silverman, 1996; Dembo & Jakubowski, 1999). Admittedly, these types of what questions are important, but if we only know the what we are handicapped in our ttempts to improve our programs and to share the results with others.

An example from one of the studies I conducted during the Spring semester of 1999 will illustrate the instructional usefulness of why questions. In this study of 53 students enrolled in history and in our Adjunct Study Strategy Seminar, we examined a variety of questions, but one of the questions concerned the students' metacognitive processing. Using a technique developed by Pressley and his colleagues (Pressley, Snyder, Levin, Murray, & Ghatala, 1987) to measure metacognitive awareness, we asked the students throughout the semester to predict their test performance in the form of a letter grade. These predictions always occurred after they took the exam and before they received the results of the history exam. At the end of the semester we found that the students' accuracy of prediction accounted for 28% of the variance in their overall performance in the history course [adjusted $R2 = .284$, $F(2, 32) = 7.73, p = .002, d = .487$]. That analysis provided us a specific, albeit partial, explanation as to why some students succeeded in history and some did not. Consequently, I made use of that why information by making sure that all the ASSC leaders spent time after each exam teaching students how to reflect and evaluate on their performance in the targeted course. Had I only collected the students' grades in the targeted history course, a what piece of data, I never would have known why some students did better than others.

There are a variety of why questions that can guide program evaluation studies and the search for appropriate measures to answer those questions. As noted by Weinstein (1994) and others, one of the most common why questions focuses on students' growth or change over a period of time. For example, in one of my earlier studies I posed several questions, one of which examined students' growth and change in terms of their self-regulated learning. To measure this, I asked the ASSC students to complete a Likert-type scale, the Learning Strategy Inventory (LSI), an instrument that had been piloted the semester before and validated by a panel of experts in reading. The LSI was grounded in self-regulation theory and measured five areas considered important to strategic learning: planning, monitoring, text processing, rehearsing, and reviewing (Zimmerman, 2000). The 176 students enrolled in biology, chemistry, and history and in ASSC completed the LSI at the beginning and end of the Fall semester of 2000. The paired samples tests revealed significant differences between the students' pre- and posttest scores, $t(176) = 8.52, p < .001$. In other words, the ASSC students changed and improved in the ways they were reading, studying, and learning.

I decided to follow up on these gain scores in order to identify some more answers as to why. Thus, I conducted a correlational analysis to determine if there was a relationship between the 176 ASSC students' LSI posttest scores and their grades in the targeted classes. The results indicated that all the correlations were significant, but not particularly strong (e.g., chemistry, $r = .227$). The one exception to that pattern occurred in history where the correlation of .317 was moderately strong for those 53 students, suggesting that there was a relationship between students' reported behaviors and strategies and their performance in history. This was an important piece of information for the students and for me.

I used another type of why question to examine potential differences in students' performance across the academic disciplines. According to Alexander and Jetton (2000), educators have tended to overlook the role that an academic discipline can play in learning from text. Because I wanted to determine if there were any differences in students' performance across the core classes that were targeted for ASSC, I made sure throughout the four years of research that I consistently asked these questions using a variety of instruments. One of these instruments, the Getting Acquainted Activity (GAA), measured students' beliefs about learning in a particular academic discipline. As with the LSI, the GAA had been embedded in theory, validated by a panel of experts, and piloted with similar students. In my analysis of the GAA data collected from 176 ASSC students enrolled in biology, chemistry, and history, I discovered that there were significant differences between the students' scores on the GAA pretests and posttests, $t(176) = 19.33, p = .0001$. The post-hoc multiple comparisons indicated that the 53 students in the history ASSC scored significantly higher ($p = .046$) on the posttest GAA than the students in the biology or chemistry ASSC. Hence, it appeared that all the students made gains or growth in their belief systems, but the history students made the most.

Because this finding has held true for three years, I have made sure that we target at least one history course per semester for an ASSC. In sum, it appears that program evaluation studies become more useful when there is a concerted attempt to answer both the what and the why questions in a variety of ways.

Suggestion 2: Use a Combination of Theory-Based Qualitative and Quantitative Measures

Boylan, Bonham, White, and George (2000) and others (e.g., Strauss & Corbin, 1990) have noted that it is important to use a variety of theory-based qualitative and qualitative instruments when conducting research. Too often, however, academic assistance professionals are hesitant to use qualitative measures such as open-ended questionnaires because they have read of the countless limitations of self-report data (e.g., Garner, 1988; Pajares, 1992). What is often forgotten in these attacks is the fact that quantitatively oriented measures are not perfect either because the data they depend on can be narrow in scope. Although the numbers involved in grades, grade point averages, attendance, or retention appear to be clean data, they, too, are fraught with limitations (Merriam, 1998; Strauss & Corbin, 1990). Students' grade point averages are a case in point. That is, there are so many reasons for the grade point averages students earn (e.g., course load, classes selected) that a mere number cannot reveal all the nuances involved in their growth and learning.

The ASSC leaders and I found this to be true when we examined the ASSC students' course grades during the 1st year of our program. At least 22 of 80 ASSC students in biology, who earned a final course grade of C in the targeted course, received an F on their first two or three exams. However, these students ended the semester with a strong B on their last exam and/or final. Obviously, these students were not able to earn a B in the targeted course given most biology professors' grading systems, but they did improve significantly and did learn how to be more strategic learners. Had these data not been collected and examined, these important trends detailing students' improvement would have been camouflaged by the quantitative data collected at the end of the semester.

An added advantage to using a combination of qualitative and quantitative instruments is that the data from one can often be used to triangulate and provide additional substantiation for the data gleaned from the other. When researchers employ multiple sources of data they also enhance the internal validity and reliability of their findings (Merriam, 1998). For example, I have been able to use the ASSC students' answers to several open-ended probes as a way of triangulating the quantitative data that we collect on their final course grades in the targeted class.

More specifically, when I wrote my summary for the Fall semester of 2001, I reported that 89% of the 80 ASSC students in biology received a grade of B or above. I also pointed out that 90% of them (72 students) reported on an open-ended questionnaire that they believed that ASSC influenced their performance in biology. Even more important than these statistics are the students' explanations as to why ASSC influenced their performance, facts hidden by mere tallies of grades. After doing a qualitative content analysis of the students' responses, I discovered that the 80 biology students reported that ASSC influenced their course performance because they learned a variety of test preparation methods (e.g., self-questioning and mapping) and because they learned how to plan and distribute their reading and studying.

Obviously, there are a variety of ways to address program evaluation questions. Two of the most promising and creative ways rely on open-ended probes and scenarios. Because these two mechanisms can strengthen any research endeavor, it is important to review how they might be developed, analyzed, or used.

Open-ended questions and probes. Open-ended questions or probes are excellent ways to answer a variety of program evaluation questions. More importantly, they can be used to determine students' viewpoints and suggestions on strategy courses or paired courses, an important aspect in any program evaluation endeavor (Mealey, 1991). For example, in order to access students' viewpoints on our program (i.e., ASSC), at the end of each semester I ask them to respond to this probe: Would you recommend ASSC to a friend? Why or why not? Over a period of four years, 83% of the 1,283 ASSC students from 1998 to 2002 have reported "yes" to that question. More important than the percentages have been the students' answers to the "why or why not" probe. Thus far, the most common explanation offered by the students has focused on the usefulness of the planning strategies they learned in ASSC.

Also, open-ended probes have been used to determine whether students have transferred and modified the targeted strategies to their other academic tasks, an extremely important question that should be asked of any strategic learning delivery model (Hofer et al., 1999). For example, Randall (2002) used a combination of open-ended probes and questions to determine whether or not her former students were transferring the strategies they had learned in her course to the courses that they were taking one semester later. Randall's instruments had been piloted with similar students and had been reviewed by a panel of reading experts so that she knew she had clear, unambiguous, valid, and reliable probes and questions. In her descriptive study of 64 former students, Randall determined for one of her research questions that 47% of the students had chosen to annotate their textbooks and that 80% of them did so in the margins of their textbook. For the other students who did not choose to annotate or who did not use the margins of their text for their annotations, Randall also learned their reasons or explanations as to why and their modifications of the strategy (e.g., yellow sticky notes). Probes and questions, creatively written, elicited that type of useful information.

Having touted the usefulness of open-ended questions and probes, it is equally important to point out that these instruments require a more time intensive method of scoring. These methods include the use of rubrics and a qualitative content analysis (Altheide, 1987). I have used the former to score students answers on a variety of open-ended probes. The rubric (see Table 1) was codeveloped by a doctoral student in history (i.e., the ASSC leader) and myself. I have found the rubric to be an efficient and reliable way of scoring students' answers to open-ended probes. Qualitative content analysis, on the other hand, requires a search for overall patterns or trends. For example, when I read the students' answers to the probe asking them to explain whether or not they were using the strategies from ASSC in their other classes — one question I pose to determine strategy transfer — I have been able to group the answers from the students who answered "yes" in three distinct ways. Those groups include the following: (a) I am using self-testing, (b) I am breaking up my reading, and (c) I am annotating my textbook.

Scenarios or case studies. Scenarios or case studies are context-specific problems for which students provide a written solution or answer (Nist & Holschuh, 2000). Scenarios can be broad-based, covering an entire semester of instruction, or they can be specific and relevant to a problem, such as procrastination or the lack of concentration. I like the broad-based scenario because it allows me to evaluate whether or not the ASSC students have grasped the idea that there is no generic method of study, a basic tenet of strategic learning theory. That is, the ASSC leaders teach their students that strategic learners have a reper-

Table 1. Sample Scoring Rubric for Open-Ended Probes

Question 1. What do you believe is important to understand and learn in history?

3 (BEST) *At least two of these:* trends and changes over time, causes/effects, the significance of events or certain individuals, themes and patterns

2 *One of the above answers and one of these or something similar:* the hows and whys, key events, key people, legislation, relevance of past to the future

1 *The emphasis is on:* names, dates, events, legislation, battles, people

Question 2. What do you do when you read your history assignments?

3 (BEST) *At least two of these:* make notes in margin of text, pause and think about key points, note key events or people, look for cause/effect and significance, predict possible questions, make connections between ideas, read headings first, compare ideas to lecture.

2 *One of the above answers and one of these or something similar:* underline or highlight, outline, focus on important facts and boldface words

1 *The emphasis is on:* reading to remember, reading slowly, highlighting, focusing on dates, battles, people, trying to memorize

toire of strategies and processes and that their use of them depends on the task required in a specific course, their background knowledge, and an informed decision on how they learn best. See the Appendix, on page 405, for an illustrative scenario describing a cultural geography course taught at our university.

The scenario explains the academic tasks required by the geography professor and describes a typical student, Jennifer, as she works through the tasks. At the beginning and end of the semester we ask the ASSC geography students to read the scenario and then write their solutions for the character Jennifer, as if they were talking to her. Students are told at the end of the semester that they are expected to write more and to be far more task-specific with their suggestions. For example, it is not atypical for students at the beginning of the semester to answer question two by suggesting "Jennifer should read her book." However, after a semester of instruction, the ASSC leaders and I expect the ASSC students enrolled in geography to recommend to Jennifer that she should break up the reading into smaller parts, to use the geography professors' Web site as a preview for the reading, and to annotate their texts with a focus on theories, visual aids, and the relationships between ideas.

The advantages of using a scenario are quite compelling. First, because scenarios do not provide students prompts for their answers, they have the potential of fully tapping students' beliefs and their strategy knowledge at a conditional and procedural level (Nist & Holschuh, 2000). Second, students' answers to scenarios tend to be more detailed than their answers to open-ended probes, especially after they realize the expectations inherent in their answers. Third, the ASSC leaders and I have found that students tend to complete the scenario in a more diligent fashion. Unlike checklists or Likert-type scales where students often circle down the middle just to complete the task (Pajares, 1992), scenarios tend to engage students in more active thinking and writing. Finally, students' answers to a pretest scenario can help academic assistance instructors understand the beliefs and approaches of undergraduates. I know our ASSC leaders look forward to reading what their students have written and routinely incorporate that information into their lesson plans. Because of these four reasons, I replaced the LSI, my Likert-type scaled instrument, with the scenario and have used these content-specific scenarios for three years with considerable success.

One limitation to the use of scenarios is that they require sophisticated methods of analysis. In addition to using rubrics or a content analysis to score a scenario, another possibility has been explored by Holschuh (1998). She set up her scenarios with problems or situations, but added another paragraph in which an imaginary student (e.g., Jennifer in geography) solves the stated problem, usually with some positive decisions and some negative decisions. Hence, the students reading the scenario do not write out their own answers, but reply to the imaginary student's solutions using a 5-point Likert-type scale (i.e., Strongly Agree to Strongly Disagree). For example, in Holschuh's scenario about a character named Chris in biology, students read the scenario about Chris and respond to these statements:

11. Chris' plan of taking good notes and trying to memorize facts should be all it takes to get a good grade in Biology 103.

12. If Chris tried to understand every theory it would take him too much time to read a chapter. (Holschuh, 1998, p. 154)

Hence, using the Likert-type scale with the scenario reduces the scoring burden and produces numbers rather than the patterns that emerge from a content analysis. Regardless of the scoring procedures chosen, the most important thing to remember is to use a variety of qualitative and quantitative theory-based instruments.

Suggestion 3: Assess the Perceptions of the Major Stakeholders

Although students are the major stakeholders in their educational experiences, they rarely are asked for their perceptions about a new program or innovation. As Maxwell (1997) and Mealey (1991) have pointed out, students have unique insights into the academic challenges they encounter which academic assistance professionals often cannot fully understand. Students can also tell us which component or part of a particular program or course has had the most impact on them and which components need improving.

Using an open-ended questionnaire that asked students about their ASSC experiences, for example, I learned from them that they resented the time spent at the beginning and end of the semester completing program evaluation instruments. Consequently, I modified and shortened the instruments and omitted one of them so that the time spent in class completing instruments was drastically reduced. On the positive side, a resounding majority of the ASSC students told me that they loved the ASSC class because it was small and informal, allowing them time and a context that encouraged them to communicate with each other and with their ASSC leader. Had I not collected this information, I would not have been able to convince administrators that these ASSC courses needed to be small (i.e., less than 25) in order to build that sense of community so often missing from the typical lecture class of 300. In short, it is always advantageous to listen to the voices of our students.

Suggestion 4: Conduct Program Evaluation Studies
Over a Sustained Period of Time

As noted by the American Association for Higher Education (1992) and numerous experts (e.g., Boylan et al., 2000; Elifson, Pounds, & Stone, 1995), academic assistance professionals should carefully plan their program evaluation studies to insure that they collect data over a sustained period of time. When studies are replicated or longitudinal in nature, we gain the advantages of strengthening the internal reliability of our findings, increasing confidence that we draw reasonable conclusions and avoid erroneous decisions (Merriam, 1998). An example from my own experiences will aptly illustrate the importance of collecting data over a period of time.

After the first year of data collection it seemed to me that the biology ASSC students were not performing well in the targeted course (i.e., biology), nor were they employing the strategies that we taught them. At the end of the first year I could have decided to seek other core courses for the ASSC instruction, but I decided, instead, to try one more year of targeting this introductory biology course that troubled so many freshmen and sophomores. Luckily, my hunches paid off because the second, third, and fourth years of ASSC for biology have reversed the trends from the initial year and have become an extremely positive experience for everyone involved: the students, the ASSC leaders, and the biology professor. Interestingly, this past year the biology ASSC students outperformed the other ASSC students in that not one of the

43 students received a course grade lower than a B in biology. In retrospect, the findings from the first year were probably an aberration caused by the newness of the program and by my tentativeness in helping the biology ASSC leaders identify appropriate strategies and classroom management techniques.

Collecting data about a program over a period of time is important. But equally important is following, over a period of time, the students who participate in a strategic learning delivery model (Boylan et al., 2000). Given the difficulty of locating students and encouraging them to participate in a program evaluation study several semesters after they have taken a learning strategy or paired course, it makes sense that academic assistance professionals resort to short-term data collection. However, it is possible to collect the follow-up data from students, especially if incentives are provided. For example, Randall (2002) has reported providing several incentives to her former students for their participation in her study. For one of these incentives the researcher has described offering a drawing for a considerable amount of money in order to insure her students' active participation. Thus, I would urge academic assistance professionals to collect data over time and to be creative in finding ways to enlist students' participation in these important studies.

Suggestion 5: Systematically Collect Information
Throughout the Semester

At first glance, this fifth suggestion may appear to be a repeat of the fourth suggestion. However, the essence of this suggestion is different in that I am stressing the importance and usefulness of collecting formative data from the students that can be used to modify and enhance instruction. Experts would certainly concur with this suggestion (e.g., Boylan et al., 2000; Payne, 1994). Data such as students' test scores in the targeted course or their evaluations about the strategies they used when studying for the tests can help academic assistance instructors understand why students are performing as they are. Moreover, this information, if organized creatively, can assist students in improving how they go about reading, studying, and learning. For example, our ASSC leaders prepare a report and class presentation for the students after each exam that describes the strategies and plans of the students receiving an A or B and the strategies and plans of the students receiving a D or F.

I remember one dramatic classroom session that occurred in the chemistry ASSC in which students learned that A and B students were studying less but using more strategies than the other students. When they entered the classroom, these chemistry students were prepared to hear that they "just had not studied long enough." Once they left class they realized that they had to alter the number and type of strategies they were using and that they needed to be studying throughout the unit, not countless hours the night before the exam. Had the ASSC leaders not collected, analyzed, and reported these data, many students would have continued to use their high school techniques.

These data can also become, in a serendipitous fashion, useful information for final reports that must be handed in to administrators (e.g., Directors, Deans). I regularly include in my final reports the number of ASSC students who have made two or three jumps in their exam grades. For example, many ASSC students in biology and history score a D on the first exam, but jump to a B or A on the next and subsequent exams. I also report these trends for the papers and projects that ASSC students have to complete for targeted core courses such as political science and anthropology. Over the four-year period I have found that ASSC students' grades on papers and projects have been consistently higher than the class averages. Thus, whether data are used in writing a report or in designing a lesson to nudge students' beliefs and behaviors, it is important to remember to collect that information.

Suggestion 6: Train the Individuals Administering the Program Evaluation Instruments and Prepare the Students

If academic assistance professionals want the highest quality data, it is imperative that they take the time to train the individuals who will be administering the instruments and the individuals who will be completing the instruments (i.e., the students). I learned this the hard way. During the first semester of the ASSC program I gave the ASSC leaders the instruments I wanted them to administer to their students. Although I discussed the necessity of collecting data about the program, I neglected to be specific and practical in my remarks. After my observations of several classes and discussion with the leaders, I discovered that they had waited until the last five minutes of the class period to distribute the instruments to the students. Moreover, they had not discussed the importance of these evaluation instruments, nor had they conducted any type of review with the students during the class period. Naturally, the students hurried through them so they could leave class early. As I read what the ASSC students had written, I realized that we had collected information that was not particularly useful. Consequently, since that time I have methodically trained the ASSC leaders on how to administer each of the instruments and how to motivate students to complete them in a detailed and honest manner.

Suggestion 7: Highlight the Findings and Trends in Creative Ways

As Payne (1994) and others have noted, academic assistance professionals conduct program evaluation studies for a variety of reasons. Most importantly, we do so in order to improve our programs or interventions.

However, many of us conduct these studies because we also need to justify our programs to university administrators. Although both reasons stimulated my program evaluation efforts, the latter reason was particularly strong for me because I had to demonstrate success if the funding for the ASSC program were to be continued. But I also knew that I had to summarize and represent my findings in a final report that would capture the interest of a busy administrator not inclined to read lengthy prose documents.

To solve this dilemma, I scrutinized the world of business and, in particular, advertising. I examined how experts in advertising represented data and how they captured the attention of the public. After this examination I decided to implement four guidelines as I wrote my report. First, keep the findings brief and bulleted. Second, avoid the use of jargon (e.g., self-regulated learning) and technical procedures (e.g., regression analysis) because many administrators are not conversant with this language. Third, use graphics such as bar graphs or pie charts whenever possible. And finally, orchestrate situations where the customers (i.e., the students) provide testimonials about the advantages of the product (i.e., the ASSC program).

To accomplish the final guideline, I asked the ASSC leaders to identify several students in their classes who would be willing to be videotaped. I wanted males and females who had succeeded in the targeted course (i.e., an A or B) or who finally "got it" and pulled out a satisfactory grade (i.e., C). I ended up with an impressive cross-section of students and a compelling videotape and CD that I sent to the administrators responsible for funding our program. I would also add that I found it best to have a professional do the videotaping in a campus studio in order to avoid the "talking heads" syndrome that occurs when amateurs, like myself, attempt to become a producer and director. In sum, think about the audience for your data and make sure that there is some creativity in how you communicate with that audience.

In the process of writing this manuscript I have considered the possibility of an eighth suggestion: Academic assistance professionals should share the results of their program evaluation studies at conferences and in journals. However, after considerable thought I have decided that this eighth suggestion is really more of a plea. Published program evaluation studies on strategic learning delivery models are virtually nonexistent except for the work of individuals such as Weinstein and her colleagues (e.g., Weinstein, Dierking, Husman, Roska, & Powderill, 1998). Hopefully, these seven suggestions that have focused on important questions that should be asked, instruments that might be used, possible data analyses methods, and practical suggestions for writing reports will stimulate academic assistance professionals to conduct more studies of their own strategic learning models.

Appendix: Example of a Scenario

Directions: Below you will find a scenario or situation that describes your geography course. Read the situation carefully, thinking about how you would read and study for this course. After reading the situation, answer the five questions that follow. I will use the information from your responses to plan the activities for this course.

Jennifer is enrolled in her first geography course. Although she was a good geography student in high school who could memorize vast amounts of information, Jennifer is experiencing some difficulties with this course. On the first exam she received a low C even though she read and studied the chapters five hours the night before the exam. Jennifer's geography professor gives two exams that are a combination of multiple choice, short answer, and essay questions. Her geography professor writes exams that require students to understand key terms, sense relationships between concepts, apply concepts to real life situations, and interpret maps and graphs. The professor's lectures are similar to the textbook, but Jennifer often has difficulties in keeping up with the professor's lectures because of the fast pace of the class and the many overheads. However, the professor makes her overheads available on the Web. In addition to weekly lectures and assigned reading, Jennifer is required to take a map quiz and complete four lab assignments outside of class.

1. Overall, what problems do you see with Jennifer's approaches to the geography course?

2. What advice would you give her about her textbook reading?

3. What advice would you give her about taking lecture notes?

4. What advice would you give her about planning and time management?

5. What advice would you give her about studying for the geography tests?

References

Alexander, P. A., & Jetton, T. L. (2000). Learning from text: A multidimensional and developmental perspective. In M. Kamil, P. Mosenthal, P. D. Pearson, & R. Barr (Eds.), *Handbook of reading research* (Vol. III, pp. 285–310). Mahwah, NJ: Lawrence Erlbaum.

Altheide, D. L. (1987). Ethnographic content analysis. *Qualitative Sociology, 10,* 65–77.

American Association for Higher Education. (1992). *Principles of good practice for assessing student learning.* Washington, DC: Author.

Boylan, H. R., Bliss, L. B., & Bonham, B. S. (1997). Program components and their relationship to student performance. *Journal of Developmental Education, 20*(3), 2–8.

Boylan, H. R., Bonham, B. S., White, J. R., & George, A. P. (2000). Evaluation of college reading and study strategy programs. In R. Flippo & D. Caverly (Eds.), *Handbook of college reading and study strategy research* (pp. 365–401). Mahwah, NJ: Lawrence Erlbaum.

Casazza, M. E., & Silverman, S. L. (1996). *Learning assistance and developmental education*. San Francisco: Jossey-Bass.

Dembo, M. H., & Jakubowski, T. G. (1999, April). *An evaluation of a learning to learn course*. Paper presented at the annual meeting of the American Educational Research Association, Montreal, Canada.

Elifson, J. M., Pounds, M. L., & Stone, K. R. (1995). Planning for an assessment of developmental programs. *Journal of Developmental Education, 19*(1), 2–11.

Garner, R. (1988). *Metacognitive reading comprehension*. Mahwah, NJ: Lawrence Erlbaum.

Gebelt, J. L., Parilis, G. M., Kramer, D. A., & Wilson, P. (1996). Retention at a large university: Combining skills with course content. *Journal of Developmental Education, 20*(1), 2–10.

Hofer, B. K., Yu, S., & Pintrich, P. R. (1999). Teach college students to be self-regulated learners. In B. Zimmerman & D. H. Schunk (Eds.), *Self-regulated learners and academic achievement: Theory, research, and practice* (pp. 57–85). New York: Springer-Verlag.

Holschuh, J. L. (1998). *The relationship between epistemological beliefs and strategy use in introductory biology*. Unpublished doctoral dissertation, University of Georgia, Athens, GA.

Martin, D. C., & Arendale, D. (1994, January). *Review of research concerning effectiveness of SI from the University of Missouri–Kansas City and other institutions across the United States*. Paper presented at the annual conference of The Freshman Year Experience, Columbia, MO.

Maxwell, M. (1997). *Improving student learning*. Clearwater, FL: H & H Publishing.

McKeough, A., Lupart, J., & Marini, A. (1995). Preface. In A. McKeough, J. Lupart, & A. Marini (Eds.), *Teaching for transfer: Fostering generalization in learning* (pp. vii–viii). Mahwah, NJ: Lawrence Erlbaum.

Mealey, D. L. (1991). Program evaluation: The politics of developmental reading. In T. Rasinsky, N. Padak, & J. Logan (Eds.), *Reading is knowledge* (pp. 1–16). Pittsburgh, KS: College Reading Association.

Merriam, S. B. (1998). *Qualitative research and case study applications in education*. San Francisco: Jossey-Bass.

Nist, S. L., & Holschuh, J. P. (2000). *Active learning: Strategies for college success*. Boston: Allyn & Bacon.

Nist, S. L., & Simpson, M. L. (2000). College studying. In M. Kamil, P. Mosenthal, P. D. Pearson, & R. Barr (Eds.), *Handbook of reading research* (Vol. III, pp. 645–666). Mahwah, NJ: Lawrence Erlbaum.

O'Hear, M. F., & MacDonald, R. B. (1995). A critical review of research in developmental education: Part I. *Journal of Developmental Education, 19*(1), 2–6.

Pajares, M. F. (1992). Teachers' beliefs and educational research: Cleaning up a messy construct. *Review of Educational Research, 62*, 307–332.

Payne, D. A. (1994). *Designing educational project and program evaluations*. Boston: Kluwer Academic.

Pressley, M. (2000). What should comprehension be the instruction of? In M. Kamil, P. Mosenthal, P. D. Pearson, & R. Barr (Eds.), *Handbook of reading research* (Vol. III, pp. 545–561). Mahwah, NJ: Lawrence Erlbaum.

Pressley, M., Snyder, B., Levin, J., Murray, H., & Ghatala, E. (1987). Perceived readiness for examination performance (PREP) produced by initial reading of text and text containing adjunct questions. *Reading Research Quarterly, 22*, 219–236.

Randall, S. N. (2002). *Evaluation of an elective academic assistance course.* Unpublished doctoral dissertation, University of Georgia, Athens, GA.

Simpson, M. L., Hynd, C. R., Nist, S. L., & Burrell, K. (1997). College academic assistance programs and practices. *Educational Psychology Review, 9*, 39–87.

Strauss, A., & Corbin, J. (1990). *Basics of qualitative research: Grounded theory, procedures, and techniques.* Newbury Park, CA: Sage Publications.

Warkentin, R., Stallworth-Clark, R., & Nolen, M. (1999, April). *Course features that influence self-directed study practices in a college history course: Linking strategy instruction to authentic content and context.* Paper presented at the annual meeting of the American Educational Research Association, Montreal, Canada.

Weinstein, C. E. (1994). Students at risk for academic failure: Learning to learn classes. In K. W. Prichard & R. M. Sawyer (Eds.), *Handbook of college teaching: Theory and applications* (pp. 375–385). Westport, CT: Greenwood Press.

Weinstein, C. E., Dierking, D., Husman, J., Roska, L., & Powderill, L. (1998). The impact of a course in strategic learning on the long-term retention of college students. In J. Higbee & P. Dwinell (Eds.), *Developmental education: Preparing successful college students* (pp. 85–96). Columbia, SC: National Research Center for The First Year Experience and Students in Transition.

Weinstein, C. E., Husman, J., & Dierking, D. R. (2000). Self-regulation interventions with a focus on learning strategies. In M. Boekaerts, P. R. Pintrich, & M. Zeidner (Eds.), *Handbook of self-regulation* (pp. 727–747). New York: Academic Press.

Zimmerman, B. J. (2000). Attaining self-regulation: A social-cognitive perspective. In M. Boekaerts, P. R. Pintrich, & M. Zeidner (Eds.), *Handbook of self-regulation* (pp. 13–39). New York: Academic Press.

Additional Readings

Angelo, T. A. (1998). *Classroom assessment and research: An update on uses, approaches, and research findings.* San Francisco: Jossey-Bass.

Boylan, H. R., & Bonham, B. (2009). Program evaluation. In R. Flippo & D. C. Caverly (Eds.), *Handbook of College Reading Study Strategy Research* (pp. 379–407). New York: Routledge.

Butler, D. L. (2002). Qualitative approaches to investigating self-regulated learning: Contributions and challenges. *Educational Psychologist, 17*(1), 59–63.

Ercikan, K. (2006). Developments in assessment of student learning. In P. A. Alexander & P. H. Winne (Eds.), *Handbook of Educational Psychology* (pp. 929–952). Mahwah, NJ: Lawrence Erlbaum.

Griffee, D. (2005). Research Tips: Classroom data collection, Part II. *Journal of Developmental Education, 29*(2), 36.

Pintrich, P. R. (2004). A conceptual framework for assessing motivation and self-regulated learning in college students. *Educational Psychology Review, 16*(4), 385–407.

Stiggins, R. (2005). *Student-involved assessment for learning.* Upper Saddle River, NJ: Pearson.

Professional Resources

Whether you are a new member to the field or an individual with years of service, it is through our professional journals and organizations that one is able to find both opportunities for professional development and supportive camaraderie associated with day-to-day practice and quality scholarship. What follows (in alphabetical order) is a description of a number of the professional journals and organizations that support the work of individuals interested in learning and study strategy activities.

Journals

The *Journal of College Literacy and Learning (JCLL)* publishes material related to advancing the scholarship on reading, writing, and academic success at the postsecondary level. It is intended to provide a forum for the exchange of information regarding research, theory, and best practice. The College Literacy and Learning Special Interest Group of the International Reading Association (see p. 410) publishes *JCLL*. This journal is available online.

The *Journal of College Reading and Learning (JCRL)* is a national, peer-reviewed forum for the theory, research, and policy related to reading improvement and learning assistance at the two- and four-year college levels. It publishes reports of original research and articles linking theory, research, or policy to practice. *JCRL* is published in the fall and spring of each year. It is the official journal of the College Reading and Learning Association (see p. 410).

The *Journal of Developmental Education (JDE)* is published as a forum for educators concerned with the practice, theory, research, and news of the postsecondary developmental and remedial community. Its content focuses on basic skills education and includes topics such as developmental writing, developmental mathematics, reading, tutoring, assessment and placement, and program evaluation. Emphasis is placed on manuscripts that relate education theory to practical teaching and learning, expand current knowledge, or clearly demonstrate impact on the field. The *JDE* is published three times each academic year, in the fall, winter, and spring, by the National Center for Developmental Education (see p. 411). *JDE* is the official publication of the National Association for Developmental Education (see p. 411).

The *Learning Assistance Review (LAR)* seeks to foster communication among learning center professionals. Its audience includes learning center administrators, teaching staff, and tutors, as well as other faculty members and administrators who are interested in improving the learning skills of postsecondary students. The *LAR* aims to publish scholarly articles and reviews that address issues of interest to a broad range of academic professionals with primary consideration on program design and evaluation, classroom-based research, the application of theory and research to practice, innovative teaching strategies, student assessment, and other topics that bridge gaps within our diverse profession. *LAR* is published twice a year, in the spring and fall. *LAR* is an official publication of the National College Learning Center Association (see p. 411).

The ***NADE Digest*** is an official publication of the National Association for Developmental Education (see p. 411). The *Digest* publishes articles that emphasize innovative approaches, best practices, effects of meaningful research on teaching and learning, and techniques to enhance student performance. It is a valued source of information for developmental education professionals including developmental educators, learning assistance personnel, academic counselors, and tutors who are interested in the discussion of practical issues in postsecondary developmental education.

Research and Teaching in Developmental Education **(RTDE)** focuses on a variety of topics related to developmental education across the disciplines. Of particular interest are articles that address measurement and evaluation procedures; program design and implementation; research and pedagogy as they inform, or are informed by, current theory; and interdisciplinary approaches to major concerns in developmental education. The journal has a biannual publication schedule. *RTDE* is the journal of the New York State College Learning Skills Association.

Research in Developmental Education **(RiDE)** is a research-based, single-article publication designed to review and analyze current developmental education practices or to report on up-to-date research literature and studies. *RiDE* provides invaluable research and resource information for students, instructors, researchers, and administrators. It is published by the National Center for Developmental Education (see p. 411) at Appalachian State University.

Organizations

The **Association for Tutoring Profession's (ATP)** mission is to foster the advancement of tutoring to enhance student academic success. Its goals are to provide a network through which current trends in practice can be identified and innovations disseminated, to enhance the status of professionals, paraprofessionals, and students working in the field, to stimulate research in the field by offering a forum at which information can be shared, and to work collaboratively with other national, regional, and state organizations and persons having purposes supportive of, or in harmony with, the concerns of the ATP. Visit their Web site for more information at myatp.org.

The **College Literacy and Learning Special Interest Group (CLL/SIG)** exchanges information relating to reading and study skills, proposes adoption of teacher qualifications, acts as a resource center, and sponsors national conferences. It also publishes the online *Journal of College Literacy and Learning* (see p. 409). Membership is open to all members of the International Reading Association. For more information, go to reading.org and click on the Professional Communities tab.

The **College Reading and Learning Association (CRLA)** offers college reading and learning professionals with an open forum to discover and exchange the leading tools and techniques to enhance student academic success. It provides professional development for college professionals active in reading, learning assistance, writing, ESOL, learning strategies, mathematics, college success programs, mentoring, and tutoring programs. CRLA publishes the *Journal of College Reading and Learning* (see p. 409). For more information, visit their Web site at crla.net.

The **Council of Learning Assistance and Developmental Education Associations (CLADEA)** provides leadership and a unified voice to advance the profession of postsecondary learning assistance and developmental education. Through its member council it fosters mutual support among national and international organizations dedicated to postsecondary learning assistance or developmental education. Member organizations include the College Reading and Learning Association, the Association for the Tutoring Profession, the National Association for Developmental Education, the National College Learning Center Association, and the National Center for Developmental Education. See www.cladea.net online for more information.

The **National Association of Developmental Education (NADE)** seeks to improve the theory and practice of developmental education at all levels of the educational spectrum, the professional capabilities of developmental educators, and the design of programs to prepare developmental educators. In addition, NADE focuses on the academic success of students by providing professional development, supporting student learning, disseminating exemplary models of practice, and coordinating efforts with other organizations involved in facilitating communication among developmental education professionals. The organization publishes the *NADE Digest* (see p. 410), provides program certification, hosts an annual conference, and sponsors regional/state chapters and special interest groups, including one for Learning and Study Skills. Go to nade.net online to learn more.

The **National Center for Developmental Education (NCDE)**, housed at Appalachian State University, provides instruction, training programs, research, and other services consistent with the purpose of developmental education. These services are provided to a national audience of professionals dedicated to serving underprepared and disadvantaged college students. The NCDE sponsors the summer Kellogg Institute for the Training and Certification of Developmental Educators and publishes both the *Journal of Developmental Education* (see p. 409) and *Research in Developmental Education* (see p. 410). For more information, go to www .ncde.appstate.edu.

The **National College Learning Center Association's (NCLCA)** mission is to support learning center professionals as they develop and to maintain learning centers, programs, and services to enhance student learning at the postsecondary level. The organization delivers both an annual conference and the NCLCA Institute. It also sponsors the Learning Center Leadership Certification and publishes *The Learning Assistance Review* (see p. 409). For more information, go to nclca.org.

The **Studying and Self-Regulated Learning (SSRL) Special Interest Group (SIG)**, which is part of the American Education Research Association (AERA), is dedicated to promoting the development of theory and research in academic studying and self-regulated learning across the life span. The SIG brings together researchers and practitioners to share expertise in all aspects of self-regulated learning, including motivation, metacognition, learning and studying strategies, and the ways in which learners manage their emotions and environments.

About the Contributors

Kathryn Bartle Angus is an instructor at California State University, Fullerton. She teaches in both the graduate and undergraduate programs of reading education and serves as coordinator for the undergraduate program and graduate cohorts and off-campus programs. Her undergraduate teaching interests include critical thinking, active learning strategies, and academic reading and writing. She has presented on these topics frequently at the College Reading and Learning Association and the California Reading Association conferences. Her publications in these areas can be found in the *Journal of Adolescent and Adult Literacy* and the *Journal of the College Reading and Learning Association*.

David R. Arendale is an associate professor in the Postsecondary Teaching and Learning Department at the University of Minnesota, Twin Cities. He teaches an undergraduate world history course and a graduate education course about best practices for student engagement, enrichment, and academic support within college courses. His research investigates the history of postsecondary college access, developmental education, and academic interventions supporting improved student achievement and persistence.

Monica C. Bernardo has worked extensively on issues of social justice and in serving the most vulnerable in society. As an undergraduate and postgraduate, Bernardo researched the psychosocial strategies of students in the borderlands, in addition to co-teaching several courses mapping the intersection of multidisciplinary inquiry and multicultural experiences. While working on her master's degree at Columbia University's School of International and Public Affairs, Bernardo published research in the *Journal of International Affairs* on the victim/perpetrator identity and its implications for peace and reconciliation in the Basque Region of Spain. Bernardo currently serves as executive director for a community-based nonprofit providing shelter and services to homeless pregnant women and women with children.

Carol Boston is assistant director of the ERIC (Educational Resources Information Center) Clearinghouse on Assessment and Evaluation, housed in the Department of Measurement, Statistics, and Evaluation at the University of Maryland.

Hunter R. Boylan is director of the National Center for Developmental Education and a professor at Appalachian State University. He is one of the founders of the National Association for Developmental Education (NADE) and of the Council of Learning Assistance and Developmental Education Associations (CLADEA). He served as president of NADE from 1981 to1983. His recent publications include *What Works: Research-Based Practices in Developmental Education* (2002).

Melinda S. Burchard teaches math education and exceptional education courses at James Madison University. Her research focuses on professional development for K–12 Response to Intervention practices and learning strategies for postsecondary learners.

David C. Caverly has been involved in developmental education for over 35 years, teaching reading and/or directing learning centers in a community college, two different four-year colleges, and six universities. He has published extensively in the field; his writings include over 80 journal articles, 13 books, 14 grants, and 200 conference presentations. He is perhaps best known for his column TechTalk in the *Journal of Developmental Education*, the second edition of a book published in 2009 titled *Handbook of College Reading and Study Strategy Research*, and the TIDE (Technology Institute for Developmental Educators) conference that he co-directs, which is in its thirteenth year. Since 1989, he has been a professor of education at Texas State University-San Marcos, where he directs the developmental reading program and teaches reading and technology classes in a master's and a proposed doctoral program in developmental education.

Nannette Evans Commander is a professor of educational psychology at Georgia State University. Her areas of expertise are in metacognition, learning, retention, higher education, and student success.

Myron H. Dembo is professor emeritus of educational psychology at the University of Southern California. He is a fellow in the American Psychological Association and the American Educational Research Association. He specializes in the areas of learning and motivation with a focus on teaching students how to become more self-regulated learners.

Mary P. Deming is an associate professor of language and literacy at Georgia State University. She coauthored, with Marie Valeri-Gold, *Making Connections through Reading and Writing* (1994) and has had her work published in the *Journal of Basic Writing*, the *Journal of Adult and Adolescent Literacy*, and the *English Journal*. Her research interests include teacher quality, alternate teacher preparation, and university–school partnerships.

Carol W. Dochen is currently the director of the Student Learning Assistance Center at Texas State University-San Marcos and teaches undergraduate courses in both University College and the College of Education. Actively involved in state and national developmental education organizations, she served two terms as the first elected president of the Texas Association of Developmental Educators and was a founding member of the annual statewide College Academic Support Programs conference jointly sponsored by the Texas Association of Developmental Educators, the Texas chapter of the College Reading and Learning Association, and the Texas Higher Education Coordinating Board. She recently coauthored the second edition of *Academic Transformation: The Road to College Success* (2010), an educational psychology textbook written specifically for learning framework courses.

Noel Entwistle is professor emeritus of education at the University of Edinburgh. He is a Fellow of the British Psychological Society, the Scottish Council for Educational Research, and the Society for Research into Higher Education, as well as past editor of the *British Journal of Educational Psychology* and *Higher Education*. His main research interests have been in the identification and measurement of approaches to studying in higher education and in exploring the influences on those approaches in terms of the interactions between students' own characteristics and the teaching and assessment procedures that they experience.

Michelle Anderson Francis is a reading professor at West Valley College in Saratoga, California. She teaches all levels of reading, from developmental to college level. Her publications have mainly focused on the issue of vocabulary acquisition and instruction at the postsecondary level.

JoAnne Greenbaum teaches undergraduate critical reading, thinking, and writing at California State University, Fullerton. She is presently the coordinator of the online Postsecondary Reading and Learning (PRL) certificate program being offered at CSUF. Greenbaum also teaches the graduate level course that focuses on content area reading in the PRL certificate program. Her special interests include critical thinking and active collaborative learning.

Shari Harrison is an instructor in the Department of Human Development, Education, and Care at Northern Lights College. She earned her master's of education degree in curriculum and instruction, with a focus on students with special needs, from the University of Northern British Columbia. Harrison has worked as an elementary schoolteacher, an adult basic education instructor, and a college instructor. She currently teaches in an online environment, where she encourages people to understand how their brains learn best, and supports students by sharing a variety of teaching and learning techniques and strategies.

William A. Henk serves as dean of the College of Education and as professor of literacy at Marquette University. He specializes in reading and language studies, particularly assessment, cognition, and affective influences on achievement. He is most known for his work on developing instruments for assessing how children feel about themselves both as readers and writers, and another tool for conducting classroom literacy observations.

Jeanne L. Higbee has a B.S. in sociology from Iowa State University and earned both an M.S. in counseling and guidance and a Ph.D. in educational administration from the University of Wisconsin, Madison. She currently serves as professor in the Department of Postsecondary Teaching and Learning at the University of Minnesota, Twin Cities. She is the coeditor of 4 books and 16 monographs, and author of more than 100 journal articles. She is a 2007 American College Personnel Association (ACPA) Diamond Honoree and the recipient of the ACPA Voice of Inclusion Medallion (2005), the Disability Ally Award (2008), the College Reading and Learning Association (CRLA) Robert Griffin Long and Outstanding Service Award (2007), the Henry Young Award for Outstanding Individual Contribution to the National Association for Developmental Education (NADE, 2002), and NADE's Hunter R. Boylan Outstanding Research/Publication Award (1999).

Jodi Patrick Holschuh is an associate professor at Texas State University. She has presented many national and international conference papers and has written numerous articles, book chapters, and books on the topic of helping students learn in college. She is coauthor of several textbooks including *Active Learning: Strategies for College Success* (1999), *College Success Strategies* (2002, 2005, 2006, 2008), *Effective College Learning* (2006, 2010). She has also coauthored, with Sherrie L. Nist, a popular trade book on learning entitled *College Rules!: How to Study, Survive, and Succeed in College* (2002, 2007). Her research interests include students' beliefs about learning, the transition from high school to college learning, strategies for academic success, and motivation.

Keith Howard is an assistant professor of secondary education at Chapman University in Orange, California. He earned his M.A. at California State University at Dominguez Hills and his Ph.D. in educational psychology and technology at the University of Southern California. His research interests include the effects of Stereotype Threat on cognitive load and testing environments, cognitive load implications for learning, the role of working memory on cognition and achievement, and the effective use of technology in educational settings.

Kenneth A. Kiewra is professor of educational psychology at the University of Nebraska at Lincoln. Formerly, he directed the University of Nebraska's Academic Success Center and edited for the *Educational Psychology Review*. His research pertains to teaching and learning in general and to aspects of the SOAR teaching and study method, in particular. His three published books are *Learning to Learn: Making the Transition from Student to Life-Long Learner* (1997), *Learn How to Study and SOAR to Success* (2004), and *Teaching How to Learn* (2008).

Ross B. MacDonald is a lifelong social justice advocate in higher education and in international peace and justice work. His work experience spans teaching English at the community college level; creating and directing statewide, research-based curriculum development projects focused on peer tutoring; developing and directing innovative interdisciplinary programs in the College of Agricultural and Environmental Sciences at the University of California at Davis; and currently supporting economic development work in the Midwest as a senior research scientist in the Agroecosystems Management Program at Ohio State University. His four years of peace and justice work included efforts in Haiti (strengthening the legal system), Iran (civilian diplomacy curriculum), and the Basque region of Spain (victims' issues).

Velda McCune teaches at the Moray House School of Education at the University of Edinburgh. Her articles have been published in the *European Journal of Psychology of Education*, the *Educational Psychology Review*, and *Higher Education*.

Donna McKusick is dean for developmental education and special academic programs at the Community College of Baltimore County. For over three decades, she has provided leadership in programs and services for at-risk students, including developmental education, tutoring, learning communities, academic development, and special interventions to close achievement gaps. She was the founding president of the Developmental Education Association of Maryland and coauthored *Making Sense: A Guide for Readers and Writers* with Al Starr in 2002.

Irving Pressley McPhail is executive vice president and chief operating officer at the National Action Council for Minorities in Engineering (NACME). A veteran teacher, scholar, advocate, and senior executive in higher education, he has served as chancellor at the Community College of Baltimore County, president of St. Louis Community College at Florissant Valley, and president of LeMoyne-Owen College. His areas of focus include research-based best practices in developmental education and learning assistance.

Kouider Mokhtari is a professor at Iowa State University, where he teaches graduate and undergraduate literacy education courses for pre-service and in-service teachers. His research focuses on the acquisition of language and literacy by first and second language learners, with particular emphasis on children and adults at-risk of reading difficulties.

Sheila A. Nicholson is a senior lecturer of developmental reading at Texas State University-San Marcos.

Sherrie L. Nist (also known as Nist-Olejnik) received her Ph.D. from the University of Florida and taught reading and study strategy courses at the University of Georgia. For the last eight years of her career, she was the director of the Division of Academic Enhancement, a unit that provides academic support services to university students. She has authored or coauthored over 50 articles and six books focusing on reading, vocabulary development, and learning and studying at the college level, including, with Jodi Patrick Holschuh, *Active Learning: Strategies for College Success* (1999), *College Rules!: How to Study, Survive, and Succeed in College* (2002, 2007), and *College Success Strategies* (2002, 2005, 2006, 2008).

Yaacov Petscher is an associate instructor at Florida State University, where he earned his master's degrees in educational psychology and in measurements and statistics, and his Ph.D. in developmental psychology.

Paul R. Pintrich (1953–2003) was a professor of education and psychology, and chair of the Combined Program in education and psychology. He received his Ph.D. in 1982 from the University of Michigan, where he also obtained a master's degree in developmental psychology. His research focused on the development of motivation, epistemological thinking, and self-regulated learning in adolescence. He published over 110 articles, book chapters, and books in these areas, and taught courses in educational psychology, child and adolescent development, motivation, and learning.

Frances Prevatt is a professor at Florida State University. She is the director of the Adult Learning Evaluation Center, a training, research, and service facility that specializes in college students and adults with learning disabilities and ADHD. Her areas of research are assessment and interventions for adults with ADHD, as well as motivational factors that lead to success in college.

Briley Proctor is an associate professor and director of the School Psychology program at Florida State University. She was previously the co-director for research and training at FSU's Adult Learning Evaluation Center. Proctor is also a licensed psychologist.

Richard Radcliffe received his Ph.D. from the University of Denver and is currently an associate professor at Texas State University. He teaches courses in research methods, middle school programming, and learning theory. His research interests include longitudinal study of building a college-going culture for at-risk students, effective middle school pedagogy, and profiles of middle grades teachers.

Abigail Reaser received her Ph.D. from Florida State University. Her unpublished doctoral dissertation, *ADHD Coaching and College Students* (2008), was chaired by Frances Prevatt.

Leslie Rush is an associate professor at the University of Wyoming, where she teaches courses in adolescent literacy, young adult literature, and English/language arts pedagogy. Her research interests include multiliteracies, critical literacy, and content area literacy. Rush taught high school English for 12 years in California, Texas, and East Africa. An active member of NCTE and its affiliate organization, the Conference on English Education, Rush has published in *Reading Research and Instruction*, *Reading Online*, and the *Journal of Literacy Research*. In addition, she serves on the editorial review board for *Reading Research Quarterly*, the *Journal of Literacy Research*, and *The Qualitative Report*.

Helena Praks Seli is an assistant professor of clinical education at the University of Southern California. She teaches an undergraduate course in learning strategies and motivation as well as a graduate course in learning theory and social factors influencing learning. As an educational psychologist, her research interests include motivation, self-regulation, self-concept, self-worth protection, and the social psychological aspects of education. Seli also conducts research on the effectiveness of educational technology, such as the use of "clickers" in large lecture courses. Along with Dr. Myron H. Dembo, she is the author of *Motivation and Learning Strategies for College Success: A Self-Management Success*, Third Edition (2007).

De Sellers received her M.A. and her Ph.D. in curriculum and instruction from the University of Texas at Austin. Between 1973 and 1999, she taught an undergraduate course in educational psychology and graduate courses in reading and adult education at Texas State University-San Marcos. During that time, Sellers also served as director of the Student Learning Assistance Center, dean of the College of General Studies, and director of the International Office. In 2005, she became a licensed professional counselor and now owns her own practice in Austin, Texas.

Ravi Sheorey is a professor of English at Oklahoma State University, where he teaches courses in applied linguistics and Teaching English As a Second Language. His research focuses on the learning and teaching of English in nonnative contexts and the learning and reading strategies of second-language learners. His papers have appeared in a variety of international journals, and some of his books include *Learning and Teaching English in India* (2006) and the coedited volume *Reading Strategies of First and Second Language Learners* (2008). Some of his recent honors include a Fulbright Professorship in 2004 and the OSU Regents' Distinguished Teaching Award in 2007.

Peter Swerdzewski specializes in educational program evaluation and psychometrics for large-scale assessment. He received both his Ph.D. in assessment and measurement and his MEd in counseling psychology from James Madison University. He has worked with organizations including the College Board, the New York City Department of Education, and James Madison University's Center for Assessment and Research Studies.

Marie Valeri-Gold is a retired assistant professor of reading from Georgia State University.

Isaac Watts (1674–1748) is best known as the "father of English hymnody," being one of the first to compose non-biblical poetry and having written over 750 hymns, most famously "Joy to the World." Brought up in a family of nonconformists in seventeenth-century Britain, he attended the Dissenting Academy, in today's London, where he composed his first serious poems and essays on theology. After graduating, Watts found a position in the pastorate training preachers in London, although he himself was more interested in promoting education than preaching particular religious views. His writings on educational theory include *The Art of Reading and Writing English* (1721), *Logic, or The Right Use of Reason in the Enquiry After Truth With a Variety of Rules to Guard Against Error in the Affairs of Religion and Human Life, as well as in the Sciences* (1724), and *The Improvement of the Mind* (1741). He also published books of poetry and psychological theory.

Kate Wilson is a consultant in academic language and learning development and an adjunct associate professor at the University of Canberra. She was director of the Academic Skills Program at the University of Canberra for 15 years, and has taught and lectured in TESOL in Zimbabwe, Cambodia, Vietnam, Indonesia, China, and Australia. Her research focuses particularly on international students' development of academic literacies.

Barry J. Zimmerman is a distinguished professor of educational psychology at the Graduate School and the University Center of the City University of New York. He has devoted his career to investigating social cognitive and self-regulatory processes of children and youth. For his research, he has received the Senior Scientist Award of American Psychological Association Division 16 (School Psychology) for a sustained and exceptional program of scholarship, and the Sylvia Scribner Award of the American Educational Research Association for exemplary research in learning and instruction. He served as president of Division 15 of the American Psychological Association (Educational Psychology).

About the Editors

Russ Hodges is an associate professor and has worked at Texas State University-San Marcos since 1986. He currently coordinates the university's learning framework course for the Department of Counseling, Leadership, Adult Education, and School Psychology. He also teaches master- and doctoral-level courses in Developmental and Adult Education. Dr. Hodges earned his Doctorate of Education, specializing in Developmental Education, from Grambling State University in Louisiana.

Dr. Hodges is a frequent keynote speaker and presenter at national, regional, and state conferences and is actively involved in many professional organizations. He is a past president of the College Reading and Learning Association (CRLA) and currently serves as chair of the Council of Learning Assistance and Developmental Education Associations.

Dr. Hodges was the recipient of the Outstanding Article Award from the *Journal of Developmental Education* in 2001, the Robert Griffin Award for Long and Outstanding Service from CRLA in 2007, the College Academic Support Programs (CASP) Lifetime Achievement Award in 2008, the Outstanding Writing in the Field of Literacy and Learning from the International Reading Association's College Literacy and Learning Special Interest Group, and the Karen G. Smith Special Recognition Award for Outstanding Service in 2010. Dr. Hodges was also named Fellow of the Council of Learning Assistance and Developmental Education Associations in 2009 — the field's most prestigious award.

Michele L. Simpson taught a variety of reading and learning strategy courses to undergraduates over the past twenty-five years, while serving as a major professor for graduate students in reading education and coordinating faculty development programs that focused on effective teaching techniques across many academic disciplines. During her tenure at the University of Georgia she coauthored three books and coedited one book, published over 60 articles and 20 chapters, and served on eight different editorial boards. The book Dr. Simpson coauthored with Bill Brozo, *Readers, Teachers, and Learners*, is in its fifth edition. For her research endeavors Dr. Simpson received the International Reading Association's prestigious Elva Knight Research Award and several outstanding article awards from professional organizations, and was inducted as a Fellow into the Council of Learning Assistance and Developmental Education Associations. In addition to her teaching awards at the University of Georgia, she is most proud of a chapter on college studying, coauthored with Sherrie Nist, that appeared in the widely respected *Handbook of Reading Research*.

Norman A. Stahl is a professor and the chair of the Department of Literacy Education at Northern Illinois University. Over the years his research has focused on postsecondary reading instruction with particular interest in the field's history. Dr. Stahl's works include content analyses, instructional reviews, commentaries, organizational histories, and methodological pieces on documentary history and oral history. He has received honors from the National Association for Developmental Education, the College Reading and Learning Association, the College Literacy and

Learning Special Interest Group of the International Reading Association, and the Association of Literacy Educators and Researchers for his scholarship pertaining to reading and learning. He has served as President of the Literacy Research Association, President of the History of Reading Special Interest Group of the International Reading Association, Chair of the American Reading Forum, and is currently President-Elect of the College Reading and Learning Association. He is a national Fellow of the Council of Learning Assistance and Developmental Education Associations.

Acknowledgments (continued from page iv)

Kathryn Bartle Angus and JoAnne Greenbaum, "Position Statement on Rights of Adult Readers and Learners." In *Journal of College Reading and Learning*, 33, pp. 122–29. Copyright © 2003. All rights reserved. Reproduced by permission.

David R. Arendale, "A Glossary of Developmental Education and Learning Assistance Terms." In *Journal of College Reading and Learning*. All rights reserved. Reproduced by permission.

David R. Arendale, "Pathways of Persistence: A Review of Postsecondary Peer Cooperative Learning Programs." In *Best Practices for Access and Retention in Higher Education*, pp. 27–40, edited by I. Duranczyk, J. L. Higbee, and D. B. Lundell. Copyright © 2004. All rights reserved. Reproduced by permission.

Carol Boston, "The Concept of Formative Assessment." *Practical Assessment, Research, and Evaluation*, 8(9). Copyright © 2002. From http://PAREonline.net. All rights reserved. Reproduced by permission.

Hunter R. Boylan, "Exploring Alternatives to Remediation." In *Journal of Developmental Education*, 22(3), pp. 2–4, 6, 8, 10. Copyright © 1999. All rights reserved. Reproduced by permission.

Melinda S. Burchard and Peter Swerdzewski, "Learning Effectiveness of a Strategic Learning Course." Reprinted from *Journal of College Reading and Learning*, 40(1). Copyright © 2009. CRLA (College Reading and Learning Association), www.crla.net. All rights reserved.

David C. Caverly, Sheila A. Nicholson, and Richard Radcliffe, "The Effectiveness of Strategic Reading Instruction for College Developmental Readers." Reprinted from *The Journal of College Reading and Learning*, 35, pp. 25–45. Copyright © 2004 (College Reading and Learning Association), www.crla.net. All rights reserved.

R. P. Cole, C. Babcock, E. T. Goetz, and C. E. Weinstein, "An In-Depth Look at Academic Success Courses." Paper presented at the meeting of the College Reading and Learning Association, Figure 5-15: Figure 1, "Matrix of Academic Success Courses." Copyright © 1997. Adapted with permission from the authors.

Nannette Evans Commander and Marie Valeri-Gold, "The Learning Portfolio: A Valuable Tool for Increasing Metacognitive Awareness." In *The Learning Assistance Review*, 6(2), pp. 5–18. Copyright © 2001 by *The Learning Assistance Review*, the publication of The National College Learning Center Association.

Myron H. Dembo and Keith Howard, "Advice about the Use of Learning Styles: A Major Myth in Education." Reprinted from *Journal of College Reading and Learning*. Copyright © CRLA (College Reading and Learning Association), www.crla.net. All rights reserved.

Mary P. Deming, "Learning Logs: A Vehicle for Student Learning and Reflective Teaching." In *Learning Assistance Review*, 4(2), pp. 5–16. Copyright © 1999. All rights reserved. Reproduced by permission.

Noel Entwistle and Velda McCune, "The Conceptual Bases of Study Strategy Inventories." In *Educational Psychology Review*, 16, pp. 325–45. Copyright © 2004. All rights reserved. Reproduced by permission.

Shari Harrison, "Creating a Successful Learning Environment for Postsecondary Students with Learning Disabilities: Policy and Practice." Reprinted from *Journal of College Reading and Learning*, 33, pp. 131–45. Copyright © 2003 CRLA (College Reading and Learning Association), www.crla.net. All rights reserved.

Jeanne L. Higbee, "Commentary: Who Is the Developmental Student?" In *Learning Assistance Review*, 5(1), pp. 41–50. Copyright © 2000 by TLAR, the publication of The National College Learning Center Association. Reprinted by permission.

Russ Hodges, De Sellers, and Carol W. Dochen, "Implementing a Learning Framework Course." In *NADE Monograph: 2001 A Developmental Odyssey*, pp. 3–13, edited by J. L. Higbee and P. L. Dwinell. Reproduced by permission from National Association of Developmental Education.